THE BIRDS OF SOUTH DAKOTA

REVISED EDITION

by
THE SOUTH DAKOTA ORNITHOLOGISTS' UNION

Preferred citation: South Dakota Ornithologists' Union, 1991,
The Birds of South Dakota, 2d Edition.

Aberdeen, South Dakota, 1991

Copyright © 1991
by
THE SOUTH DAKOTA ORNITHOLOGISTS' UNION
All rights reserved

Text Printed in the United States of America

First revised edition, 1991

Requests for permission
to reproduce material from this work
should be sent to:

SDOU
Northern State University
Box 740
Aberdeen, SD 57401 USA

ISBN 0-9628650-0-1
LIBRARY OF CONGRESS CATALOG CARD NUMBER:
91-60391

NSU PRESS IS AN ENTITY OF THE NORTHERN STATE UNIVERSITY FOUNDATION

CONTENTS

INTRODUCTION ii
    The SDOU Checklist Committee ii
    Acknowledgements ii
    South Dakota Geography iii
    South Dakota Weather iv
    Vegetation iv
    Birds of South Dakota iv
    How Human Settlement Has Changed the Environment vii
    A Brief Ornithological History of South Dakota viii
    Species Accounts ix
    Commonly Used Abbreviations xi
    Juvenile Waterfowl Age Classifications xi
    Abundance Terminology xi
    Distribution Maps xii
    Banding Recovery Maps xiii
    Christmas Bird Counts xiii
    South Dakota Counties xiv
    South Dakota Physiography xv
    South Dakota Vegetation xvi
    Panorama of Bird Habitats of South Dakota xvii

SPECIES ACCOUNTS

Gaviidae: Loons	1	Apodidae: Swifts	184
Podicipedidae: Grebes	3	Trochilidae: Hummingbirds	186
Pelecanidae: Pelicans	10	Alecidinidae: Kingfishers	189
Phalacrocoracidae: Cormorants	12	Picidae: Woodpeckers	190
Ardeidae: Bitterns and Herons	14	Tyrannidae: Tyrant Flycatchers	201
Threskionithidae: Ibises	26	Alaudidae: Larks	217
Ciconiidae: Storks	28	Hirundinidae: Swallows	218
Anatidae: Swans, Geese, and Ducks	28	Corvidae: Jays and Crows	225
Cathartidae: American Vultures	67	Paridae: Titmice	232
Accipitridae: Hawks, etc.	68	Sittidae: Nuthatches	235
Falconidae: Falcons	86	Certhiidae: Creepers	238
Phasianidae: grouse, etc.	91	Troglodytidae: Wrens	239
Rallidae: rails and coots	102	Cinclidae: Dippers	246
Gruidae: Cranes	107	Muscicapidae: Kinglets, Thrushes	247
Charadriidae: Plovers	110	Mimidae: Mockers and Thrashers	260
Recurvirostridae: Avocets, Stilts	116	Motacillidae: Pipits	265
Scolopacidae: Sandpipers, etc.	118	Bombycillidae: Waxwings	267
Laridae: Gulls and Terns	146	Laniidae: Shrikes	269
Columbidae: Pigeons and Doves	163	Sturnidae: Starlings	271
Psittacidae: Parrots	166	Vireonidae: Vireos	272
Cuculidae: Cuckoos and Anis	166	Emberizidae: Warblers, Sparrows,	
Tytonidae: Barn Owl	169	Blackbirds, etc	279
Strigidae: Typical Owls	170	Fringillidae: Finches	370
Caprimulgidae: Goatsuckers	181	Passeridae: Weaver Finches	383

REFERENCES CITED 384

SPECIES INDEX AND CHECKLIST 407

THE SOUTH DAKOTA ORNITHOLOGISTS' UNION 411

INTRODUCTION

This edition of *The Birds of South Dakota* is completely revised since it first appeared in 1978. The book is written by the checklist committee of the South Dakota Ornithologists' Union, an organization formed in 1949 under the leadership of Herman Chapman. Since its inception, the SDOU has published the quarterly journal, *South Dakota Bird Notes*.

The Birds of South Dakota attempts to integrate into one systematic list the available information on the occurrence of birds in South Dakota. Most of the data were extracted from the contributions to *South Dakota Bird Notes*, supplemented by records contained in other journals and publications, and by unpublished records of competent observers. Readers are encouraged to add records to this account of South Dakota birds by bringing their data to our attention.

THE SDOU CHECKLIST COMMITTEE

The SDOU Checklist Committee was first appointed in 1963 by President L. J. Moriarty and consisted of Nathaniel R. Whitney, Jr., Chairman, James W. Johnson, Nelda Holden, Herman Chapman, Herbert Krause, and Alfred Peterson. The latter three members were replaced by Paul Springer (1966), Bruce Harris (1967), B. J. Rose (1967), and Byron Harrell (1971). For the second edition, the committee, reconstituted in 1982, included Jocelyn Baker, past president SDOU, Dr. Gilbert Blankespoor, Biology Department, Augustana College, Dr. Byron Harrell, Biology Department, University of South Dakota, Bruce Harris, SD Department Game, Fish and Parks (retired), Nelda Holden, past president SDOU, Dr. Paul Springer, former leader, Cooperative Wildlife Research Unit, South Dakota State University, Dr. Dan Tallman, Biology Department, Northern State University, and Dr. Nathaniel Whitney, past president SDOU.

ACKNOWLEDGEMENTS

Most of the drawings in the text are by E. W. Steffens; one is by Francis Lee Jaques, and two are by Larry McQueen. The cover is by Wayne Trimm. The habitat photographs are by D. George Prisbe. The map of physiographic areas was provided through the courtesy of the South Dakota Geological Survey, Iowa University Press, and Dr. Theodore Van Bruggen.

Special recognition is made of the many contributions of Herbert Krause. Several other past and present members of the S.D.O.U. that we wish to mention expressly for their many observations included in this book are: Donald Adolphson, Les Baylor, Herman F. Chapman, Herman Chilson, Lowery Elliott, J. Scott Findley, Willis Hall, June Harter, Adrian Larson, L. J. Moriarty, Alfred Peterson, Charles and Gladyce Rogge, Dennis Skadsen, and William Youngworth.

The many other contributors to this text cannot be adequately acknowledged here; their names are in the following accounts. Staff members of the South Dakota Department of Game, Fish and Parks, and the U.S. Fish and Wildlife Service, have been generous in supplying data. Personnel of the National Wildlife Refuges and National Parks and Monuments within the state have contributed either directly or through the availability of their organizations' files. Special thanks are directed also to U.S. Fish and Wildlife Service biologists Harold F. Duebbert, Harold Kantrud, and John Loekmoen, whose work in north-central South Dakota has been a valuable addition for that part of the state. Richard Rosche provided records from southwestern South Dakota.

Review of the manuscript to provide current information on the status of birds in certain parts of the state, particularly the Black Hills and West River areas, were provided by Michael Melius and Richard Peterson.

For the first edition, we appreciate the aid of the Department of Biology of the University of South Dakota for secretarial assistance. Margot Moller provided great care in the preparation for publication of the distribution maps. Joyce Harrell did the final transformations of the manuscript to the printed page. The second edition was prepared as a computer-generated, camera-ready manuscript by Dan Tallman. Strategic Mapping, Inc., graciously allowed us to reproduce maps generated by their Atlas-MapMaker desktop mapping system.

The W. H. Over Museum, which was responsible in past years for the two editions of Over and Thoms' *Birds of South Dakota*, has continued its interest in the birdlife of South Dakota by partially supporting the cost of publication of the first edition with funds provided to them by the Friends of the W. H. Over Museum. For preparation of the second edition, Northern State University provided travel funds and Title II Federal funds to enhance our adoption of computer-generated copy, and granted Tallman release time from teaching assignments.

SOUTH DAKOTA GEOGRAPHY

South Dakota extends from about Latitude 96° 30'W to 104° W, and from Latitude 43° N to near 46° N, with slight irregularities at the northeast and southeast corners, and includes 77,047 square miles. A general increase in altitude exists from the southeast (about 1100 feet) to the northwest (about 3500 feet), although the lowest spot is on the Minnesota River (960 feet) and the highest is Harney Peak (7242 feet) in the Black Hills. South Dakota counties are portrayed in Figure 1.

The distribution of physiographic areas in South Dakota is shown in Figure 2. About 75% of the natural land forms of South Dakota are in the Great Plains physiographic province (Rothrock 1943; Flint 1955). The boundary between the Great Plains and Central Lowlands coincides with the western margin of the James Basin. East of the boundary, the region is characterized by a glaciated topography with tall grass, low rolling hills, and lake-filled depressions. West of the boundary lies an area of high semiarid mixed grass prairie with deep valleys and broad upland flats and buttes.

INTRODUCTION

The Great Plains province includes the Black Hills section near the southwestern corner of the state, the High Plains section along the south edge of the state, Cretaceous and Tertiary Table Lands, and the Missouri River Valley separating the Pierre Hills to the west and the Coteau du Missouri to the east. Almost all the area east of the Missouri and some west of the river was glaciated.

The Central Lowland includes the Minnesota Valley in the northeast, the James Basin including the Lake Dakota Plain, a small area of James River Highlands, and the section known since the time of the early French fur traders as the Coteau des Prairies, or Prairie Hills country, which includes most of the drainage of the Big Sioux River and the undrained lakes and potholes of eastern South Dakota. A great variety of glacial deposits covers essentially the whole of the Central Lowlands.

SOUTH DAKOTA WEATHER

Average annual precipitation is about 22 inches in the eastern third, decreasing to about 16 inches in the western third; extremes are from less than 13 inches in the northwestern corner to about 26 inches in the southeastern corner of the state. The higher elevations of the Black Hills, with 18–26 inches, enjoy precipitation levels above that of the surrounding country. Most of the precipitation falls during the April-to-September growing season, and there are great variations in the state from year to year. Periods of successive dry years or years that are wetter than normal are frequent. The state has a typical continental climate, with extremes of summer heat and winter cold. The lowest temperature on record is -58° F at McIntosh on Feb. 17, 1936, and the highest observed was 120° F five months later at Gann Valley on July 5, 1936. The average annual temperature for the state is approximately 46°; the range of January averages is 10–22°, and for July, is 68–78°.

VEGETATION

The distribution of the native vegetation is shown in Figure 3. Outliers of eastern deciduous forest are found in the east and outliers of Rocky Mountain conifer forest are found in the west in this primarily prairie state. Rivers crossing the plains provide a forest corridor westward aided in more recent times by windbreaks and wooded towns. Coniferous outliers extend in a spotty distribution half way across the state. Thus the state lies in a transition of east and west.

BIRDS OF SOUTH DAKOTA

Since most of South Dakota is in the northern Great Plains, grassland birds are predominant and conspicuous in the bird life across the state. The most conspicuous species in dry grasslands is the Western Meadowlark, which breeds in every county of the state. West of Longitude 99°, the Lark Bunting becomes conspicuous. Other nesting species widely distributed in dry grasslands throughout the state include the Northern Harrier, Killdeer,

Upland Sandpiper, Burrowing Owl, Common Nighthawk, Horned Lark, Dickcissel, Vesper Sparrow, Lark Sparrow, Lark Bunting, Grasshopper Sparrow, and Chestnut-collared Longspur. Other grassland species of more limited distribution are the Greater Prairie Chicken in south-central South Dakota and the Sharp-tailed Grouse which occurs most commonly in the west. Where trees occur, either naturally in stream bottoms or in planted shelterbelts, the Swainson's Hawk, Red-tailed Hawk, American Kestrel, Great Horned Owl, Mourning Dove, Northern Flicker, Western and Eastern Kingbirds, American Crow, Black-capped Chickadee, American Robin, Gray Catbird, Brown Thrasher, Yellow Warbler, American Redstart, Rufous-sided Towhee, Common Grackle, and Orchard Oriole may be found in some numbers, with some of these species inhabiting brushy draws rather than tall trees. The Mallard, Blue-winged Teal, and Spotted Sandpiper breed around marshes and ponds.

Eastern South Dakota, especially the more northern portion, is dotted with potholes and lakes that provide breeding habitat for a number of species of water, marsh, and shore birds. Especially noteworthy are the Horned Grebe, Red-necked Grebe (Waubay National Wildlife Refuge and vicinity), Western Grebe (most larger lakes), American White Pelican, Double-crested Cormorant, Great, Snowy, and Cattle Egrets, American Avocet, Franklin's Gull, Ring-billed Gull, and Black Tern. The Marbled Godwit is widespread in the tall grass prairies.

Extreme southeastern South Dakota has more deciduous forest and attracts a few species, including Whip-poor-will, whose main ranges are in the deciduous forests of the eastern United States. Other eastern deciduous forest species that in South Dakota reach their western limit in the eastern part of the state include the American Woodcock, Ruby-throated Hummingbird, Yellow-bellied Sapsucker, and Yellow-throated Vireo.

Throughout the grassland portion of the state, and especially east of the Missouri, towns constitute an important and distinct habitat. Features of towns include trees, usually deciduous and quite large, along with ornamental shrubs and buildings, but essentially no ground cover suitable for nesting or roosting. Important nesting species among town birds include the Mourning Dove, Eastern Screech-Owl, Chimney Swift, Red-headed Woodpecker, Downy Woodpecker, Northern Flicker, Purple Martin (mostly east of the Missouri River), Blue Jay, American Robin, Starling, House Sparrow, Northern Oriole, Common Grackle, Cardinal (East River), and American Goldfinch.

The Missouri River Valley averages a little over a mile in width with the valley floor 300 to 600 feet below the tops of the bluffs. This section has species that are found uncommonly elsewhere in the state. The sandbars of the Missouri River offer nesting habitat for the Piping Plover and Least Tern, and the chalk cliffs on the lower reach of the river provide nesting sites for the Barn Owl and Cliff Swallow. Large bodies of water have been formed by four dams on the Missouri River and have inundated trees, which provide nesting sites for the Double-crested Cormorant and Great Blue Heron.

Most of the birds breeding in the mixed grass plains west of the Missouri River are among those listed above as having statewide distribution. Widespread in the West River area are the Ferruginous Hawk and Long-billed Curlew, while the Sprague's Pipit and Baird's Sparrow nest in more restricted ranges to the north. Black-billed Magpies nest in brush-filled draws that are tributaries to the western drainages, and Eastern Meadowlarks breed in lowland meadows in the sandhill prairie of Bennett and Todd counties. The sage prairie of parts of extreme west South Dakota is the eastern limit of several western species, including the Sage Grouse, Sage Thrasher, and Brewer's Sparrow.

The very striking erosion forms of the White River Badlands, or as they are often called, "The Big Badlands" (Badlands National Park and adjacent regions of Pennington, Jackson, and Shannon counties), the High Plains area to the south of the Badlands, and the pine-covered buttes in the northwestern part of the state, provide nesting sites for the Golden Eagle, Prairie Falcon, a feral population of Rock Dove, Great Horned Owl, White-throated Swift, Rock Wren, and Mountain Bluebird.

Finally, the pine forests and spruce stands of the Black Hills are the home of one restricted subspecies, the White-winged form of Dark-eyed Junco, and are about as far east as many Rocky Mountain species breed, including the Lewis' Woodpecker, Red-naped Sapsucker, Dusky Flycatcher, Canyon Wren, American Dipper, Townsend's Solitaire, Audubon's form of Yellow-rumped Warbler, MacGillivray's Warbler, Western Tanager, and Cassin's Finch. Pettingill and Whitney (1965) describe this distribution in more detail.

The above account refers to the breeding birds of South Dakota. In addition, the state provides a seasonal area of rest for a variety of birds that nest in the arctic or in the transcontinental conifer forest. The two largest of these groups are shorebirds and warblers. A small number of eastern deciduous forest species whose breeding range does not reach South Dakota may also appear as migrants or casual visitors in the east.

The winter avifauna is much smaller than that of the other seasons. While a few species are common in winter, a larger number may be found on a regular basis in limited populations in protected areas. Others have only a casual or accidental status in winter. Some water birds remain late when open water freezes late, and some remain where water stays open all year. The reservoir system on the Missouri River now provides large water areas for migrants and areas of open water through the winter. These areas support large populations of wintering Bald Eagles, and also supply places for birds previously unknown in the state, such as the Black-legged Kittiwake and Glaucous Gull.

HOW HUMAN SETTLEMENT HAS CHANGED THE ENVIRONMENT

When Lewis and Clark (1904–1905) explored the newly-acquired Louisiana Purchase in 1804, they found tall-grass prairie to the east of the Missouri River, mixed-grass prairie to the west, and floodplain forest along the river. At that time the major Indian culture was that of the Dakota, with their many subdivisions, all of whom followed primarily a hunting culture based on the bison (*Bison bison* (Linnaeus)). Other Indian tribes, notably the Arapaho, Cheyenne, and Sutaio on the West River plains, and the Arikara along the Missouri River, had occupied parts of South Dakota earlier, but were not contacted by Lewis and Clark in this region (Swanton 1953). For several more years, hunting and trapping remained the only significant uses of the land.

Toward the middle of the nineteenth century, white settlement began, first along the eastern edge of the state in the valleys of the Big Sioux and James rivers and the Red River of the north, and later, with the discovery of gold in the Black Hills, in the western part of the state. The soil and topography of the tall-grass prairie is eminently suited to crop-farming, and so grain crops displaced tall-grass prairie and, with it, the bird-life that was limited in its ability to adapt to disturbed conditions. As farmers cultivated more land, they drained potholes and thus displaced the water birds and the marsh-nesting birds. Further, as they built villages and towns, they planted trees for shade and bushes for ornament, thus providing habitat suitable for other species that had formerly been confined to stream bottoms.

Thus, a major result of white settlement of eastern South Dakota was to restrict the habitat available for birds that nested in the potholes and the tall prairie, and to extend the nesting sites available for tree- and brush-nesting species. These tree- and brush-nesting species, however, are essentially birds of the forest edge and not the species of extensive or mature deciduous forest. This trend to extend the range of forest-edge species was accelerated between 1932 and 1940 when the federal government encouraged, by financial subsidy, the planting of shelterbelts on farms.

Human changes in the West River area came more slowly. Land that under natural conditions supports mid-grass prairie is often not suitable for grain farming. Broken prairie is especially susceptible to erosion. The extermination of the tremendous bison herds resulted in the subjugation of the Dakotas and other plains Indian tribes whose entire way of life depended on bison hunting. Subsequently, as white settlers moved into the West River region, they found that the only agricultural use for which the plains were suitable was livestock grazing. The result has been a replacement of bison by domestic cattle. The floristic composition of the grasslands may be different now, since evidence indicates that in the mid-nineteenth century, grasses such as buffalo grass and the gramas predominated, while currently the main grasses are needlegrasses and western wheatgrass (L. M. Berner, pers. comm.). If this supposition is correct, there may well have been some significant concurrent changes in the bird life.

More recently, modification of the Missouri River has been carried out by the U.S. Corps of Engineers, with evidence of drastic effects on the bird life. For purposes of flood control and power production, a series of dams were constructed from 1953–64 along the Missouri River in South Dakota, thus converting most of the free-flowing river into a series of large reservoirs. The most important immediate effect has been to eliminate most of the stream bottom forests and brush which formerly were important both for migrating and for nesting birds. Another effect that we have not completely evaluated is that the large lakes attract more water birds, especially during migration and winter. Most of the records of vagrant saltwater gulls have been near the Missouri River dams.

Construction of numerous stock watering ponds West River provided greatly expanded habitat for water birds in a region that formerly had only intermittent waterways and a few natural ponds to attract such species.

Much human activity has been detrimental to South Dakota's birds. Much mixed grass prairie has been lost to wheat and other crops. Sage prairie has been reduced by overgrazing, use of herbicides, and agriculture. Cutting of timber along rivers and streams, overgrazing, the advent of Dutch Elm Disease, and the failure to replace aging shelter belts have reduced habitat for woodland birds. Pesticide use has contaminated land and water, as has the improper disposal of mining wastes. The use of fertilizers and improper sewage disposal is causing eutrophication of many aquatic habitats. Finally, poor soil management is causing erosion of productive top soil and the filling of streams and ponds. South Dakota faces more environmental challenges in the future, as its citizens debate various proposals for radioactive and other dumping in the state.

A BRIEF ORNITHOLOGICAL HISTORY OF SOUTH DAKOTA

Four exploratory expeditions stand out during the first half of the nineteenth century. In 1804, Lewis and Clark (1904–1905), while exploring the Missouri River and the Louisiana Territory, noted several species of birds. Duke Paul Wilhelm of Wurttemberg (1835) traveled as far as Big Bend in 1824 and reported a few birds, most notably a specimen of Mississippi Kite. In 1833 and 1834 Prince Maximilian of Wied (1843) traveled through South Dakota, recording several species. John James Audubon visited much of the Missouri Valley in 1843, including South Dakota (Audubon 1897). The explorations before Audubon are described more fully by Krause (1956).

During the second half of the nineteenth century several expeditions sponsored by the U.S. Government crossed the state (Baird 1858, Hayden 1862). These and other reports as well as a few personal observations are summarized by Coues (1874) in his book on the Birds of the Northwest; he includes specific mention of 125 species in South Dakota. In 1874, General George H. Custer explored the Black Hills; George B. Grinnell (1875) who was with the expedition wrote a detailed report of his observations during the trip. In the same period, settlement was under way in the eastern half of the state. Two early observers in the northeast were Dr. B. Knickerbocker in 1868–1869 (Chilson 1968) and C. E. McChesney (1879) in 1875–1878. Dr. G. S. Agersborg (1885), a veterinarian at Vermillion for many years, provides a glimpse into the bird life of the late 1800's in the southeast.

The outstanding student of the first decades of the twentieth century was Stephen Sargent Visher, who between 1900 and 1915 published significant studies of the birds of Sanborn Co. (1913a), Clay Co. (1915), Harding Co. (1914), and other western portions of the state (1909, 1912a, 1912b). The first book on the birds of the whole state of South Dakota was published in 1921, although the manuscript was completed in 1916, by William H. Over and Craig S. Thoms as a publication of the University of South Dakota at Vermillion. They listed 288 species on the present list and seven others now considered synonyms or hypothetical. The number of still-accepted species later was raised to 309 (Over and Thoms 1932). A revised edition of the *Birds of South Dakota*, also published by the University, listed 336 species including 327 currently recognized (Over and Thoms 1946)

The latest phase coincides with the existence of the South Dakota Ornithologists' Union and its journal, *South Dakota Bird Notes*. In the eighth year, the checklist committee of that time prepared a seven-page tabular checklist including 342 species and six others now considered synonyms (SDOU 1956). An extensive summary of the birds of the Black Hills region by Olin S. Pettingill, Jr., and Nathaniel R. Whitney, Jr., (1956) added six more species. The first edition of *The Birds of South Dakota* recognized 377 species. The time since publication of the first edition has witnessed continued taxonomic upheaval by the American Ornithologists' Union. As a result of lumping and splitting of various species and of additions to our state bird list, this revised edition contains 395 species, plus one additional species considered likely but hypothetical.

SPECIES ACCOUNTS

The list of species is divided for convenience by family headings. The names used and the sequences followed are those of the A.O.U. Checklist of North American Birds and Supplements (American Ornithologists' Union 1983, 1985, 1989). Names that appear in the principal field guides and that differ significantly from present-day usage appear in brackets following the scientific names.

Information on ecology, nesting, food habits, etc. is available from many sources and is omitted here. Descriptions of birds themselves are also omitted, since several excellent field guides are available. For those who desire more comprehensive descriptions of plumages, such information on most of our species can be found in Thomas Sadler Roberts (1958). Subspecies cannot usually be distinguished in the field and are mostly not mentioned in this book. Exceptions are made for species only recently merged: Red-tailed Hawk, Northern Flicker, Yellow-rumped Warbler, and Dark-eyed Junco.

The criteria by which species have been accepted for admission to the list are as follows: 1. Most species are represented by one or more specimens, which are known to be in specific collections where they can be examined currently. They have not necessarily been examined by the authors. 2. Many species have been photographed within the state. A clearly recognizable photograph, accurately labeled as to locality and date, is considered to be as acceptable as a specimen record. 3. A few species have been listed on the basis of sight records without either specimens or photographs. In each case, the consensus of opinion in the Checklist Committee was that the observation was valid when consideration was given to the experience and judgment of the observer, the risk of confusion with similar species, and other pertinent factors. In a number of cases, birds in this category were caught for banding, providing an excellent opportunity of examination. In each case pertinent information, including the names of the observers, is listed. A Rare Bird Records Committee of the South Dakota Ornithologists' Union was formed in 1987 (Springer 1988) to judge the accuracy of reports. Observers are urged to submit records of rare or unusual birds to the committee in care of the editor of *South Dakota Bird Notes*.

One species, the Mute Swan meets the above criteria but is included in the main text as hypothetical species. This record of is probably correct but may be of a bird that escaped from captivity. Several other species, listed in Table 1, have been reported

Table 1. Reports of species from South Dakota that are probably erroneous or of escapes from captivity.

Species	Source	Remarks
Emperor Goose	Binger et al. in Chilson (1973)	Probable escape
Egyptian Goose	Harris (1977c)	Probable escape
Eurasian Wigeon	Harter (1967)	Probable error
Black Vulture	Over and Thoms (1921, 1946)	Probable error
Inca Dove	Sowell et al. (in Seasons 1984)	Probable escape
Ringed Turtle Dove	Harris	Probable escape
Smooth-billed Ani	Elliott (1968)	Probably a Groove-billed Ani
Lesser Nighthawk	Edwards (1969)	Probable error
Brown-headed Nuthatch	Eckert (in Seasons 1977b)	Originally reported as Pygmy Nuthatch
Northern Wheatear	Blankenship et al. (1953)	Probable error
Golden-crowned Sparrow	Nelson (1963)	Probable error

INTRODUCTION xi

in the state literature, but the Checklist Committee feels that these reports probably are erroneous or of escapes from captivity.

Except in cases with very limited data, the material under each species is organized under several headings. ***Status*** is a general statement of the numerical, geographical, and seasonal occurrence. Occasionally other information, such as historical references, is added. Information on hybrids, introductions, and reintroductions may also be included. ***Habitat*** is a very brief statement on the environment where the species may be found in the state. ***Nesting*** provides data to indicate the time of year of reproduction and occasionally other matters. ***Summer*** gives data on birds found in this season but for which we lack breeding data. ***Spring migration*** and ***fall migration*** provide information on average and extreme dates of arrival and departure. ***Winter*** adds details of occurrence roughly from late December through February.

COMMONLY USED ABBREVIATIONS

CBC — Christmas Bird Count
Co.— County
C — Central
E — Eastern
NP — National Park
NWR — National Wildlife Refuge
N — Northern
NE — Northeastern
NW — Northwestern
PSA — Public Shooting Area
S — Southern
SDBBA — South Dakota Breeding Bird Atlas
SE — Southeastern
SW — Southwestern
SP — State Park
SRA — State Recreation Area
USFWS — U. S. Fish and Wildlife Service
W — Western
[] — information lacking or species hypothetical

JUVENILE WATERFOWL AGE CLASSIFICATIONS

Class I (downy young)
Class II (partly feathered)
Class III (fully feathered)
subclasses a, b, c for the first two classes; details of this system are given in Taber (1971)

ABUNDANCE TERMINOLOGY

Terminology to indicate degrees of abundance is necessarily subjective, for the status of a bird is a complex phenomenon. There are problems related to size, to conspicuousness, to the kind of bird, to the capabilities and judgement of the observer, and to the time spent in the field. Colonial nesting species and flocking species present their own problems. With these considerations in mind, the following definitions should provide a guideline to what the authors intended when they prepared the species accounts. The definitions in words are from Phillips et al. (1964). In parentheses we have indicated first the numbers that might be seen during migration, and second, the numbers that might be seen in breeding season or winter.

CATEGORY	IN MIGRATION	OTHER SEASONS
Abundant Seen in large numbers	50 or more per day	15 or more per day
Common always seen but not in large numbers	25–50 per day	8–14 per day
Fairly common very small numbers, or not always seen	0–15 per day;	3–7 per day
Uncommon seldom seen, but not a surprise	5–10 per day	1–2 per day
Rare always a surprise, but not out of range	1 per season	1 per season
Casual out of normal range (one each 2 or 3 years)		
Accidental far from normal range and not to be expected again (a few scattered records		
Regular species probably occurs somewhere in the state at some time each year. Regular species may be in any category from *abundant* to *rare*		

DISTRIBUTION MAPS

The distribution map for each species is intended to provide a quick visual indication of the seasonal and geographic distribution. Courses of the Missouri, White, and Cheyenne rivers and outlines of the Black Hills and the Coteau des Prairies are included in our base map as generalized landmarks. With few exceptions, we have followed Pettingill and Whitney (1965) in considering Rapid City within the confines of the Black Hills. The area of shading is usually our best estimation, and represents an extrapolation from more limited data. The scale of the map is too small to show ecological limitations; thus a shaded area means that the bird may be present in suitable habitat. All of western South Dakota might be shaded for an aquatic species, although appropriate habitat is rather sparse within that region. Breeding area and wintering areas are shown, and outside of these, areas of regular migration are shown. **We have used the Missouri River rather arbitrarily as a boundary between eastern and western species;** thus, for example, western species might well be expected on the eastern side of the river. Special symbols indicate other breeding records, breeding season records, winter records, or other records. An additional symbol is used for very old records (usually those before 1920 and especially where there has been dramatic status change). The key to the symbols is given below.

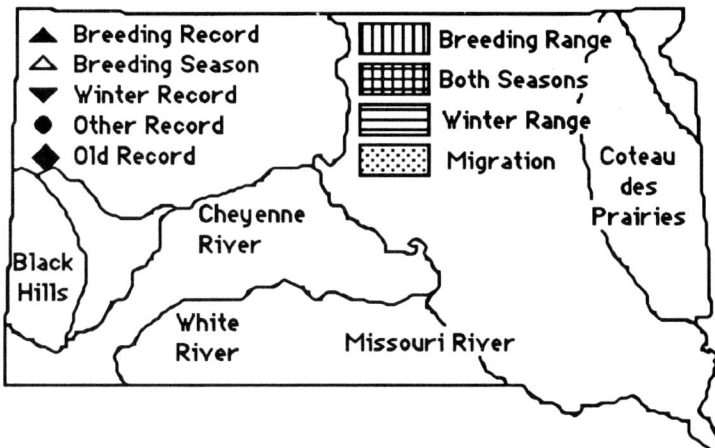

BANDING RECOVERY MAPS

The maps of banding recoveries are for birds (except for some repetitious data) that have been banded either outside or within South Dakota and that have subsequently crossed the state border. Banding locations are marked with an "o" and points of recovery are signified by an "x." The arrow on the map indicates direction of movement. However, the arrows are somewhat misleading since the birds may have wandered widely during the interval between banding and recovery and may have made several north and south migrations in that time. Birds banded and recovered within the state are not included. Also omitted are waterfowl, since data on these species can be obtained elsewhere. Species maps not available at the time this edition went to press include White Pelican, Double-crested Cormorant, and Mourning Dove. These charts first began appearing in a series of *South Dakota Bird Notes* articles, which include more information on the maps (Tallman 1990).

CHRISTMAS BIRD COUNTS

Christmas Bird counts are not cited individually. Their original publication can be found in issues of either *Audubon Field Notes* and *American Birds*, or *South Dakota Bird Notes*.

Figure 1. South Dakota countes.

Figure 2. South Dakota's physiographic divisions (after VanBruggen 1976).

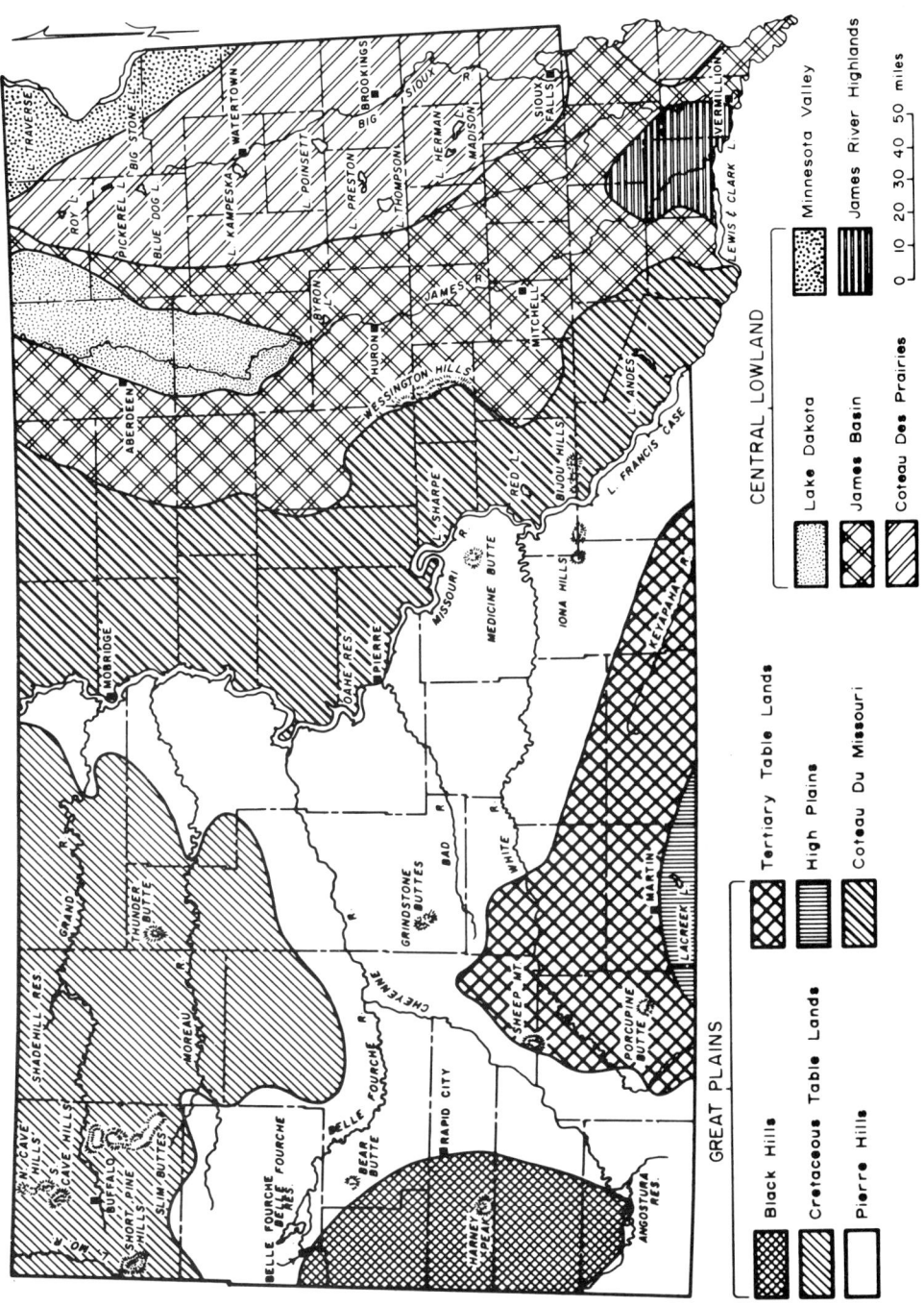

Figure 3. South Dakota's natural vegetation.

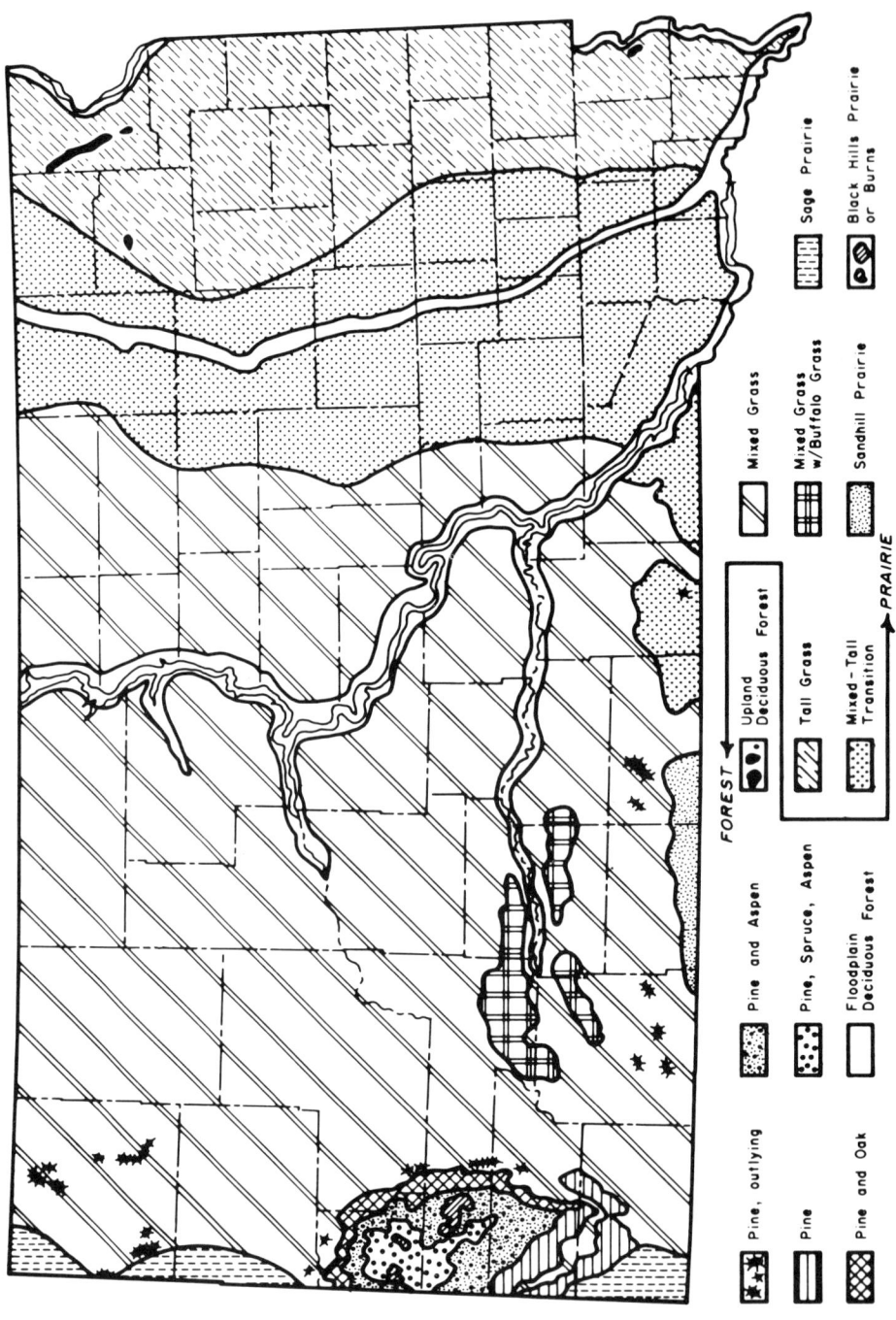

PANORAMA OF BIRD HABITATS OF SOUTH DAKOTA

The accompanying photographs were taken by Douglas George Prisbe to give a sample of the variety of habitats available to birds in all parts of the state. The photographs are roughly arranged from west to east. Because of the wide variety of habitats in the state, the photographs are not intended to be exhaustive but, rather, will give the reader a taste for the South Dakota environment.

The legends identify the habitat shown, give the area or specific location of the photograph, and occasionally add a special ornithological feature.

Figure 4. White Spruce is distributed in stands at higher elevations at Crook's Tower in the Black Hills National Forest and elsewhere in higher canyonlands.

Figure 5. Ponderosa Pine forest predominates in most of the Black Hills; These rocky pinnacles are along the Needles Highway in Custer State Park.

Figure 6. Fast flowing mountain streams, such as in Spearfish Canyon in the northern Black Hills, are good places for dippers. A rich vegetation occurs in these deep mountain canyons and many contain high cliff edges.

Figure 7. Aspen stands are usually indications of past fire disturbance in the Black Hills. Extensive open areas can remain 25 years after a forest fire.

Figure 8. The pine forests of the Black Hills meet the mixed grass prairie at Custer State Park.

Figure 9. The lakes in the Black Hills were created by dams; Pactola Lake is west of Rapid City.

Figure 10. Limited areas of sage prairie can be found along the extreme western edge of the state.

Figure 11. Some aquatic areas in the arid western plains have been managed by controlling water levels, such as at Angostora Reservoir.

Figure 12. The larger buttes of Harding County, such as in the Custer National Forest at the Slim Buttes, have pine forest on their slopes.

Figure 13. Most Missouri tributaries, such as the Grand, Cheyenne, and White Rivers, are lined with cottonwood trees.

Figure 14. Even the simple farm dugout provides a body of water for both aquatic and land birds. This Dugout is surrounded by the shorter mixed grass prairie that covers much of the West River region.

Figure 15. The Badlands National Park is characterized by low rainfall and little vegetation on the eroded slopes

Figure 16. In the badlands, where accumulated moisture exists, red cedar can be found.

Figure 17. Lacreek NWR lies within the small area of sandhills that extend north into South Dakota from Nebraska.

Figure 18. Western streams are often lined with trees, which allow woodland birds into the plains, such as along the Keya Paha River at Turtle Butte, the easternmost site of Ponderosa Pine.

Figure 19. Extensive areas of the Missouri River floodplain have been lost to reservoirs. Little remains of the original riparian growth along the Missouri.

Figure 20. Bare areas of dunes or sand bars have been formed by the shifting Missouri River and now support nesting habitat for the endangered Least Tern and Piping Plover.

Figure 21. This scene from Potter Co. is typical of the longer mixed grass prairie of eastern South Dakota.

Figure 22. Especially East River, agricultural crops have replaced much native vegetation.

Figure 23. Across the state, overgrazed pasture has also replaced native vegetation.

Figure 24. Most of South Dakota was covered with prairie; an excellent example is the Nature Conservancy's Samuel H. Ordway Prairie, an area on the Coteau du Missouri that has abundant potholes.

Figure 25. Like the other eastern north-south running rivers, the James River offers tree-lined shelter for many forest-inhabiting migratory birds.

Figure 26. Tall grass prairie in the east was converted to fertile cropland, now little native tall grass prairie remains except where protected by state and private conservation organizations.

Figure 27. Each spring and fall, Sand Lake NWR serves as a staging area for waterfowl. In the summer, the refuge is a rich wildfowl production area.

Figure 28. Oak forest at the Waubay NWR was probably protected from prairie fires by its location between lakes. Before the time of Western settlement, these forests were much more extensive.

Figure 29. Many small pothole marshes and sloughs have been preserved as Waterfowl Production Areas.

Figure 30. Although some prairie lakes lack trees along their shores, most permanent lakes in the glacial lakes region, such as Red Iron Lake, are edged with trees that make for fine birding.

Figure 31. Good upland deciduous forest sites are found in the coulees of the eastern slope of the Coteau des Prairies, such as this area of Sica Hollow State Park.

Figure 32. The woodlands of Hartford Beach State Park lie on the northeast border of South Dakota and attract eastern species such as Pileated Woodpeckers and Whip-poor-wills.

Figure 33. Trees in towns and in State Parks, such as Oak Wood Lakes, are wooded oasis that attract migrants and nesting species.

Figure 34. Upland deciduous forest is limited in the southeast to such areas as Newton Hills State Park.

SPECIES ACCOUNTS

GAVIIDAE: Loons

RED-THROATED LOON Gavia stellata (Pontoppidan)

Status. Accidental.
Only records:
  7 May 1989, Angostura Reservoir (Rosche in Berkey 1989a)
  19 Oct 1985, Fall River Co., Angostura Reservoir (Rosche in Seasons 1986a)
  22 Oct 1976, Lake Yankton (Rosche)

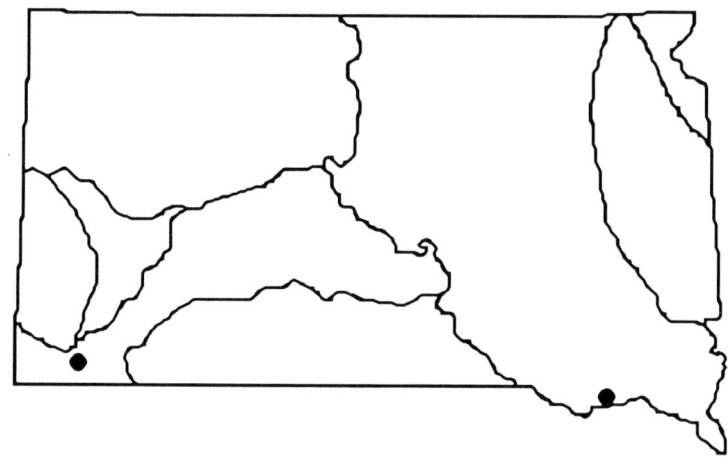

COMMON LOON Gavia immer (Brunnich)

Status. Uncommon migrant E; most common NE and along Missouri River. W River records from Perkins, Bennett, Butte, Fall River, Jackson, Meade, and Tripp counties, and the Black Hills. May be a fairly common migrant in Fall River Co. and the Black Hills (R. Peterson).
Habitat. Larger lakes and reservoirs.
Spring Migration. Mid-Apr.
  Earliest dates:
    20 Mar 1986, Yankton Co. (Hall in Seasons 1986c)
    27 Mar 1989, Oahe Dam (Harris in Seasons 1989c)
    28 Mar 1987, Yankton Co. (Hall in Seasons 1987c)
  Latest dates:
    4 Jun 1986, Day Co. (Lundie in Seasons 1986d)
    4 Jun 1987, Pennington Co. (Melius in Seasons 1987d)
    7 Jun 1983, Day Co. (Harris and Husmann in Seasons 1983c)
Summer. No definite nesting records. Loons breed in North Dakota only on the Canadian border and in Minnesota S to Big Stone Lake. Loons are usually silent in South Dakota but Harris found 2 birds calling excitedly on 16 June 1967 on Big Stone Lake adjacent to Roberts Co. and speculated that young might be nearby. Springer observed a breeding-plumaged bird at Deerfield Reservoir on 18 Jun 1990.

Summer birds along the Missouri River, in the NE, and Black Hills are probably nonbreeders; most are in nonbreeding plumage.

Fall Migration. Late Oct, a few stragglers present into early winter.

Earliest dates:
1 Aug 1982, Hyde Co. (Prieksat in Seasons 1982d)
29 Aug 1939, Roberts Co. (Harris)

Latest dates:
30 Nov 1982, Yankton Co. (Hall in Seasons 1983a)
1 Dec 1982, Yankton Co. (Hall in Seasons 1983b)
2 Dec 1973, Deuel Co. (Harris)

Winter.
14 Feb 1983, Davison Co. (Rogers and McLaird in Seasons 1983b)

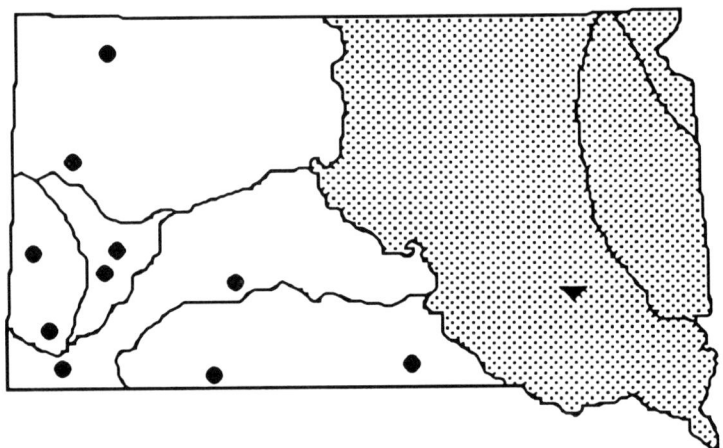

PODICIPEDIDAE: Grebes

PIED-BILLED GREBE *Podilymbus podiceps* (Linnaeus)
Status. Common summer resident; less numerous W.

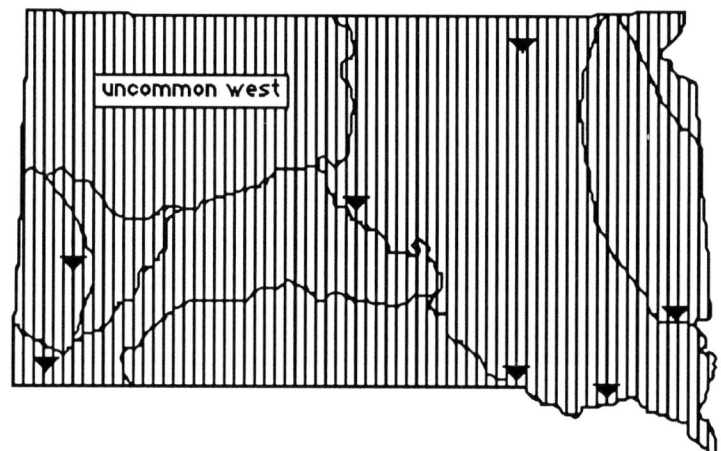

Habitat. Lakes and marshes with emergent vegetation.
Spring Migration. Last half of Apr.
  Earliest Dates:
    12 Mar 1986, Charles Mix Co. (Skadsen in Seasons 1986c)
    13 Mar 1986, Yankton Co. (Hall)
    16 Mar 1986, Codington Co. (Gilman in Seasons 1986c)
Nesting. Middle of May.
  Earliest dates:
    1 May 1963, Lake Preston, nest with 4 eggs (Hart and Twedt 1963)
    11 May 1964, near Hayti, adult on nest (Springer)
    19 May 1987, Yankton Co., adult on nest (Springer in Seasons 1987d)
  Latest dates:
    15 Jul 1978, Harding Co., adult on nest (Springer)
    29 Jul 1966, Roberts Co., brood of 6 (Harris)
    13 Aug 1976, Harding Co., 1 streaked young (Springer)
Fall Migration. Mid-Oct. Possibly some late dates represent birds crippled during hunting season. Unusual concentrations: 23 Sep 1979, Roberts Co., 106 (Harris and Monson in Seasons 1980a); 27 Sep 1976, Gregory Co., 200 (Steffen in Seasons 1977a).

Pied-billed Grebe banding recoveries

Latest dates:
  26 Nov 1975, Deuel Co. (Harris in Seasons 1975d)
  27 Nov 1971, Deuel Co. (Harris)
  3 Dec 1983, Fall River Co. (Peterson in Seasons 1984c)

Winter.
  CBC Reports:
  Canyon Lake, Hot Springs, Lake Andes, Sand Lake, Sioux Falls, and Yankton
  Other records:
  11 Jan 1976, Pierre (Hall)
  7 Feb 1973, Pierre (Rose)
  27 Feb 1977, Yankton Co. (Hall)

HORNED GREBE *Podiceps auritus* (Linnaeus)

Status. Fairly common migrant in E third of state; rare elsewhere. Nesting numbers appear to fluctuate greatly. During migration, scattered W River records. Accidental winter. Probably breeds regularly in Edmunds and McPherson counties; recent reports of nesting in Day, Marshall, Roberts and Dewey counties. Reported in the 1880's and 1890's to breed as far S as Beadle, Miner, and Bennett counties (Duebbert and Lokemoen 1973, Whitney 1955).

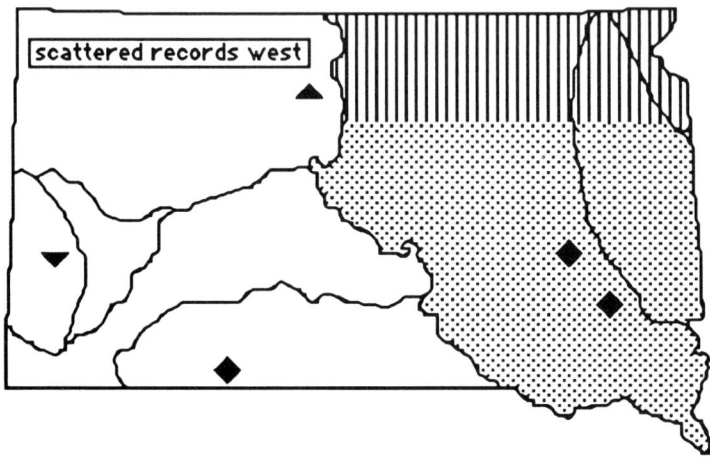

Habitat. Deep water lakes during migration. Nests in seasonally flooded wetlands and small ponds (Duebbert and Lokemoen 1973).

Spring migration. Last half of Apr. Unusual concentration: 20 Apr 1978, 45 at Clear Lake and 40 at Coteau Lake (Harris in Seasons 1978c).

Earliest dates:
  25 Mar 1977, Yankton Co. (Hall in Seasons 1977c)
  25 Mar 1987, Yankton Co. (Hall in Seasons 1987c)
  27 Mar 1910, Sioux Falls (Larson 1925)
  27 Mar 1989, Oahe Dam (Harris in Seasons 1989c)

Nesting. Late May – mid-Jul.
Earliest dates:
  20 May 1978, McPherson Co., 3 nests (Duebbert, Lokemoen, and Harris)
  20 May 1978, Edmunds Co., nest (Montgomery)
  22 May 1972, McPherson Co., nest construction (Duebbert and Lokemoen 1973)
Latest dates:
  27 Jul 1972, 12 miles SE of Eureka, pair with 2 young two-thirds grown (Duebbert and Lokemoen)
  1 Jun – 31 July 1979, Dewey Co., 6 adults and 13 young (Bjerke in Seasons 1979d)

Fall migration. Mid-Oct.
Earliest dates:
  19 Sep 1970, Beaver Lake (Krause and Blankespoor)
  5 Oct 1972, Deuel Co. (Harris)
  6 Oct 1985, Meade Co. (Baker in Seasons 1986a)
Latest dates:
  22 Nov 1983, Yankton Co. (Hall in Seasons 1984a)
  25 Nov 1987, Yankton Co. (Hall in Seasons 1988a)
  29 Nov 1982, Yankton Co. (Hall in Seasons 1983a)

Winter.
Records:
  26 Dec 1960, Rapid City (Pettingill and Whitney 1965)

RED-NECKED GREBE *Podiceps grisegena* (Boddaert)

Status. Uncommon to rare local summer resident in NE; regular in small numbers (2–7 pairs) only at Waubay NWR. Described by Lundquist (1952) as "never abundant but nests on many larger lakes in the lake region." Rare migrant in E third and few records W; formerly considered a common migrant in Sanborn Co. (Visher 1913a). Black Hills record: 9 Nov 1960, immature banded and photographed (Pettingill and Whitney 1965). An immature specimen exists from Belle Fourche Reservoir, 31 Aug 1913 (Over and Thoms 1924)

6 GREBES

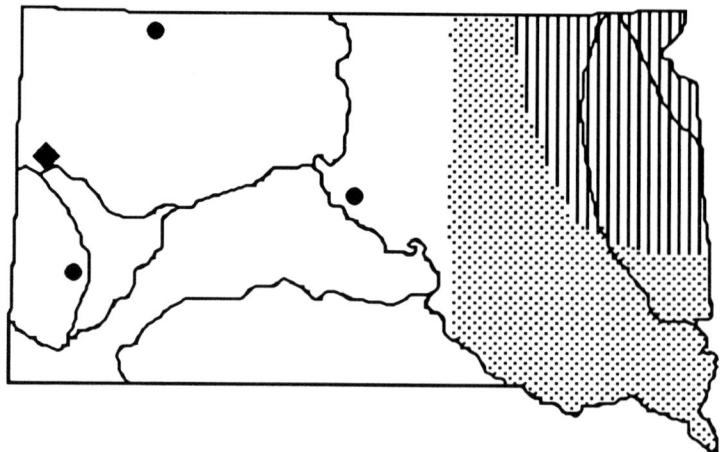

Habitat. Nests on sloughs with emergent vegetation; frequents larger lakes during migration.

Spring migration. Early May.
Earliest dates:
2 Apr 1986, Yankton Co. (Hoeger in Seasons 1986c)
2 Apr 1988, Waubay NWR (Skadsen in Seasons 1988c)
8 Apr 1987, Day Co. (Koerner in Seasons 1987c)

Nesting. Late May – mid-Jul.
Earliest dates:
20 Apr 1985, Waubay NWR, building nest (Eubank and Burke in Seasons 1985d)
6 May 1983, Waubay NWR, 2 nesting pairs (Rabenberg in Seasons 1983c)
14 May 1981, Waubay NWR, on nest (Montgomery in Seasons 1981c)
Latest dates:
4 Jul 1972, Deuel Co., bird on nest but not found after severe storm (Harris in Seasons 1972c)
7 Jul 1962, Waubay NWR, 2 nests with 6 eggs (Greer and Greer)
17 Jul 1964, Marshall Co., female and 2 half-grown young (Springer)

Fall migration.
Latest dates:
16 Sep 1951, Union Co. (Stephens et al. 1955)
27 Oct 1985, Perkins Co. (Griffiths and Griffiths)
9 Nov 1960, Rapid City (Pettingill and Whitney 1965)

EARED GREBE *Podiceps nigricollis* Brehm.

Status. Common migrant in E; fairly common migrant elsewhere. Common to abundant, but local, summer resident E; much less common elsewhere. Breeding colonies can number in the 100's. W River nesting known at Lacreek NWR, Meade, Butte, and Dewey counties.

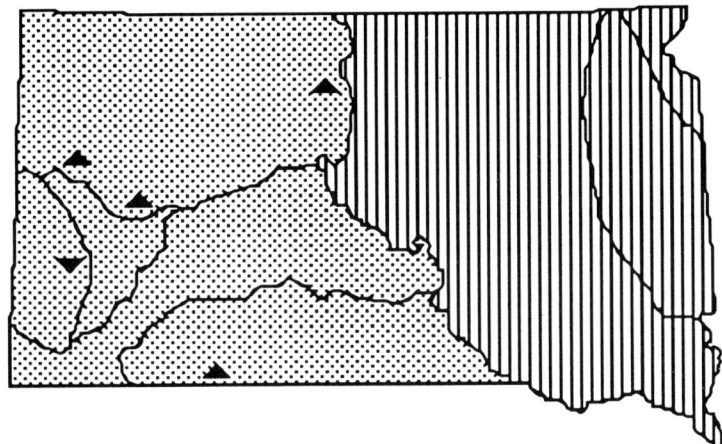

Habitat. Sloughs and marshes with emergent vegetation.
Spring migration. Late Apr.
  Earliest dates:
    16 Mar 1985, Charles Mix Co. (Kronner in Seasons 1985c)
    20 Mar 1953, Lacreek NWR, 3 of 5 banded (Krumm)
    26 Mar 1968, Sanborn Co. (Harris)
Nesting. Early Jun – mid-Jul. Unusual concentrations: 22 Jun 1981, Whitewood Lake, 112 nests and 200 birds (Harris and Husmann in Seasons 1981d); 23 Jun 1984, Piyas Lake colony with 500 nests (Husmann and Rabenburg in Seasons 1984d); summer 1984, 625 nests at Lake Andes NWR (Jave); 31 Jul 1979, 50 adults, 75 young at Eagle Butte Ponds, Dewey Co. (Bjerke in Seasons 1979d).
  Earliest dates:
    2 Jun 1972, near Hosmer, nest building (Harris)
    4 Jun 1909, Sioux Falls, nest with eggs (Parks)
    8 Jun 1902, Hamlin Co., nest with 6 eggs (Whitney 1955)
  Latest records:
    8 Jul 1969, Peever Slough, 3 adults with 10 young (Harris)
    26 Jul 1967, Lake Newell, 1 adult with 2 young (Baylor and Rosine)
    16 Aug 1971, Beaver Lake, 2 adults with 1 young (Krause and Blankespoor)
Fall migration. Mid-Oct.
  Latest dates:
    14 Nov 1975, Roberts Co. (Harris in Seasons 1975d)
    19 Nov 1962, Lacreek NWR (refuge files)
Winter.
  Records:
    29 Dec 1957, and several preceding days, Rapid City (Pettingill and Whitney 1965)

8 GREBES

WESTERN GREBE *Aechmophorus occidentalis* (Lawrence)

Status. Common to abundant summer resident in NE; less common or local elsewhere. Nesting W River only in Lacreek NWR, where breeding numbers vary greatly (100 young produced in 1965).

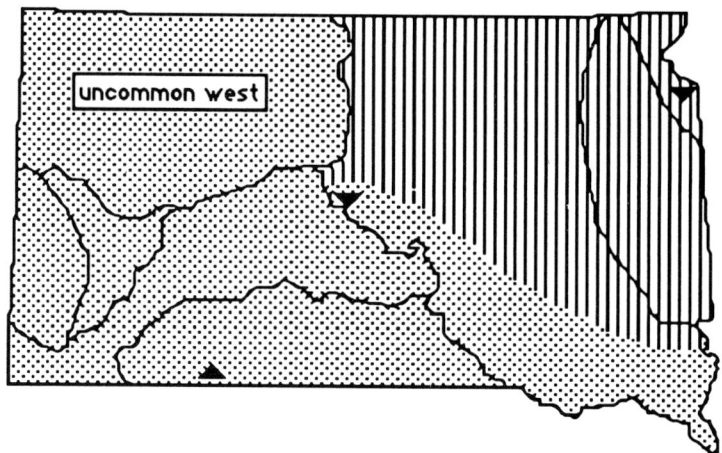

Habitat. Sloughs and shallow lakes with emergent vegetation.
Spring migration. Late Apr.
  Earliest dates:
    29 Mar 1986, Minnehaha Co. (Blankespoor and Skadsen in Seasons 1986c)
    29 Mar 1990, Butte Co. (Backlund in Seasons 1990c)
    6 Apr 1978, Lake Co. (Buckman in Seasons 1978c)
    6 Apr 1986, Codington Co. (Gilman in Seasons 1986c)
Nesting. Late May – mid-July. Reported at Lacreek NWR. Unusual concentrations: 13 Jun 1979, colony of 160 nests on 50-acre wetland near Buffalo Lake (Harris and Husmann in Seasons 1979d); Lundquist (1952) estimated 200 nests in a colony at Rush Lake.
  Earliest dates:
    26 May 1978, Beadle Co., 50+ nests (Gray)
    31 May 1973, Grass Lake, Minnehaha Co., 6 birds on nests (Krause and Baylor)
    6 Jun 1930, Day Co., 1 female on 6 eggs (Youngworth 1953)
  Latest dates:
    12 Jul 1987, Day Co., 7 nests with eggs (Skadsen in Seasons 1987d)
    16 Jul 1955, Day Co, egg hatching (photos by C. Johnson and Findley)
    21 Jul 1971, Walworth Co., 15 broods (Kantrud)
Fall migration. Early Oct.
  Latest dates:
    21 Nov 1985, Yankton Co. (Hall in Seasons 1986a)
    21 Nov 1985, Charles Mix Co. (Skadsen in Seasons 1986a)
    28 Nov 1979, Yankton Co. (Hall in Seasons 1980a)
    30 Nov 1986, Yankton Co. (Hall in Seasons 1987a)

Winter.
CBC reports:
Big Stone City and Pierre, the former still present 24 Mar 1978 (Harris).

CLARK'S GREBE *Aechmophorus clarkii* (Lawrence)

Status. This recently recognized species' status is not well documented in South Dakota. Storer and Neuchterlein (1985) state that about 1% of *Aechmophorus* grebes in North Dakota are Clark's Grebes.

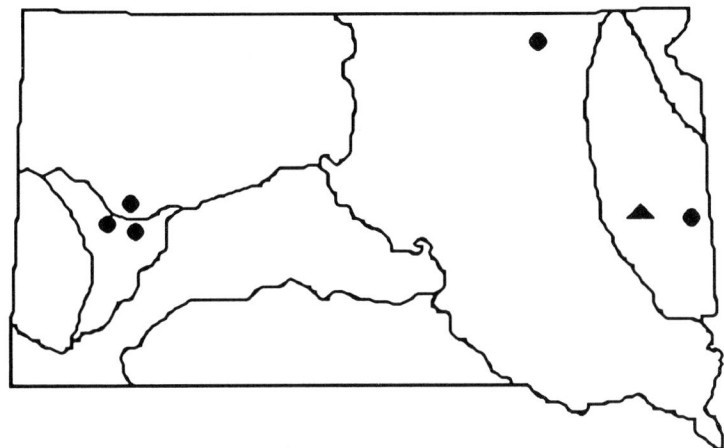

Habitat. Sloughs and shallow lakes with emergent vegetation.
Spring Migration.
Earliest dates:
18 Apr 1986, Brown Co. (Prisbe in Seasons 1986c)
19 Apr 1986, Brookings Co. (Holden and Tallman in Seasons 1986c)
8 May 1983, Meade Co. (Whitney)
Nesting. Probably late May – mid-July.
Only record:
30 Jun 1987, Kingsbury Co., nest with eggs (Harris in Seasons 1987d)
Fall migration.
Latest dates:
11 Nov 1981, Meade Co. (Whitney)
15 Nov 1987, Meade Co. (Whitney)

PELECANIDAE: Pelicans

AMERICAN WHITE PELICAN *Pelecanus erythrorhynchos* Gmelin

Status. Common to abundant summer resident, with well-established colonies in Day, Marshall, Codington, Roberts, and Bennett counties. Formerly bred at Sand Lake NWR. Colonies may be abandoned but reestablished several years later. Estimated breeding populations show marked yearly fluctuations. Histories of South Dakota nesting can be found in Adolphson and Adolphson (1968), McCrow (1974), and Sloan (1982). Nonbreeding birds occur during the summer at many locations.

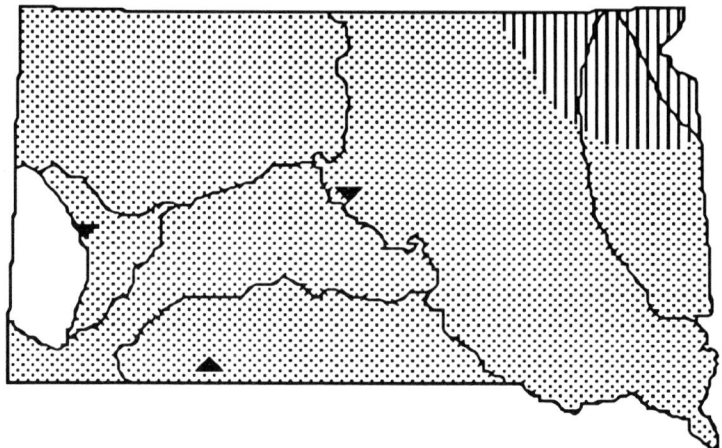

Habitat. Larger bodies of water. Nesting is on small isolated islands and sandbars, with gentle slopes free of bushes.

Spring migration. Early Apr.
Earliest dates:
   6 Mar 1987, Codington Co. (Schroeder in Seasons 1987c)
   26 Mar 1978, Brookings Co. (Holden in Seasons 1978c)
   27 Mar 1982, Orman Dam (Bjerke in Seasons 1982c)
   27 Mar 1989, Oahe Dam (Harris in Seasons 1989c)

Nesting. May – Aug. 1987 surveys found 3265 nests at Waubay and Bitter Lakes in Day Co. and at Lacreek NWR; nesting was also reported at various locations in the NE (Harris).
Earliest dates:
   10 Apr 1985, Codington Co., 100 nests with eggs (Eubank and Burke in Seasons 1985c)
   14 May 1981, Codington Co., Grass Lake, 5 young and most nests with full clutches; egg-laying must have begun about 15 April (Harris and Husmann)
Latest date:
   19 Aug 1956, estimated total of 200 flightless young at Lacreek NWR (Krumm and Whitney)

Fall migration. Mid-Sep.
Latest dates:
24 Nov 1982, Yankton Co., 2 (Hall in Seasons 1983a)
24 Nov 1983, Deuel Co. (Stava in Seasons 1984a)
29 Nov 1986, Deuel Co. (Harris in Seasons 1987a)
Winter. All winter birds are probably crippled.
CBC reports:
Pierre and Rapid City.
Other records:
8 Feb 1985, Yankton Co., cripple (Hall in Seasons 1985b)

BROWN PELICAN *Pelecanus occidentalis* Linnaeus

Status. Accidental. No specimens.
Records:
16–18 Apr 1955, Lacreek NWR (Krumm and Brook in Krumm 1955a)
28 Apr 1941 and following 2 months, Lacreek NWR (Craven in Over and Thoms 1946; Krumm 1955a)
26 Aug 1931, Oakwood Lakes (Reed in Larson 1931)

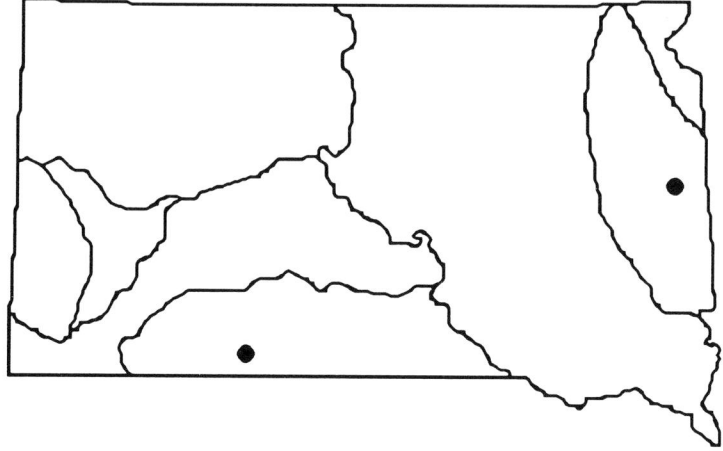

PHALACROCORACIDAE: Cormorants

DOUBLE-CRESTED CORMORANT *Phalacrocorax auritus* (Lesson)

Status. Common migrant E, less common W River. Locally common to abundant summer resident at Lacreek NWR (and elsewhere locally W River in suitable habitat), along the Missouri River, and in the NE. Colonies are fairly stable and can be expected to persist, since most breeding sites are protected and others are remote.

Habitat. Lakes and rivers. Partially submerged tree snags along the Missouri River and islands, sandbars, and in trees along lakes in NE.

Spring migration. Early Apr.
  Earliest dates:
    22 Mar 1977, Yankton Co. (Hall in Seasons 1977c)
    23 Mar 1957, Minnehaha Co. (Chapman and Krause)
    24 Mar 1946, Roberts Co. (Harris 1964)

Nesting. Mid-May – Aug.
  Earliest date:
    16 May 1981, Piyas Lake, 707 nests, 20 with young (Harris and Husmann)
  Latest date:
    Mid-Aug 1929, Waubay Lake colonies, new nests (Lundquist 1949)

Fall migration. Early Oct. Early winter records are probably late or crippled migrants.
  Latest dates:
    6 Dec 1982, Charles Mix Co. (Husmann in Seasons 1983b)
    16 Dec 1984, Waubay NWR (Bryant in Seasons 1985b)
    23 Dec 1966, Lake Andes CBC

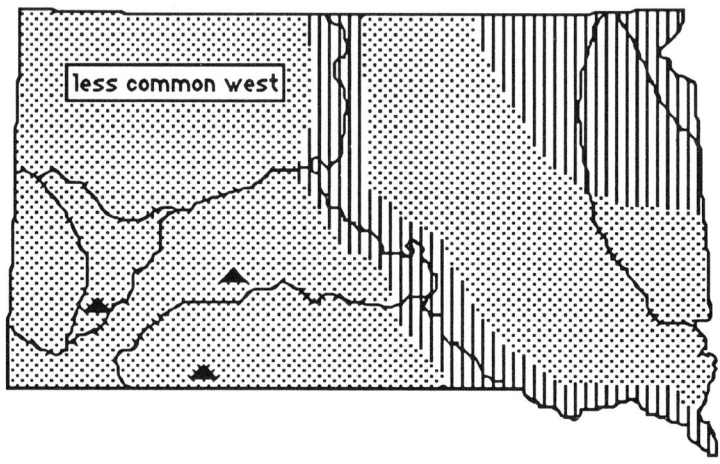

OLIVACEOUS CORMORANT *Phalacrocorax olivaceus* (Humboldt)
Status. Accidental.
Only records:
13-21 Jul 1985, Pierre (Oleson in Seasons 1985d, Purdy et al. 1985)
11 Jun 1987, Pierre (Tallman in Seasons 1987d); still present 23 June (Harris in Seasons 1987d)

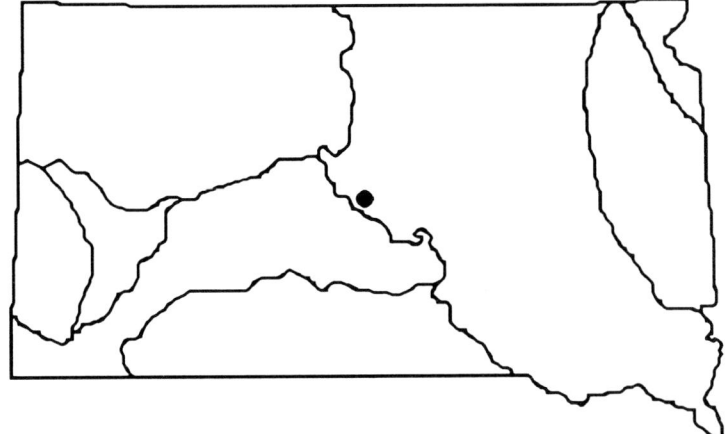

ARDEIDAE: Bitterns and Herons

AMERICAN BITTERN *Botaurus lentiginosus* (Rackett)

Status. Uncommon to locally common summer resident; not known in Black Hills. Very few W River reports but, since Hinds (1968) reported regular nesting in Perkins Co. and Baker (1980) reported courtship near Rapid City, the species probably nests elsewhere in favorable habitat.

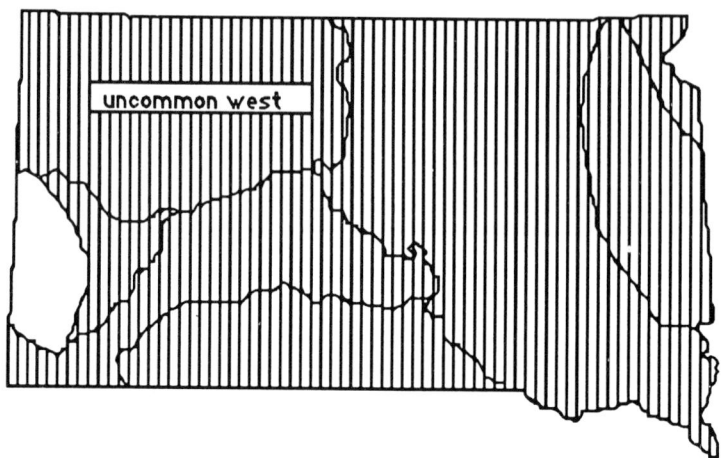

Habitat. Sloughs, marshes, and meadows.
Spring migration. Late Apr.
  Earliest dates:
    27 Mar 1977, Bon Homme Co. (Hall in Seasons 1977c)
    5 Apr 1958, Minnehaha Co. (Krause)
    9 Apr 1986, Codington Co. (Gilman in Seasons 1986c)
Nesting. Mid-June – late July. 17 nests in Edmunds Co. in 1972 (Duebbert).
  Earliest dates:
    1 Jun 1921, Sanborn Co., nest with 4 eggs (Whitney 1955)
    12 Jun 1967, Perkins Co., eggs in nest, hatched 20 Jul (Hinds 1968)
    14 Jun 1965, Perkins Co. (Hinds 1968)
  Latest dates:
    22 Jul 1983, Brookings Co., nest with eggs (Holden in Seasons 1983d)
    12 Aug 1987, Day Co., 7 nests (Getman in Seasons 1987d)
Fall migration. Mid-Oct.
  Latest dates:
    17 Nov 1983, Turner Co., alive in trap (Anderson in Seasons 1984a)
    20 Nov 1910, Sioux Falls (Larson 1925)
    20 Nov 1984, Sand Lake NWR (Waldstein in Seasons 1985a)

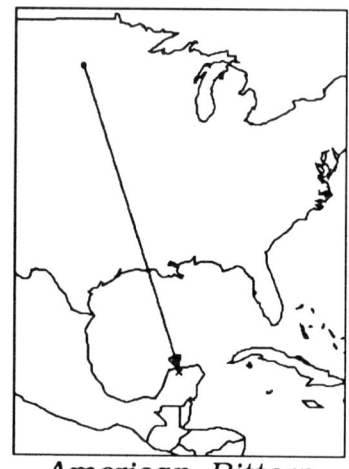

American Bittern banding recoveries

LEAST BITTERN *Ixobrychus exilis* (Gmelin)

Status. Uncommon migrant and summer resident in E; rare W. Probably more common than records indicate.

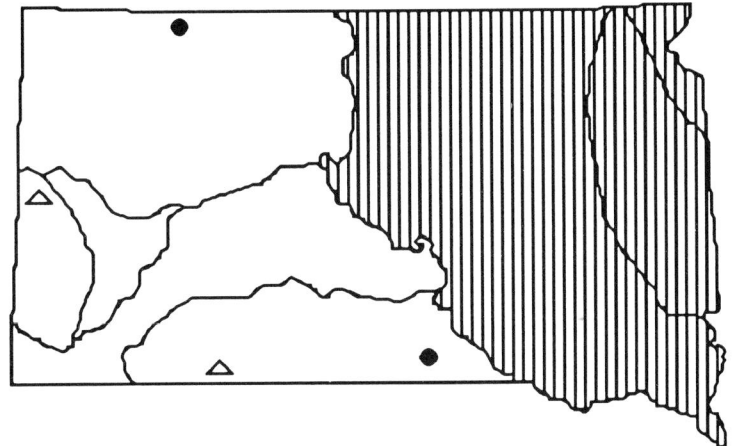

Habitat. Marshes and sloughs with dense emergent vegetation.
Spring migration. Probably late May.
  Earliest dates:
    21 Apr 1966, Faulk Co. (Rose 1967)
    11 May 1908, Sioux Falls (Larson 1925)
    11 May 1975, Deuel Co. (Harris in Seasons 1975b)
Nesting. Early Jun – mid-Jul.
  Earliest dates:
    3 Jun 1923, Sanborn Co., nest with 2 eggs (Over in Whitney 1955)
    6 Jun 1931, Rush Lake, nest (Youngworth 1935)
    9 Jun 1976, Lincoln Co., nest with 4 eggs hatching 25 Jun (Oolman and Blankespoor 1977)
  Latest dates:
    27 Jun 1972, Minnehaha Co., brooding bird with eggs (photos by Blankespoor and Krause)
    13 Jul 1984, Lake Andes NWR, downy young in nest (Jave)
    19 Aug 1971, Deuel Co., immature collected (Harris)
Fall migration. Probably late Sep, but few dates available.
  Latest dates:
    21 Sep 1965, near Sinai (Springer)
    8 Oct 1911, Sioux Falls (Larson 1925)
    12 Oct 1962, Lake Andes NWR (refuge files)
W River records.
    25 May 1986, Perkins Co. (C. Griffiths)
    16 Jun 1947, Little Spearfish Creek (Sutton in Pettingill and Whitney 1965)
    Jul 1966 and 1967, Lacreek NWR (refuge files)
    27 Jul 1955, Lacreek NWR (Krumm 1955d)
    28 Sep 1976, Gregory Co (Steffen 1977)

GREAT BLUE HERON *Ardea herodias* Linnaeus

Status. Common migrant E; uncommon W. Locally common resident in breeding colonies, most along the Missouri River, on plains adjacent to Black Hills, and in NE. Feeding flights and postbreeding dispersal take birds to areas without colonies. Scattered breeding season records for the Black Hills (Pettingill and Whitney 1965).

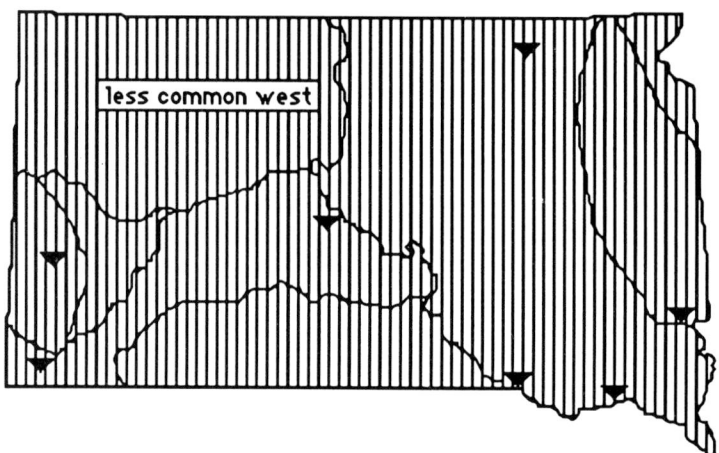

Habitat. Ponds, larger streams, and lakes; also upland pastures and grasslands.

Spring migration. Early Apr.
Earliest dates:
10 Mar 1985, Bon Homme Co. (Kronner in Seasons 1985c)
16 Mar 1986, Davison Co. (Rogers and McLaird in Seasons 1986c)
20 Mar 1986, Yankton Co. (Van Sickle in Seasons 1986c)
20 Mar 1987, Deuel Co. (Harris in Seasons 1987c)

Nesting. Apr and May. Normally nests in tree colonies with cormorants but single nests exist; rarely on ground. Nest-building evidently begins soon after arrival on breeding grounds.
Earliest dates:
16 Mar 1986, Davison Co., 5 at rookery (Rogers and McLaird in Seasons 1986c)
22 Mar 1985, Charles Mix Co., 3 on nests (Skadsen in Seasons 1985d)
22 Mar 1986, Charles Mix Co., 6 at nests (Skadsen in Seasons 1986c)
Latest dates:
9 Jul 1972, Pennington Co., young in nests (Black Hills Audubon Society in Seasons 1972c)
10 Jul 1984, Gregory Co., 6 nests (Steffen)
20 Jul 1986, Jackson Co., 14 young (Graupmann in Seasons 1986d)

Fall migration. Late Oct. The average date (2 years) when last seen was 26 Oct in Minnehaha Co. (Larson 1925).

Latest dates:
   27 Nov 1982, Fall River Co. (Rosche in Seasons 1983a)
   28 Nov 1981, Deuel Co. (Harris in Seasons 1982a)
   30 Nov 1978, Rapid City (Baker in Seasons 1979a)
Winter. About a dozen records.
   CBC reports:
   Hot Springs, Lake Andes, Pierre, Rapid City, Sioux Falls, and Yankton.
   Other records:
   4 Jan 1981, Yankton Co. (Hall in Seasons 1981b)
   7 Jan 1987, Brown Co. (Schultze in Seasons 1987b)
   22 -24 Jan 1983, Yankton Co. (Hall in Seasons 1983b)
   31 Jan 1987, Yankton Co. (Hall in Seasons 1987b)

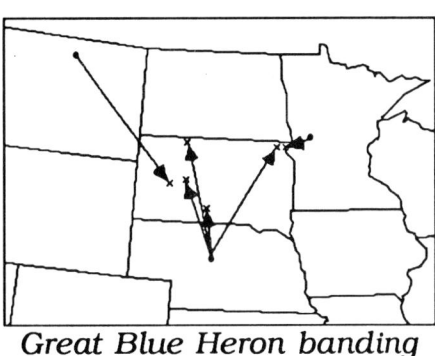

Great Blue Heron banding recoveries

GREAT EGRET *Casmerodius albus* (Linnaeus)

Status. Uncommon to common visitor during spring, summer and fall in E; W River only in Bennett, Fall River, Pennington, Gregory and Tripp counties. The first state record: Rush Lake, 4 Jun 1929 (Kubichek in Over and Thoms 1932). Common but local breeder in NE and at Lake Andes NWR. Usually solitary or in small groups in spring but flocks up to 80 birds in early fall.

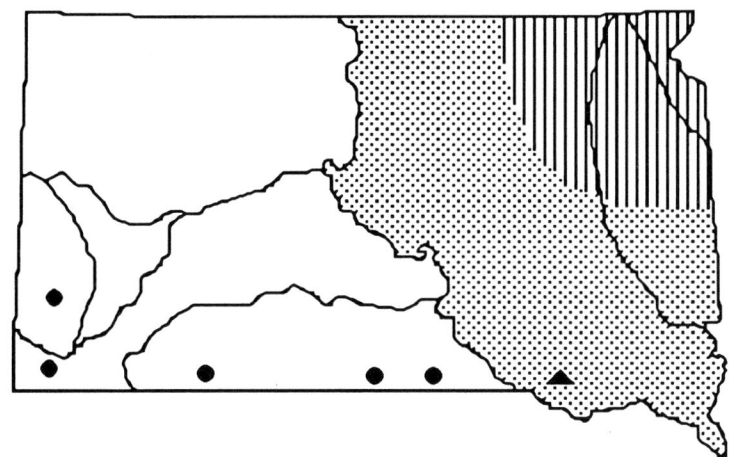

Habitat. Sloughs, marshes, and flooded pastures.
Spring migration. Mid-June – July.
   Earliest dates:
   6 Apr 1973, Deuel Co. (Harris)
   6 Apr 1980, Hutchinson Co. (L. Anderson)
   9 Apr 1985, Codington Co. (Harris in Seasons 1985c)
   9 Apr 1985, Charles Mix Co (Skadsen in Seasons 1985c)

Nesting. Mid-Jun – Jul. First breeding record: 29 Jun 1978, Sand Lake NWR, (Harris and Husmann in Seasons 1978d; Harris 1982a).

Earliest dates:
23 May 1987, Kingsbury Co., 100 in nesting colony (Springer in Seasons 1987c)
16 Jun 1987, Marshall Co., 10+ nests with young (Skadsen et al. in Seasons 1987d)

Latest dates:
10 Jul 1982, Brown Co., Stratford Slough, ca. 200, with dead young under colony (Tallman and Carrels in Seasons 1982d)
14 Jul 1981, Kingsbury Co., nest with fledgling (Harris and Husmann in Seasons 1981d)
1 Aug 1979, Sand Lake NWR, downy young (Colonial Bird Registry)

Fall migration. Sep.

Latest dates:
21 Oct 1985, Kingsbury Co. (Wells in Seasons 1986a)
21 Oct 1986, Day Co. (Skadsen in Seasons 1987a)
25 Oct 1983, Brown Co. (Montgomery in Seasons 1984a)
25 Oct 1986, Kingsbury Co. (Wells in Seasons 1987a)

W River Records:
14 Aug 1980, Tripp Co. (Strom 1981)
21 Aug 1981, Gregory Co. (Steffen 1982a)

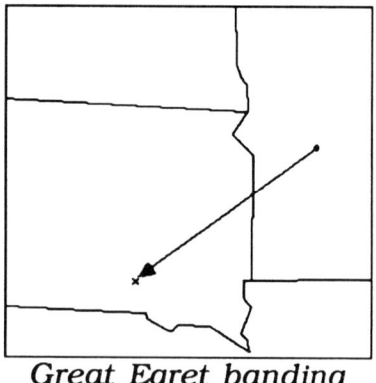
Great Egret banding recoveries

SNOWY EGRET *Egretta thula* (Molina)

Status. Rare to uncommon migrant E River; casual W. First reported 2 May 1940 near Sand Lake NWR (Over and Thoms 1946). Since the early 1980's, has become a locally common breeder in Brown, Kingsbury (Harris et al. in Seasons 1981d; Harris in Seasons 1983d), and Day counties (Husmann et al. in Seasons 1982d, 1983d, 1984d), and at Lake Andes NWR (Jave in Seasons 1985d and 1987d).

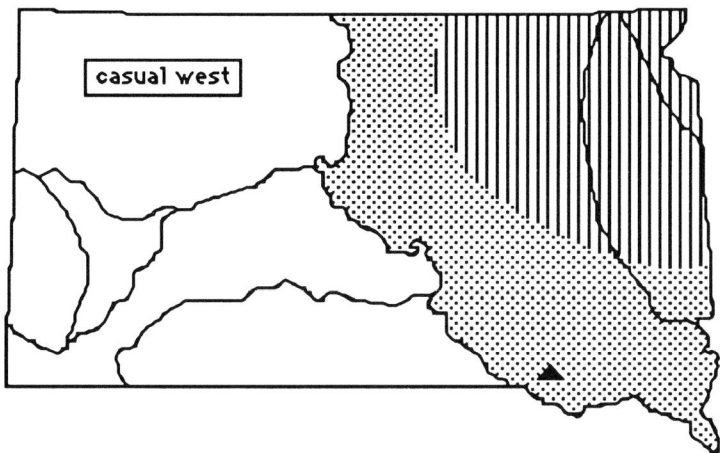

Habitat. Marshes and sloughs.
Spring migration. Late Apr.
  Earliest dates:
    7 Apr 1974, near Madison (Haglund 1974)
    10 Apr 1986, Bon Homme Co. (Kronner in Seasons 1986c)
    10 Apr 1988, Minnehaha Co. (Hoeger in Seasons 1988c)
Nesting. Early Jun – Mid-July. Possibly nesting since 10 Aug 1972 when Fredrickson (1973) found 12 birds near Lake Preston. First confirmed nesting reported at Sand Lake NWR, 27 Jun – 22 Jul 1977 (Waldstein 1977).
  Earliest date:
    9 May 1987, Kingsbury Co., adults on 10 nests (Skadsen in Seasons 1987d)
  Latest dates:
    17 Jul 1983, Kingsbury Co., 30 nests (Harris et al. in Seasons 1983d)
    24 Jul 1980, Brown Co., young in nest (Schultze)
    29 Jul 1987, Lake Andes NWR, 40 nests (Jave in Seasons 1987d)
Fall migration. Mid-Sep.
  Latest dates:
    17 Oct 1967, Lake Andes NWR (refuge files)
    21 Oct 1985, Kingsbury Co. (Wells in Seasons 1986a)
    25 Oct 1986, Kingsbury Co. (Wells in Seasons 1987a)

LITTLE BLUE HERON *Egretta caerulea* (Linnaeus)

Status. Increasingly common visitor E, now with yearly records. Accidental W. First breeding record: 9 Jun 1980, Sand Lake NWR (Schultze in Colonial Bird Registry). Rare breeder at Sand Lake, Lake Andes and Lake Preston.

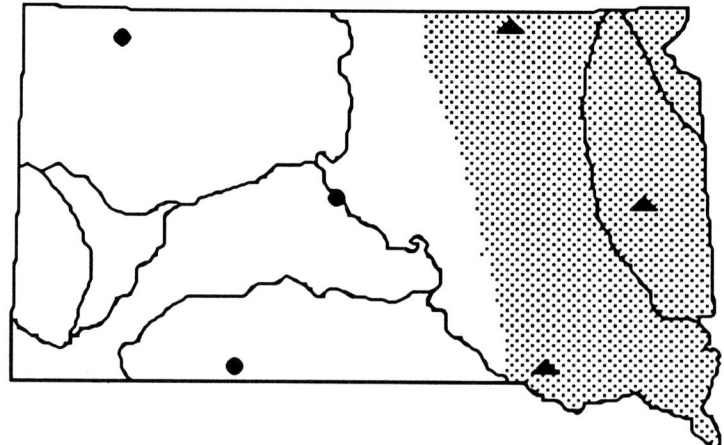

Habitat. Large marshes with dense but open stands of cattails, bulrushes and other emergent vegetation.

Spring migration. Late May.
  Earliest dates:
    17 Apr 1973, Waubay NWR (refuge files)
    1 May 1988, Perkins Co. (Griffiths and Griffiths in Seasons 1988c)
    7 May 1970, Sand Lake NWR (Russell and Eckert)

Nesting. Mid-Jun – Jul.
  Earliest dates:
    9 Jun 1980, Sand Lake NWR, adults incubating eggs (Schultze in Colonial Bird Registry)
    11 Jun 1987, Lake Preston Creek, 1 nest (Springer)
  Latest dates:
    1 Jul 1985, Lake Andes NWR, 3 nests (Jave in Seasons 1985d)
    7 Jul 1986, Lake Andes NWR, 1 nest with feathered young (Jave in Seasons 1986d)
    26 Jul 1986, Lake Preston Creek, nest with young (Skadsen in Seasons 1986d)
  Other records:
    19 May 1975, Farm Island (Backlund)
    2–6 Jul 1975, Bennett Co. (Burgess 1976)

Fall migration. Probably late Sep.
  Latest dates:
    2–6 Oct 1959, Day Co., Blue Dog Lake (Chilson)
    7 Oct 1984, Sanborn Co. (Rogers in Seasons 1985a)
    8 Nov 1988, Day Co. (Getman in Seasons 1989a)

TRICOLORED HERON *Egretta tricolor* (Muller)

Status. Casual visitor and breeder.

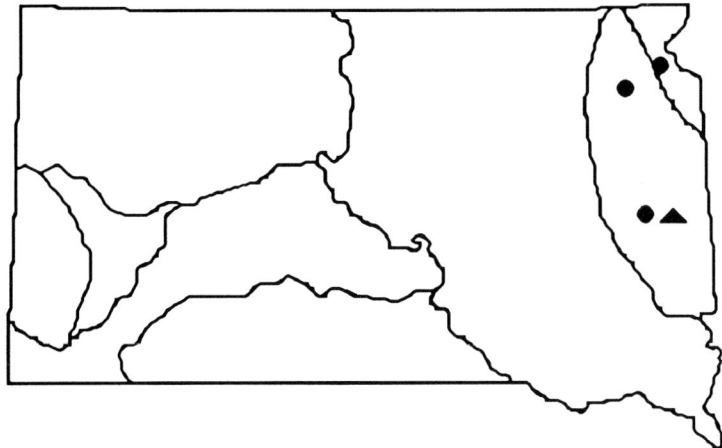

Habitat. Marshes and sloughs.
Records.
  28 Jun 1980, Peever Slough (Harris 1980b)
  7 Jun 1983, Day Co., Rush Lake (Harris in Seasons 1983d)
  14 Jul 1981, Kingsbury Co., Whitewood Lake (Harris and Husmann in Seasons 1981d)
Nesting record:
  13–26 Jul 1986, Kingsbury Co., Lake Preston Creek, 2 nests with young (Skadsen 1986) (First nesting record)

CATTLE EGRET *Bubulcus ibis* (Linnaeus)

Status. Uncommon visitor to E during spring, summer and fall; only 4 W River records (Bennett, Fall River, and Jackson counties). Fairly common to abundant breeder in colonies in Brown, Faulk, Kingsbury, Codington, Charles Mix, and Day counties. First state record: 17 Jul 1961, Sand Lake NWR (Schoonover 1962).

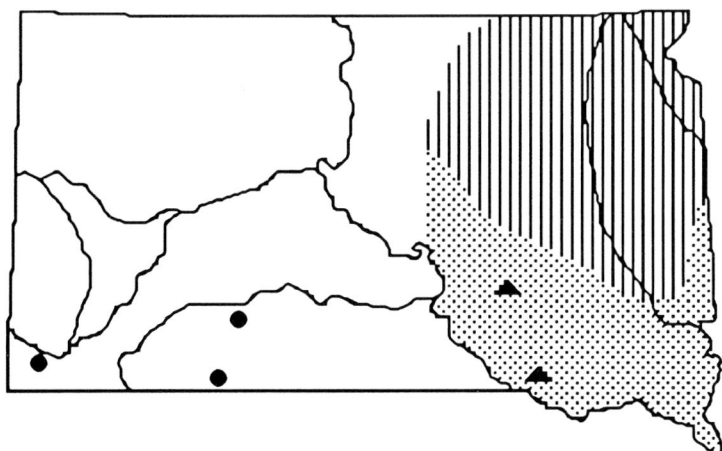

Habitat. Pastures and wetland edges; breeds in large wetlands with dense but open areas of cattails and bulrushes.

22 BITTERNS AND HERONS

Spring migration. Early May.
Earliest dates:
16 Apr 1989, Day Co. (Prisbe in Seasons 1989c)
17 Apr 1982, Brookings Co. (Holden in Seasons 1982c)
18 Apr 1985, McCook Co., 3 (Anderson in Seasons 1985c)
Nesting. Early Jun – mid-July. First record: 27 Jun – 22 Jul 1977, Sand Lake NWR (Waldstein 1977), although sightings suggest the species may have bred as early as 1969. Nesting colonies have since been found in Faulk Co., N Scatterwood Lake by Linehan (Harris and Husmann in Seasons 1978d), at various lakes in Kingsbury Co. (Harris and Husmann in Seasons 1981d, Harris et al. in Seasons 1982d, Harris et al. in Seasons 1983d, Wells and Wells 1983), in Day Co. at Rush Lake (Husmann in Seasons 1983d, Harris and Skadsen in Seasons 1984d), and at Lake Andes NWR (Jave 1984). Probably also nested at Goose Lake and Grass Lake in Codington Co., at Milwaukee Slough in Lake Co., White Lake in Aurora Co., and elsewhere. Colonies occasionally number in the hundreds.
Earliest date:
11 Jun 1987, Kingsbury Co., 8 nests (Springer)
Latest date:
26 Jul 1986, Kingsbury Co., fledged young (Skadsen in Seasons 1986a)
Fall migration. Early Oct.
Latest dates:
29 Oct 1982, Day Co. (Smith and Waddel in Seasons 1983a)
31 Oct 1975, Spink Co. (Lind 1976)
5 Nov 1977, Angostura Reservoir (Rosche 1982)

GREEN-BACKED HERON *Butorides striatus* (Linnaeus)

Status. Uncommon to fairly common breeder E River and probably Gregory Co. Scattered W River records in Harding, Pennington, Custer, Fall River, and Bennett counties.

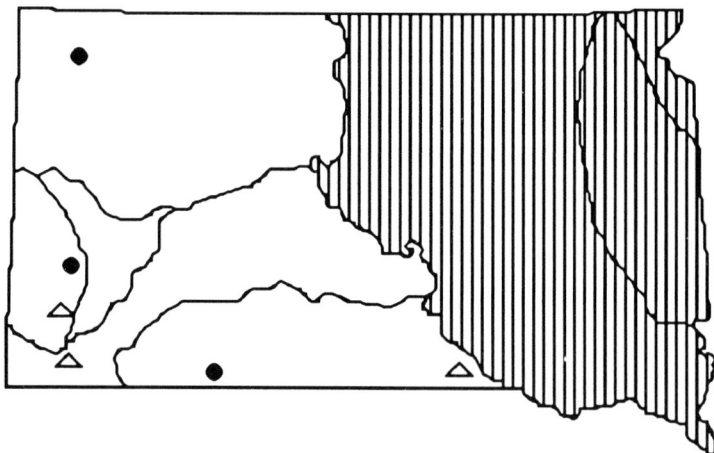

Habitat. Creeks, rivers and lakes with heavy willow or other brushy cover; slough edges.

Spring migration. Mid May.
  Earliest dates:
    15 Apr 1987, Day Co. (Russell in Seasons 1987c)
    16 Apr 1976, Roberts Co. (Harris)
    18 Apr 1982, Hutchinson Co. (Anderson in Seasons 1982c)
Nesting. Mid-May – Jun.
  Earliest dates:
    8 May 1973, Oakwood Lakes, nest later abandoned (Harris)
    30 May 1984, Codington Co., nest with eggs (Harris and Gilman in Seasons 1984d)
  Latest dates:
    7 Jul 1980, Brookings Co., nest with 5 downy young (McPhillips 1981)
    11 Aug 1980, Gregory Co., adults and immatures (Steffen 1981c)
Fall migration. Late Sep.
  Latest dates:
    19 Oct 1969, Miner Co. (Harris)
    26 Oct 1971, Deuel Co. (Harris)

BLACK-CROWNED NIGHT-HERON *Nycticorax nycticorax* (Linnaeus)

Status. Fairly common migrant E River; rare W. Abundant breeding species in many E colonies; W River breeding known only at Lacreek NWR (Lohoefener and Ely 1978). Rarely winters.

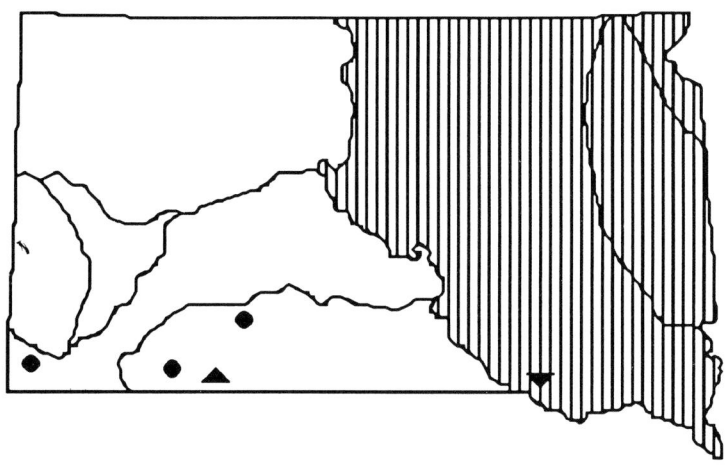

Habitat. Rivers, streams, lakes and potholes for feeding. Breeds in trees and in large cattail and bulrush marshes; wetland colonies are more stable than those in trees (Adolphson).

Spring migration. Mid-Apr.
  Earliest dates:
    26 Mar 1988, Faulk Co. (Williams in Seasons 1988c)
    31 Mar 1981, Deuel Co. (Stava in Seasons 1981c)
    4 Apr 1946, Roberts Co. (Harris)
    4 Apr 1956, Minnehaha Co. (Chapman and Krause)
    4 Apr 1982, Deuel Co. (Harris)

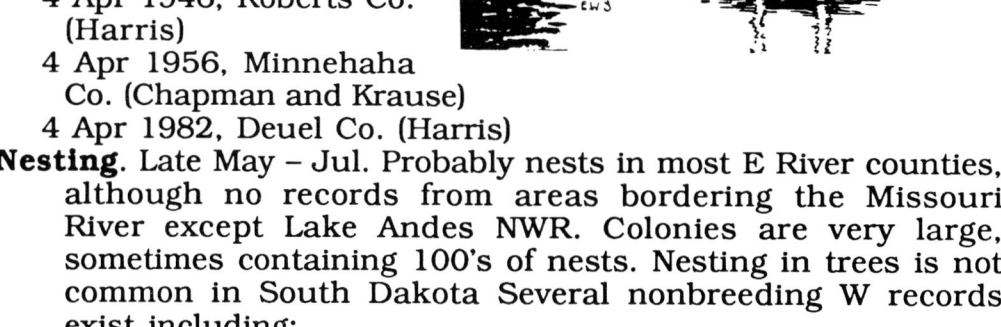

Nesting. Late May – Jul. Probably nests in most E River counties, although no records from areas bordering the Missouri River except Lake Andes NWR. Colonies are very large, sometimes containing 100's of nests. Nesting in trees is not common in South Dakota Several nonbreeding W records exist including:
  2 May 1985, Fall River Co. (Peterson in Seasons 1985c)
  23 May 1985, Shannon Co. (Springer)
  30 Oct 1982, Jackson Co. (Graupmann in Seasons 1983a).

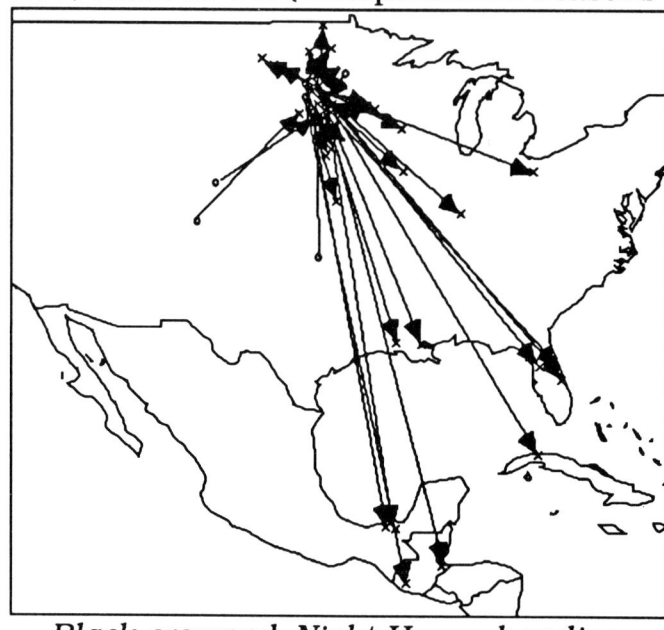

Black-crowned Night-Heron banding recoveries

Earliest dates:
  16 May 1981, Piyas Lake, Marshall Co., nest on ground with 2 eggs and 2 young (Harris and Husmann in Seasons 1981d)
  22 May 1924, Aurora Co., nests (Lee in Whitney 1955)
Latest dates:
  14 Jul 1977, Lacreek NWR, 1 egg and 1 young (Lohoefener and Ely 1978)
  14 Jul 1978, Sand Lake NWR, nesting colony of 2000 (Waldstein in Seasons 1978d)
  27 Jul 1983, Rush Lake, young in nests (Husmann in Colonial Bird Registry)
Fall migration. Mid-Oct.
Latest dates:
  13 Nov 1984, Sand Lake NWR (Waldstein in Seasons 1985a)
  20 Nov 1910, Minnehaha Co. (Larson 1925)
  7 Dec 1985, Turner Co. (Anderson in Seasons 1986b)
Winter.
Record:
  5–19 Jan 1963, Lake Andes NWR (refuge files)

YELLOW-CROWNED NIGHT-HERON *Nyctanassa violacea* (Linnaeus)

Status. Rare visitor during spring, summer and fall, primarily in E counties but several records W. Most records are in May, Jun, and Jul.

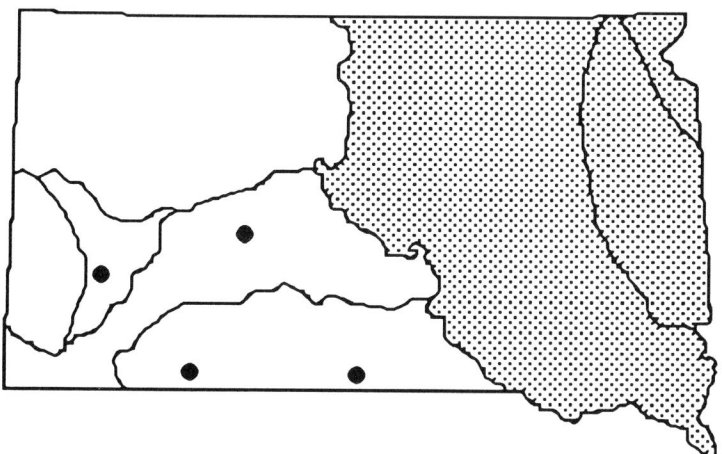

Habitat. Rivers, streams, lakes and marshes.
Spring migration. Mid-May.
  Earliest dates:
    4 Apr 1989, Brown Co. (Montgomery and Montgomery)
    6 Apr 1963, Beadle Co. (Johnson 1963a)
    13 Apr 1958, Union Co. (Felton and Nicholson)
Summer records. At least 10 observations during the breeding season may imply nesting but birds have been solitary and nesting has not been confirmed.

Fall migration. Sep.

Latest dates:
13 Sep 1978, Sand Lake NWR (Waldstein et al. in Seasons 1979a)
13 Sep 1986, Brown Co. (Tallman in Seasons 1987a)
Oct 1955, Beadle Co., dead (Kouf in Harris 1968d)
12-13 Nov 1984, Yankton Co., photographed (Kronner in Seasons 1985b)

THRESKIORNITHIDAE: Ibises

WHITE IBIS *Eudocimus albus* (Linnaeus)

Status. Accidental.
Records:
May 1879, Clay Co., 12 miles N of Missouri River, 1 of 2 shot (Agersborg 1885)
Summer 1890, Clay Co., 1 seen often (Agersborg in Over and Thoms 1946)
31 Jul 1986, Bennett Co. (Brashears and Lanier)

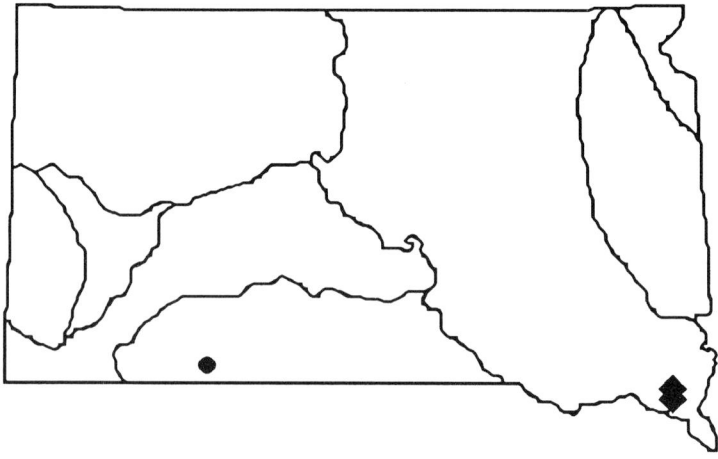

WHITE-FACED IBIS *Plegadis chihi* (Vieillot)

Status. Rare to uncommon visitor E River; very rare W (records only from Pennington, Bennett, Shannon, and Fall River counties). Breeding locally in Kingsbury, Codington, Day, and Brown counties; unconfirmed breeder at Lake Andes NWR and several other sites. First state record: 7 Jun 1962, Sand Lake NWR (Schoonover 1962).

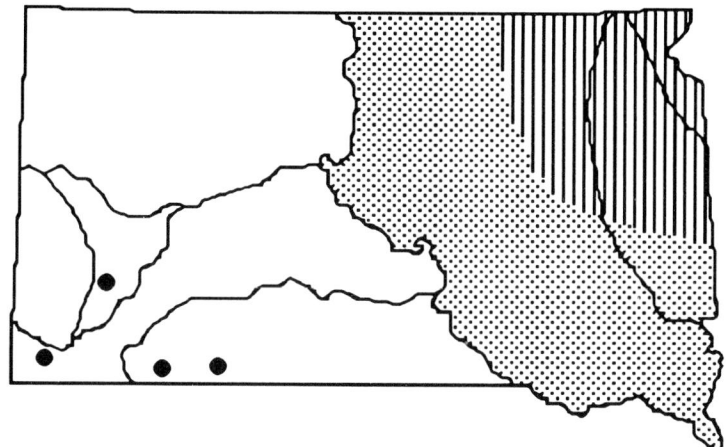

Habitat. Often in shallow, open marshes but nests in deeper marshes among cattails and bulrushes.

Spring migration. Early May.

Earliest dates:
  16 Apr 1975, Clay Co. (Siljenberg 1975)
  20 Apr 1970, Lake Co., 7 (Buckman in Seasons 1984c)
  22 Apr 1975, Sand Lake NWR (Fuller 1976)

Nesting. Jun – Jul. Nesting first reported at Sand Lake NWR, 28 Jun 1978, and subsequently in 1979 (2 nests, 10 adults), in 1981, 1983 (2 nests), and 1984 (Waldstein in Seasons 1978d, 1983d, 1984d). Since 1984, this species has nested at Whitewood Lake, Lake Preston, and, after the Preston colony flooded in 1984, possibly Lake Thompson (Harris 1983, Harris in Seasons 1982d, Wells and Wells 1983, Harris in Seasons 1984d)

Earliest dates:
  4 Jun 1979, Sand Lake NWR, 2 nests (Waldstein in Seasons 1979d)
  15 Jun 1987, Day Co., 9 nests with eggs (Skadsen in Seasons 1987d)

Latest dates:
  11 Jul 1986, Goose Lake, 4 nests with eggs (Harris et al. in Seasons 1986d)
  14 Jul 1981, Kingsbury Co., 2 nests with eggs (Harris and Husmann in Seasons 1981d)
  1 Aug 1979, Sand Lake NWR, nests with young (Kessler in Colonial Bird Registry)

Fall migration. Probably late Sep but few records.

Latest dates:
  10 Oct 1975, Sand Lake NWR (Fuller 1976)
  14–15 Oct 1975, Minnehaha Co. (Rogge and Rogge 1976)
  9 Nov 1986, Day Co. (Koerner in Seasons 1987a)

28 SWANS, GEESE, AND DUCKS

CICONIDAE: Storks

WOOD STORK *Mycteria americana* Linnaeus
Status. Accidental.
Only Record:
    17 Aug 1964 and several days prior, Hanson Co., 14 miles NE of Mitchell, photographed (Law 1964)

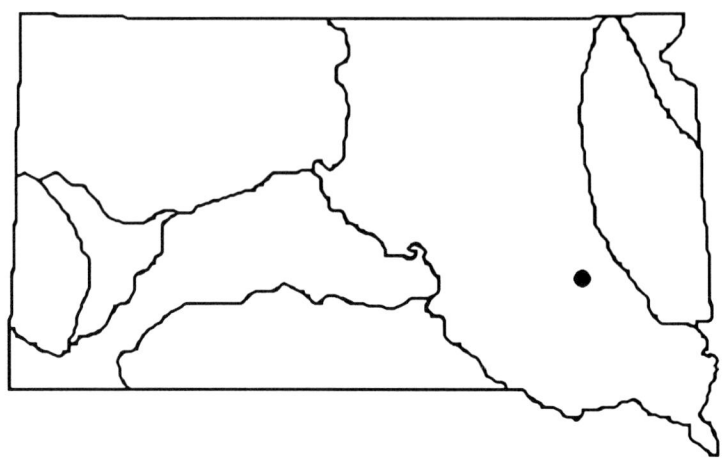

ANATIDAE: Swans, Geese, and Ducks

FULVOUS WHISTLING-DUCK *Dendrocygna bicolor* (Vieillot)
Status. Accidental visitor.
Records:
    Late Oct 1948, 3 miles SE of Salem, specimen (Bechtold in Hills 1949)
    14 Jun 1967, Miner Co., Twin Lakes (Harris 1968e)

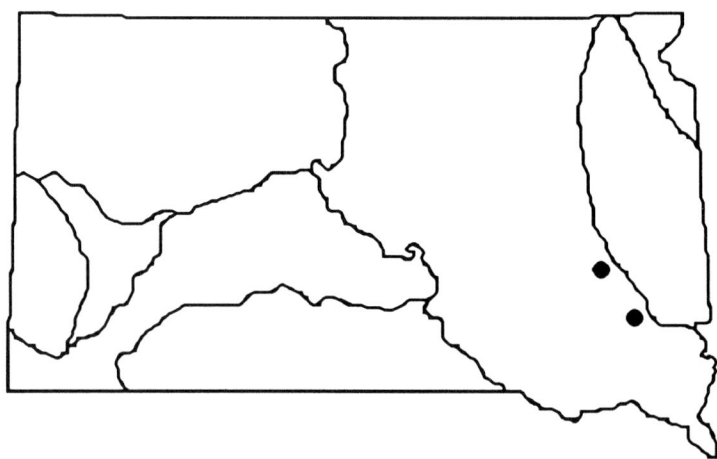

TUNDRA SWAN *Cygnus columbianus* (Ord)

Status. Fairly common migrant E, especially along Minnesota border; common to abundant migrant in NE lake country. Rare W River.

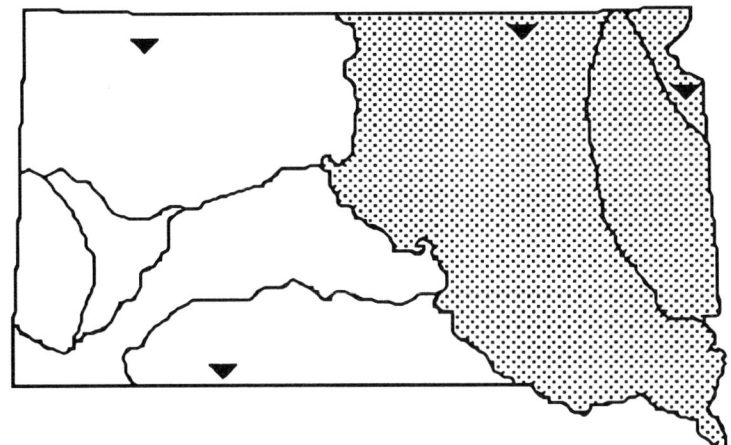

Habitat. Larger lakes and wetlands.

Spring migration. First half of Apr. An estimated 2500 birds stopped at Bullhead Lake for most of the week of 10 Apr 1938 (*Wilmot Enterprise*, 14 Apr 1938). Most flocks are small (fewer than 30), but Harris found concentrations of 165 – 400 in Roberts and Deuel counties on 4 Apr 1982.

Earliest dates:
13 Mar 1979, Yankton Co. (Hall in Seasons 1979c)
14 Mar 1987, Yankton Co. (Hall in Seasons 1987c)
15 Mar 1985, Hutchinson Co. (Skadsen in Seasons 1985c)

Latest Dates:
3 May 1969, Grant Co. 8 birds (Harris)
Mid-May 1905, Sanborn Co. (Visher 1913a); possibly Trumpeter Swans, but Visher was a careful observer.

Fall migration. Late Oct. Concentrations often number several hundred birds; peak numbers at Sand Lake and Waubay NWR have been 3500 to 4500. Birds stay in the NE into late Nov and early Dec if open water is available.

Earliest dates:
18 Sep 1985, McPherson Co. (Tallman in Seasons 1986a)
20 Sep 1985, Waubay NWR (Bryant in Seasons 1986a)
29 Sep 1965, Sand Lake NWR (refuge files)

Winter.
CBC report:
Sand Lake NWR.

Other records:
16 Dec 1970, 2 (1 crippled) captured and moved from Perkins Co., Sorum Dam, to Canyon Lake near Rapid City (GFP)
30 Dec 1977, Lacreek NWR (refuge files)
Late Dec 1975, 1976 (until 15 Feb 1977), and 1979 (until 1 Feb 1980), S end of Big Stone Lake (Harris)

30 SWANS, GEESE, AND DUCKS

TRUMPETER SWAN *Cygnus buccinator* Richardson

Status. Introduced at Lacreek NWR in 1960–1963 from cygnets transferred from Red Rocks Lakes NWR, Montana. The refuge population in Fall 1987 was 268 swans (Brashears). In recent years breeding birds have spread to Bennett, Shannon, Jackson, Pennington, Meade, Ziebach, Mellette, Todd, and Harding counties. Most winter at Lacreek. Although records are lacking, the Trumpeter Swan undoubtedly nested in South Dakota during the last century. Over and Thoms (1946) state that it "nested in South Dakota in the eighties," but give no substantiating evidence. Definite records are available in the late 1800's for Iowa, Nebraska, Minnesota, and North Dakota (Banko 1960).

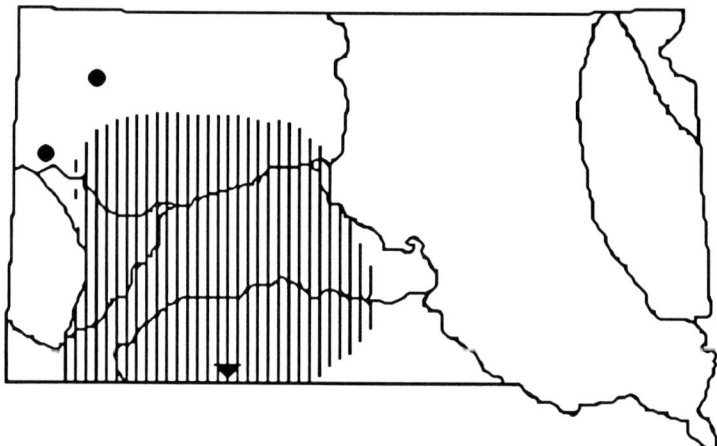

Habitat. Shallow lakes and open marshes (Banko 1960).
Nesting. Mid-Apr – Jul. No nests established by Lacreek birds until 1963, when 2 breeding pairs hatched 14 eggs and fledged 2 cygnets. At Lacreek NWR from 1976–1987 there was an average of 6 pairs and 5 broods. In 1987, 86 cygnets were counted on Lacreek NWR after the breeding season (Brashears).
Earliest dates:
  Mid-Apr 1976, Lacreek NWR, egg laying began (Leach 1977)
  30 Apr 1987, Meade Co., nesting (E. Miller)
Latest dates:
  12 Jun 1987, Lacreek NWR, hatching (Brashears)
  Early Aug 1976, Lacreek NWR, fledging (Leach 1977)
  9 Sep [year], Lacreek NWR, fledging (Brashears)
Migration. Local migration from peripheral areas to Lacreek NWR. On 24 Nov 1983, 2 Trumpeter Swans were seen at Orman Dam, Butte Co. (Bjerke 1984).
Winter. 1987/88 winter population at Lacreek NWR was 268 on 4 Jan and 192 on 20 Jan, indicating that winter migration may be occurring (Brashears).

[**MUTE SWAN** *Cygnus olor* (Gmelin)]

Status. Hypothetical. A free flying bird observed 13–14 Jul 1988 at Long Lake, Lake Co. (Buckman et al. in Seasons 1988d) may have escaped from captivity.

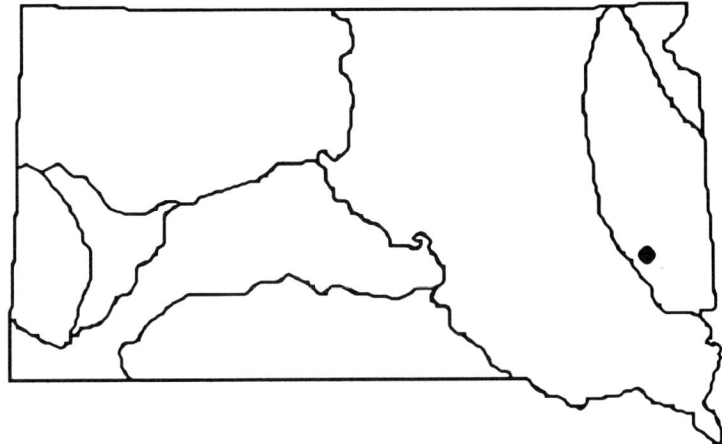

GREATER WHITE-FRONTED GOOSE *Anser albifrons* (Scopoli)

Status. Common to abundant migrant in E half, particularly in the spring; main flight is between Aberdeen and the Missouri River, less common W.

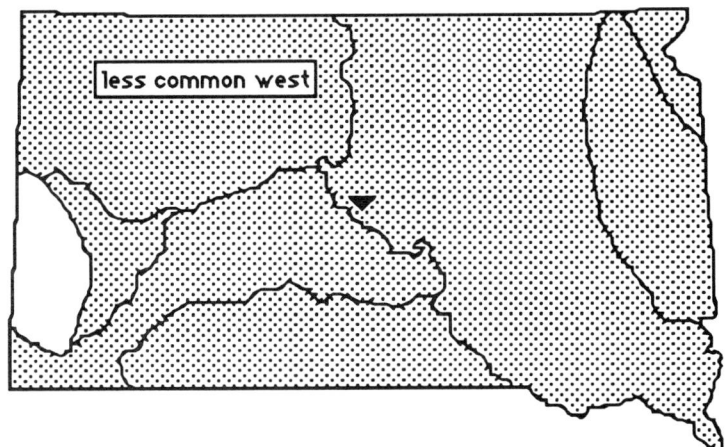

Habitat. Larger wetlands with emergent vegetation, often feeding in surrounding fields.

Spring migration. Third week of Mar at Lake Andes and Sand Lake NWR. Unusual concentration: 18 Mar 1964, Lake Andes NWR, 5,500 (refuge files).

Earliest dates:
  1 Mar 1983, Gregory Co. (Lengkeek in Seasons 1983c)
  2 Mar 1986, Charles Mix Co. (Skadsen and Skadsen in Seasons 1986c)
  3 Mar 1974, Lacreek NWR (Burgess 1976)

Latest dates:
  13 May 1990, Day Co. (Harris in Seasons 1990c)
  14 May 1981, Codington Co. (Harris in Seasons 1981c)
  18 May 1989, Hamlin Co. (Harris in Seasons 1989c)
Summer dates:
  14 Jun 1962, Pelican Lake (Moriarty 1962c)
  30 Jun 1975, Harding Co. (Grant)
  6 Jul 1965, Waubay Lake, molting (Springer)
  20 Jul 1965, near Crandall (Springer)
Fall migration. Oct. Unusual concentration: 23 Oct 1975, Lyman Co., 2000 (Hill).
  Earliest dates:
  28 Aug 1986, Yankton Co. (Kronner in Seasons 1987a)
  15 Sep 1938, Lacreek NWR (refuge files)
  15 Sep 1960, Sand Lake NWR (Podoll 1963)
  Latest dates:
  4 Nov 1984, Roberts Co. (Harris in Seasons 1985a)
  6 Nov 1982, Jackson Co. (Graupmann in Seasons 1983a)
  1 Dec 1968, Lyman Co. near Chamberlain (Harris)
Winter. Individuals rarely remain into early winter.
  CBC report:
  Pierre.

SNOW GOOSE *Chen caerulescens* (Linnaeus)

Status. Common to abundant migrant in E River counties. Uncommon elsewhere, but major flyway is evidently shifting W; more birds observed each year along the Missouri River where formerly considered rare. Common spring and rare fall migrant in SW (Rosche 1982). The spring migration is a spectacular sight in E South Dakota. Birds concentrate in fall in Lake, Kingsbury, Day and Brown counties. Accidental nester.

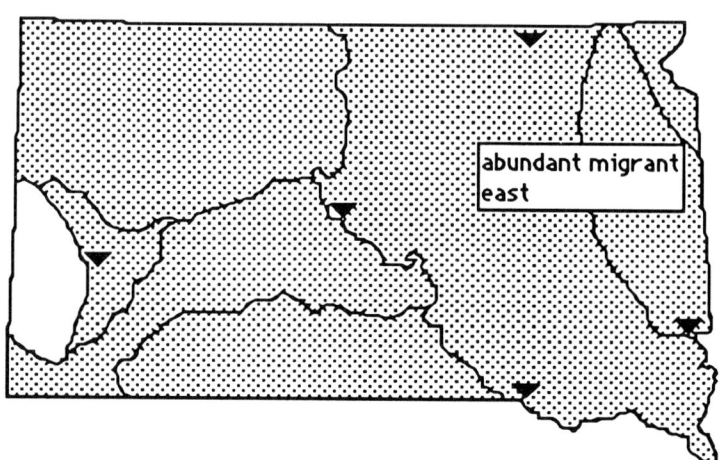

Habitat. Large wetlands with emergent vegetation; feed in grain stubble and newly-planted fields.
Spring migration. Late Mar and early Apr. Peak concentrations: 5 Apr 1982, Sand Lake NWR, 240,000 (Waldstein in Seasons

1982c); 7 Apr 1978, Turner Co., 100,000 (Spomer); 12 Apr 1964, Lake Preston, 180,000 (ground count) (Springer);

Earliest dates:
14 Feb 1981, Clay Co. (Hoover in Seasons 1981b)
14 Feb 1984, McCook Co. (Anderson in Seasons 1984b)
15 Feb 1984 Minnehaha Co. (Anderson in Seasons 1984c)

Latest Dates:
23 May 1984, Waubay NWR (Rabenberg in Seasons 1984c)
25 May 1981, Shannon Co. (Mitten)
28 May 1985, Union Co. (Springer in Seasons 1985c)
28 May 1990, Lake Co. (Buckman in Seasons 1990c)

Summer. Although this species normally breeds in the arctic, stragglers have been seen in summer. On 19 May 1976, a captive crippled bird nested with an apparently healthy mate at Sand Lake NWR and produced 3 young (Bair).

Fall migration. Third week of Oct. Peak concentrations: 30 October 1988, Sand Lake NWR, 220,000 (Schultze in Seasons 1989a); 2 Dec 1980, Deuel Co., 200 (Stone). An unusual late concentration: 9 Nov 1986, Gregory Co, 50,000 (Steffen in Seasons 1986c).

Earliest dates:
3 Sep 1911, Sioux Falls (Larson 1925)
15 Sep 1982, Deuel Co. (Kreger)
18 Sep 1979, Deuel Co. (Harris)

Winter. Very rarely winter. Most early winter records are of fall stragglers.

CBC reports:
Aberdeen, Lake Andes, Pierre, Rapid City, and Sioux Falls.

Other records:
1982–83, Sand Lake NWR, 30 wintered (refuge files)
3 Feb 1987, Oahe Dam (Tallman in Seasons 1987b)

ROSS' GOOSE *Chen rossii* (Cassin)

Status. Uncommon but regular migrant during fall migration in E, most records from Sand Lake NWR; fewer spring records, and casual winter. Casual migrant W. Apparently becoming more common in recent years; most observations are since 1946.

34 SWANS, GEESE, AND DUCKS

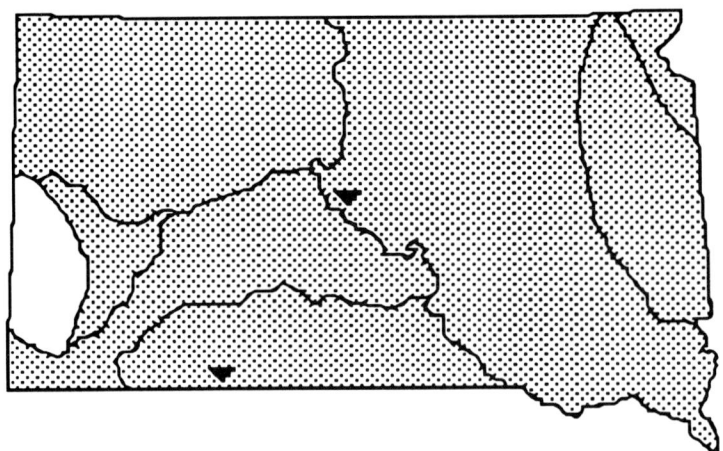

Habitat. Lakes; feeds in stubble fields.

Spring migration. Late Mar. Peak numbers: 30 Mar 1984, Turner Co., 5 with many Snow Geese; 31 Mar 1984, Hutchinson Co., 6 (also 1 collected on 27 Mar 1984 and 1 reported by GFP several days later in Kingsbury Co.) (Anderson 1984).

Earliest dates:
12 Mar 1985, Turner Co. (Anderson in Seasons 1985c)
16 Mar 1974, Pierre, Capitol Lake (Rose)
17 Mar 1986, Turner Co. (Anderson in Seasons 1986c)

Latest dates:
13 Apr 1986, Pennington Co. (Baker 1987)
16 Apr 1971, Lacreek NWR (Hall 1971)
20 Apr 1990, Pennington Co. (Whitney in Seasons 1990c)

Fall migration. Oct. Totals at Sand Lake NWR from hunter kills and refuge surveys in fall: 6 (1964), 12 (1966), 9 (1967) (GFP). A hybrid Snow-Ross' Goose was found dead on 2 Nov 1981 in Deuel Co. (Harris in Seasons 1982a).

Earliest dates:
25 Sep 1973, Lacreek NWR (Burgess in Fjetland 1973)
30 Sep 1979, Sand Lake NWR (refuge files)
1 Oct 1958, Sand Lake NWR (refuge files)

Latest dates:
31 Oct 1967, Sand Lake NWR (refuge files)
1 Nov 1966, Sand Lake NWR (refuge files)

Winter.
Records:
20 Dec 1981–27 Feb 1982, Pierre (Coonrod et al.)
Dec 1977, Lacreek NWR (Burgess)
6 Jan 1974, Lacreek NWR (refuge files)
30 Jan 1987, Oahe Dam (Harris in Seasons 1987b)

BRANT *Branta bernicla* (Linnaeus)

Status. Casual migrant. Old reports of "brant" often refer to Snow Geese, or Hutchin's Canada Geese, as market hunters called any small goose a "brant." All but 1 record are of the Black Brant subspecies. Most observations are from Sand Lake NWR, where first confirmed state record was a bird killed 31 Oct 1956 (banded Jul 1954 in Alaska) (GFP).

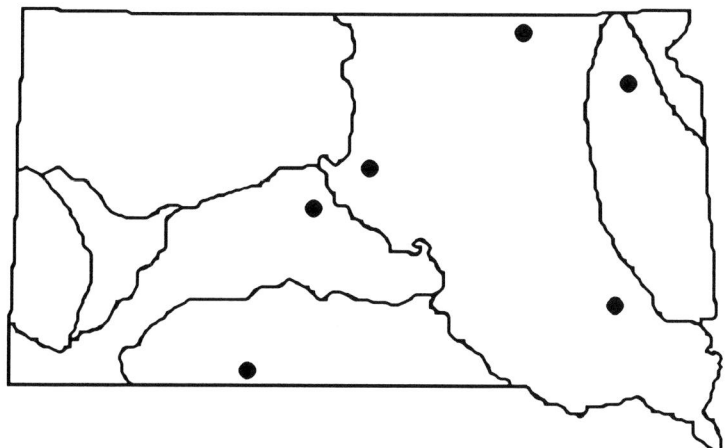

Spring migration. Only 4 records; first 3 photographed.
Records:
3 Feb 1984 and 25 Mar–1 Apr 1984, Stanley Co. (Riis in Seasons 1984d)
12 Apr 1983, Sand Lake NWR (Waldstein in Seasons 1983c)
19–23 Apr 1971, Lacreek NWR (Hall 1971)
14 Jun 1962, Bitter Lake (Moriarity 1962c)

Fall migration. 5 records. Early winter birds are probably fall stragglers.
Earliest dates:
9 Oct 1967, Sand Lake NWR (Prevett)
27 Oct 1965, Sand Lake NWR, banded "American Brant" (Schoonover)
4 Nov 1972, Sully Co. (Summerside)
Latest date:
12 Dec 1958, near Emery, Hanson Co., 1 (banded 22 Jul 1954 in Yukon Delta, Alaska) (GFP)

CANADA GOOSE *Branta canadensis* (Linnaeus)

Status. Abundant migrant E; common W. Several races, which show a great range in size, occur during migration. The Giant Canada Goose (*B. c. maxima*), the large breeding subspecies, is common in NE (including McPherson Co.); uncommon elsewhere E and in W where introduced by GFP. Historically, geese were reported breeding in Corson Co. (Hoffman 1877), Day Co. (Drewien and Johnson 1968), Deuel Co. (W. Rose), possibly Marshall Co. (McChesney 1879), and sparingly in the S (Agersborg 1885, Cooke

1906). By the early 1900's, settlers caused the near extinction of the Giant Canada Goose. The last known nesting then was in 1910 at Bitter Lake (Drewien and Johnson 1968). Offspring from captive-reared birds were released on the Waubay NWR from 1937-1945, and successful nesting first occurred in 1943, continuing in small numbers through the early 1960's. In 1962, GFP began to restore the Giant Canada to its former range in South Dakota. Through this program, 9 W River counties received 3450 geese (1967-1980) and 5704 geese were released in 12 E River counties (1977-1987). By 1987 the population was 10,000 birds W River and 12,500 E River (Mammenga). The extreme SE has little suitable habitat for breeding geese, but various landowners have introduced flocks on their property.

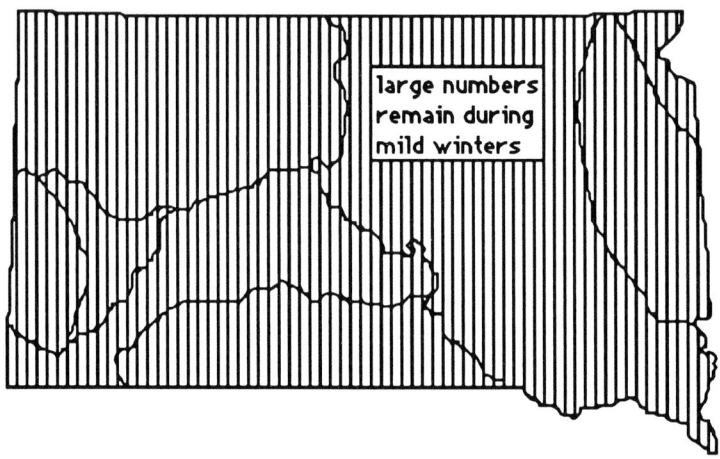

Habitat. Larger wetlands, shallow lakes with emergent vegetation, and large stockponds and dugouts for nesting; concentrations along the Missouri River use mud flats and sand bars for loafing and roosting sites; regularly feed in fields. The species winters in areas with open water and food.

Spring migration. Early Mar for Giant Canadas, last week of Mar for others. Peak concentrations: 2 Mar 1983, Sand Lake NWR, 5000 (refuge files); 2 Apr 1978, Sand Lake NWR, 7500 (Seasons 1978c). Earliest spring dates are reported for Feb but may represent wintering birds.

Nesting. Late Mar – late May.
 Earliest dates:
  4 Apr 1989, Day Co., 8 eggs (Ray)
  13 Apr 1988, Codington Co., 6 eggs (Ray)

Fall migration. Early Oct, but breeding populations make most dates difficult to interpret. Kuck reports that migrants arrive in the NE in late Sep. Peak concentrations: 40,000, Sand Lake NWR; Missouri River, 250,000; NE, 20,000 (GFP).

Winter. Large numbers remain during mild winters. In 1984-85, 3000 wintered at Shadehill Reservoir in Perkins Co. and 50,000 in the Pierre area (GFP), in 1982-83, 350 were at

Sand Lake NWR and 6000 remained at the Big Stone Power Plant in Grant Co. (D. Skadsen).

WOOD DUCK *Aix sponsa* (Linnaeus)

Status. Common migrant and summer resident E, especially along the James and Big Sioux rivers. Uncommon W, sporadic in Black Hills. Has increased since 1930's in all parts of the state.

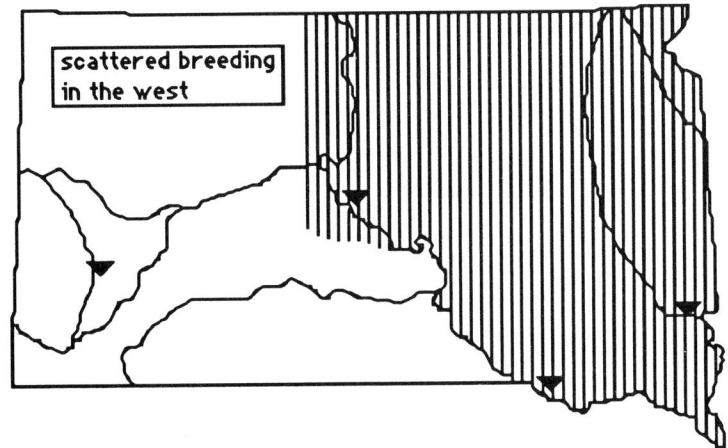

scattered breeding in the west

Habitat. Wooded lakes, ponds, rivers and streams that provide large trees for nesting cavities.

Spring migration. First 2 weeks of Apr. Unusual concentration: 7 Apr 1963, Roberts Co., flocks of up to 40 (Dusing).
Earliest dates:
   2 Mar 1988, Yankton Co. (Hall in Seasons 1988c)
   7 Mar 1981, Davison Co. (McLaird in Seasons 1981c)
   7 Mar 1985, Charles Mix Co. (Kronner in Seasons 1985c)
   9 Mar 1987, Sanborn Co. (Rogers in Seasons 1987c)

Nesting. Mid-Apr – Jun. June 1980, 15 nests in 28 boxes along Big Sioux River, Brookings Co. (SDSU). 13 Jul 1974, Deuel Co., at least 15 broods on large wetland (Harris).
Earliest dates:
   19 Apr 1964, Brown-Spink Co. line, nest with 9 eggs (Rose)
   8 May 1971, Roberts Co., nest with 8 eggs (M. Harris)
   19 May 1987, Yankton Co., female with 2 Class I young (Springer)
Latest dates:
   1 Aug 1972, Minnehaha Co., 3 young not able to fly (Krause and Blankespoor)
   1 Aug 1982, Gregory Co., 5 broods (Steffen in Seasons 1983a)
   9 Aug 1964, Brookings Co., females with 2 Class I young (Springer)

Fall migration. First half of Oct. Unusual concentrations: 1 Oct 1978, Deuel Co., 50 (Kreger); 21 Sep 1979, Deuel Co., 58 (Harris in Seasons 1980a).

38 SWANS, GEESE, AND DUCKS

Latest dates:
16 Nov 1975, Waubay NWR (refuge files)
16 Nov 1985, Turner Co. (Anderson in Seasons 1986a)
23 Nov 1987, Yankton Co. (Hall in Seasons 1988a)

Winter. Sporadic winter observations in Rapid City; some, but not all, released stock (Whitney).

CBC reports:
Charles Mix, Hughes, Minnehaha, and Pennington counties.

GREEN-WINGED TEAL *Anas crecca* Linnaeus

Status. Locally common migrant; rare to uncommon local breeding species in widely separated areas, primarily in NE, but also in Jones, Harding, and Jackson counties. Pairs and apparently unmated males occur elsewhere during summer. Rated a rare breeder in Sanborn County by Visher (1913a).. Restricted winter distribution.

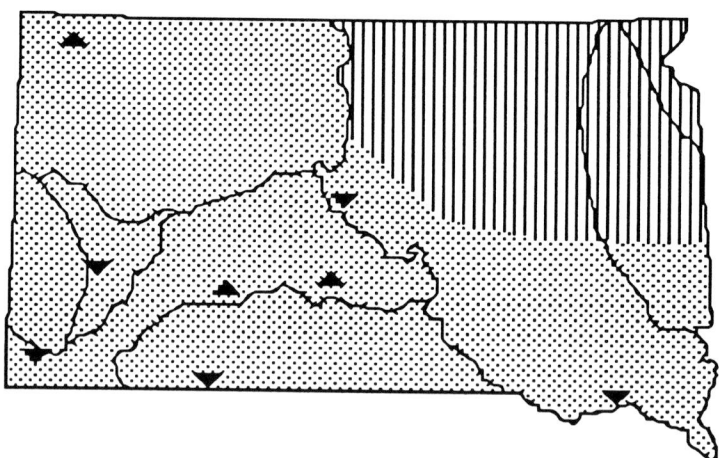

Habitat. Marshes, ponds, and lakes.
Spring migration. Mid-Mar.
Earliest dates:
22 Feb 1982, Yankton Co. (Hall in Seasons 1983b)
27 Feb 1986, Yankton Co. (Anderson in Seasons 1986b)
28 Feb 1978, Pierre (Hill in Seasons 1978b)
28 Feb 1978, Yankton (Hall in Seasons 1978b)

Nesting. Late May and early Jun.
Earliest dates:
4 May 1969, Edmunds Co., nest (Duebbert)
6 May 1968, Edmunds Co., nest (Duebbert)
14 May 1968, Edmunds Co., nest with 8 eggs (Duebbert)

Latest Dates:
13 Jul 1978, Harding Co., brood of Class I young (Springer)
First week Aug 1972, Jackson Co., broods (K. Evans and Kerbs)

Fall migration. Mid Oct. Peak concentrations: 300 on 17 Oct 1969 and 150, 3 Nov 1969, Sanborn Co. (Harris); 6 Oct 1974, Deuel Co., 90 (Harris); 8 Sep 1988, Day Co., 500 (Springer in Seasons 1989a).

Latest dates:
   20 Nov 1983, Pennington Co. (Paulson in Seasons 1984a)
   21 Nov 1967, Davison Co. (Harris)
   23 Nov 1977, Yankton Co. (Hall in Seasons 1978a)
Winter. Winters in small numbers at Canyon Lake in Rapid City (Whitney), and at Hot Springs (Rosche 1982), rare elsewhere with open water. 4 records for Lacreek NWR (1966, 1972, 1976, and 1977-78) (refuge files).
   CBC reports:
      Hot Springs, Lacreek NWR, Pierre, and Rapid City.
   Other records:
      11 Jan 1964, Gavin's Point (Springer)
      31 Jan 1982, Pierre (Coonrod in Seasons 1982b)

AMERICAN BLACK DUCK *Anas rubripes* Brewster

Status. Rare migrant E; very rare W. Possibly a rare breeder. Black Duck x Mallard hybrids are sometimes reported.

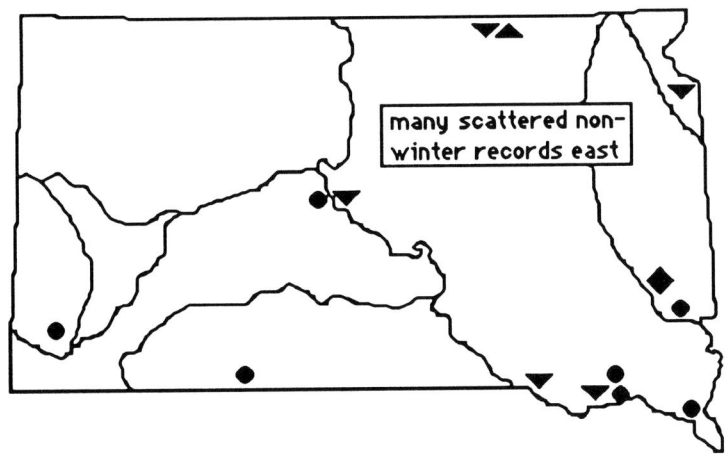

Habitat. Marshes and wooded ponds.
Spring migration. Probably early Apr.
   Earliest dates:
      26 Feb 1978, Gavin's Point (Hall)
      2 Mar 1904, Union Co. (Stephens 1918)
      14 Mar 1939, Lacreek NWR (refuge files)
Nesting. Over 15 summer E River reports suggest nesting. However, most are of single birds that probably hybridize with Mallards.
   Records:
      1922, near Lake Madison (Over and Thoms 1946)
      7 Jul 1981, Sand Lake NWR, brood of 5 (Waldstein in Seasons 1981d)
Fall migration. Mid-Oct.
   Earliest dates:
      12 Aug 1979, Lacreek NWR (Rosche and Rosche)
      13 Aug 1963, Oahe Dam (Springer)
      28 Aug 1934, Wind Cave NP (Cahalane in Anon. 1962)

40 SWANS, GEESE, AND DUCKS

Latest dates:
  17 Nov 1985, Yankton Co. (Hall in Seasons 1986a)
  23 Nov 1950, Union Co. (Stephens et al. 1955)
  27 Nov 1928, Union Co. (Stephens et al. 1955)
Winter. Jan and Feb reports from Lake Andes NWR, Gavin's Point, and Pierre.
CBC reports:
  Big Stone Lake, Pierre, and Sand Lake.

MALLARD *Anas platyrhynchos* Linnaeus

Status. Common to abundant migrant and common breeder. Fall concentrations occur along Missouri River from Pierre to Vermillion. Winters along Missouri River and elsewhere in mild winters. Pintail x Black Duck hybrids are sometimes reported.

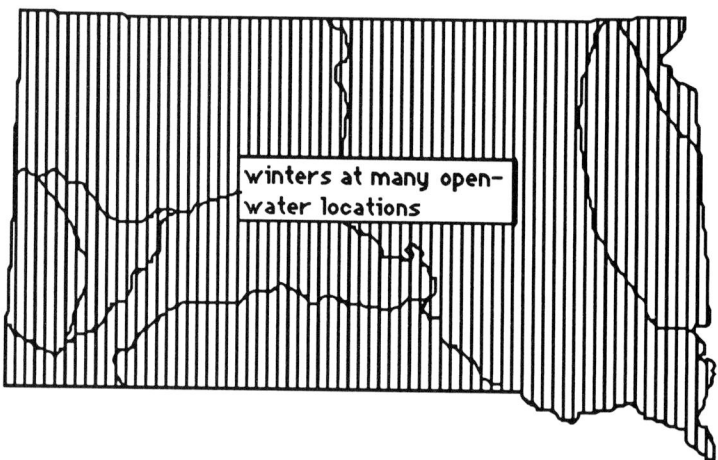

winters at many open-water locations

Habitat. Lakes, ponds, marshes and flooded ditches. Nests often in upland fields.
Spring migration. Last of Mar. Early records in SE and along Missouri River may be of feeding flights of wintering birds.
  Earliest dates:
    10 Feb 1985, Douglas Co., 1000 (Skadsen in Seasons 1985b)
    16 Feb 1983, Jackson Co. (Graupmann in Seasons 1983b)
    19 Feb 1981, Aurora Co. (Harris)
    19 Feb 1983, Miner Co. (Rogers in Seasons 1983b)
Nesting. Mid-Apr – Aug.
  Earliest dates:
    26 Apr 1974, Deuel Co., nest with 11 eggs (Harris)
    29 Apr 1952, Day Co., nest (Evans and Black 1956)
  Latest dates:
    7 Aug 1964, Campbell Co., female and 6 Class III young (Springer)
    7 Aug 1965, Brookings Co., female and 4 Class I young (Springer)
    9 Aug 1964, Brookings Co., female and 4 Class I young (Springer)
    22 Aug 1971, Harding Co., 2 broods Class II (Springer)

Fall migration. Late Oct at Sand Lake NWR; peaks the third week of Nov at Lake Andes NWR. Mallards are extremely hardy, and will remain in an area as long as food and water are available. Peak concentrations: 1 Nov 1966, Sand Lake NWR, 115,000 (refuge files); 1 Nov 1984, Sand Lake NWR, 160,000 (refuge files).

Winter. Large numbers along Missouri River from Pierre S, at Lacreek NWR and at Hot Springs; lesser numbers near Rapid City and S end of Big Stone Lake. Based on aerial surveys in the winter of 1968–1969, Bean (1973) reported Mallards made up 98% of 40,000 wintering ducks along Missouri River in Yankton, Clay and Union counties. An unusual outbreak of duck viral enteritis resulted in the loss of 40,000 Mallards at Lake Andes NWR during Jan–Mar 1973 (refuge files). Peak concentrations: Jan 1970, Lake Andes NWR, 120,000 (refuge files); 17 Dec 1974, on Missouri River from Pierre to Vermillion, 267,500 (GFP); 27 Dec 1972, Lacreek NWR, 5000 (refuge files).

CBC records:
Lake Andes NWR averaged 106,000 Mallards from 1965 to 1972; also reported at many other CBC during years with open water.

NORTHERN PINTAIL *Anas acuta* Linnaeus

Status. Common to abundant migrant; common nesting species E and fairly common W. Rare or casual in winter. Hybrid pintail x Mallard are sometimes reported.

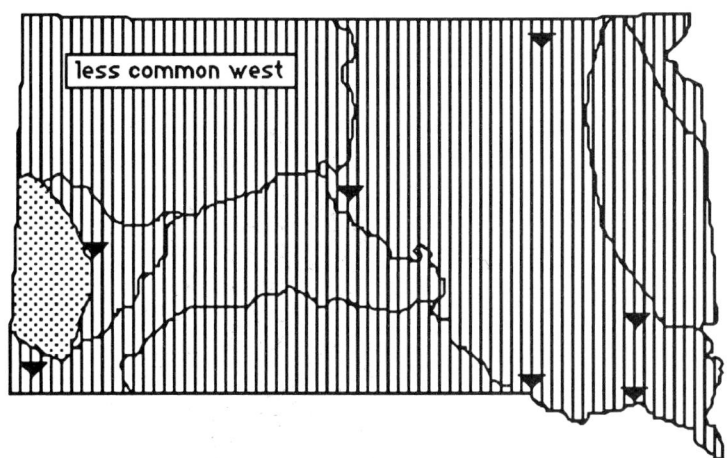

Habitat. Marshes, shallow lakes, and ponds with emergent vegetation. Nests often in upland fields.

Spring migration. Mid-Mar. Peak concentration: 10 Apr 1978, Sand Lake NWR, 45,000 (Waldstein in Seasons 1978c).

Earliest dates:
15 Feb 1962, Lacreek NWR (refuge files)
16 Feb 1984, Hutchinson Co. (Anderson in Seasons 1948b)
17 Feb 1983, Haakon Co. (Bjerke in Seasons 1983b)

Nesting. Mid-Apr – Jun.
  Earliest dates:
    18 Apr 1951, Day Co., nest (Evans and Black 1956)
    18 Apr 1967, Edmunds Co., nest (Duebbert)
    16 May 1967, Edmunds Co., Class Ia brood (Duebbert)
  Latest dates:
    22 Jul 1974, near Camp Crook, female and 6 Class II young (Springer)
    24 Jul 1973, near Ralph, female and 5 Class III young (Springer)
    31 Jul 1911, Fall River Co., brood (Visher 1912b)
Fall migration. Third week of Sep at Lake Andes NWR. Unusual concentration: 29 Aug 1966, Sanborn Co., 200–300 birds (Harris). Early winter dates are probably late fall migrants.
  Latest dates:
    4 Dec 1983, Butte Co., 6 (Bjerke in Seasons 1984b)
    5 Dec 1954, Minnehaha Co. (Chapman and Krause)
    22 Dec 1952, Lake Andes NWR (refuge files)
Winter. Regularly found in small numbers at Rapid City. Rosche (1982) reported records until 24 Jan in Fall River Co.
  CBC reports:
    Aberdeen, Hot Springs, Lake Andes, Mitchell, Pierre, and Yankton.
  Other record:
    11 Jan 1964, Lake Andes NWR (Springer)

BLUE-WINGED TEAL *Anas discors* Linnaeus

Status. Abundant migrant and breeder, rare winter.
Habitat. Flooded ditches, marshes, ponds and shallow lakes. Nests in upland fields.

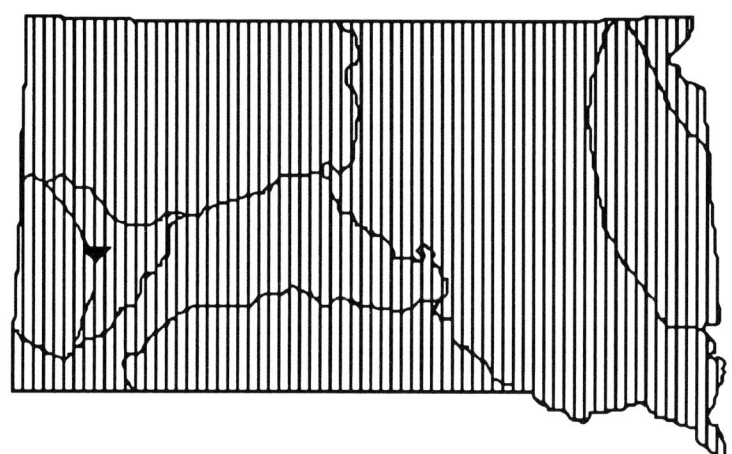

Spring migration. The second week of Apr. Peak concentrations: 30 Apr 1978, Sand Lake NWR, 20,000 (Waldstein in Seasons 1978c); 26 May 1978, Lacreek NWR, 3000 (Burgess in Seasons 1978c).
Earliest dates:
   3 Mar 1983, Aurora Co. (Rogers and McLaird in Seasons 1983c)
   11 Mar 1986, Charles Mix Co. (Skadsen in Seasons 1986b)
   15 Mar 1978, Lacreek NWR (Burgess in Seasons 1978c)
Nesting. Late Apr – Jul.
Earliest dates:
   30 Apr 1952, Day Co., egg laying (Evans and Black 1956)
   31 May 1910, Charles Mix Co., nest with 5 eggs (Zolnosky)
   1 Jun 1922, Sanborn Co., nest with 12 eggs (Patton)
Latest dates:
   3 Aug 1911, Fall River Co., brood (Visher 1912b)
   9 Aug 1964, Brookings Co., 2 broods (Springer)
   13 Aug 1976, Harding Co., 2 broods of Class II young (Springer)
Fall migration. Mid-Sep. Peak concentrations: 14 Aug 1975, Waubay NWR, 18,200 (Fromelt in Seasons 1975d); 10 Aug 1977, Deuel Co., 1000, 1500, and 2000 on 3 wetlands (Harris in Seasons 1978a).
Latest dates:
   14 Nov 1984, Waubay NWR (Bryant in Seasons 1985a)
   15 Nov 1963, Brookings Co. (Springer)
   25 Nov 1905, Sioux Falls (Larson 1925)
   25 Nov 1954, Minnehaha Co. (Chapman and Krause)
Winter.
CBC report:
   Rapid City

CINNAMON TEAL *Anas cyanoptera* Vieillot

Status. Probably regular in W River counties. Considered rare in E, but reported nearly every year. Male Cinnamon Teal with unidentified female teal during the breeding season W River, particularly at Lacreek NWR, suggest nesting.

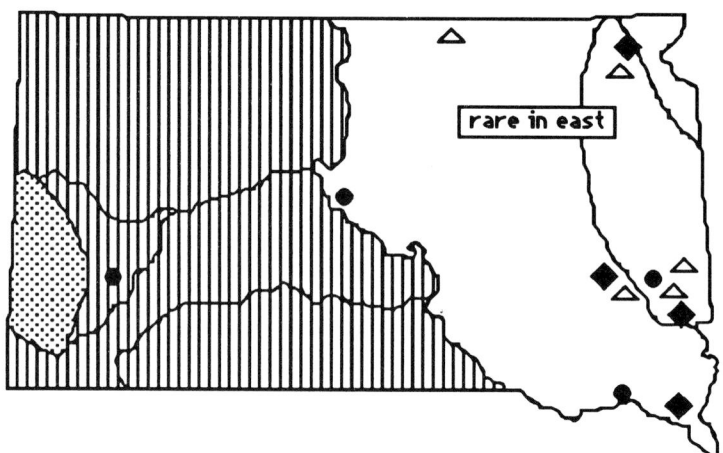

Habitat. Shallow lakes and ponds.
Spring migration. First half of Apr.
  Earliest dates:
    24 Mar 1985, Yankton Co. (Hall and Wilcox in Seasons 1985c)
    1 Apr 1976, Lake Co. (Buckman 1976)
    2 Apr 1911, Union Co., specimen (Stephens et al. 1955),
    2 Apr 1972, Pierre (Rose)
Nesting. Nest reported in Day Co. (Over and Thoms 1921) and broods reported at Lacreek NWR in 1965, 1972, and 1973 (refuge files), but no positive identification of females.
  Assumed pairs have been reported W River as follows:
    1939, Lacreek NWR (Krumm 1955c)
    Spring 1953, Lacreek NWR, pair on territory (Krumm 1955c)
    7 May 1967, Pennington Co. (Rose)
    23 May 1986, Edgemont (R. Peterson)
    29 May 1955, Lacreek NWR (Krumm 1955c)
    4 Jun 1967, Meade Co. (Rose)
    Jul 1965, Lacreek NWR, 6 pairs (Russell 1966)
  Assumed pairs have been reported E River as follows:
    1896, Miner Co. (Patton in Over and Thoms 1921)
    24 Apr 1968, Miner Co., male Cinnamon Teal courting unidentified female and fighting off male Blue-winged Teal (Harris 1968e)
    12 May 1988, Day Co. (R. Peterson)
    14 May 1962, Miner Co. (E. Anderson and Twedt)
    20 May 1964, near Brookings (Springer)
    22 May 1972, McPherson Co. (Duebbert and Lokemoen)
    16 Jun 1983, Lake Co., male Cinnamon Teal courting unidentified female and fighting off male Blue-winged Teal (Wittmeir in Seasons 1983d)
    20 Jun – 26 Jul 1950, Day Co. (Evans and Black 1956)

Fall migration.
Only records:
5 Sep 1984, Pennington Co. (Paulson and Coons in Seasons 1985a)
16 Sep 1979, Pennington Co. (Baker et al. in Seasons 1980a)
8 Oct 1911, Sioux Falls, 1 shot (Larson 1925)
23 Nov 1981, Pierre, hunter kill (Coonrod in Seasons 1982b)

NORTHERN SHOVELER *Anas clypeata* Linnaeus

Status. Common to abundant migrant and common breeder E; less common W. Rare winter.

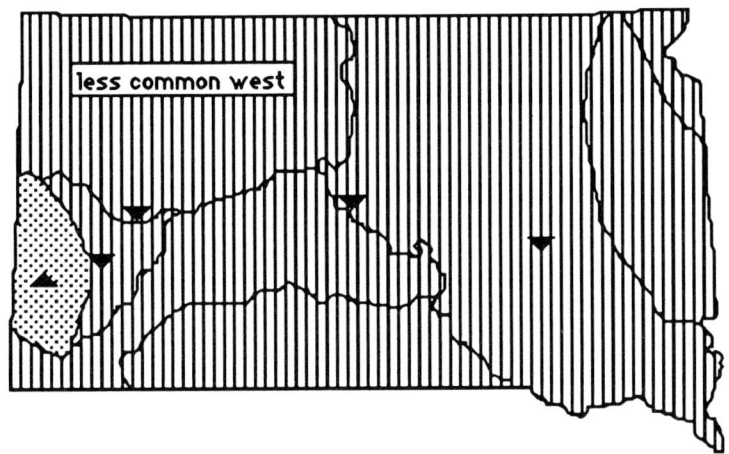

Habitat. Roadside ditches and marshes. Nests in upland fields.
Spring migration. First week of Apr. Peak concentration: 3 May 1981, Deuel Co., 155 (80 males) (Harris).
Earliest dates:
27 Feb 1983, Gregory Co. (Steffen in Seasons 1983b)
4 Mar 1987, Sanborn Co. (Rogers in Seasons 1987c)
8 Mar 1911, Sioux Falls (Larson 1925)
8 Mar 1987, Deuel Co. (Kreger in Seasons 1987c)
Nesting. May – Jul.
Earliest dates:
29 Apr 1968, Edmunds Co., nest (Duebbert)
18 May 1985, Day Co., nest with 11 eggs (Harris)
24 May 1971, Edmunds Co., nest with 11 eggs (Duebbert)
Latest dates:
24 Jul 1973, Harding Co., female with 2 Class I young (Springer)
22 Aug 1971, near Ludlow, 6 young able to fly (Springer)
29 Aug 1967, Sanborn Co., broods (Harris)
Black Hills Record:
5 Jun 1987, Deerfield Reservoir, brood (R. Peterson)
Fall migration. Sep–Oct. Among the early migrants, but a later wave definitely moves through NE (Harris). Peak concentrations: 13 Sep 1977, Clear Lake, over 200; 16 Oct 1977, Round Lake PSA, 200; 20 Nov – 3 Dec 1987, Lake Poinsett,

46 SWANS, GEESE, AND DUCKS

1000 (Lundquist et al. in Seasons 1986d); 8 Sep 1988, Bitter Lake, 3000 (Springer in Seasons 1989a).

Latest dates:
23 Nov 1977, Big Stone Lake (Harris in Seasons 1978a)
28 Nov 1915, Sioux Falls (Larson 1925)
28 Nov 1987, Corson Co. (Griffiths in Seasons 1988a)

Winter. Early winter dates may be of fall stragglers.

CBC reports:
Pierre and Rapid City.

Other records:
11 Dec 1968, Sanborn Co. (Harris)
Winter 1967–68, near Rapid City (Rose)
Jan and Feb 1983, Meade Co. (Miller in Seasons 1983b)

GADWALL *Anas strepera* Linnaeus

Status. Fairly common to common migrant; common breeder E, uncommon on W plains, does not breed in Black Hills. Winters regularly, including in Black Hills, on open water.

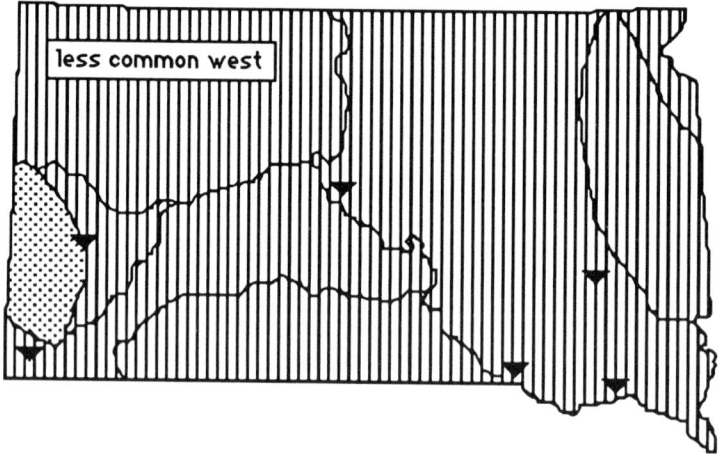

Habitat. Marshes, lakes with emergent vegetation and stock ponds. Nests often in upland fields, and on dikes and islands.

Spring migration. Last week of Mar and early Apr. Peak concentrations: 30 Apr 1978, Sand Lake NWR, 9000 (Waldstein in Seasons 1978c); 29 Mar 1978 Lacreek NWR, 940 (Burgess in Seasons 1978c).

Earliest dates:
21 Feb 1981, Davison Co., 4 (McLaird in Seasons 1981c)
24 Feb 1981, Harding Co., 24 (Rogers in Seasons 1981c)
25 Feb 1985, Yankton Co. (Anderson in Seasons 1985b)

Nesting. May – Jul.

Earliest dates:
2 May 1969, Edmunds Co., nest (Duebbert)
27 May 1922, Kingsbury Co., nest with 9 eggs (Patton)
3 Jun 1969, Edmunds Co., nest with 11 eggs (Duebbert)

Latest dates:
   13 Aug 1976, Harding Co., 4 broods of Class I and II young (Springer)
   13 Aug 1988, Deuel Co., 2 broods of Class II and III young (Springer)
   15 Aug 1986, Day Co., late hatch (Lundie in Seasons 1986d)
Fall migration. First week of Oct; irregular peaking at Lake Andes NWR from the last of Oct to 21 Nov. Peak concentration: 25 Nov 1967, Rapid City, 200 (Baylor). Due to wintering birds, late fall dates are difficult to interpret.
Winter. Regular at Canyon Lake, Rapid City, where up to 150 have been observed (Baylor et al.) and Fall River Co. (Rosche 1982). Regular on Missouri River near Yankton and Pierre.
   CBC records:
   Hot Springs, Lake Andes, Pierre, and Yankton.
   Other records:
   23 Dec 1969, Sanborn Co. (Harris)
   11 Jan 1964, Lake Andes NWR (Springer)

AMERICAN WIGEON *Anas americana* Gmelin

Status. Common migrant E; less common W. Rare to uncommon but evidently widespread nesting species. Rare winter except at Canyon Lake in Rapid City where locally common.

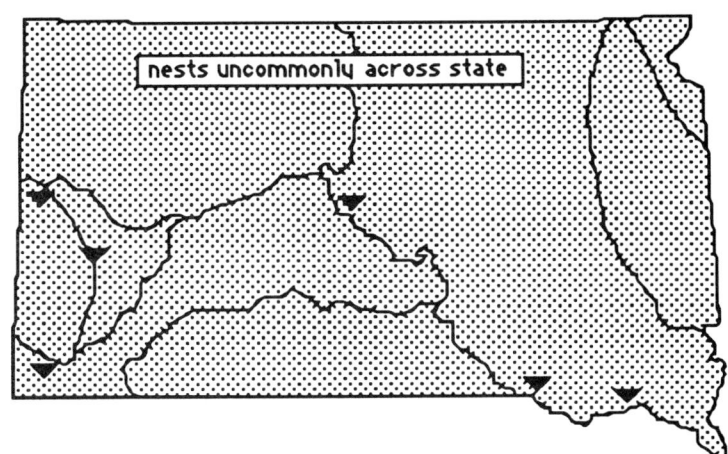

Habitat. Wetlands (often saline) E; stockponds with emergent vegetation W.
Spring migration. Late Mar. Peak concentration: 15 Apr 1978, Sand Lake NWR, 5000 (Waldstein in Seasons 1978c).
   Earliest dates:
   17 Feb 1985, Yankton Co. (Kronner in Seasons 1985c)
   22 Feb 1976, Custer Co. (Baker in Seasons 1976c)
   27 Feb 1984, Turner Co. (Anderson in Seasons 1984c)
Nesting. Jun–Jul.
   Earliest dates:
   20 May 1968, Edmunds Co., nest (Duebbert)
   27 May 1922, Kingsbury Co., nest with 5 eggs (Patton)

1 Jun 1970, Edmunds Co., 3 nests with clutch sizes of 10 and 11 eggs (Duebbert)

Latest dates:
24 Jul 1973, Gardner Lake near Buffalo, 3 broods of Class I and II young (Springer)
13 Aug 1976, Harding Co., 4 broods of Class I and II young (Springer)
21 Aug 1972, Deuel Co., broods (Harris)

Fall migration. First week of Oct. Peak concentrations: 1 Oct 1975, Waubay NWR, 5200 (Fromelt and Hall in Seasons 1975d); 3 Oct 1981, Lake Francis PSA, 1000 (Harris); 12 Sep 1967, Miner Co., 1000+ (Harris).

Latest dates:
20 Nov 1910, Sioux Falls (Larson 1925)
20 Nov 1983, Pennington Co. (Paulson in Seasons 1984a)
20 Nov 1983, Custer Co. (Paulson in Seasons 1984a)
28 Nov 1976, Pierre (Baker in Seasons 1977a)
1 Dec 1983, Davison Co. (McLaird in Seasons 1983b)

Winter. Regular in Fall River Co. (Rosche 1982) and Rapid City area; otherwise uncommon S. A possible hybrid Wigeon x Gadwall, initially reported as a Eurasian Wigeon, was photographed near Rapid City during the winters of 1967–68 and 1968–69 (Rose).

CBC reports:
Hot Springs, Lake Andes, Pierre, Spearfish, Rapid City, and Yankton.

Other records:
23 Jan–26 Feb 1987, Yankton Co. (Hall in Seasons 1987b)
30 Jan 1987, Oahe Dam (Harris in Seasons 1987b)

CANVASBACK *Aythya valisineria* (Wilson)

Status. Fairly common migrant E, where locally abundant on preferred lakes during fall migration. Abundant spring and common fall migrant in Fall River Co. (Rosche 1982), but uncommon elsewhere W. Fairly common breeding species in NE, but uncommon to rare elsewhere S to Lincoln Co. and W to Bennett and Harding counties. Much reduced population during recent years.

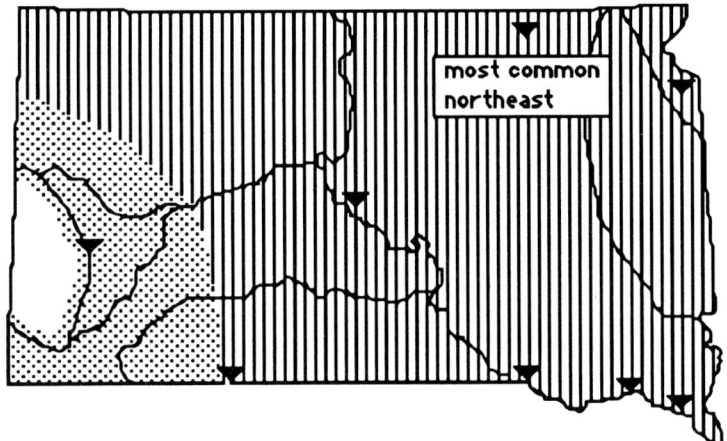

Habitat. Shallow lakes and ponds with bulrush and cattail nesting cover; deep water lakes in migration.

Spring migration. Last week of Mar. Seldom over 300 per flock in NE (Harris). Early spring dates from the Missouri River may be wintering birds.

Earliest dates:
13 Feb 1981, Deuel Co. (Kreger in Seasons 1981c)
13 Feb 1987, Yankton Co. (Hall in Seasons 1987b)
17 Feb 1984, Yankton Co. (Hall in Seasons 1984b)

Nesting. May – Jul. Has low reproductive potential, with narrow ecological tolerance, and is very slow to recover after unsuccessful nesting seasons.

Earliest date:
5 May 1971, Brookings Co., nest (hatching 1 June) (Vaa)
26 May 1888, Miner Co., nest with 8 eggs (Patton)
1 Jun 1893, Douglas Co., nest with 9 eggs (Hewitt)

Latest dates:
19 Jul 1967, Edmunds Co., nest with 6 eggs (Duebbert)
20 Jul 1973, Lincoln Co., hen with 10 young (Krause)
2 Aug 1965, Kingsbury Co., hen with 3 class II young (Springer)

Fall migration. Oct. Band recovery data from 1951–1966 South Dakota kills show 29% of the birds taken from 1–10 Oct, 33% from 11–20 Oct, 24% from 21–31 Oct, and 13% from 1–30 Nov (Stoudt 1968).

Latest dates:
17 Nov 1979, Deuel Co. (Harris in Seasons 1980a)
18 Nov 1972, Deuel Co. (Harris)
26 Nov 1988, Yankton Co. (Hall in Seasons 1989a)

Winter. Occasionally winters at Pierre and along Missouri River near Yankton.

CBC reports:
Big Stone Lake, Lake Andes, Sand Lake, and Vermillion.

Other records:
3 records of single birds on Canyon Lake (Pettingill and Whitney 1965).
Dec 1978, Lacreek NWR (refuge files)

50 SWANS, GEESE, AND DUCKS

REDHEAD *Aythya americana* (Eyton)

Status. Fairly common to common migrant and breeder E, with fall concentrations in McPherson, Brown, Marshall, Codington, and Deuel counties; less common migrant and breeder elsewhere; does not nest in Black Hills.

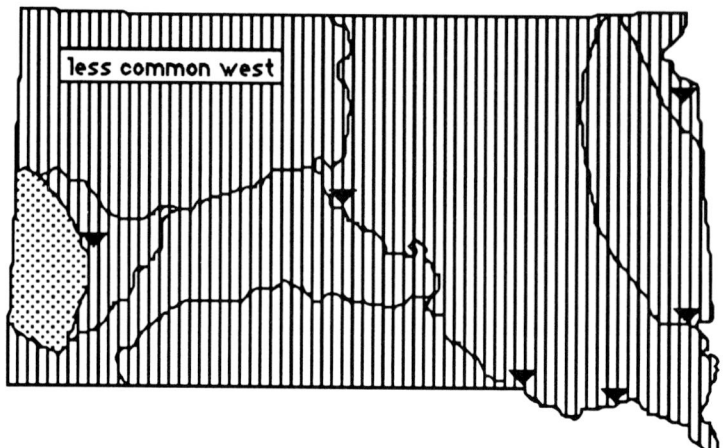

Habitat. Lakes and larger ponds with emergent vegetation.

Spring migration. Last week of Mar at Sand Lake and Lake Andes NWR. Early spring dates from Missouri River may be of wintering birds.
Earliest dates:
1 Feb 1987, Pierre (Harris in Seasons 1987b)
3 Feb 1984, Pierre (Baker et al. in Seasons 1984b)

Nesting. May–Jul.
Earliest dates:
26 May 1922, Kingsbury Co., nest with 11 eggs (Patton)
27 May 1981, Deuel Co., brood of 3 downy young (Harris)
3 Jun 1968, Edmunds Co., nest (Duebbert)
Latest dates:
10 Jul 1965, Brookings Co., 2 broods, Class I young (Springer)
2 Aug 1965, Brookings Co., 2 broods, Class I young (Springer)

Fall migration. Last half of Oct. Remain late into Nov if open water is available. Peak count: 21 Oct 1975, Waubay NWR, 6500 (Fromelt and Hall in Seasons 1975d). Band returns indicate a split migration, as with nationwide populations; most birds go to the Gulf Coast but a few to the E coast from New Jersey to Florida (Hammond, USFWS files).
Latest dates away from Missouri River:
28 Nov 1915, Sioux Falls (Larson 1925)
28 Nov 1968, Sanborn Co. (Harris)

Winter. A few usually winter at Canyon Lake in Rapid City (Whitney); scattered reports from Pierre, Big Stone City, and Charles Mix Co.
CBC reports:
Big Stone City, Pierre, Rapid City, and Sioux Falls.

Other records:
   1-13 Dec 1982, Missouri River near Yankton (Hall in Seasons 1983b)

RING-NECKED DUCK *Aythya collaris* (Donovan)

Status. Common migrant E; fairly common W; uncommon to fairly common breeder NE, S to Deuel Co., including McPherson and Edmunds counties; nonbreeding males found elsewhere during breeding season, occasionally S to Turner and Charles Mix counties.

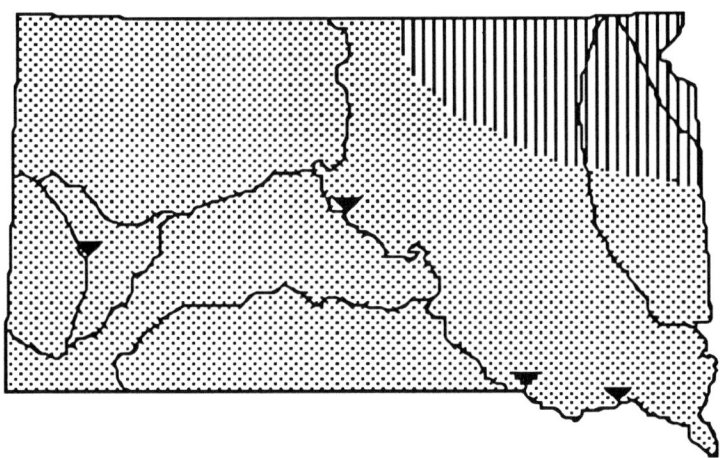

Habitat. Wetlands and smaller lakes, often bordered with trees or shrubs.
Spring migration. Last week of Mar.
   Earliest dates:
      1 Feb 1983, Pierre (Whitney in Seasons 1983b)
      13 Feb 1987, Yankton Co. (Hall in Seasons 1987b)
      15 Feb 1962, Lacreek NWR (refuge files)
Nesting. Jun–Jul. No nest records, but a number of broods have been reported from the Coteau areas of Marshall, Roberts, Day and Deuel counties. The center of the breeding population is probably W Roberts Co., where Springer and Harris recorded 12 pairs, 35 males and 6 females, 21 Jun 1970. Only record W of Marshall Co.: 18 Jul 1973, Edmunds Co., brood of 13 (Lokemoen).
   Earliest dates:
      19 Jun 1987, Marshall Co., female with 6 Class I young (Springer)

28 Jun 1969, Roberts Co., female with 6 Class I young and 2 Class I Redhead young (Springer)
4 Jul 1987, Roberts Co., nest with 10 eggs (Skadsen and Skadsen in Seasons 1987d)

Latest dates:
21 Jul 1971, Marshall Co., 3 broods, Class I and II young, (Springer)
30 Jul 1979, Deuel Co., 1/3-grown young (Harris in Seasons 1979d)
22 Sep 1960, Marshall Co., female and 12 Class II young (Reeves 1961)

Fall migration. Second and third weeks of Oct in NE, when often quite common. 300, Deuel Co., 6 Nov 1983 (Harris in Seasons 1984a).

Latest dates:
29 Nov 1982, Yankton Co. (Hall in Seasons 1983a)
30 Nov 1983, Yankton Co. (Hall in Seasons 1984a)
10 Dec 1982, Yankton Co. (Hall in Seasons 1983b)

Winter. Frequently reported in winter in Rapid City, Pierre, and Yankton. Early winter dates may be fall stragglers.

CBC reports:
Lake Andes, Pierre, and Yankton.

Other record:
10 Dec 1982, Yankton Co. (Hall in Seasons 1983c)

GREATER SCAUP *Aythya marila* (Linnaeus)

Status. Rare to uncommon migrant E and along the Missouri River, most records from fall migration. Status needs clarification.

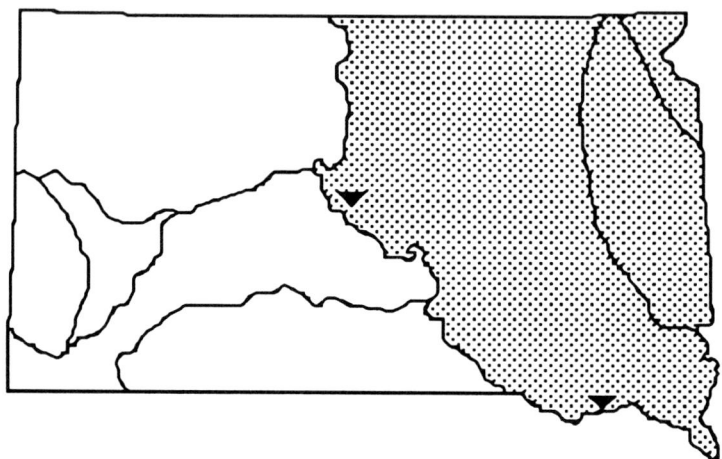

Habitat. Larger lakes and reservoirs.
Spring migration. Early Apr.
Earliest dates:
21 Feb 1986, Pierre (Prisbe in Seasons 1986b)
28 Feb 1984, Yankton Co. (L. Anderson)
2 Mar 1988, Yankton Co. (Hall in Seasons 1988c)

Latest date:
   22 Apr 1972, Lake Alice, pair (Harris)
Fall migration. Late Oct and early Nov.
   Earliest date:
   8 Oct 1972, shot near Pierre on Missouri River (Rose).
   Latest dates:
   26 Nov 1988, Hughes Co. (Rosche and Rosche)
   27 Nov 1966, Yankton Co., shot (banded in Maryland 25 Jan 1965) (USFWS files).
   28 Nov 1915, Sioux Falls (Larson 1925)
Winter.
   CBC report:
   Pierre.
   Other records:
   Mid-Dec throughout winter, Pierre (Rose in Seasons 1975a)
   1 Dec 1966, Gavin's Point Dam, specimen (B. Anderson)
   30 Jan 1987, Pierre (Prisbe et al. in Seasons 1987b)

LESSER SCAUP *Aythya affinis* (Eyton)

Status. Common to abundant migrant E; less common elsewhere. Rare to uncommon breeder in Marshall, Day, Deuel, Codington, Edmunds, and McPherson counties; probably nests in Roberts Co. Nesting in Jones Co. in 1978 (Mack). Uncommon winter, most often seen along Missouri River.

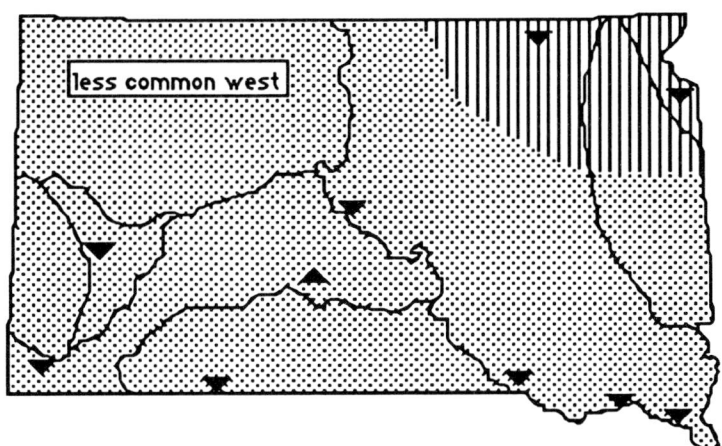

Habitat. Larger lakes and wetlands.
Spring migration. Last week of Mar. Sometimes concentrates in very large masses during migration, especially on larger lakes. Early spring dates along the Missouri River may be of wintering birds.
   Earliest dates:
   11 Feb 1983, Pennington Co. (Whitney in Seasons 1983b)
   16 Feb 1984, Yankton Co. (Hall in Seasons 1984b)
   21 Feb 1986, Pierre (Prisbe in Seasons 1986b)
Nesting. Jun – Jul. Upland nests: 25 Jun 1984, Codington Co., with 12 eggs, 200 yards from water (Rabenberg in Seasons

1984d); 9 Jul 1986, Marshall Co., 4 nests on small island (Skadsen et al. in Seasons 1986d).

Earliest dates:
12 Jun 1988, Day Co., nest with eggs (Skadsen et al. in Seasons 1988d)
15 Jun 1980, Day Co., hen with nest of 13 eggs (Harris in Seasons 1980d)
21 Jun 1973, near Hosmer, nest with 9 eggs (Lokemoen)

Latest dates:
11 Jul 1972, Edmunds Co., 5 Class I broods (Duebbert and Lokemoen)
16 Jul 1964, Bitter Lake, 2 nests with 10 and 6 hatching eggs (Springer and Drewien)
16 Jul 1972, McPherson Co., 2 broods of downy young (Duebbert and Lokemoen)
17 Jul 1964, Day Co., female and 4 Class I young (Springer)

Fall migration. Last week of Oct, remaining until water freezes.

Latest dates away from Missouri River:
27 Nov 1979, Deuel Co., 29 (Harris in Seasons 1980a)
28 Nov 1984, Gregory Co. (Steffen in Seasons 1985a)
30 Nov 1984, Hutchinson Co. (Anderson in Seasons 1985a)

Winter. Regular in small numbers along Missouri River in Clay and Yankton counties and in Pierre. Occasionally at Canyon Lake in Rapid City.

CBC reports:
Big Stone, Hot Springs, Lake Andes, Pierre, and Rapid City.

Other records away from Missouri River:
12 Dec 1980, Sand Lake NWR (Waldstein in Seasons 1981b)
Dec 1977, Lacreek NWR (Burgess in Seasons 1978b)
18 Dec 1976 and 10 Dec 1978, Fall River Co. (Rosche 1982)

COMMON EIDER *Somateria mollissima* (Linnaeus)

Status. Casual fall migrant.

Records:
- 4 Nov 1911, Madison Pass, verified specimen (Visher 1912c)
- 7 Nov 1940, Lake Poinsett, 1 shot (Berchtold in Spawn 1950)
- Nov 1970, Stanley Co., specimen discarded (McDaniel, verified by Rose)

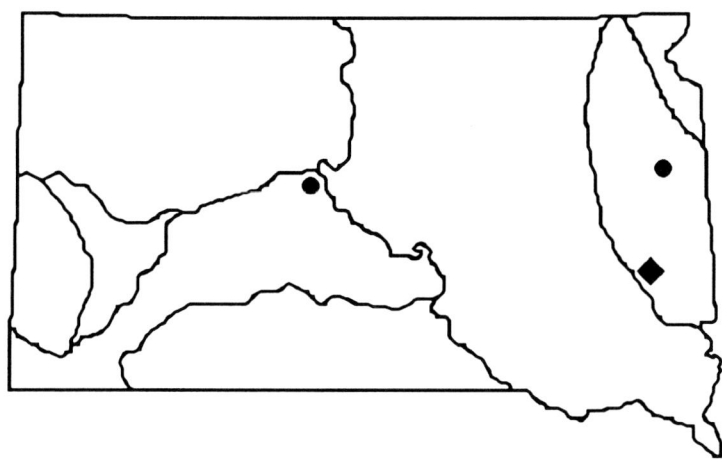

OLDSQUAW *Clangula hyemalis* (Linnaeus)

Status. Rare fall migrant, very rare spring migrant and in winter along the Missouri River and E. Accidental W (Bennett, Perkins, Meade, and Pennington counties). The first state record: fall 1878, a hunter kill in SE (Agersborg 1885), but the next report 72 years later at Sand Lake NWR on 8 Nov 1950 (Rollings). Perhaps more common in some years than in others. Most have been females or immatures, with most reports in Nov.

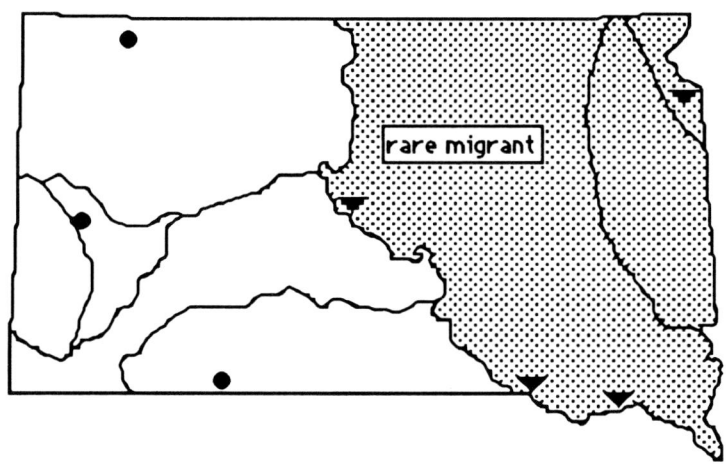

Spring migration.
Only records:
2 Mar 1980, Oahe Dam (Spomer 1980)
5 Apr 1981, Yankton Co., photo (Hall in Seasons 1981c)
11–13 Apr 1987, Oahe Dam (Tallman et al. in Seasons 1987c)
27 Apr 1988, Perkins Co. (Griffiths and Griffiths in Seasons 1988c)

Fall migration. Late Oct – Nov. Late dates may be of birds attempting to winter.
Earliest dates:
20 Oct 1954, Union Co. (Felton in Stephens et al. 1955)
28 Oct 1973, Deuel Co. (Harris 1973b)
29 Oct 1976, Deuel Co. (Harris in Seasons 1977a)

Winter.
CBC report:
Pierre.
Other records:
4 Dec 1967, Lake Andes NWR (Town 1968)
1–6 Dec 1984, Yankton Co. (Hall in Seasons 1985b)
15 Dec 1973, Big Stone City (Harris)
9 Jan 1988, Pickstown (Harris et al.)

BLACK SCOTER *Melanitta nigra* (Linnaeus)

Status. Casual fall migrant; only 2 spring records. 12 records, most since 1974; 7 from Missouri River and 3 from Deuel Co. No winter records.

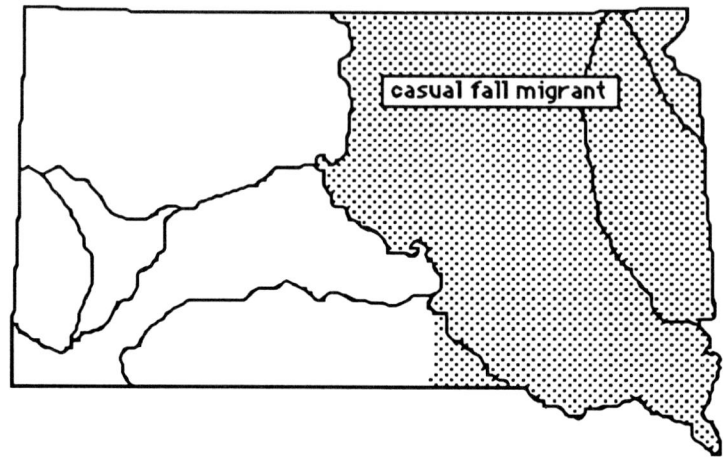

Habitat. Larger lakes and reservoirs.
Spring migration.
Records:
16–17 Apr 1981, Gregory Co. (Steffen 1982)
26–28 Apr 1985, Yankton Co. (Kronner in Seasons 1985c)
Fall migration. Late Oct. Fall observations are evenly divided in Oct and Nov.

Earliest dates:
  10 Oct 1976, Lake Oahe near Pierre (Hill in Seasons 1977a)
  18 Oct 1975, near Pierre, 3 (Rose in Seasons 1975d)
  19 Oct 1974, Yankton Co., 2, photo (Hall 1975)
Latest dates:
  15 Nov 1983, Deuel Co. (Harris and Stava in Seasons 1984a)
  16 Nov 1983, Yankton Co. (Hall in Seasons 1984a)
  17 Nov 1980, Clay Co. (Hall in Seasons 1981a)

SURF SCOTER *Melanitta perspicillata* (Linnaeus)

Status. Casual fall migrant, accidental spring migrant, but recent observations suggest more regular occurrence. 19 records, most during fall hunting season, with 7 specimens. Accidental W River (2 records in Perkins Co. (Griffiths and Griffiths)).

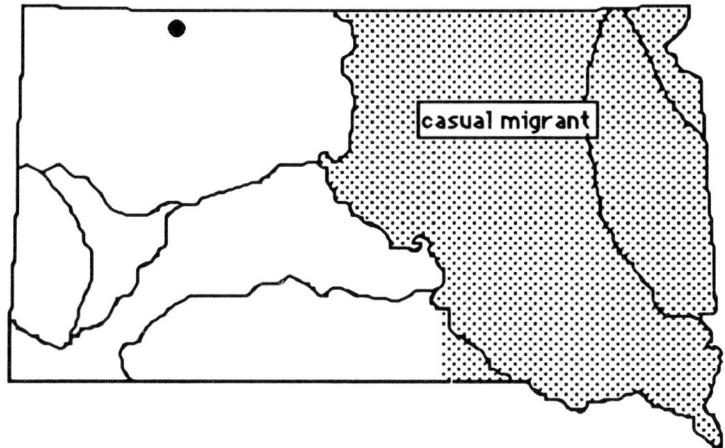

Habitat. Larger lakes and reservoirs.
Spring migration.
  Only records:
    1 Apr 1988, Yankton Co. (Hall in Seasons 1988c)
    23 Apr 1990 Yankton Co. (Hall in Seasons 1990c)
Fall migration. Mid-Oct. Migrates earlier than other scoters, resulting in few Nov records.
  Earliest dates:
    11 Oct 1976, Deuel Co. (Harris in Seasons 1977a)
    14 Oct 1966, Lake Hendricks, specimen (B. Anderson)
    16 Oct 1977, Lake Oahe near Pierre (Hill in Seasons 1978a)
  Latest dates:
    11-13 Nov 1985, Gregory Co. (Steffen 1986)
    24 Nov 1982, Gavin's Point (Hall in Seasons 1983a)
    12 Dec 1981, Missouri River, Yankton Co. (Hall in Seasons 1982b)

WHITE-WINGED SCOTER *Melanitta fusca* (Linnaeus)

Status. Rare to uncommon migrant during Oct and Nov; very rare spring migrant. Rarely winters. Most records are from E and are of female or immature birds; Accidental W River (Lacreek NWR, Fall River, Perkins, and Pennington counties, and Bear Butte Lake).

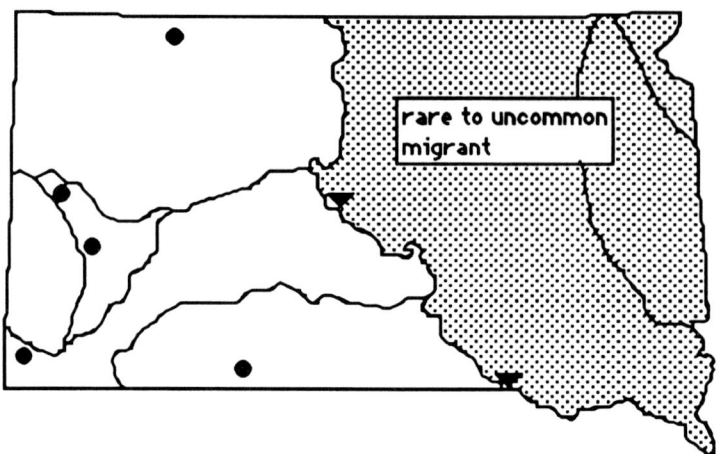

Habitat. Larger lakes and reservoirs.

Spring migration.
  Earliest dates:
    5 Apr 1982, Yankton Co. (Hall in Seasons 1982c)
    12 Apr 1986, Brookings Co. (Holden in Seasons 1986c)
    26 Apr 1985, Yankton Co. (Kronner in Seasons 1985c)
  Latest date:
    1 Jun 1983, Waubay NWR (Rabenburg in Seasons 1983c)

Fall migration. Late Oct and Nov. Individuals or small groups usually observed, but flocks of 11 and 6 at Lake Alice on 30 Oct 1976 and 12 Nov 1980, respectively (Harris in Seasons 1977a and 1981a).
  Earliest dates:
    3 Oct 1974, Lacreek NWR (Burgess 1976)
    11 Oct 1976, Deuel Co. (Harris)
    22 Oct 1968, McPherson Co. (Squire and Rinke, misidentified as a Black Scoter in Wallenstrom 1968)
  Latest dates:
    24 Nov 1975, Pierre, hunter kill (Rose in Seasons 1975d)
    27 Nov 1974, Lacreek NWR (Burgess 1976)
    30 Nov 1976, Lake Yankton (Hall)

Winter.
  Records:
    6 Dec 1982, Charles Mix Co. (Husmann in Seasons 1983b)
    7 Dec 1974, Lake Oahe Dam (Lokemoen and Duebbert)
    8–26 Dec 1974, Pierre (Rose in Seasons 1975a)
    14 Dec 1978, Pierre (Spomer in Seasons 1979b)

COMMON GOLDENEYE *Bucephala clangula* (Linnaeus)

Status. Uncommon to fairly common migrant E; uncommon W of the Missouri River. May have bred in Day Co. until 1965. Winters regularly in Black Hills and along Missouri River.

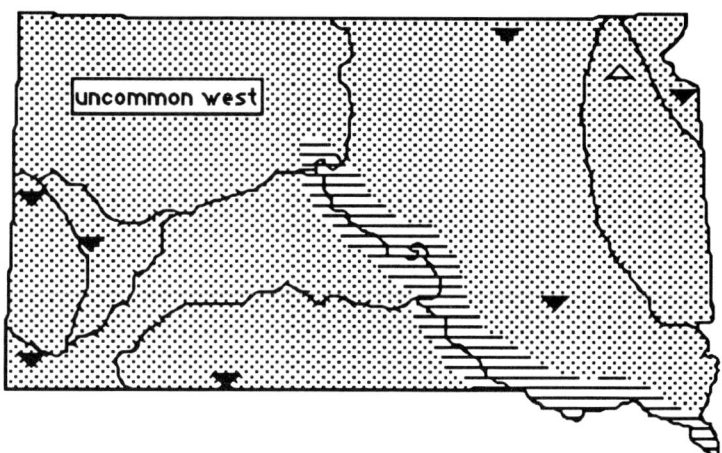

Habitat. Larger lakes and reservoirs.
Spring migration. Last 2 weeks of Mar.
  Earliest dates:
    16 Feb 1984, Big Stone Lake (Skadsen in Seasons 1984b)
    19 Feb 1984, Jackson Co. (Graupmann in Seasons 1984b)
    24 Feb 1983, Davison Co. (Anderson in Seasons 1983b)
  Latest dates:
    8 May 1974, Roberts Co. (Harris)
    16 May 1969, Clark Co. (Jonkel)
    20 May 1974, Deuel Co. (Harris)
Nesting. Breeding records of questionable reliability at Rush Lake (Lundquist in Youngworth 1935) and at the Waubay NWR in most years between 1937 and 1965 (Waubay NWR files).
Fall migration. Late Oct, leaving only when water freezes.
  Earliest date:
    7 Oct 1907, Sioux Falls (Larson 1925).
Winter. Regular in varying numbers at Canyon Lake (200 on 24 Nov 1967, and 250 during winter 1968–69 (Baylor), in the Hot Springs area (Rosche 1982), and along the Missouri River from Oahe Dam S (500 at Gavin's Point Dam on 11 Jan 1964 (Springer); 131 at Pierre on 29 Dec 1974 (Rose)). Occasionally at Spearfish and in Davison Co.
  CBC reports:
    Big Stone Lake, Hot Springs, Lacreek, and Sand Lake.

BARROW'S GOLDENEYE *Bucephala islandica* (Gmelin)

Status. Casual.

Rapid City records: 29 Nov 1970 to 21 Mar 1971, 7 Nov 1971–10 Mar 1972, Canyon Lake, 1 male (Baylor 1971a, 1975); no subsequent observations at Canyon Lake until 17 Dec 1978 (Baker and Whitney in Seasons 1979b), after which 1 adult male observed regularly each winter through 1989/90 (many observers); the earliest observation being 8 Nov 1986 (Baker in Seasons 1987a).

Other records:
21 Mar 1953, Minnehaha Co. (Findley and Findley 1953a)
24 Mar 1955, Minnehaha Co. (Rosine and Krause)
24 Mar 1959, Sand Lake NWR (Rose)
8 Apr 1984, Deuel Co. (Harris in Seasons 1984c)
15 Apr 1957, Douglas Co. (Crutchett 1957)

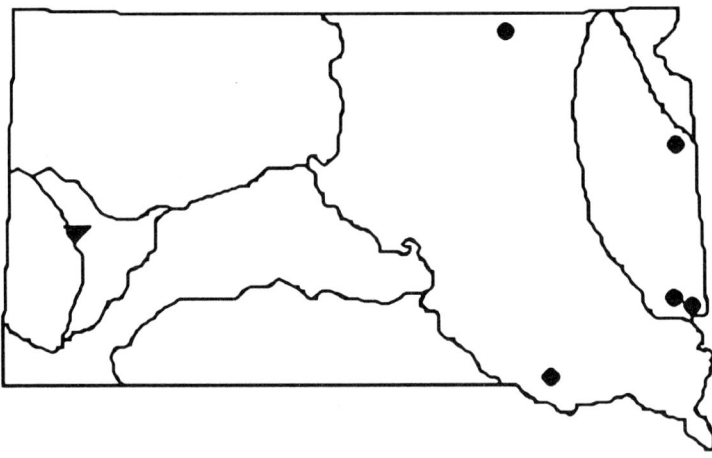

BUFFLEHEAD *Bucephala albeola* (Linnaeus)

Status. Uncommon to fairly common spring migrant E; locally abundant fall migrant NE. Less common W River. Regular winter at Canyon Lake in Rapid City since 1979, but uncommon elsewhere.

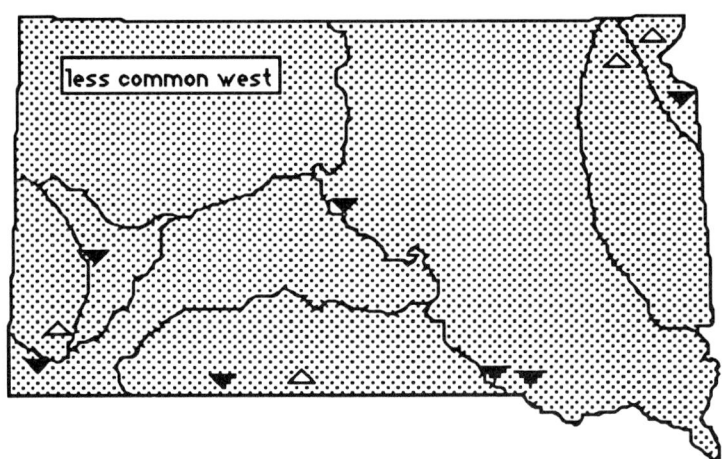

Habitat. Lakes, wetlands, stockponds.

Spring migration. First week of Apr. The latest dates are well within the breeding period for the species, but most likely represent slow migrants or non-breeders. Peak concentration: 6 Apr 1971, near Sioux Falls 150 (Krause).

Earliest dates:
23 Feb 1981, Lacreek NWR (Brashears in Seasons 1981b)
24 Feb 1981, Yankton Co. (Hall in Seasons 1981c)
27 Feb 1984, Yankton Co. (Hall in Seasons 1984b)

Latest dates:
26 May 1990, Perkins Co. (Springer in Seasons 1990c)
29 May 1981, Fall River Co. (Rosche in Seasons 1981c)
31 May 1986, Roberts Co. (Skadsen and Skadsen in Seasons 1986c)

Summer observations:
23 Jun 1978, Roberts Co. (Harris in Seasons 1978d)
4 Jul 1989, Todd Co. (Springer)
10 Aug 1974, Custer Co. (Rosche and Rosche)
15 Aug 1966, Day Co. (Sewall in Chilson 1968)

Fall migration. Late Oct. Peak concentrations: 10 Nov 1940, Lake Andes NWR, 2000; 5–10 Nov 1968, Sisseton, 200–300 (Harris); 6 Nov 1975, Waubay NWR, 625 (Fromelt in Seasons 1975d).

Earliest dates:
20 Sep 1985, Waubay NWR (Bryant in Seasons 1986a)
2 Oct 1980, Deuel Co. (Harris in Seasons 1981a)
5 Oct 1973, Deuel Co. (Harris)

Latest dates:
27 Nov 1983, Pennington Co. (Baker in Seasons 1984a)
29 Nov 1982, Yankton Co., 3 (Hall in Seasons 1983a)
30 Nov 1984, Yankton Co. (Hall in Seasons 1985a)

Winter. Regular at Rapid City since 1979. Also recorded Lacreek NWR, Pierre, Charles Mix and Fall River counties.

CBC reports:
Big Stone City, Hot Springs, Lake Andes NWR, and Pierre.

HOODED MERGANSER *Lophodytes cucullatus* (Linnaeus)

Status. Uncommon migrant E; few records W (including Perkins, Butte, and Lawrence counties). Rare breeder along Big Sioux River and possibly elsewhere E. Regularly winters near Rapid City; occasionally E.

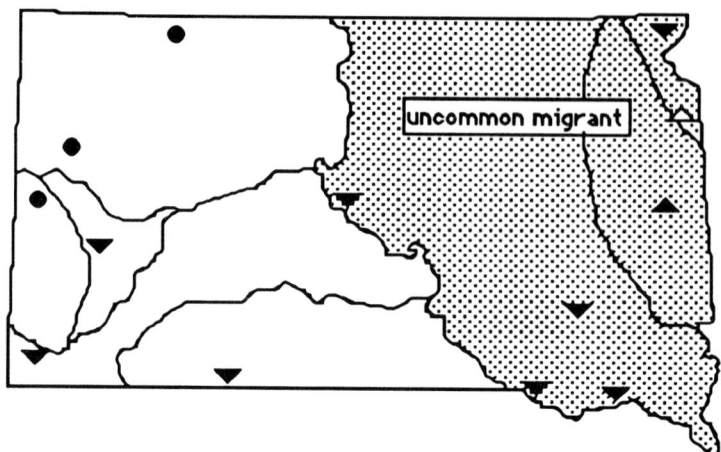

Habitat. Lakes, larger streams and open wetlands; prefers wooded ponds during breeding season.

Spring migration. Early Apr.
Earliest dates:
  1 Mar 1988, Yankton (Hall)
  4 Mar 1986, Yankton Co. (Van Sickle in Seasons 1986c)
  12 Mar 1955, Yankton Co. (Findley)

Nesting. 3 records, all in 1 mile of Big Sioux River in Brookings Co. in Wood Duck nesting boxes. A few records suggest breeding in NE: summer 1971-74, Deuel Co., females, including 1 at the same wooded pond on 3 occasions, but no evidence of nest or broods (Harris); 29 Aug 1974, Lake Alice, 2 full-grown, apparently immatures (Harris).

Records:
  22 May 1980, Brookings Co., nest with 10 eggs, hatched during first week of June (Smith 1981)
  1981, Brookings Co., 2 nests, each with 11 eggs, all of which hatched (Smith 1982)

Fall migration. Due to summering birds, earliest dates are questionable.

Latest dates:
  26 Nov 1966, Yankton Co. (Springer)
  26 Nov 1987, Corson Co. (Griffiths in Seasons 1988a)
  27 Nov 1983, Pierre (Paulson in Seasons 1984a)
  28 Nov 1909, Sioux Falls (Larson 1925)
Winter. Regular in Pierre and Rapid City.
  CBC reports:
  Pierre and Hot Springs
  Other records:
    16 and 18 Dec 1976, Fall River Co. (Rosche 1982)
    19 Dec 1986, Yankton Co. (Hall in Seasons 1987b)
    Winter 1950–51 and 1968–69, Lacreek NWR (refuge files)
    Winter 1964–65, Sanborn Co. (C. Backlund)
    12 Jan 1986, Charles Mix Co. (Skadsen and Skadsen in Seasons 1986b)
    26 Jan 1985, Charles Mix Co. (Skadsen et al. in Seasons 1985b)
    11 Feb 1984, Roberts Co. (Skadsen in Seasons 1984b)

COMMON MERGANSER *Mergus merganser* Linnaeus

Status. Fairly common to common migrant through-out, locally abundant on the Missouri River in fall and winter. Very rare breeder in Black Hills and along Missouri River.

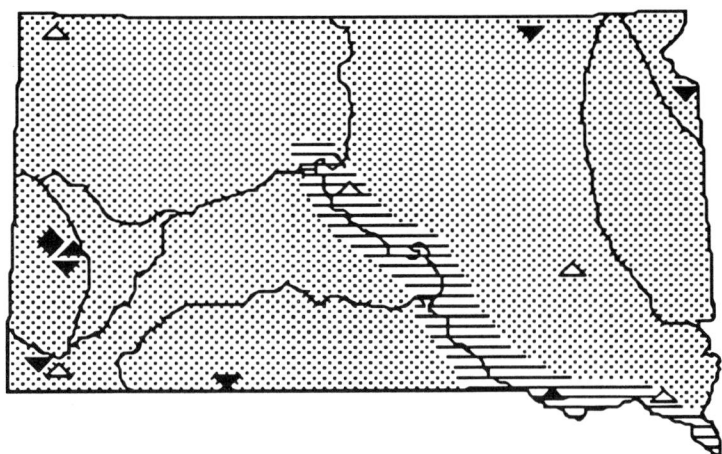

Habitat. Larger lakes and river systems.
Spring migration. Late Mar to mid-Apr.
  Earliest dates:
    15 Feb 1984, Jackson Co. (Graupmann in Seasons 1984b)
    16 Feb 1984, Big Stone Lake (Skadsen in Seasons 1984b)
    21 Feb 1987, Gregory Co. (Steffen in Seasons 1987b)
  Latest dates (outside breeding area):
    21 May 1987, Clay Co. (Springer in Seasons 1987c)
    10 Jun 1987, Pierre (Tallman)
    21 Jun 1975, Harding Co. (Eckert)
Nesting. May–Jul. Since 1984, 8 broods have been reported in the Rapid City area (Baylor et al. 1987). The only previously recorded nestings there were 110 and 90 years earlier

(Grinnell 1875, *Rapid City Journal* 1897). Nonbreeding birds casually occur in the summer.

Earliest dates:
26 May 1990, Rapid City, female and 2 young (Bjerke)
6 Jun 1984, Canyon Lake, brood of ducklings (Baylor in Seasons 1984d)
9 Jun 1989, Rapid Creek, female with 6 young (Crawford)

Latest dates:
1 Aug 1968, near Pickstown, female with young about 3/4 grown on Missouri (Timken)
16 Aug 1986, Pennington Co., 2 adults and 6 young (Thorson, Hillager, and Speiser)

Summer nonbreeding records:
10 Jun 1987, Stanley Co. (Tallman)
18 Jun 1978, Fall River Co. (Rosche)
21 Jun 1975, Harding Co. (Eckert)
25 Jun 1969, Vermillion (Polcyn)
21 Jul 1969, Sanborn Co. (Olson)

Fall migration. Mid-Nov. Late dates may be birds attempting to winter. Peak concentrations: 22 Nov 1980, Charles Mix Co., 7600 (Hall in Seasons 1981a); 27 November 1982, Yankton Co., 8000 (Wilcox in Seasons 1983a).

Earliest dates:
17 Sep 1976, Fall River Co. (Rosche)
13 Oct 1974, Fall River Co. (Rosche)
23 Oct 1976, Deuel Co. (Harris)

Winter. Common, often abundant, on Missouri River from Oahe Dam S; regular at Canyon Lake and in Fall River Co. About 50 usually winter at Lacreek NWR. Peak concentrations: 11 Jan 1964, Gavin's Point Dam, 500 (Springer); Lake Andes CBC show counts of 3000, 1302, 985, and 300 during recent years.

CBC reports:
Big Stone, Hot Springs, Lake Andes, Pierre, Rapid City, Sand Lake, and Yankton.

RED-BREASTED MERGANSER *Mergus serrator* Linnaeus

Status. Rare to uncommon migrant E and along Missouri River. Rare migrant in Fall River (Rosche 1982), Jackson (Graupmann in Seasons 1989c) and Perkins (Griffiths) counties.. Rarely winters.

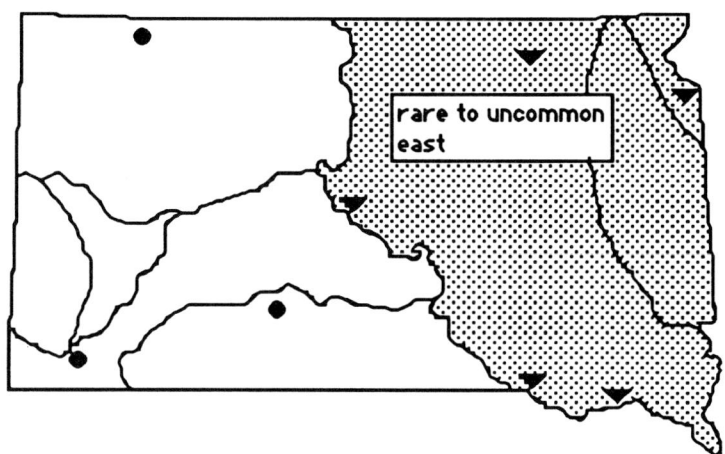

Habitat. Larger lakes and drainages.
Spring migration. Early Apr.
  Earliest dates:
    14 Mar 1981, Yankton Co. (Hall and Wilcox in Seasons 1981c)
    14 Mar 1985, Minnehaha Co., 4 (Rogers in Seasons 1985c)
    18 Mar 1977, Clay Co. (Hoover in Seasons 1977c)
  Latest dates:
    19 May 1983, Yankton Co. (Hall in Seasons 1983c)
    22 May 1973, Pierre (Rose)
    29 May 1972, Pierre (Rose)
Fall migration. Early Nov. Late fall dates on Missouri River probably refer to wintering birds.
  Earliest dates:
    16 Oct 1965, Sand Lake NWR (Springer)
    28 Oct 1984, Deuel Co., shot by hunter (Harris in Seasons 1985a)
  Latest dates:
    18 Nov 1972, Deuel Co. (M. Harris)
    26 Nov 1966, Yankton Co. (Springer)
    4 Dec 1988, Perkins Co. (Griffiths and Griffiths)
Winter.
  CBC reports:
    Aberdeen, Big Stone, Lake Andes, and Pierre.
  Other records:
    12 Jan 1986, Charles Mix Co. (Skadsen in Seasons 1986b)
    26 Jan 1985, Charles Mix Co. (Skadsen and Skadsen in Seasons 1985b)
    25 Feb 1967, Yankton Co., specimen (Timken)
    Winter 1982–83, Yankton Co. (Anderson in Seasons 1983b)

RUDDY DUCK *Oxyura jamaicensis* (Gmelin)

Status. Fairly common to common migrant; locally abundant in fall. Fairly common summer resident NE, nesting S to Turner Co.; less common elsewhere; in SE seldom nests S of Davison and Minnehaha counties. Not known to breed in the Black Hills. Sporadic in early winter.

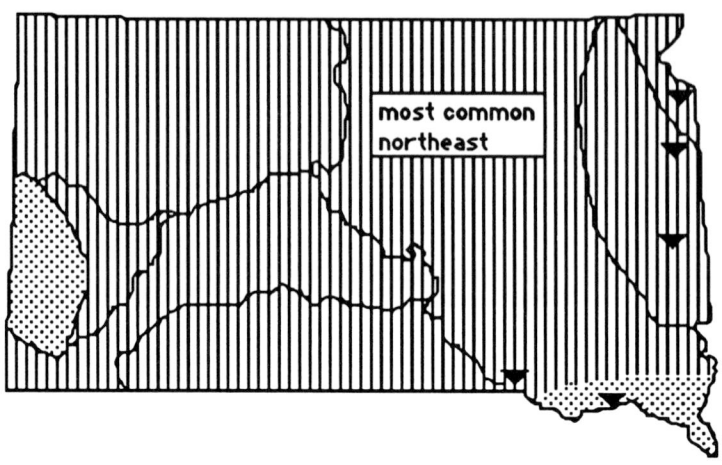

Habitat. Deepwater wetlands and marshes.
Spring migration. Mid-Apr.
Earliest dates:
27 Feb 1986, Yankton Co. (Anderson in Seasons 1986b)
5 Mar 1987, Sanborn Co. (Rogers in Seasons 1987c)
8 Mar 1974, Brookings Co. (Holden)
Nesting. Jun.
Earliest dates:
24 May 1941, Codington Co., nest with 2 eggs (Johnson 1956a)
10 Jun 1922, Kingsbury Co., nest collected with 10 eggs (Patton in Whitney 1955)
16 Jun 1987, Campbell Co., female on nest (Springer)
Latest dates:
3 Sep 1966, Brookings Co., Class II brood (Springer)
5 Sep 1986, Deuel Co., female with 3 small downy young (Harris in Seasons 1987a)
6 Sep 1965, Brookings Co., Class I brood (Springer)
Fall migration. Late Oct – first week of Nov. Fall concentrations:
1 Oct 1972, Deuel Co., 500 and 400 (Harris).
Latest date:
28 Nov 1915, Minnehaha Co. (Larson 1925)
Winter. Wintering birds may be cripples.
CBC reports:
Big Stone, Brookings, and Lake Andes.
Other records:
1 Dec 1984, Yankton Co. (Hall in Seasons 1985b)
2 Dec 1982, Yankton (Hall in Seasons 1983b)
31 Dec 1979, Deuel Co. (Harris)

CATHARTIDAE: American Vultures

TURKEY VULTURE *Cathartes aura* (Linnaeus)

Status. Fairly common to common summer resident in local areas along the Missouri River and W. Uncommon migrant and summer visitor E River; formerly bred in the Ft. Sisseton area (McChesney 1879), in Clay Co. (Agersborg 1885), and Sioux Falls (Larson 1925). "Very abundant" on the plains during Custer expedition of 1874 (Grinnell 1875). Probably declined with the disappearance of the bison herds.

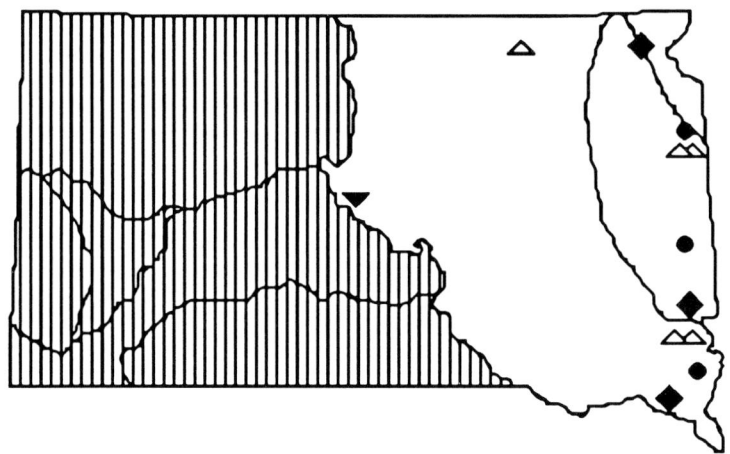

Habitat. W River prairies and Badlands, and the Black Hills. Roost of about 60 on Sheep Mountain Table on 20 Aug 1969 (Whitney, Yarger and Yarger).

Spring migration. Late Mar–May.
  Earliest dates:
    15 Mar 1964, Brookings (Holden 1964)
    21 Mar 1987. Brookings and Deuel counties (Harris in Seasons 1985c)
    29 Mar 1985, Fall River Co. (Miller in Seasons 1985c)

Nesting. Probably May – Jul.
  Only records:
    Late Jun 1969, Gregory Co., nest with at least 2 young (Eberly)
    3 Jul 1988, Custer Co., chick in nest (Peterson and Peterson for SDBBA)
  E River summer records away from Missouri River:
    31 May 1979, Deuel Co. (Harris)
    10 Jun 1987, Lincoln Co. (Springer in Seasons 1987d)
    14 Jun 1971, Deuel Co. (Stava)
    14 Jun–25 Aug 1985, Lincoln Co., 1–2 flying immatures 3–25 Aug (Springer and Skadsen 1986).
    28 Jun 1987, Brown Co. (Prisbe and Carrels)

Fall migration. Sep.
  Latest dates:
    4 Nov 1950, Union Co. (Stephens et al. 1955)
    16 Nov 1934, Wind Cave NP (Cahalane in Pettingill and Whitney 1965).

Winter. Formerly in Clay Co., a few seen occasionally in winter (Agersborg 1885).
  CBC report:
  Pierre

ACCIPITRIDAE: Kites, Eagles, and Hawks

OSPREY *Pandion haliaetus* (Linnaeus)

Status. Uncommon migrant. Formerly nested in SE, now casual summer visitor at scattered locations throughout the state.

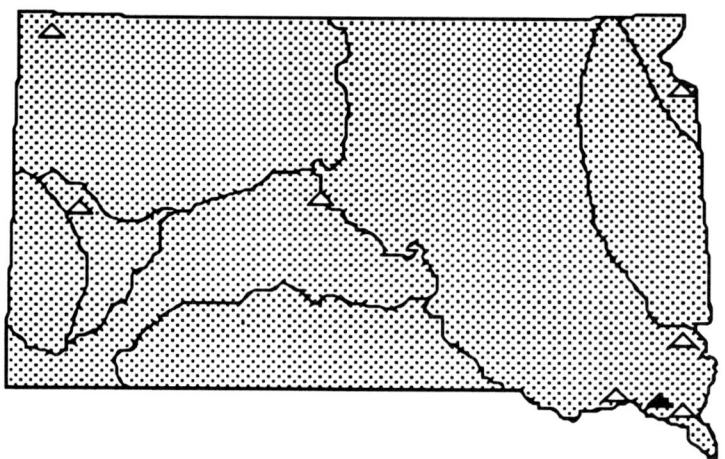

Habitat. Lakes and larger drainages.
Spring migration. Mid-Apr – Mid-May.
  Earliest dates:
  29 Feb 1964, Yankton Co. (Rogge 1964)
  18 Mar 1969, below Oahe Dam (Rose)
Summer records:
  1 Jun 1986, Stanley and Yankton counties (Kronner in Seasons 1986d)
  2 Jun 1984, Meade Co. (Miller in Seasons 1989d)
  10 Jun 1963, Sodak Park (Harris 1963)
  20 Jun 1981, Harding Co. (Grant)
  29 Jun 1989, Clay Co. (Reinking in Seasons 1989d)
  4 Jul 1989, Lincoln Co. (Reinking in Seasons 1989d)
Nesting.
  Only record:
  May 1883, Clay Co., along Vermillion River (Agersborg 1885)
Fall migration. Sep.
  Earliest dates:
  24 Aug 1981, Laframbois Island (Castor and O'Brien)
  25 Aug 1982, Gregory Co. (Lengkeek)
  26 Aug 1981, Gregory Co. (Steffen 1983a)
  Latest dates:
  7 Nov 1986, Yankton Co. (Hall in Seasons 1987a)
  13 Nov 1984, Gregory Co. (Steffen 1985)
  19 Nov 1950, Union Co. (Stephens et al. 1955)

AMERICAN SWALLOW-TAILED KITE *Elanoides forficatus* (Linnaeus)

Status. Extirpated; no records since the summer of 1910 when 1 was collected near Vermillion (Visher 1915). Agersborg (1885) reported a few in the summer in the SE and thought they nested in Nebraska. McChesney (1878; also in Coues 1878) reported this species all winter in 1877–1878 at Ft. Sisseton and wrote that Indians reported them along the James River in the winter and early spring. Since the species now winters in South America and casually north only to southern Florida, McChesney's winter records must be considered highly questionable.

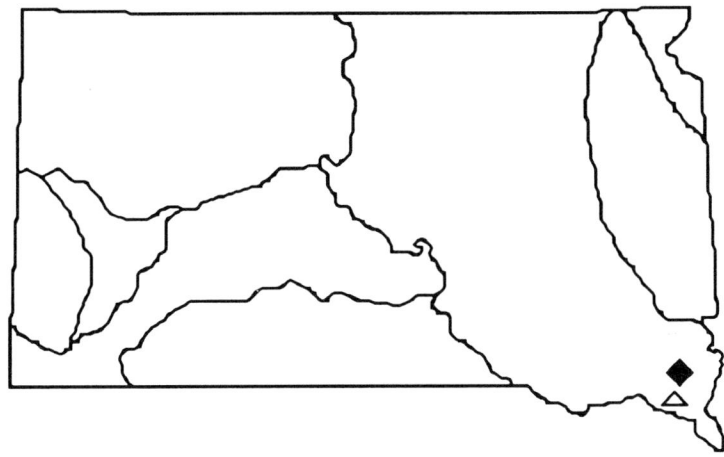

BLACK-SHOULDERED KITE *Elanus caeruleus* (Desfontaines)

Status. Accidental.
Only record:
9–10 Jul 1978, Jones Co., photographed (Mack 1979)

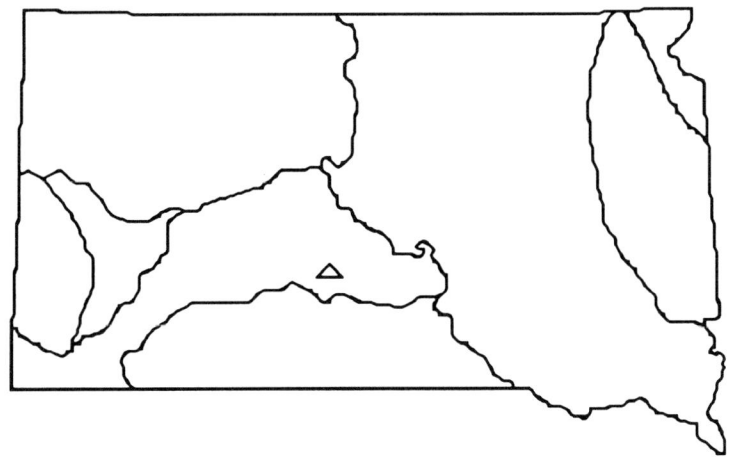

70 KITES, EAGLES AND HAWKS

MISSISSIPPI KITE *Ictinia mississippiensis* (Wilson)

Status. Accidental. After declining in the early 1900's, this species' range has been expanding in the S Great Plains; thus, future SD records may be expected.

Records:
   30 Aug 1823, near Bijou Hills, specimen (present location unknown) (Wilhelm 1835)
   12 May 1983, Minnehaha Co. (Blankespoor 1984)

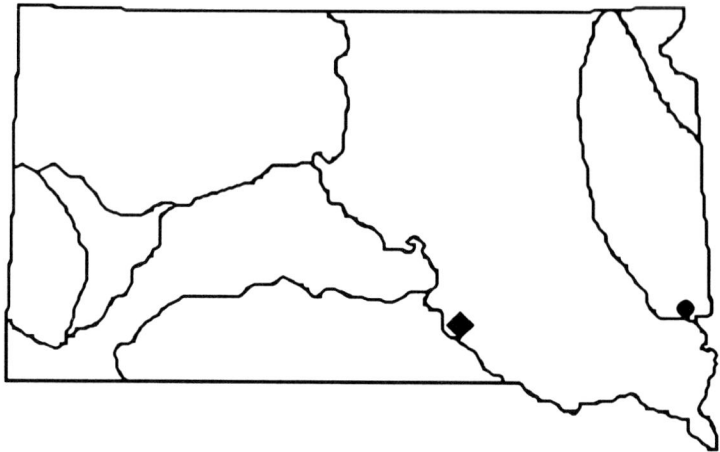

BALD EAGLE *Haliaeetus leucocephalus* (Linnaeus)

Status. Uncommon migrant throughout, more common in the NE lake country, especially during fall migration. Winters regularly in large numbers along the Missouri River below the reservoirs from Pierre to Yankton and at scattered locations across the state. Formerly a rare breeder in the SE (Agersborg 1885); no other reports of nesting.

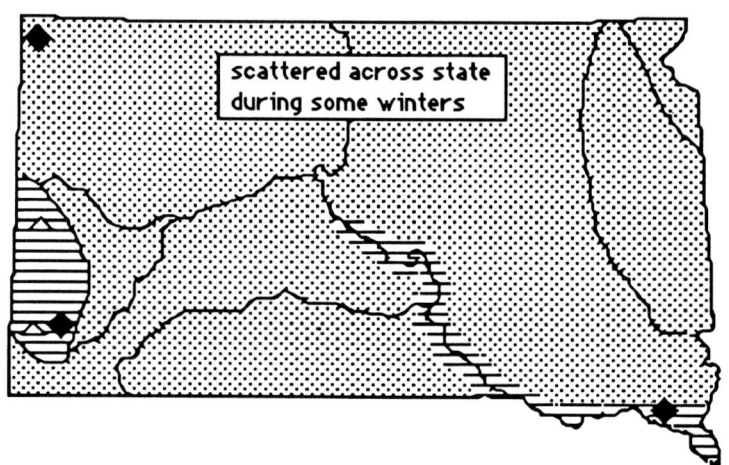

Habitat. Missouri River reservoirs and tributaries; large lakes in the NE; open valleys in the Black Hills. In winter roosts at night in stands of large floodplain trees; habitat in Gregory and Charles Mix counties described by Steenhof et al. (1980).

Spring migration. Mar, peaks probably in latter half of the month.

Earliest dates:
25 Feb 1967 along James River near Forestburg (Loveday)
4 Mar 1951, Canyon Lake by Behrens (Pettingill and Whitney 1965).

Latest dates:
20 Apr 1978, Lacreek NWR (Seasons 1978c)
21 May 1979, Custer Co. (Hagen and Hanson in Seasons 1979c)
28 May 1916, Centerville (Anderson in Stephens 1918)

Summer observations. Because nesting occurs in North Dakota (Stewart 1975) and was attempted in Nebraska 4 miles SW of Yankton (Lock and Schuckman 1973), future nesting is expected in the ideal habitat offered by recent impoundments and reservoirs.

Records:
2 Jul 1969, near Black Fox Camp Ground (Rose)
7-24 Jul 1888, near Custer (Bailey in Anon. 1962)
20 Jul 1910, Little Missouri River (Visher 1914)
10 Aug 1962, Custer Co. (Clark in Anon. 1962)

Fall migration. Oct – Dec.

Earliest dates:
28 Aug 1983, Brown Co. (Tallman et al. in Seasons 1984a)
1 Sep 1978, Brown Co. (Seasons 1979a)
2 Sep 1988, Deuel Co. (Harris and Rose in Seasons 1989a)

Winter. Statewide winter populations from 1961–85 ranged from 81 in 1970 to 476 in 1983, and averaged 286 (mid-winter inventories). Most birds occur along the Missouri River reservoirs. In years when open water is available outside of the regular wintering areas, Bald Eagles are widespread. 28 eagles fed on offal from dead bison in Dec 1955 during the herd reduction at Custer SP (Berner in Pettingill and Whitney 1965). A wintering bird in Clay Co. was color-marked in Saskatchewan (Terry 1976).

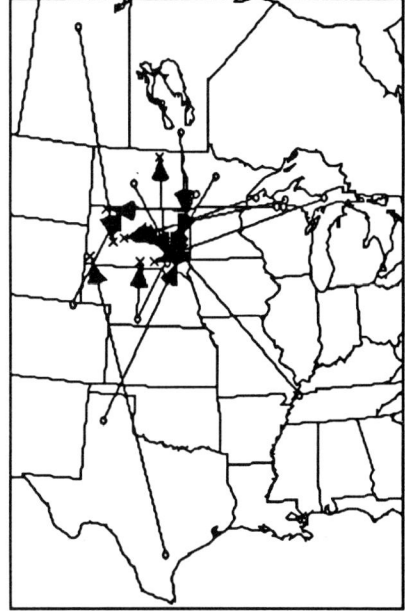

Bald Eagle banding recoveries

NORTHERN HARRIER *Circus cyaneus* (Linnaeus)

Status. Fairly common to common migrant and summer resident, more common W River. Winters regularly in small numbers in S, and sparingly during mild winters farther N. Call (1975) reported 33% of wintering hawks 1966–67 in Clay Co. were Northern Harriers.

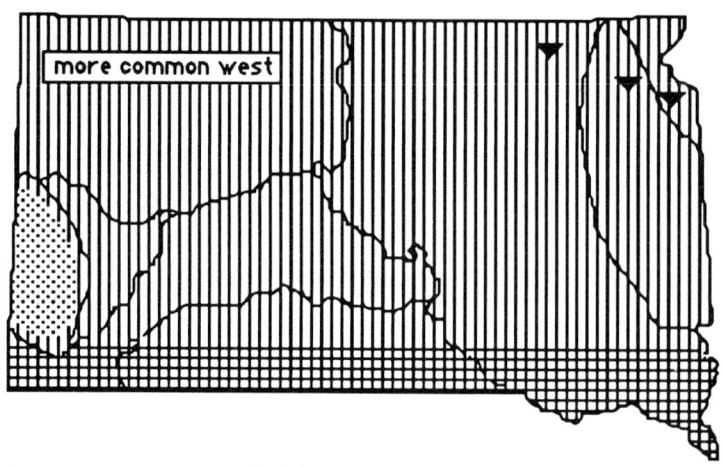

Habitat. Prairies, open fields and marshes.

Spring migration. Last 2 weeks of Mar.

Earliest dates:
19 Feb 1987, Sanborn Co. (Rogers in Seasons 1987c)
25 Feb 1983, Marshall Co. (Smith in Seasons 1983c)
26 Feb 1987, Deuel Co. (Harris in Seasons 1987c)

Nesting. Courtship late Apr – first week of May, with eggs hatching in Jun.

Earliest dates:
13 May 1967, Clay Co. nest with 2 eggs (Call 1967)
30 May – 4 Jun, near Watertown, 5 eggs pipped (Moriarty 1962a)

Latest dates:
13 Jul 1978, Harding Co., 2 fledged young (Springer)
19 Jul 1977, Lacreek NWR, 3 eggs (Lohoefener and Ely 1978)
29 Aug 1978, Deuel Co., adult and 1 fledged young in nest (Harris)

Fall migration. Last 2 weeks of Sep and first half of Oct.

Winter. In Dec 1962, 40 individual Marsh Hawks were reported on 7 CBC, N to Milbank, Sand Lake, and Webster.

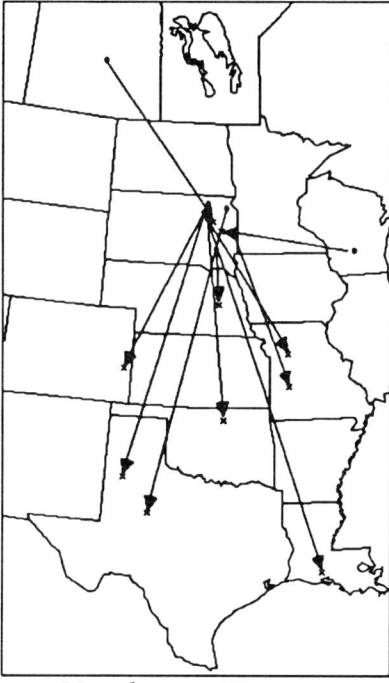

Northern Harrier banding recoveries

SHARP-SHINNED HAWK *Accipiter striatus* Vieillot

Status. Fairly common migrant and uncommon winter resident. Uncommon permanent resident in the Black Hills and a rare nester in the buttes of Harding Co. Formerly resident E of the Missouri, especially SE where said to be common (Agersborg 1885, Visher 1915) and at Ft. Sisseton where not uncommon (Youngworth 1935).

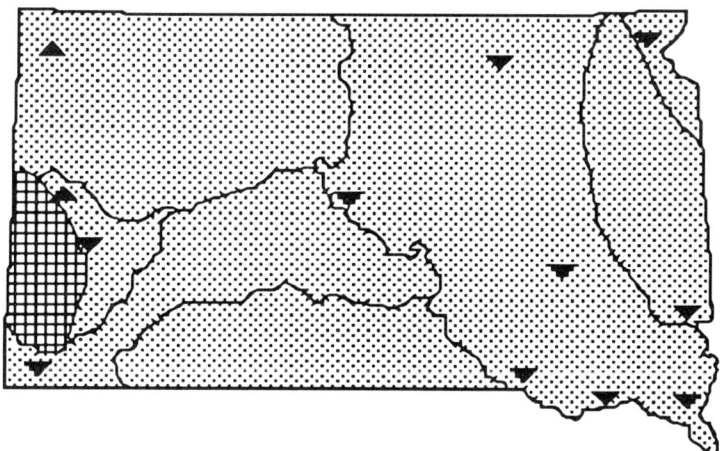

Habitat. Trees. Found in streamside forests and shelterbelts. In Black Hills: riparian forests and conifers.

Spring migration. Apr and May. Early migrants may be wintering birds.

Latest dates:
  16 May 1968, Presho (Springer)
  29 May 1960, Milbank (Elliott 1967a)
Nesting. May – Jul.
  Earliest dates:
    17 May 1983, Harding Co., nest (Hodorff)
    1 Jun 1980, Custer Co., nest with 2 young (Hagen and Hanson in Seasons 1980d)
    8 Jun 1899, Gillette Canyon, nest with 2 newly laid eggs (Cary 1901)
  Latest dates:
    3 Jul 1985, Pennington Co., female on nest (Peterson in Seasons 1985d)
    21 Jul 1984, Meade Co., adult and 2 fledged young (Miller in Seasons 1984d)
    29 Jul 1990, Pennington Co., pair and 1 young (Riner)
Fall migration. Sep and Oct. Very early dates may represent nesting birds. Regularly reported into early winter.
  Earliest dates:
    Late Aug 1911, Bennett Co. (Visher 1912a)
    22 Aug 1910, Harding Co. (Visher 1914)
    28 Aug 1964, Badlands NM (Springer)
Winter.
  CBC reports:
    Aberdeen, Hot Springs, Lake Andes, Pierre, Rapid City, Roberts Co., Sioux Falls, and Union Co.
  Other records:
    13 Jan 1968 and 11 Feb 1970, Sanborn Co. (Harris)
    29 Feb 1964, Yankton (Hall)

COOPER'S HAWK *Accipiter cooperii* (Bonaparte)

Status. Uncommon to rare breeder in Black Hills; rare summer resident elsewhere. Uncommon to fairly common migrant throughout, with more fall observations. Rare to uncommon winter.

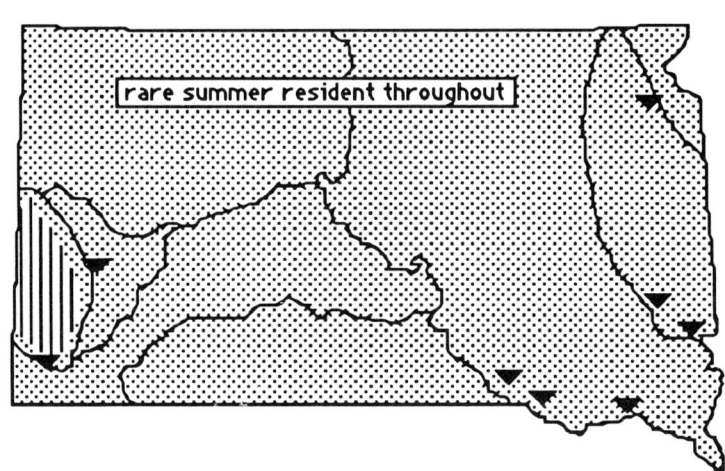

Habitat. Shelterbelts and streamside forests.
Spring migration. Apr. Early spring dates may be of wintering birds.
Nesting. Late Apr – May.
  Earliest dates:
    22 Apr 1982, Roberts Co., nesting (Skadsen in Seasons 1982c)
    7 May 1982, Marshall Co., nest with eggs (Harris in Skadsen 1988)
    15 May 1975, Roberts Co., nest (Harris 1977a)
    15 May 1983, Marshall Co., nest with 2 eggs (Harris and D. Skadsen)
  Latest dates:
    1 Jul 1985, Pennington Co., nest with 4 young (Melius in Seasons 1985d)
    1 Jul 1987, Meade Co., nest with excited adult (Springer in Seasons 1987d)
    14 Jul 1984, Jackson Co., nest with young, fledged 20 Jul (Graupmann in Seasons 1984d)
    18 Jul 1985, Jackson Co., nest with fledglings (Graupmann in Seasons 1985d)
Fall migration. Sep. Late fall dates may represent wintering birds.
Winter.
  CBC reports:
    Hot Springs, Lake Andes, Madison, Platte, Rapid City, Sioux Falls, Waubay, and Yankton.
  Other record:
    7 Feb 1969, Rapid City (Rose)

NORTHERN GOSHAWK *Accipiter gentilis* (Linnaeus)

Status. Rare to uncommon permanent resident especially at higher elevations in the Black Hills. Rare breeder in Harding Co. Uncommon winter visitor elsewhere. Both breeding and wintering populations show marked fluctuations.

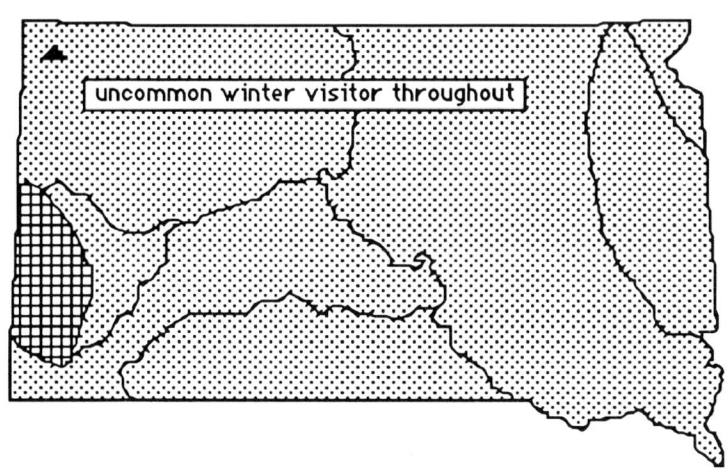

Habitat. In the Black Hills in Ponderosa Pine stands, especially even age old growth stands (Bartelt 1977; Peterson 1986; Erickson 1987), usually near openings, sometimes in mixed spruce and aspen; elsewhere, streamside forests and shelterbelts.

Spring migration.
Latest dates:
30 Mar 1985, Gregory Co. (Steffen in Seasons 1985c)
8 Apr 1973, Deuel Co. (Harris)
8 Apr 1982, Gregory Co. (Steffen 1983b)

Nesting. Mid-Mar – Jun.
Earliest dates:
27 Mar 1972, near Nemo, nest in construction (Wild 1973)
9 Jun 1985, Custer Co., nest with 2 young (Peterson in Seasons 1985d)
Latest dates:
27 Jul 1986, Pennington Co., nest with young (Peterson in Seasons 1986d)
28 Jul 1973, Lawrence Co., nest with 1 young (Wild 1973)
8 Aug 1975, Lawrence Co., young ready to leave nest (Bartelt 1977)

Fall migration. Oct or Nov.
Earliest dates:
23 Aug 1960, Milbank (Elliott 1967a)
15 Sep 1965, Lyman Co. (Springer)
7 Oct 1972, Deuel Co. (Harris)

RED-SHOULDERED HAWK *Buteo lineatus* (Gmelin)

Status. Rare migrant, casual winter resident, and possible breeder. Most records E River.

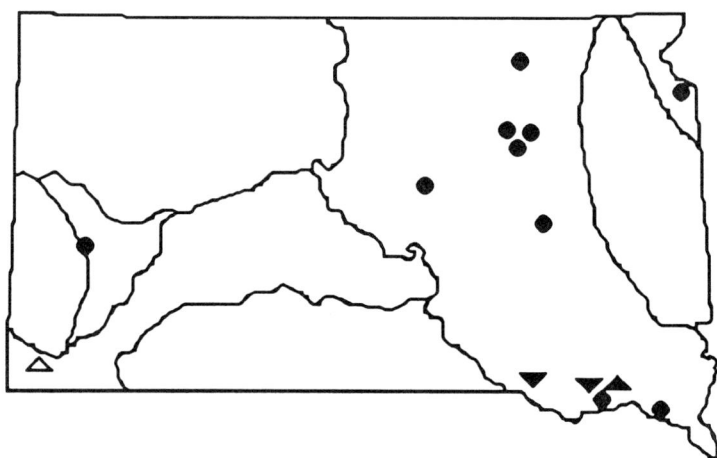

Habitat. River-bottom forests.

Spring migration.
Earliest dates:
14 Mar 1914, Rapid City, specimen (Lee)
16 Mar [year], Huron (Bent 1937)
23 Mar 1973, Spink Co. (Martsching 1984)
Nesting. Several summer records exist, including 1 found dead, 18 Apr 1975 near Big Stone City (Strum) and an immature, 3 Jun 1980, Fall River Co. (Rosche 1982).
Only nesting date:
1-11 Mar 1986, Yankton Co., building nest (Hall in Seasons 1986c)
Fall migration.
Earliest dates:
6 Sep 1975, Spink Co. (Martsching 1984)
9 Sep 1984, Brown Co. (Tallman and Donaldson in Seasons 1985a)
17 Sep 1955, Hyde Co. (Harter 1969)
Latest dates:
4 Oct 1980, Clay Co. (Hall in Seasons 1981a)
7 Oct 1972, Spink Co. (Martsching 1984)
14 Nov [year], Yankton (Bent 1937)
Winter.
Only dates:
8 Jan - Mar 1986, Yankton Co. (Hall in Seasons 1986c)
4 Jan 1986, Charles Mix Co. (Hall in Seasons 1986c)

BROAD-WINGED HAWK *Buteo platypterus* (Vieillot)

Status. Fairly common migrant E River; uncommon migrant W. All breeding records are from Roberts and Lawrence counties. Other breeding season records from Hughes, Bon Homme, Minnehaha, and Lincoln counties. Formerly bred in Bon Homme Co. (Johnson 1958) and seen in summer in Sanborn Co. (Visher 1913a).

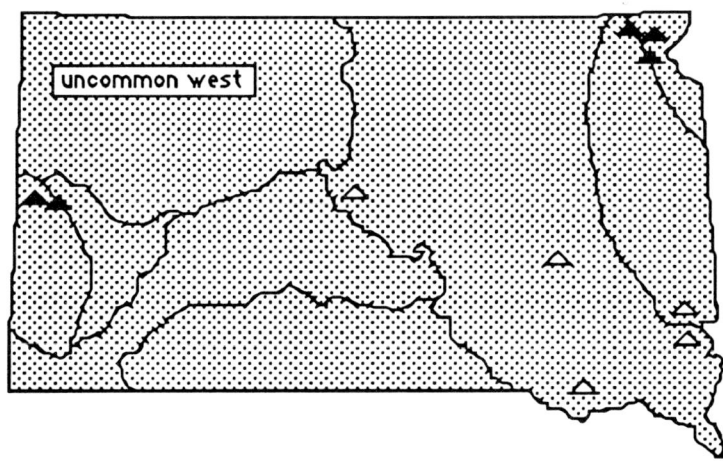

Habitat. Deciduous woodlands.
Spring migration. Mid-Apr - Mid-May. Peak migrations at Pierre between 15 and 25 Apr (Rose). Unusual numbers: 57 during a half-hour period on 27 Apr 1968 in Roberts Co. (Harris).

78 KITES, EAGLES AND HAWKS

Earliest dates:
   25 Mar 1906, Pierre (Lee in Burns 1911)
   26 Mar 1923, Yankton Co. (Halverson)
   31 Mar 1931, Yankton Co. (Halverson)
Nesting. May – July.
Earliest dates:
   11 May 1940, Sodak Park, nest (Harris)
   11 May 1990, Pennington Co. (Whitney)
   24 May 1942, Sodak Park, nest (Harris)
   25 May 1972, Lawrence Co., young left nest (Scott and Whitney 1977)
Latest dates:
   3–24 Jul 1981, Sica Hollow SP, nest with 2 young (Giusti 1982)
   21 Jul 1986, Lawrence Co., 1 young in nest (Ring et al. 1987)
Fall migration. Last half of Sep. Unusual concentration: 16 Sep 1959, Sioux Falls, ca. 400–500 (Krause 1959).
Earliest dates:
   2 Aug 1986, Brown Co. (Griffiths and Griffiths)
   23 Aug 1923, Yankton Co. (Halverson)
   25 Aug 1973, Lacreek NWR (Burgess)
Latest dates:
   30 Sep 1987, Brown Co. (Tallman)
   3 Oct 1925, Yankton Co. (Halverson)
   6 Oct 1978, Deuel Co. (Harris)

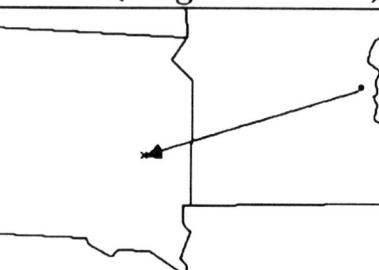
Broad-winged Hawk banding recoveries

SWAINSON'S HAWK *Buteo swainsoni* Bonaparte

Status. Fairly common to common summer resident, most common in C and W, except rare in Black Hills. Abundant during migration. Reports of winter sightings probably are erroneous.

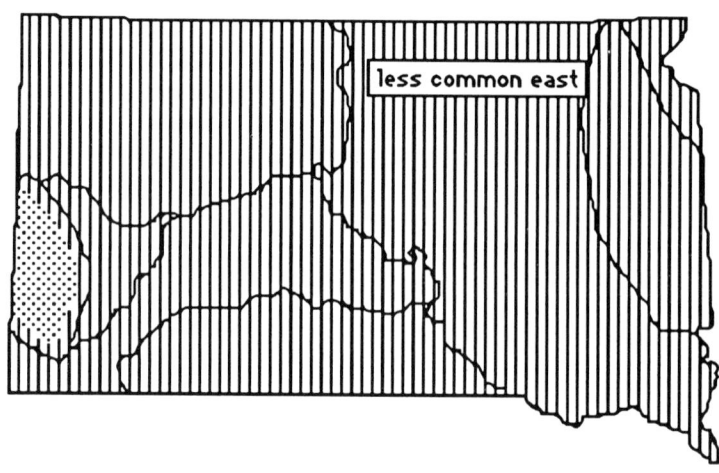

Habitat. Prairies and farmlands.

Spring migration. Last half of Apr. Unusual numbers: 24 Apr 1979, Custer Co., 128 (Nordstrom in Seasons 1979c).

Earliest dates:
  22 Mar 1976, Lyman Co. (McDaniel)
  28 Mar 1986, Codington Co. (Gilman in Seasons 1986c)
  31 Mar 1979, Hutchinson Co. (L. Anderson)

Nesting. On territories by late Apr, incubating by mid-May, with young fledged by the end of Jul. Most nests are in trees, but some are on the ground or cliffs.

Earliest dates:
  23 Apr 1981, Brown Co., building nest (Spomer in Seasons 1987d)
  24 Apr 1987, Day Co., adult on nest (Skadsen in Seasons 1987d)
  1 May 1964, Brown Co., copulating (Springer)

Latest dates:
  19 Jul 1966, Spink Co., 2 young ready to fledge (Adolphson 1966b)
  24 Jul 1966, Beadle Co., 3 young ready to fledge (Adolphson 1966b)
  2 Aug 1985, Badlands NP, nest with 2 young (Glass)

Fall migration. Last 2 weeks of Sep. During fall, large numbers pass through the state, usually in small

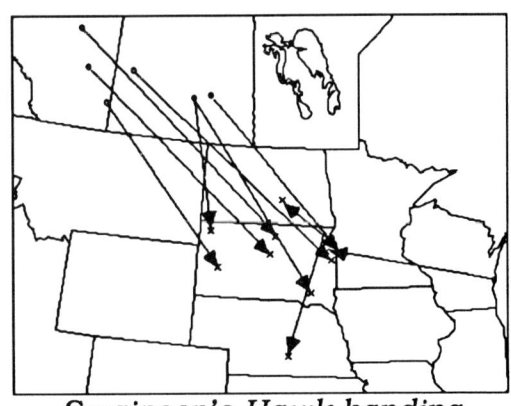

Swainson's Hawk banding recoveries

groups, but sometimes in larger numbers. Flocks of over 25 have been reported across the state. Peak concentrations: 22 Sep 1964, Spink Co., estimated 100 roosting, with some Broad-winged Hawks in the group (Johnson 1965); 25 Sep 1986, Clay Co., over 100 on ground (Jungeman); 18 Sep 1988, Fall River Co., 350 (Peterson in Seasons 1989a); 24 Sep 1988, Stanley Co., 500 on ground (Miller in Seasons 1989a).

Latest dates:
25 Oct 1986, Kingsbury Co. (Wells in Seasons 1987a)
1 Nov 1980, Gavin's Point (Hall in Seasons 1979a)
22 Nov 1980, Bon Homme Co. (Wilcox in Seasons 1981a)

RED-TAILED HAWK *Buteo jamaicensis* (Gmelin)

Status. Fairly common to common migrant throughout; fairly common to common summer resident. Most numerous in the SE. Winters in small numbers throughout, especially in the S. They made up 15% of the wintering hawks in Clay Co. in 1966–67 (Call 1975). The Harlan's Hawk, *B. j. harlani*, is a rare migrant and winter resident in the W (earliest fall date: 19 Sep 1965, near Ipswich (Springer); latest spring date: 30 Apr 1972, below Oahe Dam (Rose and Whitney)). The status of the 3 other races that occur in SD requires clarification.

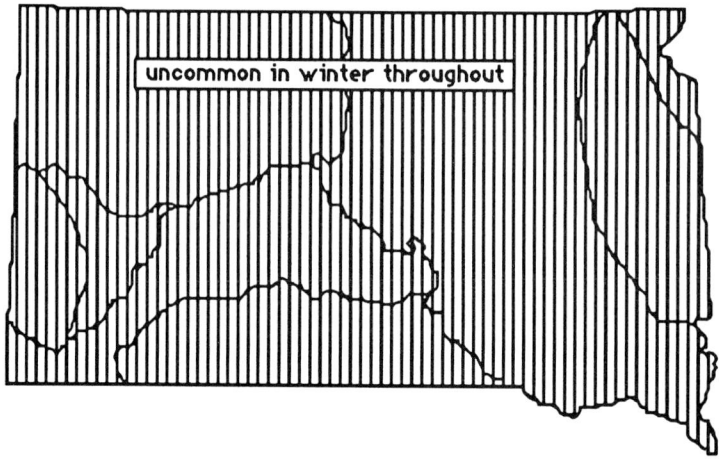

Habitat. Wooded areas, prairie, croplands.

Spring migration. First 2 weeks of Mar in S; later N. Frequently winters, thus early spring sightings are not listed.

Nesting. Mar – Jun. Most young hatch between mid-May and early Jun. In Clay Co. eggs usually laid between 10 and 20 Mar and hatch about 15 Apr (Dunstan and Harrell 1973). Nests usually placed in trees, but also on cliffs and canyon walls in W (see Hereford 1982).

Earliest dates:
17 Mar 1967, Clay Co., apparently incubating (Call 1967)
20 Mar 1985, Miner Co., nest (Anderson in Seasons 1985d)
2 Apr 1985, Codington Co., bird on nest (Harris)

Latest dates:
12 Jun 1964, Yankton Co., young fledged (Hall 1965)
12 Jun 1968, Harding Co., 2 downy young (Baylor and Rosine 1970)
6 Jul 1963, Harding Co., nest with 3 flight-capable young (Grant)

Fall migration. First 2 weeks of Oct.

Winter. A few winter regularly in the S, but also sparingly in NE and in Black Hills. Most numerous at Lake Andes and along the Missouri River impoundments.

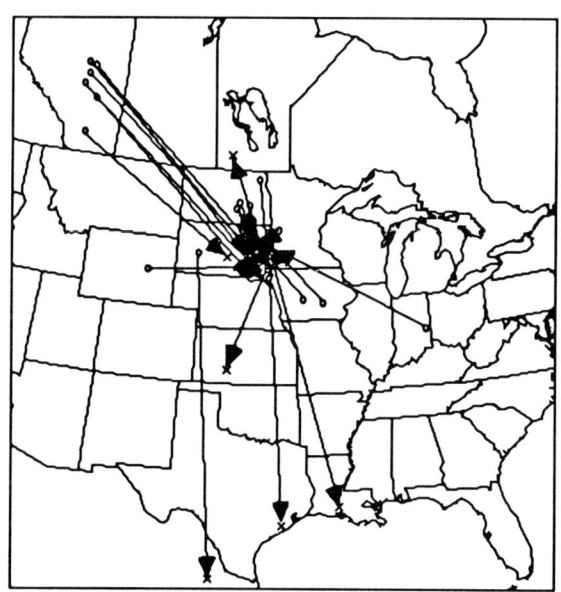

Red-tailed Hawk banding recoveries

FERRUGINOUS HAWK *Buteo regalis* (Gray)

Status. Uncommon to fairly common summer resident in prairies, chiefly in the W, but also in NE counties across the N tier to Roberts and Deuel counties and S to Buffalo Co. Rare in winter. Breeding population averaged 1 pair/412 km^2 for 2 years in Harding Co. (Blair and Schitoskey 1982) and 1 pair/17.4 km^2 in McPherson Co. (Lokemoen and Duebbert 1976).

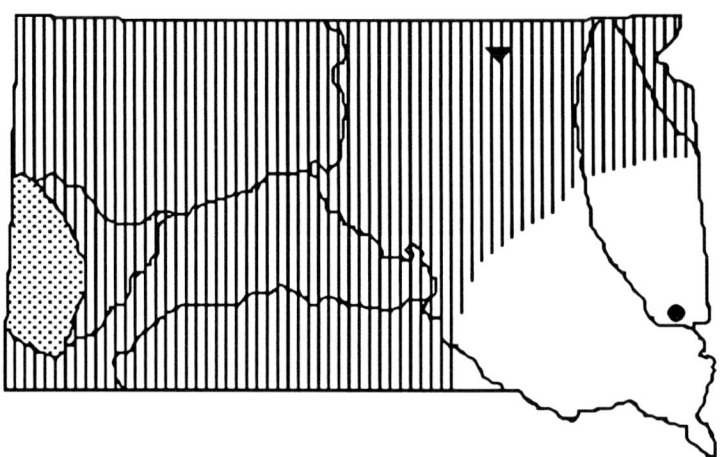

Habitat. Prairies, prairie dog towns during migration and winter in W.

Spring migration. Late Mar or early Apr. Frequently winters, thus early spring sightings are not listed.

Nesting. Apr–Jun. Nests may be in trees, on the ground, on haystacks, or on cliffs. Tree nests may be up to 50 feet above the ground. Nonbreeding or young birds can be observed in the summer outside of breeding range (e.g., 15 Jun 1985, Minnehaha Co. (Springer in Seasons 1985d).

Earliest dates:
  9 Apr 1981, Walworth Co. nest with 1 egg (Spomer in Seasons 1981d)
  12 Apr 1973, McPherson Co., first eggs (Lokemoen and Duebbert 1976)
  13 Apr 1976, Harding Co., first egg laid (Blair and Schitoskey 1982)

Latest dates:
  5 Jul 1974, McPherson Co., nest with young (Lokemoen)

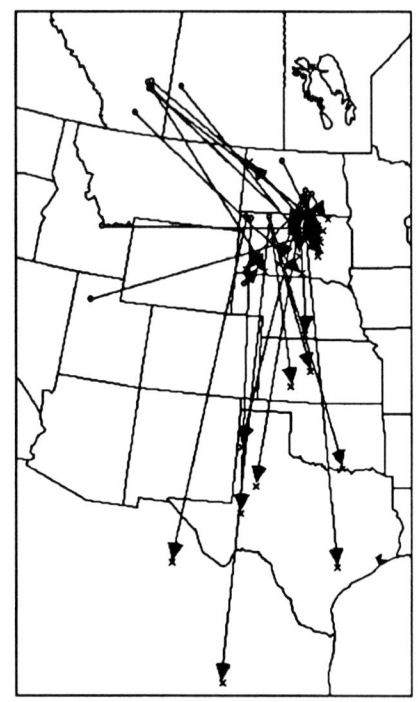

Ferruginous Hawk banding recoveries

10 Jul 1977, Harding Co., last fledgling (Blair and Schitoskey 1982)

12 Jul 1976, Harding Co., last fledgling (Blair and Schitoskey 1982)

Fall migration. Sep. Late fall dates may refer to wintering birds.

Winter. A few winter in the S and further N in mild winters.

Other records:
26 Jan 1966, Brown Co. (Rose 1967)

ROUGH-LEGGED HAWK *Buteo lagopus* (Pontoppidan)

Status. Uncommon to common migrant. Fairly common winter resident, most common in SE. Uncommon winter resident in the Black Hills, less numerous than in surrounding plains.

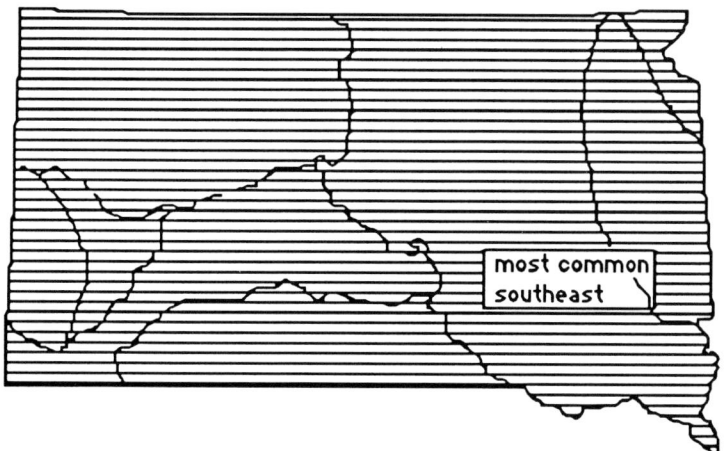

Habitat. Prairies and open fields.

Spring migration. Late Mar – first half of Apr.

Latest dates:
14 May 1987, Badlands NM (Consolo)
15 May 1960, NE SD (Elliott 1967a)
17 May 1985, Deuel Co. (Harris in Seasons 1985c)

Fall migration. Last half of Oct, with peaks in mid-Nov.

Earliest dates:
1 Sep 1987, Pennington Co. (Glass in Seasons 1988a)
2 Sep 1988, Jackson Co. (Graupmann in Seasons 1989a)
7 Sep 1985, Bennett Co. (Steffen and Baker 1986)

Winter. Most common Buteo in winter, especially along the S edge of state. Call (1975) found it represented 31% of the winter hawks in Clay Co. in 1966–1967.

84 KITES, EAGLES AND HAWKS

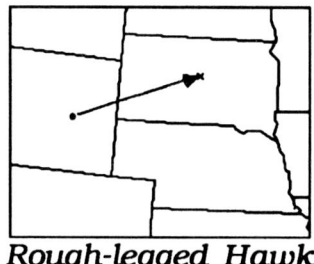

Rough-legged Hawk banding recoveries

GOLDEN EAGLE *Aquila chrysaetos* (Linnaeus).

Status. Fairly common permanent resident far W, uncommon to rare elsewhere W. Uncommon winter E. Formerly rare resident and breeder along the Missouri River in the SE (Agersborg 1885).

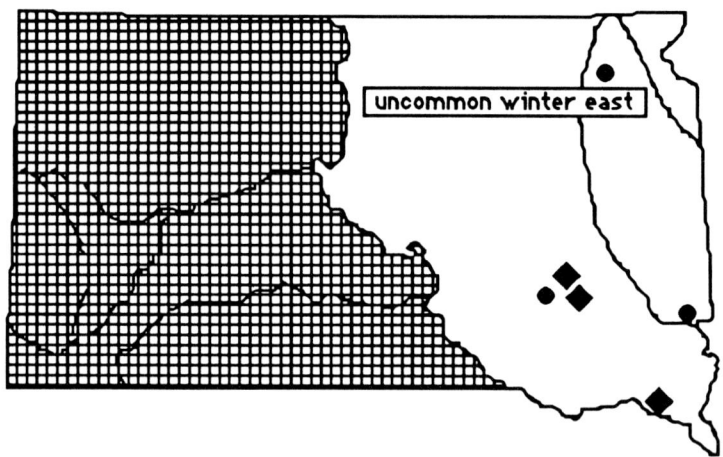

Habitat. Nesting: in Black Hills: on sandstone and limestone cliffs (Pettingill and Whitney 1965; Adolphson); in Harding Co.: on a wide variety of sites, including rocky outcrops, mud buttes, and banks, and in trees along streams (Pulkrabek and O'Brien 1974). Winter: prairies and, along the Missouri River, bottomland forests.

Spring migration. Late Mar.
Latest dates:
  28 Apr 1979, Day Co. (Watters in Seasons 1979c)
  2 May 1909, Emery (Stephens 1918)
  17 May 1909, Alexandria (Stephens 1918)

Nesting. Mar – Jun. Pulkrabek and O'Brien (1974) found 19 active nests in Harding Co. in 1973 and 1974, and estimated 25 to 35.
Earliest dates:
  28 Feb 1981, Fall River Co., nest building (Rosche and Rosche in Seasons 1981d)
  6 Mar 1968, Butte Co., adult incubating in a tree nest (Rose)
  26 Apr 1986, Custer Co., adult on nest (Melius)

Latest dates:
29 Jun 1972, Harding Co., nest with 1 flight-capable young (Grant)
3 Jul 1967, Harding Co., nest with 2 half-grown young (Grant)
18 Jul 1970, Harding Co., adult at nest (Grant)

Fall migration. Late Oct.
Earliest date:
21 Oct 1966, Aurora Co. (Harris)

Winter. Statewide winter populations from 1962–85 ranged from 52 in 1970 to 298 in 1982, and averaged 147 (midwinter inventories). The proportion of adults varied from 80% West River to 64% East River. One young banded during the spring of 1966 in Meade Co. was shot the following winter in N Clay Co. Recorded on many CBC across the state.

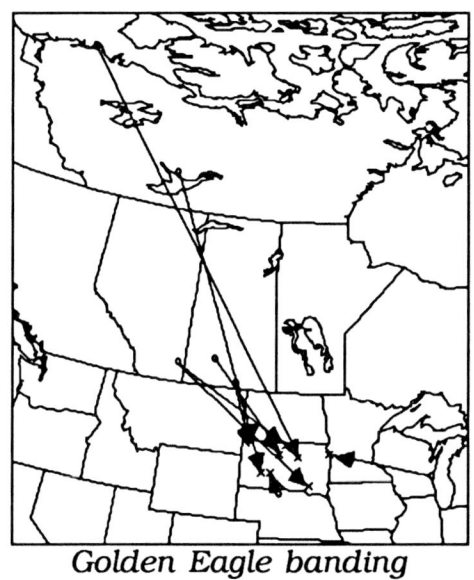

Golden Eagle banding recoveries

FALCONIDAE: Falcons

AMERICAN KESTREL *Falco sparverius* Linnaeus

Status. Fairly common summer resident. Numbers now are apparently down, since rated abundant by Over and Thoms (1946) and Visher (1913a). Uncommon winter resident S. Widespread in mild winters. In the winter of 1966–67 in Clay Co., kestrels were 4% of the hawks seen (Call 1975).

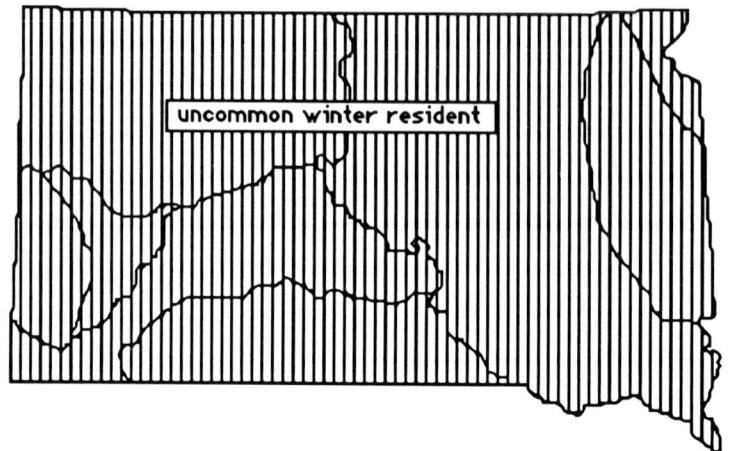

Habitat. Open country, but usually with access to trees large enough to provide nesting cavities. Nests in rocky outcrops in Badlands NP and also in Harding Co. and may be found far from trees in such areas.

Spring migration. Apr. Unusual concentrations: 4 May 1969, 35 in Shannon Co. (Adolphson).

Nesting. May – Jul.
  Earliest dates:
    8 May 1964, Harding Co., nest (Grant)
    14 May 1911, Minnehaha Co., nest with eggs (Larson 1925)
    7 Jun 1977, Day Co., nest in nest box (Husmann)
  Latest dates:
    10 Jul 1965, Brookings Co., flying young (Springer)
    10 Jul 1971, Deuel Co. fledgling out of nest (Harris)
    19 Jul 1970, Harding Co., nest (Grant)
    26 Jul 1977, Deuel Co., flying young (Harris)

Fall migration. Late Aug through Oct. Late fall birds may be attempting to winter.

Winter. Recorded on most CBC.

MERLIN *Falco columbarius* Linnaeus

Status. Rare to uncommon permanent resident in the Black Hills (Pettingill and Whitney 1965) and NW and possibly to E Meade Co. (Tallman et al. 1983) and Jackson Co. (R. Peterson). Pulkrabek and O'Brien (1974) estimated 52 pairs in Harding Co. in 1974. Uncommon migrant and winter visitor elsewhere.

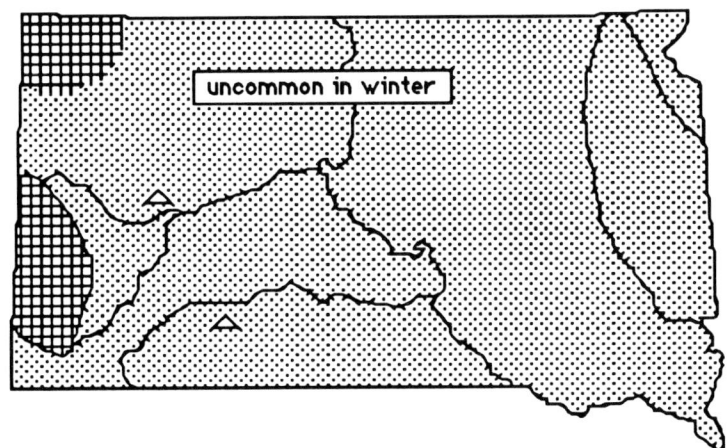

Habitat. Nesting: open pine forests and woodland edges. Migration and winter: prairies and lake shores.

Spring migration: Late Apr and early May. Early spring birds may have wintered in the state.

Latest dates:
  9 May 1952, Union Co. (Felton and Youngworth)
  13 May 1923, Union Co. (Spiker in Stephens et al. 1955)
  16 May 1987, Bennett Co. (Baker in Seasons 1987c)

Nesting. Late Apr through Jun. Pulkrabek and O'Brien (1974) give no specific dates, but indicate that most Harding Co. nests contained young in Jun.

Earliest dates:
  25 May 1975, Harding Co., nest (Grant)
  11 Jun 1948, Pennington Co., nest with 5 newly-hatched young (Pettingill and Whitney 1965)
  16 Jun 1970, Harding Co., nest (Grant)

Latest dates:
  2 Jul 1972, Harding Co., 3 nests with 4 young, 1 nest with 3 eggs and 1 young (Grant)
  14 Jul 1982, Wind Cave NP, pair and 2 fledged young (Weaver 1982)

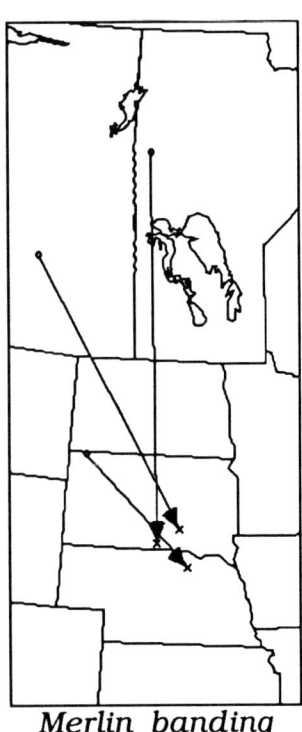

Merlin banding recoveries

Fall migration. Mid-Sep – Nov.
   Earliest dates:
   4 Sep 1989, Marshall Co. (Harris in Seasons 1990a)
   10 Sep 1968, Hyde Co. (Harter 1969)
   12 Sep 1957, Fall River Co. (Whitney)
Winter. The breeding race, *F. c. richardsoni*, was present in Vermillion from 23 Nov – 27 Dec 1984 (Jungeman) and was banded in Aberdeen on 10 Feb 1988 (Tallman in Seasons 1988b); thus both this and the nominate race occur in winter. Merlins are occasionally reported on many CBC.

PEREGRINE FALCON *Falco peregrinus* Tunstall

Status. Uncommon migrant throughout, with more observations E River. Formerly rare summer resident in the Black Hills (Pettingill and Whitney 1965) and Slim Buttes (Patton 1926). McChesney (1879) reported that a few remained through the summer in the Ft. Sisseton area; 1 was also seen at Ft. Sisseton on 5 Jun 1931 (Youngworth 1935). Probably no longer breeds in SD. In 1979 in the Black Hills 2 were cross-fostered and fledged in a Prairie Falcon nest (Sharps and O'Brien 1984). Listed by the USFWS as endangered.

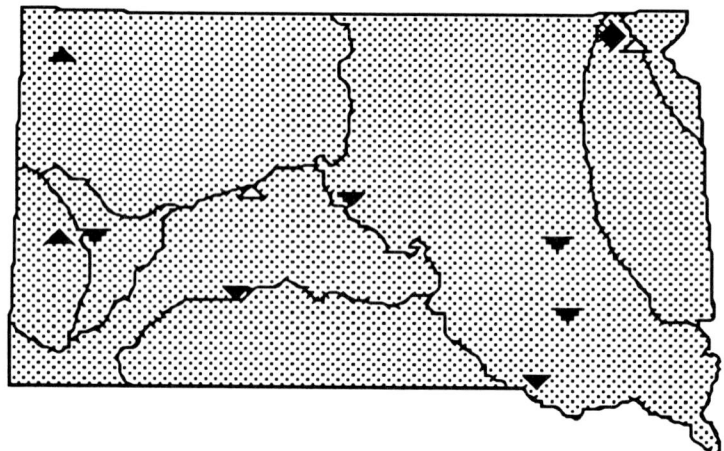

Habitat. Nesting: rocky cliffs. Migration: larger bodies of water. Usually stays close to waterfowl and shorebird concentrations.
Spring migration. Early May.
   Earliest dates:
   15 Mar 1955, Wall Lake (Krause and Rosine 1955)
   18 Mar 1983, Brookings Co. (Husmann in Seasons 1983c)
   Latest dates:
   17 May 1985, Brookings Co. (Flake and Linder 1985)
   18 May 1968, Hyde Co. (Jonkel and Harris)
   22 May 1987, Brown Co. (Tallman and Prisbe in Seasons 1987c))
Nesting. May through Jul. Breeding season observation: 16 Jun 1976, Haakon Co., along Cheyenne River (fide R. Hill).

Only dates:
9 May 1925, Slim Buttes, nesting (Patton 1926)
18 Jun 1945, Pennington Co., occupied nest, stage undetermined (Dilger in Pettingill and Whitney 1965)
Fall migration. Probably latter half of Sep. Very few observations.
Earliest dates:
2 Sep 1965, Badlands NP (Russell 1966)
2 Sep 1989, Marshall Co. (Harris in Seasons 1990a)
23 Sep 1979, Roberts Co. (Harris and Monson)
25 Sep 1981, Brown Co. (Harris et al.)
Latest dates:
20 Nov 1982, Turner Co., dead on road (L. Anderson)
25 Nov 1977, Oahe Dam (Hill)
25 Nov 1979, Hughes Co. (Smith in Seasons 1980a)
Winter. Winter records are unusual.
CBC reports:
Huron, Pierre, and Rapid City.
Other records:
2 Jan 1985, Charles Mix Co. (Skadsen in Seasons 1985b)
8 Feb 1981, Davison Co. (McLaird in Seasons 1981b)
16 Feb 1985, Jackson Co. (Graupmann in Seasons 1985b)

GYRFALCON *Falco rusticolus* Linnaeus
Status. Rare winter visitor.

Habitat. Open prairies.
Spring migration.
Latest date:
23 Apr 1955, Wall Lake (Krause 1955a)
Fall migration.
Earliest dates:
8 Sep 1949, Grant Co. (Donahoe 1950)
4 Oct 1986, Butte Co. (Miller in Seasons 1987a)
8 Oct 1972, Deuel Co. (Harris 1973)

PRAIRIE FALCON *Falco mexicanus* Schlegel

Status. Rare permanent resident W, except uncommon in far W. Uncommon migrant E, more common during winter. The 1874 Custer Expedition records indicate that the Prairie Falcon was "abundant everywhere on the plains, but was not seen in the Black Hills. Its breeding places were found on almost every high butte" (Grinnell 1875).

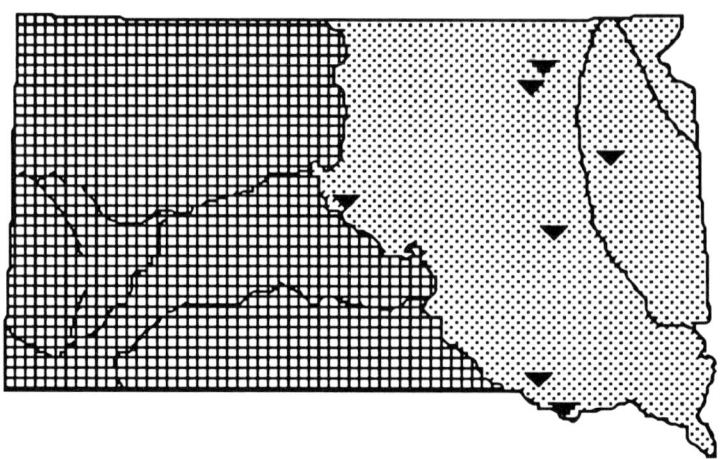

Habitat. Plains and open areas, with cliffs for nesting.
Spring migration. Only E River dates are given.
　Latest dates:
　　27 Apr 1960, Milbank (Elliott 1967a)
　　30 Apr 1983, Day Co. (Koerner in Seasons 1983c)
　　5 May 1912, Minnehaha Co. (Larson 1925)
Nesting. Mid-Apr – Jul. In N Cave Hills cliff sites, nests averaged 1.5 km apart (Maher 1982). 2 occupied nests at Wind Cave in July 1937 (Suter in Pettingill and Whitney 1965).
　Earliest dates:
　　24 Apr 1926, Harding Co., nest with 3 eggs (Abbey)
　　19 May 1925, Black Hills, nest with 4 eggs (Abbey)
　　10 Jun 1981, Fall River Co., nest (Whitney)
　Latest dates:
　　22 Jun 1969, Wind Cave NP, nest with 2 young (Weaver 1982)
　　26 Jun 1978, Custer SP, nest with 3 eggs (Spomer in Seasons 1978d)
　　2 Jul 1966, Harding Co., nest with 5 flight-capable young (Grant)
Fall migration. Only early E River fall dates are given.
　Earliest dates:
　　8 Aug 1946, Milbank (Elliott)
　　10 Aug 1986, Day Co. (Skadsen 1986)
　　15 Aug 1976, Cottonwood Lake (Martsching 1984)
Winter. Numerous records across the state. All observations in winter in Clay Co. from 1979–1984 were females (Jungeman)

CBC records:
Aberdeen, Huron, Lacreek, Lake Andes, Pierre, Rapid City, Sand Lake, Springfield, and Watertown.

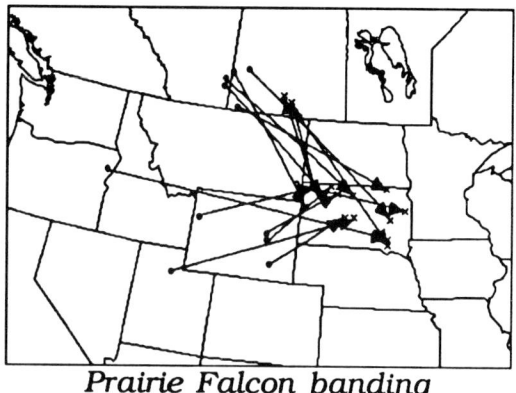
Prairie Falcon banding recoveries

PHASIANIDAE: Partridge, pheasant, grouse, turkey, and quail

GRAY PARTRIDGE *Perdix perdix* (Linnaeus).

Status. Introduced. Common permanent resident N and E; uncommon to fairly common elsewhere, except rare or absent in the SW. In Dec 1983 Harris found about 1 covey per mile in the Watertown area.

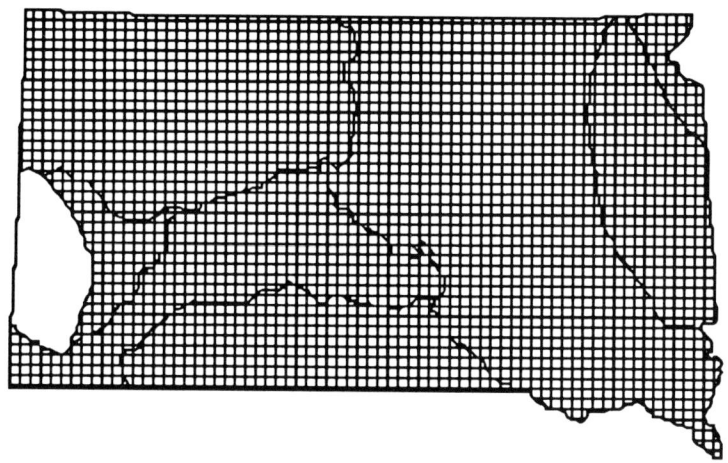

History of Introduction. In 6 introductions between 1923 and 1941 the GFP and private parties released about 2500 pairs over the state; most were acquired from Canada (Rose 1968).
Habitat. Agricultural fields, pastures, and grassy roadsides.
Nesting. Egg-laying in May – Jul.
Earliest dates:
6 Jun 1988, Meade Co., nest with 11 eggs (E. Miller)
8 Jun 1974, Walworth Co., nest with 20 partridge eggs and 2 pheasant eggs (hatched 20 Jun) (L. Smith)
10 Jun 1974, Hand Co., nest with 23 partridge eggs and 1 pheasant egg (Schuurmans)

Latest dates:
  3 Jul 1966, Harding Co., pair with several young (Grant)
  20 Jul 1970, Harding Co., 3 adults with 16 1/3-grown young (Grant)
  25 Jul 1978, Deuel Co., nest with 9 eggs (Harris)

CHUKAR *Alectoris chukar* (Gray)

Status. Introduced widely across state. No nesting records. Formerly uncommon permanent resident in local areas in Harding and Jackson counties.

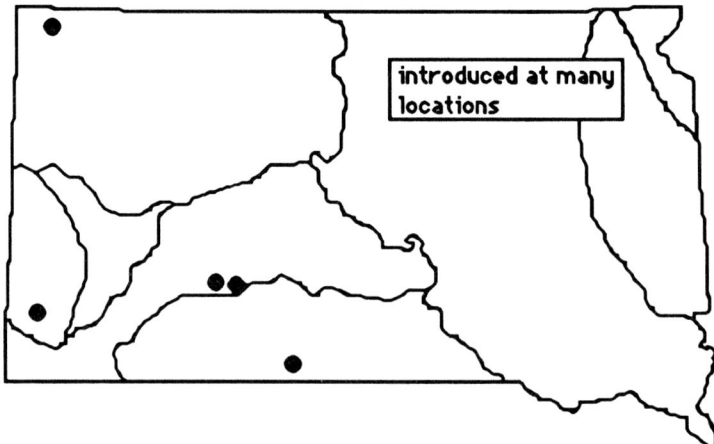

History of introduction. The GFP released 198 wild-trapped Chukars from Wyoming and Nevada in the Cave Hills during Mar 1960 and Apr 1961. Pulkrabek and Rose encountered about 45 Chukars on 24 Oct 1968 on Table Mountain, about 7 miles W of North Cave Hills, and Pulkrabek reported birds in the same area in 1973 and 1975. In Apr 1964, the GFP released 174 Chukars from Nevada into the Badlands area of Jackson Co., S of Kadoka (Rose 1968). Rose photographed 1 of 5 birds found there on 9 Jan 1968. McDaniel observed 2 birds in Todd Co. on 5 Mar 1981 and Weber (in Seasons 1986b) found 1 in Custer Co. on 7 Feb 1986, although the latter was likely a locally escaped caged bird (R. Peterson). Also released unsuccessfully in Brown and Day counties in 1937 and more recently and in the Black Hills in 1940. Records from other areas of the state probably represent local releases or escapes.

Habitat. Rocky and rough terrain.

RING-NECKED PHEASANT *Phasianus colchicus* Linnaeus

Status. Introduced. Common to abundant permanent resident E, uncommon to common W, except absent Black Hills.

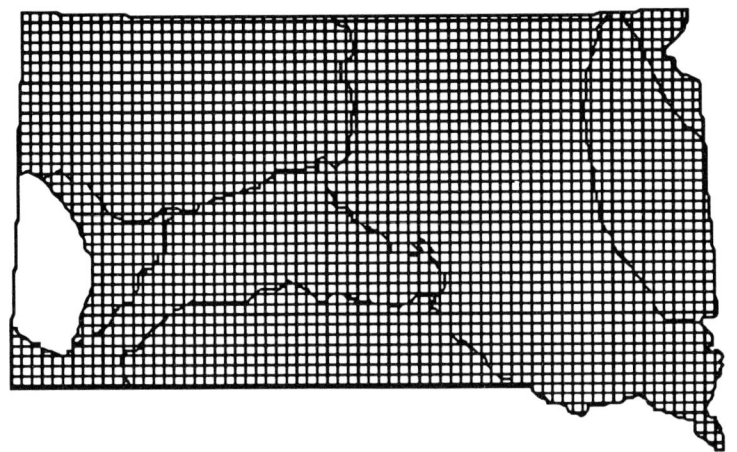

History of introduction. Oregon birds were released near Sturgis in 1891 and Illinois stock was released in Minnehaha Co. in 1899 and 1903; both introductions eventually failed. In 1908 and 1909, several people released birds in Spink Co., and soon afterwards the Redfield Chamber of Commerce made a large release. These introductions were successful. In 1911, the GFP released about 500 pheasants along the James River in Spink and Beadle counties. The GFP released an additional 7,660 pheasants between 1914 and 1919 and, between 1926 and 1941, trapped and transplanted more than 33,000 birds into Corson, Fall River, Lawrence, Meade, Pennington, Perkins, and Zieback counties (GFP files, Rose 1968).

Habitat. Almost all upland habitats in E. In W, found in cultivated fields and along river and stream bottoms.

Nesting. 1 May – mid-Jun. Main hatching period extends from first week of Jun through about first week of Jul. Nests most frequently along fencerows where nests per acre averaged 11.6 in 1958 and 13.0 in 1959. Roadsides averaged 1.87 nests per acre in 1958 and 2.82 in 1959. Among field habitats, alfalfa had the highest density: 1.31 in 1959 and 1.57 in 1959. Sloughs, wild hay, field margins, and railroad rights-of-way had nest densities greater than 1 per acre (Trautman 1960).

Earliest dates:
early Apr, egg production begins (Trautman 1960)
24 May 1985, Gregory Co., 10 downy young (Springer)

Latest dates:
11 Aug 1988, Bennett Co., 7 half-grown young (Springer)
19 Sep 1965, Kingsbury Co., 2 young (Springer)
15 Oct 1964, Brookings Co., 2 half-grown young (Springer)

BLUE GROUSE *Dendragapus obscurus* (Say)

Status. Formerly occurred in Black Hills. 4 specimens were collected in the Black Hills on 2 and 3 Aug 1856, and 9 Aug 1857 (Wood in Baird 1858). Grinnell (1875) reported a single bird in dense pine forests of the higher portions of Black Hills in summer 1874. Probably extirpated in the late 1800's. Cary (1901) wrote that ranchers frequently shot these grouse in the higher Black Hills. However, because he did not list the more common Ruffed Grouse as occurring in the Black Hills, these reports likely refer to gray-phased Ruffed Grouse. Between 18 and 30 Jul 1969, the GFP released near Black Fox Campground, W of Rochford, 22 mixed-age Blue Grouse from Colorado. In May 1971, 1 of these, an adult female when released, was found by Barrett as a road kill E of Belle Fourche, about 40 miles N of the release site and outside the Black Hills. On 15 Aug 1974, 10 Blue Grouse from Colorado were released in the Harney Peak area. These introductions are presumed to have been unsuccessful and no other observations have been reported.

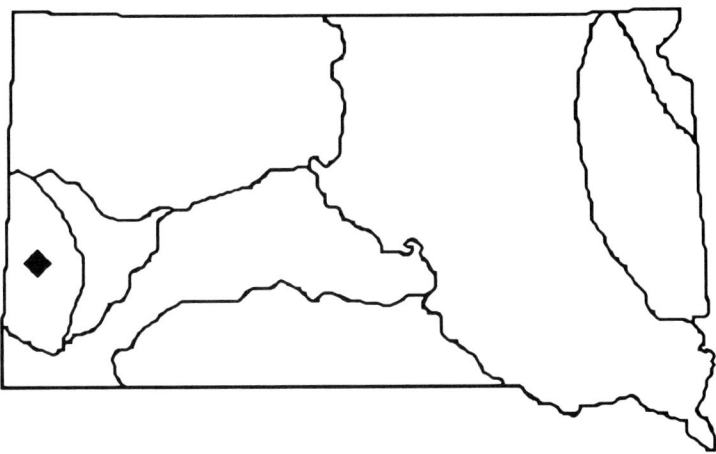

RUFFED GROUSE *Bonasa umbellus* (Linnaeus)

Status. Uncommon permanent resident in Black Hills, more numerous in the N half. Grinnell (1875) considered it to be abundant in 1874. Also formerly occurred in the buttes of NW Harding Co. (Visher 1914), questionably rarely on the old Rosebud Indian Reservation (Reagan 1908), and in the NE (Over and Thoms 1946).

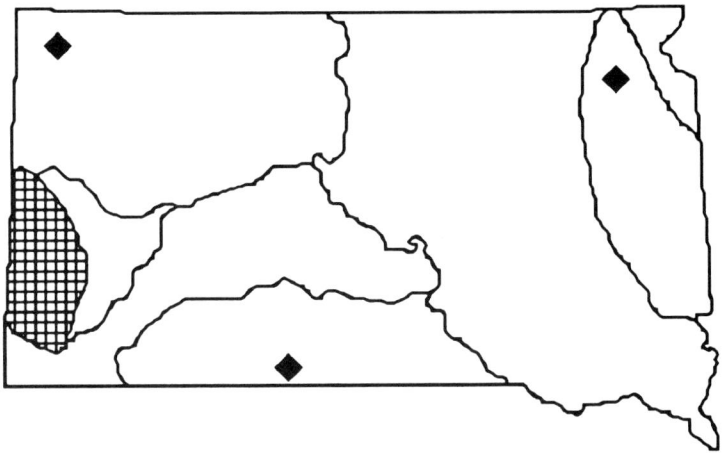

Habitat. Young to medium age stands of aspens, other hardwoods, and open pine forests. Fire protection has resulted in loss of optimum habitat.

Nesting. May – Jul.

Earliest dates:
2 May 1963, near Black Fox Campground, nest with 13 eggs (Richardson in Pettingill and Whitney 1965)
6 May 1958, Harney Peak region, nest with 10 eggs (Richardson in Pettingill and Whitney 1965)

Latest dates:
16 Aug 1959, Reno Gulch, adult with 2 downy young (Richardson in Pettingill and Whitney 1965)
22 Aug 1989, Pennington Co., adult with 3 young (Meader)

SAGE GROUSE *Centrocercus urophasianus* (Bonaparte)

Status. Locally common permanent resident in Harding, Butte, and W portions of Perkins, Meade (numbers greatly reduced along eastern edge of range), and Fall River counties. Formerly found in many W River areas (Visher 1914, Over and Thoms 1946). Visher (1914) stated that they occupied the Sage Creek Basin in the Badlands until 1907. Reported in what is now Corson Co. by Hoffman (1877).

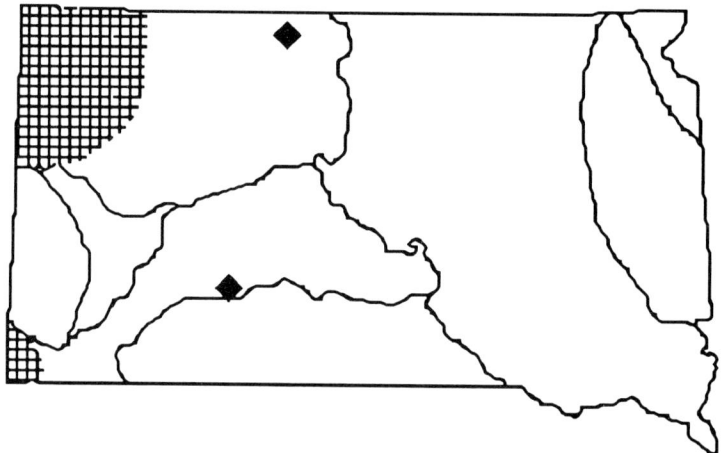

Habitat. Sagebrush prairies. Destruction of sagebrush areas is a continuing threat to this species.

Nesting. Mid-May – early Jun.
  Earliest dates:
    23 Mar 1969, W of Belle Fourche, courtship (Whitney et al.)
    14 Apr 1984, Fall River Co., 8 males courting (Peterson in Seasons 1984c)
    15 Apr 1985, Fall River Co., 6 males courting (Peterson in Seasons 1985c)
  Egg dates:
    14 May 1925, Harding Co., nest with 8 eggs (Patton)
    21 May 1969, NE Butte Co., nest with 9 eggs (Photograph by Rose)
    1 Jun 1954, SE Harding Co., nest with 6 eggs and 2 young, and another brood (Chapman and Chapman 1954)
  Latest dates:
    17 Jul 1978, Harding Co., female and 3 2/3-grown young (Springer)
    20 Jul 1970, Harding Co., female and 5 young (Grant)
    26 Jul 1967, Harding Co., brood (Baylor and Rosine 1970)

PARTRIDGES, PHEASANT, GROUSE, TURKEY, AND QUAIL

GREATER PRAIRIE CHICKEN *Tympanuchus cupido* (Linnaeus)

Status. Fairly common permanent resident in S-central South Dakota. Most of the population is within an area about 4 counties wide from the Nebraska border N to Dewey, Walworth, and Edmunds counties. In recent years seen regularly in the fall and winter in Brown, Marshall, Day, and Clark counties, where it breeds in small numbers. Recently reported nesting in Grant Co. and wintering in the E central and SE. Originally the species occurred only in the SE (Coues 1874), although Audubon (1897) saw 1 at the Big Bend of the Missouri River below Pierre in 1843. Cooke (1888) noted that this species moved W with settlements, following the planting of grain. At that time it occupied the whole length of the E part of the state in a strip 30 to 60 miles wide. The species moved as a breeder as far as SW Harding Co. (Visher 1914), but is now absent from that area, and no longer nests in the SE.

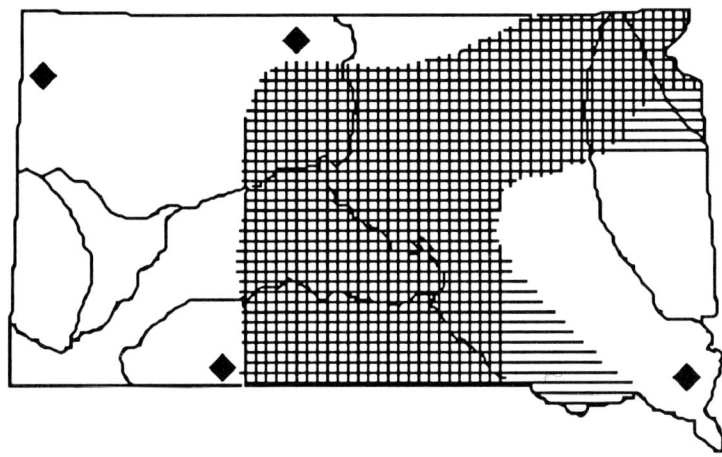

Habitat. Tall-grass and mid-grass prairies.
Nesting. Mid-May – Jun.
  Earliest dates:
    6 May 1911, Douglas Co., nest with 10 eggs (Walker)
    7 May 1889, Sanborn Co., nest with 10 eggs (Patton)
    14 May 1889, Flandreau, nest with 15 eggs (Patton)
  Latest dates:
    22 May – 13 Jun 1974, Lyman and Jones counties, 5 nests (Carter and Rice)
    2 Jun 1882, Flandreau, nest with eggs (H. Bailey)
    9 Jun 1884, Vermillion, nest with 16 fresh eggs (Agersborg in Cooke 1888)
    26 Jun 1987, Grant Co., adult with brood (Koerner and Getman in Seasons 1987d)

SHARP-TAILED GROUSE *Tympanuchus phasianellus* (Linnaeus)

Status. Permanent resident W to E-central, formerly in SE where it occurred primarily in winter (Coues 1874, Agersborg 1885, Visher 1913a, 1915). Common along Missouri River and in prairies W through Corson, Ziebach, and Bennett counties; present but less common farther W. Recently present in Grant, Codington, Marshall and Roberts counties. Hillman and Jackson (1973) summarized information on this species in South Dakota.

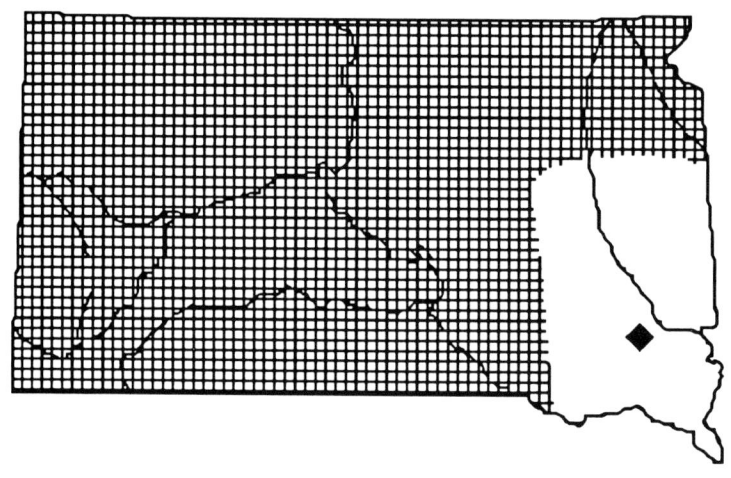

Habitat. Short-grass and mid-grass prairies. Most numerous in grassland habitats that include brushy draws and thickets.
Nesting. Mid-May – Jun.
 Earliest dates:
  6 Feb 1987, Bennett Co., birds on lek (Seasons 1987b)
  10 May 1925, Lyman Co., nest (Lee in Whitney 1955)
  13 May 1987, Grant Co., 4 nests with eggs (Getman in Seasons 1987d)
 Latest dates:
  12 Jul 1978, Mellette Co., female and 16 3/4-grown young (Springer)
  17 Jul 1978, Harding Co., female and 10 1/3-grown young (Springer)
  24 Jul 1973, Harding Co., female and 3 half-grown young (Springer)

WILD TURKEY *Meleagris gallopavo* Linnaeus

Status. Reintroduced. Fairly common permanent resident in Black Hills, Fall River Co., timbered areas in Harding and Jackson counties, along W rivers, and in timbered areas E River.

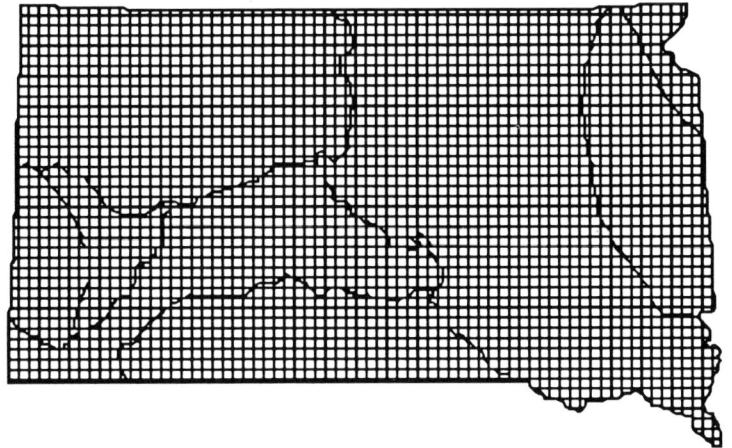

History of reintroduction. At the time of first exploration, the subspecies *silvestris*, the Eastern Wild Turkey, was found along the Missouri River and its tributaries N to the Grand River (Lewis and Clark in Burroughs 1961, Long in Wright 1915), but the last native bird was killed before 1920. Between 1948 and 1951, the GFP released 49 Merriam's Turkeys (*M. g. merriami*), acquired from Colorado and New Mexico, in the Black Hills (Rose 1968). Thereafter until present, birds, including Rio Grande Turkeys (*M. g. intermedia*), have been released by GFP nearly every year in almost all suitable parts of the state (Fowler 1987).
Habitat. Coniferous and deciduous woodlands. Nests are placed on the ground under some form of cover, such as pine slash or junipers (Peterson and Richardson 1975).
Nesting. Apr – Aug. Peak hatching first 2 weeks of Jun.

Earliest dates:
- 19 Apr 1971, Black Hills, nest with 4 eggs (Sallee in Peterson and Richardson 1975)
- 20 Apr 1968, near Rapid City, nest with 3 eggs (Can in Peterson and Richardson 1975)
- 29 Apr 1971, near Belle Fourche, nest with 7 eggs (Marchiando in Peterson and Richardson 1975)

Latest dates:
- 12 Aug 1988, Todd Co., 2 females with half-grown young (Springer)
- 13 Sep 1988, Pennington Co., 2 adults and 6 small young (Biltoft)
- 4 Oct 1986, Yankton Co., 21 half-grown young (Hall)

NORTHERN BOBWHITE *Colinus virginianus* (Linnaeus)

Status. Uncommon to common permanent resident along S edge of E SD. Range fluctuates N and W along major drainages. Formerly more widespread. Coues (1874) stated that Bobwhite spread N and W with the advance of settlement, that the species was abundant at Fort Randall, and that according to Hayden it followed the Missouri River to the White River. In 1871, McChesney (1879) observed birds as far N as Ft. Sully. Cooke (1888) reported that in "southeastern Dakota it is abundant and has advanced north in the state to about latitude 44° 30'." (Brookings and Beadle counties). Has been introduced elsewhere. Recent records from Brown and Day counties and earlier reports from Shannon, Marshall, Haakon, and Faulk counties, Lacreek NWR, Rapid City, and Wind Cave NP are probably the result of introductions.

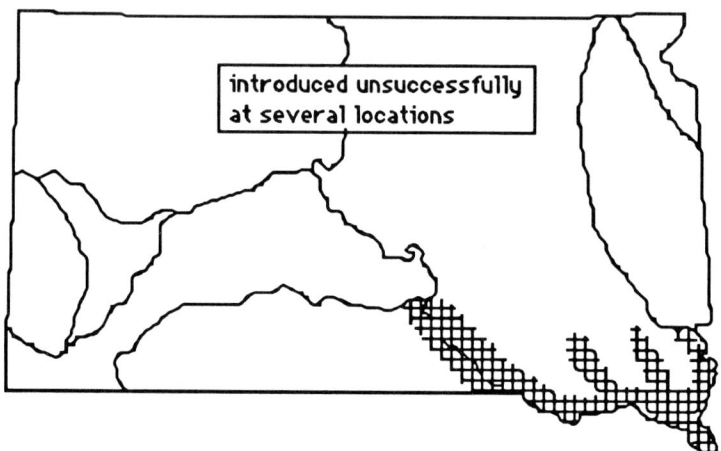

Habitat. Mixed habitat. Especially numerous in bottomland croplands and brushy borders along the Missouri River.

Nesting.
Only record:
- 4 Jun 1987, Union Co., 2 nests with 4 eggs (Beck)

PARTRIDGES, PHEASANT, GROUSE, TURKEY, AND QUAIL

CALIFORNIA QUAIL *Lophortyx californicus* (Shaw)

Status. Unsuccessfully introduced in the Cascade Valley of Fall River Co.

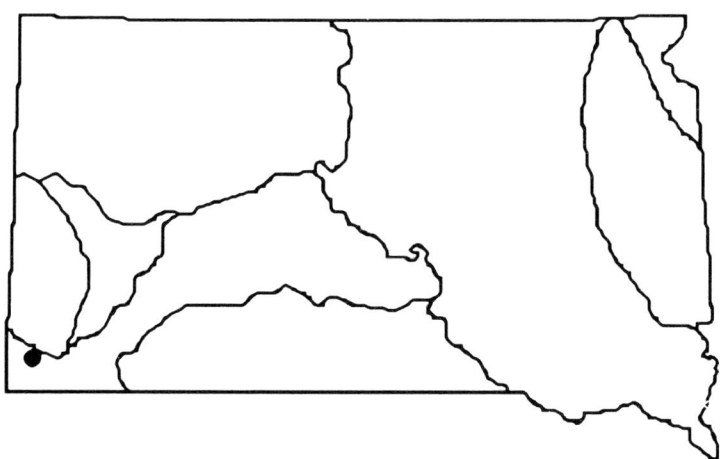

History of introduction. In 1961 the GFP released 100 wild-trapped birds from Oregon near Cascade Falls. Pairs with young were reported annually around nearby ranches for several years thereafter (Pettingill and Whitney 1965). Rose observed individuals S of Cascade Falls in May 1967 and on 21 Apr 1969. Coveys have also been reported in weedy areas in the upper reaches of Angostura Reservoir. Recent observations may indicate private releases.

Habitat. Brushy and weedy areas.

Nesting.
  Only record:
    27 Jun 1963, Cascade Springs, female with 11 small chicks (Richardson in Pettingill and Whitney 1965).

RALLIDAE: Rails, Gallinules, and Coots

YELLOW RAIL *Coturnicops noveboracensis* (Gmelin).

Status. Uncertain. Probably a rare summer resident, and rare spring and fall migrant.

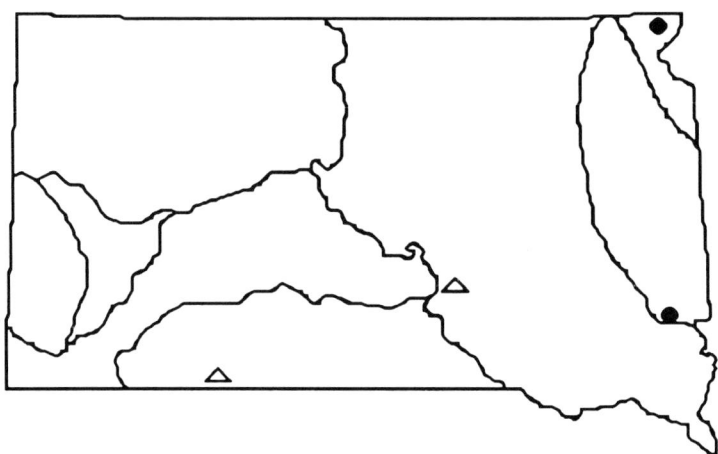

Habitat. Marshes.
Records.
- 11 May 1976, Roberts Co., near New Effington (Hall 1976) (only record with verifying details)
- 3 Jun 1975, Lacreek NWR (Ridgway in Burgess 1976)
- 24 Jun 1948, Brule Co. (Packard 1949)
- 26 Aug 1950, near Wall Lake (Findley and Findley)

KING RAIL *Rallus elegans* Audubon

Status. Rare summer resident E and Lacreek NWR. Observed in E Mellette Co. (Reagan 1908).

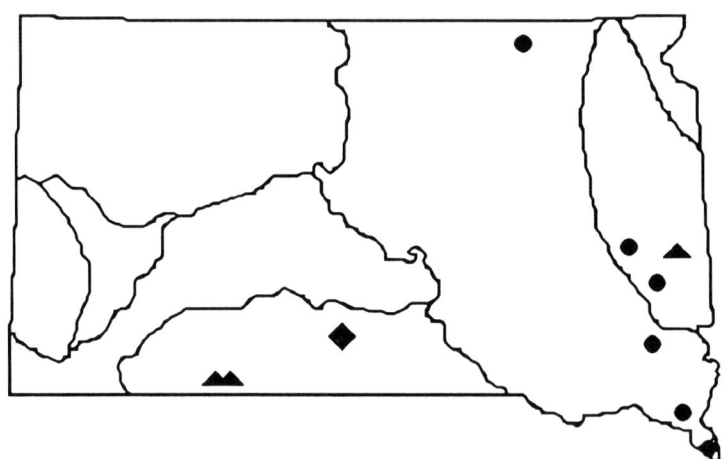

Habitat. Marshes.
Spring migration. Second week of May.
  Only dates:
    25 Apr 1950, McCook Lake (Chapman and Peterson)
    6 May 1951, Vermillion (Chapman 1951)
    14 May 1947, Madison (Habeger 1950)
    19 May 1966, Sand Lake NWR (Rose 1967)
Nesting. Probably the last week of May – mid-Jul.
  Only records:
    29 Jun 1952, 14 miles S Brookings in Moody Co., adult with 3 downy young (Spawn 1952)
    7 Jul 1974, Lacreek NWR, pair with at least 1 hatchling (Burgess)
    1977, Lacreek NWR, young (USFWS in Seasons 1978a)
Fall migration. Aug and first week of Sep.
  Only dates:
    29 Aug 1952, near Freeman (Chapman 1952)
    14 Sep 1925, Lake Preston (Peterson)
    Early Nov 1925, Union Co. (Stephens et al. 1955)

VIRGINIA RAIL *Rallus limicola* Vieillot

Status. Common summer resident E; W River, found wherever suitable habitat occurs.

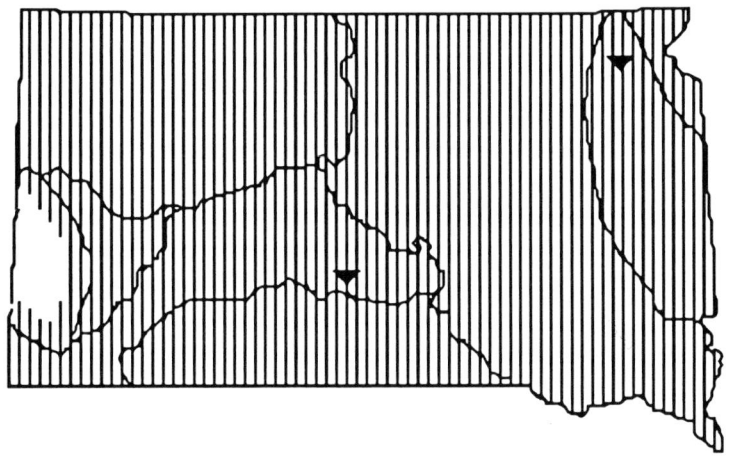

Habitat. Marshes and meadows.
Spring migration. Probably the first 3 weeks of May.
  Earliest dates:
    2 May 1977, Lacreek NWR (Nissen in Seasons 1977c)
    7 May 1971, Pierre (Rose)
Nesting. Late May – mid-Aug.
  Earliest dates:
    17 May 1987, Brown Co., adult with 6 young (Springer in Seasons 1987d)
    24 May 1890, Aberdeen, nest with eggs (M. Johnson)
    4 Jun 1922, Sanborn Co., set of 8 eggs collected (Patton in Whitney 1955)

Latest dates:
   6 Aug 1949, SW of Sioux Falls, 1 juvenile (Findley)
   6 Aug 1986, Yankton Co., 1 juvenile (Hall)
   14 Aug 1975, Deuel Co., 3 immatures (Harris in Seasons 1975d)

Fall migration. Last half of Sep and first half of Oct.
Latest dates:
   19 Oct 1951, Union Co. (Felton)
   3 Nov 1975, Gavin's Point (Hall in Seasons 1975d)
   7 Nov 1987, Brown Co. (Montgomery)

Winter.
Records.
   27 Dec 1972, Day Co., in muskrat trap (Thuringer)
   25 Jan 1976, Jones Co., near warm spring (Hill 1976)

SORA *Porzana carolina* (Linnaeus)

Status. Common summer resident.

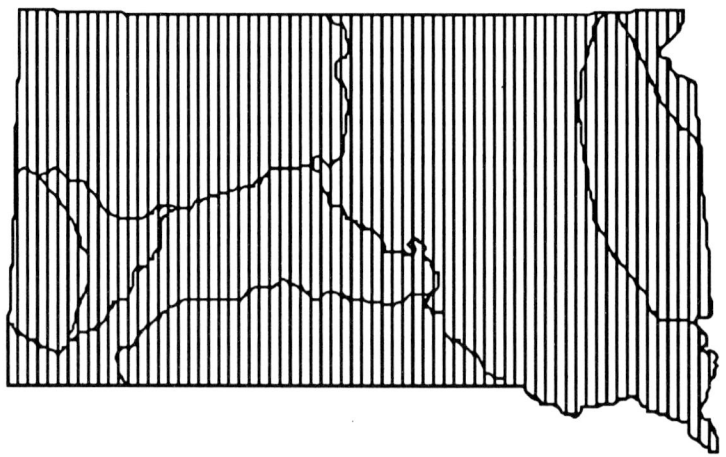

Habitat. Marshes.
Spring migration. Second week of May.
Earliest dates:
   22 Apr 1979, Hutchinson Co. (Spomer in Seasons 1979c)
   22 Apr 1981, Brown Co. (Tallman in Seasons 1981c)
   22 Apr 1990, Stanley Co. (Whitney in Seasons 1990c)
   29 Apr 1976, Day Co. (Hall in Seasons 1976c)
   29 Apr 1978, Deuel Co. (Harris in Seasons 1978c)
   29 Apr 1986, Sanborn Co. (Rogers in Seasons 1986c)
Nesting. Jun to Aug.
Earliest dates:
   29 May 1886, Beadle Co., nest with 10 eggs (Cheney)
   31 May 1911, Charles Mix Co., nest with 12 eggs (Walker)
   1 Jun 1888, Pitrodia, eggs collected (Cheney in Cooke 1914)

Latest dates:
 20 Jul –20 Aug 1951, Stanley Co., 10 nests on 5 ponds; 5 successful nests produced 51 young (Blankenship et al. 1953)
 1 Aug 1986, Yankton Co., 1 juvenile (Hall)
Fall migration. Last half of Sep.
Latest dates:
 11 Oct 1932, Union Co. (Youngworth)
 15 Oct 1976, Burke Lake (Steffen in Seasons 1977a)
 17 Oct 1909, Sioux Falls (Larson 1925)

COMMON MOORHEN *Gallinula chloropus* (Linnaeus)

Status. Casual visitor, possibly rare summer resident E; accidental W. Reported in the Ft. Sisseton area by Knickerbocker in 1869 (Chilson 1968) and considered a summer resident there by Youngworth (1935a). Peterson reported 1 shot at Wentworth Slough in 1918. Considered accidental at Waubay and Lacreek NWR (FWS records); undated specimen in Over Museum from Lake Norden.

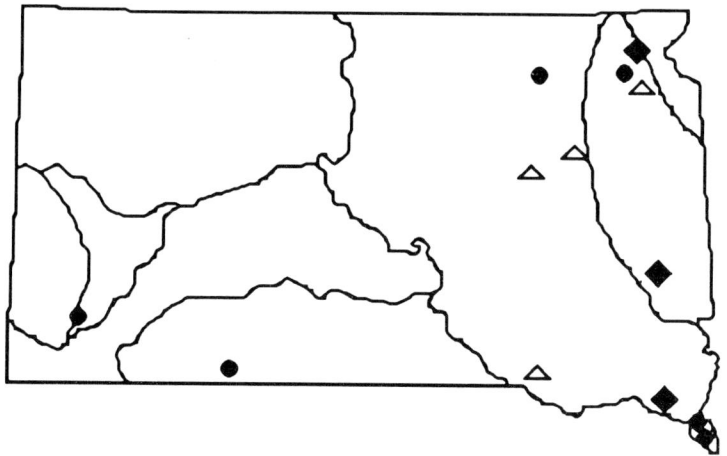

Habitat. Edges of deepwater marshes.
Records:
 15 Apr 1899, near Vermillion, 1 shot (Sweet in Visher 1915)
 30 May 1975, Brown Co. (Fjetland 1975)
 9 Jun 1979, Lake Andes NWR, photograph (Hilley 1980a)
 Summer, Day Co., Lundquist (1950)
 Summer 1950, Beadle Co. (Dahlgren fide Lundquist 1950)
 3 Jul 1971, Clark Co. (Nelson 1971a)
 18 Sep 1977, Buffalo Gap (Lynch and Lynch in Rogge and Rogge 1978)
 6 Oct 1950, Union Co., 1 shot (Felton in Stephens et al. 1955)
 20 Oct 1951, Union Co. (Felton in Stephens et al. 1955)

AMERICAN COOT *Fulica americana* (Linnaeus).

Status. Abundant summer resident E River. Abundant locally W where suitable habitat is available. Rare winter when water is open.

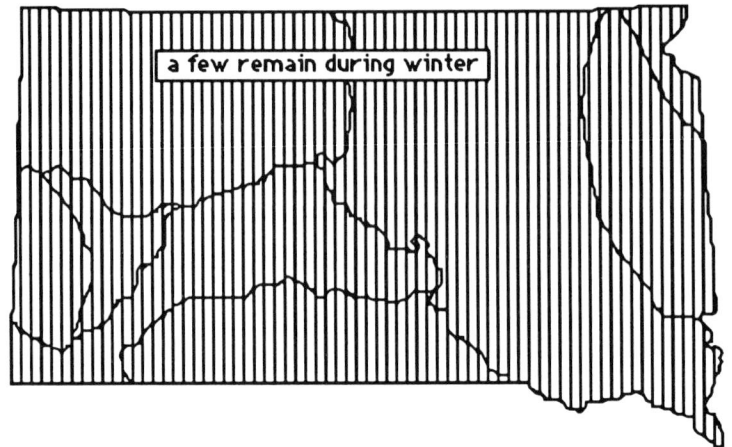

Habitat. Deep marshes. Floating nests are built.
Spring migration. First week of Apr E; later W.
  Earliest dates:
    4 Mar 1986, Yankton Co. (Van Sickle in Seasons 1986c)
    9 Mar 1986, Gregory Co. (Steffen in Seasons 1986c)
    12 Mar 1987, Yankton Co. (Hall in Seasons 1987c)
Nesting. Third week of May – first week of Jul (Moriarty 1964b).
  Earliest dates:
    1 May 1963, nest with 8 eggs at Lake Preston (Hart and Twedt 1963)
    27 May 1985, Union Co., adult on nest (Springer)
    11 Jun 1987, Lake Co., adult feeding 2 downy young (Springer)
  Latest dates:
    24 Jul 1973, NE Harding Co., 1 adult and 3 small downy young, (Springer)
    27 Jul 1986, Yankton Co., 6 young (Hall)
    13 Aug 1976, Harding Co., adults and 7 half-grown young, (Springer)
Fall migration. Last half of Sep – early Nov; some remain throughout winter. Unusual concentration: 26 Sep 1955, Bear Butte Lake, ca. 12,000 (Whitney).
Winter. Under favorable conditions can be seen in small numbers all winter. Many CBC records statewide.

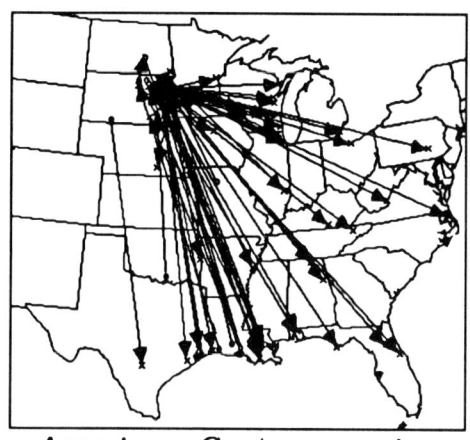
American Coot recoveries within the United States

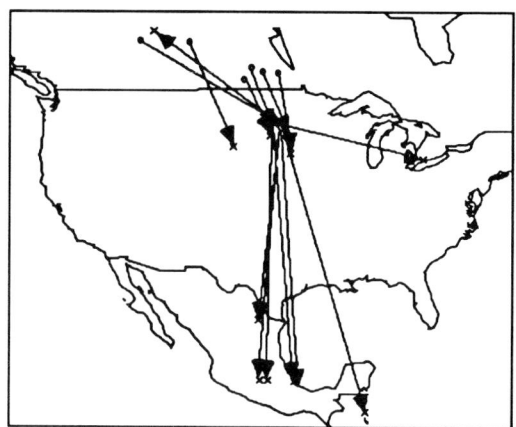
American Coot foreign recoveries

GRUIDAE: Cranes

SANDHILL CRANE *Grus canadensis* (Linnaeus)

Status. Locally abundant spring and fall migrant in central and W, although less common in spring in far W; migrates sparingly E. Apparently a common migrant in E prior to 1900. Formerly nested at Lacreek (Tullsen in Visher 1912a), occurred rarely in Sanborn Co. (Visher 1910), a few reported on the Coteau des Prairies (McChesney 1879), and in SE (Agersborg 1885, Stephens et al. 1955).

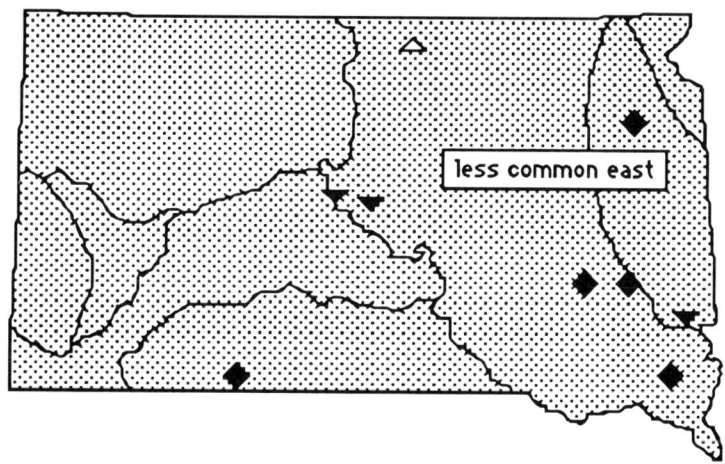

Habitat. Usually seen overhead. Assemble and feed in lowlands, wet fields, meadows, and shallow lakes.

Spring migration. Late Mar and early Apr. Unusual concentration: 11 Apr 1989, Faulk Co., 2200 feeding (Melius in Seasons 1989c).

Earliest dates:
   2 Mar 1986, Shannon Co. (Dagelen)
   10 Mar 1987, Shannon Co. (Dagelen)
   22 Mar 1967, Hyde Co. (Harter)

Latest dates:
- 6 Jun 1983, Jackson Co. (Graupmann in Seasons 1983d)
- 6 Jun 1985, McPherson Co. (Harris in Seasons 1985d)
- 9 Jun 1979, Charles Mix Co. (Hilley 1980)

Nesting. Visher (1910) reported a nest in a moist meadow in Sanborn Co. Over and Thoms (1946) listed 2 sets of eggs from Miner Co, 22 May 1887, without any further details.

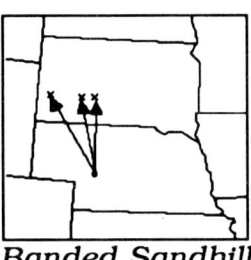
Banded Sandhill Crane sightings

Other summer records:
- 19 Jul 1961, McPherson Co. (Pulliam 1961)
- 18 Aug 1911, near Lacreek (Visher 1912a)

Fall migration. Mid-Sep – early Nov. Buller (1967) stated that they arrive in the Pollock region in early Sep and build up to a peak concentration of 10,000 to 18,000 in late Oct.

Earliest dates:
- 8 Sep 1891, SE South Dakota (Cooke 1914)
- 8 Sep 1988, Brown Co. (Young in Seasons 1989a)
- 10 Sep 1977, Hughes Co. (Hill in Seasons 1977a)

Latest dates:
- 25 Nov 1975, Deuel Co. (Harris)
- 26 Nov 1985, Jackson Co. (Parker in Seasons 1986a)
- 4 Dec 1967, Lake Andes NWR (refuge files)

Winter.
- 16 Dec 1981, Hughes Co. (Prickart)
- 20 Dec 1975, Sioux Falls (Scott and Davis in Anon. 1976)
- 9 Feb 1981, Oahe Dam, 1 immature able to fly (Jobman)

WHOOPING CRANE *Grus americana* (Linnaeus)

Status. Rare spring and fall migrant. Accidental summer. Statewide records, although majority W. Seen most often at Pollock, Lacreek, and near Pierre (Blankespoor 1985). Since 1957, 10 of 14 probable and/or confirmed sightings in the E third of the state have been in the spring (USFWS Whooping Crane Monitoring Project). Although no nesting records known, it probably nested in NE, since it bred within 25 miles of state line in both SE North Dakota (Stewart 1975) and W-central Minnesota (Roberts 1932) and within 70 miles in NW Iowa (Cooke 1914). However, McChesney (1879) in the Ft. Sisseton area found it only in spring and fall migration in small numbers.

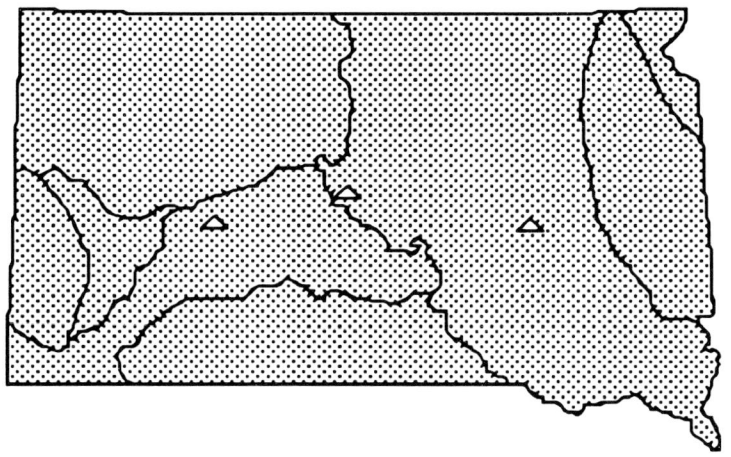

Habitat. Fields and shallow wetlands.
Spring migration. Last 2 weeks of Apr.
  Earliest dates:
    25 Mar 1890, near Harrison (Cooke 1914)
    5 Apr 1893, Ipswich, 2 collected (Allen 1952)
    6 Apr 1888, Grandview near Valley (Bent 1926)
  Latest dates:
    11 May 1962, Hyde Co. (Shepherd)
    17–21 May 1982, Dewey Co. (Lesmeister)
    18 May 1962, near Martin (Hughlett 1962)
Summer.
  Records:
    13 Jun 1973, Haakon Co., 1 immature (McDaniel and Sandall)
    22 Jun 1973, Hughes Co. (Hollis)
    30 Jul 1936, near Wolsey, nonbreeding bird (Moos 1937)
Fall migration. Sep and Oct.
  Earliest dates:
    8 Sep 1891, SE South Dakota (Cooke 1914)
    10–15 Sep 1964, Pollock, 2 (Springer 1965b)
    18 Sep 1972, Butte Co. (GFP)
  Latest dates:
    20 Oct–11 Nov 1969, Campbell Co. (W. Larson)
    8–9 Nov 1983, Stanley Co. (Goossen)
    11 Nov 1972, Dewey Co. (Rehm)

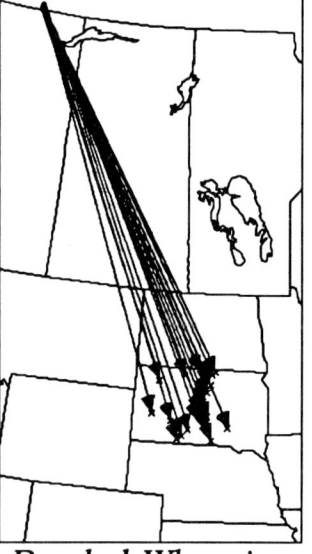

Banded Whooping Crane sightings

CHARADRIIDAE: Plovers

BLACK-BELLIED PLOVER *Pluvialis squatarola* (Linnaeus)

Status. Uncommon spring and fall migrant in appropriate habitat. Rare in Black Hills.

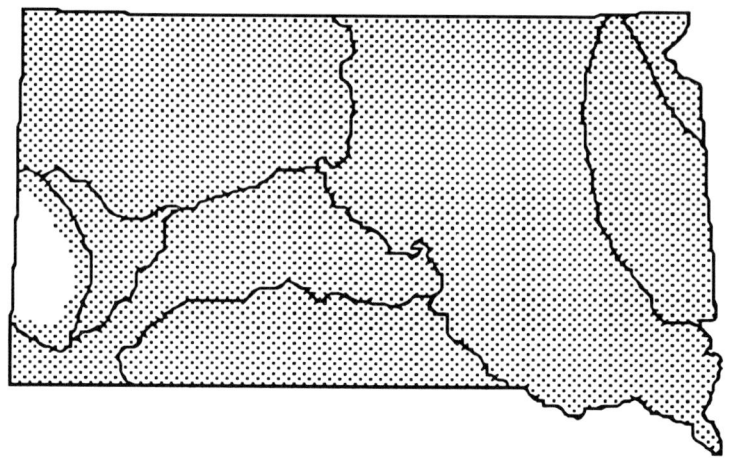

Habitat. Mud flats and wet fields.
Spring migration. Third week of May.
  Earliest dates:
    29 Apr 1976, Meade Co. (Miller in Seasons 1976c)
    1 May 1981, Fall River Co. (Rosche and Rosche in Seasons 1981c)
    4 May 1960, Deuel Co, Lake Alice (Peterson 1965)
  Latest dates:
    3 Jun 1972, Dewey Co. (Harris)
    9 Jun 1955, Salt Lake (Peterson 1962a)
    18 Jun 1985, Day Co. (Springer in Seasons 1985d)
    18 Jun 1987, Roberts Co. (Springer in Seasons 1987d)
Fall migration. Sep and Oct.
  Earliest dates:
    10 Aug 1955, Clear Lake (Peterson 1960a)
    14 Aug 1975, Waubay NWR (Hall in Seasons 1975d)
    15 Aug 1955, Florence (Peterson 1962a)
  Latest dates:
    3 Nov 1976, Day Co. (Harris in Seasons 1977a)
    5 Nov 1957, Lake Mary (Peterson 1960a, 1961a, 1964)
    8 Nov 1975, Bon Homme Co. (Baker in Seasons 1975d)

LESSER GOLDEN-PLOVER *Pluvialis dominica* (Muller)

Status. Common to abundant spring migrant, and less common fall migrant E; no spring and few fall records W.

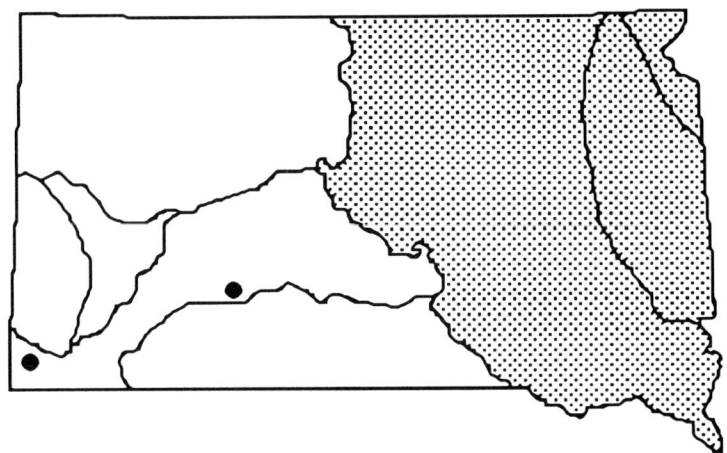

Habitat. Fields, preferably with grass stubble. Prefers drier areas than most shorebirds.

Spring migration. Second and third weeks of May.
Earliest dates:
  10 Apr 1986, Sanborn Co. (Rogers in Seasons 1986c)
  12 Apr 1953, North Hartford (Findley)
  13 Apr 1978, Deuel and Hamlin counties (Harris in Seasons 1978c)
Latest dates:
  29 May 1957, Kranzburg (Peterson 1957, 1960b)
  30 May 1976, Deuel Co. (Harris)
  3 Jun 1965, Florence (Springer)

Fall migration. Last week of Sep and most of Oct.
Earliest dates:
  5 Aug 1957, Brookings Co. (Peterson 1964)
  7 Aug 1981, Fall River Co. (Rosche in Seasons 1982a)
  13 Aug 1985, Jackson Co. (Graupmann in Seasons 1986a)
Latest dates:
  8 Nov 1926, Lake Whitewood (Peterson in Roberts 1932)
  8 Nov 1976, Roberts Co. (Harris in Seasons 1977a)
  11 Nov 1958, Day Co. (Peterson 1963b)
  14 Nov 1958, Clear Lake (Peterson 1963b)

SNOWY PLOVER *Charadrius alexandrinus* Linnaeus

Only record:
 1 May 1976, Fall River Co., Angostura Reservoir (Rosche 1982)

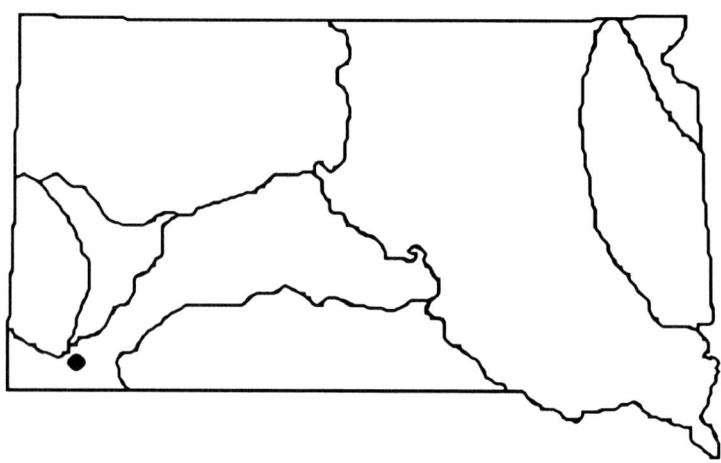

SEMIPALMATED PLOVER *Charadrius semipalmatus* Bonaparte

Status. Fairly common spring and fall migrant, but only 1 record from Black Hills (Pettingill and Whitney 1965).

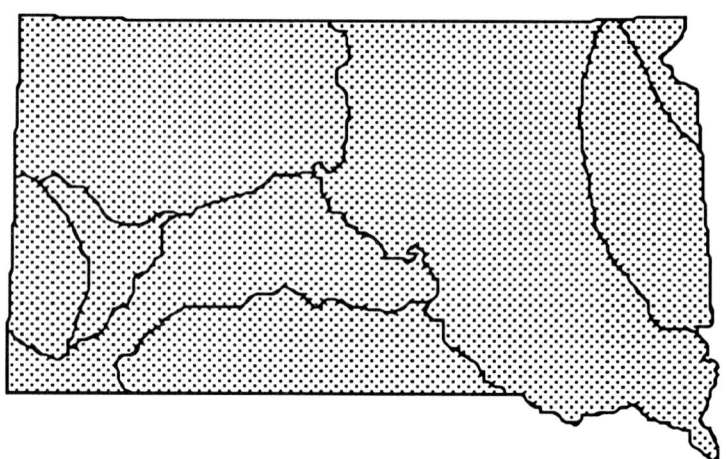

Habitat. Mudflats and shallow ponds.
Spring migration. Second and third weeks of May.
 Earliest dates:
  6 Apr 1986, Corson Co. (Griffiths and Griffiths)
  16 Apr 1982, Fall River Co. (Rosche)
  19 Apr 1987, Yankton Co. (Hall in Seasons 1987c)
 Latest dates:
  5 Jun 1957, NE SD (Peterson 1960a)
  6 Jun 1978, Day Co. (Harris)
  14 Jun 1988, Perkins Co. (Griffiths and Griffiths in Seasons 1988d)

Fall migration. Aug and first half of Sep.
  Earliest dates:
    7 Jul 1985, Charles Mix Co. (Skadsen in Seasons 1986a)
    12 Jul 1985, Sioux Falls (Hoeger in Seasons 1986a)
    16 Jul 1958, Oakwood Lakes (Peterson 1960a, 1963b)
  Latest dates:
    30 Sep 1979, Minnehaha Co. (Buckman 1979)
    10 Oct 1957, NE SD (Peterson 1961a, 1960b)
    24 Oct 1984, Yankton Co. (Hall and Bregelmeier in Seasons 1985a)

PIPING PLOVER *Charadrius melodus* Ord.

Status. Locally common summer resident, primarily in the Missouri Valley and its W tributaries. Nests rarely in Day and Codington counties. Uncommon migrant across state. The species is listed as a Threatened Species by the USFWS.

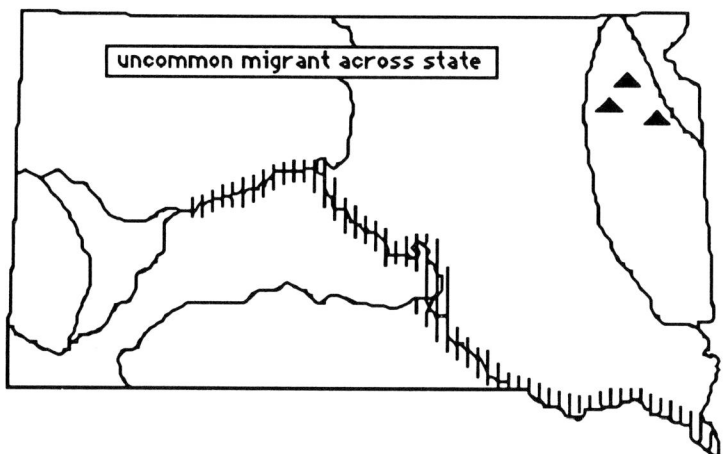

Habitat. Nests on open sand and gravel beaches.
Spring migration. Last week of Apr and first half of May.
  Earliest dates:
    11 Apr 1989, Yankton Co. (Hall in Seasons 1989c)
    13 Apr 1986, Yankton Co. (Hall in Seasons 1986c)
    13 Apr 1988, Jackson Co. (Graupmann in Seasons 1988c)
    14 Apr 1979, Yankton Co. (Wilcox in Seasons 1979c)
Nesting. May through Jul. Nesting status summarized by Schwalbach et al. (1986)
  Earliest dates:
    6 May 1987, Yankton Co., 2 nests (Schwalbach)
    17 May 1959, Yankton Co., nest with 4 eggs (Jobman and Findley 1959)
    17 May 1986, Yankton Co., 2 courting (Kronner in Seasons 1986c)
    18 May 1985, Day Co., nest with 4 eggs (Harris and Gilman in Seasons 1985c)

Latest dates:
    25 Jul 1986, Gavin's Point, 11 nests (Schwalbach)
    29 Jul 1987, Yankton Co., 3 nests (Schwalbach)
    7 Aug 1955, Day Co., adult with 3 young, and 10 and 15 Aug, 4 young with adult (Peterson 1955)
Fall migration.
  Latest dates:
    28 Aug 1987, Union and Clay counties (Schwalbach)
    4 Sep 1978, Aberdeen (Lynch in Seasons 1979a)
    8 Sep 1979, Clay Co. (Hall in Seasons 1980a)

KILLDEER *Charadrius vociferus* Linnaeus

Status. Very common to abundant summer resident. Rare winter.

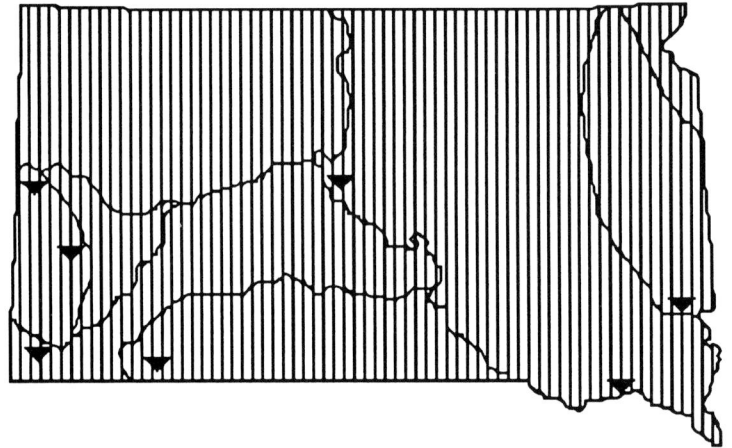

Habitat. Nests in dry fields but feeds in wet, grassy and muddy areas. In winter found along shores of open water.
Spring migration. Second and third weeks of Mar.
  Earliest dates:
    6 Feb 1982, Pennington Co. (Baker in Seasons 1982b)
    28 Feb 1981, Hutchinson Co. (L. Anderson)
    3 Mar 1975, Sturgis (Miller in Seasons 1975a)
    3 Mar 1983, Deuel Co. (Harris in Seasons 1983c)
Nesting. Jun.
  Earliest dates:
    18 May 1968, Hyde Co., nest with 4 eggs (Harris)
    19 May 1933, Harding Co., 4 eggs collected, incubation advanced (Lee and McIntosh in Whitney 1955)
    19 May 1987, Lake Andes NWR, adults and 3 young (Springer)
  Latest dates:
    22 Jul 1974, Harding Co., 1 downy young (Springer)
    23 Jul 1964, Grenville, 1 downy young (Springer)
    25 Sep 1952, Wall Lake, young (Findley)
Fall migration. Late Sep – mid-Oct. Individuals linger until water freezes.

Latest dates where wintering unexpected:
  14 Nov 1976, Roberts Co. (Harris in Seasons 1977a)
  18 Nov 1975, Waubay NWR (Hall in Seasons 1975d)
  28 Nov 1968, Aurora Co. (Harris)
Winter. 5 Jan records exist from the Rapid City/N Black Hills region.
  CBC reports:
  Pierre, Sioux Falls, Yankton, Rapid City, and Hot Springs.
  Other record:
  1 Jan – 19 Mar 1980, Pine Ridge (Homoya)

MOUNTAIN PLOVER *Charadrius montanus* Townsend

Status. Formerly rare breeder W, occurring casually farther E in migration. Bred in "SW Dakota, in the vicinity of the Black Hills," (Coues 1874), E to Edgemont (Bent 1929). Over and Thoms (1946) noted that small flocks were seen in prairie dog towns in W. Bent's (1929) report of an earliest arrival on 16 Apr at Huron and the latest departure date of 20 Sep at Forestburg suggests a former casual occurrence in the E during migration.
Recent record:
  1-12 Jul 1977, Bennett Co., N of Little White River (Lohoefener 1978)

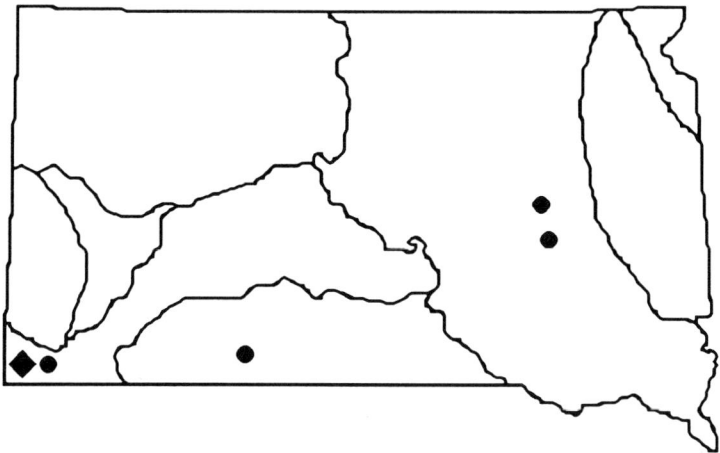

RECURVIROSTRIDAE: Stilts and avocets

BLACK-NECKED STILT *Himantopus mexicanus* (Muller)

Status. Casual visitor. No specimens.

Records.
- 8 May 1987, Bennett Co. (Brashears in Seasons 1987c)
- 18 May 1951, near McCook-Hutchinson county line (Keck 1952)
- 6 Jun – 29 Jul 1977, Spearfish Lagoons (Hays in Seasons 1977d)
- 3 Jul 1949, near Bitter Lake, (Chapman 1949)
- 13 Jul 1971, McPherson Co., S of Long Lake (Duebbert)
- 2 Aug 1978, Charles Mix Co. (Good et al. in Seasons 1979a)
- 17 Sep 1978, Orman Dam, 26 (Ross and Bjerke in Seasons 1979a)

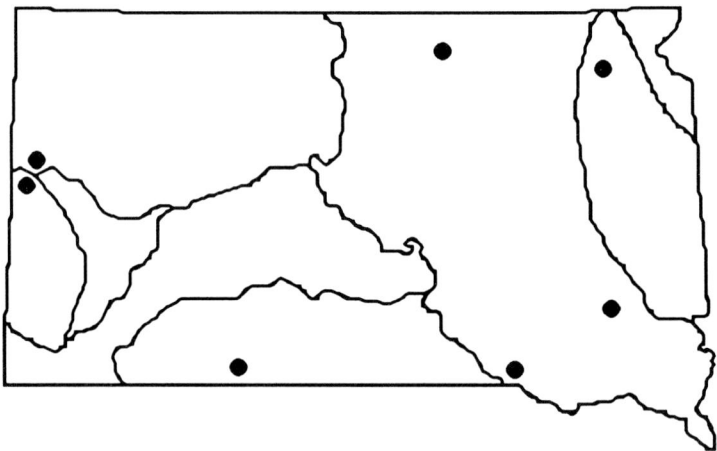

AMERICAN AVOCET *Recurvirostra americana* Gmelin

Status. Common summer resident in appropriate habitat. Less common W.

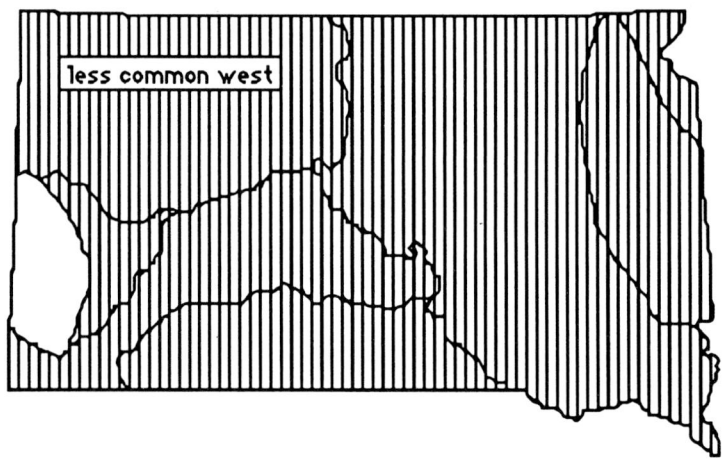

Habitat. Alkaline lakes, breeding on the shores and feeding in shallow water.

Spring migration. Last week of Apr and first half of May. Unusual concentration: 3 May 1968, Crow Lake, 80+ (Harris).
  Earliest dates:
    21 Mar 1986, Turner Co. (Anderson in Seasons 1986c)
    9 Apr 1981, Faulk Co. (Montgomery in Seasons 1981c)
    9 Apr 1987, Pennington Co. (E. Miller)
Nesting. Last third of May through first half of Jul.
  Earliest dates:
    19 May 1985, Roberts Co., pair with nest (Harris in Seasons 1985d)
    26 May 1984, Roberts Co., nest with 4 eggs (Harris)
    27 May 1956, Bitter Lake, nest with eggs photographed (Whitney)
  Latest dates:
    10 Jul 1981, Fall River Co., 4–6 adults and downy young (Rosche and Rosche in Seasons 1981d)
    14 Jul 1978, Harding Co., adults feigning injury (Springer)
    24 Jul 1959, near Milbank, 3 young almost full-grown (Elliott 1959)
Fall migration. Mid-Sep.
  Latest dates:
    27 Oct 1951, Union Co. (Wannerholm and Hanson in Stephens et al. 1955)
    31 Oct 1975, Waubay NWR (Hall in Seasons 1975d)
    4 Nov 1903, McCook Lake (Stephens et al. 1955)

SCOLOPACIDAE: Sandpipers and phalaropes

GREATER YELLOWLEGS *Tringa melanoleuca* (Gmelin)

Status. Common spring and fall migrant, except absent in Black Hills.

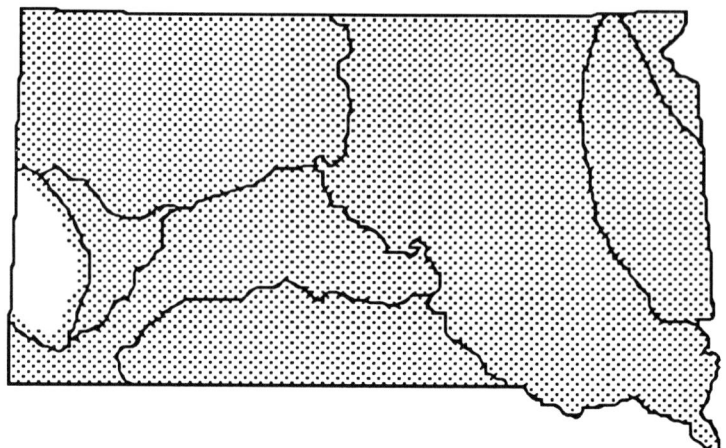

Habitat. Marshes and shallow water; mud flats and flooded meadows.

Spring migration. Second half of Apr.
   Earliest dates:
      16 Mar 1986, Davison Co. (McLaird in Seasons 1986c)
      19 Mar 1955, Minnehaha Co. (Chapman and Krause)
      23 Mar 1987, Lincoln Co. (Skadsen in Seasons 1987c)
   Latest dates:
      22 May 1968, Meade Co. (Whitney)
      29 May 1963, near Milbank (Peterson 1963c)
      20 Jun 1987, Day Co. (Springer)

Summer observations. Summer observations can represent either late spring or early fall migrants.

Fall migration. Aug – Oct.
   Latest dates:
      9 Nov 1985, Deuel Co. (Harris)
      10 Nov 1967, Sanborn Co. (Harris)
      13 Nov 1984, McCook Co. (Anderson in Seasons 1985a)

LESSER YELLOWLEGS *Tringa flavipes* (Gmelin)

Status. Abundant spring and fall migrant except absent in Black Hills. Rare summer.

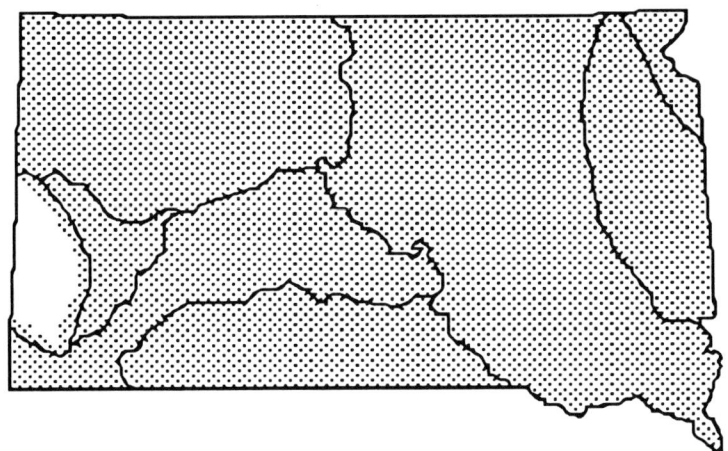

Habitat. Flooded meadows, mud flats, and shallow ponds.

Spring migration. Last half of Apr and first 3 weeks of May.
  Earliest dates:
    8 Mar 1953, Minnehaha Co. (Chapman and Krause)
    24 Mar 1976, Bon Homme Co. (Yankton Bird Club in Seasons 1976c)
    25 Mar 1989, Minnehaha Co. (Skadsen in Seasons 1989c)

Jun observations. Many summer observations can represent either late spring or early fall migrants. Unusual concentration: 29 Jun 1987, Clark, Potter, and Dewey counties, 81 total (Springer).

Fall migration. Jul – first half of Sep.
  Latest dates:
    11 Nov 1986, Yankton Co. (Hall in Seasons 1987a)
    17 Nov 1985, Charles Mix Co., (Skadsen in Seasons 1986a)
    20 Nov 1975, Waubay NWR, (Hall in Seasons 1975d)

Lesser Yellowlegs banding recoveries

SOLITARY SANDPIPER *Tringa solitaria* Wilson

Status. Fairly common spring and fall migrant.

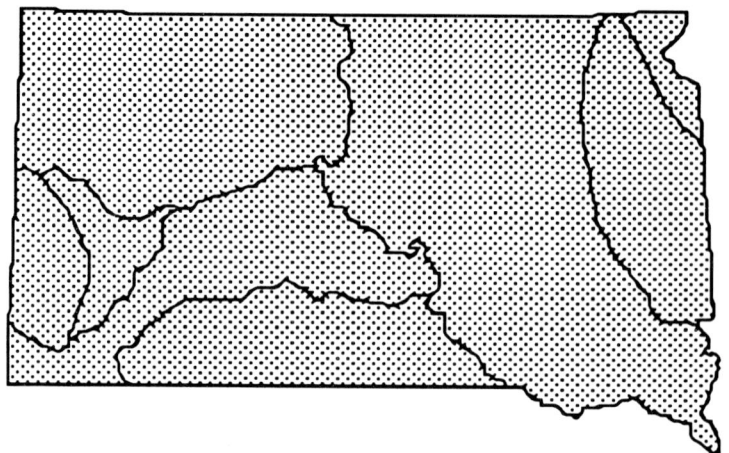

Habitat. Streams, wooded ponds, and flooded meadows.
Spring migration. First 2 weeks of May.
Earliest dates:
  15 Apr 1971, Pierre (Rose)
  16 Apr 1982, Turner Co. (Anderson in Seasons 1982c)
  22 Apr 1981, Brown Co. (Tallman in Seasons 1981c)
  22 Apr 1981, Wind Cave NP (Delaney)
  22 Apr 1989, Edmunds Co. (Williams in Seasons 1989c)
Latest dates:
  2 Jun 1990, Butte Co. (Springer)
  7 Jun 1963, near Milbank (Elliott and Harris)
  12 Jun 1969, Miner Co. (Harris)
Fall migration. Last half of Jul and first 3 weeks of Aug.
Earliest dates:
  24 Jun 1981, Fall River Co. (Rosche and Rosche in Seasons 1982a)
  27 Jun 1971, near Tripp (Holden)
  29 Jun 1989, Hutchinson Co. (Springer)
Latest dates:
  6 Oct 1950, Dell Rapids (Findley)
  7 Oct 1979, Pennington Co. (Whitney in Seasons 1980a)
  25 Oct 1986, Deuel Co. (Harris et al. in Seasons 1987a)

WILLET *Catoptrophorus semipalmatus* (Gmelin)

Status. Fairly common spring and fall migrant. Fairly common breeder in NE, less common or rare SE and W. Absent from higher Black Hills.

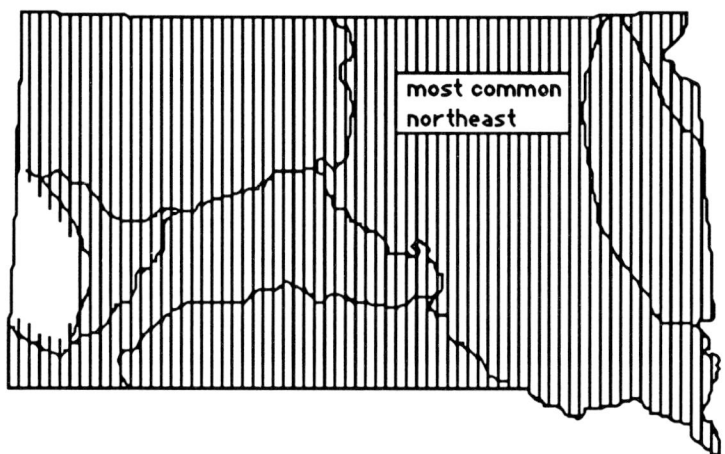

Habitat. Mud flats and wet meadows.
Spring migration. Late Apr – early May.
  Earliest dates:
    7 Apr 1978, Yankton Co. (Hall in Seasons 1978c)
    11 Apr 1985, Waubay NWR (Getman in Seasons 1985c)
    13 Apr 1977, Lacreek NWR (Nissen in Seasons 1977c)
Nesting.
  Earliest dates:
    29 May 1985, McPherson Co., nest with 4 eggs (Harris and Baker)
    11 Jun 1978, Buffalo Gap NG, territorial pair (Rosche 1982)
    15 Jun 1973, Roberts Co., 2 pair and 3 chicks (Harris)
    15 Jun 1987, Sully Co, pair and 2 young (Springer)
  Latest dates:
    22 Jun 1971, SW of Roscoe, nest with 4 eggs, pipping (Kantrud)
    22 Jul 1975, Waubay NWR, 3 young (Hall in Seasons 1975c)
Fall migration. Late Aug – early Sep.
  Latest dates:
    26 Sep 1955, Bear Butte Lake (Whitney)
    17 Oct 1982, Hamlin Co. (Harris in Seasons 1983a)
    26 Oct 1951, Union Co. (Stephens et al. 1955)

SPOTTED SANDPIPER *Actitis macularia* (Linnaeus)

Status. Fairly common summer resident.

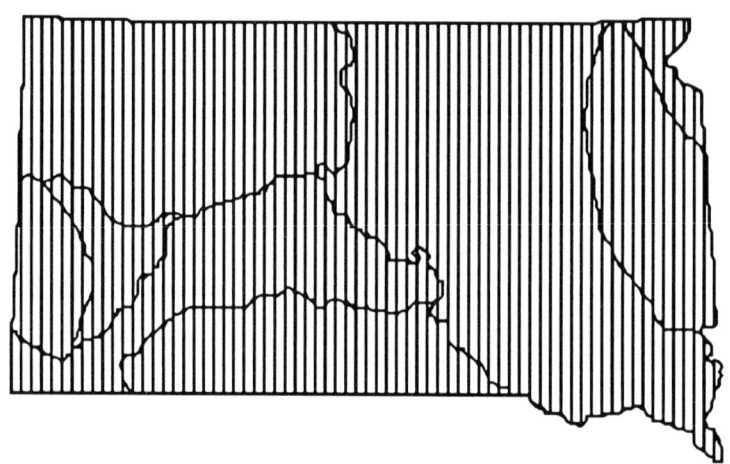

Habitat. Lakes and stream shores, prefers rocky areas if available.
Spring migration. Second and third weeks of May.
  Earliest dates:
    10 Apr 1910, Sioux Falls area (Larson 1925)
    24 Apr 1971, Minnehaha Co. (Krause and Blankespoor)
    27 Apr 1989, Pennington Co. (Backlund in Seasons 1989c)
Nesting. Jun and Jul.
  Earliest dates:
    3 Jun 1972, Pierre, completed clutch of 4 eggs (Rose)
    8 Jun 1972, Pierre, completed clutch of 4 eggs (Rose)
    13 Jun 1930, Rapid City, fresh eggs collected (Whitney 1955)
  Latest dates:
    19 Jul 1977, Little White River RA, 1 adult with 2 young (Lohoefener and Ely 1978)
    19 Jul 1977, Roberts Co., adult with 2 fledglings (Harris)
    22 Jul 1974, Harding Co., adult with 1 young just able to fly (Springer)
    22 Jul 1975, Waubay NWR, nest with 4 eggs (Husmann in Seasons 1975c)
Fall migration. Last half of Aug and first week of Sep.
  Latest dates:
    23 Oct 1976, Meade Co. (Baker in Seasons 1977a)
    28 Oct 1972, Deuel Co. (Harris)
    16 Nov 1983, Turner Co. (Anderson in Seasons 1984a)

UPLAND SANDPIPER *Bartramia longicauda* (Bechstein)

Status. Common summer resident, except in Black Hills where local.

Habitat. Dry prairies.

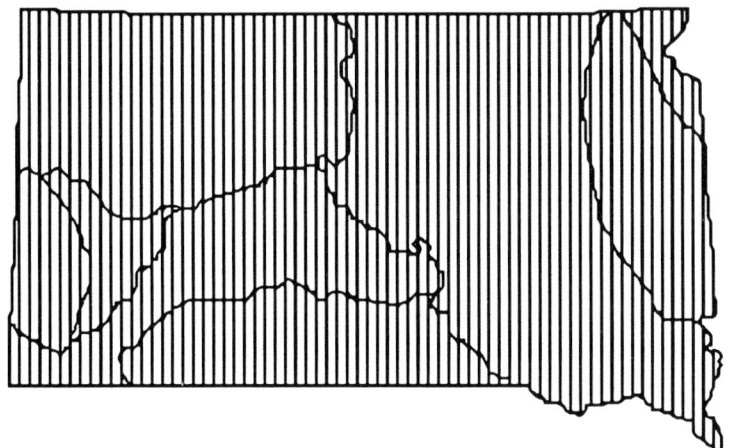

Spring migration. First 2 weeks of May.
Earliest dates:
10 Apr 1885, Grand View (Blanchard in Cooke 1888)
15 Apr 1981, Brookings Co. (Holden in Seasons 1981c)

Nesting. Last week of May through first 3 weeks of Jul.
Earliest dates:
13 May 1987, Grant Co., 19 nests with eggs (Getman in Seasons 1987d)
14 May 1980, Deuel Co., nest with 4 eggs (Harris in Seasons 1980d)
15 May 1902, Hamlin Co., nest with 2 eggs (Lee)
Latest dates:
9 Jul 1971, near Roscoe, 4 young hatched (Kantrud)
14 Jul 1953, Spink Co., young of various ages to 3/4 grown (Padrnos 1953b)
25 Jul 1966, Sanborn Co., downy young (Harris 1967d)

Fall migration. First half of Aug.
Latest dates:
8 Sep 1982, Deuel Co. (Harris in Seasons 1983a)
8 Sep 1966, near Artesian (Harris)
10 Sep 1977, Brookings Co. (Froiland in Seasons 1978a)
16 Sep 1967, Hyde Co. (Harter)

ESKIMO CURLEW *Numenius borealis* (Forster)

Status. Formerly a common to abundant spring migrant (at least E River); now nearly extinct. The species was very abundant in spring in the SE (Agersborg 1885; Over and Thoms 1921, 1946); during the second week of May 1873, Coues (1874) observed numerous flocks of 50 to several hundred between Ft. Randall and Yankton. The earliest record was 16 Apr in Brown Co. (Bent 1929). Agersborg collected 2 specimens at Vermillion on 3 and 5 May 1879 (Hahn 1963), and the bulk arrived at the same location on 3 May 1884 (Cooke 1888). Bent (1929) gave a date of 10 May at Harrison.

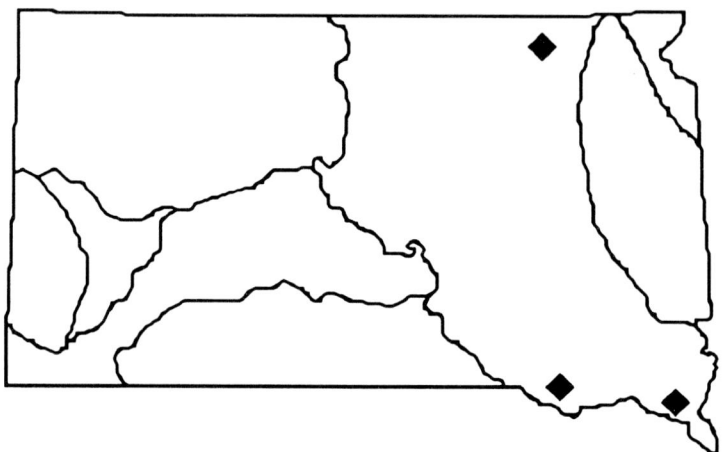

WHIMBREL *Numenius phaeopus* (Linnaeus)

Status. Rare spring migrant.

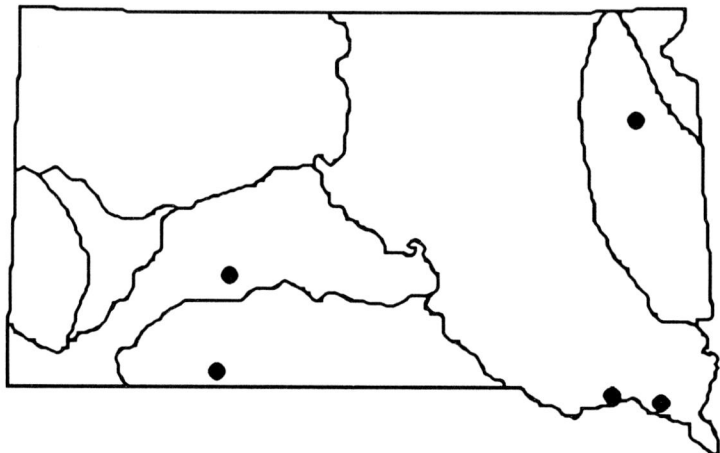

Spring migration. May.
  Earliest dates:
    29 Apr 1985, Codington Co. (Harris et al. in Seasons 1985c)
    6 May 1985, Codington Co. (Harris in Seasons 1985c)
    15 May 1958, Lacreek NWR (Whitney 1958)

Latest dates:
   23 May 1982, Yankton Co. (Hall in Seasons 1982c)
   25 May 1974, Clay Co. (Hoover 1975)
   28 May 1990, Brown Co. (Miller in Seasons 1990c)

LONG-BILLED CURLEW *Numenius americanus* Bechstein

Status. Fairly common W River summer resident in suitable habitat. Former abundant summer resident and migrant in SE (Agersborg 1885). Also recorded in the Ft. Sisseton area by Knickerbocker in 1869 (Chilson 1968). Greatly decreased in last 50 years.

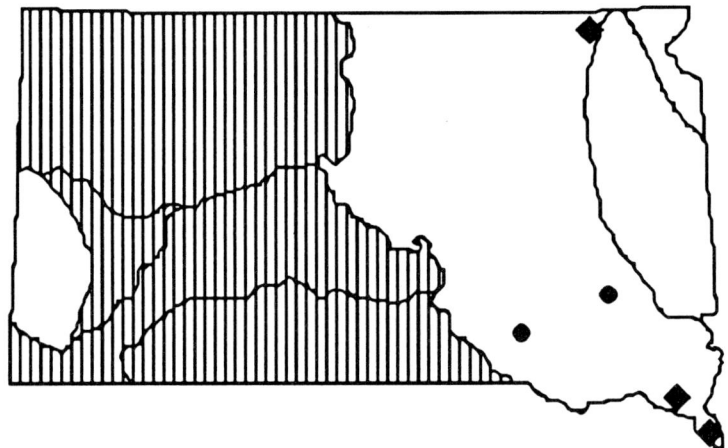

Habitat. Mid-grass prairies.
Spring migration. Third and fourth weeks of Apr.
   Earliest dates:
   28 Mar 1986, Custer Co. (Melius in Seasons 1986c)
   1 Apr 1968, Stanley Co (Rose)
   1 Apr 1977, Lacreek NWR (Nissen in Seasons 1977b)
Recent E Records:
   11 Apr 1982, McCook Co. (L. Anderson)
   25 May 1979, Douglas Co. (Hall in Seasons 1979c)
Nesting. May and Jun.
   Earliest dates:
   1 May 1934, Meade Co., nest with 4 eggs (Whitney 1955)
   3 May 1982, Perkins Co., nest with 4 eggs (Hinds in Seasons 1982c)
   Latest dates:
   11 Jul 1981, Stanley Co., adult and 3 young (Spomer 1981)
   15 Jul 1975, Meade Co., pair with 3 young (Rose in Seasons 1975c)
   15 Jul 1983, Perkins Co., adult with 4 young (Hinds in Seasons 1983d)

Late summer concentrations.
  21 Jul 1966, Jackson Co., 34 (Evans and Kerbs 1967)
  23 Jul 1978, Meade Co., 50 (Serr et al. in Seasons 1978d)
  28 Jul 1960, near Scenic, 30 (Whitney)
Fall migration. First week of Aug.
  Latest date:
    25 Oct 1914, Union Co., 2 along the Missouri River (Anderson in Stephens 1918)

HUDSONIAN GODWIT *Limosa haemastica* (Linnaeus)

Status. Fairly common spring migrant E and at Lacreek NWR (Fjetland). Only 1 fall record: 29 Oct 1977, Yankton Co., flock of 14 (Hall in Seasons 1978a).

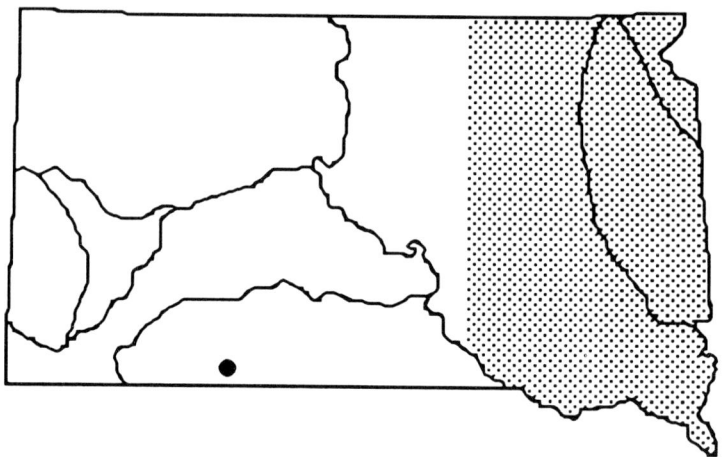

Habitat. Marshes, mud flats, and wet fields.
Spring migration. Last third of Apr and May.
  Earliest dates:
    10 Apr 1989, Brown Co. (Tallman in Seasons 1989c)
    13 Apr 1978, Hamlin Co. (Harris in Seasons 1978c)
    14 Apr 1982, McCook Co. (Anderson in Seasons 1982c)
  Latest dates:
    5 Jun 1986, Roberts Co. (Harris in Seasons 1986d)
    6 Jun 1979, Deuel Co. (Harris in Seasons 1979c)
    7 Jun 1983, Day Co. (Harris)

MARBLED GODWIT *Limosa fedoa* (Linnaeus)

Status. Fairly common summer resident, N of Brookings Co. and W to Haakon and SE Shannon counties. Reported nesting at Lacreek NWR (Burgess in Seasons 1978) and considered an uncommon to fairly common migrant in Fall River Co. (Rosche 1982).

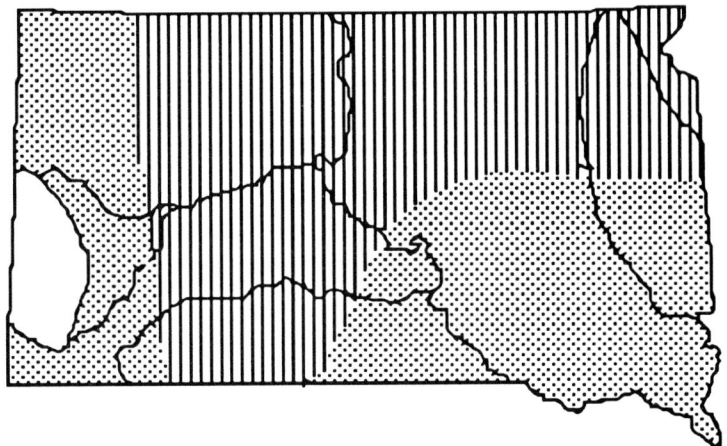

Habitat. Nests in dry grassland; feeds in wet fields and on mud flats.
Spring migration. Last half of Apr and first half of May.
  Earliest dates:
    5 Apr 1978, Yankton Co. (Hall in Seasons 1978c)
    8 Apr 1979, Yankton Co. (Hall in Seasons 1979c)
    8 Apr 1986, Sanborn Co. (Rogers in Seasons 1986c)
    8 Apr 1989, Minnehaha Co. (Skadsen in Seasons 1989c)
Nesting. Last third of May into Jul. Unusual concentration: 13 Jul 1953, Andover, 41 (Peterson 1953).
  Earliest dates:
    14 May 1945, Codington Co., nest with 4 eggs (photo by J. Johnson)
    27 May 1956, near Bitter Lake, nest with 4 eggs (Krause, photographed by Whitney)
  Latest dates:
    21 Jun 1990, Sully Co. pair with 4 young (Springer)
    16 Jun 1966, Bitter Lake, young photographed (Rose)
    3 Jul 1964, Bitter Lake, 4 downy young (Springer)
Fall migration. Aug and Sep. Unusual concentration: 16 Aug 1978, Brown Co., 60 (Montgomery)
  Latest dates:
    3 Oct 1971, Deuel Co. (Harris)
    11 Oct 1953, NE SD (Peterson 1953, 1960b)

RUDDY TURNSTONE *Arenaria interpres* (Linnaeus)

Status. Fairly common spring migrant in the Coteau des Prairies, but uncommon or rare elsewhere. Uncommon fall migrant.

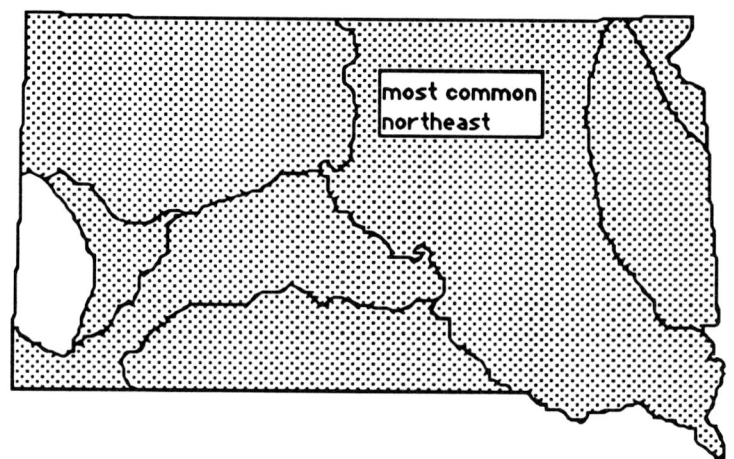

Habitat. Mudflats, shallow ponds, and plowed fields.
Spring migration. Last half of May.
  Earliest dates:
    21 Apr 1968, S Meade Co. (Rose)
    2 May 1939, Whetstone Valley (Harris 1964)
    4 May 1974, Lacreek NWR (Burgess)
  Latest dates:
    6 Jun 1964, Lake Poinsett (Springer)
    7 Jun 1987, Day Co. (Harris et al. in Seasons 1987c)
    11 Jun 1979, Douglas Co. (Hall in Seasons 1979d)
Fall migration. Second week of Aug.
  Earliest dates:
    26 Jul 1988, Hamlin Co. (Harris in Seasons 1988d)
    29 Jul 1977, Deuel Co. (Harris)
    6 Aug 1973, Lacreek NWR (Burgess)
  Latest dates:
    16 Sep 1934, Lake Herman (Spawn 1935)
    16 Sep 1980, Clay Co. (Husmann in Seasons 1981a)
    17 Sep 1976, Fall River Co. (Rosche 1982)

RED KNOT *Calidris canutus* (Linnaeus)

Status. Casual migrant. No specimens.

Records.
9 May 1981, Harding Co. (Rogers in Seasons 1981c)
15 May 1983, Yankton Co. (Hall in Seasons 1983c)
26 May 1974, Clay Co. (Harris 1975a)
5 Sep 1986, Deuel Co. (Harris 1987d)
11 and 13 Sep 1957, Fox Lake (Peterson 1958, 1960b, 1961a)

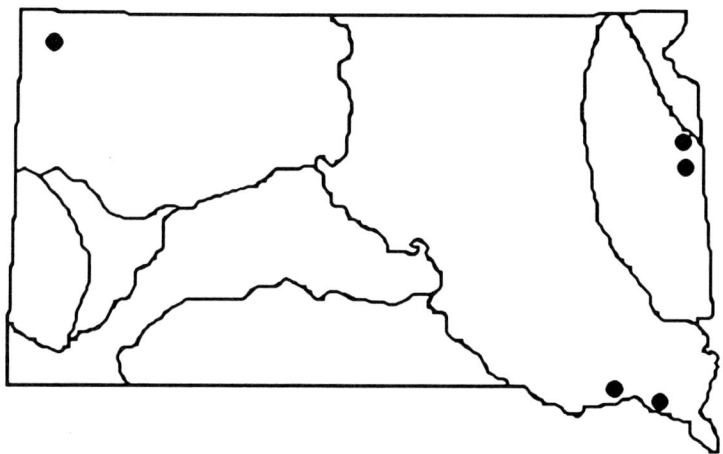

SANDERLING *Calidris alba* (Pallas)

Status. Uncommon spring and fall migrant E. Rare to uncommon W, depending on availability of habitat.

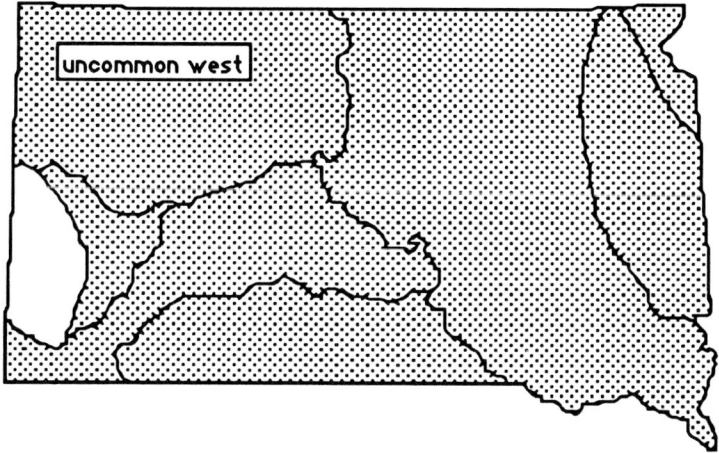

Habitat. Sand flats and sandy shores, rarely on mud.
Spring migration. Fourth week of May.
 Earliest dates:
  16 Apr 1979, Deuel Co. (Harris and Husmann in Seasons 1979c)
  24 Apr 1976, Beadle Co. (Baker in Seasons 1976c)
  27 Apr 1959, near Lake Alice (Peterson 1960a, 1964)
 Latest Dates:
  7 Jun 1955, Dry Lake, Hamlin Co. (Peterson 1959, 1960b, 1962a)
  7 Jun 1958, Fox Lake (Peterson 1959, 1960b, 1962a)
  7 Jun 1987, Day Co. (Harris et al. in Seasons 1987c)
Fall migration. Sep.
 Earliest dates:
  3 Jul 1981, Fall River Co. (Rosche 1982)
  12 Jul 1911, Pine Ridge Indian Reservation (Visher 1912a)
  16 Jul 1964, Lake Poinsett (Springer)
 Latest dates:
  25 Oct 1974, Roberts Co. (Harris)
  28 Oct 1980, Yankton Co. (Hall in Seasons 1981a)
  4 Nov 1984, Waubay NWR (Bryant in Seasons 1985a)

SEMIPALMATED SANDPIPER *Calidris pusilla* (Linnaeus)

Status. Abundant spring and fall migrant E. Uncommon migrant W.

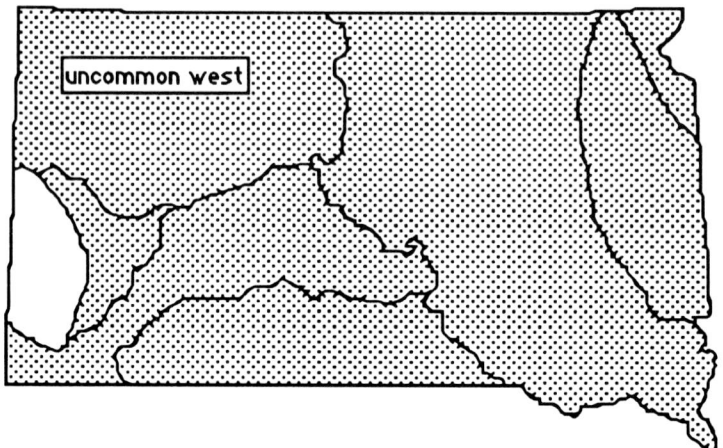

Habitat. Mud flats and shallow ponds.
Spring migration. Last 3 weeks of May.
 Earliest dates
  2 Apr 1986, Yankton Co. (Hall)
  4 Apr 1989, Moody Co. (Prisbe in Seasons 1989c)
  6 Apr 1981, Brown Co. (Tallman in Seasons 1981c)
 Latest dates:
  15 Jun 1985, Sioux Falls (Springer)
  18 Jun 1985, Bitter Lake (Springer)
  19 Jun 1985, Edmunds Co. (Springer)

Fall migration. Aug, tapering off through Sep. Rosche's (1982) Fall River Co., 24 Jun 1981, record could be an early fall bird.
Earliest dates:
  2 Jul 1971, McPherson Co. (Springer)
  2 Jul 1989, Todd Co. (Springer in Seasons 1989d)
  6 Jul 1989, Lacreek NWR (Springer)
Latest dates:
  16 Oct 1959, Lake Marsh and Lake Mary (Peterson 1960a, 1964)
  27 Oct 1960, Lake Albert (Peterson 1965)
  31 Oct 1957, NE SD (Peterson 1960a, 1961a)

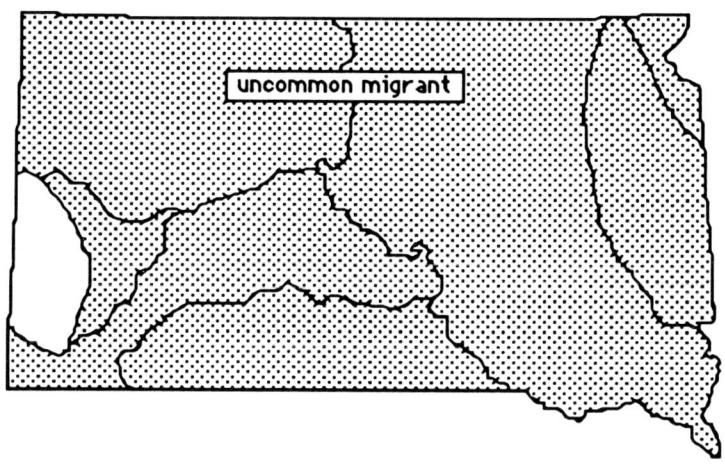

Semipalmated Sandpiper banding recoveries

WESTERN SANDPIPER *Calidris mauri* (Cabanis)

Status. Uncommon spring and fall migrant except absent in Black Hills.

Habitat. Mud flats and shallow ponds.
Spring migration. Late Apr – May
  Earliest dates:
    6 Apr 1985, Bon Homme Co. (Kronner in Seasons 1985c)
    12 Apr 1971, Lacreek NWR (Fjetland 1973)
    13 Apr 1928, Lyman Co. (Thietje in Over and Thoms 1932)
  Latest dates:
    30 May 1981, Sioux Falls (Whitney)
    6 Jun 1964, Volga (Springer)
    15 Jun 1985, Sioux Falls (Springer in Seasons 1985d)
Fall migration. Aug.
  Earliest dates:
    6 Jul 1989, Lacreek NWR (Springer in Seasons 1989d)
    10 Jul 1981, Fall River Co. (Rosche and Rosche in Seasons 1982a)

17 Jul – 2 Aug 1973, Lacreek NWR, 4 captured (Fjetland 1973)
Latest dates:
14 Sep 1960, Deuel Co., collected (Breckenridge)
22 Sep 1984, McPherson Co. (Tallman in Seasons 1985a)

LEAST SANDPIPER *Calidris minutilla* (Vieillot)

Status. Uncommon to fairly common spring and fall migrant.
Habitat. Shallow marshes and ponds, mud flats, and flooded meadows.
Spring migration. Second and third weeks of May.
Earliest dates:
16 Apr 1982, Fall River Co. (Rosche in Seasons 1982c)
17 Apr 1977, Fall River Co. (Rosche)
18 Apr 1981, Pennington Co. (Baker in Seasons 1981c)
Latest dates:
6 Jun 1970, near Bison (Springer)
6 Jun 1978, Day Co. (Harris)
6 Jun 1986, Yankton Co. (Kronner)
8 Jun 1958, Fox Lake (Peterson 1959)
Fall migration. Aug and Sep.
Earliest dates:
2 Jul 1989, Todd Co. (Springer in Seasons 1989d)
3 Jul 1981, Fall River Co. (Rosche and Rosche in Seasons 1982a)
11 Jul 1966, Sanborn Co. (Harris)
Latest dates:
23 Oct 1956, Fox Lake (Peterson 1960a)
5 Nov 1957, Fox Lake (Peterson 1960a, 1961b)
10 Nov 1969, Sanborn Co. (Harris)

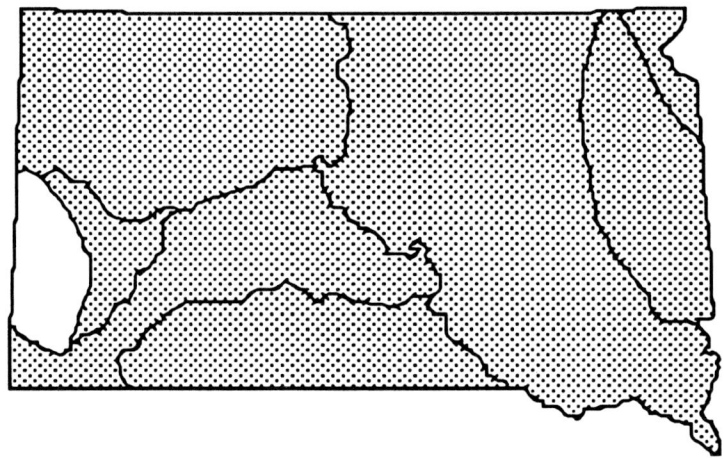

WHITE-RUMPED SANDPIPER *Calidris fuscicollis* (Vieillot)

Status. Common spring and rare fall migrant E; much less common W, where not recorded in the fall.

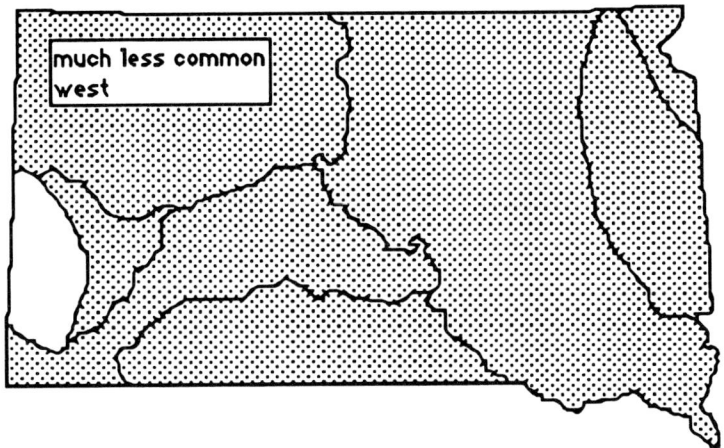

Habitat. Shallow ponds and marshes.

Spring migration. Second and third weeks of May. Peak numbers: 21 May 1931, Union Co, 250 (Stephens et al. 1955); 5 Jun 1968, Mound City, 80 (Springer); 6 Jun 1970, near Bison, 75 (Springer).

Earliest dates:
  17 Apr 1966, Brown Co. (Rose 1967)
  26 Apr 1961, Rush Lake (Peterson 1961b)
  29 Apr 1960, Rush Lake and near Milbank (Peterson 1965)

Latest dates:
  21 Jun 1958, Fox Lake (Peterson 1960a, 1963b)
  29 Jun 1989, Hutchinson Co. (Springer)
  30 Jun 1989, Clark Co. (Harris in Seasons 1989d)

Fall migration. Sep.

Earliest dates:
  2 Aug 1959, Clear Lake (Peterson 1960a, 1964)
  9 Aug 1964, Estelline (Springer)
  11 Aug 1984, Minnehaha Co. (M. Skadsen)

Latest dates:
  14 Oct 1957, Fox Lake (Peterson 1960a, 1961a, 1963a)
  18 Oct 1956, Fox Lake (Peterson 1960a, 1961a, 1963a)

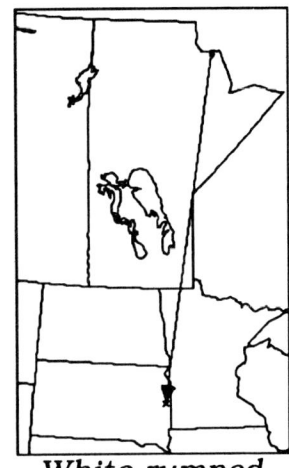

White-rumped Sandpiper banding recoveries

BAIRD'S SANDPIPER *Calidris bairdii* (Coues)

Status. Common spring and fall migrant.

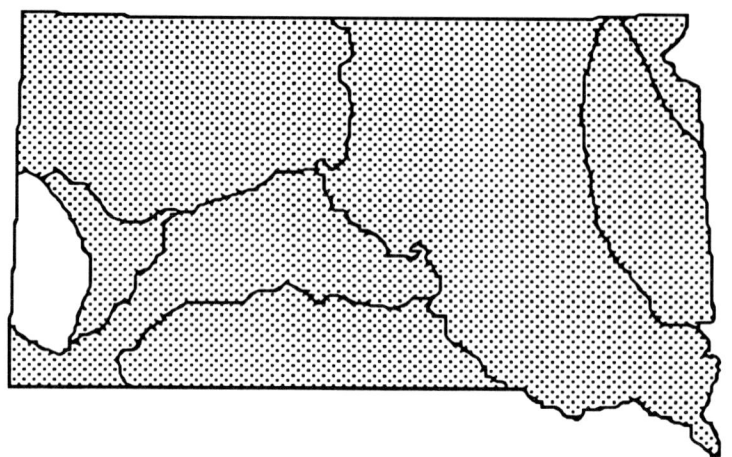

Habitat. Mud flats and shallow ponds.

Spring migration. Second and third weeks of Apr.
  Earliest dates:
    18 Mar 1968, Sanborn Co. (Harris)
    19 Mar 1959, Lake Campbell (Holden)
    21 Mar 1989, Roberts Co. (Harris in Seasons 1989c)
  Latest dates:
    11 Jun 1911, Sioux Falls area (Larson 1925)
    11 Jun 1987, Kingsbury Co. (Springer in Seasons 1987d)
    18 Jun 1987, Roberts Co. (Springer)

Fall migration. Last week of Aug and first half of Sep. Unusual concentration: 19 Aug 1980, Lacreek NWR, 1500 (Rosche and Rosche in Seasons 1981a). Observation on 24 Jun 1981, Fall River Co. (Rosche 1982) may represent summering birds.
  Earliest dates:
    2 Jul 1989, Todd Co. (Springer in Seasons 1989d)
    10 Jul 1981, Fall River Co. (Rosche and Rosche in Seasons 1982a)
    10 Jul 1988, Perkins Co. (Griffiths and Griffiths in Seasons 1988d)
  Latest dates:
    19 Oct 1966, Bitter Lake (Springer)
    28 Oct 1965, Bitter Lake (Springer)
    10 Nov 1969, Sanborn Co. (Harris)

PECTORAL SANDPIPER *Calidris melanotos* (Vieillot)

Status. Common spring and fall migrant E; rare spring, uncommon fall migrant W.

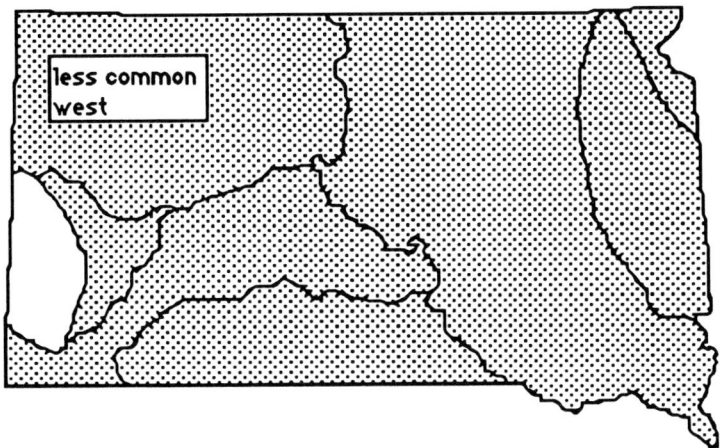

Habitat. Flooded meadows and shallow ponds.

Spring migration. Last week of Apr and first half of May. Unusual concentration: 29 Apr 1989, Grant Co., 300 (Harris in Seasons 1989c).

Earliest dates:
29 Mar 1988, Day Co. (Harris in Seasons 1988c)
1 Apr 1953, Lake Hendricks (Peterson 1953, 1960b)
4 Apr 1964, near Volga (Springer)

Latest dates:
11 Jun 1911, Sioux Falls area (Larson 1925)
11 Jun 1987, Kingsbury Co. (Springer)
12 Jun 1985, Union Co. (Springer in Seasons 1985d)
19 Jun 1985, Edmunds Co. (Springer)

Fall migration. Last half of Jul – first week of Sep.

Earliest dates:
10 Jul 1988, Perkins Co. (Griffiths and Griffiths in Seasons 1988d)
10 Jul 1989, Brookings Co. (Reinking in Seasons 1989d)
11 Jul 1956, Fox Lake (Peterson 1960a, 1963b)

Latest dates:
5 Nov 1911, Sioux Falls area (Larson 1925)
6 Nov 1975, Davison Co. (Baker in Seasons 1975d)
26 Nov 1988, Stanley Co. (Rosche and Rosche in Lambeth 1989)

DUNLIN *Calidris alpina* (Linnaeus)

Status. Fairly common spring and rare fall migrant E. Casual on Missouri River and only 1 W River record: 5 May 1984, Lacreek NWR (Baker and Paulson in Seasons 1984c).

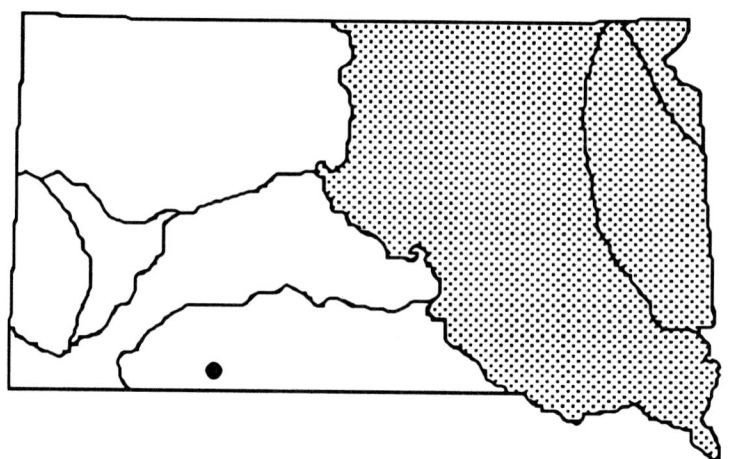

Habitat. Mud flats and shallow ponds.
Spring migration. Last 2 weeks of May.
  Earliest dates:
    24 Apr 1968, Miner Co. (Harris)
    24 Apr 1976, Deuel Co. (Harris)
    25 Apr 1981, Deuel Co. (Harris in Seasons 1981c)
  Latest dates:
    6 Jun 1964, Volga, (Springer)
    6 Jun 1978, Day Co. (Harris)
    6 Jun 1986, Yankton Co. (Kronner in Seasons 1986d)
    20 Jun 1975, Deuel Co. (Harris)
Fall migration. May not be a regular fall migrant.
  Earliest date:
    22 Jul 1988, Deuel Co. (Harris in Seasons 1988d)
    17 Aug 1978, McPherson Co. (Kesseler in Seasons 1979a)
  Latest dates:
    5 Nov 1957, Fox Lake (Peterson 1960a, 1961b)
    19 Nov 1985, Minnehaha Co. (Blankespoor in Seasons 1985a)
    23 Nov 1985, Minnehaha Co. (Blankespoor in Seasons 1985a)

STILT SANDPIPER *Calidris himantopus* (Bonaparte)
Status. Fairly common spring and fall migrant.

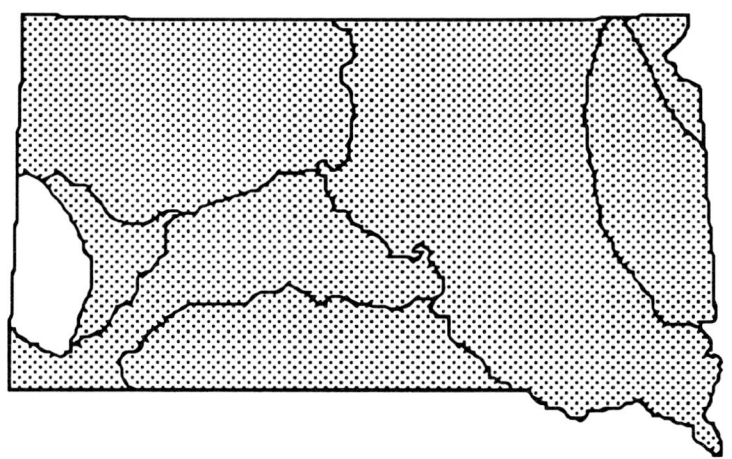

Habitat. Mud flats and shallow ponds.
Spring migration. Last 3 weeks of May.
  Earliest dates:
    18 Apr 1955, near Lake Poinsett (Peterson 1960a, 1962b)
    25 Apr 1981, Deuel Co. (Harris in Seasons 1981c)
    29 Apr 1960, near Lake Poinsett (Peterson 1960a, 1962b)
  Latest dates:
    5 Jun 1930, Day Co. (Youngworth 1935)
    5 Jun 1968, near Mound City (Springer)
    14 Jun 1967, Miner Co. (Harris)
Fall migration. Aug – Sep.
  Earliest dates:
    29 Jun 1987, Day Co. (Skadsen and Skadsen in Seasons 1987d)
    2 Jul 1971, McPherson Co. (Springer)
    6 Jul 1989, Lacreek NWR (Springer in Seasons 1989d)
  Latest Dates:
    22 Oct 1973, Deuel Co. (Harris)
    27 Oct 1960, Lake Albert (Peterson 1965)
    2 Nov 1986, Perkins Co. (Griffiths in Seasons 1987a)

BUFF-BREASTED SANDPIPER *Tryngites subruficollis* (Vieillot)

Status. Rare spring and fall migrant, most observations E. All W River records from fall.

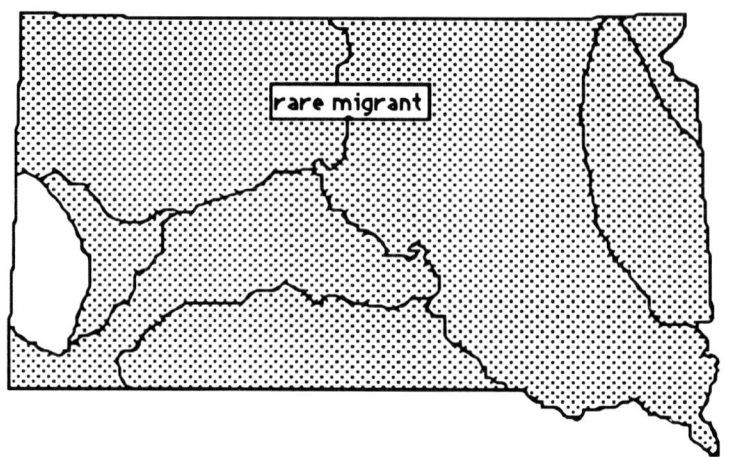

Habitat. Plowed and newly-planted fields, wet meadows, mowed hayfields, and spring-burned uplands.

Spring migration. Third week of May. Unusual concentration: 19 May 1966, Brown Co., 175 (Rose 1967).
Earliest dates:
10 May 1955, Grant Co. (Elliott 1955)
12 May 1912, Sioux Falls area (Larson 1925)
Latest dates:
22 May 1876, near Ft. Sisseton (McChesney 1879)
27 May 1990, Brookings Co. (McLaird in Seasons 1990c)

Fall migration. Last half of Aug and first week of Sep.
Earliest dates:
2 Aug 1987, Deuel Co. (Harris in Seasons 1988a)
7 Aug 1977, Fall River Co. (Rosche)
10 Aug 1982, Potter Co. (S. Harris)
Latest dates:
10 Sep 1976, Fall River Co. (Rosche)
15 Sep 1934, Brant Lake, specimen (Spawn 1935)
18 Sep 1982, Jackson Co. (Graupmann in Seasons 1983a)

RUFF *Philomachus pugnax* (Linnaeus)
Only record:
  8 Apr 1977, Bennett Co. (Rosche)

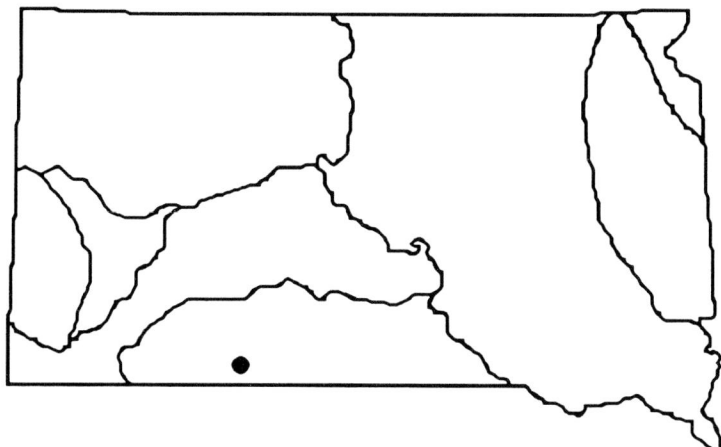

SHORT-BILLED DOWITCHER *Limnodromus griseus* (Gmelin)

Status. Probably a fairly common migrant through-out the state, although most records E.

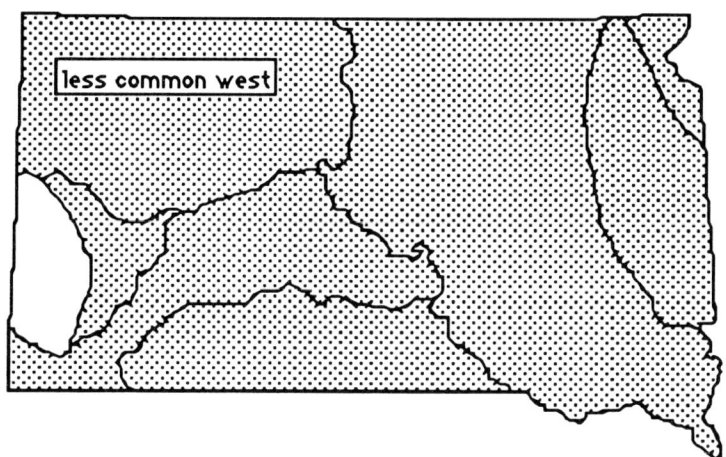

Habitat. Mud flats and shallow ponds.
Spring migration.
  Earliest dates:
    25 Apr 1971, Lacreek NWR (Rose in Fjetland 1973)
    4 May 1986, Sand Lake NWR (Prisbe in Seasons 1986c)
    4 May 1989, Edmunds Co. (Prisbe in Seasons 1989c)
  Latest dates:
    20 May 1989, Jackson Co. (Springer et al. in Seasons 1989c)
    21 May 1988, Day Co. (Skadsen et al. in Seasons 1988c)
    22 May 1974, Meade Co. (Whitney)

140 SANDPIPERS AND PHALAROPES

Fall migration.
  Earliest dates:
    28 Jun 1968, Sanborn Co. (Harris 1975b)
    7 Aug 1981, Fall River Co. (Rosche and Rosche in Seasons 1982a)
    12 Aug 1979, Lacreek NWR (Rosche and Rosche)
  Latest dates:
    28 Sep 1985, Minnehaha Co. (Martsching in Seasons 1986a)
    28 Sep 1985, Charles Mix Co. (Skadsen in Seasons 1986a)

LONG-BILLED DOWITCHER *Limnodromus scolopaceus* (Say)

Status. Common to abundant spring and fall migrant, except Black Hills.

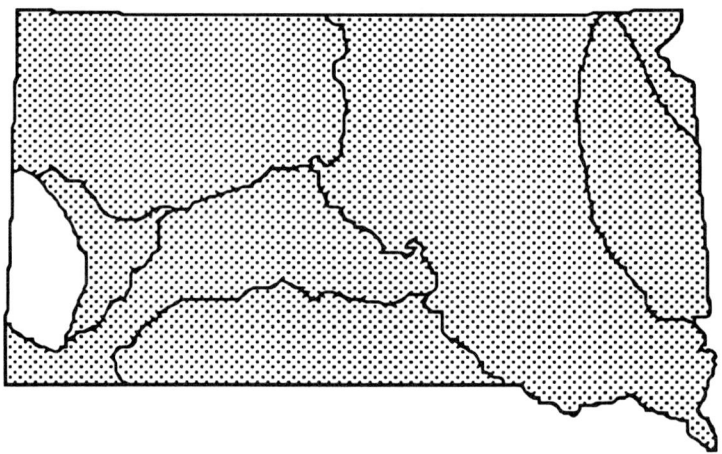

Habitat. Mud flats and shallow ponds.
Spring migration. First 3 weeks of May.
  Earliest dates:
    25 Mar 1967, near Lennox (Springer)
    1 Apr 1960, near Brandt (Peterson 1960a)
    15 Apr 1956, Fox Lake (Peterson 1960a)
  Latest dates:
    27 May 1974, Deuel Co. (Harris)
    27 May 1955, [Bitter Lake] (Peterson 1960a, 1962a)
    27 May 1978, Bennett Co. (Faanes in Seasons 1978c)
Fall migration. Sep and first half of Oct. Unusual concentration: 5 Oct 1968, Sanborn Co. 300+ (Harris).
  Earliest dates:
    28 Jun 1968, Sanborn Co. (Harris)
    29 Jun 1966, Miner Co. (Harris)
    30 Jun 1965, Grenville (Springer)
  Latest dates:
    2 Nov 1959, Lake Mary (Peterson 1960a, 1964)
    2 Nov 1969, Sanborn Co. (Harris)
    26 Nov 1985, Minnehaha Co. (Blankespoor in Seasons 1986a)

COMMON SNIPE *Gallinago gallinago* (Linnaeus)

Status. Common spring and fall migrant. Breeding status uncertain, may be fairly common in appropriate habitat. Winters in small numbers where open water is available.

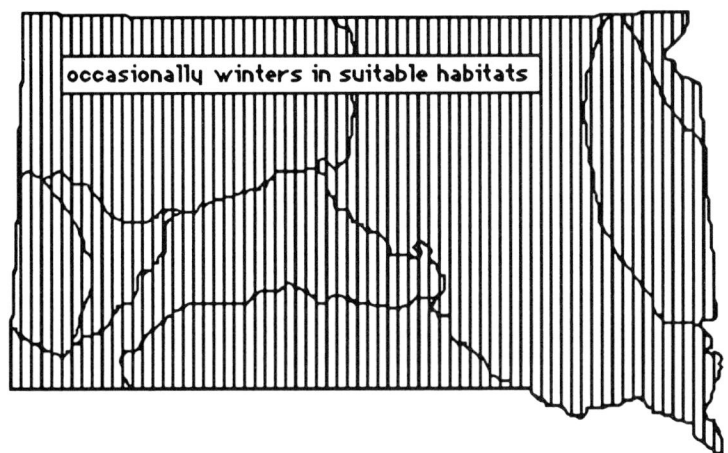

Habitat. Wet meadows and pastures, borders of marshy ponds and along streams.

Spring migration. Last 2 weeks of Apr. Early dates are assumed to be nonwintering birds.

  Earliest dates:
   3 Mar 1975, Sturgis (Miller in Seasons 1975a)
   6 Mar 1989, Lawrence Co. (Backlund in Seasons 1989c)
   15 Mar 1908, Sioux Falls area (Larson 1925)

Nesting. Only a few records for this elusive nester. Numerous reports of courting or territorial birds exist. Burgess reported it breeding every year at Lacreek.

  Nesting dates:
   13 May 1986, Day Co., nest with 4 eggs (Skadsen in Seasons 1986c)
   13 May 1987, Bennett Co., nest with 2 eggs (Brashears in Seasons 1987d)
   22 May 1984, Minnehaha Co., nest with 4 eggs photographed (Blankespoor 1986)
   24 May 1979, Codington Co., 1 adult with young (Husmann in Seasons 1979c)

Fall migration. Mid-Aug – Oct. Latest dates are omitted because of birds attempting to winter during mild falls.

Winter. Attempts to winter near open water, with most birds probably dying by midwinter.

  CBC reports:
   Rapid City, Spearfish, Lacreek, Hot Springs, Sioux Falls, Madison, Lake Co., Aberdeen, Wilmot, and Yankton.

AMERICAN WOODCOCK *Philohela minor* (Gmelin)

Status. Fairly common but local summer resident in extreme E, casual migrant elsewhere. W River record from Gregory Co.

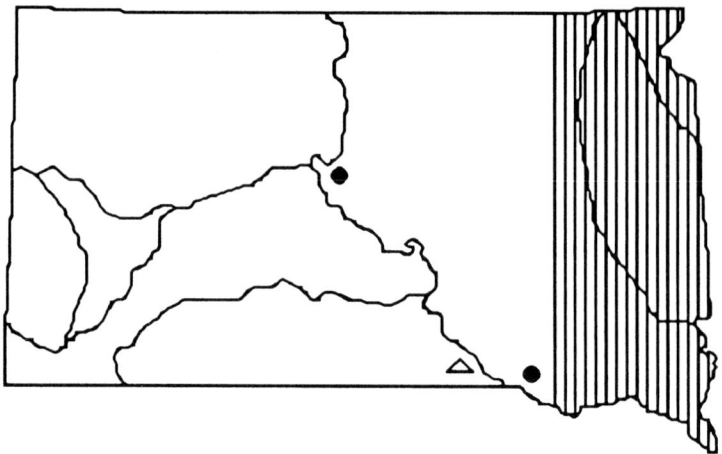

Habitat. Moist thickets and forest edges.
Spring migration.
Earliest dates:
18 Mar 1977, Brookings Co., dead bird (Harris)
19 Mar 1985, Charles Mix Co. (Kronner in Seasons 1985c)
20 Mar 1985, Lincoln Co. (Skadsen in Seasons 1985c)
Nesting. Many summer observations in E, but few nests found.
Early dates:
21 Apr 1884, Clay Co., nest with eggs (Agersborg in Cooke 1912)
27 Apr 1972, Oakwood Lakes State Park, nest with 4 eggs and downy young next day (Gates 1973)
3 May 1989, Gregory Co., nest with 2 young (Clawson 1989)
Latest dates:
16 Jun 1980, Brookings Co., nest and eggs (McPhillips 1980)
20 Jun 1985, Waubay NWR, adult with 5 young (Rabenberg in Seasons 1985d)
Fall migration.
Latest dates:
28 Oct 1983, Lincoln Co. (Bradwisch)
14 Nov 1975, Marshall Co. (Opitz in Seasons 1975d)
14 Nov 1985, Sully Co. (Johnson in Seasons 1986a)

WILSON'S PHALAROPE *Phalaropus tricolor* (Vieillot)

Status. Fairly common summer resident, except in the Black Hills and SE. Accidental winter.

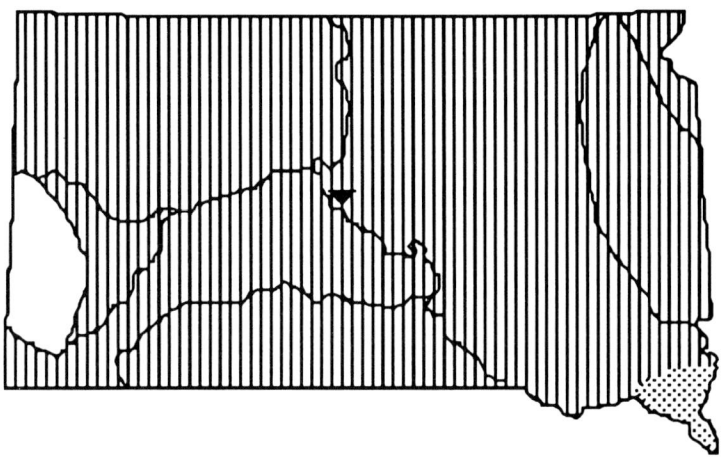

Habitat. Marshes and shallow ponds.

Spring migration. Second and third weeks of May. Unusual concentration: 17 May 1987, Todd Co., 600 on 1 pond (Springer in Seasons 1987c).

  Earliest dates:
    6 Mar 1970, Lake Andes (Krause)
    25 Mar 1967, near Madison (Springer)
    2 Apr 1989, Brown Co. (Prisbe in Seasons 1989c)

Nesting. Late May and Jun. In Stanley Co., 10 nests were found between 23 May and 18 Jun 1951, with hatching dates 29 May to 2 Jun (Blankenship et al. 1953).

  Earliest dates:
    17 May 1984, Codington Co., nest (Rabenberg in Seasons 1984d)
    20 May 1969, Miner Co., nest with 4 eggs (Harris)

  Latest dates:
    3 Jul 1981, Fall River Co., nest (Rosche and Rosche in Seasons 1981d)
    3 Jul 1987, Day Co., nest with 4 eggs (Skadsen and Skadsen in Seasons 1987d)
    6 Jul 1978, Harding Co., adults with 1/2-grown young (Springer)

Fall migration. Aug.

  Latest dates:
    11 Oct 1985, Kingsbury Co. (Wells in Seasons 1986a)
    13 Oct 1908, Sioux Falls area (Larson 1925)
    2 Nov 1959, NE SD (Peterson 1960a)

Winter.

  Only record:
    21 Feb 1976, Pierre (Mortimer in Seasons 1976b)

RED-NECKED PHALAROPE *Phalaropus lobatus* (Linnaeus)

Status. Fairly common, locally abundant, spring and fall migrant. Often associated with the more numerous Wilson's Phalaropes. Accidental winter.

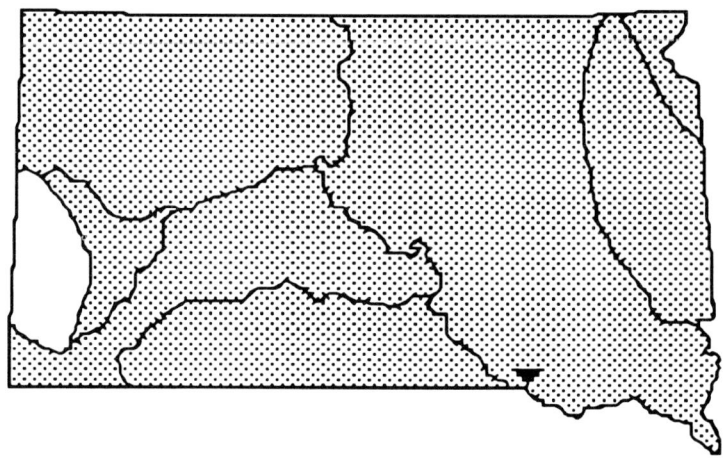

Habitat. Shallow ponds and marshes.

Spring migration. Third and fourth weeks of May. Unusual concentration: 2 Jun 1931, Bitter Lake, 4000 (Youngworth 1935).
Earliest dates:
7 May 1962, near Highmore (Harter 1968a)
10 May 1966, Brown Co. (Rose 1967)
11 May 1967, near Rapid City (Rose)
Latest dates:
6 Jun 1958, NE SD (Peterson 1960a)
6 Jun 1970, near Bison (Springer)
12 Jun 1968, Sanborn Co. (Harris)

Fall migration. Last week of Aug and first week of Sep.
Earliest dates:
2 Jul 1971, near Leola (Springer)
21 Jul 1988, Deuel Co. (Harris in Seasons 1988d)
9 Aug 1978, Deuel Co. (Harris)
Latest dates:
2 Oct 1981, Deuel Co. (Harris in Seasons 1982a)
2 Oct 1970, Deuel Co. (Harris)
10 Oct 1953, NE SD (Peterson 1953)
11 Oct 1976, Fall River Co. (Rosche)

Winter.
Only record:
1 Feb 1967, Lake Andes, female photographed (Town 1967)

RED PHALAROPE *Phalaropus fulicarius* (Linnaeus)

Status. Accidental.
Records:
- 27 May 1904, near Rapid City (Behrens in Visher 1909)
- ca. 28 Nov 1912, near McCook Lake, collected (Anderson in Stephens 1914, 1916)
- 27 May 1982, near Madison (Haertel and Haertel in Seasons 1982c)

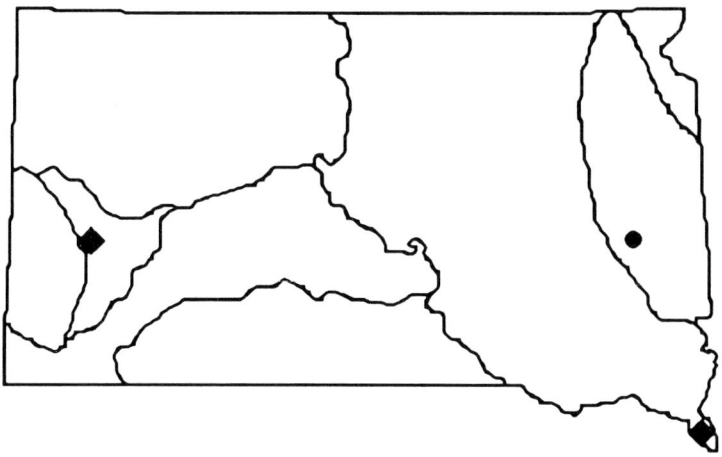

LARIDAE: Jaegers, Gulls, and Terns

POMARINE JAEGER *Stercorarius pomarinus* (Temminck)

Only record:
9 Oct 1932, near Madison, specimen (Hyde in Breckenridge 1933)

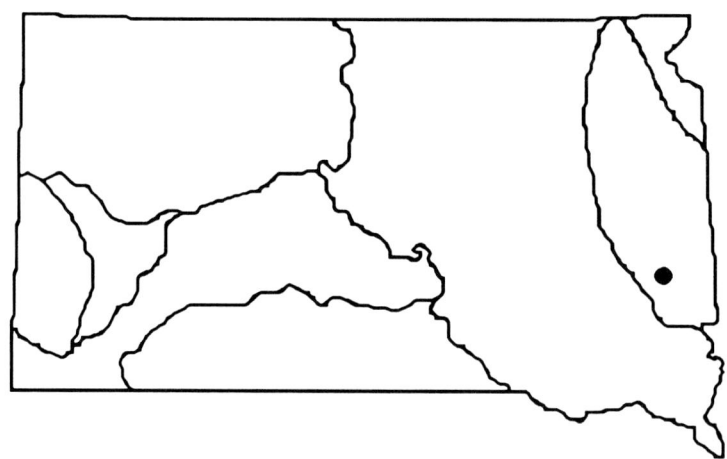

LONG-TAILED JAEGER *Stercorarius longicaudus*(Linnaeus)

Only record:
3 Oct 1975, Lacreek NWR (fide Ritts et al. in Burgess 1975)

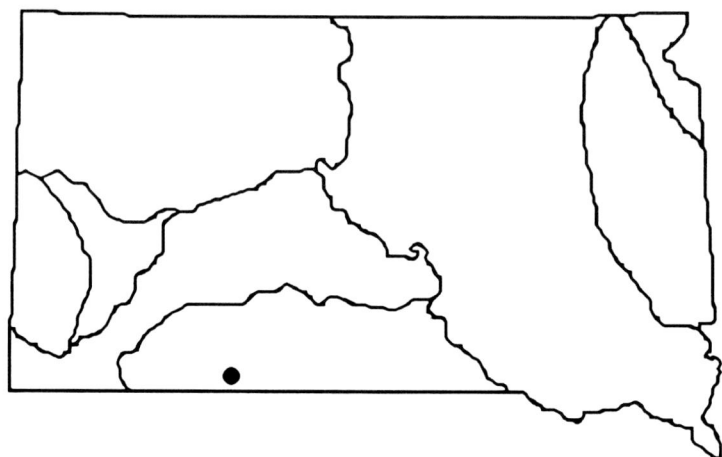

LAUGHING GULL *Larus atricilla* (Linnaeus)

Only records:
29 Sep 1919, near Lake Goodenough, specimen (Allen in Stephens 1920, Stephens et al. 1955)

10 Jan – 28 Apr 1990, Yankton Co., photographed (Harris and Van Sickle in Seasons 1990b; Van Sickle in Seasons 1990c)

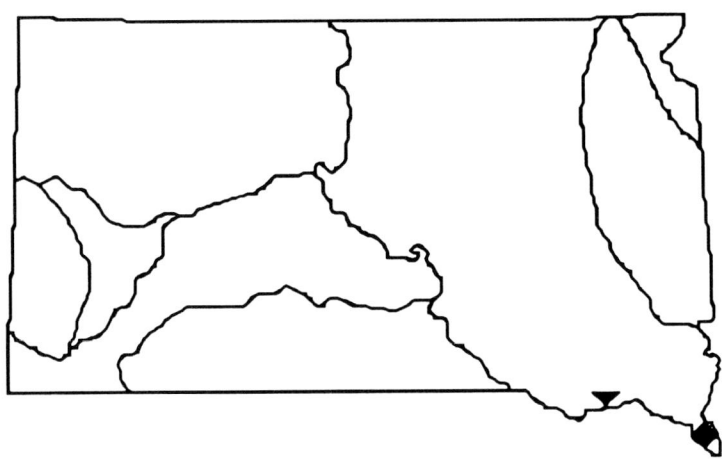

FRANKLIN'S GULL *Larus pipixcan* Wagler.

Status. Abundant summer resident but breeding colonies very local in Codington, Lake, Roberts and Kingsbury counties. Uncommon migrant and summer visitor W River. Often found in spectacular concentrations during fall.

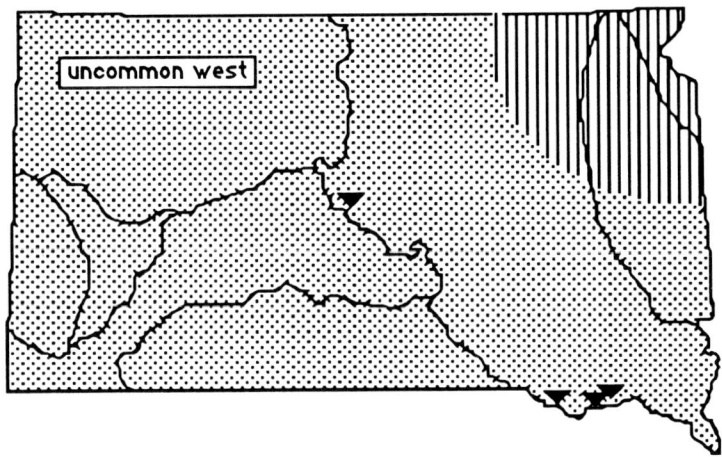

Habitat. Nests in marshes. Feeds around water, and in plowed fields.

Spring migration. Late Mar – Apr. Early dates may represent wintering birds. Unusual concentration: 21 Apr 1968, Seavey's Lake, flock of 100 (Rose and Whitney).

Earliest dates:
1 Mar 1983, Yankton Co. (Hall in Seasons 1983a)
6 Mar 1983, Stanley Co. (Coonrod in Seasons 1983c)
6 Mar 1987, Hamlin Co. (Harris in Seasons 1987c)

Nesting. Last week of May – Jun. Colonies not stable from year to year.

Earliest date:
21 May 1903, Hamlin Co., nest with 4 eggs (Lee)
25 May 1922, Kingsbury Co., nest with 3 eggs (Patton)
1 Jun 1902, Lake John, 5 sets of eggs collected (Lee in Whitney 1955)

Latest dates:
8 Jul 1970, Peever Slough, young just flying and 1 downy in nest (Harris 1970d)
8 Jul 1981, Lake Co., fledgling (Harris et al. in Seasons 1981c)
11 Jul 1986, Codington Co., flightless young (Harris et al. in Seasons 1986d)

Fall migration. Sep. Unusual concentrations: 29 Sep 1978, Yankton Co., 40,000 (Hall in Seasons 1979a); 24 Sep 1979, Day Co., 40,000 (Watters in Seasons 1980a).

Latest dates (away from Missouri River):
15 Nov 1967, Roberts Co. (Harris)
21 Nov 1982, Davison Co. (Rogers in Seasons 1983b)
24 Nov 1909, Sioux Falls area (Larson 1925)

Winter.
CBC report:
Pierre. The latter bird still present 1 Feb 1987 (Harris et al.)

Other records:
13–24 Dec 1988, Yankton Co. (Hall et al. in Seasons 1989b)
14 Dec 1983, Yankton Co. (Hall in Seasons 1984b)

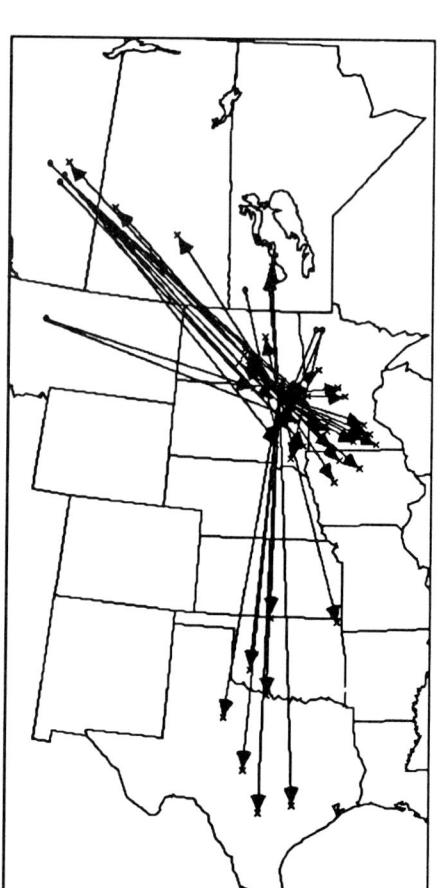

North American Franklin's Gull banding recoveries

27 Feb 1983, Yankton Co. (Hall and Wilcox in Seasons 1983a)
28 Feb 1983, Bon Homme Co. (Hall in Seasons 1983a)

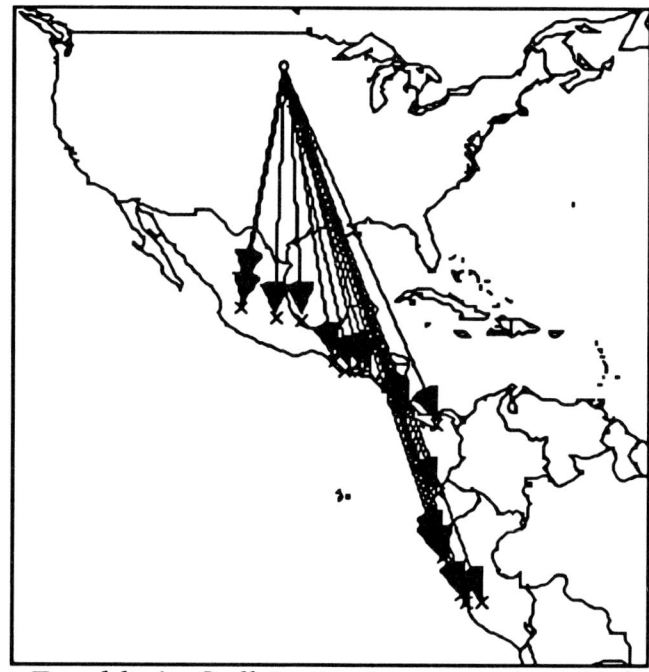

Franklin's Gull Latin American banding recoveries

BONAPARTE'S GULL *Larus philadelphia* (Ord)

Status. Fairly common spring and fall migrant E, primarily along Coteau des Prairies and Missouri River. Rare winter along Missouri River. Casual W River (Fall River, Pennington, Perkins, and Jackson counties).

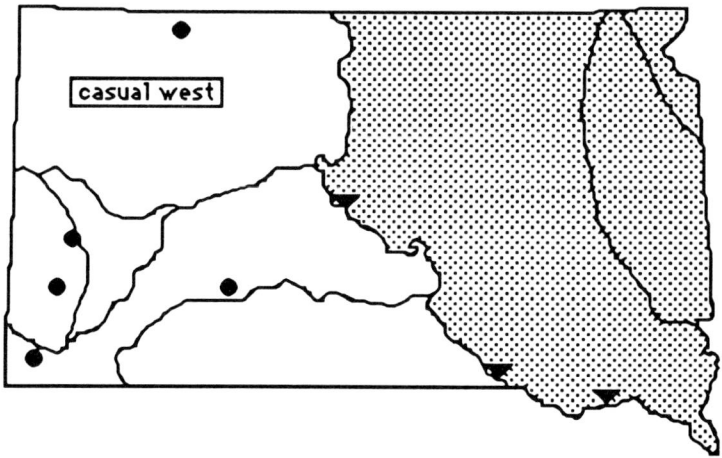

Habitat. Rivers, lakes, and marshes.
Spring migration. Last week of Apr and the first week of May. Unusual concentration: 19 Apr 1976, Yankton Co., 160 (Holden).

Earliest dates:
- 31 Mar 1981, Turner Co. (L. Anderson)
- 2 Apr 1986, Yankton Co. (Hoeger in Seasons 1986c)
- 5 Apr 1981, Yankton Co. (Hall in Seasons 1981c)
- 5 Apr 1978, Yankton Co. (Hall in Seasons 1978c)
- 5 Apr 1990, Yankton Co. (Hall in Seasons 1990c)

Latest dates:
- 28 May 1982, Hughes Co. (Montgomery and Tallman in Seasons 1982c)
- 10 Jun 1974, Deuel Co. (Harris)
- 30 Jun 1975, Roberts Co. (Harris)

Fall migration. Sep and Oct. Birds on the Missouri River linger into early winter.

Earliest dates:
- 10 Aug 1990, Day Co. (Hoogendoorn)
- 14 Aug 1977, Deuel Co. (Harris in Seasons 1978a)
- 16 Aug 1967, Jerauld Co. (Harris)

Latest dates away from Missouri River:
- 2 Nov 1986, Perkins Co. (Griffiths and Griffiths in Seasons 1987a)
- 28 Nov 1968, Canyon Lake (Baylor 1969)

Winter.

CBC reports:
Pierre

Other records:
- 1 Dec 1983, Yankton Co. (Hall in Seasons 1984b)
- 7 Dec 1985, Charles Mix Co. (Skadsen and Skadsen in Seasons 1986b)

RING-BILLED GULL *Larus delawarensis* (Ord)

Status. Common spring and fall migrant, more common E. Breeds in single colonies in Day and Roberts counties. Non-breeding birds summer along the Missouri River and elsewhere. Winters regularly along the Missouri River.

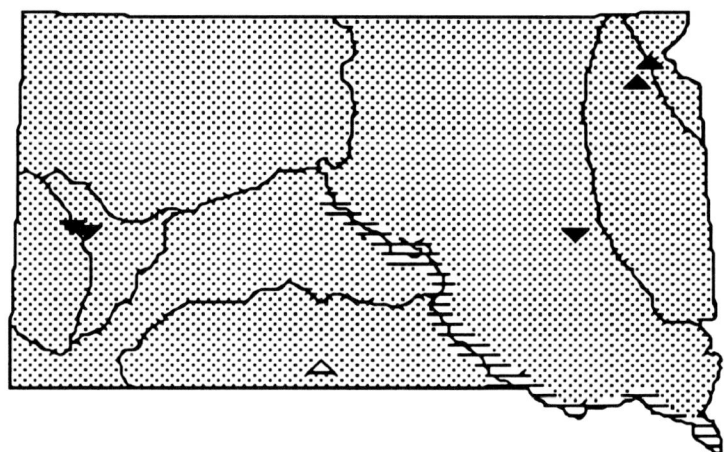

Habitat. Lakes, marshes, and large rivers.
Spring migration. Late Mar – Apr. Large concentration: 28 Mar 1989, Minnehaha Co., 2000 (Skadsen in Seasons 1989c).
 Earliest dates (away from Missouri River):
  2 Mar 1981, Deuel Co. (Harris in Seasons 1981c)
  3 Mar 1983, Deuel Co. (Harris in Seasons 1983c)
  6 Mar 1987, Hamlin Co. (Harris in Seasons 1987c)
  6 Mar 1987, Day Co. (Skadsen in Seasons 1987c)
Nesting. Mid-May – Jun. Springer reported a nesting season record on 2 Jun 1989 in Todd Co.
 Earliest dates:
  8 May 1985, Day Co., 2504 nests, most with full clutches (Harris et al.)
  13 May 1984, Day Co., 1964 nests (Harris et al.)
  16 May 1981, Day Co., 1013 nests (Harris and Husmann in Seasons 1981d)
 Latest dates:
  3 Jul 1960, Day Co., 24 young banded (Findley)
  3 Jul 1987, Day Co., 149 nests with eggs (Skadsen and Skadsen in Seasons 1987d)
  5 Jul 1978, Day Co., eggs and young (Wells and Wells in Seasons 1978d)
Fall migration. Oct.
 Latest dates (away from Missouri River):
  24 Nov 1983, Pennington Co. (Bjerke 1984)
  26 Nov 1973, Deuel Co. (Harris)
  27 Nov 1968, Sanborn Co. (Harris)
Winter. Fairly common, although not annual, along Missouri River.
 CBC reports:
  Huron, Pierre, and Yankton.

Other records (away from Missouri River):
  7 Dec 1954, Rapid City (Pettingill and Whitney 1965)
  7 Dec 1958, Rapid City (Pettingill and Whitney 1965)

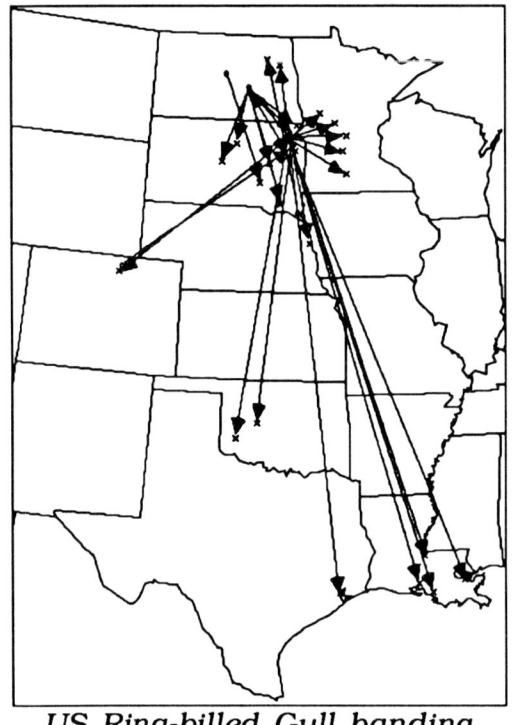

US Ring-billed Gull banding recoveries

Ring-billed Gull recoveries outside of the USA

CALIFORNIA GULL *Larus californicus* Lawrence

Status. Regular breeder in small numbers in Day and Marshall counties, uncommon migrant elsewhere.

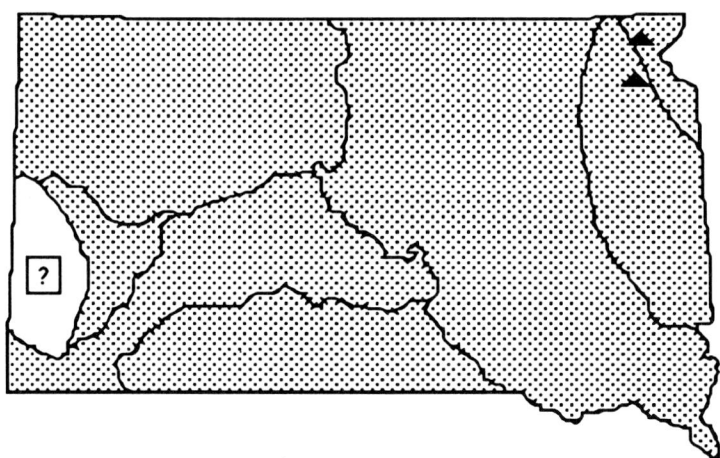

Habitat. Open water and large wetlands.

Spring migration.
Earliest dates:
  29 Mar 1988, Day Co. (Harris in Seasons 1988c)
  14 Apr 1989, Day Co. (Skadsen in Seasons 1989c)
  16 Apr 1966, Brown Co. (Rose 1967)
Latest dates:
  19 May 1984, McPherson Co. (Harris et al. in Seasons 1984c)
  20 May 1973, Pierre (Rose)
  22 May 1985, Fall River Co. (Springer in Seasons 1985c)

Nesting.
Earliest dates:
  28 May 1984, Day Co., 23 nests with full clutches (Harris and Skadsen in Season
  5 Jun 1986, Marshall Co., 2 nests (Skadsen 1987e)
  6 Jun 1983, Day Co., chicks (Harris et al. in Seasons 1983c)
Latest dates:
  3 Jul 1981, Day Co., 3 nests with eggs and young (Harris 1982b)
  3 Jul 1987, Day Co., 5 nests with eggs (Skadsen and Skadsen in Seasons 1987d)

Fall migration.
Earliest dates:
  11 Jul 1981, Pierre (Missouri Breaks Audubon Society)
  25 Jul 1977, Pierre (Hays in Seasons 1977d)
  29 Jul 1984, Pierre (Riis in Seasons 1984b)
Latest dates:
  20 Sep 1980, Lacreek NWR (Rosche and Rosche in Seasons 1981c)
  22 Sep 1984, Charles Mix Co. (Harris et al. in Seasons 1985a)
  19 Nov 1967, Big Bend Dam (Rose)

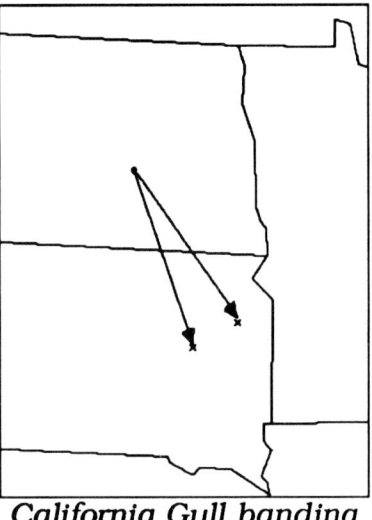

California Gull banding recoveries

HERRING GULL *Larus argentatus* Pontoppidan

Status. Fairly common spring and fall migrant. Common winter resident, although locally absent some years, along Missouri River; rare in W third.

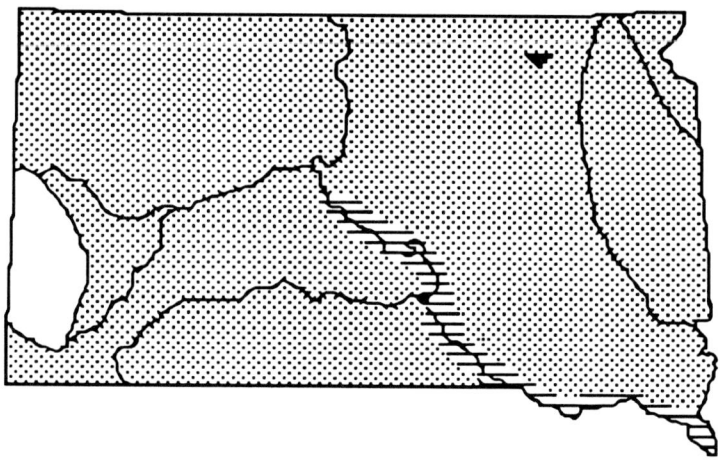

Habitat. Rivers and lakes.

Spring migration. Last half of Mar – early Apr, as soon as the ice begins to break up.
  Earliest dates:
   2 Mar 1988, Brookings Co. (Sandell in Seasons 1988c)
   3 Mar 1962, Sand Lake NWR (Podoll 1963)
   6 Mar 1987, Yankton Co. (Hall)
  Latest dates:
   6 May 1978, Roberts Co. (Harris)
   20 May 1987, Yankton Co. (Springer in Seasons 1987c)
   29 May 1981, Fall River Co. (Rosche and Rosche in Seasons 1981c)

Fall migration. Nov.
  Earliest dates:
   1 Sep 1974, Pierre (Rose)
   11 Sep 1963, Sand Lake NWR (Springer)
   14 Sep 1975, Yankton Co. (Hall in Seasons 1975d)

Winter. Winters regularly along Missouri River, especially at Pierre.
  CBC reports:
   Lake Andes, Pierre, and Yankton.
  Other records:
   23 Dec 1985, Brown Co. (Bryant in Seasons 1986b)

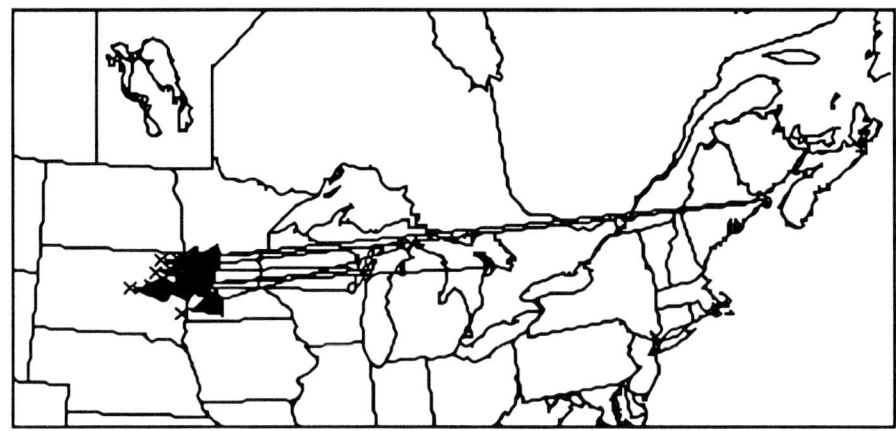
Herring Gull banding recoveries

THAYER'S GULL *Larus thayeri* Brooks

Status: Rare winter visitor, primarily along Missouri River. First reported: 30 Jan 1987, Oahe Dam, photographed (Tallman, Harris, et al.).

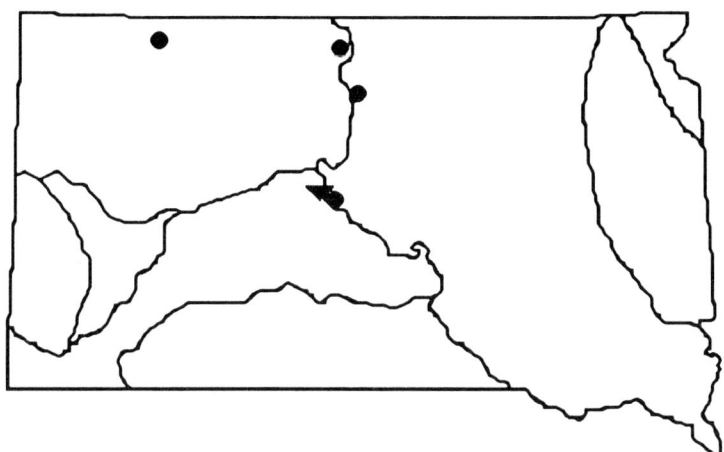

Habitat. Open water.
Spring migration.
  Latest dates:
    6 Mar 1987, Oahe Dam, photographed (Tallman et al.)
    21 Mar 1987, Perkins Co. (Griffiths and Griffiths)
    7 May 1987, Walworth Co. (Griffiths and Griffiths in Seasons 1987c)
Fall migration.
  Earliest dates:
    28 Nov 1987, Corson Co. (Griffiths and Griffiths in Seasons 1988a)
    9 Dec 1988, Oahe Dam, (Tallman, Montgomery, and Harris)

156 JAEGERS, GULLS, AND TERNS

ICELAND GULL *Larus glaucoides* Meyer

Only record.
11 Dec 1988, Gavin's Point Dam, photographed (Rose and Bray)

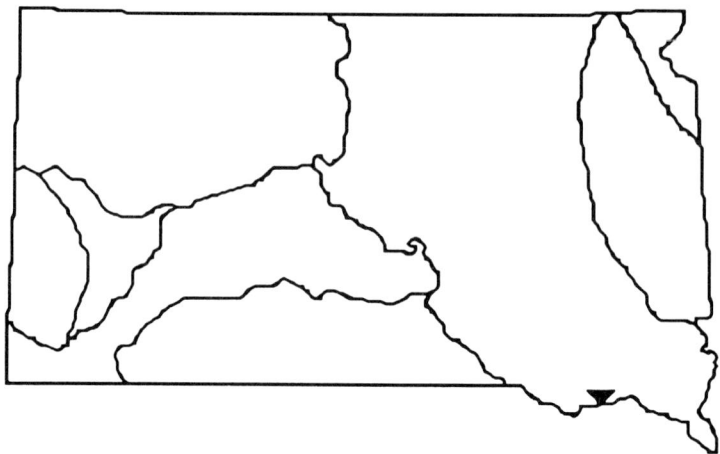

GLAUCOUS GULL *Larus hyperboreus* Gunnerus

Status. Irregular, uncommon winter visitor along Missouri River and NE (Hamlin, Deuel, Kingsbury, and Roberts counties). Rare elsewhere. Reported from Lacreek NWR, 7 Apr 1979 (Rosche and Rosche).

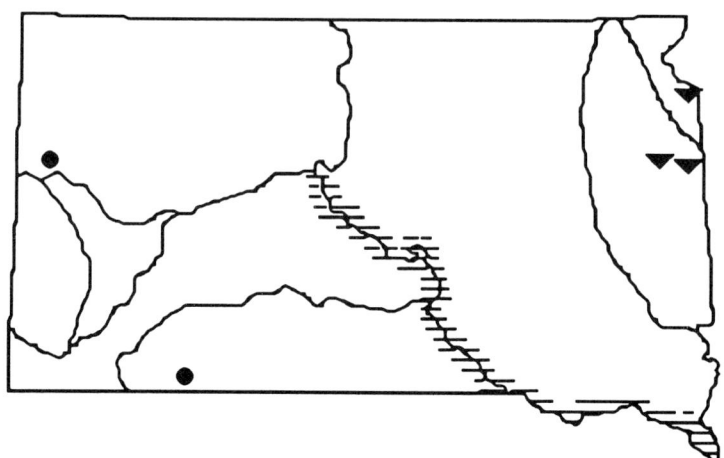

Habitat. Open water.
Spring migration.
  Latest dates:
    2 May 1974, Pierre (Rose 1974)
    7 May 1981, Hughes Co. (Spomer in Seasons 1981c)
    10 May 1972, Pierre (Rose 1974)
Fall migration.
  Earliest dates:
    11 Nov 1973, Pierre (Rose 1974)
    24 Nov 1983, Butte Co. (Bjerke 1984)

BLACK-LEGGED KITTIWAKE *Rissa tridactyla* (Linnaeus)

Status. Rare migrant and winter visitor.
Habitat. Large lakes and rivers, especially the Missouri.

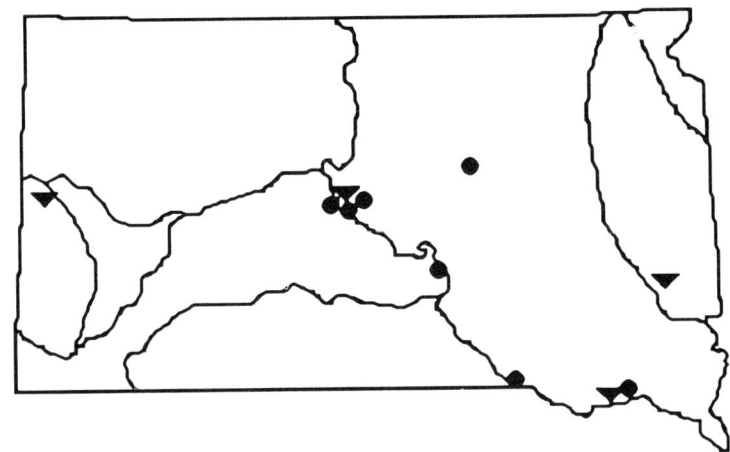

Spring Migration.
  Latest dates:
    2 May 1972, Pierre (Rose)
    2 May 1982, Yankton Co. (Hall in Seasons 1982c)
    10 May 1972, Pierre (Rose 1974)
    6 Jun 1987, Hand Co. (Van Dyk 1989)
Fall migration. Nov.
  Earliest dates:
    3 Nov 1967, Big Bend Dam (Harris 1967)
    11 Nov 1973, Pierre, specimen (Rose)
    15 Nov 1985, Fort Randall Dam (Skadsen 1986a)
Winter.
  CBC reports:
    Pierre.
  Other records:
    1 Dec 1982, Yankton Co. (Hall in Seasons 1983d)
    1-20 Dec 1988, Yankton Co. (Hall in Seasons 1989b)
    5 Dec 1969, Lake Co. (Harris)
    20 Dec 1969, Sturgis (Schroeder 1970)

SABINE'S GULL *Xema sabini* (Sabine)

Status. Casual migrant, most often observed in fall.
Habitat. Lakes and large rivers.
Spring migration.
  Only record:
    15 May 1967, Perkins Co. (Hinds 1968)
Fall migration.
  Records:
    17 Sep 1988, Butte Co. (Springer in Seasons 1989a)
    4 Oct 1966, Brown Co. (Rose 1967)
    22 Oct 1976, Yankton Co. (Rosche)

23 Nov 1967, Buffalo Co., Big Bend Dam, mummified specimen (Rose)

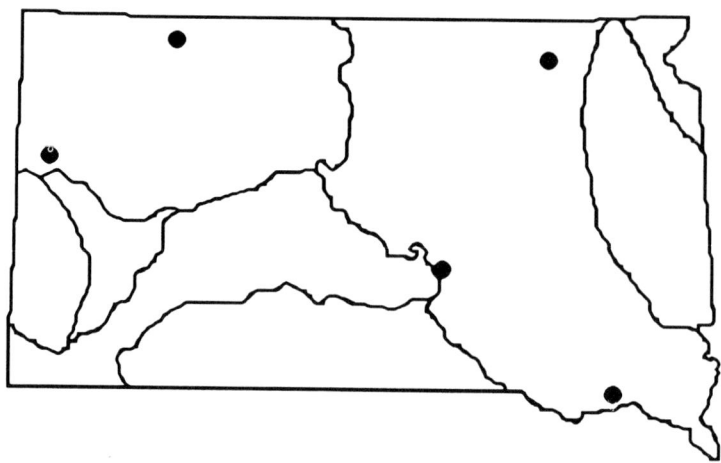

CASPIAN TERN *Sterna caspia* Pallas

Status. Rare migrant and summer visitor NE. Casual W River. No specimens.

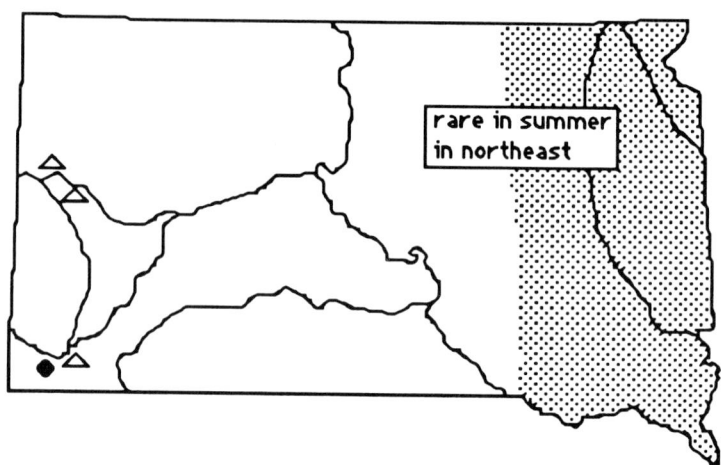

Habitat. Marshes and lakes.
Spring migration. Because of summer birds in NE, late dates are not given.
  Earliest dates:
    27 April 1951, Union Co. (Stephens et al. 1955)
    1 May 1976, Fall River Co. (Rosche 1982)
    3 May 1953, Union Co. (Stephens et al. 1955)
Summer. Many summer sightings exist E. W records in Butte and Meade counties. A particularly noteworthy record was of a copulating pair, 25 Jun 1989 at Angostura Reservoir (Rosche in Berkey 1989b).
Fall migration. Because of summer birds, early dates are not given. Unusual concentration: 15 Sep 1976, Deuel Co., 23 (Harris).

Latest dates:
 23 Sep 1980, Miner Co. (L. Anderson)
 26 Sep 1986, Brookings Co. (Van Sickle in Seasons 1987a)
 27 Sep 1976, Deuel Co. (Harris 1977b)

COMMON TERN *Sterna hirundo* Linnaeus

Status. Fairly common spring migrant. Uncommon summer resident NE, rare W in suitable habitat.

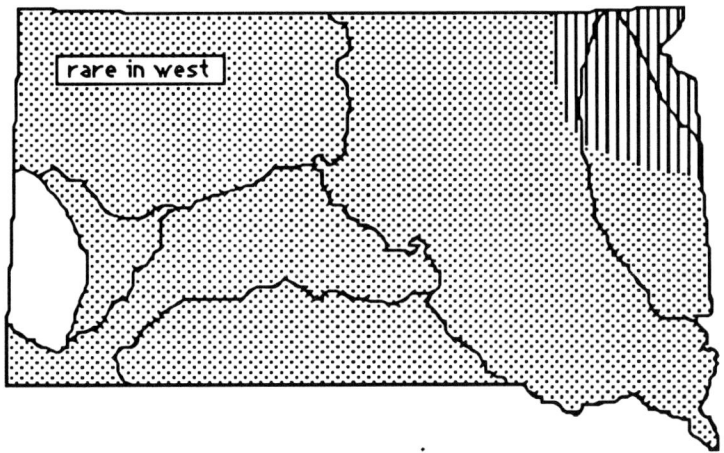

Habitat. Lakes, preferably with sandy or rocky islands.
Spring migration. First 3 weeks of May.
 Earliest dates:
  1 Apr 1986, Yankton Co. (Kronner in Seasons 1986c)
  4 Apr 1953, Sand Lake (Podoll 1963)
  6 Apr 1977, Yankton Co. (Hall in Seasons 1977c)
Nesting. Late May – Jun. Breeds only in Roberts, Day, and Marshall counties.
 Earliest dates:
  28 May 1983, Roberts Co., eggs (Skadsen et al. in Seasons 1983d)
  28 May 1984, Roberts Co., eggs (Harris et al. in Seasons 1984d)
  1 Jun 1986, Roberts Co., eggs (Skadsen et al. in Seasons 1986d)
 Latest dates:
  9 Jul 1986, Marshall Co., nests with eggs (Skadsen in Colonial Bird Registry)
  3 Aug 1930, Lake Poinsett, nonflying young (Peterson 1960b)
Fall migration. Last half Sep.
 Latest dates:
  4 Oct 1985, Gregory Co. (Skadsen 1986a)
  8 Oct 1983, Codington Co. (Harris and Gilman in Seasons 1984a)
  15 Oct 1975, Day Co. (Hall in Seasons 1975d)

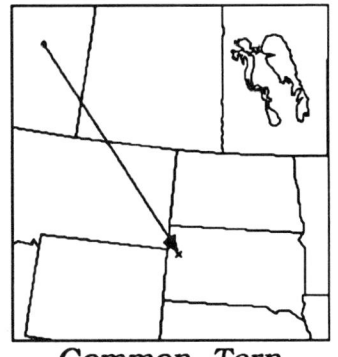

Common Tern banding recoveries

FORSTER'S TERN *Sterna forsteri* Nuttall

Status. Common summer resident E and Lacreek NWR. Otherwise an uncommon visitor W.

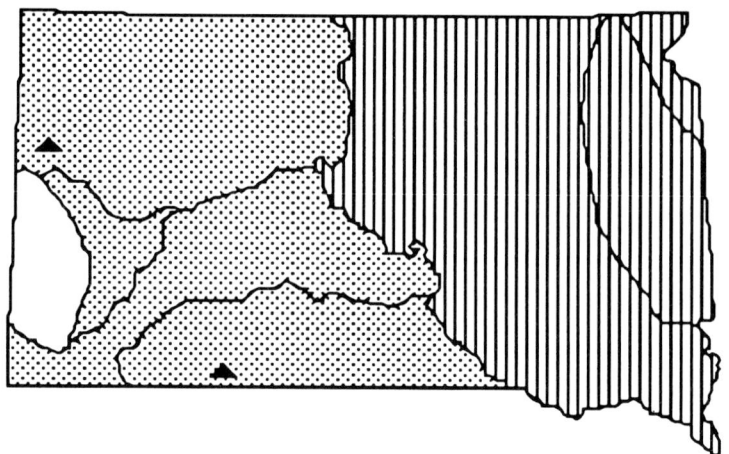

Habitat. Lakes and marshes.
Spring migration. Last week of Apr and first half of May.
  Earliest dates:
    31 Mar 1986, Yankton Co. (Hall in Seasons 1986c)
    9 Apr 1916, Union Co. (Stephens et al. 1955)
    9 Apr 1986, Turner Co. (Anderson in Seasons 1986c)
Nesting. Jun and first week of Jul.
  Earliest dates:
    5 Jun 1981, Roberts Co., 7 nests with eggs (Harris and Husmann in Seasons 1981d)
    7 Jun 1922, Kingsbury Co., nest with 3 eggs (Patton)
    7 Jun 1983, Day Co., 1 egg in nest (Harris and Husmann)
  Latest dates:
    13 Jul 1986, Day Co., nests with eggs (Harris and D. Skadsen)
    22 Jul 1977, Lacreek NWR (Lohoefener and Ely 1978)
    16 Aug 1986, Butte Co., 4 young (Baker in Seasons 1987a)
Fall migration. Mid Sep.
  Latest dates:
    25 Sep 1976, Yankton Co. (Hall in Seasons 1977a)
    26 Sep 1985, Codington Co. (Harris in Seasons 1986a)
    28 Sep 1985, Charles Mix Co. (Skadsen in Seasons 1986a)

LEAST TERN *Sterna antillarum* (Lesson)

Status. Local summer resident of Missouri and Cheyenne rivers. Observed 14 Jun 1988, Perkins Co. (Griffiths and Griffiths in Seasons 1988d). Listed as endangered by USFWS in 1985.

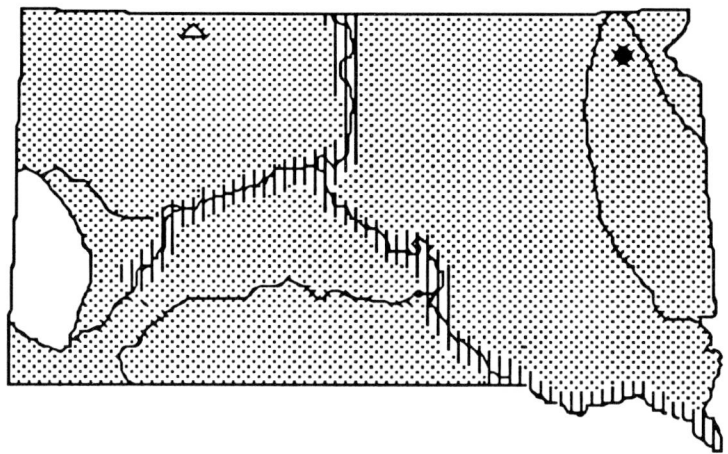

Habitat. Sandbars, beaches and islands.
Spring migration. Late May.
  Earliest dates:
    18 May 1985, Bon Homme Co. (Kronner in Seasons 1985c)
    19 May 1987, Bon Homme Co. (Schwalbach)
    20 May 1987, Yankton Co. (Schwalbach)
Nesting. May – Jul. Nesting status summarized by Youngworth (1960a) and Schwalbach et al. (1986), who censused 372 individuals.
  Earliest dates:
    20 May 1987, Yankton Co., 5 nests (Schwalbach)
    29 May 1987, Sully Co., 3 nests (Schwalbach)
    7 Jun 1986, Cheyenne River, nest (Schwalbach)
  Latest dates:
    30 Jul 1986, Oahe Reservoir, 11 nests (Schwalbach)
    31 Jul 1987, Union and Clay counties, 5 nests (Schwalbach)
    4 Aug 1987, Cheyenne River, 2 nests (Schwalbach)
Fall migration. Last weeks of Aug and first week of Sep.
  Latest dates:
    28 Aug 1987, Union and Clay counties (Schwalbach)
    7 Sep 1961, Rush Lake (Elliott 1961b)
    8 Sep 1932, Union Co. (Youngworth)

BLACK TERN *Chlidonias niger* (Linnaeus).

Status. Abundant migrant and common summer resident E, uncommon W in suitable habitat.

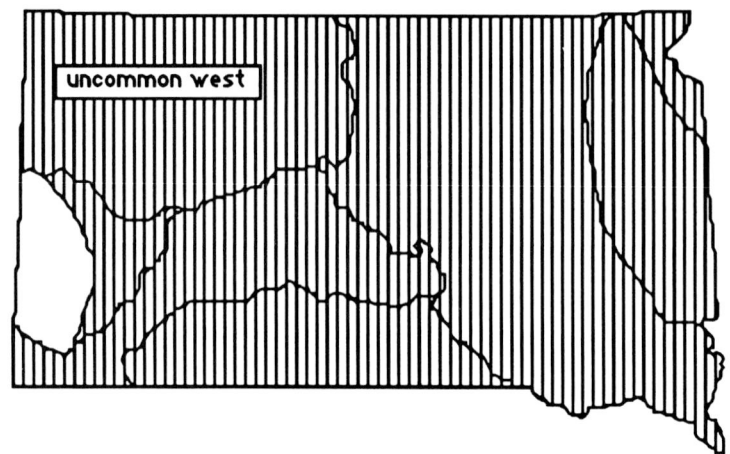

Habitat. Marshes and flooded fields.

Spring migration. Second and third weeks of May.
Earliest dates:
   10 Apr 1954, Wall Lake (Findley)
   27 Apr 1964, Hyde Co. (Harter 1968a)
   1 May 1978, Clay Co. (Hoover in Seasons 1978c)

Nesting. Jun. Unusual concentration: 5 Jul 1980, Walworth Co., 800 (Hall in Seasons 1980c).
Earliest dates:
   31 May 1986, Roberts Co., nests (Skadsen 1987b)
   4 Jun 1971, Deuel Co., nest with 3 eggs (Harris)
   6 Jun 1969, Lacreek, 3 nests (Harris)
Latest dates:
   26 Jun 1895, Todd Co., nests with eggs (Trostler)
   29 Jun 1910, Douglas Co., nest with 3 eggs (Walker)
   19 Jul 1977, Lacreek NWR, nest with 2 eggs (Lohoefener and Ely 1978)

Fall migration. Late Aug and first half of Sep.
Latest dates:
   29 Sep 1946, Roberts Co. (Harris)
   29 Sep 1986, Yankton Co. (Hall)
   2 Oct 1977, Yankton Co. (Hall in Seasons 1981a)
   4 Oct 1908, Sioux Falls area (Larson 1925)

COLUMBIDAE: Pigeons and Doves

ROCK DOVE *Columba livia* Gmelin

Status. Feral populations occur in canyons in the Black Hills, Badlands NP, Sheep Mountain Table, and sandstone buttes of Harding Co. Occur in varying degrees of independence in most cities and towns and some farms. Probably nonmigratory.

Habitat. Feral populations usually found around rock cliffs and bridges.

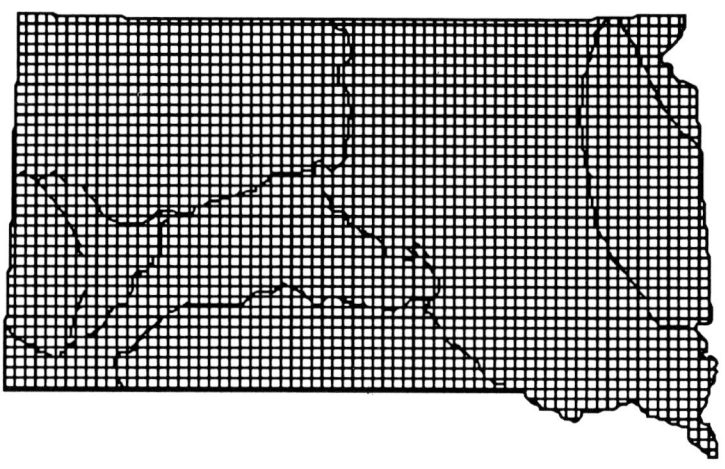

BAND-TAILED PIGEON *Columba fasciata* Say

Status. Accidental.
Records.
  20 Apr 1979, Lawrence Co. (Hoffman)
  20 Apr 1981, Fall River Co. (Twomey 1981)
  3 May 1981, Pierre (Coonrod 1981)
  15 May 1969–1 Aug 1969, 30 miles E of Sturgis, specimen (Whitney)
  13 Jun 1964, Spearfish Canyon (Pettingill and Whitney 1965)
  30 Jul 1983, Custer SP (Goebel)

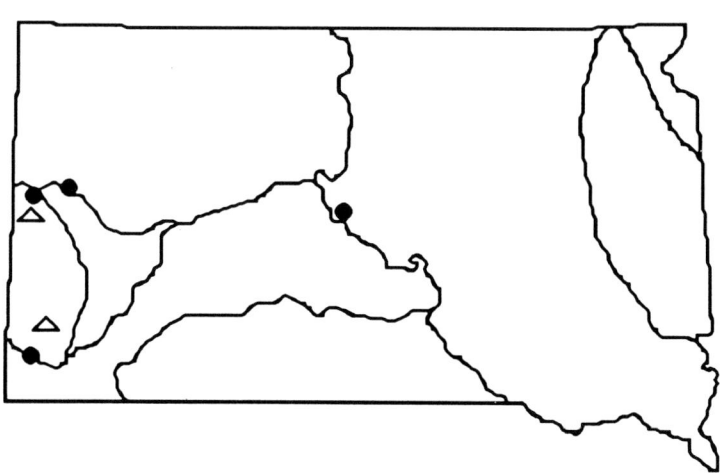

MOURNING DOVE *Zenaida macroura* (Linnaeus)

Status. Abundant summer resident, less common in higher Black Hills. Uncommon winter resident, especially S.

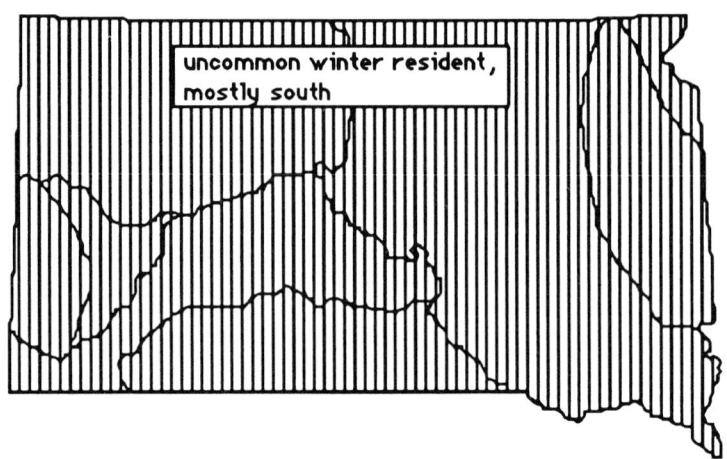

Habitat. Found in all upland habitats.

Spring migration. First half of Apr E, and last half Apr W. Early spring dates may be wintering birds.

Nesting. Late Apr – mid-Sep. For nesting studies see Adolphson and Adolphson (1966) and Drewien and Sparrowe (1966).

Earliest dates:
6 Apr 1990, Day Co., nest with eggs (Skadsen in Seasons 1990c)
17 Apr 1985, Turner Co., nest with eggs (Anderson in Seasons 1985d)
19 Apr 1981, Brown Co., nest with 2 eggs (Steffen et al. 1981)

Latest dates:
14 Sep 1981, Yankton, nest with fledglings (Hall in Seasons 1982a)
15 Sep 1983, Bon Homme Co., incubating eggs (Anderson in Seasons 1984a)
19 Sep 1963, Brookings, 1 young unable to fly (Springer)

Fall migration. Sep and first week of Oct. Flocking begins in late Jul and in Aug. Late fall dates may be of birds attempting to winter.

Winter. Many winter records from all regions, although most commonly seen S. Has been recorded in nearly all CBC.

PASSENGER PIGEON *Ectopistes migratorius* (Linnaeus)

Status. Extinct. Formerly a fairly common to common migrant in woodlands in the E and along the Missouri River and its tributaries; was less common as a breeding bird (Over and Thoms 1921, 1946). Many nests reported along the upper Missouri River N of Pierre (Cooper 1869). McChesney (1879) considered it an occasional visitor near Ft. Sisseton and noted they were taken in numbers at the head of the Coteau des Prairies in the fall of 1877 and near it in Jul 1878. Hoffman (1877) saw only 1 small flock at Grand River Agency between Oct 1872 and Jun 1873. Partch recorded arrival at White on 4 May 1884 (Cooke 1888).

Other records:
- 3–6 Sep 1843, along the Missouri near the Moreau River, flocks (Audubon in Audubon 1897)
- 3 May 1856, mouth of the Big Sioux River (Hayden in Baird 1885)

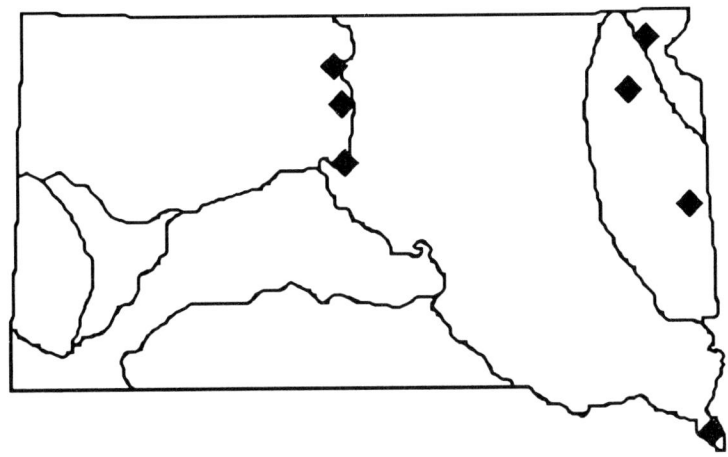

PSITTACIDAE: Parrots

CAROLINA PARAKEET *Conuropsis carolinensis* (Linnaeus)

Status. Extinct. Formerly occurred along Missouri River to central South Dakota. Rarely seen N of the present Iowa-South Dakota line (Wurttemberg 1853). No breeding evidence.

Only record:
16 Sep 1843, E Stanley Co., N of Big Bend on Missouri River (Bell in Audubon 1897)

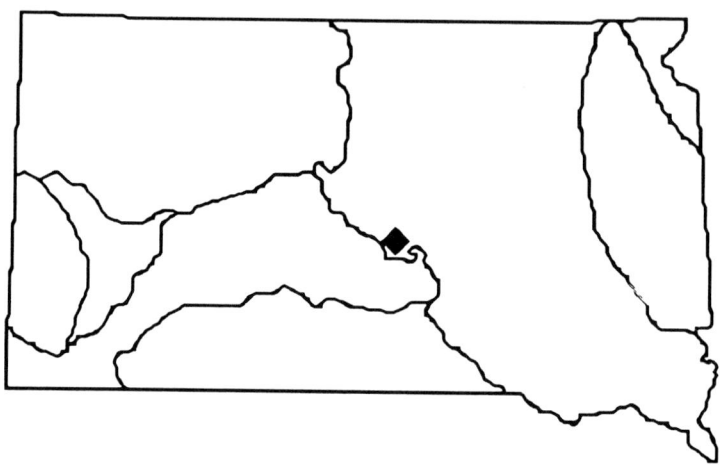

CUCULIDAE: Cuckoos and Anis

BLACK-BILLED CUCKOO *Coccyzus erythropthalmus* (Wilson)

Status. Uncommon summer resident, except absent in higher Black Hills.

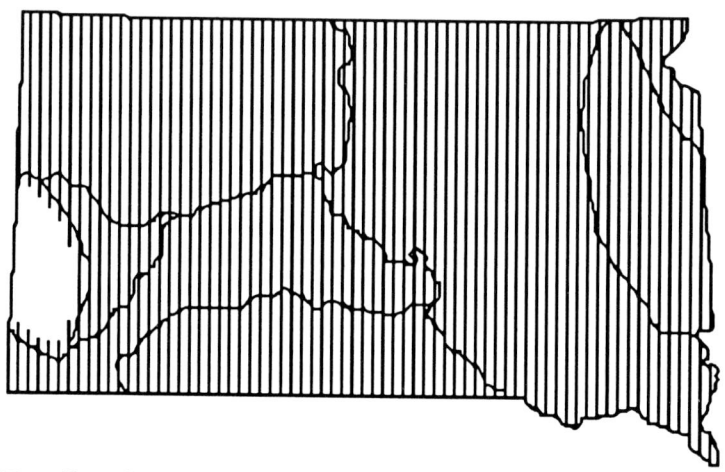

Habitat. Woodlands.
Spring migration. Mid May E, Last week of May W.
Earliest dates:
1 May 1938, Whetstone Valley (Harris 1964)
4 May 1988, Brookings Co. (Kieckhefer in Seasons 1988c)
9 May 1977, Clay Co. (Hoover in Seasons 1977c)

Nesting. Jun and Jul.
  Earliest dates:
    30 May 1940, Sodak Park, nest (Harris)
    9 Jun 1891, Brown Co., nest with 2 eggs (Johnson 1891)
    24 Jun 1956, Rapid City, nest with 3 young (Bachmann in Pettingill and Whitney 1965)
  Latest dates:
    14 Jul 1958, near Edgemont (Carter 1958a)
    17 Jul 1977, Lacreek NWR, nest with 2 eggs (Lohoefener and Ely 1978)
Fall migration. Aug.
  Latest dates:
    13 Sep 1976, Badlands (Wilt in Seasons 1977a)
    22 Sep 1907, Sioux Falls area (Larson 1925)
    29 Sep 1981, Hyde Co. (Harter in Seasons 1982a)

YELLOW-BILLED CUCKOO *Coccyzus americanus* (Linnaeus)

Status. Uncommon summer resident, primarily SE; scattered records in SW, accidental in Harding Co. and absent in higher Black Hills.

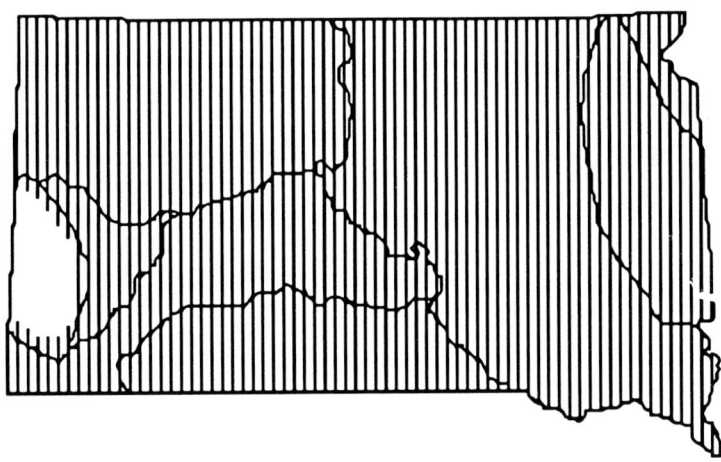

Habitat. Woodlands.
Spring migration. Last half of May.
  Earliest dates:
    6 May 1952, Union Co. (Felton and Nickolson in Stephens et al. 1955)
    7 May 1932, Dell Rapids (Wagar 1958)
    12 May 1959, Union Co. (Youngworth 1949)
Nesting.
  Earliest dates:
    9 Jun 1891, Brown Co. (Johnson 1891)
    1 Jul 1987, Haakon Co. (Melius in Seasons 1987d)
    6 Jul 1911, Douglas Co., nest with 3 eggs (Walker and Silletto)

Latest dates:
- 31 Jul 1949, Minnehaha Co., nest with 2 eggs (contained young, 7 Aug) (Chapman et al.)
- 12 Sep 1960, Huron, adult feeding full-grown young (Johnson 1960)

Fall migration. Aug.
Latest dates:
- 27 Sep 1986, Sanborn Co. (Rogers in Seasons 1987a)
- 28 Sep 1986, Day Co. (Skadsen and Skadsen in Seasons 1987a)
- 30 Sep 1976, Clay Co. (Lemons fide Hall in Seasons 1977a)

GROOVE-BILLED ANI *Crotophaga sulcirostris* Swainson

Status. Accidental in fall.
Records:
- 22 Sep 1984, Gregory Co. (Steffen in Seasons 1985a)
- 29 Sep 1982, Huron (Johnson 1983)
- 13 Oct 1982, Pierre (Larsen 1983)
- 23 Oct 1968, Milbank (Elliott 1968)
- 27 Oct– 18 Dec 1972, near Pickstown, specimen (Rose)

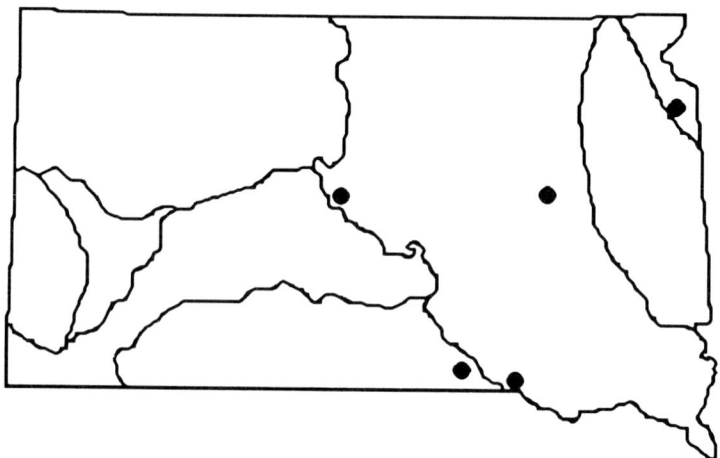

TYTONIDAE: Barn Owls

BARN OWL *Tyto alba* (Scopoli)

Status. Rare summer resident, mostly along S half of Missouri River. Additional records away from Missouri from Fall River, Harding, Jackson, Lawrence, and Minnehaha counties. Status in Black Hills uncertain.

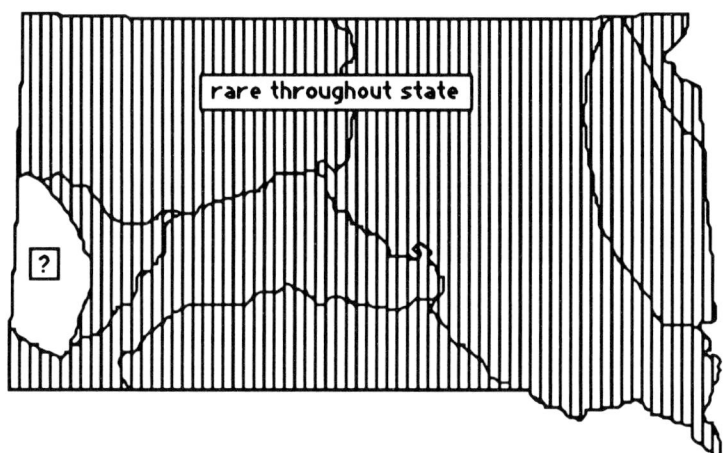

Habitat. Chalk cliffs and shale bluffs. Nests in river banks below Big Bend Dam. Also old barns, silos, and churches.

Nesting. May – Sep.

Earliest dates:
  25 May 1974, Chamberlain, nesting along Missouri River (Marroue and Linde)
  27 May 1990, Fall River Co., nest with 9 eggs (Black Hills Audubon Society)
  10 Jun 1969, Fall River Co., young banded in nest (found Apr 1969) (Adolphson)

Latest dates:
  26 Jul 1987, Jackson Co., nest with young (Graupmann in Seasons 1987d)
  11 Sep 1961, Sioux Falls, 3 small young at nest (Findley 1961)
  17 Sep 1931, Yankton Co., young present (Larrabee 1932)

Migration. Too few records exist to ascertain normal movements.

Barn Owl banding recoveries

STRIGIDAE: Typical Owls

EASTERN SCREECH-OWL *Otus asio* (Linnaeus)

Status. Permanent resident, ranging from common in the SE to uncommon W. Absent from higher Black Hills. In Missouri River floodplain forest in Clay Co., densities are about 1.7 pairs per square mile (Johnson 1969).

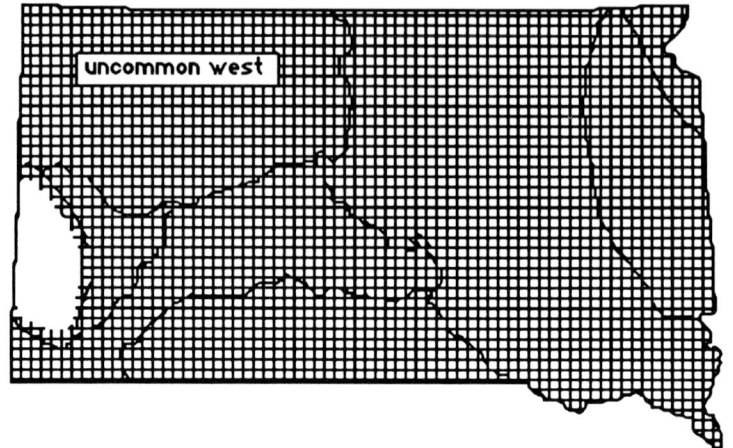

Habitat. Open deciduous forest, including along streams W River. Frequently found in towns with mature trees.

Nesting. Apr and May.

Earliest dates:
  27 Mar 1988, Yankton Co., copulating (Van Sickle 1989)
  18 Apr 1909, Minnehaha Co., nest with eggs (Larson 1925)
  17 May 1969, Sanborn Co., downy young (Harris)

Latest dates:
  30 Jun 1977, Roberts Co., 4 young out of nest (Harris)
  6 Jul 1978, Roberts Co., 3 young out of nest (Harris)
  15 Jul 1981, Pierre, 8-week old young (R. Wilson)

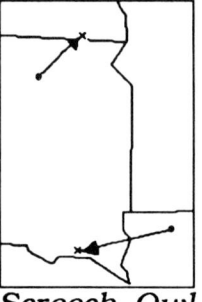

Screech Owl banding recoveries

GREAT HORNED OWL *Bubo virginianus* (Gmelin)

Status. Common permanent resident. In Clay Co., pairs were spaced at 1.1 miles apart along the Missouri River (Johnson 1969) and 0.4 mile apart along the Vermillion River (Behrends 1966). The pale arctic race occurs in winter (perhaps only in response to low snowshoe hare populations in Canada) (17 Jan 1984, Burke (Steffen 1984d), 31 Mar 1983, Brown Co. (Tallman 1983), 3 Apr 1983, Brookings Co. (Holden and Vaa in Seasons 1983c)).

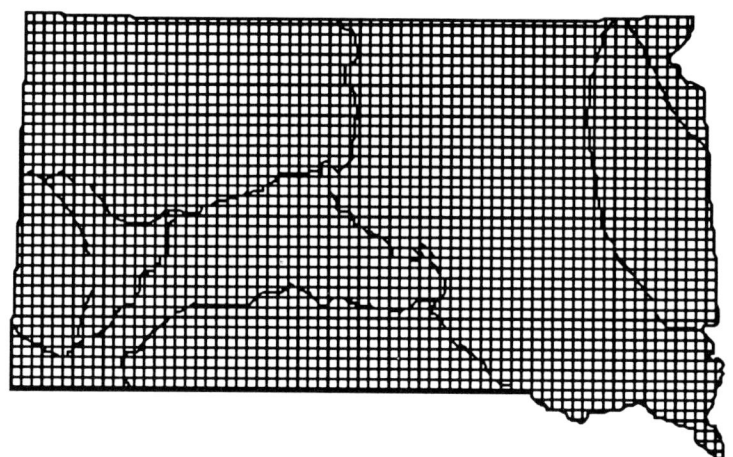

Habitat. Woodlands including stream-bottom forests in the prairies and pine forests in the Black Hills.

Nesting. Late Jan – May. In Clay Co. eggs are usually laid about 10 Feb, hatching about 20 Mar and fledging about 1 May (Dunstan 1970; Dunstan and Harrell 1973). At Buffalo Gap, egg laying is usually complete by 15 Mar and young fledge in early May (Adolphson).

Earliest dates:
  28 Jan 1969, Clay Co., egg laying with hatching 3 Mar (Dunstan 1970; Dunstan and Harrell 1973)
  15 Feb 1986, Codington Co., bird on nest (Harris)
  17 Feb 1970, Sanborn and Jerauld counties, nests (Harris)

Latest dates:
  4 Jul 1979, Wind Cave NP, adult and 2 young (Jervis)
  15 Jul 1947, Spearfish Canyon, fledged downy young collected (Lea in Pettingill and Whitney 1965)
  27 Jul 1977, Waubay NWR, nests with young (Husmann in Seasons 1979c)

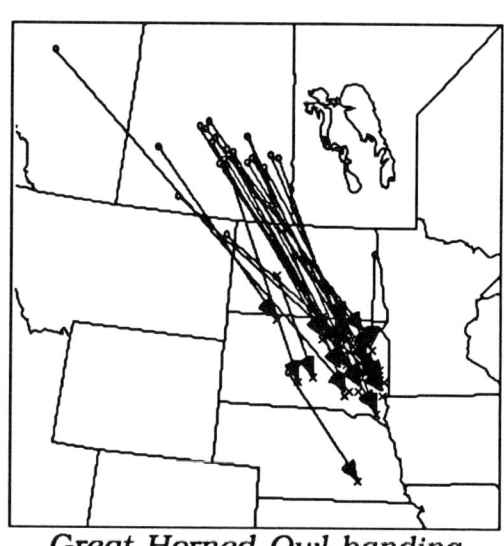

Great Horned Owl banding recoveries

SNOWY OWL *Nyctea scandiaca* (Linnaeus)

Status. Irregular winter visitor, heavy flights some years. During the winter of 1949–50, a total of 643 individuals was reported for 23 counties (Rogge 1950). Seen most frequently in Brown Co. and through the James River valley. Recorded in all parts of the state except Black Hills. Spomer (in Seasons 1982b) counted 46 in 18 counties. Detailed data are summarized by Adolphson and Jonkel (1965) and Adolphson (1965, 1966a, 1967, 1969b).

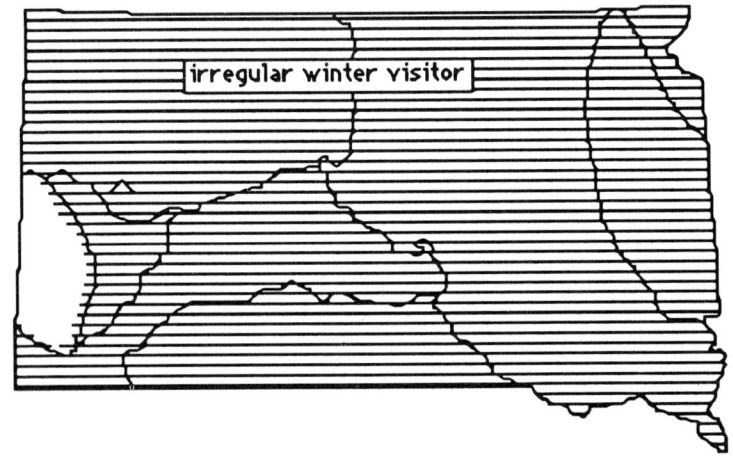

Habitat. Marshes, lakes and lowland. Noted frequently around refuges, where they feed on injured waterfowl.

Seasonal occurrence. Of the reported sightings, 1% have been in Oct, 14% in Nov, 25% in Dec, 36% in Jan, 18% in Feb, 6%

in Mar, and less than 1% in Apr (Adolphson and Jonkel 1965).

Earliest date:
  15 Oct 1964, Beadle Co. (Adolphson 1965)
Latest dates:
  25 Apr 1979, Deuel Co. (Kreger in Seasons 1979c)
  26 Apr 1965, Grenville (Drewien)
  28 Apr 1965, Day Co. (Moriarity 1965a)
Summer record:
  2 Jul 1988, Meade Co. (Miller and Whitney in Seasons 1988d)

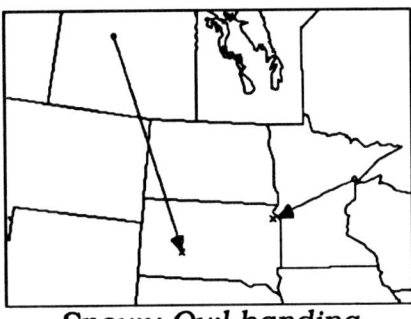
Snowy Owl banding recoveries

NORTHERN HAWK OWL *Surnia ulula* (Linnaeus)

Status. Accidental winter. No specimens.
Only record:
  12–26 Jan 1978, Brookings Co. (Peterson 1978)

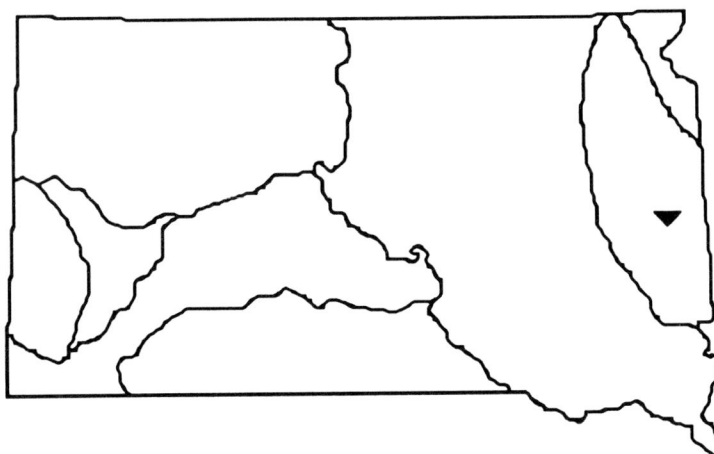

BURROWING OWL *Athene cunicularia* (Molina)

Status. Locally common summer resident W, except rare in the Black Hills; Uncommon E. Casual winter.

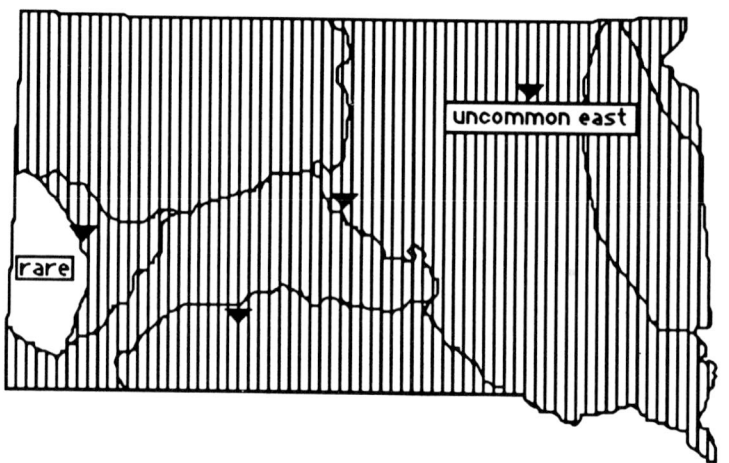

Habitat. Dry prairies. Usually associated with colonies of Black-tailed Prairie Dogs (*Cynomys ludovicianus*) W or Richardson's Ground Squirrels (*Spermophilus richardsoni*) E.

Spring migration. Apr.
Earliest dates:
17 Mar 1977, Brule Co. (L. Anderson)
4 Apr 1989, Custer Co. (Melius in Seasons 1989c)
5 Apr 1974, Sanborn Co. (Harris)

Nesting. May – mid-Jul. Bent (1938) gives egg dates for the Dakotas between 1 May and 13 Jun.
Earliest dates:
16 May 1911, Douglas Co., nest with 10 eggs (Walker)
5 Jun 1960, Minnehaha Co., nest, 7 young seen during first half of Jul (Hall 1961)
7 Jun 1981, Custer Co., carrying food to burrow (Hetlet)
Latest dates:
10 Jul 1978, Wind Cave NP. adults with 2 young (Klukas)
11 Jul 1978, Mellette Co., adult with 3 young (Springer)
27 Jul 1987, Badlands NP, 3 fledglings (Glass)

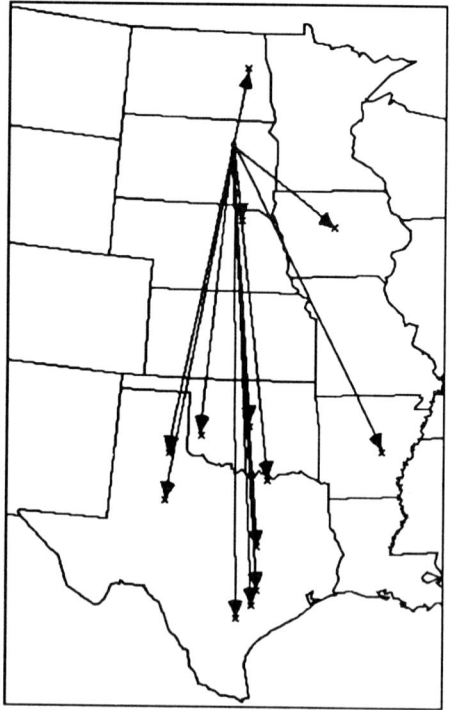

Burrowing Owl banding recoveries

Fall migration. Late Sep.
Latest dates:
5 Oct 1966, Hyde Co. (Harter 1969)
13 Oct 1979, Brown Co. (Montgomery and Tallman in Seasons 1980a)
26 Oct 1979, Pennington Co. (Whitney in Seasons 1980a)

Winter. Agersborg (1885) reported as many as 20 using 1 hole in the winter in Clay Co.
CBC Reports:
Rapid City and Aberdeen.
Other record:
27 Feb 1977, Jackson Co. (Ghering)

BARRED OWL *Strix varia* Barton

Status. Uncertain. Most records in NE, SE, and Black Hills. May be an permanent resident in the SE and Black Hills. Formerly uncommon to rare permanent resident in SE (Agersborg 1885, Visher 1915).

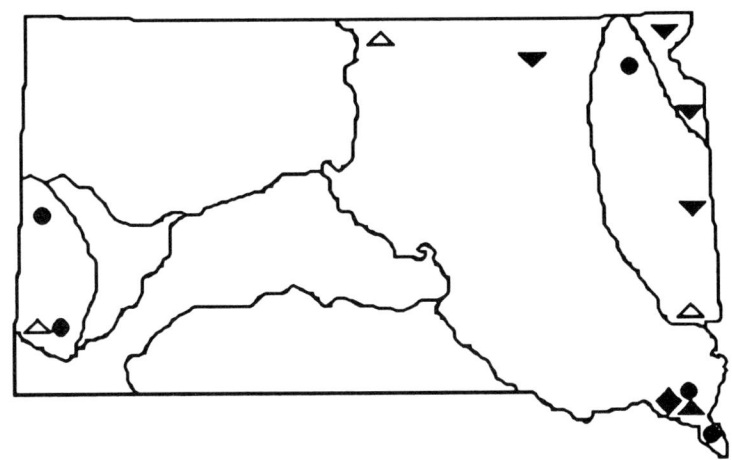

Nesting.
Only records
1912, Clay Co. (Visher 1915)
Apr 1987, Vermillion, courtship and nest site (Jungeman)

Other records.
14 Jan 1973, Deuel Co. (Harris)
14 Jan 1988, Brookings Co. (Reinking and Sandel in Seasons 1988b)
29 Jan 1925, 16 Apr 1931, and 11 May 1929, Union Co. (Stephens et al. 1955)
16 Mar 1964, Clay Co. (Twedt and Hart in Anon. 1964)
6 Apr 1986, Day Co. (Skadsen and Skadsen in Seasons 1986d)
25 Jun 1935 and 1 Oct 1945, Custer Co. (Pettingill and Whitney 1965)
14 Jun 1967, Custer Co. (B. Anderson and Getman)

Jul 1955, Campbell Co. (Short 1961)
2 Jul 1988, Minnehaha Co. (Hoeger in Seasons 1988d)
10 Aug 1986, Lawrence Co., heard (Harris in Seasons 1987a)
29 Nov 1964 and 22 Jan 1973, Day Co. (Johnson 1965 and Olson)
17 Dec 1988, Brown Co. (Antonides 1989)
27 Dec 1966, Roberts Co. (Harris 1968c)

GREAT GRAY OWL *Strix nebulosa* Forster

Status. Accidental in winter. Over and Thoms (1921, 1946) included Coues' statement that this owl strayed S in winter to Dakota; however, this geographical term also includes North Dakota.

Only record:
25 Jan 1984, near Dell Rapids, found dead (Bradwisch)

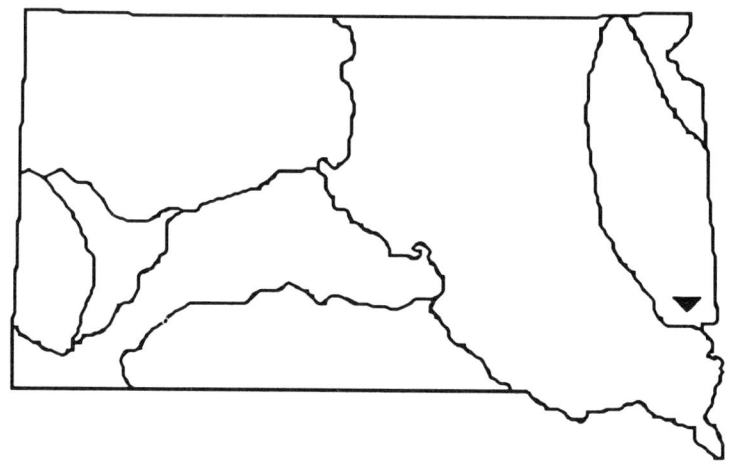

LONG-EARED OWL *Asio otus* (Linnaeus)

Status. Rare to uncommon permanent resident. May migrate, since more winter records exist.

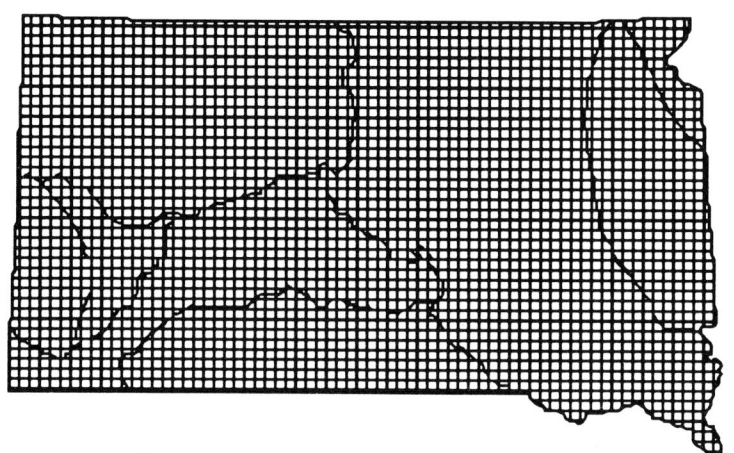

Habitat. Dense forests of ponderosa pines in the Black Hills. Woodlands, often of juniper, and thickets elsewhere.

Nesting. Apr – Jun.

Earliest dates:
  14 Mar 1983, Badlands NP, nest (Hodorff in Paulson and Sieg 1984)
  4 Apr 1982, Badlands NP, adult and half-grown young (Hodorff in Paulson and Sieg 1984)
  26 Apr 1983, Badlands NP, nest with egg and broken egg (Paulson and Sieg 1984)

Latest dates:
  28 Jun 1981, Badlands NP, adult with half-grown young (Paulson and Sieg 1984)
  4 Jul 1948, South Canyon, 2 immatures collected (Dilger in Pettingill and Whitney 1965)
  20 Jul 1977, Badlands, nest with young (Witt in Seasons 1977d)

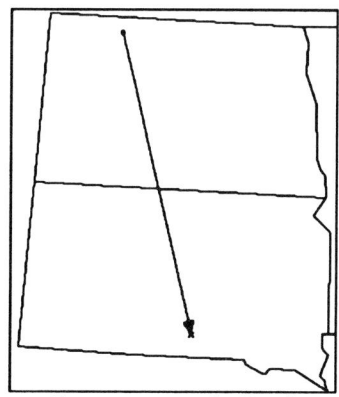

Long-eared Owl banding recoveries

SHORT-EARED OWL *Asio flammeus* (Pontoppidan)

Status. Uncommon to fairly common permanent resident, except absent in Black Hills. Rarely nests in NE (Harris). Populations are variable, with many seen during some years (e.g., 1978 in NE (Harris 1980a)), and few or none in others.

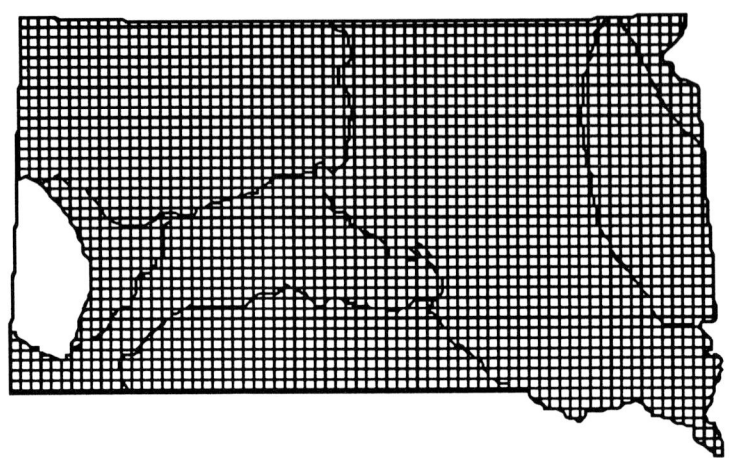

Habitat. Prairies and cultivated fields, particularly in moist lowland areas.

Nesting. May – Jun. 20 nests observed at Lacreek NWR in 1987 (Brashears in Seasons 1987d).

Earliest dates:
  10 May 1968, 8 miles N of Belle Fourche, nest in sagebrush, contained 5 eggs on 10 May, and 1 young with 1 infertile egg on 11 Jun (Adolphson 1969a)
  12 May 1894, Miner Co., nest with eggs (Patton)
  14 May 1978, Deuel Co., nest with 6 eggs (Harris 1980a)

Latest dates:
  24 May 1891, Miner Co., nest with 5 eggs (Patton and Raine)
  30 May 1972, Edmunds Co., recently hatched young (Duebbert and Lokemoen)
  4 Jun 1960, Douglas Co., young hatching in nest (Crutchett 1961)

Winter. Noted regularly on CBC's.

BOREAL OWL *Aegolius funereus* (Linnaeus)

Status. Casual visitor.

Records.
Mar 1913, near Clear Lake, specimen SDSU (Gustavson in Rose and Springer 1975)
6 Dec 1957, Freeman, live bird in hand (Kaufman 1957)
16 Aug 1949, Watertown (Moriarty 1951)

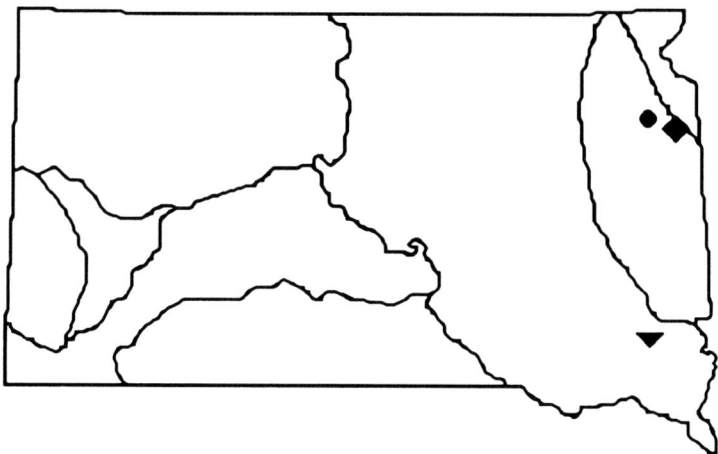

NORTHERN SAW-WHET OWL *Aegolius acadicus* (Gmelin)

Status. Uncommon permanent resident in Black Hills and probably Shannon, E Meade, and Harding counties; 1 recent breeding record from Roberts Co. Possibly regular but overlooked migrant and irregular winter visitor E. Formerly reported as a very rare resident in SE (Agersborg 1885).

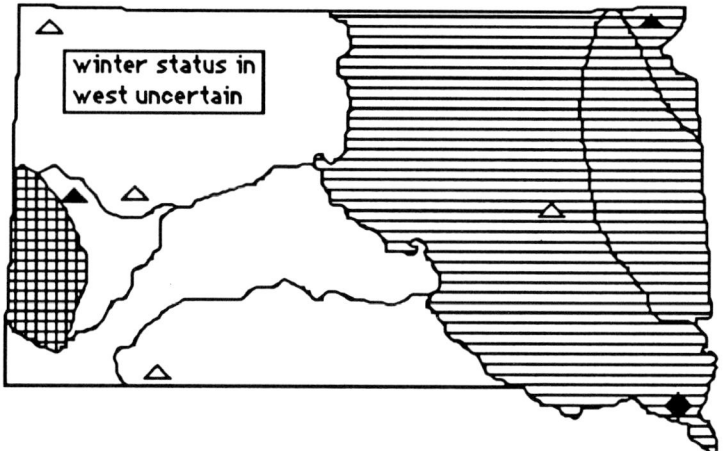

Habitat. Pine and spruce forests, other woodlands during migration.

Nesting. 10 Apr 1968, Custer Co., hole, bird remained through most of May and reoccupied hole in 1969 (Rose, Whitney, and L. Yarger). Breeding season record: 30 Jun 1972, Harding Co. (Grant et al.).

Earliest dates:
  29 May 1978, Roberts Co., 1 adult and 2 immatures (Spinner and Spinner 1978)
  8 Jun 1988, Meade Co., 3 fledglings (Sieg 1990)
Latest dates:
  11 Jun 1900, Gillette Canyon, immature specimen (Cary 1901)
  20 Jun 1983, E Meade Co., immature banded (Tallman et al. 1983)

E River records. May be a sporadically uncommon but overlooked fall migrant (Tallman 1987, Tallman in Seasons 1988a). Records scattered in Edmunds, Brown, Roberts, Codington, Hand, Huron, Deuel, Brookings, Douglas, and Clay counties, primarily between Oct and Apr. In addition to the May breeding record in Roberts Co., Johnson and Johnson (1985) reported this owl in Huron on 15 Aug 1985.

CAPRIMULGIDAE: Goatsuckers

COMMON NIGHTHAWK *Chordeiles minor* (Forster)

Status. Common to abundant summer resident.

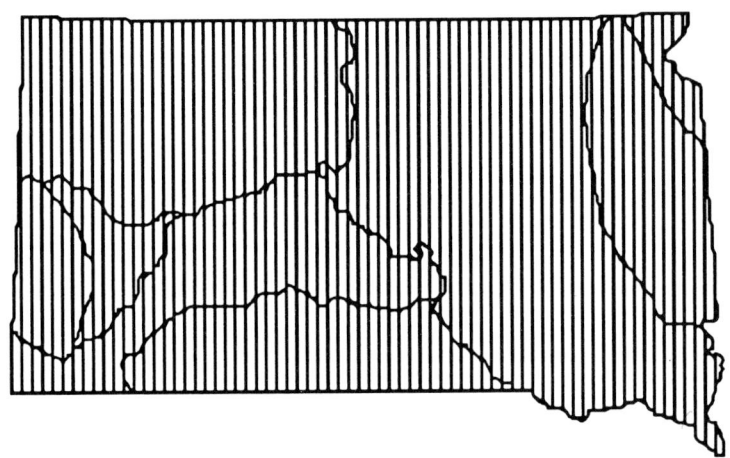

Habitat. Aerial. Nests on the ground in open grasslands, open forests, and, in towns, on flat roofs.

Spring migration. Last third of May, earlier in E than W.
  Earliest dates:
    26 Apr 1989, Jackson Co. (Graupmann in Seasons 1989c)
    27 Apr 1980, Brookings Co. (Taylor in Seasons 1980c)
    28 Apr 1984, Brookings Co. (Husmann)

Nesting. Jun and the first 3 weeks of Jul.
  Earliest dates:
    9 Jun 1911, Douglas Co., nest with 2 eggs (Walker)
    10 Jun 1925, Custer Co., nest with 2 eggs (Patton)
    17 Jun 1973, near Buffalo, nest with 2 eggs (Springer)
  Latest dates:
    18 Jul 1957, Rapid City, nest with 2 eggs (Pettingill and Whitney 1965)
    21 Jul 1965, Sioux Falls, 2 young banded on roof (Findley)
    22 Jul 1954, Rapid City, recently hatched young (Pettingill and Whitney 1965)

Fall migration. Second and third weeks of Aug.
  Latest dates:
    4 Oct 1962, Milbank (Elliott)
    4 Oct 1963, Brookings Co. (Springer)
    5 Oct 1986, Minnehaha Co. (Hoeger in Seasons 1987a)
    7 Oct 1979, Brookings Co. (Taylor in Seasons 1980a)

COMMON POORWILL *Phalaenoptilus nuttallii* (Audubon)

Status. Common summer resident W River, especially in the Badlands, the lower slopes of the Black Hills, the buttes of Harding Co., and the wooded valleys of the Pine Ridge (Roberts and Roberts 1951) and Rosebud (Visher 1912a, Rosche, Springer) Indian Reservations. Formerly nested in SE (Agersborg 1885).

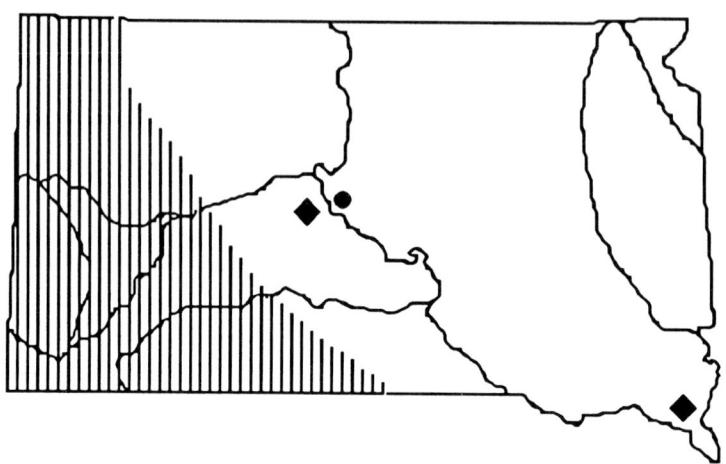

Habitat. Canyons and rock outcrops.
Spring migration. Second and third weeks of May.
  Earliest dates:
    27 Apr 1987, Custer Co. (Parker in Seasons 1987c)
    3 May 1963, Rapid City (Pettingill and Whitney 1965)
    3 May 1977, Rapid City (Whitney in Seasons 1977c)
    3 May 1985, Rapid City (Whitney in Seasons 1985c)
Nesting.
  Only records:
    6 Jun 1990, Tripp Co., nest with 2 eggs (Backlund 1990)
    14 Jun 1980, Harding Co., nest with 2 eggs (Erickson)
    23 Jun 1989, Harding Co., nest with 1 young (Melius in Seasons 1989d)
    28 Jun 1985, Harding Co., nest with 2 young (Springer in Seasons 1985d)
Fall migration. Late Sep.
  Earliest dates:
    21 Aug 1987, Pierre (Riis)
    7 Sep 1843, along Missouri River N of Ft. Pierre (Audubon in Audubon 1897)
  Latest dates:
    6 Oct 1955, Rapid City (Pettingill and Whitney 1965)
    7 Oct 1962, Rapid City (Pettingill and Whitney 1965)
    7 Oct 1985, Fall River Co. (Parker in Seasons 1986a)

CHUCK-WILL'S WIDOW *Caprimulgus carolinensis* Gmelin
Status. Accidental.
Habitat. Bottomland forest.
Records:
   17–18 May 1986, Stanley Co., below Oahe Dam (Schumacher)
   1 Jun 1967, Brookings Co. (Holden and Holden 1968)
   11 Jun 1988, Stanley Co., below Oahe Dam (Clinton)
   13 Jun – early Aug 1987, Stanley Co., below Oahe Dam (Springer et al. in Seasons 1987d)

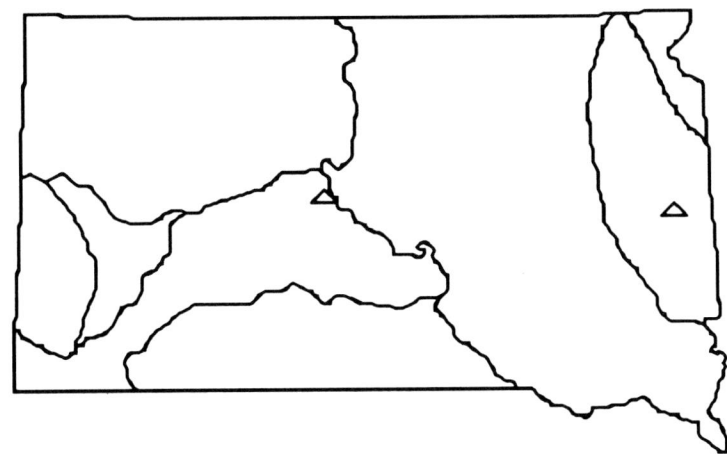

WHIP-POOR-WILL *Caprimulgus vociferus* Wilson
Status. Common summer resident in Lincoln, Clay, Union, and Yankton counties. Rare migrant elsewhere E; accidental W.

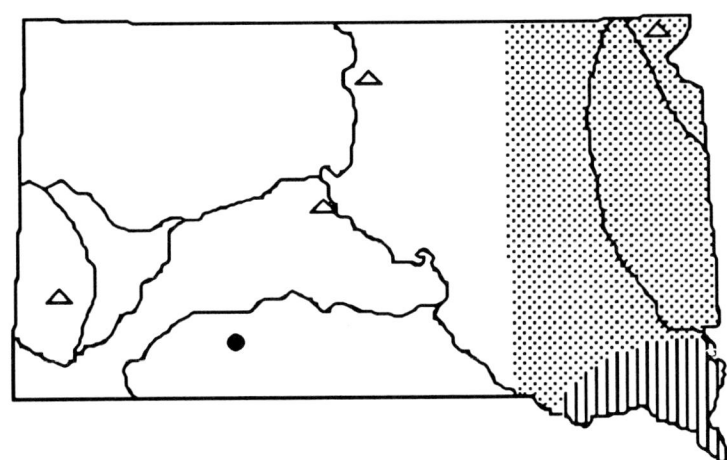

Habitat. Forests of river bottomlands.
Spring migration. Last half of May.
   Earliest dates:
      17 Apr 1982, Yankton Co. (Wilcox in Seasons 1982c)
      18 Apr 1981, Brookings Co. (Holden in Seasons 1981c)
      20 Apr 1987, Brown Co. (Tallman in Seasons 1987c)
   Latest date:
      8 Jun 1970, Hiddenwood SP (Rogge and Rogge 1970)
Nesting. No nesting data.

Summer: Called all summer 1989 in Roberts Co. (Stewart in Seasons 1989d).
 17 Jun 1984, Roberts Co. (Skadsen in Seasons 1984d)
 18 Jun 1988, Lincoln Co., calling (Harris in Seasons 1988d)
Fall migration. Sep.
 Latest date:
  8 Oct 1961, Brookings, banded (Holden 1962)
  14 Oct 1984, Minnehaha Co. (Skadsen in Seasons 1985a)
W River records.
 29 May 1960, near Hill City (Gates 1960)
 10 Jul – early Aug 1987, below Oahe Dam (Vance and Hanten)
 25 Aug 1988, Jackson Co, banded (Graupmann)

APODIDAE: Swifts

CHIMNEY SWIFT *Chaetura pelagica* (Linnaeus)

Status. Abundant summer resident E. Scattered breeding colonies at lower elevations in the Black Hills and elsewhere W (except NW where migrant).

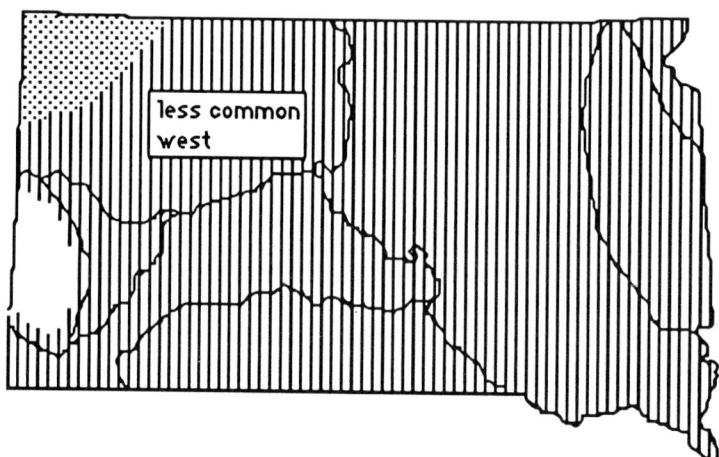

Habitat. Cities and towns. Usually nests in chimneys, but may rarely nest in hollow trees.
Spring migration. First half of May.
 Earliest dates:
  15 Apr 1986, Brown Co. (Montgomery in Seasons 1986c)
  21 Apr 1979, Hutchinson Co. (Spomer in Seasons 1979c)
  21 Apr 1987, Yankton Co. (Van Sickle in Seasons 1987c)
Nesting. The few records do not reflect actual abundance.

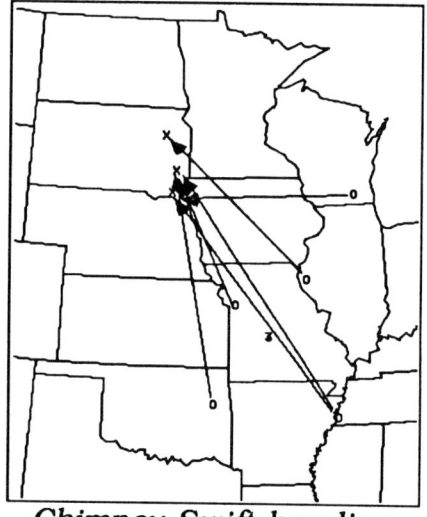

Chimney Swift banding recoveries.

Only records:
- 4 Jul 1891, Milbank, nest and eggs collected (Flett in Moriarty 1960)
- 8 Jul 1989, Brookings Co., 3 nests, 2 with eggs, 1 with young (Reinking in Seasons 1989d)

Fall migration. First half of Aug. 18 Aug 1952, Sioux Falls, flock of 1000 not found next day (Chapman).

Latest dates:
- 3 Oct 1977, Yankton Co. (Hall in Seasons 1978a)
- 9 Oct 1983, Lake Co. (SDOU in Seasons 1984a)
- 10 Oct 1983, Minnehaha Co. (Blankespoor in Seasons 1984a)

WHITE-THROATED SWIFT *Aeronautes saxatalis* (Woodhouse)

Status. Common summer resident in the Badlands, Black Hills, and buttes of Harding Co.

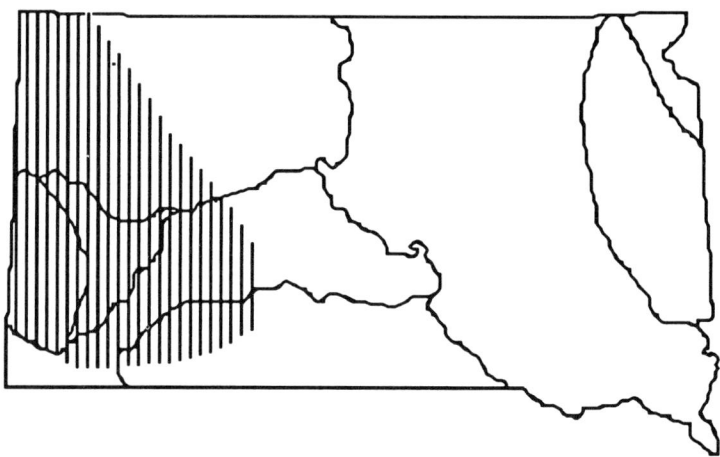

Habitat. Rock cliffs.

Spring migration. Last week of Apr and the first week of May.

Earliest dates:
- 5 Apr 1976, Badlands (Wilt in Seasons 1976c)
- 10 Apr 1981, Fall River Co. (Rosche in Seasons 1981c)
- 12 Apr 1989, Fall River Co. (Peterson in Seasons 1989c)

Nesting. Jun and Jul.

Earliest dates:
- 9 May 1925, Harding Co., nesting sites observed (Patton 1926)
- 9 May 1961, Rapid City, copulating pairs (Whitney)

Latest dates:
- 29 Jun 1979, Custer Co., 5 nests (Bjerke)
- 24 Jul 1948, Loveland Canyon, adult carrying food to nest (Dilger in Pettingill and Whitney 1965)

Fall migration. Last half of Aug and the first week of Sep.

Latest dates:
- 13 Sep 1960, Rapid City (Pettingill and Whitney 1965)
- 23 Sep 1983, Lawrence Co. (Hall in Seasons 1984a)
- 4 Oct 1975, Stanley Co. (Hill in Seasons 1975d)

TROCHILIDAE: Hummingbirds

RUBY-THROATED HUMMINGBIRD *Archilochus colubris* (Linnaeus)

Status. Rare to uncommon migrant E; rare breeder in extreme NE. Current breeding status in extreme SE uncertain. Few summer records elsewhere. No definite W River records except for Rosebud Indian Reservation (Reagan 1908) and Gregory Co.

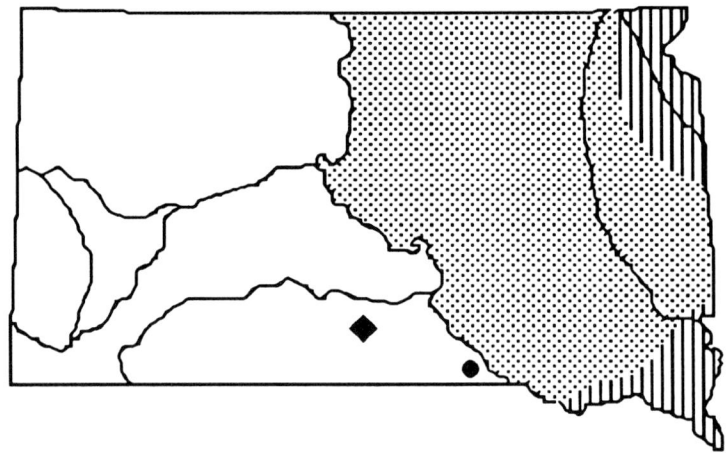

Habitat. Towns, shelterbelts, and stream-bottom woodlands.
Spring migration. Mid-May.
  Earliest dates:
    2 May 1965, Brookings (Springer)
    8 May 1949, Union Co. (Youngworth 1949)
    10 May 1959, Brookings (Holden)
Nesting. Summer records in NE and SE.
  Only records:
    29 Jul 1986, Roberts Co., female on nest (Harris 1987a)
    27 Jun 1988, Roberts Co., female on nest (Harris in Seasons 1988d)
Fall migration. Early Sep.
  Latest dates:
    13 Oct 1975, Gregory Co. (Steffen in Seasons 1975d)
    18 Oct 1981, Hughes Co. (Coonrod in Seasons 1982a)
    31 Oct 1986, Grant Co. (Prisbe)

CALLIOPE HUMMINGBIRD *Stellula calliope* (Gould)

Status. Casual late summer and early fall migrant in Black Hills.

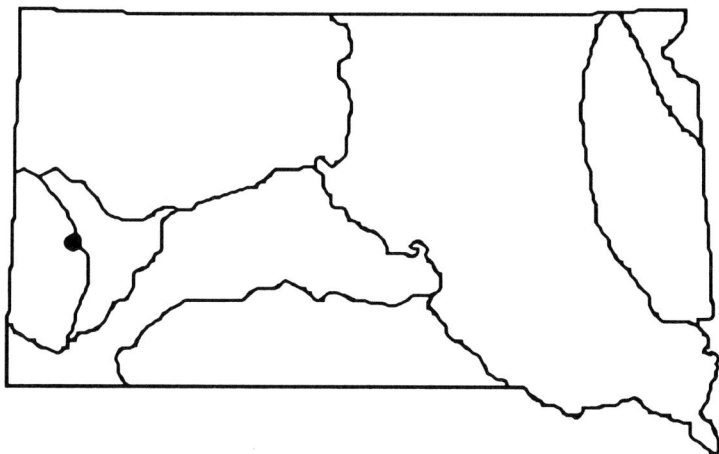

Habitat. Gardens in towns.

Records.
- 23 Jul 1980, Rapid City, (Baylor in Seasons 1980d)
- 8 Aug 1978, Rapid City, specimen (Whitney)
- 19 Aug 1964, Rapid City, specimen (Behrens in Pettingill and Whitney 1965)
- 21 Aug 1983, Rapid City (Whitney)

BROAD-TAILED HUMMINGBIRD *Selasphorus platycercus* (Swainson)

Status. In Black Hills, possibly casual fall migrant, and rare summer resident.

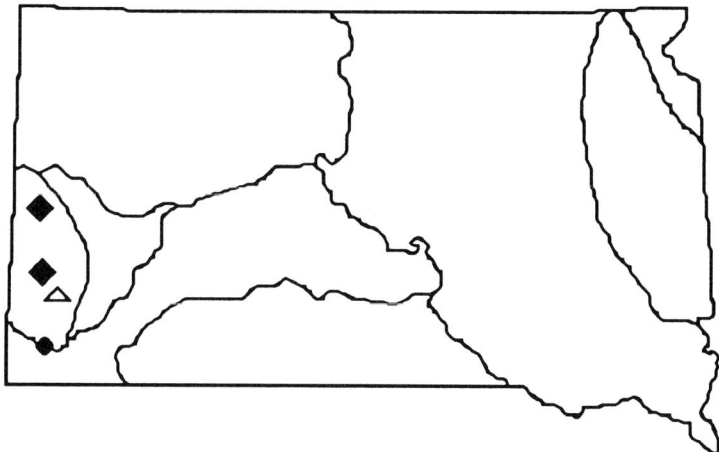

Nesting. Young were seen in Lead in 1929 (Over and Thoms 1946). A nest with 2 young in the Black Hills, where the birds were said to be common, was reported by Holden to Coues (1874). Reported from Pennington Co. on 8–13 Jun 1990 (Gifford in Seasons 1990d). No recent observation of nests.

Fall migration.
Only record.
Late May 1880, Gillette Canyon (Cary 1901)
Fall migration.
Only record.
7 Aug 1977, Hot Springs (Rosche)

RUFOUS HUMMINGBIRD *Selasphorus rufus* (Gmelin)

Status. Regular late summer migrant in Black Hills region. No specimens and no spring records.

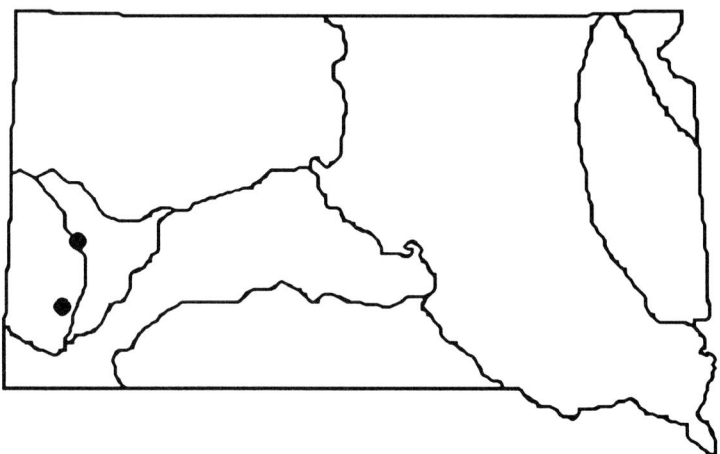

Habitat. Gardens in towns.
Fall migration.
Earliest dates:
26 Jun 1977, Rapid City (Hays in Seasons 1977d)
16 Jul 1988, Custer Co. (Parker in Seasons 1988d)
30 Jul 1980, Rapid City (Baylor in Seasons 1980d)
Latest dates:
13 Aug 1984, Rapid City (Whitney)
17 Aug 1986, Rapid City (Whitney in Seasons 1987a)
8 Sep 1988, Custer Co. (Parker in Seasons 1989a)

ALCEDINIDAE: Kingfishers

BELTED KINGFISHER *Ceryle alcyon* (Linnaeus)

Status. Fairly common summer resident, rarely wintering where water remains open.

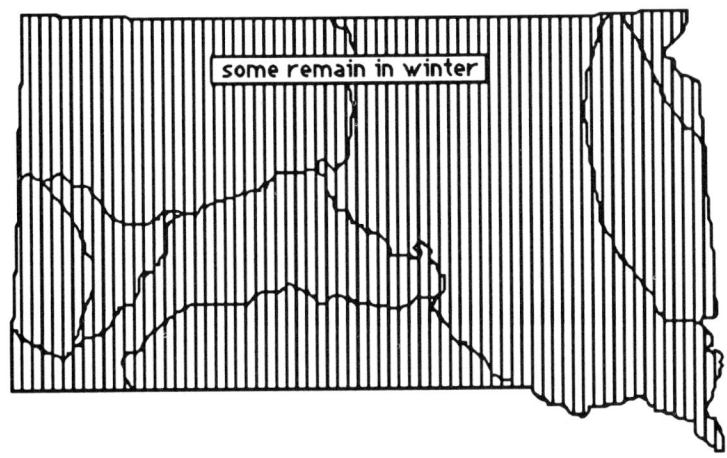

Habitat. Streams, lakes, and marshes. Nests in mud banks.

Spring migration. Apr. Early dates are in Mar but may refer to wintering birds.

Nesting.
  Earliest dates:
    9 May 1982, Custer Co., nest (Goebel)
    13 May 1990, Butte Co., adults with 4 young (Palmer)
    15 May 1927, Fall River Co., nest (McIntosh in Whitney 1955)
  Latest dates:
    10 Jul 1965, near Brookings, adult with 2 full-grown young (Springer)
    19 Jul 1956, Lawrence Co., nest with young (Szalay in Pettingill and Whitney 1965)

Fall migration. Oct. Late dates may be of birds attempting to winter.

Winter. Has occurred on many CBC's in winters with open water.

PICIDAE: Woodpeckers

LEWIS' WOODPECKER *Melanerpes lewis* (Gray)

Status. Locally uncommon summer resident in Black Hills, and locally rare permanent resident of adjacent stream bottoms. Casual in buttes of Harding Co., and near Pine Ridge, Shannon Co. Casual visitor E.

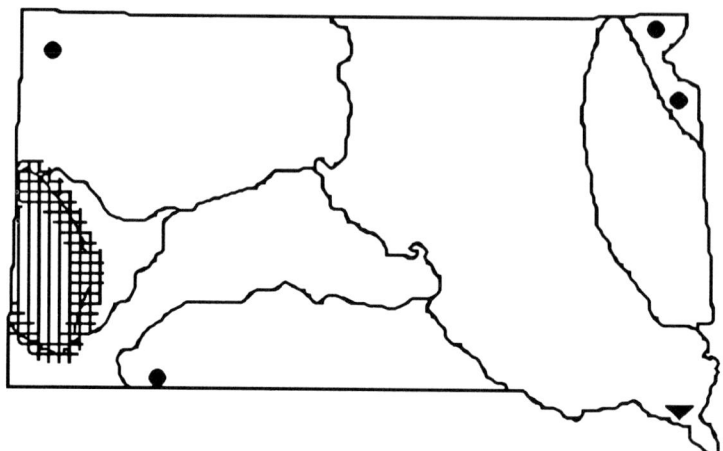

Habitat. Dead trees in burned areas. Oaks and cottonwoods of stream bottoms or open areas.

Spring migration. Probably the last half of May, but early reports could be wintering individuals.

Nesting. Jun and Jul in the Black Hills.
  Earliest dates:
    19 Apr 1988, Meade Co., pair copulating (G. Levine)
    23 May 1959, McVey Burn, courtship (Pettingill and Whitney 1965)
    23 May 1990, Pennington Co., adult feeding young in nest (Kober)
    9 Jun 1988, Sturgis, feeding young (E. Miller)
  Latest dates:
    10 Jul 1986, Fall River Co., pair carrying food (Parker in Seasons 1986d)
    13 Jul 1979, Lawrence Co., 2 pair nesting (Bjerke in Seasons 1979d)
    27 Jul 1965, Deadwood, young nearly ready to leave nest (Rose)

Fall migration. Last half of Aug and Sep. Leaves higher elevations, such as the McVey Burn, by the end of Aug, but may remain all winter at lower elevations.

Winter. Irregular resident in lower Black Hills.
  CBC reports:
    Spearfish.

E River records:
19 Jan 1919, Union Co. (Stephens et al. 1955)
4 Mar 1957, Milbank (Elliott)
6 Apr 1940, Roberts Co. (Harris)

RED-HEADED WOODPECKER *Melanerpes erythrocephalus* (Linnaeus)

Status. Fairly common summer resident. Rare winter.

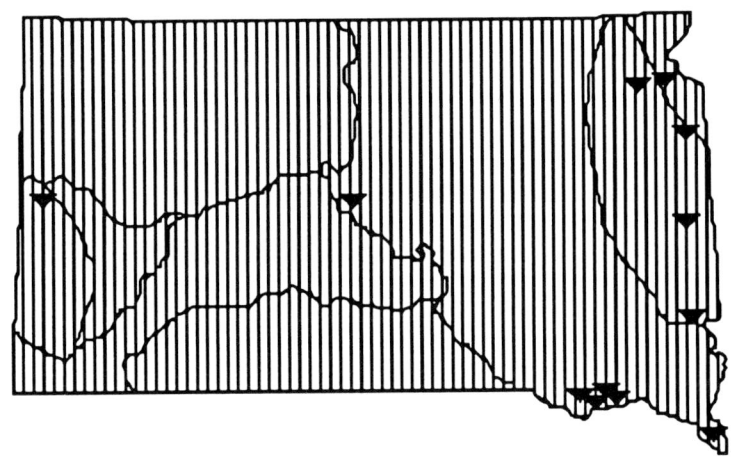

Habitat. Woodlands and wood fenceposts along roadsides in otherwise treeless areas.

Spring migration. First and second weeks of May. Early reports could be wintering individuals.
Earliest dates:
19 Mar 1938, Wilmot (Harris 1963)
25 Mar 1963, Brookings Co. (Froiland)
1 Apr 1967, Chamberlain (Harris)

Nesting. Jun and first half of Jul.
Earliest dates:
11 Jun 1911, Douglas Co., nest with 5 eggs (Walker)
13 Jun 1985, Vermillion, pair copulating (Springer)
14 Jun 1958, Caputa, nest with 7 eggs (Whitney)

Red-headed Woodpecker banding recoveries.

Latest dates:
26 Jul 1962, Brookings Co., immature banded (Holden)
7 Aug 1966, Milbank, partly grown young (Elliott 1967b)
13 Aug 1976, Gregory Co., 6 adults and immatures (Steffen in Seasons 1977b)

Fall migration. First half of Sep. Late fall dates may represent birds attempting to winter.

Winter. Has wintered in Union Co. (Stephens et al. 1955).
CBC reports:
Sturgis, Deuel Co., Wilmot, Yankton, Sioux Falls, Pierre, Brookings, and Waubay.

Other reports:
18 Jan 1981, Deuel Co. (Kreger in Seasons 1981b)
11–26 Feb 1982, Yankton Co. (Hall in Seasons 1982b)
23 Feb 1985, Yankton Co. (Hall and Wilcox in Seasons 1985b)

RED-BELLIED WOODPECKER *Melanerpes carolinus* (Linnaeus)

Status. Uncommon permanent resident in E, less common N. More widespread in winter. Casual farther W.

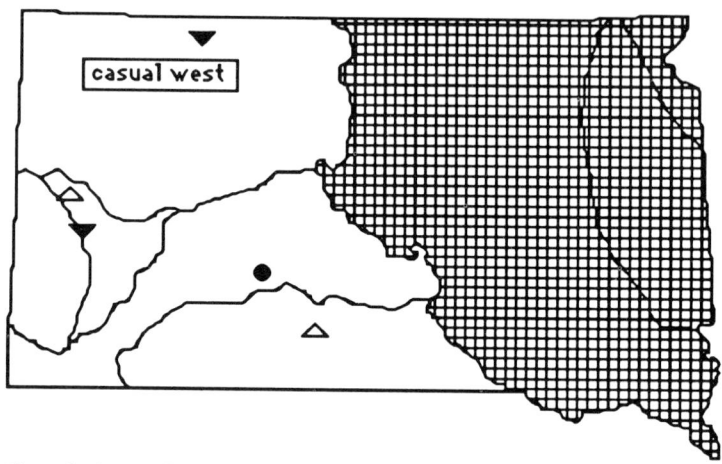

Habitat. Floodplain forests.
Nesting.
Earliest dates:
13 Apr 1990, Sanborn Co., pair copulating (Rogers)
18–21 May 1954, near Yankton, young being fed (Hall 1969)
25 May – 12 Jun 1958, near Yankton, young being fed (Hall 1969)
Latest dates:
20 Jun 1980, Brookings Co., pair bringing food to hole (Parrish 1980)
26 Jun 1982, Hartford Beach State Park, nesting (Skadsen in Seasons 1982d)
West River Records.
21 May 1989, Jackson Co. (Springer et al.).
3 Jun 1966, White River (Springer)
15 Jun 1990, Meade Co. (Levine)
Winter. Has occurred sporadically on most CBC's W to Pierre with many other winter records. Single records in Perkins and Pennington counties.

YELLOW-BELLIED SAPSUCKER *Sphyrapicus varius* (Linnaeus)

Status. Uncommon summer resident in E border counties, although fairly common in Newton Hills SP.. Formerly, at least, a rare summer resident in Clay Co. (Visher 1915) and Bon Homme Co. (Johnson 1958). Elsewhere in E, a rare to uncommon spring and fall migrant. Casual winter. Pre1987 records from the Black Hills are assumed to be of the Red-naped Sapsucker. Springer thought immatures in Sep in Harding and Perkins counties were this species.

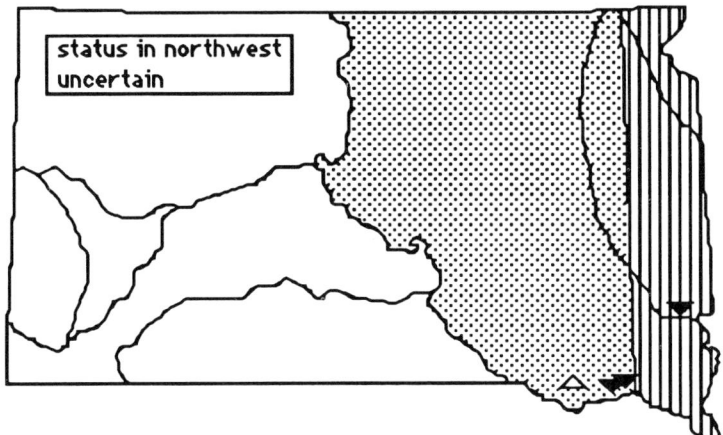

Habitat. Woodlands.

Spring migration. Second half of Apr. Late dates may be breeding birds.
Earliest dates:
19 Mar 1987, Yankton Co. (Van Sickle in Seasons 1987c)
22 Mar 1987, Brown Co. (Tallman in Seasons 1987c)
28 Mar 1976, Pierre (McDaniel fide Hill in Seasons 1976b)

Nesting. Jun – Jul.
Earliest dates:
26 May 1985, Lincoln Co., nesting (13 Jun, feeding young) (Springer and Skadsen 1986)
2 Jun 1985, Lincoln Co., feeding young (Springer and Skadsen 1986)
7 Jun 1981, Big Stone Lake, nest with young (Harris in Seasons 1981d)
Latest dates:
9 Jul 1969, Roberts Co., nests with young (Harris)
20 Jul 1970, Roberts Co., nest with young (Harris 1971a)
22 Jul 1975, Brookings Co., adults with young (Holden in Seasons 1975c)

Fall migration. Sep.
  Latest dates:
    2 Nov 1984, Codington Co. (Gilman)
    20 Nov 1977, Brookings Co. (Taylor in Seasons 1978a)
    1 Dec 1975, Turner Co. (Breen in Seasons 1976b)
Winter.
  Records:
    Jan 1977, Sioux Falls (fide Eckert in Seasons 1977b)
    4 Jan 1982, Yankton Co. (Hall in Seasons 1982b)
    19 Jan 1985, Yankton Co. (Hall in Seasons 1985b)

RED-NAPED SAPSUCKER *Sphyrapicus nuchalis* Baird

Status. Uncommon summer resident in Black Hills. Accidental winter.

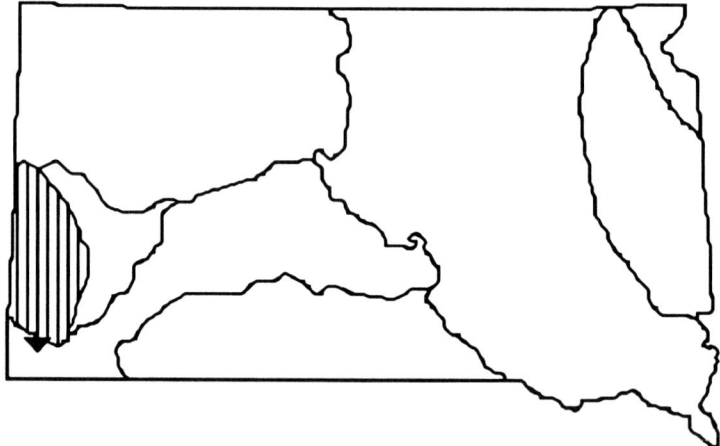

Habitat. Aspen groves and mixed pines and aspens.
Spring migration. First half of May.
  Earliest dates:
    17 Mar 1986, Custer Co. (Parker in Seasons 1986c)
    13 Apr 1969, Piedmont (Rose)
    20 Apr 1968, Hill City (Rose)
Nesting. Jun and Jul.
  Earliest dates:
    12 Jun 1947, Limestone Flats, 2 nests, probably with eggs (Sutton in Pettingill and Whitney 1965)
    13 Jun 1947, Spearfish Canyon, nest with eggs (Pettingill and Whitney 1965)
    18 Jun 1990, Black Fox Campground, pair feeding young in nest (Springer)
  Latest dates:
    16 Jul 1988, Custer Co., 2 breeding pairs (Whitney in Seasons 1988d)
    18 Jul 1952, Pennington Co., 3 young (Pettingill and Whitney 1965)
    24 Jul 1952, Palmer Gulch, 3 young (Behrens in Pettingill and Whitney 1965)

Fall migration.
  Latest dates:
    15 Sep 1957, Rapid City (Whitney)
    18 Sep 1986, Rapid City (Whitney)
    5 Oct 1963, Pennington Co. (Krause)
Winter.
  CBC report:
    Hot Springs.

WILLIAMSON'S SAPSUCKER *Sphyrapicus thyroideus* (Cassin)

Status. Accidental.
Only record:
  23 Apr – 1 May 1975, Pierre, State Capitol grounds, male photographed (Hill in Seasons 1975b)

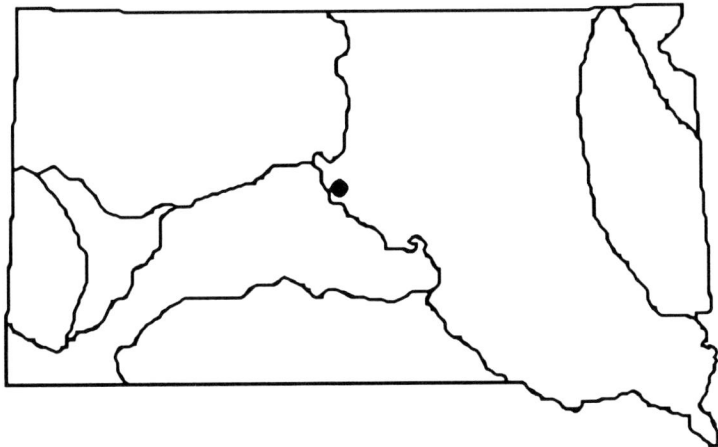

DOWNY WOODPECKER *Picoides pubescens* (Linnaeus)

Status. Common resident, although less numerous in Black Hills.

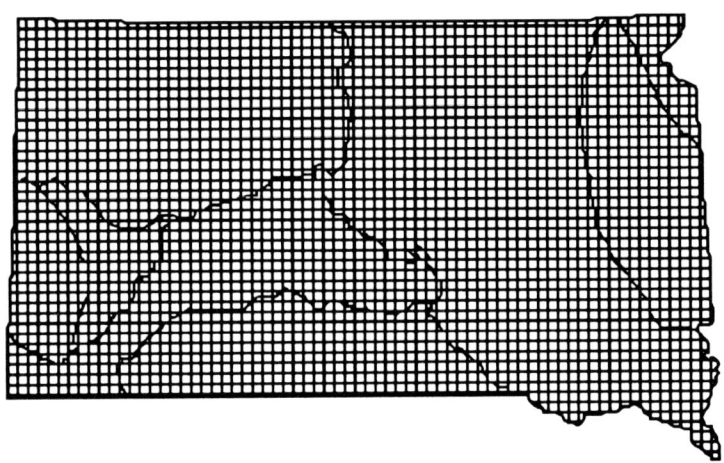

Habitat. Woodlands; primarily riparian forest in Black Hills.
Nesting. May – Jul. Territorial drumming begins in Jan or Feb.

Earliest dates:
  10 Apr 1968, Sanborn Co., active nest (Harris)
  23 Apr 1988, Meade Co., copulating (G. Levine)
  11 May 1968, Roberts Co., nest (Harris)
Latest date:
  27 Jul 1957, Rapid City, female feeding full-grown fledgling (Whitney)

Migration. Although Downy Woodpeckers are present all year, a specimen from Rapid City was identified as *D. p. nelsoni*, the Canadian Rockies population, by Hubbard (Pettingill and Whitney 1965). Banding studies may show further evidence of migration.

HAIRY WOODPECKER *Picoides villosus* (Linnaeus)

Status. Common permanent resident of Black Hills. Uncommon to fairly common permanent resident elsewhere.

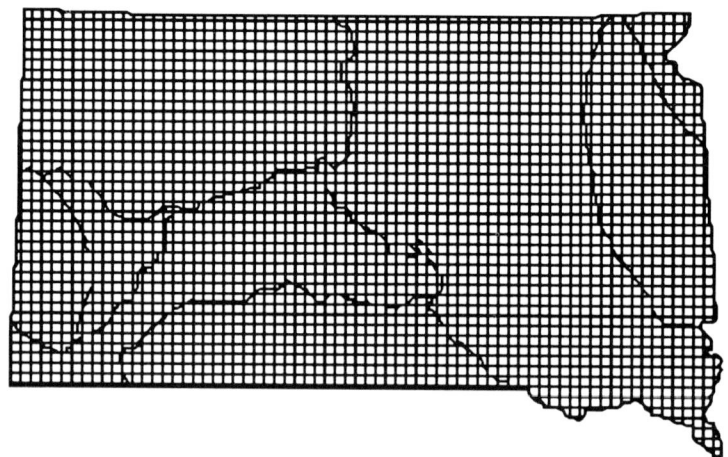

Habitat. Woodlands; conifer forests in Black Hills.
Nesting. Last week of May – first half of Jul. Courtship begins in Mar.
Earliest dates:
  21 May 1988, Meade Co., nesting (E. Miller)
  24 May 1984, Codington Co., adult feeding young in nest (Harris).
  26 May 1968, Forestburg, adults feeding young (Harris)
Latest dates:
  19 Jul 1975, Pennington Co., 1 nestling in cavity (Hill in Seasons 1975c)
  19 Jul 1975, Perkins Co., feeding 5 young (Hinds in Seasons 1975c)
  20 Jul 1988, Pennington Co., female feeding young (R. Peterson)

THREE-TOED WOODPECKER *Picoides tridactylus* (Linnaeus)

Status. Rare permanent resident at higher elevations in Black Hills. May also be found at lower elevations, especially in winter.

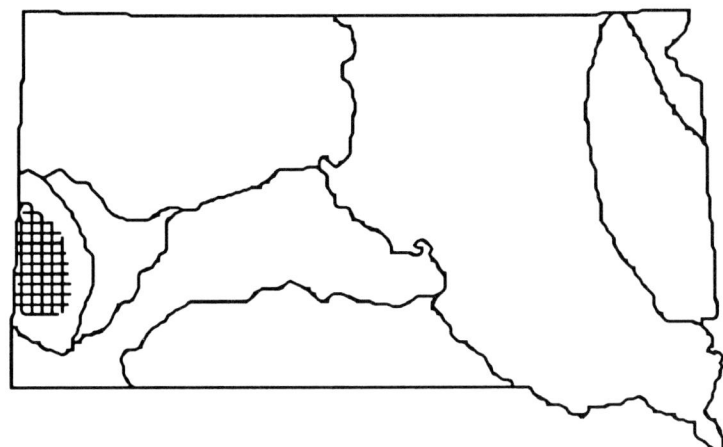

Habitat. Coniferous forests, especially spruce.
Nesting. May – Jul.
  Earliest dates:
    1 Jun 1979, Custer Co., building nest cavity (Holden in Seasons 1979d)
    12 Jun 1947, Spearfish Canyon, nest with 3 eggs (Sutton in Pettingill and Whitney 1965)
    18 Jun 1990, Lawrence Co., copulating pair (Springer)
  Latest date:
    9 Aug 1986, Lawrence Co., adult feeding young in nest (Harris in Seasons 1986d)

BLACK-BACKED WOODPECKER *Picoides arcticus* (Swainson)

Status. Uncommon permanent resident at higher elevations in Black Hills.

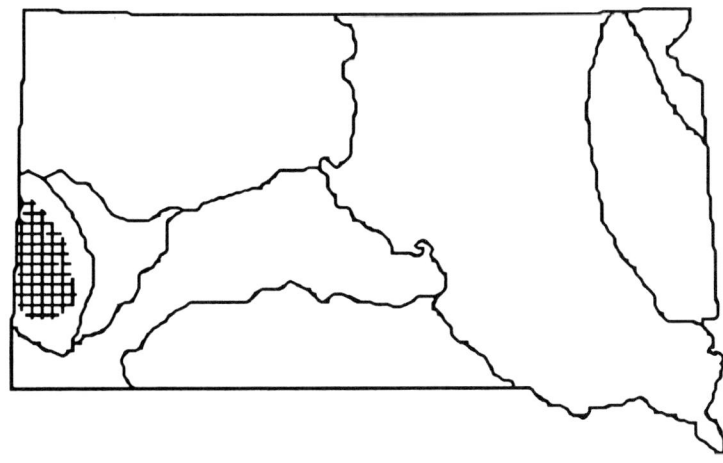

Habitat. Coniferous forests, especially with numerous dead trees and tall stumps, such as are found in recently burned areas.

Nesting. May – Jul.

Earliest dates:
  24 Apr 1982, Custer SP, pair excavating hole (Jackson)
  20 Jun 1954, Custer Co., nest with young (Levi and Levi 1954)
  27 Jun 1978, Custer Co., nest (Spomer)

Latest dates:
  7 Jul 1958, Jewel Cave NM, adult male feeding fledgling (Carter 1958b)
  25 Jul 1952, Palmer Gulch, 2 young out of nest (Behrens in Pettingill and Whitney 1965)
  9 Aug 1986, Lawrence Co., pair feeding young (Harris and Harris in Seasons 1987a)

NORTHERN FLICKER *Colaptes auratus* (Linnaeus)

Status. Very common summer resident. Uncommon in winter. Pure red-shafted birds are extremely rare, even though some individuals may appear in the field to be very red. Anderson (1969, 1971) found no pure red-shafted flickers among 511 breeding specimens, mostly collected in the W. Pettingill and Whitney (1965) cited few pure red-shafted birds among 25 specimens from the Black Hills. Birds appearing red-shafted are more often seen in winter E River, although in summer individuals show more orange, salmon, or reddish as one moves W. E River yellow-shafted birds often contain a few salmon-shafted feathers.

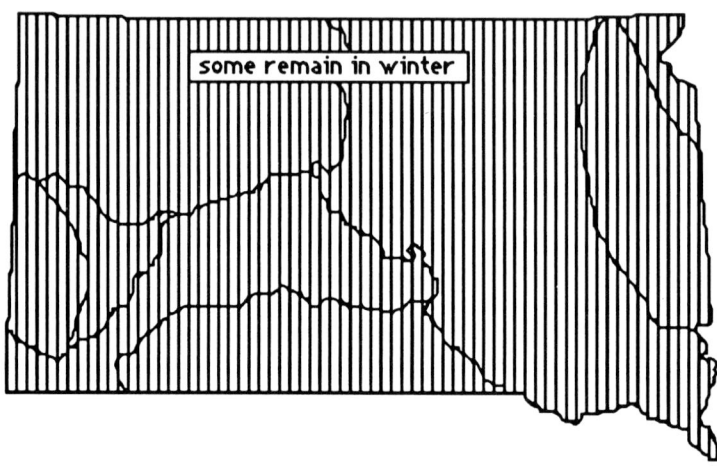

Habitat. Woodlands.
Spring migration. Last third of Mar. Early dates may represent wintering individuals.
Nesting. Last week of May – mid-Jul.
  Earliest dates:
    24 Apr 1954, Rapid City, nest excavation (Whitney)
    28 Apr 1963, Belvidere, courtship (DeVries 1963)
  Latest dates:
    17 Jul 1975, Perkins Co., brood of 5 left nest (Hinds in Seasons 1975c)
    20 Jul 1975, Clay Co., young in yard (Hoover in Seasons 1975c)
    4 Sep 1950, Hill City, young just out of nest (Behrens)
Fall migration. Oct. On 17 Oct 1960, Pickstown, between 200 and 300 (Youngworth and Youngworth)
Winter. Normally reported on many CBC during the last week of Dec and first week of Jan..
  Other records:
    22 Jan 1981, Davison Co. (McLaird in Seasons 1981b)
    8 Feb 1980, Turner Co. (L. Anderson)

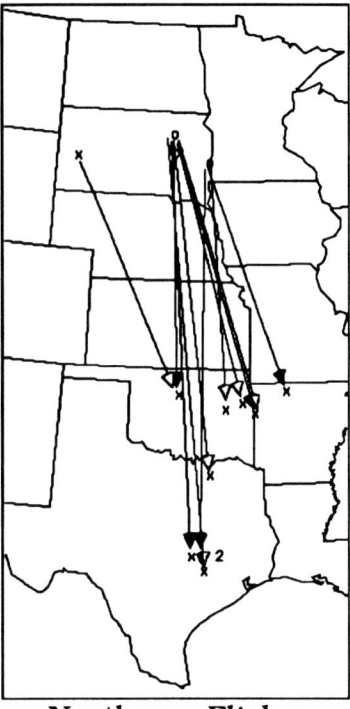

Northern Flicker banding recoveries.

PILEATED WOODPECKER *Dryocopus pileatus* (Linnaeus)

Status. Rare visitor NE. Breeding possible but unconfirmed. Post-breeding dispersal (early date: 12 Aug 1986, Roberts Co. (Cole fide Harris 1987b) brings birds up the Minnesota River Valley (or south through the Red River Valley) into Deuel, Grant, and Roberts counties. These birds stay into winter and the species may be establishing itself in breeding season (Harris 1987b). Earliest and latest records suggestive of possible breeding range from 13 Mar 1989, Roberts Co. (Tallman and Prisbe in Seasons 1989c) and 10 Apr 1986, Roberts Co. to 27 Jun 1987, Roberts Co. (Harris 1987b, Harris in Seasons 1987d). Formerly in the SE (Hayden 1863, Audubon 1897, Stephens et al. 1955); Agersborg (1885) thought it only a possible winter visitor along Missouri River in the SE. Reported once at Oahe Dam (Russell 1968).

Habitat. Large bottomland trees.

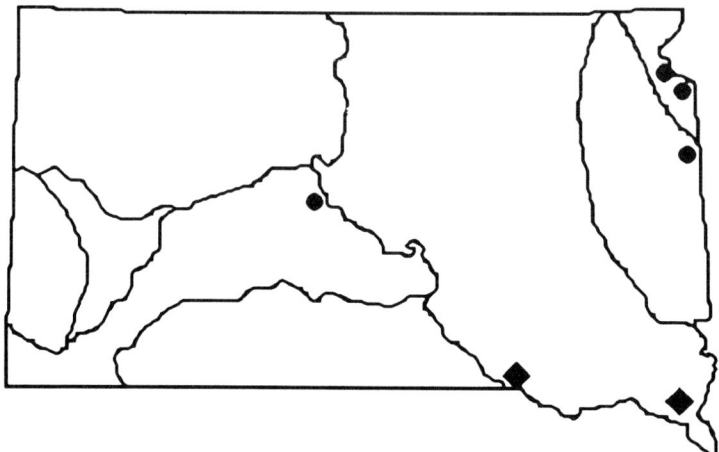

TYRANNIDAE: Tyrant Flycatchers

OLIVE-SIDED FLYCATCHER *Contopus borealis* (Swainson)

Status. Casual migrant and possible breeder in Black Hills. Uncommon migrant E.

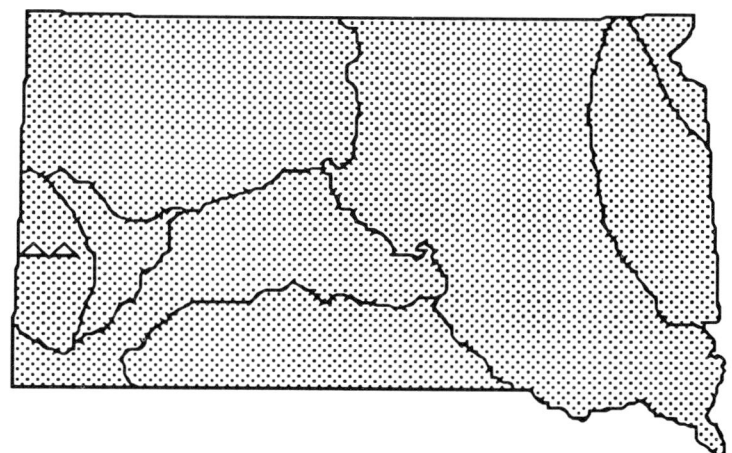

Habitat. Woodlands. Often perch in dead tops of large trees.
Spring migration. Second week of May.
  Earliest dates:
    12 May 1949, Union Co. (Youngworth)
    14 May 1990, Brookings Co. (Rogers in Seasons 1990c)
    17 May 1984, Codington Co. (Harris)
  Latest dates:
    2 Jun 1990, Brown Co., banded (Tallman)
    2 Jun 1918, McCook Lake (Stephens et al. 1955)
    13 Jun 1986, McPherson Co. (Tallman and Prisbe in Seasons 1986d)
Nesting. No definite records despite at least 5 nesting season observations ranging from 21 Jun 1931 at Mystic (Dille in Pettingill and Whitney 1965) to 30 Jul 1948 at Loveland Canyon (Dilger in Pettingill and Whitney 1965).
Fall migration. Third week of Aug.
  Earliest dates:
    6 Aug 1984, Gregory Co. (Steffen in Seasons 1985a)
    9 Aug 1981, Gregory Co. (Steffen in Seasons 1982a)
    10 Aug 1987, Brown Co. (Prisbe in Seasons 1988a)
  Latest dates:
    16 Sep 1982, Hanson Co. (Anderson in Seasons 1983a)
    16 Sep 1985, Brown Co. (Prisbe in Seasons 1986a)
    22 Sep 1931, Union Co. (Stephens et al. 1955)
    30 Sep 1984, Yankton Co. (Van Sickle in Seasons 1985a)

WESTERN WOOD-PEWEE *Contopus sordidulus* Sclater

Status. Common summer resident at all elevations in Black Hills, especially between 5000 and 6000 feet (Pettingill and Whitney 1965). Uncommon summer resident on Little Missouri River and in W Short Pines of Harding Co. (Springer). Also nests along Cheyenne River and its tributaries in Fall River Co. (McIntosh 1928; Springer), S Shannon Co (Homoya and Rosche), Lacreek NWR (Lohoefener and Ely 1978), SE Mellette Co. (Reagen 1908) and Todd Co. (Springer). Migrant through W River. Silent birds W are considered to be this species.

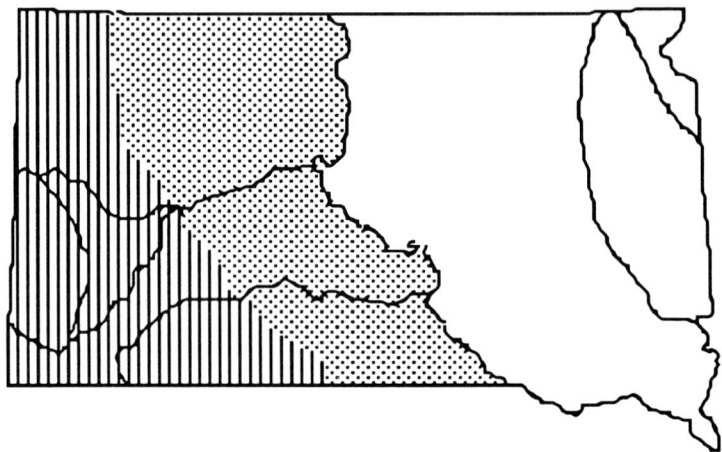

Habitat. Pine forests; mature cottonwoods along river bottomland.
Spring migration. Last half of May.
  Earliest dates:
    5 May 1989, Lawrence Co. (Backlund in Seasons 1989c)
    14 May 1961, Rapid City (Bachmann in Pettingill and Whitney 1965)
    15 May 1957, Rapid City (Bachmann in Pettingill and Whitney 1965)
Nesting. Jun and Jul (in the Black Hills).
  Earliest date:
    9 Jun 1956, Rapid City, nest under construction (Bachmann in Pettingill and Whitney 1965)
  Latest dates:
    23 Jul 1988, Rapid City, 2 fledglings (Slaughter)
    26 Jul 1958, Jewel Cave NM, adult feeding juvenile (Carter 1958b)
    2 Aug 1979, Wind Cave NP, nest with young (Jervis)
Fall migration. Last half of Aug.
  Latest dates:
    10 Sep 1989, Fall River Co. (Black Hills Audubon Society)
    26 Sep 1975, Badlands (Wilt in Seasons 1975d)

EASTERN WOOD-PEWEE *Contopus virens* (Linnaeus)
Status. Fairly common summer resident E. Casual W.

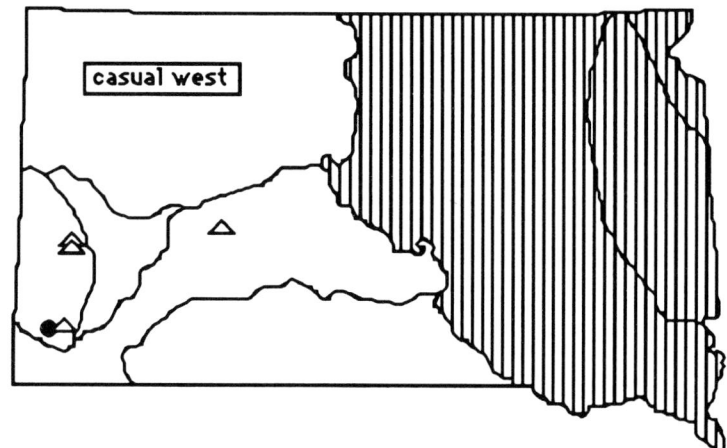

Habitat. Woodlands, orchards, and groves.
Spring migration. Second week of May.
  Earliest dates:
    18 Apr 1986, Codington Co. (Gilman in Seasons 1986c)
    2 May 1938, Sodak Park (Harris 1964)
    4 May 1964, Hyde Co. (Harter)
Nesting. Jun and Jul.
  Earliest dates:
    4 Jun 1967, Rapid City (Rose)
    17 Jun 1940, Sodak Park, nest with 2 eggs (Harris)
  Latest dates:
    28 Jul 1986, Roberts Co., adult feeding 3 fledged young (Harris in Seasons 1986d)
    28 Jul 1988, Yankton Co., feeding young in nest (Hall in Seasons 1988d)
    17 Sep 1989, Minnehaha Co., adults feeding fledged young (Hoeger in Seasons 1990a)
Fall migration. Late Aug.
  Latest dates:
    20 Sep 1982, Deuel Co. (Harris in Seasons 1983a)
    22 Sep 1984, Minnehaha Co. (Hoeger in Seasons 1985a)
    22 Sep 1985, Minnehaha Co. (Blankespoor in Seasons 1986a)
W River Records.
    summer 1955, NW Haakon Co. (Short 1961)
    6 Jul 1977, Pennington Co. (Baker)
    3 Jul 1978, Pennington Co. (Baker)
    8 Aug 1979, Wind Cave NP (Jervis)
    23 Jun 1982 in Custer Co. (Whitney in Seasons 1982d)

YELLOW-BELLIED FLYCATCHER *Empidonax flaviventris* (Baird and Baird)

Status. Rare migrant E; casual W.

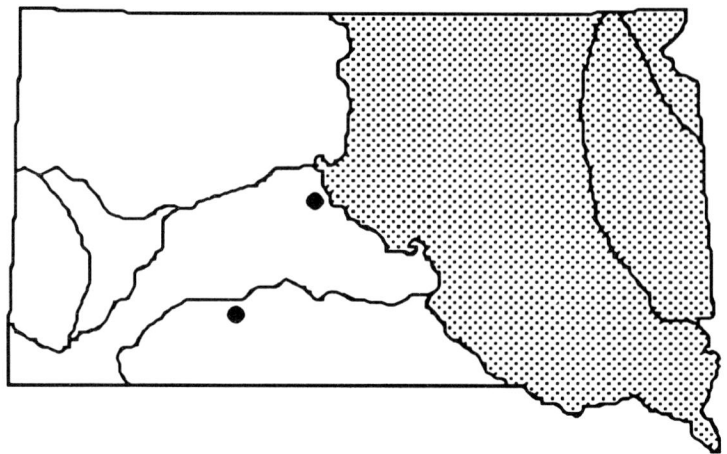

Habitat. Deciduous woods.
Spring migration. Last half of May.
Earliest dates:
  16 May 1988, Brookings Co. (Sandell in Seasons 1988c)
  16 May 1990, Turner Co. (Lauritzen in Seasons 1990c)
  17 May 1946, Chamberlain (Randall 1953)
  17 May 1981, Waubay NWR (Husmann in Seasons 1981c)
Latest dates:
  1 Jun 1956, Milbank, banded (Elliott 1967c)
  4 Jun 1983, Brown Co., banded (Tallman in Seasons 1983c)
  9 Jun 1986, Brown Co., banded (Tallman in Seasons 1986d)
Fall migration. Last half of Aug.
Earliest dates:
  5 Aug 1985, Jackson Co., banded (Graupmann)
  16 Aug 1933, Brown Co. (George)
  24 Aug 1988, Jackson Co., banded (Graupmann in Seasons 1989a)
Latest date:
  14 Sep 1959, Milbank, banded (Elliott 1967c)

ACADIAN FLYCATCHER *Empidonax virescens* (Vieillot)

Status. Not known if this species now occurs in South Dakota. Only observations are at McCook Lake in Union Co. before 1922 (Stephens et al. 1955). A specimen taken 2 Jun 1918 by Anderson and Stephens was confirmed by H. C. Oberholser, another taken on 30 May 1919 by Stephens was identified as an Acadian, and 4 were reported on 29 May 1921 by Stephens et al.

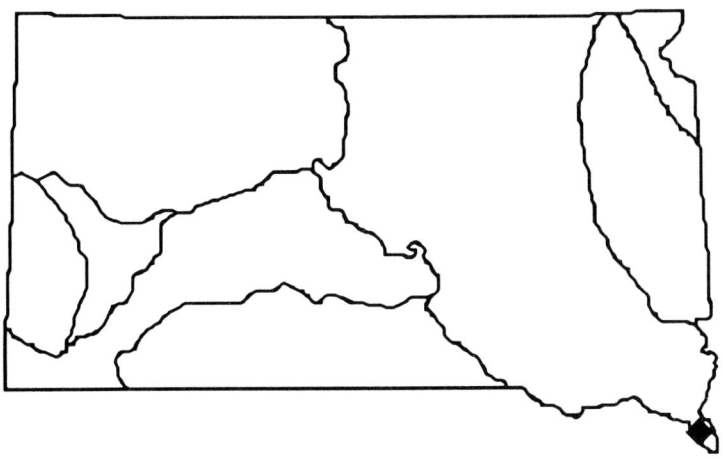

ALDER FLYCATCHER *Empidonax alnorum* Brewster

Status. Migrant of uncertain status E; status elsewhere unknown because, unless singing its "fee-bee-o" call, this species is impossible to separate from the Willow Flycatcher. Silent birds are best named Traill's Flycatchers, the name given to Willow and Alder Flycatchers when both were considered conspecific. See Willow Flycatcher account for late fall dates.

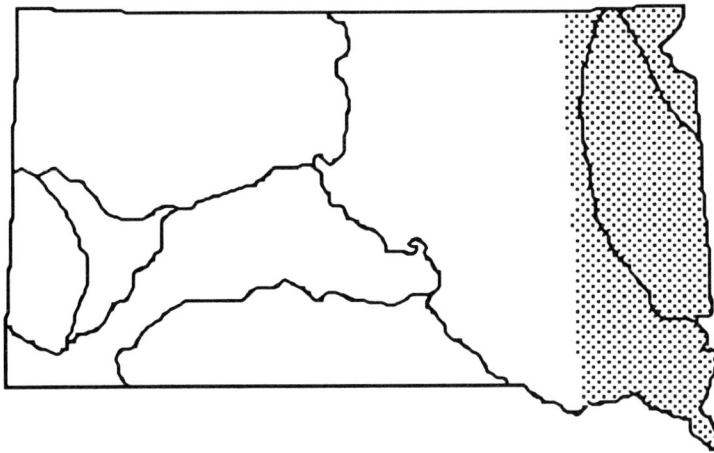

Habitat. Shrubbery and small trees.
Spring migration. Late May. All records calling birds.
  Earliest dates:
    16 May 1982, Brookings Co. (Holden in Seasons 1982c)
    16 May 1984, Codington Co. (Harris in Seasons 1984c)
  Latest dates:
    31 May 1986, Roberts Co. (Harris in Seasons 1986c)
    1 Jun 1986, Roberts Co. (Harris et al. in Seasons 1986c)
    2 Jun 1984, Lake Co. (Evanich in Seasons 1984d)

WILLOW FLYCATCHER *Empidonax traillii* (Audubon)

Status. Uncommon to locally common summer resident. Status in the Black Hills is unknown. Only birds calling "fitz-bew" should be identified as Willow Flycatchers; as explained in the previous account, silent individuals should be called Traill's Flycatchers.

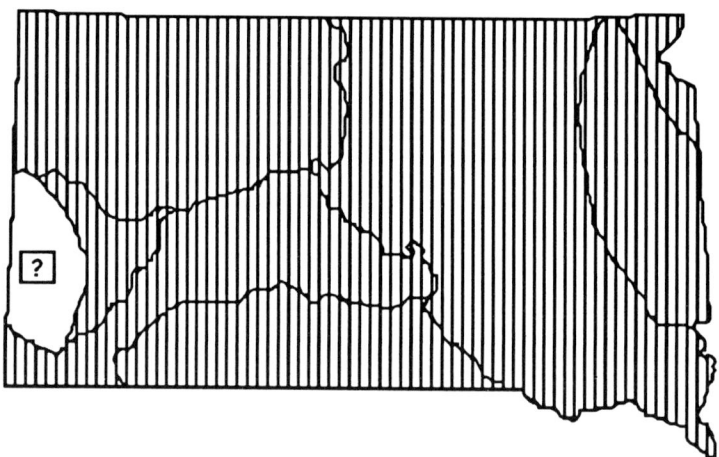

Habitat. Shrubbery and small trees, often near water.
Spring migration. Middle – third week of May.
  Earliest date:
    5 May 1971, Highmore (Harter)
Nesting. Jun and Jul.
  Earliest dates:
    4 Jul 1987, Roberts Co., nest with 2 young (Skadsen and Skadsen in Seasons 1987d)
    5 Jul 1974, Deuel Co., nest with 4 naked young (Harris)
    7 Jul 1971, Deuel Co., nest (Harris)
  Latest dates:
    15 Jul 1977, Lacreek NWR, nest with 4 young found and adults' calls confirmed (Lohoefener and Ely 1978)
    29 July 1985, Charles Mix Co., nest with 2 young (Skadsen in Seasons 1985d)

Fall migration. Late Jul – Aug. Records refer to "Traill's" Flycatchers.
Latest dates:
7 Sep 1967, Highmore (Harter)
21 Sep 1987, Brown Co. (Prisbe in Seasons 1988a)
14 Oct 1967, Brown Co. (Harris)

LEAST FLYCATCHER *Empidonax minimum* (Baird and Baird)

Status. Uncommon summer resident E; rare along Missouri River, its tributaries, and Little Missouri River in NW Harding Co., and Meade Co. Common migrant in the prairies and E. Uncommon migrant in Black Hills where breeding status uncertain.

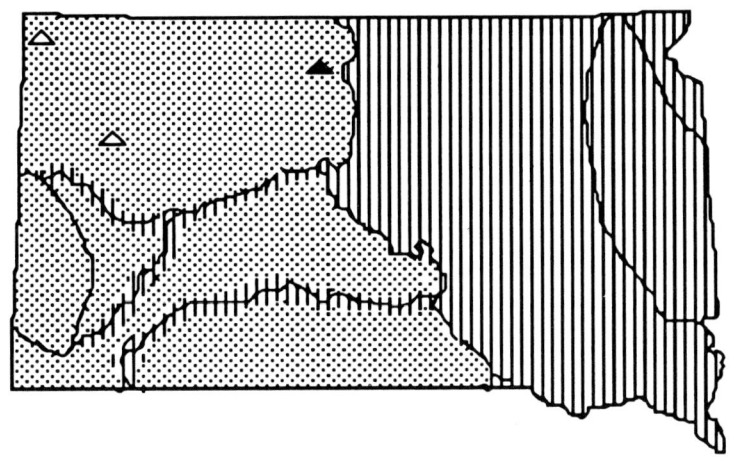

Habitat. Open deciduous woodlands.
Spring migration. First half of May.
Earliest dates:
28 Apr 1976, Day Co. (Chilson in Seasons 1976c)
30 Apr 1975, Hyde Co. (Harter in Seasons 1975c)
1 May 1986, Codington Co. (Gilman in Seasons 1986c)
1 May 1990, Brown Co. (Stanford in Seasons 1990c)
Nesting. Jun.
Earliest dates:
31 May 1968, Roberts Co., nest building (Harris)
8 Jun 1942, Sodak Park, with eggs (Harris)
Latest dates:
29 Jun 1968, Farm Island, nest (Harris)
2 Jul 1984, Turner Co., nest building, by 19 Jul a second nest with 1 egg and 3 newly-hatched young (Anderson in Seasons 1984d)

Least Flycatcher banding recoveries

15 Jul 1985, Dewey Co., adults feeding fledged young (Husmann and Harris)

Fall migration. Last half of Sep.
Latest dates:
24 Sep 1983, Jackson Co., banded (Graupmann in Seasons 1984a)
25–26 Sep 1965, Farm Island, banded (Holden 1966)

DUSKY FLYCATCHER *Empidonax oberholseri* Phillips

Status. Uncommon summer resident in Black Hills of Pennington and Custer counties.

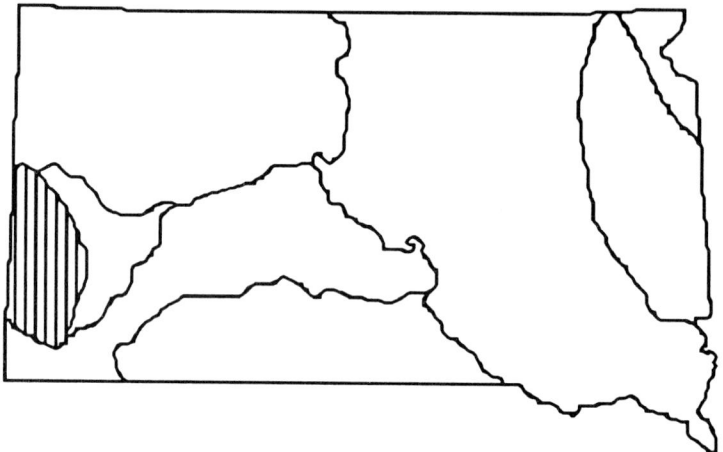

Habitat. Deciduous shrubbery, aspen groves, and open woods.
Spring migration. Mid-May.
Earliest dates:
11 May 1986, Pennington Co. (Whitney in Seasons 1986c)
20 May 1984, Willow Creek Horse Camp in Black Hills, 4–5 singing (Paulson and Coons in Seasons 1984c)
25 May 1986, Wind Cave NP (Whitney in Seasons 1986c)
Nesting. Jun and Jul.
Earliest dates (all records from Pettingill and Whitney 1965):
11 Jun 1948, about 4 miles N Pactola Reservoir, female in laying condition collected (Pettingill)
13 Jun 1947, Spearfish Canyon, nest with 3 eggs (Edwards)
Latest dates:
22 Jun 1985, Pennington Co., nest with 4 eggs (Springer in Seasons 1985d)
17 Jul 1988, Custer Co., nest with 3 young (R. Peterson)
Fall migration. Aug.
Only record:
17 Aug 1986, Lawrence Co. (Baker in Seasons 1987a)

CORDILLERAN FLYCATCHER *Empidonax occidentalis* Nelson

Status. Common summer resident in Black Hills. Only record elsewhere: 23 May 1965, Pierre (Rogge and Rogge). Previously known as Western Flycatcher, *E. difficilis.*

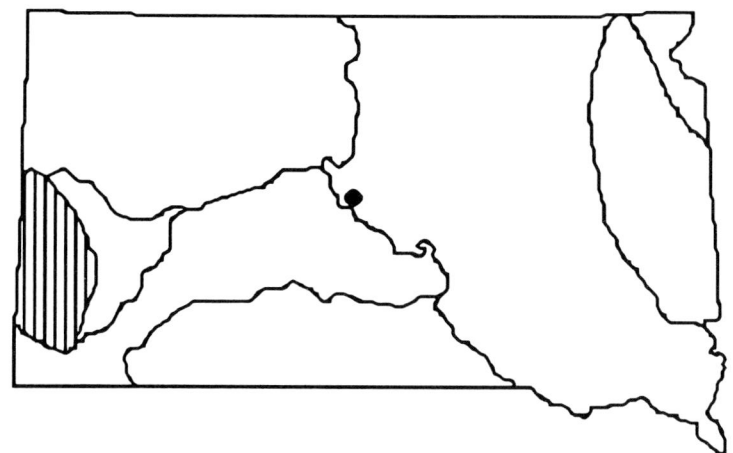

Habitat. Gulches, canyons, mountain slopes, invariably well-shaded by coniferous or mixed forest, usually near streams or moist areas.

Spring migration. Mid-May.
Earliest dates:
  5 May 1960, Rapid City (Bachmann in Pettingill and Whitney 1965)
  9 May 1955, Rapid City (Bachmann in Pettingill and Whitney 1965)
  13 May 1961, Rapid City (Bachmann in Pettingill and Whitney 1965)

Nesting. Jun and Jul.
Earliest date:
  9 Jun 1948, Little Elk Creek, female in egg-laying condition collected (Pettingill in Pettingill and Whitney 1965)
Latest date:
  2 Aug 1961, Sheridan Lake, 2 young fledged (Pettingill and Whitney 1965)

Fall migration. Aug.
Latest dates:
  8 Aug 1976, Lawrence Co. (Baker)
  15 Aug 1934, Wind Cave NP (Cahalane in Pettingill and Whitney 1965)

EASTERN PHOEBE *Sayornis phoebe* (Latham)

Status. Uncommon summer resident, except rare in Black Hills.

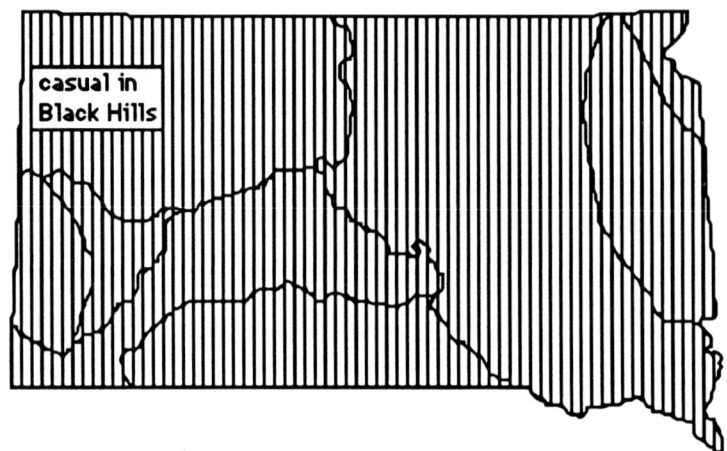

casual in Black Hills

Habitat. Wooded areas to open agricultural and farm communities, nesting in sheds and under bridges.

Spring migration. Second week of Apr. On 13 Apr 1984, 17 were seen in a small area in Roberts Co. (Skadsen in Seasons 1984c).

Earliest dates:
28 Mar 1946, Sodak Park (Harris 1964)
29 Mar 1986, Lincoln Co. (Skadsen in Seasons 1986c)
2 Apr 1989, Lincoln Co. (Skadsen in Seasons 1989c)

Nesting. Last week of Apr – mid-Jul.

Earliest dates:
11 Apr 1976, Sodak Park, nest building (Harris)
28 Apr 1968, Sodak Park, nest almost complete (Harris)
9 May 1946, Lawrence Co., nesting (Pettingill and Whitney 1965)

Latest dates:
10 Jul 1955, Perkins Co., second nest started (Hinds 1968)
2 Aug 1954, Perkins Co., young left nest (Hinds 1968)

Fall migration. Mid-Sep.

Latest dates:
3 Nov 1984, Brown Co. (Tallman in Seasons 1985a)
3 Nov 1984, Minnehaha Co. (Hoeger in Seasons 1985a)
1 Dec 1912, Clay Co. (Visher 1915)

SAY'S PHOEBE *Sayornis saya* (Bonaparte)

Status. Fairly common summer resident W. Rare migrant E where occasionally breeds.

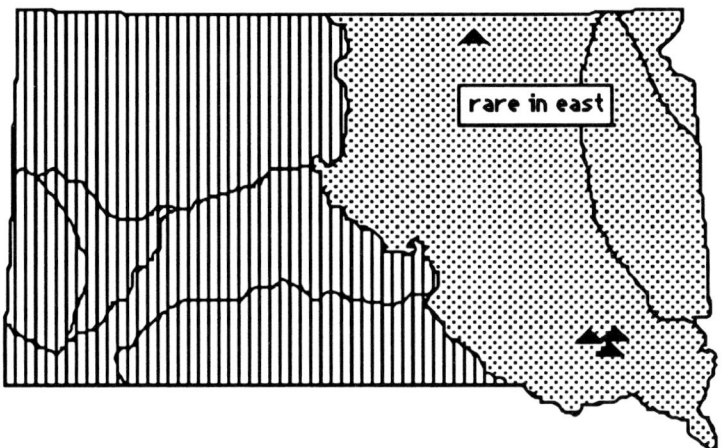

Habitat. Prairies and badlands, nesting on or in the vicinity of buildings, and unshaded canyons. Prefers drier and more open country than the Eastern Phoebe.

Spring migration. Late Apr and early May.
  Earliest dates:
    20 Mar 1978, Wind Cave NP (Klukas)
    1 Apr 1982, Yankton Co. (Hall in Seasons 1982c)
    5 Apr 1982, Gregory Co. (Steffen 1983a)

Nesting. Middle of May – Jul.
  Earliest W River dates:
    13 May 1987, Shannon Co., nest with 5 eggs (Rosche and Springer)
    15 May 1985, Perkins Co., forced out of nest by Barn Swallow (Hinds in Seasons 1985d)
    19 May–31 Jul 1987, Pennington Co., 3 broods fledged (Glass in Seasons 1987d)
  Latest W River dates:
    24 Jul 1973, Buffalo, nest with 4 eggs (Springer)
    4 Aug 1986, Badlands NP, second clutch fledged (Glass in Seasons 1986d)
    9 Aug 1934, Wind Cave NP, adults feeding young (Cahalane in Pettingill and Whitney 1965)
  E River Records: Several nesting records ranging from late May 1977 to 23 June 1979 are cited for Hutchinson Co. (Spomer 1979)
    21 May 1980, Hutchinson Co., nest with 5 eggs (L. Anderson)
    29 May 1985, McPherson Co. nest and young (Harris and Baker in Seasons 1985d)
    10 Jul 1984, Hutchinson Co., 2 fledged juveniles (Anderson in Seasons 1984d).

Fall migration. Sep.
Latest dates:
18 Sep 1968, Yankton Co. (Harris and Bradwisch)
20 Sep 1975, Yankton Co. (Hall in Seasons 1975d)
28 Oct 1986, Brown Co. (Tallman in Seasons 1987a)

VERMILION FLYCATCHER *Pyrocephalus rubinus* (Boddaert)

Status. Accidental
Only records:
12 May 1990, Day Co. (Skadsen in Seasons 1990c)
24 May 1958, Mitchell (Baylor 1959)
27 Sep 1986, Sand Lake NWR (Prisbe 1987)

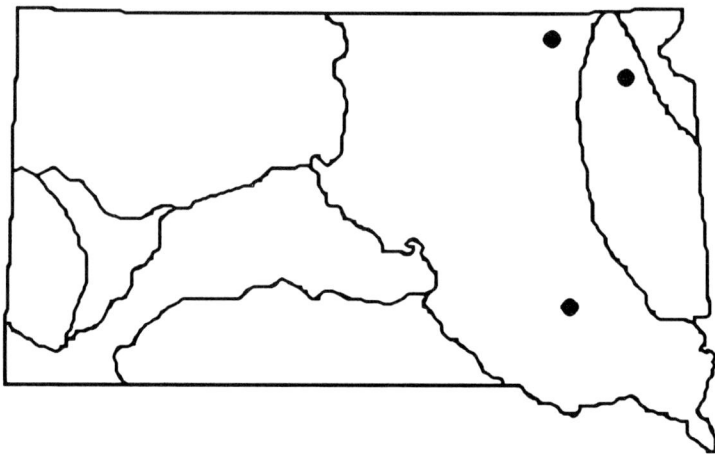

GREAT CRESTED FLYCATCHER *Myiarchus crinitus* (Linnaeus)

Status. Uncommon to fairly common migrant and summer resident E; less common in suitable habitat W; casual in Black Hills.

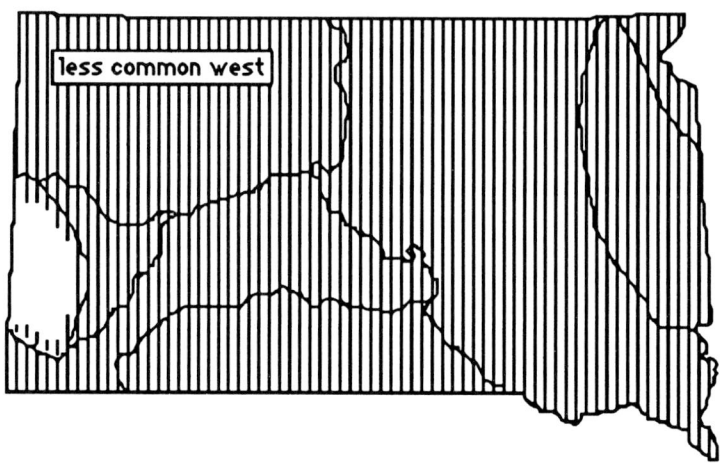

Habitat. Mature deciduous woodlands.
Spring migration. Second and third weeks of May.
Earliest dates:
1 May 1980, Brookings Co. (Taylor in Seasons 1980c)
1 May 1986, Bon Homme Co. (Kronner)
4 May 1952, Wilmot (Harris 1964)
6 May 1986, Gregory Co. (Steffen in Seasons 1986c)
Nesting. Last week of May into Jun. In Pennington Co. near Wall on 4 Jul 1983, Baylor et al. (1983) watched 2 birds intermittently gather food and fly into a woodland, perhaps to feed nestlings. Also 2 observed 12 June 1985 in E Pennington Co. (Baker)
Earliest dates:
26–27 May 1956, Waubay, pair building nest (Elliott 1957b)
6 Jun 1968, Mission, nest (Rose)
Latest dates:
19 Jun 1969, Sodak Park, nest hole (Harris)
26 Jun 1941, Sodak Park, nest hole (Harris)
Fall migration. Late Aug into Sep.
Latest dates:
22 Sep 1968, Huron (Johnson)
22 Sep 1971, Huron (Johnson)
24 Sep 1970, Deuel Co. (Harris)
27 Sep 1986, Brown Co. (Prisbe and Carrels in Seasons 1987a)

CASSIN'S KINGBIRD *Tyrannus vociferans* Swainson

Status. Rare or casual migrant SW. Rare breeder in Bennett and probably Shannon counties. Rosche (1982) states "locally fairly common to common autumn transient [in Shannon Co.] ...reaches its peak of abundance well after most of the Eastern and Western Kingbirds have left." No specimens or photographs.

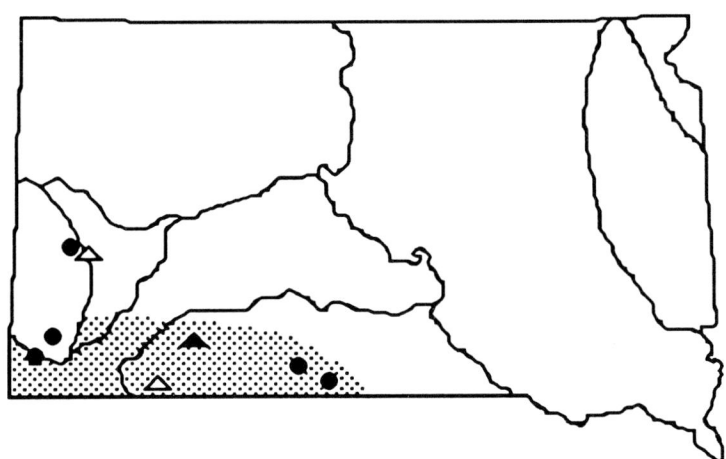

Spring migration.
Earliest dates:
18 May 1974, Rapid City (Serr, verified by Frazelle and Whitney)
22 May 1981, Wind Cave NP (Hetlet)
Latest date:
8 Jun 1969, near Rapid City in Meade Co. (Rose 1969b)
Nesting. Recorded 10 Jul 1989, Shannon Co. (R. Peterson)
15 Jun 1990, Bennett Co., nest with 4 eggs (Peterson and Peterson)
Fall migration.
Earliest dates:
10 Sep 1976, S of Cascade Springs (Rosche)
17 Sep 1988, near St. Francis (Rosche)
17 Sep 1989, near Pine Ridge (R. Peterson)
18 Sep 1988, near Parmelee (Rosche in Lambeth 1989)
Latest date:
22 Sep 1973, near Ardmore (Rosche)

WESTERN KINGBIRD *Tyrannus verticalis* Say

Status. Common summer resident, less common in Black Hills.

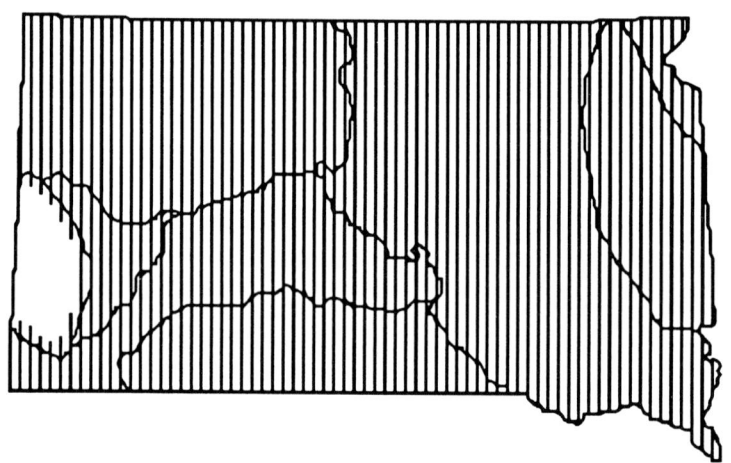

Habitat. In towns, farms, and open country.
Spring migration. Mid May.
Earliest dates:
16 Apr 1986, Bon Homme Co. (Kronner in Seasons 1986c)
21 Apr 1949, Sand Lake NWR (Podoll 1963)
26 Apr 1979, Stanley Co. (Hill in Seasons 1979c)
Nesting. Jun and Jul.
Earliest dates:
19 May 1986, Rapid City, building nest (Barnes)
22 May 1985, Edgemont, gathering nesting material (Springer)
26 May 1914, Lincoln Co., nest (Mallory 1915)

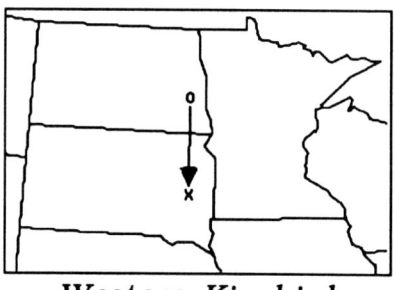

Western Kingbird banding recoveries.

Latest dates:
 19 Jul 1954, Huron, young fledged (Johnson 1970a)
 24 Jul 1973, NE Harding Co., pair feeding young (Springer)
 26 Jul 1985, Charles Mix Co., nest with 2 young (D. Skadsen in Seasons 1985d)

Fall migration. Last half of Aug. Nearly all are gone by the end of the month.
Latest dates:
 26 Sep 1989, Pennington Co. (Meader)
 29 Sep 1969, Sanborn Co. (Harris)

EASTERN KINGBIRD *Tyrannus tyrannus* (Linnaeus)

Status. Common summer resident, but with yearly local population fluctuations. Less common in higher Black Hills. Huntley (1970) in a study throughout Clay Co., found 3.5 times as many Eastern as Western Kingbirds during nesting, and 9 times as many in Aug.

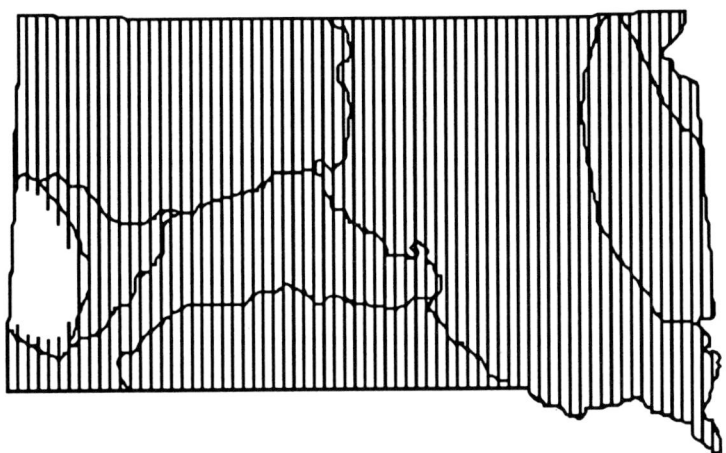

Habitat. Open woodlands, shelterbelts, and scattered trees.
Spring migration. Second and third week of May.
Earliest dates:
 9 Apr 1939, Yankton Co. (Youngworth)
 27 Apr 1981, Day Co. (Harris in Seasons 1981c)
 28 Apr 1952, Union Co. (Stephens et al. 1955)
Nesting. First week of Jun into Jul.
Earliest dates:
 18 May 1987, Tripp Co., building nest (Springer)
 20 May 1987, Clay Co., building nest (Springer)
 22 May 1985, Edgemont, gathering nesting material (Springer)
Latest dates:
 30 Jul 1956, Rapid City, adult feeding fledgling (Pettingill and Whitney 1965)
 6 Aug 1973, Deuel Co., 3 young in nest (Harris)
 13 Aug 1976, Harding Co., adults with 2 fledged young (Springer)

Fall migration. Last week of Aug – first half of Sep. 102 in quarter-mile, Clay Co., 27 Aug 1980 (Hall in Seasons 1981a).

Latest dates:
16 Sep 1984, Custer Co. (Peterson in Seasons 1985a)
18 Sep 1985, Moody and Lincoln Co. (Anderson in Seasons 1985a)
29 Sep 1946, Wilmot (Harris)

SCISSOR-TAILED FLYCATCHER *Tyrannus forficatus* (Gmelin)

Status. Casual visitor. No specimens.
Records:
18 May 1979, Brookings Co. (Spomer 1981)
24 May 1972, Deuel Co. (Harris 1972)
9 Jun 1989, Bennett Co. (Kippes)
18 Jun 1962, Lyman Co. (Bever 1962)
26 Jun 1988, Todd Co. (Brashears in Seasons 1988d)
27 Jul 1969, Custer Co., photographed (Rose 1969a)
Aug 1915, Sanborn Co. (Visher in Anon. 1956)

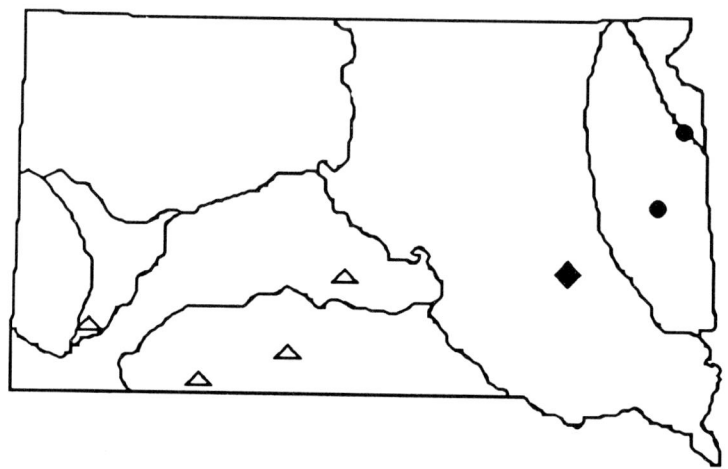

ALAUDIDAE: Larks

HORNED LARK *Eremophila alpestris* (Linnaeus)

Status. Abundant summer resident and winter visitor, sometimes in flocks of thousands.

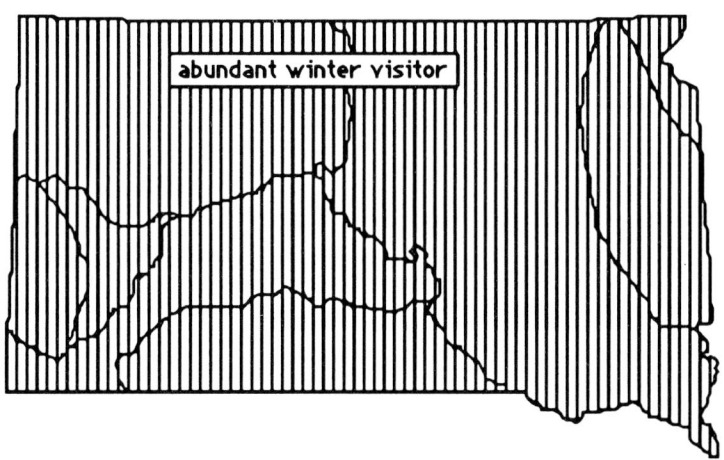

Habitat. Fields, pastures and prairies.

Spring migration. Mar – early Apr. Early dates are not applicable for this winter resident.

Nesting. Apr to Jun.
  Earliest dates:
   9 Apr 1980, Day Co., bird on nest (Harris in Seasons 1980d)
   17 Apr 1990, Deuel Co., fledgling (Harris in Seasons 1990c)
   19 Apr 1965, Rifle Lake, nest with 3 eggs, 2 hatched 23 Apr (Kuck in Olson 1965)
  Latest dates:
   15 Jul 1910, Harding Co., nest with 4 eggs (Visher 1914)
   1 Aug 1978, fledglings at Lacreek NWR (Lohoefener and Ely 1979).

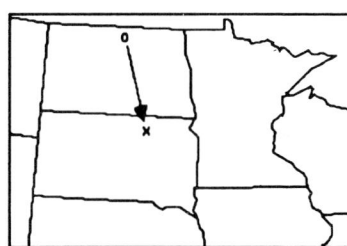

Horned Lark banding recoveries.

Fall migration. Sep – Oct. Huge flocks of mixed races can occasionally be seen moving during this period, although, as in spring, large wintering populations make actual migration dates difficult to ascertain.

HIRUNDINIDAE: Swallows

PURPLE MARTIN *Progne subis* (Linnaeus)

Status. Common summer resident E. Breeds W to Martin and to Thunder Hawk (Stewart 1975). A few occur in spring migration W to Pine Ridge and the Black Hills. Formerly common in the Black Hills (Grinnell 1875, Visher 1909).

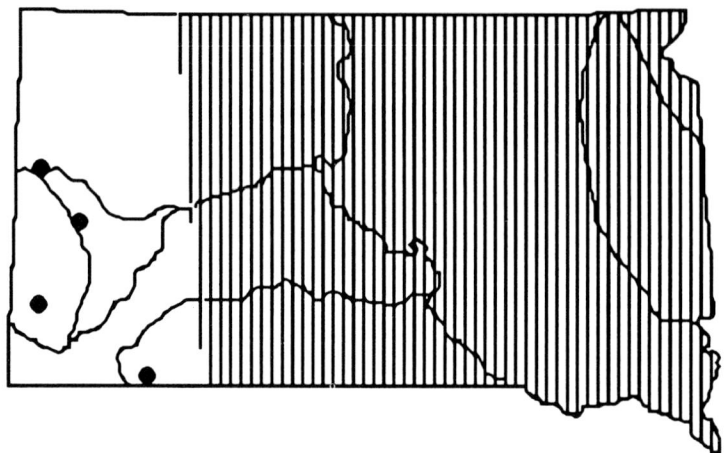

Habitat. Nesting largely determined by availability of martin houses.

Spring migration. Apr into May. Substantial arrivals late into last week of May. Probably the earliest arrivals fail to survive the rain and cold of some years.

Earliest dates:
27 Mar 1988, Burke (Steffen in Seasons 1988c)
30 Mar 1977, Burke (Steffen in Seasons 1977c)
1 Apr 1981, Gregory Co. (Steffen in Seasons 1981c)

Nesting. First week of May – Jun.

Earliest Date:
12 May 1987, Gregory Co., building nest (Steffen)
19 May 1959, Huron, building nests (Johnson 1967)

Latest dates:
3 Aug 1959, Huron, young fledged (Johnson 1967)
26 Aug 1980, Gregory Co., young fledged (Steffen)

Fall migration. Last week of Aug, though pairs with early-fledged young disappear earlier.

Latest dates:
8 Sep 1980, Gregory Co. (Steffen)
25 Oct 1982, Deuel Co. (Kreger in Seasons 1983a)

Purple Martin banding recoveries

Far W Records.
11 Jun 1904, Kyle (Tullsen 1911)
26 May 1964, Custer Co. (Springer)
May 1969, Butte Co. (Weyler)
19 May 1969, Rapid City (Rose)

TREE SWALLOW *Tachycineta bicolor* (Vieillot)

Status. Uncommon summer resident, locally more common NE, decreasing W. Rare NW.

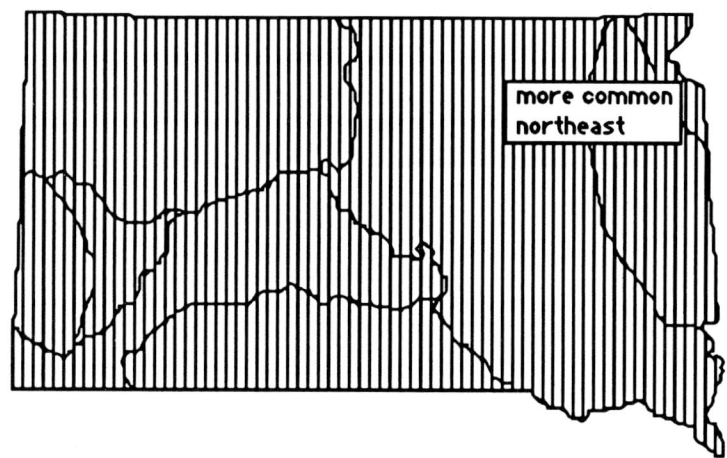

Habitat. Wherever groves near water or dead trees in water provide natural cavities for nesting. Often uses bluebird houses.
Spring migration. Last week of Apr – first week of May. Unusual concentration: 3 May 1984, Hill City, 50 (Whitney).
  Earliest dates:
    2 Apr 1978, Pierre (Hill in Seasons 1978c)
    6 Apr 1984, Brookings Co. (Jensen in Seasons 1984c)
    7 Apr 1976, Deuel Co. (Harris)
    7 Apr 1986, Day Co. (Prisbe)
    7 Apr 1987, Day Co. (Koerner in Seasons 1987d)
Nesting. Mid-May – mid-Jun.
  Earliest dates:
    12 May 1987, Day Co., nest with egg (D. Skadsen)
    15 May 1986, Day Co., nest with 2 eggs (D. Skadsen)
    16 May 1985, Custer Co., pair at hole (Whitney)
  Latest dates:
    22 Jun 1985, Pennington and Lawrence counties, 3 nests (Springer)
    28 Jun 1932, Union Co. (Stephens et al. 1955)
    31 Jul 1986, Day Co., nest with 5 eggs (D. Skadsen)

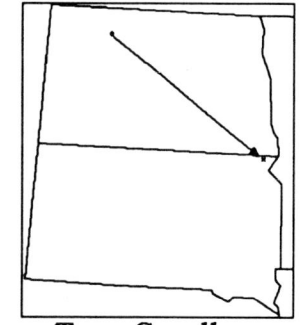

Tree Swallow banding recoveries

Fall migration. Late Aug – Sep. Large concentrations occur.
  Latest dates:
    15 Oct 1964, near Lake Preston, Kingsbury Co. (Springer)
    21 Oct 1963, Codington and Day counties (Springer)
    22 Oct 1976, Deuel Co. (Harris in Seasons 1977a)

VIOLET-GREEN SWALLOW *Tachycineta thalassina* (Swainson)

Status. Fairly common summer resident at all elevations of Black Hills and adjacent areas, the buttes of Harding Co., and the Badlands (Visher 1912a). Late summer records on Pine Ridge Indian Reservation but breeding not documented (Springer).

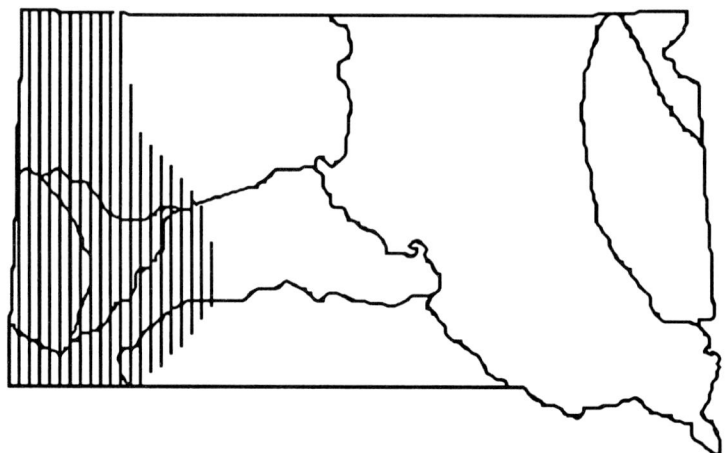

Habitat. Steep-walled canyons; less frequently open woods and near buildings, meadows, and water.
Spring migration. Second week of May.
  Earliest dates:
    16 Apr 1987, Custer Co. (Whitney in Seasons 1987c)
    16 Apr 1989, Meade Co. (Miller in Seasons 1989c)
    17 Apr 1977, Rapid City (Baker and Hays in Seasons 1977c)
Nesting. Jun and Jul.
  Earliest dates:
    11 Jun 1959, near Hill City, pair building a nest (Pettingill and Whitney 1965)
    13 Jun 1948, Rochford, pair nesting (Pettingill and Whitney 1965).
    14 Jun 1947, Spearfish Canyon, nest with young (Lea and Edwards in Pettingill and Whitney 1965)
  Latest dates:
    24 Jul 1948, Loveland Canyon, nest with young (Dilger in Pettingill and Whitney 1965)
    24 Jul 1958, Jewel Cave NM, nest with young (Whitney and Carter in Pettingill and Whitney 1965)
Fall migration. Aug. Carter (in Pettingill and Whitney 1965) noted a large breeding population departed Jewel Cave NM 26 Jul 1958.

Latest dates:
   30 Aug 1960, Canyon Lake (Pettingill and Whitney 1965)
   5 Sep 1975, Rapid City (Whitney in Seasons 1975a)

NORTHERN ROUGH-WINGED SWALLOW *Stelgidopteryx serripennis* (Audubon)

Status. Fairly common summer resident, rare in Black Hills, except in the Rapid City area.

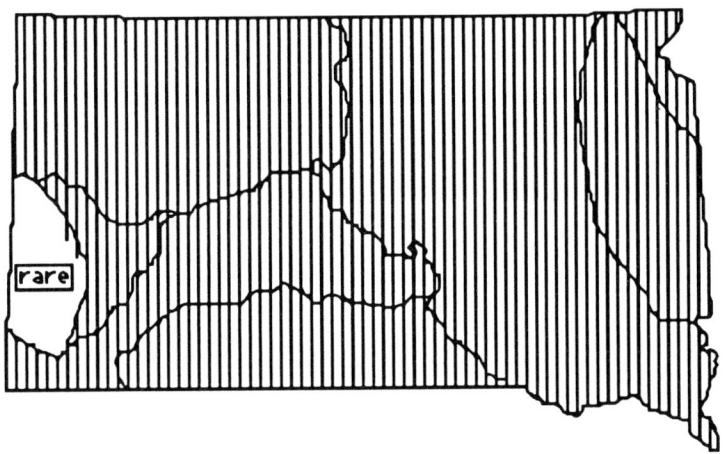

Habitat. Any excavatable steep bank may become a colony site; also use crevices under bridges.
Spring migration. Mid-May.
   Earliest dates:
      10 Apr 1981, Yankton Co. (Hall in Seasons 1981c)
      11 Apr 1981, Gregory Co. (Steffen in Seasons 1981c)
      17 Apr 1971, Pierre (Rose)
      17 Apr 1982, Shannon Co. (Rosche in Seasons 1982c)
Nesting. Late May and Jun. Husmann (1981) found nests in 1978 and 1979 in a shed in Day Co.
   Earliest dates:
      13 May 1965, Marshall Co., nests (Springer)
      16 May 1964, Farm Island, nesting (Whitney)
      20 May 1967, Belvidere, nesting (Whitney)
      20 May 1987, Yankton Co., nesting (Springer)
   Latest dates:
      22 Jul 1974, Harding Co., feeding young in nests (Springer)
      24 Jul 1973, Harding Co., fledged young (Springer)
Fall migration. Aug.
   Latest dates:
      28 Sep 1980, Brookings Co. (SDOU in Seasons 1981a)
      29 Sep 1969, Sanborn Co. (Harris)
      12 Oct 1977, Yankton Co. (Hall in Seasons 1978a)

BANK SWALLOW *Riparia riparia* (Linnaeus)

Status. Common summer resident in Missouri Valley and E; less common W; status in Black Hills uncertain.

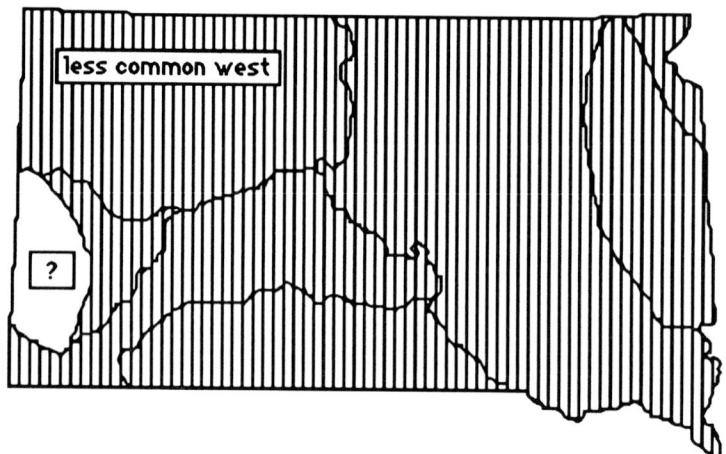

Habitat. Nests in colonies in steep banks of sand, dirt or gravel.
Spring migration. Middle of May.
  Earliest dates:
    15 Apr 1974, Capitol Lake, Pierre (Rose)
    19 Apr 1986, Gregory Co. (Steffen in Seasons 1986c)
    20 Apr 1987, Yankton Co. (Van Sickle in Seasons 1987c)
Nesting. Mid-May – mid-Jun.
  Earliest dates:
    18 May 1957, Lacreek NWR, 2 fledglings (Elliott 1957a)
    20 May 1987, Union Co., nesting (Springer)
  Latest date:
    24 Jul 1973, Ralph, fledgling (Springer)
Fall migration. Late Aug.
  Latest dates:
    27 Sep 1981, Brown Co. (Rogge and Rogge in Seasons 1982a)
    10 Oct 1967, Jerauld Co. (Harris)

CLIFF SWALLOW *Hirundo pyrrhonota* Vieillot

Status. Locally abundant summer resident.

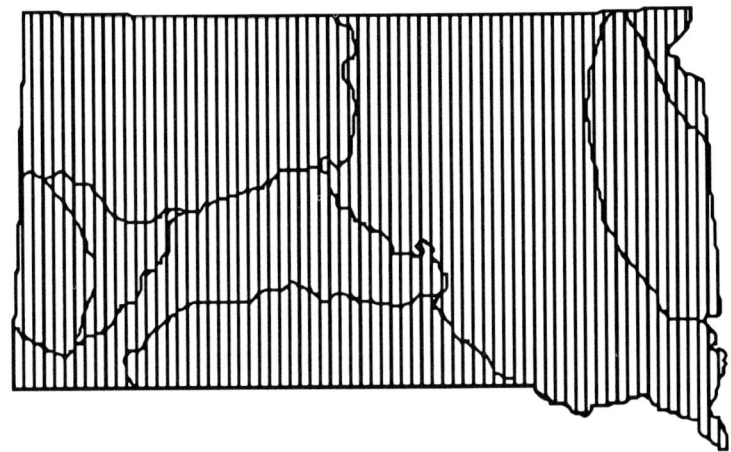

Habitat. Colonies form at suitable nesting sites under eaves of barns, under highway bridges, in highway culverts, and on steep-walled cliffs.

Spring migration. Mid-May.
Earliest dates:
20 Apr 1987, Lacreek NWR (Edinger)
22 Apr 1984, Hanson Co. (Anderson in Seasons 1984c)
26 Apr 1964, Hyde Co. (Harter)

Nesting. Late May – mid-Jul.
Earliest dates:
12 May 1987, Shannon Co., newly completed nests (Springer)
12 May 1987, Roberts Co., nests (Skadsen in Seasons 1987d)
13 May 1982, Deuel Co., nests (Harris)
Latest dates:
11 Jul 1981, Aberdeen, young in nests (Tallman)
13 Jul 1978, Scenic, nesting on church (Springer)
16 Jul 1978, Harding Co., feeding fledged young (Springer)

Fall migration. Aug.
Latest dates:
22 Sep 1973, Deuel Co. (Harris)
27 Sep 1964, Hyde Co. (Harter)
15 Oct 1962, Hyde Co. (Harter)

Cliff Swallow banding recoveries

BARN SWALLOW *Hirundo rustica* Linnaeus

Status. Common summer resident.

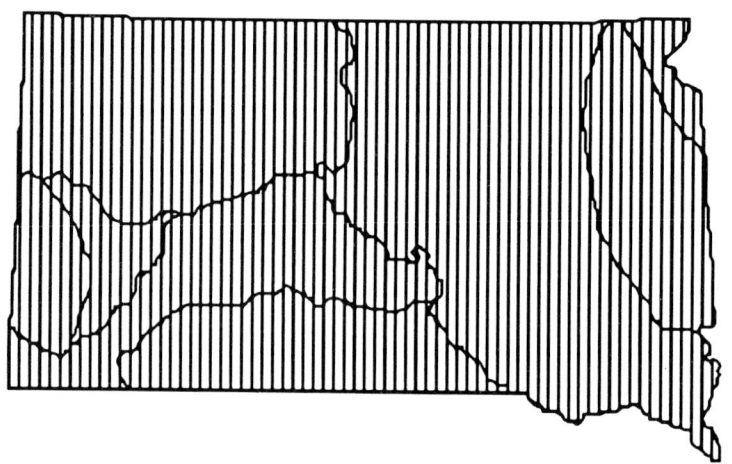

Habitat. Nests in or on barns, houses, under highway bridges, and in culverts.

Spring migration. First week of May.
  Earliest dates:
    10 Apr 1982, Yankton Co. (Hall in Seasons 1982c)
    10 Apr 1982, Gregory Co. (Steffen in Seasons 1982c)
    11 Apr 1984, Hanson Co. (Anderson in Seasons 1984c)

Nesting. Late May, into late Jun.
  Earliest dates:
    13 May 1987, Shannon Co., 2 nests with 2 eggs (Springer and Rosche)
    19 May 1987, Lake Andes NWR, building nest (Springer)
    23 May 1987, Badlands NP, 5 nests (Glass)
  Latest date:
    15 Sep 1906, Shannon Co., nest with 3 young just flying (Tullsen 1911)

Fall migration. Late Sep. On 25 Sep 1984, 40 dead on 9 mi of highway after 2-inch snow (Harris in Seasons 1985a).
  Latest dates:
    20 Oct 1951, Union Co. (Felton)
    20 Oct 1966, Sand Lake NWR (Springer)
    21 Oct 1963, Codington and Day counties (Springer)
    26 Oct 1980, Deuel Co. (Harris in Seasons 1981a)

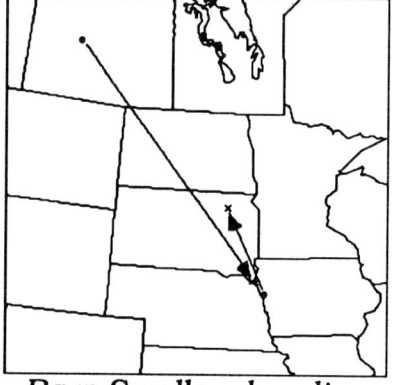

Barn Swallow banding recoveries

CORVIDAE: Jays, Magpies, and Crows

GRAY JAY *Perisoreus canadensis* (Linnaeus)

Status. Common permanent resident in Black Hills at elevations above 4000 ft.; ranges lower in nonbreeding season (Hot Springs, Rapid City). Rare visitor elsewhere.

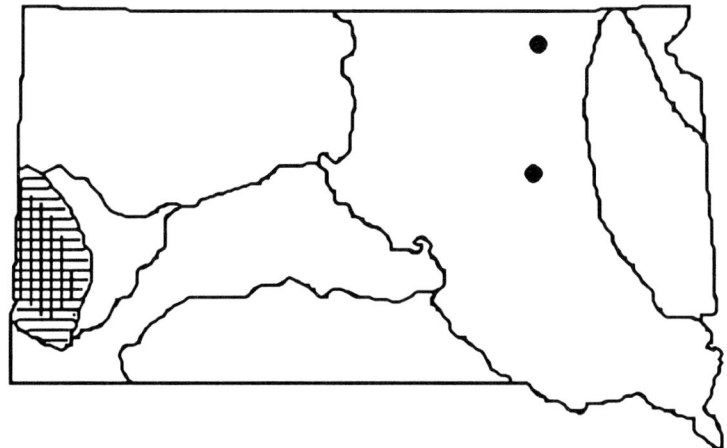

Habitat. Dense pine or spruce forests, occasionally mixed woodland.

Nesting. Jun.

Earliest dates:
- 27 Feb 1985, Custer Co., nest building; 2 Apr, incubating eggs; 24 Apr, 3 downy young; 29 Apr, young hopping about in nest tree (Peterson et al. in Seasons 1985c)
- 4 May 1983, Custer Co., adult carrying food (Whitney)
- 19 May 1982, Custer Co., family group of at least 3 full-grown but recently fledged young (Whitney)

Latest dates:
- 26 May 1964, Deerfield, 2 adults with 3 flying young (Springer)
- 9 Jun 1958, Rochford, 3 eggs and nest collected in pine tree (Behrens)
- 13 Jun 1964, Lawrence Co., 4 fledged young begging food from parents (Pettingill and Whitney 1965)

E River records.
- 6 Nov 1960, Huron (Jonkel and Jonkel 1960)
- 27 Sep 1986, Sand Lake NWR (Prisbe 1987)

BLUE JAY *Cyanocitta cristata* (Linnaeus)

Status. Fairly common summer resident E and lower Black Hills, otherwise uncommon W and absent from higher Black Hills. Uncommon to common winter. Winter populations may be migrants from the N.

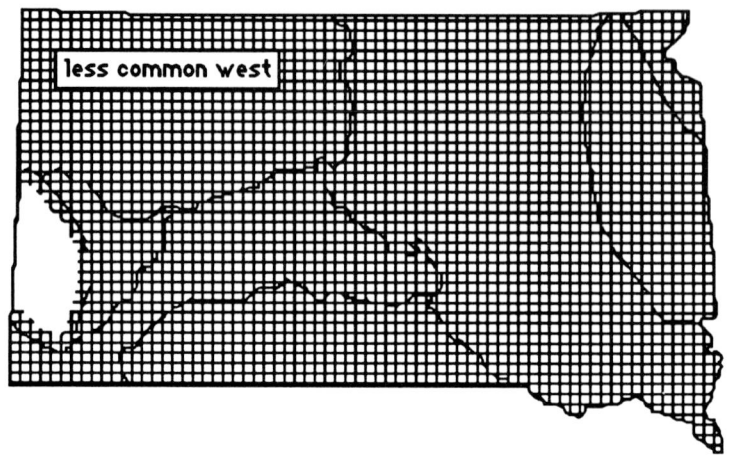

Habitat. Woods and residential areas.

Migration. Because jays are present all year, spring and fall migration dates are hard to ascertain. However, flocks of migrating jays are occasionally observed during migrations. Migrating birds were noted in the first week of Sep in Hyde Co. (Harter 1969).

Nesting. May–Jun.

Earliest dates:
7 May 1973, Roberts Co., nest building (Harris)
13 May 1977, Roberts Co., bird on nest (Harris)
24 May 1942, Wilmot, nest (Harris)

Latest dates:
3 Jul 1970, S Slim Buttes, 2 adults and 3 fledged young (Springer)
4 Jul 1988, Rapid City, 2 adults and 2 fledged young (Speiser)
13 Jul 1988, Rapid City, 1 adult with 4 fledged young (E. Miller)

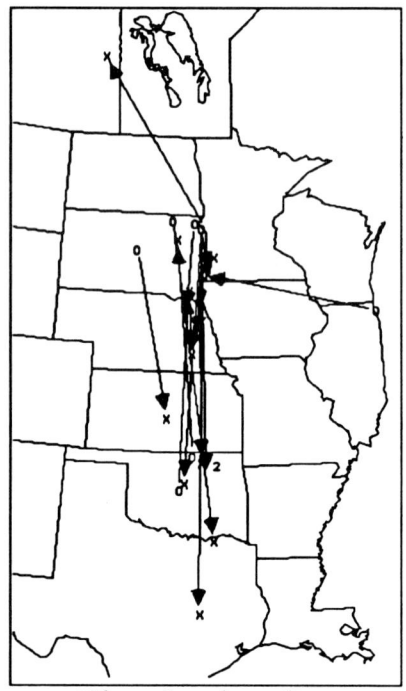

Blue Jay banding recoveries

STELLER'S JAY *Cyanocitta stelleri* (Gmelin)

Status. Accidental. Reported as casual in SW South Dakota (AOU 1957), but the basis for this ascertation is undetermined. No specimens or photographs.

Only record. 22 Jul 1948, Loveland Canyon, 2 "for certain and possibly a third" among Blue Jays (Dilger in Pettingill and Whitney 1965).

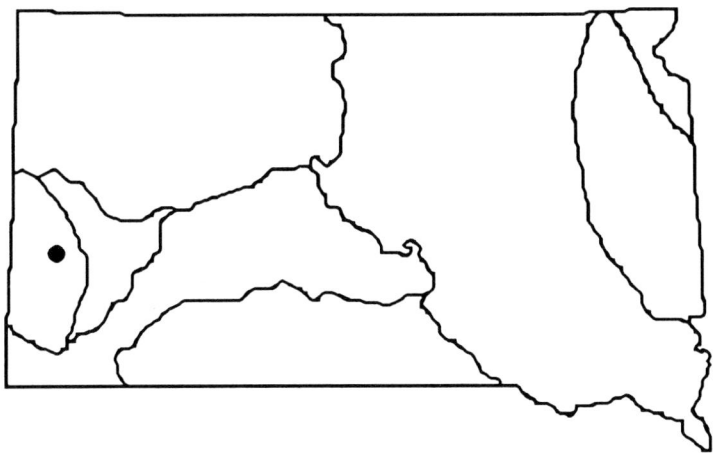

PINYON JAY *Gymnorhinus cyanocephalus* Wied

Status. Common permanent resident in Black Hills from 3200 to 4500 feet. Also in Short Pines, Cave Hills, Long Pines of Harding Co., and in Shannon Co. Visher (1912a) reported 2 on Sheep Mountain on 14–16 Jul 1911. Casual wanderer elsewhere. See Whitney (1982).for banding study.

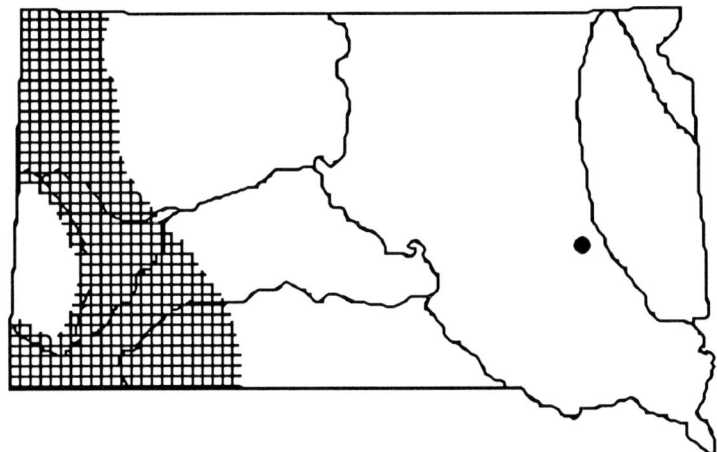

Habitat. Pine forest with dry soil (where the trees are small and relatively far apart).
Nesting. Apr – Jun.
  Earliest dates:
    12 May 1982, Rapid City, fledglings (Whitney in Seasons 1982d)
    16 May 1986, Custer Co., adults with young (Parker)
    18 May 1924, Black Hawk, set of 2 eggs (Whitney 1955)

Latest dates:
  28 Jun 1971, East Short Pines, flock of 60 adults and young (Springer)
  1 Jul 1978, Wind Cave NP, adults with 1 newly fledged young (Jervis)
  18 Jul 1953, Custer, 5 young (Behrens in Pettingill and Whitney 1965)
E River records:
  28 Jun 1959, Huron (Johnson and Johnson 1959)
  5 Sep 1959, Huron (Johnson and Johnson 1959)
  28 Sep 1983, Huron (Johnson 1984)

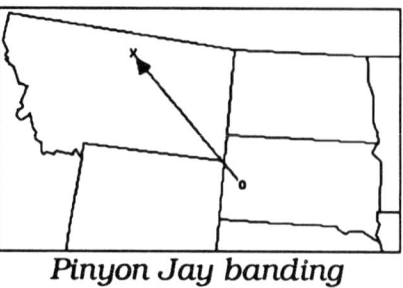

Pinyon Jay banding recoveries

CLARK'S NUTCRACKER *Nucifraga columbiana* (Wilson)

Status. Uncommon invasive fall and winter visitor to Black Hills, occasionally nesting after peak invasion years. Casual further E. Recorded on Rapid City CBC in Dec 1987.

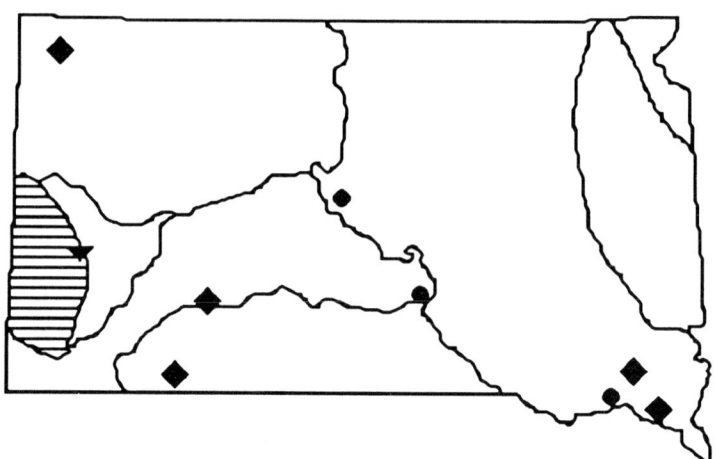

Habitat. Pine forests.
Nesting. Said to be a frequent summer resident in the Short Pines of Harding Co. (Visher 1914) but no nests found; perhaps occurring after an invasion.
  Records:
    7 Apr 1987, Custer Co., nest with 2 young (Peterson 1988)
    16 Apr 1987, Custer Co., 2 nests with 2 young each (Peterson 1988)
    29 Apr 1985, Custer Co., recently fledged young (Peterson 1985)
Records outside Black Hills: Reported frequently between 1857 and 1860 in Badlands (Hayden 1863), once between 1901 and 1908 in Shannon Co. (Tullsen 1911), in fall 1903 in Hutchinson Co. (Sweet in Visher 1909), and a rare winter visitor in 1932 in Bon Homme Co. (Johnson 1958).
  Specific dates:
    18 Oct 1883, Clay Co., 2 seen and 1 shot (Agersborg 1885)

24 Nov 1969, Lyman Co. across bridge from Chamberlain (Harris)
17 Jul 1985, Hughes Co. (Riis in Seasons 1985d)

BLACK-BILLED MAGPIE *Pica pica* (Linnaeus)

Status. Fairly common resident in counties bordering Missouri River and W. Rare SE. Regular winter visitor in the Wessington Hills S of Miller, the Highmore area, and in small numbers in NE counties (Harris 1974b, 1963), where invasions occur in some falls and winters. The 1972–73 winter irruption in NE was unusually large (Harris 1974b). Formerly irregular winter visitor in Union Co. (Stephens et al. 1955), Sioux Falls (Larson 1925), and Clay Co. (Agersborg 1885).

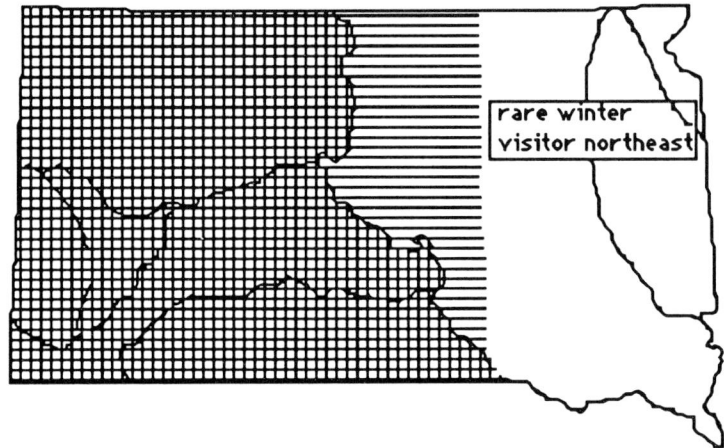

Habitat. Streamside woodlands and thickets, prairie groves, and open pine forests.
Nesting. Late Apr – mid-Jul. Nested in the Wessington Hills S of Miller in 1969 (Harris)
Earliest dates:
17 Apr 1978, near Wind Cave NP, nesting (Buitron)
28 Apr 1925, near Rapid City, 2 sets of eggs (McIntosh in Whitney 1955)
28 Apr 1987, Pennington Co., nest with eggs (Melius in Seasons 1987d)
Latest dates:
27 Jun 1956, Rapid City, fledglings (Whitney)
27 Jun 1957, Rapid City, fledglings (Whitney)
28 Jun 1972, Harding Co, 2 newly fledged young (Grant)

AMERICAN CROW *Corvus brachyrhynchos* Brehm

Status. Common resident and migrant, congregating in winter flocks, especially in SE.

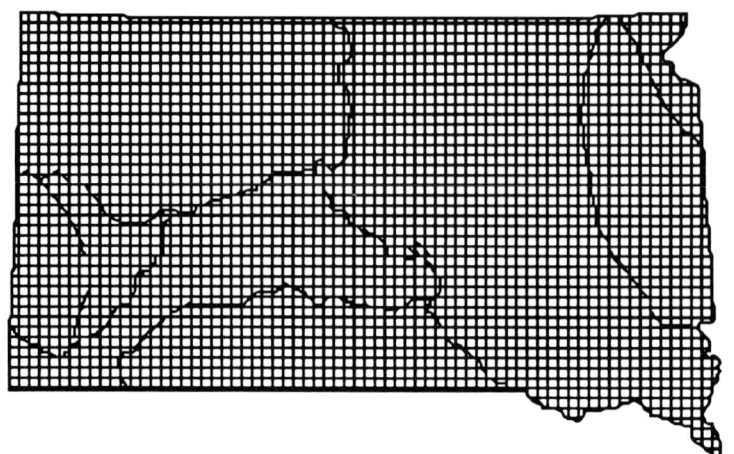

Habitat. Forest and woodland with adjacent open country.

Spring migration. Mar – early Apr. Definite migration dates are difficult to determine, except when large flocks move north (e.g., 11 Mar 1970, Sanborn Co., 80–150 (Harris).

Nesting. Early Apr – Jun.
Earliest dates:
31 Mar 1911, Douglas Co, nest with 4 eggs (Walker)
9 Apr 1985, Turner Co., carrying nesting material (Anderson in Seasons 1985d)
14 Apr 1940, Wilmot (Harris)
Latest dates:
24 May 1941, Wilmot (Harris)
1 Jun 1972, Corson Co., nest with 4 young (Hall in Seasons 1972c)
14 Jun 1985, Newton Hills SP, 2 fledged young (Springer)

Fall migration. First half of Oct. Migration dates are difficult to ascertain except when large flocks are obviously flying south, as on 2 October 1977, Hughes Co., 400 (Harris).

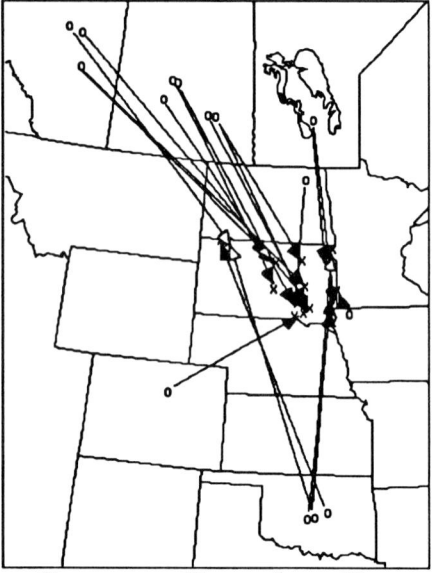

Common Crow banding recoveries.

Winter. Often reported, occasionally in 100's, on CBC throughout the state.
Other records:
13 Dec 1980, Brookings Co., 134 (Harris in Seasons 1981b)
8 Jan 1981, Gregory Co., 250 in scattered flocks (Steffen in Seasons 1981b)

COMMON RAVEN *Corvus corax* Linnaeus

Status. Accidental. Probably regular resident prior to the disappearance of the buffalo. Plentiful at the Great Bend of the Missouri River in 1853 (Cooper (1860). In summer 1874, "observed in the Black Hills" by Custer Expedition (Grinnell 1875); observed "almost every day" and "bred on many of the lofty buttes that we passed," but the locations are uncertain since much of the route was in North Dakota. Wintered commonly before 1880 in Clay Co., but disappeared thereafter (Agersborg 1885). No recent breeding records.

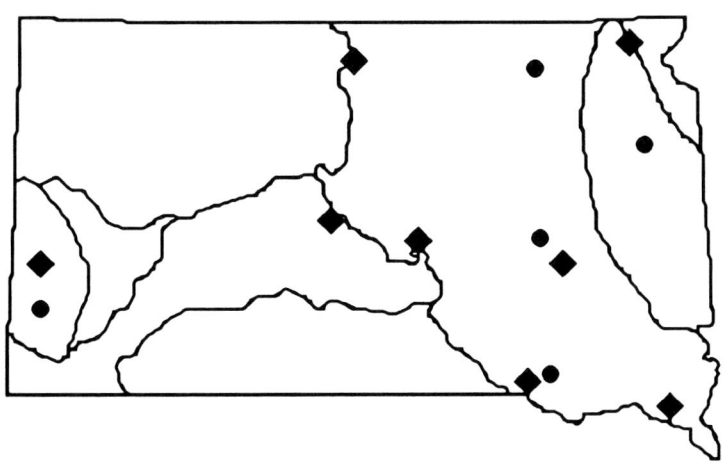

Older records:
  5 Oct 1856, Ft. Pierre and 18 Oct 1856, Ft. Randall (Hayden in Baird 1858); hovered over travelers in the Badlands (Hayden 1863)
  1872–1873, near Mobridge, seen infrequently (Hoffman 1877)
  9 Jul 1876, near Ft. Sisseton, 2 young birds (McChesney 1877)
  Fall 1906, Sanborn Co., "tolerably common" (Visher 1913a)
Recent records:
  19 Aug 1934, over Silvertop Peak, 3 birds flying and calling (Cahalane in Pettingill and Whitney 1965)
  Oct 1957, N of Wolsey, injured (R. Dahlgren)
  3 Oct and 9 Nov 1987, Brown Co. (Montgomery; photographed by Waldstein)
  12 Nov 1954, Dry Lake, specimen (W. Rose)
  24 Nov 1967, Lake Andes, dead (Olsen 1968)

PARIDAE: Titmice

BLACK-CAPPED CHICKADEE *Parus atricapillus* Linnaeus

Status. Common resident. Local populations may be irregularly migratory, as has been found in other parts of the country (Bull 1974).

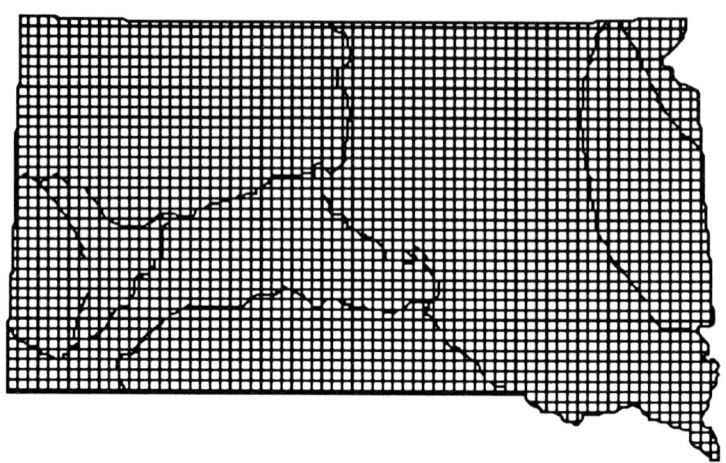

Habitat. Woodlands, thickets, and towns.
Nesting. Late Apr – mid-Jul.
Earliest dates:
   24 Apr 1970, Sanborn Co., carrying nesting material into hole (Harris)
   28 Apr 1988, Day Co., constructing nest in bluebird box (Skadsen in Seasons 1988d)
   7 May 1988, Brookings Co., young fledged from wren box (Kieckhefer in Seasons 1988d)
Latest dates:
   2 Jul 1970, Harding Co., adults feeding 2 young (Springer)
   4 Jul 1967, along Harney Peak Trail, nest in hollow aspen (Whitney)
   14 Jul 1978, S Slim Buttes, 2 adults and 4 fledged young (Springer)

MOUNTAIN CHICKADEE *Parus gambeli* Ridgway

Status. Casual visitor in Black Hills. No specimens.
Records.
- 11–16 Apr 1977, Rapid City (Brodsky in Seasons 1977c)
- 19 Nov 1966, Rapid City (Bachmann, confirmation by Whitney (Anon. 1967)) and photographed in Feb 1967 (Rose)
- 23 Dec 1972–3 Jan 1973, Rapid City, regular at feeder (Baylor 1973)

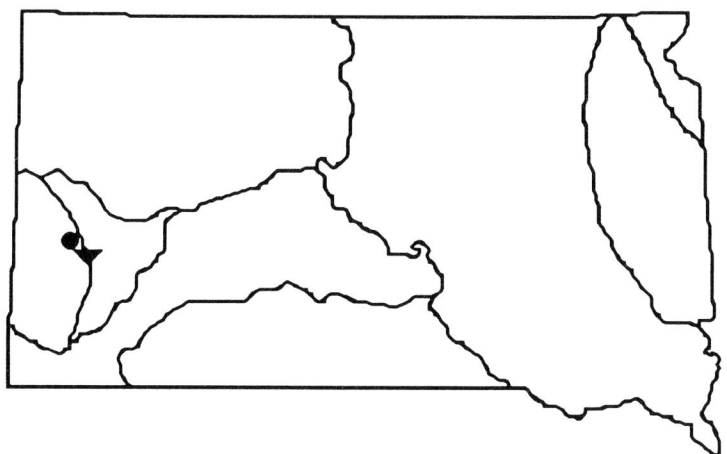

BOREAL CHICKADEE *Parus hudsonicus* Forster

Status. Casual. No specimens.
Records:
- 2–3 Nov 1972, Deuel Co. (Harris 1972)
- 12–18 Nov 1972, Brookings Co., banded and photographed (Holden 1972)

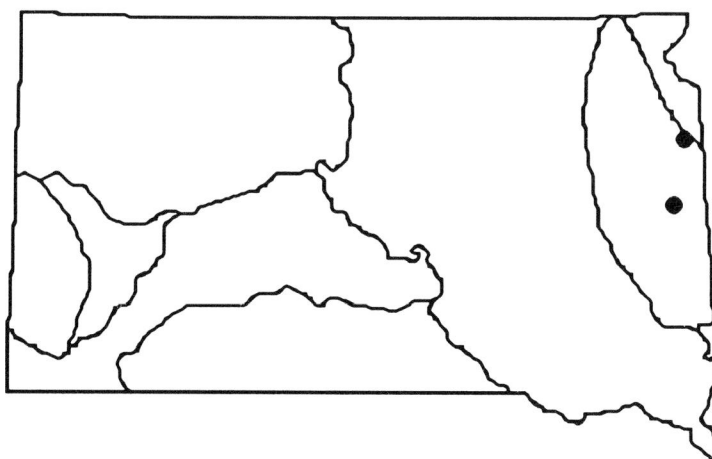

TITMICE

TUFTED TITMOUSE *Parus bicolor* Linnaeus

Status. Casual spring, fall and winter visitor, in E quarter of state. Accidental breeder. No specimens.

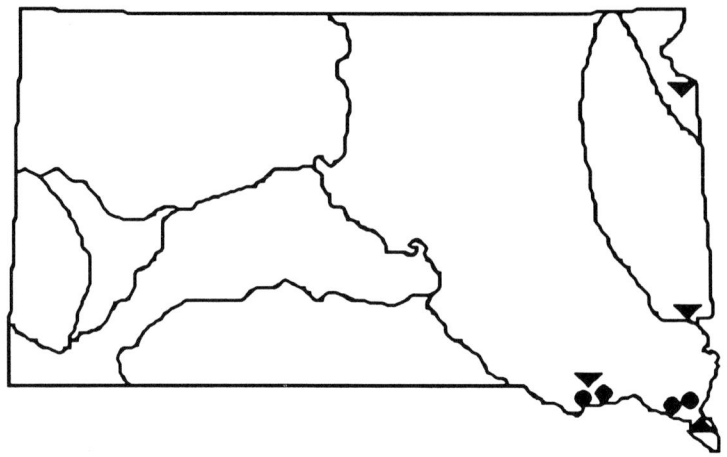

Habitat. Woodland and towns.
Nesting.
  Only record:
    27 Aug 1931, Union Co., adults feeding nearly full-grown young (Youngworth in Stephens et al. 1955).
Other records:
  23 Jan 1977, Yankton (Wilcox 1977)
  15 May 1925, Union Co. (Spiker in Stephens et al. 1955)
  17 May 1960, Union Co. (Youngworth)
  21 May 1922, Yankton (Halverson)
  18 Oct 1921, Yankton (Halverson)
  20 Nov 1962–21 Feb 1963, Big Stone City, banded 27 Nov (Elliott 1963b, 1963c)
Winter.
  CBC report: Sioux Falls.

SITTIDAE: Nuthatches

RED-BREASTED NUTHATCH *Sitta canadensis* Linnaeus

Status. Common migrant and regular but uncommon winter visitor E. Common permanent resident in Black Hills. Fairly common resident in buttes of Harding Co. Nests in Pine Ridge Indian Reservation (Visher 1912a and Homoya).

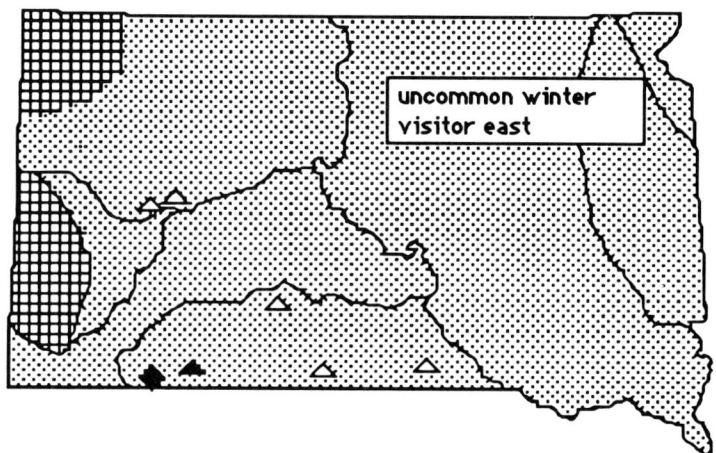

Habitat. Breeding: pine and spruce forests, occasionally in deciduous trees. Wintering: pine forests and deciduous stands. Visits feeders.

Spring migration.
   Latest dates (E River):
      22 May 1985, Brown Co. (Prisbe in Seasons 1985c)
      24 May 1985, Codington Co. (Gilman in Seasons 1985c)
      30 May 1990, Brown Co., banded (Tallman)

Nesting. May – Jul. Recorded, but with no evidence of nesting, late Jun 1983 and 1 July 1987, E Meade Co. (Tallman et al. 1983, Springer), late Jul 1985, Jackson Co. (Graupmann in Seasons 1985d), 12 Jul 1969, Todd Co. (Timken), and 19 and 22 Jul 1980, Gregory Co. (Steffen 1981a).
   Earliest dates:
      19 Apr 1963, Steamboat Rock Campground, pair copulating (Pettingill and Whitney 1965)
      21 May 1988, Meade Co., incubating (E. Miller)
      25 May 1985, Harding Co., birds carrying food into nest hole (Martin in Berkey 1985)
   Latest dates:
      5 Jul 1987, Harding Co., pair feeding 3 fledged young (Springer)
      7 Jul 1956, Palmer Gulch, pair feeding young (Eastman in Pettingill and Whitney 1965)
      18 Jul 1987, Rapid City, 4 fledged young (Eckmann)

Fall migration. Last week of Aug – middle of Oct. August records at Aberdeen of birds carrying food and of very young birds suggest but do not confirm breeding in the area (Tallman).

Earliest dates (E River):
  14 Aug 1985, Aberdeen, immature banded (Tallman in Seasons 1986a)
  22 Aug 1981, Aberdeen (Tallman in Seasons 1982a)

WHITE-BREASTED NUTHATCH *Sitta carolinensis* Latham

Status. Fairly permanent common resident; breeding status in NW unknown. Records from Cave Hills in summer (Griffiths) and Prairie City in winter (Hinds).

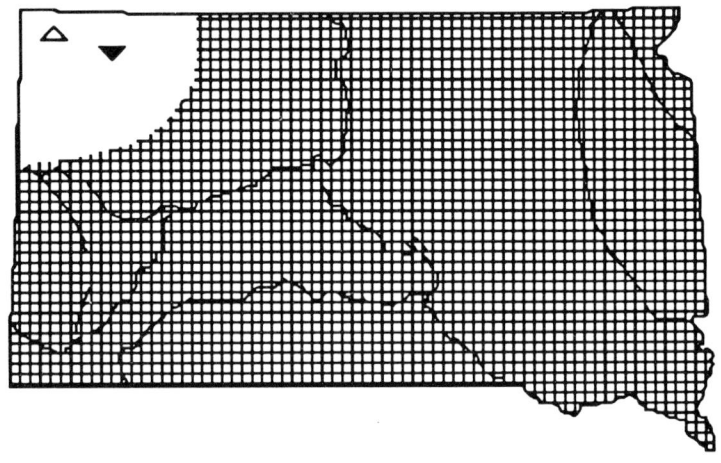

Habitat. Woodlands and towns.
Nesting. May – Jul.
  Earliest dates:
    15 Apr 1987, Wind Cave NP, excavating hole (Hetlet and Laycock)
    3 May 1988, Meade Co., pair at nest box (Schad)
    10 May 1969, S of Hill City, carrying material into hole in aspen (Rose)
  Latest dates:
    7 Jul 1956, Palmer Gulch, parents feeding juvenile (Eastman in Pettingill and Whitney 1965)
    19 Jul 1958, Jewel Cave NM, adults feeding juvenile (Carter 1958b)
    25 Jul 1989, Black Hawk, young fledged (Schad)

PYGMY NUTHATCH *Sitta pygmaea* Vigors

Status. Uncommon permanent resident in Black Hills (but status in higher Black Hills uncertain). Populations fluctuate yearly (Rosche 1982) but recently reported more regularly.

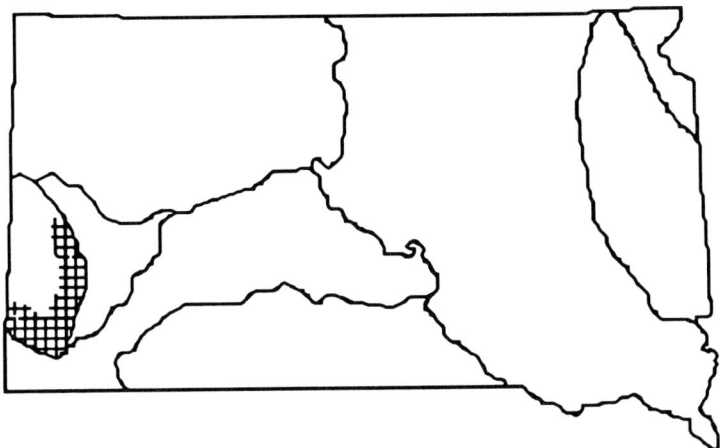

Habitat. Pine forests.

Nesting. Regular in S Black Hills.

Earliest dates:
24 Mar 1983, Fall River Co., excavating hole; 29 May, feeding young in nest (Peterson 1983)
7 Apr 1987, Custer Co., pair at nest cavity (Peterson in Seasons 1987d)

Latest dates:
12 Jul 1968, Custer Co., 2 adults and 8 fledged young (Weaver 1982)
22 Jul 1948, near Box Elder Creek, Loveland Canyon, adult female and immature collected (Dilger in Pettingill and Whitney 1965)

CERTHIIDAE: Creepers

BROWN CREEPER *Certhia americana* Bonaparte

Status. Uncommon permanent resident in Black Hills. Fairly common winter resident and migrant statewide. Formerly uncommon to rare resident in Clay Co. (Agersborg 1885, Visher 1915), in Sioux Falls area (Larson 1925), and in midsummer 1904 in Gregory Co. (Jones 1908). Present E River breeding status unknown.

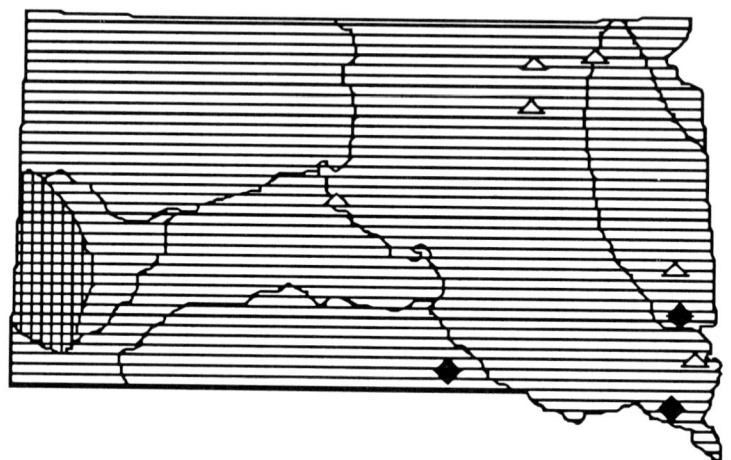

Habitat. Pine and spruce forests in Black Hills. Deciduous forests and towns in winter.

Spring migration. Apr.
Latest dates:
6 May 1984, Roberts Co. (Harris)
8 May 1983, Day Co. (Husmann in Seasons 1983c)
16 May 1984, Codington Co. (Harris)

Nesting. Mid-May – Mid-Jul in the Black Hills.
Dates:
13 Jun 1980, Rapid City, 2 broods (Kovarik fide Whitney in Seasons 1980d)
18 Jun 1980, Custer State Park, adults feeding young (Whitney)
13 Jul 1971, near Rochford, feeding young (Baylor et al. 1972)
E River breeding season records:
5 May 1985, Marshall Co., 2 singing and probably in courtship (Harris, Holden, and Meyer)
5 Jun 1972, Farm Island, 1 heard singing (Harris)
11 Jul 1989, Brown Co. (Stanford in Seasons 1989d)
17 Jun 1987, Lincoln Co. (Rogers 1989)
20 Jul 1976, Spink Co. along James River (Hill in Seasons 1976d)
10 Aug 1988, Brookings Co. (Froiland in Seasons 1989a)

Fall migration. Oct.
  Earliest dates:
    18 Sep 1987, Minnehaha Co. (Hoeger in Seasons 1988a)
    19 Sep 1987, Brown Co. (Prisbe in Seasons 1988a)
    27 Sep 1981, Aberdeen (SDOU in Montgomery 1981)
Winter. Fairly common winter resident

TROGLODYTIDAE: Wrens

ROCK WREN *Salpinctes obsoletus* (Say)

Status. Common summer resident in N Cave Hills, Slim Buttes (Baylor and Rosine 1970), Short Pines, Black Hills, and Badlands. Breeding season records near the Oahe Dam and elsewhere along Missouri River. Rare or unreported elsewhere. Accidental winter.

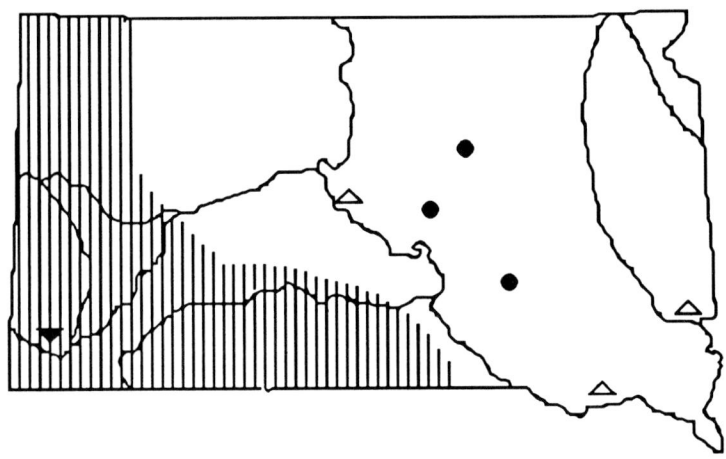

Habitat. Plains to high mountains, rocky outcrops, rough cliff walls, and sharply eroded slopes, usually in relatively dry locations.
Spring migration. Late Apr and first half of May.
  Earliest dates:
    18 Apr 1972, Pennington Co. (Whitney)
    18 Apr 1985, Jackson Co. (Graupmann in Seasons 1985c)
    24 Apr 1986, Pennington Co. (Whitney)
    24 Apr 1987, Jackson Co. (Graupmann in Seasons 1987c)
Nesting. Late May – Jul.
  Earliest dates:
    13 May 1987, Shannon Co., nesting (Springer and Rosche)
    13–17 Jun 1948, Dark Canyon, nest with young (Dilger in Pettingill and Whitney 1965)
    21 Jun 1975, Pennington Co., pair building nest (Green in Seasons 1975c)

Latest dates:
- 19 Jul 1958, Rapid City, occupied nest but contents not determined (Brodsky in Pettingill and Whitney 1965)
- 27 Jul 1975, Badlands, young being fed (Serr and Mortimer in Seasons 1975c)
- 27 Jul 1979, Wind Cave NP, newly fledged young (Jervis)

Fall migration. Sep.
Latest dates:
- 15 Sep, McVey Burn (Pettingill and Whitney 1965)
- 22 Sep 1961, Rapid City, specimen (Behrens)
- 8 Oct 1984, Pennington Co. (Skadsen and Skadsen in Seasons 1985a)

Winter.
Records:
Winter to 4 Feb 1935, Wind Cave NP (Cahalane in Anon. 1962)

E River Records:
- 10 May 1986, Faulk Co. (Melius)
- 17 May 1959, Yankton Co. (Findley 1959)
- 18 May 1968, Hyde Co. (Jonkel and Harris)
- 23 May 1968, Jerauld Co. (Harris)
- 7 Jul 1931, Yankton Co. (Youngworth 1932a)
- 20 Jul 1924, Minnehaha Co. (Bent 1948)

CANYON WREN *Catherpes mexicanus* (Swainson)

Status. Uncommon, but local, permanent resident in Black Hills.

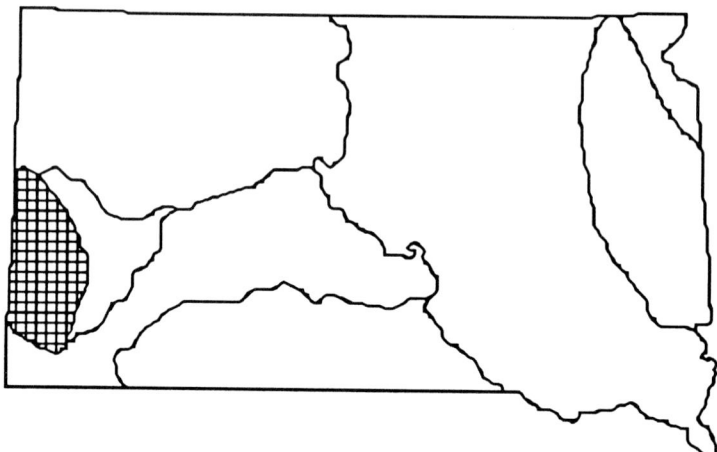

Habitat. Fairly well sheltered vertical cliff and canyon walls, usually at least 50 to 100 feet high.

Migration. Last third of Mar and first half of Apr and Oct – Nov. Early and late dates may be of wintering birds.

Nesting. Late May – Jul (Pettingill and Whitney 1965).
  Earliest date:
    1 June 1981, Fall River Co., adults feeding young (Hall in Seasons 1981d)
  Latest dates:
    29 Jul 1969, Fall River Co., pair with 5 fledged young (Weaver 1982)
    11 Aug 1965, Stagebarn Canyon, an adult carrying food (Whitney)
Winter. Numerous winter records from various canyons in the Black Hills.
  CBC reports:
    Hot Springs and Rapid City.

CAROLINA WREN *Thryothorus ludovicianus* (Latham)

Status. Casual visitor, most records in fall and winter. The basis for Bent's (1948) statement that this wren breeds north to Yankton Co. is unknown.

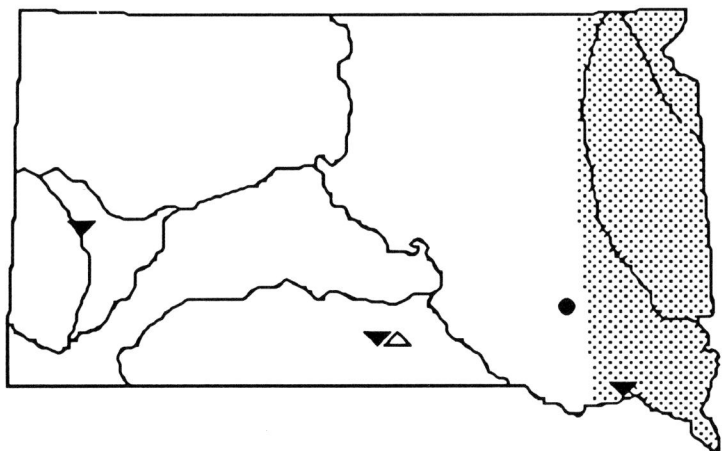

Spring migration.
  Only dates:
    27 Apr 1978, Yankton Co. (Hall in Seasons 1978c)
    9 May 1986, Deuel Co. (Harris in Seasons 1986c)
    10 May 1958, Mitchell (Baylor)
Summer record.
    1 Aug 1955, Winner, banded (Wagar)
Fall migration.
  Earliest date:
    17 Sep 1956, Milbank, banded (Elliott)
  Latest date:
    1 Nov 1974 – 18 Dec 1974, Brookings Co. (Edie 1975)
Winter.
  CBC record:
    Yankton.

242 WRENS

Other reports:
26 Dec 1965, Rapid City, specimen (Hyde)
29 Jan 1958, Winner, banded (Wagar)

BEWICK'S WREN *Thryomanes bewickii* (Audubon)

Status. Accidental.
Only record:
3 Dec 1950 – 26 Feb 1951, Sioux Falls (Krause 1951)

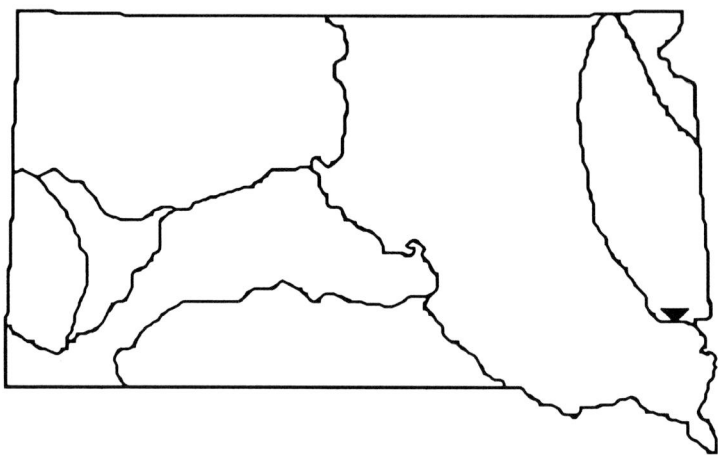

HOUSE WREN *Troglodytes aedon* Vieillot

Status. Common to abundant summer resident; status uncertain in higher Black Hills.

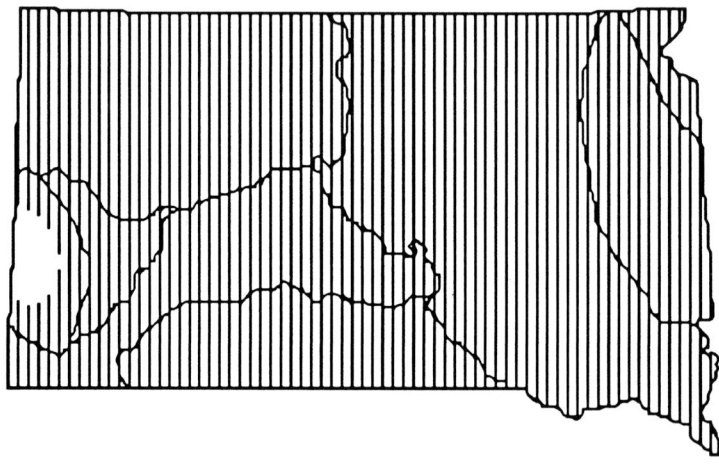

Habitat. Thickets, woodlands, and towns.
Spring migration. First half of May.
  Earliest dates:
    15 Apr 1982, Yankton Co. (Anderson in Seasons 1982c)
    15 Apr 1989, Brown Co. (Stanford in Seasons 1989c)
    17 Apr 1975, Brookings Co. (Edie in Seasons 1975b)
Nesting. Mid-May – Aug.
  Earliest dates:
    15 May 1959, Rapid City (Behrens)
    18 May 1988, Pennington Co., building nest (Lester)
    20 May 1982, Wind Cave NP, nesting (Laycook)
  Latest dates:
    5 Aug 1914, Lincoln Co., 5 young left nest (Mallory 1915)
    13 Aug 1988, Lincoln Co., adults with fledged young (Springer)
    28 Aug 1951, Rapid City, fledged young (Behrens in Pettingill and Whitney 1965)
Fall migration. Mid Sep.
  Latest dates:
    8 Oct 1962, Brookings Co., banded (Holden)
    8 Oct 1969, Sanborn Co. (Harris)
    9 Oct 1981, Brown Co., banded (Tallman)
    11 Oct 1989, Minnehaha Co. (Hoeger in Seasons 1990a)

House Wren banding recoveries

WINTER WREN *Troglodytes troglodytes* (Linnaeus)

Status. Rare to uncommon spring and fall migrant and winter resident. Recent evidence of possible breeding in N Black Hills.

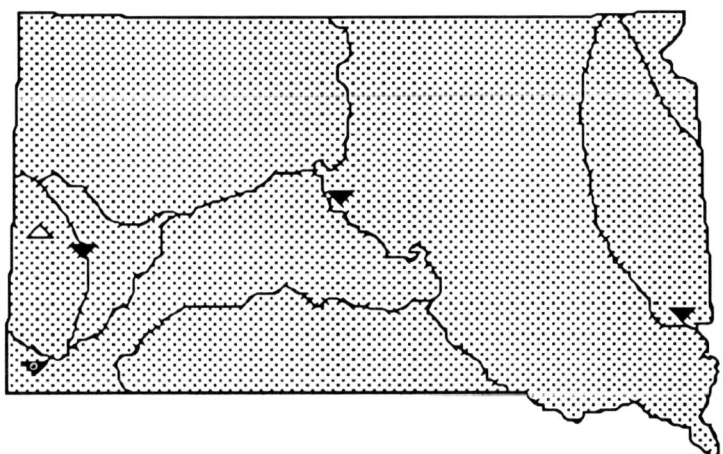

Habitat. Thickets, particularly along streams, fallen logs, and stream drift piles, town yards and gardens.
Spring migration. Late Apr.
Latest dates:
19 May 1907, Minnehaha Co. (Larson 1925)
22–23 May 1965, Farm Island, banded (Holden 1966)
26 May 1978, Yankton Co. (Hall in Seasons 1978b)
Summer records.
4 Jun 1979, Black Fox Campground (Holden 1980a)
26 Jun 1990, Black Fox Campground (Peterson and Peterson in Seasons 1990d)
29 Jun 1978, Lawrence Co., 1 singing (Rogers 1981)
Fall migration. Last half of Sep – Oct.
Earliest dates:
31 Aug 1984, Aberdeen, cat kill (Prisbe in Seasons 1985a)
4 Sep 1955, Sioux Falls (Krause 1955b)
9 Sep 1981, Aberdeen, specimen (Tallman)
Winter. Scattered winter records. Regular only near warm water springs in Fall River Co. but survival there may be low since few Feb and no Mar records (Rosche 1982).
CBC reports:
Pierre, Rapid City, and Sioux Falls.

SEDGE WREN *Cistothorus platensis* Latham

Status. Locally common summer resident E. Unrecorded W except at Lacreek NWR.

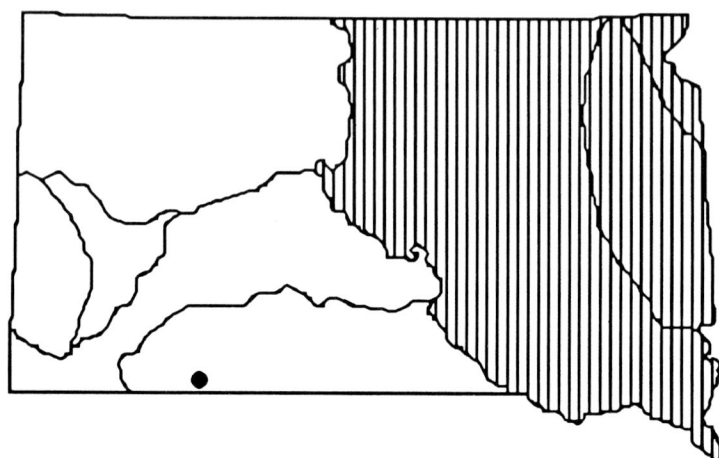

Habitat. Damp meadows and grassy marshes.
Spring migration. Mid May.
Earliest dates:
24 Apr 1964, Hyde Co. (Harter)
28 Apr 1990, Minnehaha Co. (Skadsen in Seasons 1990c)
29 Apr 1986, Sanborn Co. (Rogers in Seasons 1986c)
Nesting. No nest records, despite numerous E River summer records. Males sing during fall migration.

Fall migration. Sep.
  Latest dates:
    19 Oct 1986, Sanborn Co. (Rogers in Seasons 1987a)
    25 Oct 1982, Yankton Co. (Hall in Seasons 1983a)
    27 Oct 1986, Sanborn Co. (Rogers in Seasons 1987a)

MARSH WREN *Cistothorus palustris* (Wilson)

Status. Abundant summer resident E in areas of suitable habitat. Uncommon and local W. Absent in most of the NW, but recorded in Harding Co. (Springer). Rare winter straggler, but regular in SW.

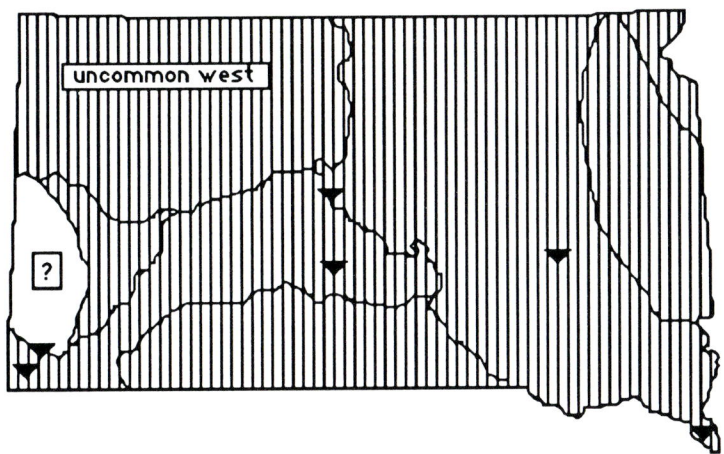

Habitat. Large marshes with tall, dense vegetation.
Spring migration. May.
  Earliest dates:
    27 Mar 1986, Rapid City (Whitney in Seasons 1986c)
    5 Apr 1967, Rapid City (Whitney)
    17 Apr 1987, Sanborn Co. (Rogers in Seasons 1987c)
Nesting. Late May – Jul.
  Earliest date:
    9 Jun 1968, Sanborn Co., Long Lake, nest with 1 egg (Harris)
  Latest dates:
    13 Jul 1967, Bullhead Lake, several empty nests (Harris)
    17 Jul 1910, Douglas Co., nest with 6 eggs (Walker)
    8 Aug 1967, Sanborn Co., adult carrying food, young calling nearby not located (Harris).
Fall migration. Oct. Nov dates possibly refer to wintering birds.
Winter. Regular along warm water stream edges in Fall River Co, especially along Cascade Creek below Cascade Springs (Rosche 1982).
  CBC record:
    Hot Springs

Other records:
  16 Dec 1951, Jefferson (Felton 1952)
  5–20 Nov and 21 Dec 1952, Union Co. (Stephens et al. 1955)
  21 Jan 1983, Sanborn Co. (Rogers and McLaird in Seasons 1983b)
  25 Jan 1976, Jones Co. (Hill in Seasons 1976b)
  3 Feb 1980, Farm Island (Backlund)

CINCLIDAE: Dippers

AMERICAN DIPPER *Cinclus mexicanus* Swainson

Status. Fairly common but local permanent resident in Spearfish Canyon, the Rapid Creek drainage, and intervening streams. Absent elsewhere.

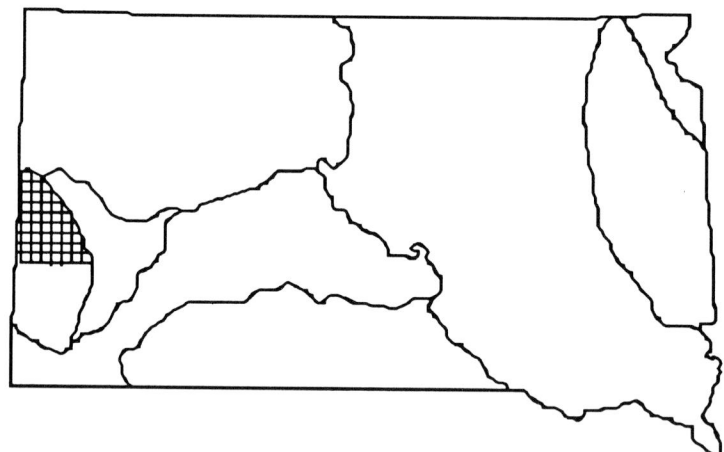

Habitat. Swift mountain streams.
Nesting. Late Apr – Jul.
  Earliest dates:
    23 Mar 1989, Roughlock Falls, pair building nest (Backlund 1989)
    13 Apr 1987, Rapid Creek, pair, 1 at nest (Melius)
    24 Apr 1965, Spearfish Canyon, pair at nest (Springer and Rosine)
  Latest dates:
    15 Jun 1928, Dark Canyon, adult incubating eggs (Lee in Whitney 1955)
    5 Jul 1926, Rapid Creek above Pactola, nest with 4 eggs (McIntosh in Whitney 1955)
    17 Aug 1975, Spearfish Canyon, 3 family groups, each containing fledged immature (Whitney)

MUSCICAPIDAE: Kinglets and Thrushes

GOLDEN-CROWNED KINGLET *Regulus satrapa* (Linnaeus)

Status. Uncommon permanent resident at higher elevations in Black Hills. Elsewhere, common spring and fall migrant. Uncommon in winter.

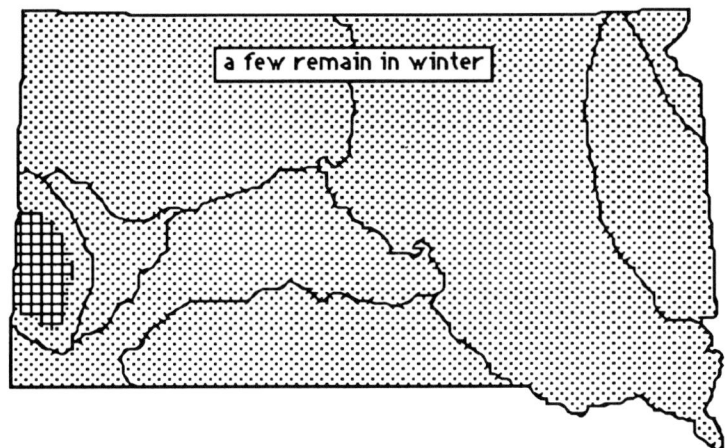

a few remain in winter

Habitat. Breeding: spruce, and occasionally pine, forests.
Migration: any type of woody vegetation.
Spring migration. Apr. Some early spring birds may be wintering individuals.
  Latest dates:
    17 May 1968, Hyde Co. (Harter)
    23 May 1953, Spearfish (Bennett in Haight 1953)
Nesting.
  Earliest date:
    9 Jun 1979, Custer Co., pair building nest (Bjerke in Seasons 1979d)
  Latest dates:
    8 Jul 1962, South Canyon, fully-grown young collected (Dilger in Pettingill and Whitney 1965)
    14 Jul 1959, near Rochford, adults carrying food (Moriarty in Pettingill and Whitney 1965)
Fall migration. Oct. Late dates may be wintering birds.
  Earliest dates:
    20 Sep 1986, Brown Co. (Tallman in Seasons 1987a)
    21 Sep 1988, Brown Co., banded (Tallman in Seasons 1989a)
    27 Sep 1981, Brown Co. (Montgomery 1981)
Winter. A few winter in scattered areas across the state. Generally found on CBC at 1 to 6 localities across state.

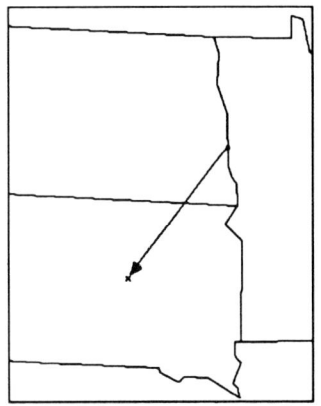

Golden-crowned Kinglet banding recoveries

KINGLETS AND THRUSHES

RUBY-CROWNED KINGLET *Regulus calendula* (Linnaeus)

Status. Fairly common summer resident in higher elevations of Black Hills. Common spring and fall migrant statewide. Rare winter.

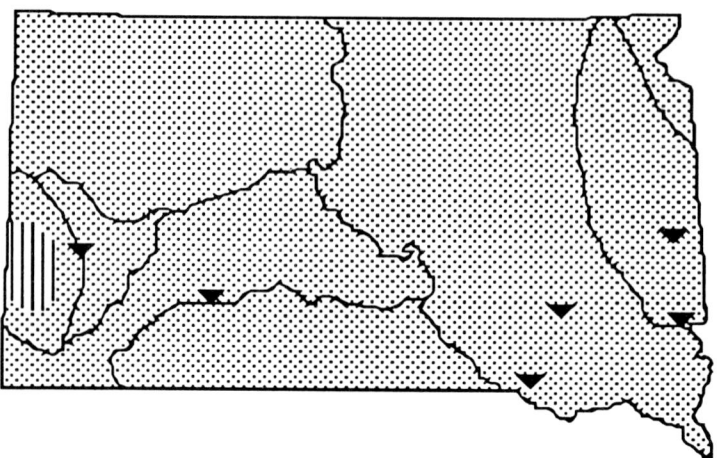

Habitat. Breeding: spruce forests. Migration: woody areas.

Spring migration. First half of May in Black Hills. Apr and first 3 weeks of May in the plains.

Earliest dates:
  22 Mar 1987, Minnehaha Co. (Hoeger in Seasons 1987c)
  28 Mar 1938, Alexandria (Wagar 1958)
  31 Mar 1981, Brookings Co. (Boecke in Seasons 1981c)
  31 Mar 1986, Codington Co. (Gilman in Seasons 1986c)

Latest dates:
  20 May 1974, Deuel Co. (Harris)
  20 May 1974, Grant Co. (Harris)
  21 May 1931, Union Co. (Youngworth)
  21 May 1990, Moody Co. (Wells in Seasons 1990c)

Nesting. Jun and Jul.

Only dates:
  8 Jul 1962, adults carrying food at Black Fox Campground (Pettingill and Whitney 1965)
  20 Jul 1988, Custer Co., feeding cowbird nestling (R. Peterson)

Fall migration. Sep and first half of Oct. Late dates may refer to wintering birds.

Earliest dates:
  31 Aug 1961, Hyde Co. (Harter 1962)
  2 Sep 1988, Deuel Co. (Harris in Seasons 1989a)
  4 Sep 1977, Hyde Co. (Harter in Seasons 1978a)

Winter.
CBC reports:
Badlands, Brookings, Lake Andes, Mitchell, Rapid City, and Sioux Falls.

BLUE-GRAY GNATCATCHER *Polioptila caerulea* (Linnaeus)

Status. Casual visitor. Rare summer resident in SE. A specimen taken in 1872 or 1873, Grand River Agency (Hoffman 1877). Williams photographed 1 in Edmunds Co. on 7 May 1988 (Springer 1990), and Harris (in Seasons 1990a) reported 1 from Deuel Co. on 24 Aug 1989.

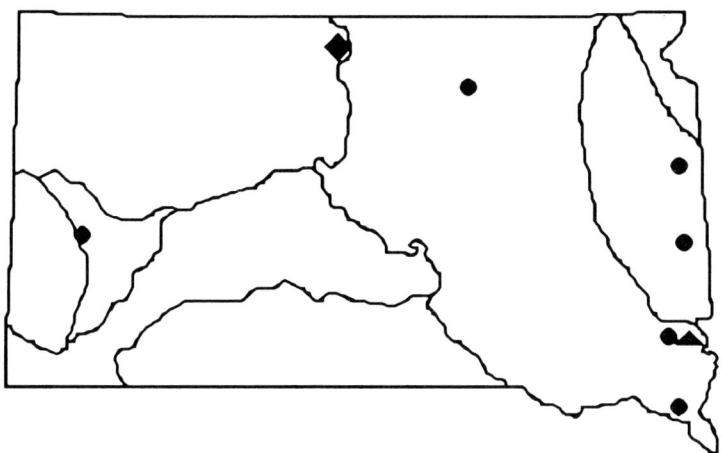

Habitat. Deciduous forests.
Spring Migration.
Earliest dates:
28 Apr 1989, Minnehaha Co. (Skadsen in Seasons 1989c)
29 Apr 1979, Rapid City (Baker 1979)
30 Apr 1989, Moody Co. (Reinking in Seasons 1989c)
Nesting.
Only record:
4–15 May 1986, Lincoln Co., nest built but quickly abandoned (Skadsen 1987)
Fall migration.
Latest dates:
1 Sep 1985, Lincoln Co. (Springer and Skadsen 1986)
12 Sep 1985, Clay Co. (Anderson in Seasons 1986a)
30 Oct 1976, Rapid City (Whitney 1977)

EASTERN BLUEBIRD *Sialia sialis* (Linnaeus)

Status. Uncommon summer resident, including Black Hills. Slightly more common from James River Valley E. Rare winter.

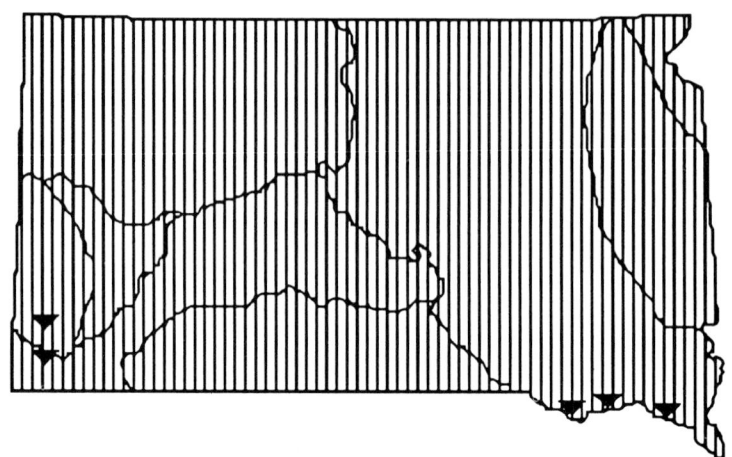

Habitat. Farmyards, and woodland edges.

Spring migration. Last week of Mar – Apr. Early dates may be wintering birds, especially in S.
  Earliest dates:
    3 Mar 1983, Deuel Co. (Harris)
    3 Mar 1988, Yankton Co. (Hall)
    5 Mar 1985, Yankton Co. (Kronner in Seasons 1985c)

Nesting. Late Apr – Jul.
  Earliest dates:
    16 Apr 1987, Day Co., nest with 2 eggs (D. Skadsen)
    5 May 1987, Day Co., nest with 6 young (D. Skadsen)
    14 May 1986, Rapid City, pair checking box (Eckmann)
  Latest dates:
    22 Jul 1986, Yankton Co., adults with fledged young (Hall)
    30 Jul 1986, Yankton Co., adults with fledged young (Hall)
    14 Aug 1987, Day Co., nest with 3 young (D. Skadsen)

Fall migration. Oct. Late dates may refer to wintering birds.

Winter. Present in Yankton Co. 50% of years 1975–1985.
  CBC reports:
    Hot Springs, Springfield, Vermillion, and Yankton.
  Other records:
    24 Dec 1934, Wind Cave NP (Cahalane in Pettingill and Whitney 1965)

MOUNTAIN BLUEBIRD *Sialia currucoides* (Bechstein)

Status. Very common summer resident in Black Hills at all elevations, common in Badlands and in Slim Buttes and Cave Hills of Harding Co. Also breeds locally near pines elsewhere in W plains. Rare migrant to E border of the state, especially in spring. Winter locally in Badlands and similar habitat SW.

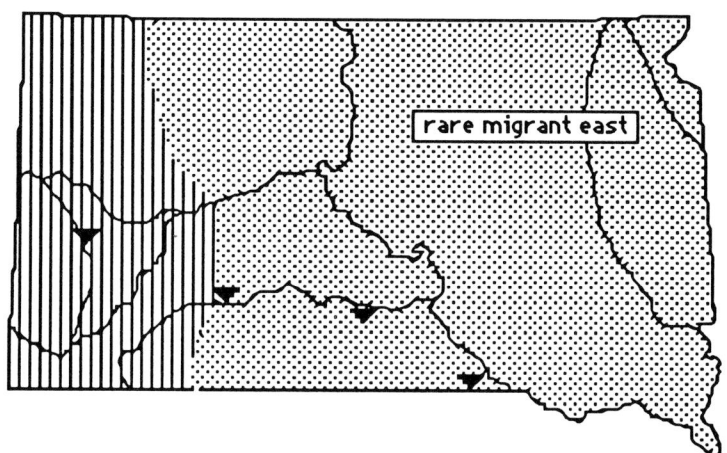

Habitat. Breeding: Open areas adjacent to pine forests; in Badlands in wide canyons with some trees. Often nests in bird houses. Migration: most open areas with suitable perches and occasional trees.

Spring migration. Mid-Mar – Apr.
  Earliest dates:
    19 Feb 1982, Fall River Co. (Rosche in Seasons 1982c)
    23 Feb 1989, Custer Co. (Parker in Seasons 1989b)
    24 Feb 1981, Pennington Co. (Laber in Seasons 1981c)

Nesting. Early May – Jul. Records for Rapid City cited by Pettingill and Whitney (1965) range from early nest building on 4 Apr 1963 to a late date for young in nest on 5 Aug 1959.

Fall migration. Mid-Aug – mid-Oct.
  Latest dates:
    18 Oct 1963, Rapid City (Pettingill and Whitney 1965)
    21 Oct 1980, Meade Co. (Miller in Seasons 1981c)
    2 Nov 1987, Pennington Co. (Whitney in Seasons 1987a)

E River records:
  Spring records range from 6 Mar 1987, Walworth Co. (Tallman) to 23 Apr, Aurora Co. (Harris).
  Summer record:
    14 Jul 1984, near Pierre, female (Riis in Seasons 1984d)

Mountain Bluebird banding recoveries

Fall records:
 15 Oct 1974, Grant Co. (Harris)
 15 Oct 1967, Marshall Co. (Harris)
 2 Nov 1967, Sanborn Co. (Harris)
 9 Nov 1979, Brown Co. (Montgomery and Tallman 1979)

Winter.
 CBC reports:
 Badlands.
 Other records:
 14 Dec 1972, Gregory Co. (Steffen 1973)
 26 Jan 1967, Mellette Co. (Springer)
 31 Jan 1978, Rapid City (Johnson in Seasons 1978b)

TOWNSEND'S SOLITAIRE *Myadestes townsendi* (Audubon)

Status. Fairly common resident in Black Hills, breeding at higher elevations and wintering lower. Observed 11 Jun 1982 near Edgemont (Rosche). Irregular migrant and winter visitor across the state.

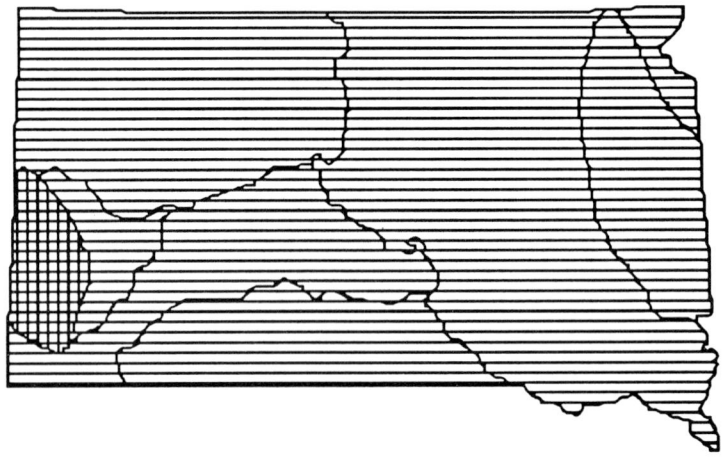

Habitat. Breeding: pine and spruce forest. Wintering: woodlands and shelterbelts.

Nesting. May into Jul.
 Earliest dates:
 4 May 1965, near Rapid City, pair carrying nesting material (Whitney)
 5 May 1989, Pennington Co., building nest (Barnes)
 17 May 1946, Horse Thief Lake, specimen containing large egg (Sutton in Pettingill and Whitney 1965)
 Latest dates:
 13 Jul 1971, near Terry Peak, nest with 4 eggs (Baylor et al. 1972)
 18 Jul 1971, near Terry Peak, nest with 4 eggs (Baylor et al. 1972)
 27 Jul 1911, near Minnekahta, fledgling (Visher 1913b)

E River records: Numerous but scattered records exist, ranging from 22 Sep 1986, Brown Co. (Ernst in Seasons 1987a) to 8 Apr 1958, Brookings Co. (Holden 1958).

VEERY *Catharus fuscescens* (Stephens)

Status. Local summer resident, common in Spearfish Canyon and Sica Hollow; rare elsewhere in Black Hills and NE. Formerly rare summer resident in Clay Co. (Agersborg 1885, Visher 1915) and was found in summer in Sioux Falls area (Larson 1912, 1925) and at Faulkton (Norton). Uncommon migrant elsewhere.

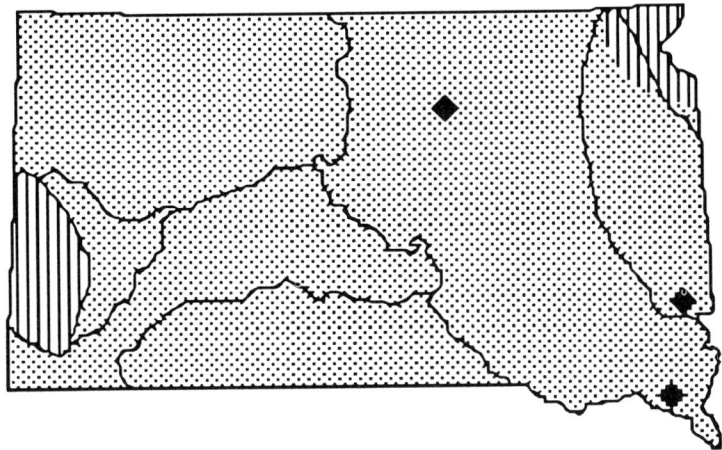

Habitat. Dense deciduous thickets.
Spring migration. Last 3 weeks of May.
  Earliest dates:
    1 May 1978, Hyde Co. (Harter in Seasons 1978c)
    2 May 1983, Brookings Co. (Vaa in Seasons 1983c)
    6 May 1988, Minnehaha Co. (Skadsen in Seasons 1989c)
  Latest dates:
    6 Jun 1983, Jackson Co., banded (Graupmann in Seasons 1983d)
    8 Jun 1981, Bon Homme Co. (Rosche in Seasons 1981d)

Nesting. Jun, probably into Jul.
  Earliest dates:
    11 Jun 1940, Sodak Park, nest (Harris 1963)
    15 Jun 1974, Sica Hollow, nest with four eggs (Harris)
    17 Jun 1966, Sica Hollow, nest with 3 young about 1 day old (Harris)
  Latest date:
    2 Jul 1971, Sica Hollow, nest recently abandoned (M. Harris)
Fall migration. Early Sep. Fewer records than spring.
  Earliest dates:
    16 Aug 1933, Brown Co., banded (Mewaldt)
    28 Aug 1969, Highmore (Harter)
    29 Aug 1933, Brown Co., banded (Mewaldt)
  Latest dates:
    12 Sep 1933, Brown Co., banded (Mewaldt)
    12 Sep 1982, Brown Co., banded (Tallman in Seasons 1983)
    18 Sep [year], Brown Co. (Bent 1949)

GRAY-CHEEKED THRUSH *Catharus minimus* (Lafresnaye)

Status. Common spring and uncommon fall migrant. More common E, rare W, absent from higher Black Hills.

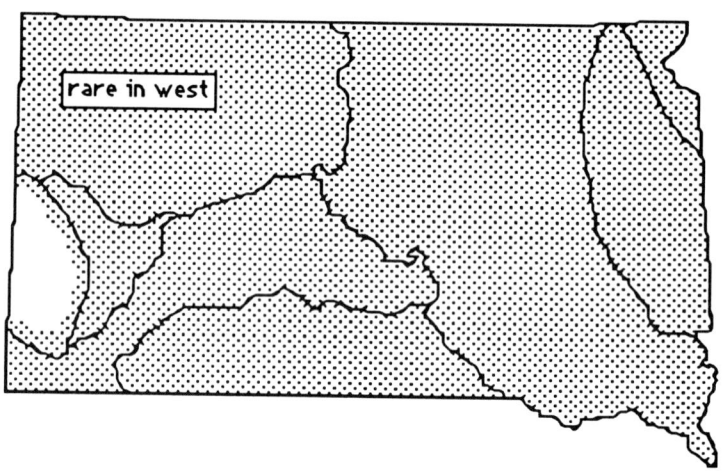

Habitat. Deciduous woods and thickets.
Spring migration. Second and third week of May.
  Earliest dates:
    20 Apr 1989, Brown Co. (Prisbe in Seasons 1989c)
    1 May 1983, Brown Co., banded (Tallman in Seasons 1983c)
    2 May 1987, Codington Co. (Gilman in Seasons 1987c)
  Latest dates:
    28 May 1984, Brown Co. (Tallman in Seasons 1984c)
    31 May 1976, Hyde Co. (Harter in Seasons 1976b)
    18 Jun 1933, Brown Co., banded (Mewaldt)
Fall migration. Last 3 weeks of Sep.
  Earliest date:
    28 Aug 1969, Huron (Johnson)
    3 Sep 1975, Badlands NP (Wilt in Seasons 1975a)

Latest dates:
   5 Oct 1969, Sodak Park (Harris)
   6 Oct 1986, Brown Co., banded (Tallman in Seasons 1987a)
   4 Nov 1970, Roberts Co. (Harris)

SWAINSON'S THRUSH *Catharus ustulatus* (Nuttall)

Status. Fairly common summer resident in higher elevations of Black Hills. Common to abundant spring and less common fall migrant elsewhere. Accidental summer visitor E.

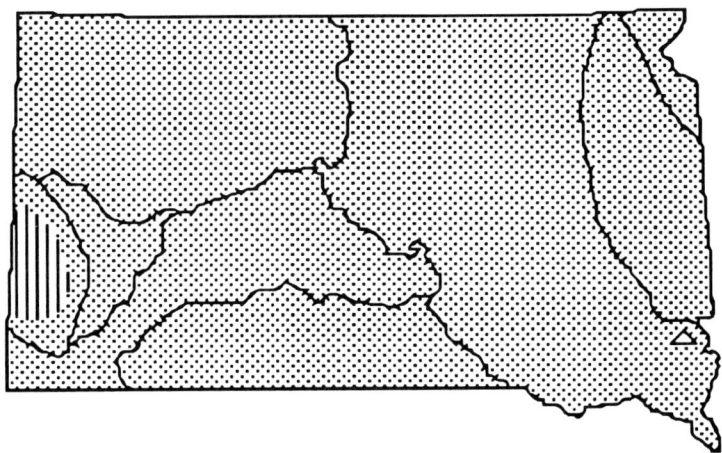

Habitat. Breeding: spruce and occasionally mixed forests. Migrants: deciduous woods and thickets.

Spring migration. First – third week of May.
   Earliest dates:
      14 Apr 1958, Brandt (Peterson)
      15 Apr 1968, Huron (Johnson)
      15 Apr 1969, Huron (Johnson)
   Latest dates:
      12 Jun 1976, Pennington Co. (Baker in Seasons 1976)
      13 Jun 1983, Hyde Co. (Harter in Seasons 1983d)
      17 Jun 1983, Meade Co. (Tallman in Seasons 1983d)

Nesting. Jun and Jul.
   Earliest dates:
      10 Jun 1947, Spearfish Canyon, collected female ready to lay egg (Edwards in Pettingill and Whitney 1965)
      11 Jun 1947, Spearfish Canyon, nest (Sutton in Pettingill and Whitney 1965)
      19 Jun 1965, along Harney Peak Trail above Sylvan Lake, newly-built nest (Whitney)

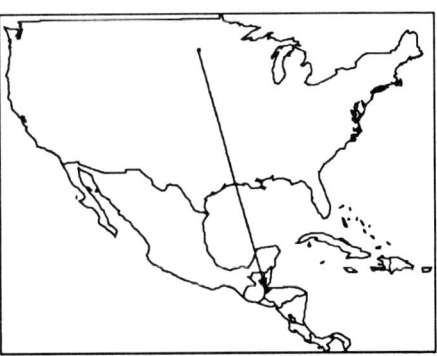

Swainson's Thrush banding recoveries

Latest date:
: 22 Jul 1971, 8 miles W of Rapid City, nest with 3 fairly large young (Baylor et al. 1972)

E River summer record:
: 5 Jul 1985, Lincoln Co., singing male, but breeding not noted (Lehman in Seasons 1985d).

Fall migration. Sep.
Earliest dates:
: 17 Aug 1987, Jackson Co., banded (Graupmann in Seasons 1988a)
: 21 Aug 1984, Harding Co. (Hodorff)
: 22 Aug 1988, Brown Co., banded (Tallman)

Latest dates:
: 18 Oct 1980, Brookings (Holden in Seasons 1981a)
: 25 Oct 1979, Huron (Johnson)
: 27 Oct 1962, Milbank (Elliott)

HERMIT THRUSH *Catharus guttatus* (Pallas)

Status. Uncommon migrant E; rare W. Accidental breeding Black Hills.

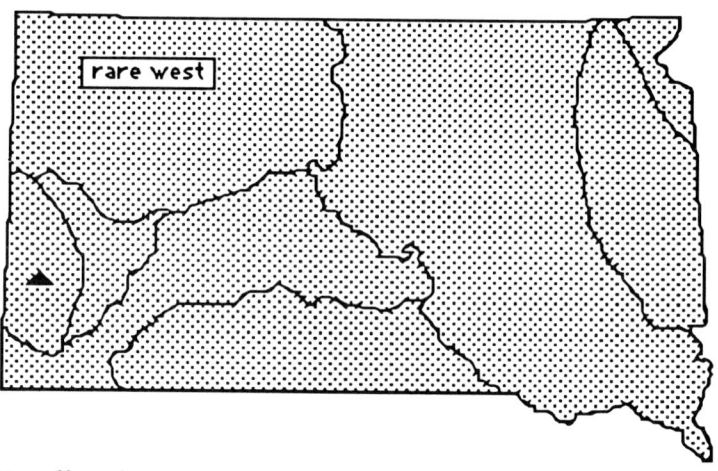

Habitat. Woodlands.

Spring migration. Last half of Apr.
Earliest dates:
: 30 Mar 1916, Sioux Falls (Larson 1925)
: 30 Mar 1977, Brookings Co. (Taylor in Seasons 1977c)
: 1 Apr 1981, Brookings Co. (Taylor in Seasons 1981c)

Latest dates:
: 13 May 1933, Brown Co., banded (Mewaldt)
: 17 May 1976, Turner Co. (Breen in Seasons 1976b)
: 19 May 1990, Brown Co. (Stanford in Seasons 1990c)

Nesting.
Only record.
: 19 Jun 1966, near Sylvan Lake (6000 feet), nest (fide Sutton) with 4 eggs and incubating adult (Greiner and Neill 1966)

Fall migration. First half of Oct.
  Earliest dates:
    28 Sep 1985, Codington Co. (Gilman in Seasons 1986a)
    29 Sep 1987, Brown Co., banded (Tallman in Seasons 1988a)
    30 Sep 1987, Brown Co., banded (Tallman)
  Latest dates:
    12 Nov 1980, Brookings Co. (Hoover in Seasons 1981d)
    25 Nov 1982, Brookings Co. (Peterson in Seasons 1983a)

WOOD THRUSH *Hylocichla mustelina* (Gmelin)

Status. Fairly common summer resident along Missouri River N to Stanley Co. and in SE; Rare breeder in Roberts Co. (Harris); uncommon migrant along the Missouri N to Mobridge (Mewaldt) and through the SE counties bordering Minnesota; still less common between these areas. Reagan (1908) considered the species rare in E Mellette Co. and observed in Todd Co., 4 Jun 1976 (Rosche).

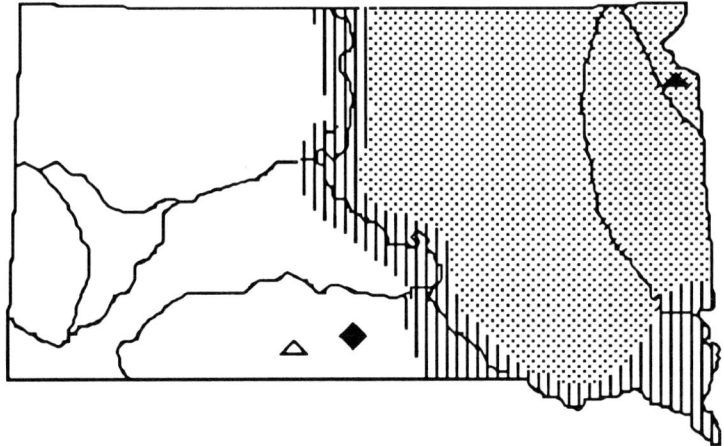

Habitat. Heavily wooded areas and underbrush as resident; also in towns as migrant.
Spring migration. May.
  Earliest dates:
    27 Apr [year], Yankton Co. (Bent 1949)
    2 May 1968, Sanborn Co. (Harris in Harter 1974a)
    5 May 1933, Brown Co., banded (Mewaldt)
Nesting. Jun.
  Earliest dates:
    26 May 1985, Newton Hills SP, nest (Buckman)
    1-6 Jun 1972, Gregory Co., 5 active nests along Missouri River (Anderson in Seasons 1972c)
    7 Jun 1969, Gregory Co., ca. 12 miles W of Pickstown, nest with 4 eggs (Anderson and Daugherty in Harris 1969)

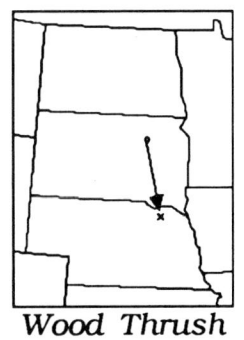

Wood Thrush banding recoveries

Latest dates:
- 10 Jun 1964, Newton Hills SP, nest with 2 hatched young found and observed through fledging and dispersal 17 Jun (Knopf 1974)
- 23 Jun 1967, Charles Mix Co., nest with 4 eggs (Anderson and Daugherty in Harris 1969)
- 23 Jun 1978, Roberts Co., nest with young (Harris)
- 15 Jul 1986, Lincoln Co., nest and young (Skadsen in Seasons 1986d)

Fall migration. Early Sep.
Latest dates:
- 17 Sep 1972, Highmore (Harter)
- 1 Oct 1978, Brookings Co., banded (Holden in Seasons 1979a)
- 11 Oct 1983, Minnehaha Co. (Blankespoor in Seasons 1984a)

AMERICAN ROBIN *Turdus migratorius* Linnaeus

Status. Abundant summer resident. Rare to common winter resident.

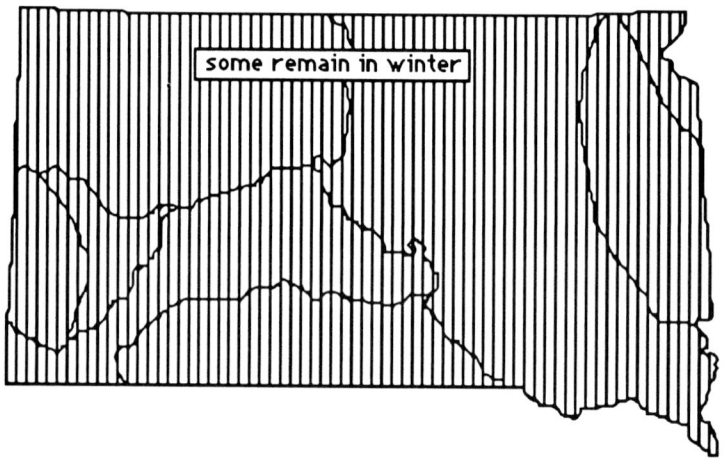

Habitat. Trees and short grass. Will nest on buildings.
Spring migration. Late Mar – mid-Apr. Varying numbers winter that are often reported as early migrants.
Nesting. Late Apr – Jul. 3 broods are common. At Huron, young robins started arriving at roosts by 10 Jun.
Earliest dates:
- 15 Apr 1969, Huron, nest started (Johnson)
- 20 Apr 1988, Meade Co., building nest (E. Miller)
- 24 Apr 1954, Rapid City, constructing nest (Pettingill and Whitney 1965)

Latest dates:
- 24 Jul 1973, near Ludlow, feeding fully grown young (Springer)
- 13 Aug 1976, Buffalo, feeding fledged young (Springer)
- 4 Sep 1987, Deuel Co., feeding recently fledged young (Harris in Seasons 1988a)

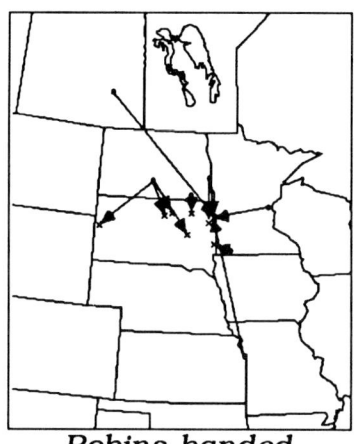 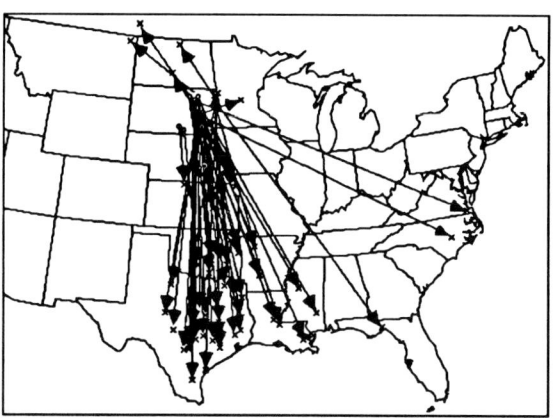

Robins banded outside of South Dakota and recovered within the state

Robins banded in South Dakota and recovered outside of the state

Fall migration. Breeding birds move out during late Aug and Sep. Large migrating flocks from farther N appear in Oct and the first half of Nov.

Winter. Winter where food and shelter are available; sometimes in large numbers.

VARIED THRUSH *Ixoreus naevius* (Gmelin)

Status. Casual visitor during migration and winter. About 3 dozen records, ranging from 29 Aug 1971 in Belle Fourche (Weyler 1971) to 26 May 1983 in Hyde Co. (Harter in Seasons 1983d), including a specimen taken at Twin Lakes SP on 29 Nov 1966 (Harris 1970a). A report on 24 June 1971 near Huron (Betts 1971) was probably a young robin.

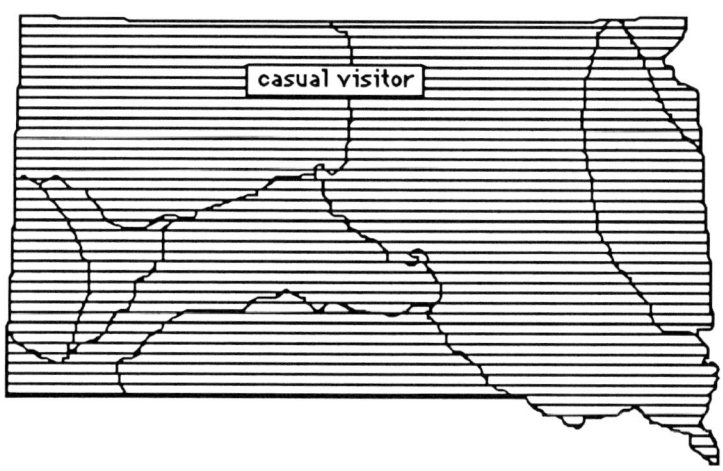

MIMIDAE: Mockingbird and Thrashers

GRAY CATBIRD *Dumetella carolinensis* (Linnaeus)

Status. Fairly common to common summer resident, including the lower levels of the Black Hills.

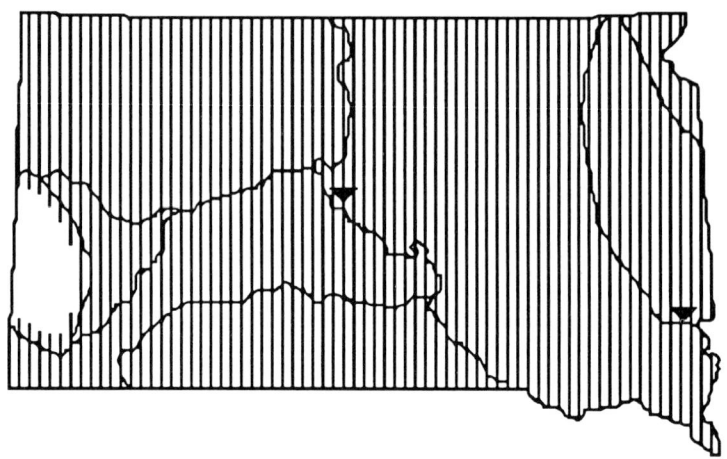

Habitat. Low thickets, undergrowth, and brush.
Spring migration. Last half of May.
  Earliest dates:
    26 Apr 1987, Codington Co. (Gilman in Seasons 1987c)
    1 May 1979, Yankton Co. (Wilcox in Seasons 1979c)
    3 May 1986, Minnehaha Co. (Hoeger in Seasons 1986c)
Nesting. Last week of May into Jul.
  Earliest dates:
    21 May 1914, Lincoln Co., nest building begun (Mallory 1915)
    21 May 1987, Union Co., nest construction (Springer in Seasons 1987d)
    24 May 1968, Sanborn Co., nest (Harris)
  Latest dates:
    26 Jul 1972, Yankton Co., nest with eggs and young (Hall in Seasons 1972c)
    10 Jul 1914, Lincoln Co., nest with 4 eggs (Mallory 1915)
    5 Aug 1958, Rapid City, dead fledgling (Pettingill and Whitney 1965)
Fall migration. Last half of Sep.
  Latest dates:
    4 Nov 1983, Brown Co. (Tallman in Seasons 1984a)
    4 Nov 1983, Yankton (Hall in Seasons 1984a)
    12 Nov 1983, Codington Co. (Gilman in Seasons 1984a)
    14 Nov 1981, Brookings Co. (Edie)
Winter.
  CBC reports:
    Pierre and Sioux Falls.

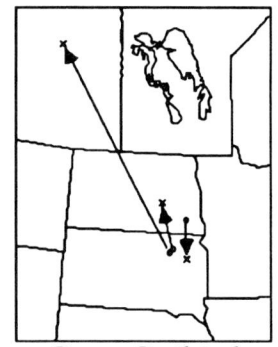

Gray Catbird banding recoveries

NORTHERN MOCKINGBIRD *Mimus polyglottos* (Linnaeus)

Status. Rare to uncommon summer resident with records scattered over the state. Status uncertain in lower Black Hills. The majority of records are in spring. Casual winter. Presence in winter in nonbreeding areas suggests a postbreeding dispersal.

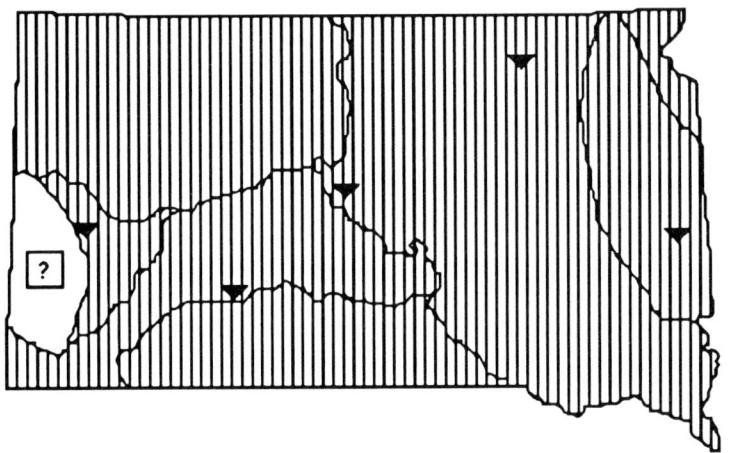

Habitat. Residential areas, thickets, and streamsides.
Spring migration. Last week of Apr – first half of May.
  Earliest dates:
    20 Apr 1983, Stanley Co. (Coonrod in Seasons 1983c)
    25 Apr 1960, Hyde Co. (Harter 1968a)
    28 Apr 1966, Brown Co. (Rose 1967)
Nesting. Jun in Sanborn Co. (Harris). Findley (1949) summarized available literature and refers to a number of breeding records, unfortunately without dates, throughout the state.
  Earliest dates:
    7 Jun 1936, Smithwick, nest with eggs (Barr 1937)
    20 Jun 1934, near Ethan, nest (Wagner in Findley 1949)
    22 Jun 1967, near Letcher, nest with 3 young (Harris 1968b)
    22 Jun 1988, Meade Co., pair with 2 young (Miller et al. in Seasons 1988d)
  Latest dates:
    10 Aug 1968, Clay Co., fledgling dead on road (Timken)
    7 Sep 1966, Sanborn Co., specimen, fledging just out of nest (Harris)
Fall migration. Last half of Sep – Oct, with stragglers into early winter.
  Earliest date:
    30 Aug 1975, Keystone (Ranier and Abel in Seasons 1975d)
  Latest dates:
    26 Sep 1979, Brown Co. (Tallman 1979a)
    1 Oct 1976, Yankton Co. (Hall in Seasons 1977a)

262 MOCKINGBIRD AND THRASHERS

Winter.
CBC reports:
Aberdeen, Brookings, Pierre, and Rapid City.
Other records:
8 Jan 1983, Jackson Co. (Graupmann in Seasons 1983b)

SAGE THRASHER *Oreoscoptes montanus* (Townsend)

Status. Uncommon summer resident in extreme W; accidental E River. An immature female collected "in the Black Hills," probably in Sep 1857, was reported in error as a Mockingbird by Hayden (1863) and Visher (1909) (Pettingill and Whitney 1965).

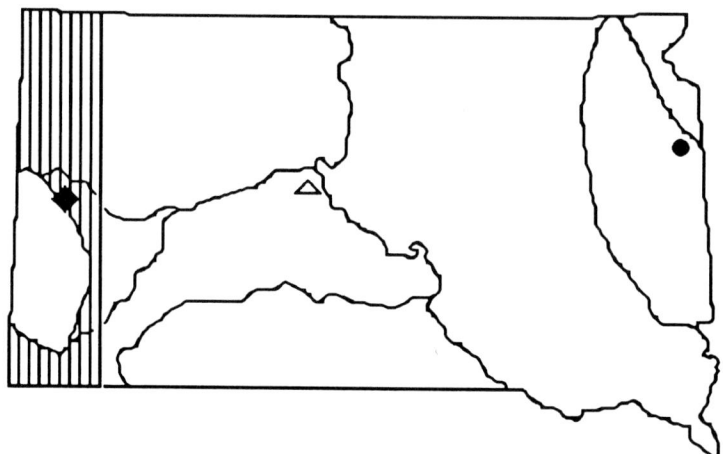

Habitat. Sagelands.
Spring migration.
Earliest date:
21 Apr 1968, Pennington Co., photographed (Rose 1969c)
Nesting. Prior to early 1960's, nesting E of Smithwick at Prairie Gem Ranch (Barr 1961).
Fall migration.
Latest dates:
12 Aug 1966, Edgemont, immature killed by car (Baylor in Whitney 1972)
16 Sep 1988, Fall River Co. (Peterson in Seasons 1989a)
Records away from far W:
9 May 1974, Deuel Co., dead (Harris)
29 Jul 1913, Stanley Co. (Bent 1948)

BROWN THRASHER *Toxostoma rufum* (Linnaeus)

Status. Common summer resident, including elevations below 4000 feet in the Black Hills.

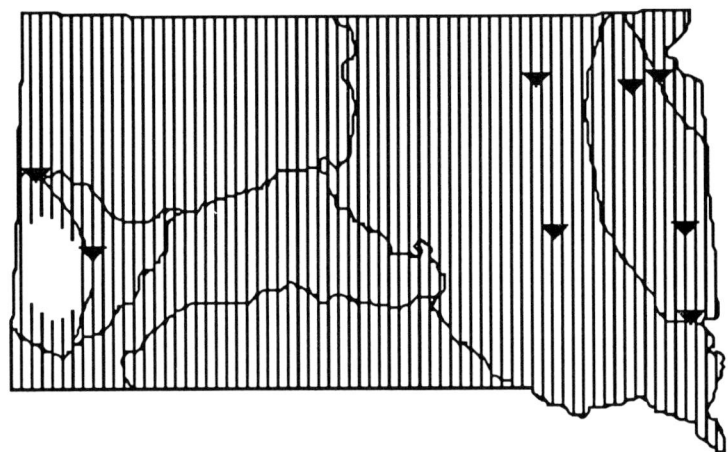

Habitat. Woodland edges, thickets and shrubbery.
Spring migration. Last week of Apr – first week of May.
  Earliest dates:
    1 Apr 1973, Huron (Johnson)
    12 Apr 1947, Rapid City (Behrens in Pettingill and Whitney 1965)
    13 Apr 1969, Wilmot (Harris)
Nesting. Mid-May – Jul.
  Earliest dates:
    9 May 1914, Lincoln Co., nest construction (Mallory 1915)
    12 May 1912, Sioux Falls, nest with eggs (Larson 1925)
    16 May 1965, Huron, pair just started nest, 4-egg clutch

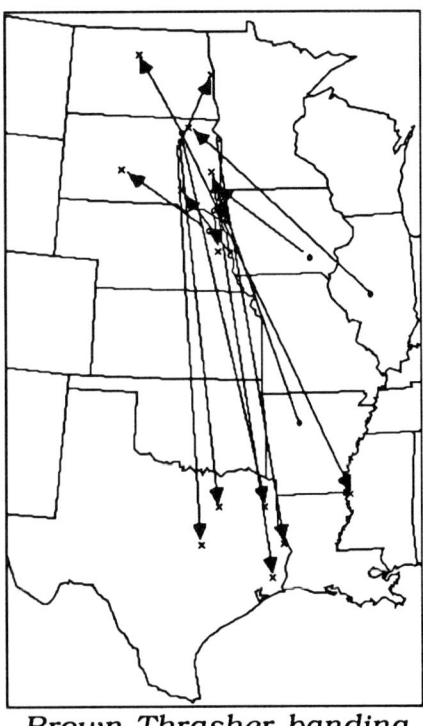

Brown Thrasher banding recoveries

completed 27 May (Johnson)
Latest dates:
1 Jul 1951, Minnehaha Co., adult incubating (Findley)
13 Jul 1978, Lacreek NWR, nest with 1 egg (Lohoefener and Ely 1978)
22 Jul 1974, NW Harding Co., feeding young (Springer)

Fall migration. Last half of Aug for locals. Migrants come through Sep – Oct.

Winter. Occasional individuals fail to migrate; most do not survive the winter.
CBC reports:
Wilmot, Brookings, Aberdeen, Webster, Sioux Falls, Huron, Belle Fourche, and Rapid City.

CURVE-BILLED THRASHER *Toxostoma curvirostre* (Swainson)

Status. Casual.
Records:
Mid-Nov 1966 – 25 Feb 1967, Fairburn (Smith 1967, photographed by Rose)
Feb 1971, Buffalo Co. (Knight in Johnson 1972 with photo); remained in vicinity all summer and through winter of 1971–72; the following spring it built another "nest" or roosting platform under the eaves of a ranch house but disappeared in mid-May and was not seen again (Johnson 1973)
25 May 1973, Lacreek NWR, photograph (Rose in Fjetland 1973)

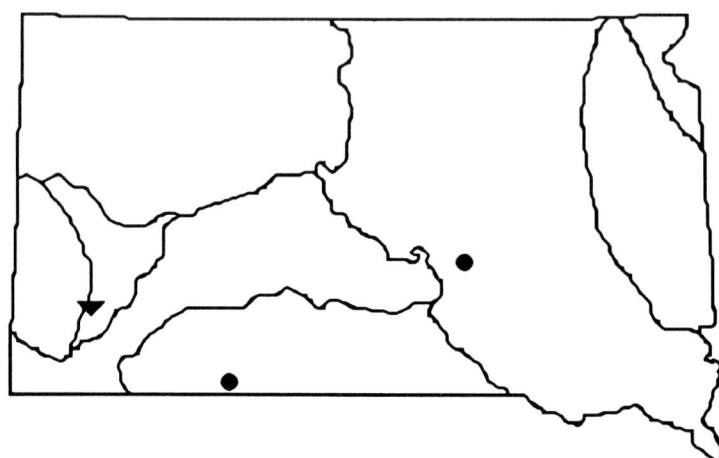

MOTACILLIDAE: Pipits

AMERICAN PIPIT *Anthus rubescens* (Tunstall)

Status. Fairly common migrant, occasionally moving in flocks. Accidental winter. Formerly known as Water Pipit, *A. spinoletta.*

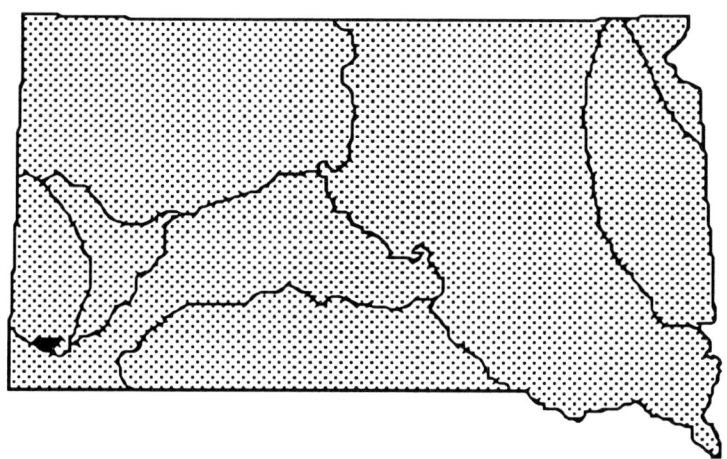

Habitat. Plains, bare fields, shores.
Spring migration. Mid-Apr – early May.
  Earliest dates:
    27 Mar 1910, Sioux Falls (Larson 1925)
    27 Mar 1977, Bon Homme Co. (Hall in Seasons 1977c)
    5 Apr 1978, Brown Co. (Kessler in Seasons 1978c)
  Latest dates:
    15 May 1987, Todd Co. (Peterson in Seasons 1987c)
    16 May 1946, Roberts Co. (Harris)
    24 May 1986, Fall River Co. (Van Sickle in Seasons 1986c)
Fall migration. Oct.
  Earliest dates:
    5 Sep 1988, Brown Co. (Tallman in Seasons 1989a)
    5 Sep 1989, Marshall Co. (Harris in Seasons 1990a)
    10 Sep 1934, Custer State Park (Cahalane in Pettingill and Whitney 1965)
    14 Sep 1988, Dewey Co. (Springer)
  Latest date:
    27 Oct 1985, Deuel Co. (Harris in Seasons 1986a)
    31 Oct 1970, Deuel Co. (Harris)
    5 Nov 1983, Deuel Co. (Harris in Seasons 1984a)
Winter.
  Only record:
    16 Dec 1976, Hot Springs (Baker)

SPRAGUE'S PIPIT *Anthus spragueii* (Audubon)

Status. Fairly common spring and fall migrant along Missouri River region; less common elsewhere. A breeding species in Harding Co. (Visher 1914), Dewey and Stanley counties; probably breeds in Corson Co. S to E Pennington Co., and possibly also in Campbell and McPherson counties.

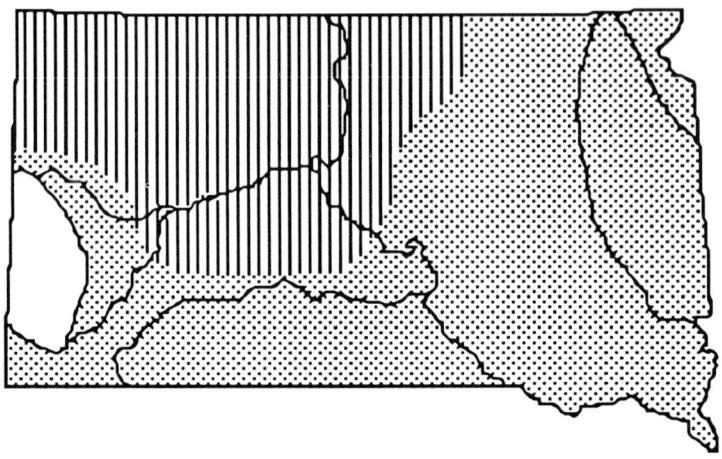

Habitat. Plains, short grass prairies.
Spring migration. Mid-Apr – mid-May.
  Earliest dates:
    30 Mar 1977, Deuel Co. (Harris)
    15 Apr 1982, Sanborn Co. (Rogers in Seasons 1982c)
    18 Apr 1967, near Phillip (Rose)
Nesting. Summer records exist but are not confirmed to be of breeders.
  Only record:
    26 May 1907, Stanley Co., nest with 5 eggs (Bingaman 1912)
Fall migration. Sep.
  Earliest date:
    3 Sep 1965, 4 miles N of Scenic (Russell 1966)
  Latest dates:
    10 Oct 1983, Bon Homme Co. (Anderson in Seasons 1984a)
    22 Oct 1985, Deuel Co. (Harris in Seasons 1986a)
    30 Oct [year], Sanborn Co. (Bent 1950)

BOMBYCILLIDAE: Waxwings

BOHEMIAN WAXWING *Bombycilla garrulus* (Linnaeus)

Status. Erratic winter visitor, frequently in flocks of several hundred in Black Hills, usually in small numbers elsewhere. Notable irruptions E in the winters of 1961–62 and 1986–87.

Habitat. Fruit-bearing trees and shrubs.
Spring migration: Apr.
  Latest dates:
    16 Apr 1962, Huron (Johnson)
    18 Apr 1915, Union Co. (Hayward in Stephens et al. 1955)
    28 Apr 1948, Madison (Habeger)
Fall migration: Nov to Jan.
  Earliest dates:
    27 Oct 1987, Day Co. (Skadsen in Seasons 1988a)
    31 Oct 1965, Huron (Johnson)
    5 Nov 1934, Wind Cave NP (Cahalane in Pettingill and Whitney 1965)

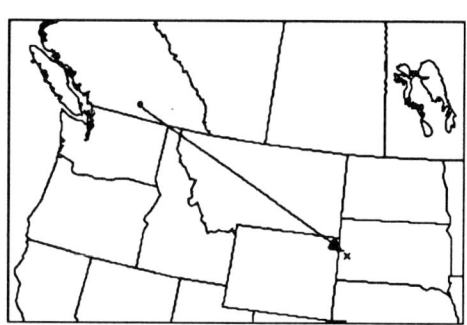

Bohemian Waxwing banding recoveries

CEDAR WAXWING *Bombycilla cedrorum* Vieillot

Status. Erratic but fairly common summer resident and winter visitor, including lower elevations of the Black Hills. Occasional winter resident in flocks of varying numbers, often with Bohemian Waxwings.

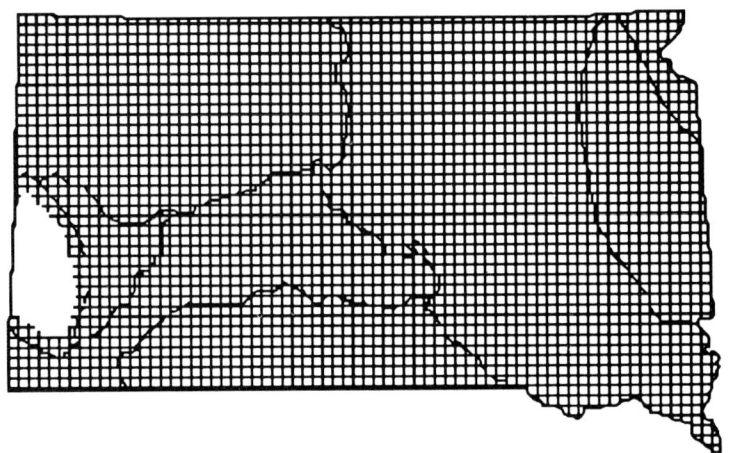

Habitat. Deciduous woodlands in summer; fruit-bearing trees and shrubs in winter.

Migrations. Movements of this species appear to be too erratic for reporting early or late dates. The species may be present any month or go unobserved for months in some years.

Nesting. Irregular and late nester.

Earliest dates:
- 1 Jun 1969, Charles Mix Co., nest, other pairs active in area (B. Anderson and Daugherty)
- 12 Jun 1986, Lincoln Co., nest building (Harris)
- 14 Jun 1968, Roberts Co., adult on nest (M. Harris)

Latest dates:
- 28 Jul 1982, Deuel Co., nest with freshly broken egg (Harris)
- 1 Aug 1919, Vermillion, full-grown young (Over and Thoms 1946)
- 7 Sep 1988, Day Co., adults with 4 fledged young (Springer)

Cedar Waxwing banding recoveries

LANIIDAE: Shrikes

NORTHERN SHRIKE *Lanius excubitor* Linnaeus

Status. Uncommon migrant and winter resident, rare in Black Hills.

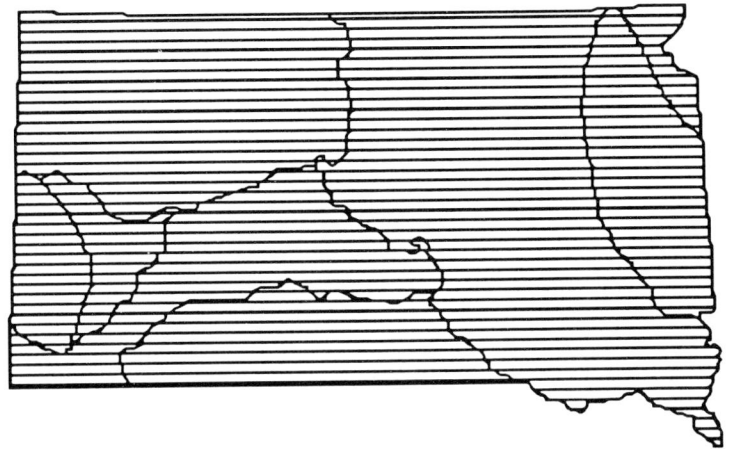

Habitat. Open country with exposed perches.
Spring migration. Early Mar.
   Latest dates:
      2 Apr 1987, Custer Co. (Parker)
      29 Apr 1980, Brookings Co. (Husmann et al. in Seasons 1980c)
      30 Apr 1989, Faulk Co. (Melius in Seasons 1989c)
Fall migration. Nov.
   Earliest dates:
      15 Oct 1968, Butte Co. (Rose)
      15 Oct 1988, Jackson Co., banded (Graupmann in Seasons 1989a)
      16 Oct 1981, Wind Cave NP (Hetlet and Lewis)

LOGGERHEAD SHRIKE *Lanius ludovicianus* Linnaeus

Status. Fairly common summer resident, less common E and rare in Black Hills. Casual winter resident.

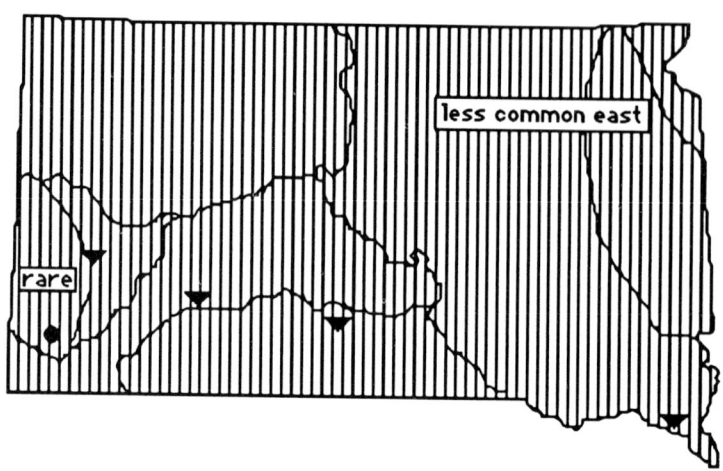

Habitat. Open country with scattered, low deciduous thickets.
Spring migration. Apr.
  Earliest dates:
    9 Mar 1978, Wind Cave NP (Klukas)
    11 Mar 1988, Yankton Co. (Hall in Seasons 1988c)
    16 Mar 1941, Pierre (Wagar 1958)
    16 Mar 1958, Rapid City (Pettingill and Whitney 1965)
Nesting. Mid-Apr – Jun.
  Earliest dates:
    18 Apr 1969, Tripp Co., 2 females on nests, no eggs (Harris)
    22 Apr 1981, Turner Co., nest with 1 egg (Anderson).
    23 Apr 1967, near Ideal, female on nest, no eggs (Harris)
  Latest dates:
    4 Jul 1977, Lacreek NWR, 4 young in nest (Lohoefener and Ely 1978)
    15 Jul 1978, Harding Co., adults with fledged young (Springer)
    13 Aug 1976, Harding Co., feeding fledged young (Springer)

Loggerhead Shrike banding recoveries

Fall migration. Late fall records may be of wintering birds.
  Latest dates:
    13 Nov 1910, Sioux Falls area (Larson 1925)
    17 Nov 1967, Miner Co. (Harris)
    19 Nov 1987, Yankton Co. (Hall in Seasons 1988a)
Winter. Undocumented CBC reports for this species are considered unreliable.
  Records:
    11 Jan 1964, Clay Co. (Springer)
    15 Jan 1964, near Rapid City (Pettingill and Whitney 1965)
    26 Jan 1967, Mellette Co. (Springer)

29 Jan 1987, Badlands NP (Tallman and Prisbe in Seasons 1987b)

27 Feb 1979, Wind Cave NP (Klukas)

STURNIDAE: Starlings

EUROPEAN STARLING *Sturnus vulgaris* Linnaeus

Status. Common permanent resident, including lower elevations of Black Hills. Introduced from Europe into New York in 1890, it spread rapidly W. First reported near Lake Minnewasta in Day Co., when Lundquist (1934) observed 1 on 14 May 1933 and shot 1 in Webster on 27 Dec 1933. "Well-established" by 1939 in E SD (Youngworth 1944) and reaching the Black Hills in 1946 (Pettingill and Whitney 1965). The population is shifting and variable, without clear pattern of migration, although migrating flocks are noted in March and October.

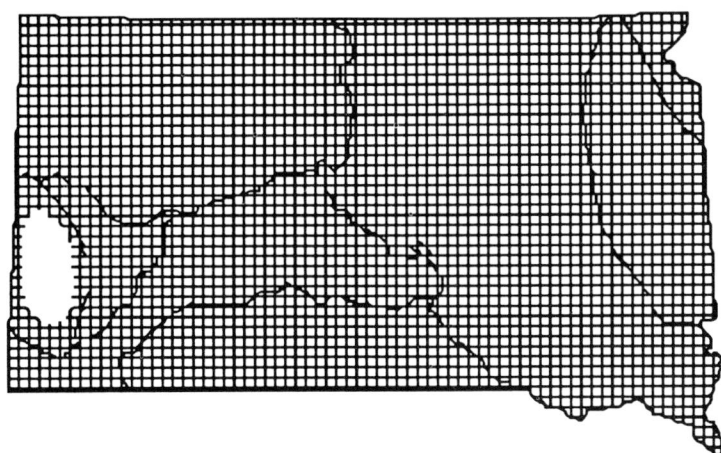

Habitat. Widespread, especially near human habitation and deciduous trees. Nests in any cavity of adequate size, preempting holes made by woodpeckers and houses made for bluebirds and flickers.

Nesting. May and Jun.

Earliest dates:
23 Apr 1967, Tripp Co., young in nest (Harris)
7 May 1976, Deuel Co., adult carrying food (Harris)
11 May 1955, Rapid City, adult carrying nesting material (Pettingill and Whitney 1965)

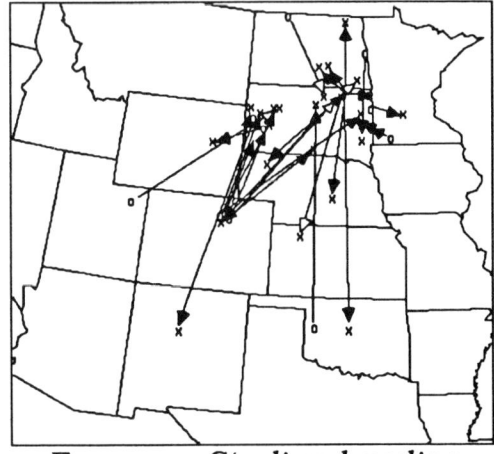

European Starling banding recoveries

Latest dates:
17 Jun 1973, Buffalo, feeding young (Springer)
14 Jul 1978, near Buffalo, adults with 2 young (Springer)
17 Jul 1978, Camp Crook, flock of 20 adults and 50 young (Springer)

VIREONIDAE: Vireos

WHITE-EYED VIREO *Vireo griseus* (Boddaerd)
Status. Casual SE.

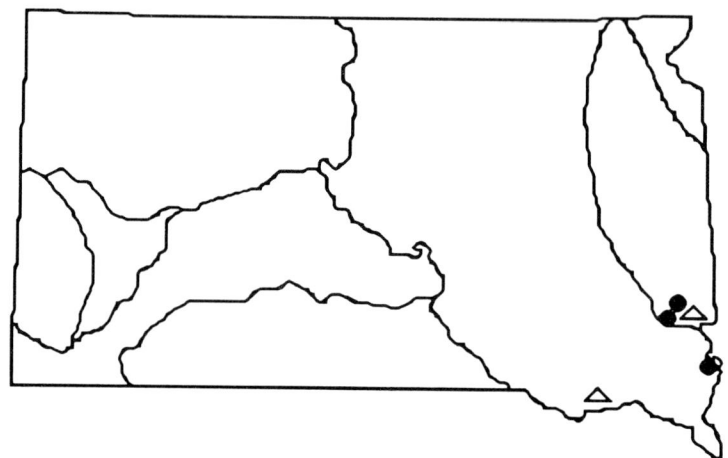

Habitat: Brushy deciduous woodlands.
Records: Reported as a summer resident in Bon Homme Co. in 1932 (Johnson 1958).
1 May 1965, Minnehaha Co. (Nelson 1972)
8 May 1987, Minnehaha Co. (Hoeger and Skadsen in Seasons 1987c)
20 May 1982, Lincoln Co. (Rogge and Rogge in Seasons 1982c)
4 Jun 1971, Minnehaha Co. (Nelson 1971b)

BELL'S VIREO *Vireo bellii* Audubon

Status. Summer resident, fairly common S half, in Missouri River Valley, and Lacreek NWR area. Much less common in Black Hills (where absent at higher elevations).

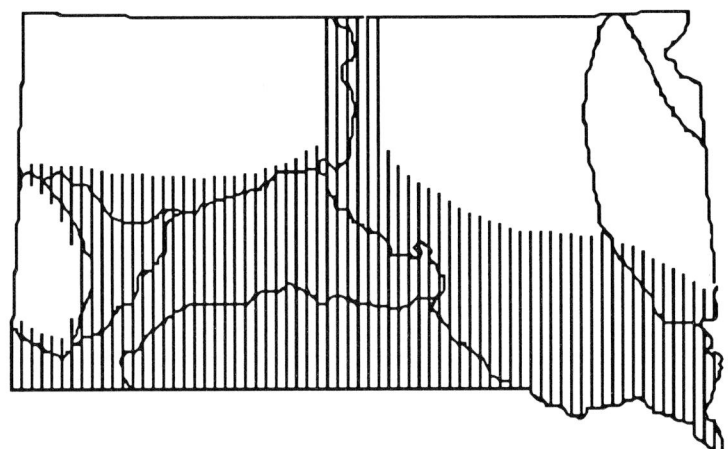

Habitat. Riparian thickets.
Spring migration. Last week of May.
Earliest dates:
   9 May 1989, Moody Co. (Reinking in Seasons 1989c)
   11 May 1967, Hyde Co. (Harter)
   13 May 1952, Union Co. (Youngworth)
Nesting. Jun and Jul.
Earliest dates:
   23 May 1970, Sanborn Co., nest , 4 eggs 1 Jun (Harris)
   3 Jun 1972, Corson Co., pair at empty nest (Harris)
Latest dates:
   8 Jul 1979, Yankton Co., nest with eggs and young (Hall)
   13 Jul 1977, Lacreek NWR, nest with 3 young (Lohoefener and Ely 1978)
   17 Jul 1985, Charles Mix Co., nest with 3 eggs (Skadsen in Seasons 1985d)
Fall migration. First half of Aug.
Latest dates:
   10 Sep 1934, Wind Cave NP (Cahalane in Pettingill and Whitney 1965)
   10 Sep 1985, Charles Mix Co. (Skadsen in Seasons 1986a)
   28 Sep 1964, Rapid City (Behrens in Pettingill and Whitney 1965)

SOLITARY VIREO *Vireo solitarius* (Wilson)

Status. Common summer resident in Black Hills. Uncommon spring and fall migrant elsewhere.

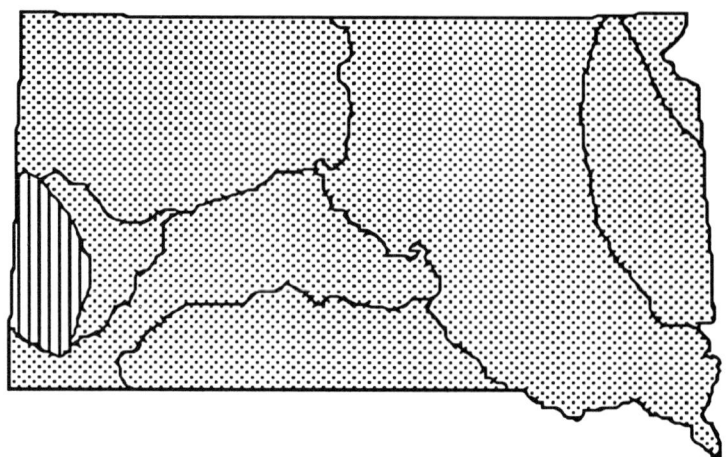

Habitat. Breeding: coniferous forest. Migration: woodlands.
Spring migration. Last half of May.
 Earliest dates:
  25 Apr 1986, Minnehaha Co. (Blankespoor in Seasons 1986c)
  29 Apr 1978, Deuel Co. (Harris in Seasons 1978c)
  29 Apr 1978, Custer Co. (Hill in Seasons 1978c)
Nesting. Last week of May – Jul.
 Earliest dates:
  24 May 1981, Lawrence Co., nest building (Harris)
  25 May 1964, Sheridan Lake, pair building nest (Springer)
  29 May 1960, Keystone, nest under construction (Pettingill and Whitney 1965)
 Latest dates:
  11 Jul 1983, Custer SP, nest with 2 young (Goebel)
  13 Jul 1971, near Rochford, nest with 4 well-developed young, nest empty 18 Jul (Baylor et al. 1972)
  23 Jul 1952, Palmer Gulch, young (Behrens in Pettingill and Whitney 1965)
Fall migration. Late Aug – early Sep.
 Earliest E River dates:
  21 Aug 1987, Lincoln Co. (Skadsen in Seasons 1987c)
  25 Aug 1976, Roberts Co. (Harris)
  28 Aug 1986, Roberts Co. (Harris)
 Latest dates:
  1 Nov 1987, Brown Co., banded (Whitney and Tallman 1988)
  3 and 5 Nov 1968, Rapid City, photo of blue-headed form (Rose)

YELLOW-THROATED VIREO *Vireo flavifrons* Vieillot

Status. Uncommon spring and fall migrant E River. Uncommon summer resident in extreme NE and SE (Yankton, Bon Homme, Lyman, and Lincoln counties) (Youngworth 1932b, Johnson 1958, Short 1961, Springer and Skadsen 1986); formerly at Sioux Falls (Larson).

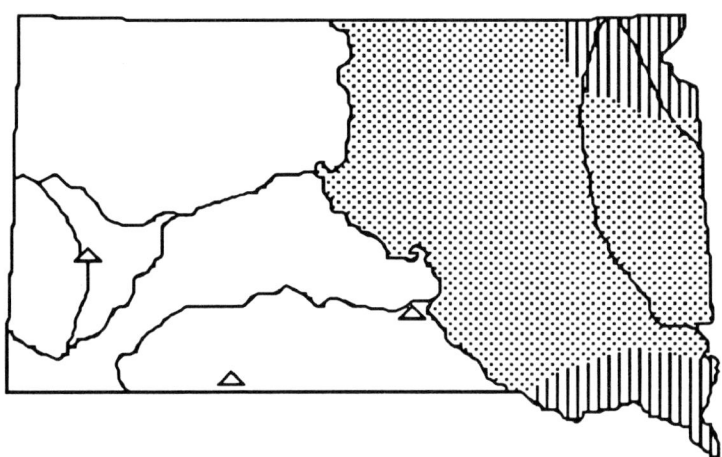

Habitat. Deciduous woodlands.
Spring migration. May.
 Earliest dates:
  30 Apr 1989, Day Co. (Skadsen in Seasons 1989c)
  2 May 1952, Roberts Co. (Harris 1964)
  4 May 1941, Union Co. (Youngworth)
Nesting. Last week of May and Jun.
 Earliest dates:
  1 Jun 1941, Sodak Park, nest (Harris)
  6 Jun 1983, Day Co., bird on nest (Husmann and Harris)
  15 Jun 1940, Sodak Park, nest (Harris)
 Latest dates:
  3 Jul 1964, Grant Co., agitated pair (Springer)
  4 Jul 1932, near Yankton, breeding bird collected (Youngworth 1932)
Fall migration. Late Aug.
 Latest Dates:
  9 Sep 1985, Roberts Co. (Harris in Seasons 1986a)
  10 Sep 1987, Roberts Co. (Harris in Seasons 1988a)
  12 Sep 1982, Minnehaha Co. (Hoeger in Seasons 1983a)
Records W of Missouri River.
  Jul 1955, Lyman Co. (Short 1961)
  18 and 19 May 1957, Lacreek NWR (Baylor and Whitney)
  5 May into Jul 1974, Rapid City (Baylor and Whitney)

WARBLING VIREO *Vireo gilvus* (Vieillot)

Status. Common summer resident, including Black Hills at all elevations.

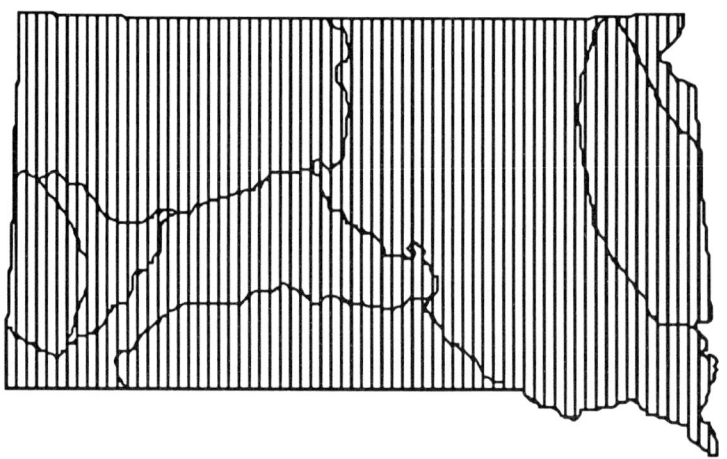

Habitat. Woodlands and residential areas.
Spring migration. Second half of May.
  Earliest dates:
    29 Apr 1986, Yankton Co. (Kronner in Seasons 1986c)
    30 Apr 1959, Rapid City (Bachmann in Pettingill and Whitney 1965)
    30 Apr 1988, Minnehaha Co. (Hoeger in Seasons 1988c)
    4 May 1986, Gregory Co. (Steffen in Seasons 1986c)
Nesting. Late May into Jul.
  Earliest dates:
    18 May 1985, Brookings Co., nest building (Meyer in Seasons 1985d)
    3 Jun 1896, McCook Lake, nest with eggs collected (Rich in Stephens et al. 1955)
    3 Jun 1966, Blunt, building nest (Springer)
  Latest dates:
    23 Jun 1957, Huron, nest with young being brooded (Johnson)
    27 Jun 1941, Roberts Co., nest (Harris)
    27 Jul 1983, Custer SP, nest with 3 young (Goebel)
Fall migration. Aug.
  Latest dates:
    24 Sep 1979, Hyde Co. (Harter in Seasons 1980a)
    29 Sep 1907, Sioux Falls (Larson 1925)
    1 Oct 1986, Brown Co. (Prisbe in Seasons 1987a)

Warbling Vireo banding recoveries (see Rogge and Rogge 1983)

PHILADELPHIA VIREO *Vireo philadephicus* (Cassin)

Status. Uncommon spring and fall migrant E. Casual W River.
Habitat. Woodlands.

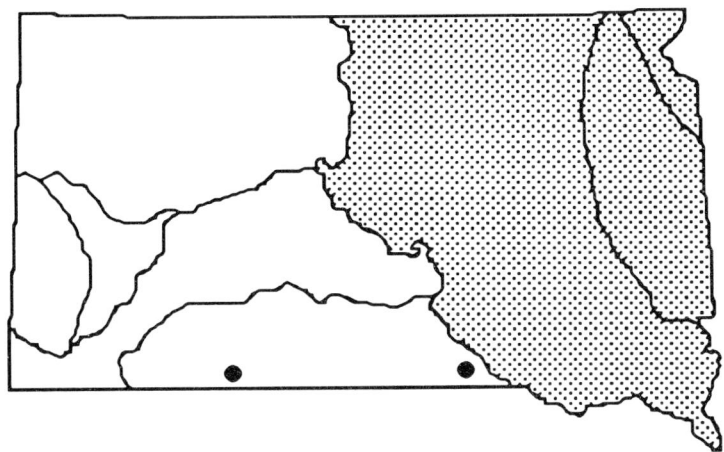

Spring migration. Last half of May.
Earliest dates:
  8 May 1979, Clay Co. (Peterson in Seasons 1979c)
  8 May 1986, Minnehaha Co. (Skadsen in Seasons 1986c)
  9 May 1986, Deuel Co. (Harris in Seasons 1986c)
Latest dates:
  31 May 1908, Sioux Falls (Larson 1925)
  4 Jun 1933, Brown Co., banded (George)
  12 Jun 1973, Lacreek NWR (Koeln in Fjetland 1973)
Fall migration. Sep.
Earliest dates:
  22 Aug 1987, Minnehaha Co. (Hoeger in Seasons 1988a)
  23 Aug 1986, Minnehaha Co. (Blankespoor and Skadsen in Seasons 1987a)
  30 Aug 1988, Brookings Co. (Rose in Seasons 1989a)
Latest dates:
  6 Oct 1983, Gregory Co., banded (Steffen in Seasons 1984a)
  7 Oct 1985, Brown Co., banded (Tallman in Seasons 1986a)
  30 Oct 1980, Edmunds Co. (Tallman 1981)

RED-EYED VIREO *Vireo olivaceus* (Linnaeus)

Status. Fairly common summer resident but with distribution scattered; common in lower elevations in the Black Hills. Fairly common spring and fall migrant throughout.

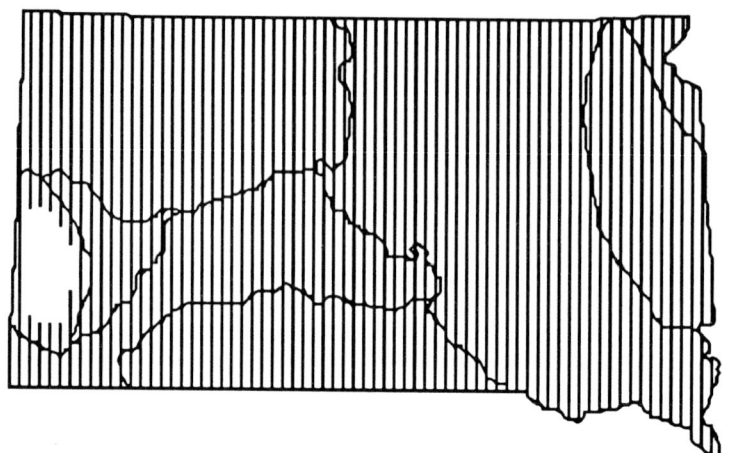

Habitat. Woodlands and residential shade trees.

Spring migration. Last half of May. First week of May, Union Co. (Stephens et al. 1955)
  Earliest dates:
    4 May 1952, Roberts Co. (Harris 1964)
    9 May 1964, Brookings (Springer)
    12 May 1912, Sioux Falls area (Larson 1925)

Nesting. Late May – mid-Jul. Birds may resume singing after nesting.
  Earliest dates:
    23 May 1985, near Rosebud, pair copulating (Springer)
    6 Jun 1946, Rapid City, nest (Behrens in Pettingill and Whitney 1965)
    9 Jun 1971, Deuel Co., nest (Harris)
  Latest dates:
    7 Jul 1948, South Canyon, nest in paper birch with 2 young nearly ready to fledge (Dilger in Pettingill and Whitney 1965)
    24 Aug 1986, Rapid City, adult feeding full-grown fledgling (Whitney)
    9 Sep 1985, Roberts Co., adult feeding begging young (Harris)

Fall migration. Mid-Aug – Mid-Sep.
  Latest dates:
    24 Sep 1911, Sioux Falls (Larson 1925)
    29 Sep 1946, Roberts Co. (Harris)
    30 Oct 1965, Huron (Johnson)

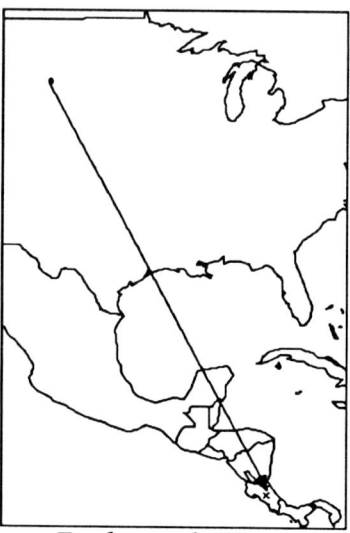

Red-eyed Vireo banding recoveries

FAMILY EMBERIZIDAE

SUBFAMILY PARULINAE: Wood-Warblers

BLUE-WINGED WARBLER *Vermivora pinus* (Linnaeus)

Status. Casual migrant E. No specimens, although 5 banded in Spink Co. between 1931 and 1944 (Brenckle). The hybrid, Lawrence's Warbler, seen 16 Jun 1954, near Waverly (Moriarty 1954); the hybrid, Brewster's Warbler, seen 23 May 1976, Huron (Johnson and Johnson 1976).

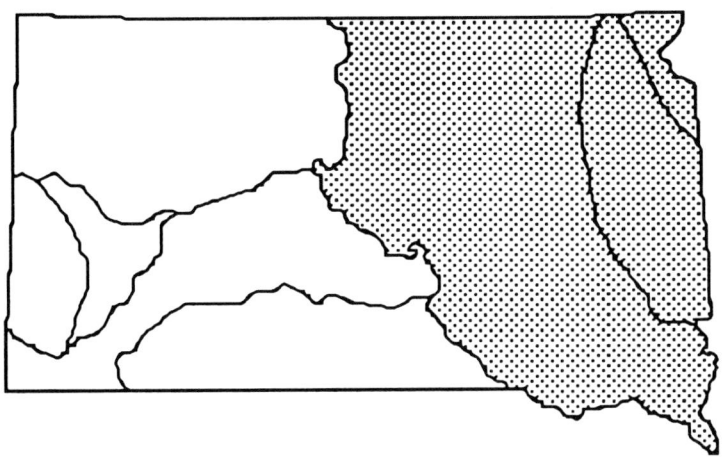

Habitat. Woodlands.
Spring migration. Second – third week of May.
  Earliest dates:
    7 May 1969, Huron (Johnson)
    7 May 1979, Hyde Co. (Harter in Seasons 1979c)
    8 May 1965, Hyde Co. (Harter 1968a)
  Latest dates:
    17 May 1952, Sioux Falls (Krause)
    18 May 1948, Sioux Falls (Krause)
    25 May 1981, Roberts Co. (Harris in Seasons 1981c)
Fall migration.
  Only date:
    4 Sep 1960, Armour (Crutchett 1962)

GOLDEN-WINGED WARBLER *Vermivora chrysoptera* (Linnaeus)

Status. A rare migrant E. More common extreme E. For hybridization, see Blue-winged Warbler.

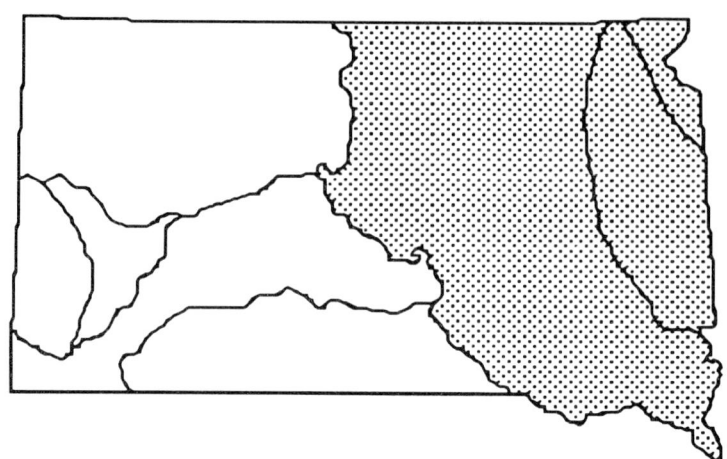

Habitat. Deciduous woodlands.
Spring migration. Second – third week of May.
  Earliest dates:
    8 May 1966, Farm Islands, banded (Holden)
    9 May 1963, Sioux Falls (Krause)
    10 May 1933, Dell Rapids, collected (Anderson 1933)
    10 May 1974, Pierre, photographed (Rose)
  Latest dates:
    23 May 1968, Wessington Hills (Harris)
    23 May 1976, Minnehaha Co. (Blankespoor in Seasons 1976c)
    23 May 1976, Huron (Johnson and Johnson 1976)
    25 May 1971, Aberdeen (Lynch in Houston 1971)
Fall migration. Late Aug and the first week of Sep
  Earliest dates:
    25 Aug 1982, Minnehaha Co. (Hoeger in Seasons 1983a)
    29 Aug 1976, Brookings Co. (Holden in Seasons 1977a)
    1 Sep 1986, Brown Co. (Tallman and Tallman in Seasons 1987a)
  Latest dates:
    16 Sep 1988, Brown Co. (Tallman in Seasons 1989a)
    20 Sep 1986, Codington Co. (Gilman in Seasons 1987a)
    30 Oct 1982, Yankton Co. (Wilcox in Seasons 1983a)

TENNESSEE WARBLER *Vermivora peregrina* (Wilson)

Status. Migrant, uncommon W, common to abundant E. Accidental summer.

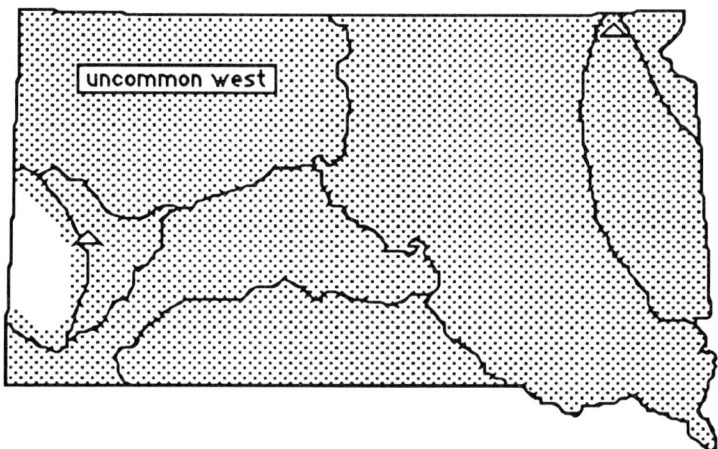

Habitat. Found chiefly in the upper half of tall trees of wooded areas.

Spring migration. Last 3 weeks of May.
  Earliest dates:
    27 Apr 1964, Hyde Co. (Harter 1968a)
    29 Apr 1986, Yankton Co. (Kronner)
    30 Apr 1955, Sioux Falls (Krause)
  Latest dates:
    10 Jun 1977, Yankton Co. (Wilcox in Seasons 1977d)
    13-14 Jun 1975, Wind Cave NP (Palmer)
    16 Jun 1941, Union Co. (Youngworth 1960b)

Summer.
  Only record: (of singing but probably nonbreeding male).
    19 Jul 1967, Buffalo Lake, 1 (Harris 1968a)

Fall migration. Sep.
  Earliest dates:
    3 Aug 1989, Day Co., banded (Skadsen in Seasons 1990a)
    11 Aug 1987, Deuel Co. (Harris in Seasons 1988a)
    19 Aug 1979, Brown Co. (Tallman 1979)
  Latest dates:
    11 Oct 1982, Brown Co, banded (Tallman in Seasons 1983a)
    14 Oct 1982, Brown Co., banded (Tallman)
    15 Oct 1983, Brown Co. (Tallman in Seasons 1984a)

ORANGE-CROWNED WARBLER *Vermivora celata* (Say)
Status. Common migrant. Accidental summer.

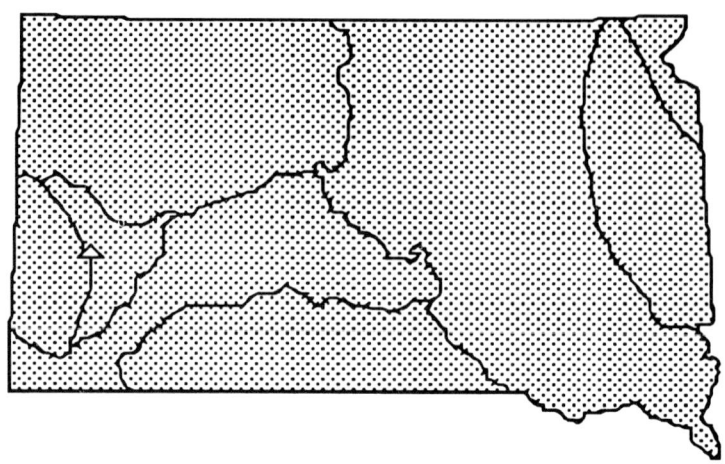

Habitat. Deciduous woodlands.
Spring migration. Last week of Apr and first 2 weeks of May.
  Earliest dates:
    16 Apr 1977, Gregory Co. (Steffen in Seasons 1977c)
    17 Apr 1964, Hyde Co. (Harter 1968a)
    18 Apr 1969, Brookings (Edie)
  Latest dates:
    31 May 1971, Rapid City (Serr in Seasons 1971c)
    2 Jun 1947, Brookings, banded (Wagar)
    14 Jun 1971, North Cave Hills (Krause, Baylor and Rosine)
Summer.
  Only record:
    25 Jul 1977, Rapid City, probably nonbreeder (Bachmann in Seasons 1977d)
Fall migration. Last 2 weeks of Sep and first 2 weeks of Oct.
  Earliest dates:
    18 Aug 1987, Jackson Co. (Graupmann in Seasons 1988a)
    23 Aug 1972, Faulk Co. (Wagar)
    27 Aug 1985, Deerfield Lake (Unitt)
  Latest dates:
    28 Oct 1983, Brown Co., banded (Tallman in Seasons 1984a)
    28 Oct 1984, Yankton Co. (Hall in Seasons 1985a)
    29 Oct 1982, Huron (Johnson and Johnson)

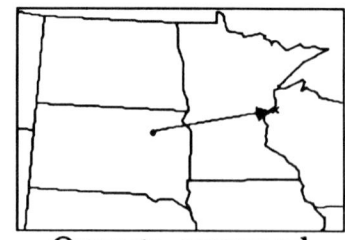

Orange-crowned Warbler banding recoveries

NASHVILLE WARBLER *Vermivora ruficapilla* (Wilson)

Status. Uncommon migrant. Very few records W. Accidental summer.

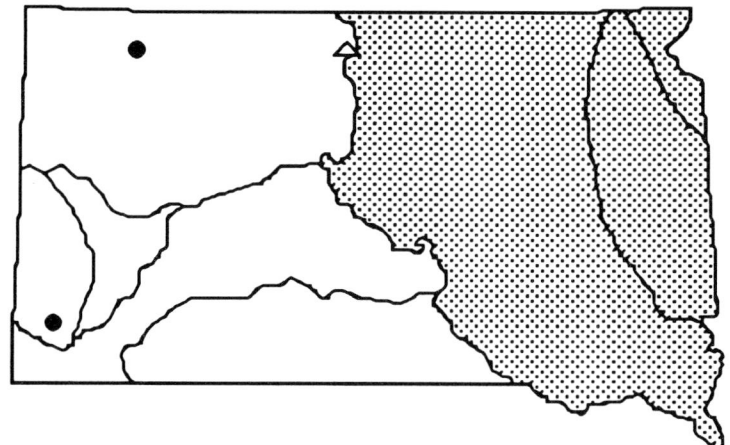

Habitat. Second-growth deciduous woodlands.
Spring migration. Second and third week of May.
  Earliest dates:
    23 Apr 1990, Fall River Co. (Peterson in Seasons 1990c)
    29 Apr 1989, Minnehaha Co. (Skadsen in Seasons 1989c)
    30 Apr 1981, Perkins Co. (Hinds and Hinds in Seasons 1981c)
  Latest dates:
    28 May 1989, Brown Co. (Prisbe in Seasons 1989c)
    28 May 1962, Hyde Co. (Harter 1968a)
    3 Jun 1933, Aberdeen (George)
Summer. Over and Thoms' (1921, 1946) record of breeding in Harding Co. is unsubstantiated.
  Only record:
    12–15 Jul 1955, Mobridge, 2 singing males (Short 1961)
Fall migration. Sep and first week of Oct.
  Earliest dates:
    12 Aug 1987, Roberts Co. (Harris in Seasons 1988a)
    18 Aug 1986, Roberts Co. (Harris in Seasons 1987a)
    24 Aug 1934, Wind Cave NP (Cahalane in Pettingill and Whitney 1965)
    24 Aug 1985, Codington Co. (Gilman in Seasons 1986a)
  Latest dates:
    28 Oct 1982, Brown Co. (Tallman in Seasons 1983a)
    31 Oct 1979, Brookings Co. (Taylor in Seasons 1980a)
    13 Nov 1970, Huron (Johnson and Johnson 1970)

NORTHERN PARULA *Parula americana* (Linnaeus)

Status. Rare to uncommon migrant E; casual to rare migrant W. Casual summer.

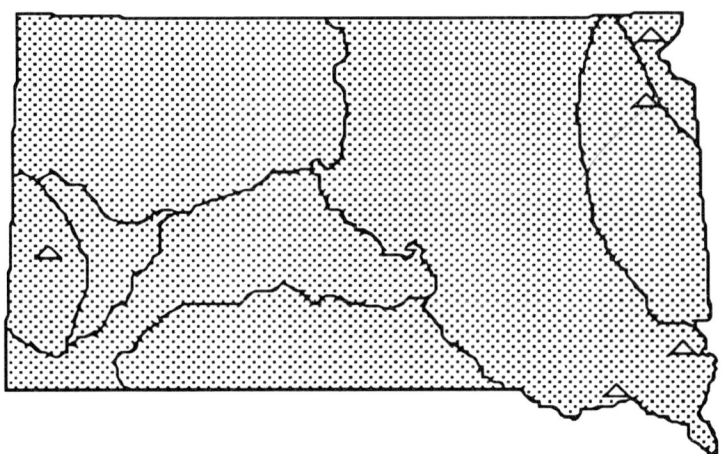

Habitat. Woodlands.

Spring migration. Last 3 weeks of May. Late dates are not listed because of summering birds.
   Earliest dates:
      2 Apr 1965, Belvidere, 1 dead (DeVries 1965)
      22 Apr 1968, Highmore, 1 dead (Harter 1968a)
      25 Apr 1987, Minnehaha Co. (Hoeger in Seasons 1987c)

Summer. Summer birds (fewer than 10 records) may breed but no nests known. Summer records are from the Black Hills, Roberts, Codington, Lincoln, and Yankton counties.

Fall migration. Last 3 weeks of Sep.
   Earliest dates:
      8 Sep 1985, Lincoln Co. (Skadsen in Seasons 1986a)
      9 Sep 1976, Hyde Co. (Harter in Seasons 1977a)
      9 Sep 1988, Hughes Co. (Harris in Seasons 1989a)
   Latest dates:
      3 Oct 1955, Minnehaha Co. (Krause 1959a)
      16 Nov 1969, Rapid City (Rose)

YELLOW WARBLER *Dendroica petechia* (Linnaeus)

Status. Common to abundant summer resident. Absent from higher Black Hills.

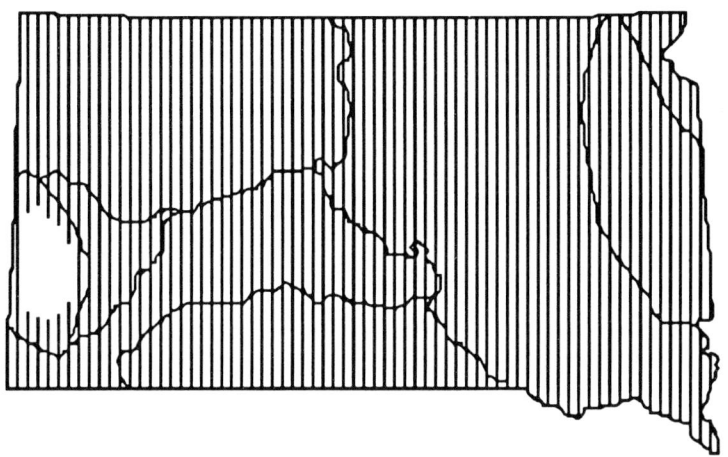

Habitat. Open woods and shrublands.
Spring migration. Second and third week of May.
  Earliest dates:
    24 Apr 1966, Yankton (Hall)
    25 Apr 1976, Day Co. (Johnson in Seasons 1976c)
    28 Apr 1981, Deuel Co. (Harris in Seasons 1981c)
Nesting. Mid-May – late Jul.
  Earliest dates:
    15 May 1924 and 31 May 1925, Rapid City, sets of 3 and 4 eggs collected (McIntosh in Whitney 1955)
    9 Jun 1969, Forestburg, nest with 4 eggs (Harris)
  Latest dates:
    21 Jul 1971, Roberts Co., adult feeding fledgling (Springer)
    22 Jul 1974, Harding Co., adults feeding 2 young (Springer)
    27 Jul 1957, Rapid City, fledglings attended by adults (Pettingill and Whitney 1965).
Fall migration. Mid-Aug – Mid-Sep.
  Latest dates:
    20 Oct 1990, Brown Co., banded (Tallman)
    20 Oct 1962, Milbank, banded (Elliott 1963a)
    6 Nov 1981, Pierre (Coonrod 1982)

CHESTNUT-SIDED WARBLER *Dendroica pensylvanica* (Linnaeus)

Status. Uncommon migrant E; casual W, absent from higher Black Hills. Accidental summer.

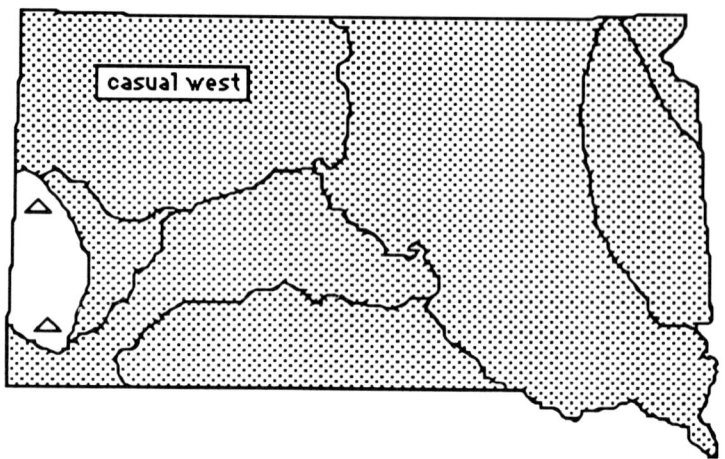

Habitat. Woodlands.

Spring migration. Third and fourth weeks of May.
  Earliest dates:
    6 May 1988, Minnehaha Co. (Hoeger in Seasons 1988c)
    9 May 1935, Union Co. (Bailey in Stephens et al. 1955)
    9 May 1986, Deuel Co. (Harris in Seasons 1986c)
  Latest dates:
    29 May 1968, Brookings (Edie)
    29 May 1970, Cresbard, banded (Wagar)
    9 Jun 1969, Rapid City (Rose 1969a)

Summer.
  Only records:
    17 Jun 1979, Custer Co. (Jervis 1979)
    16 Jul 1975, Pennington Co. (Rose in Seasons 1975c)

Fall migration. Late Aug – mid-Sep.
  Earliest dates:
    23 Aug 1977, Yankton Co. (Wilcox in Seasons 1978a)
    23 Aug 1987, Brown Co. (Tallman in Seasons 1988a)
    25 Aug 1976, Roberts Co. (Harris in Seasons 1977a)
  Latest dates:
    25 Sep 1987, Brown Co. (Tallman)
    1 Oct 1976, Hyde Co. (Harter in Seasons 1977a)
    12 Nov 1989, Brown Co. (Prisbe in Seasons 1990a)

MAGNOLIA WARBLER *Dendroica magnolia* (Wilson)

Status. Uncommon migrant E; casual migrant W. Absent from higher Black Hills.

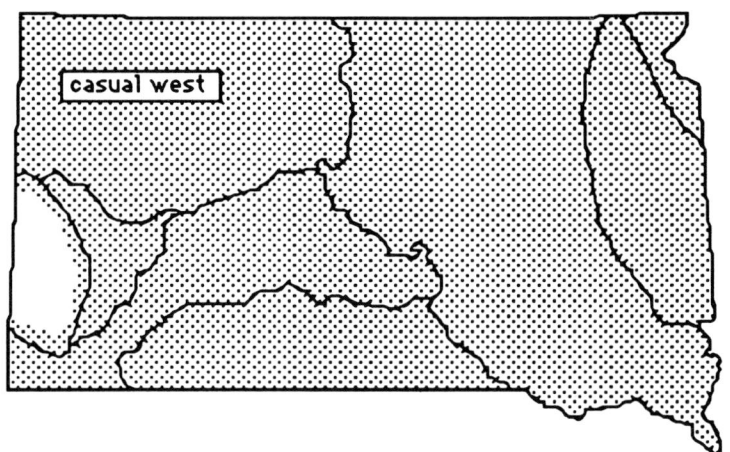

Habitat. Deciduous woodlands.
Spring migration. Third and fourth week of May.
Earliest dates:
2 May 1957, Sioux Falls (Krause)
4 May 1969, Rapid City (Southmayd)
5 May 1856, Clay Co. (Hayden in Baird 1858)
Latest dates:
1 Jun 1907, Sioux Falls area (Larson 1925)
1 Jun 1966, Brown Co. (Rose)
5 Jun 1979, Colman (Vinland)
6 Jun [year], Yankton (Bent 1953)
Fall migration. Sep.
Earliest dates:
23 Aug 1977, Brookings Co. (Taylor in Seasons 1978a)
25 Aug 1976, Roberts Co. (Harris in Seasons 1977a)
26 Aug [year], Aberdeen (Bent 1953)
Latest dates:
12 Oct 1954, Milbank, banded (Wagar)
13 Oct 1968, Brookings (Edie)
9 Nov 1981, Pierre (Coonrod 1982)

CAPE MAY WARBLER *Dendroica tigrina* (Gmelin)

Status. Rare migrant E; accidental spring migrant W.

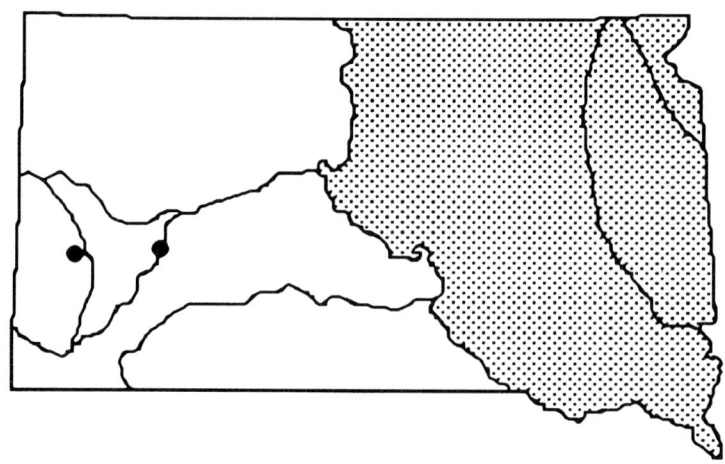

Habitat. Woodlands and residential areas.
Spring migration. Second and third week of May.
  Earliest dates:
    5 May 1952, Sioux Falls (Krause)
    6 May 1988, Minnehaha Co. (Hoeger in Seasons 1988c)
    8 May 1966, Brown Co. (Rose 1967)
    8 May 1970, Cresbard, banded (Wagar)
  Latest dates:
    26 May 1976, Wasta (Holden in Seasons 1976c)
    3 Jun 1935, near Spring Lake (Youngworth 1935)
    4 Jun 1983, Huron (Johnson and Johnson)
Fall migration. Late Aug – Sep.
  Earliest dates:
    19 Aug 1986, Roberts Co. (Harris in Seasons 1987a)
    23 Aug 1975, Deuel Co. (Harris in Seasons 1975c)
  Latest dates:
    3 Oct 1954, Sioux Falls (Findley)
    8 Oct 1967, Hyde Co. (Harter 1969)
Other W River record.
    16 May 1985, Pennington Co. (Riner in Seasons 1985c)

BLACK-THROATED BLUE WARBLER *Dendroica caerulescens* (Gmelin)

Status. Rare migrant E; accidental W.

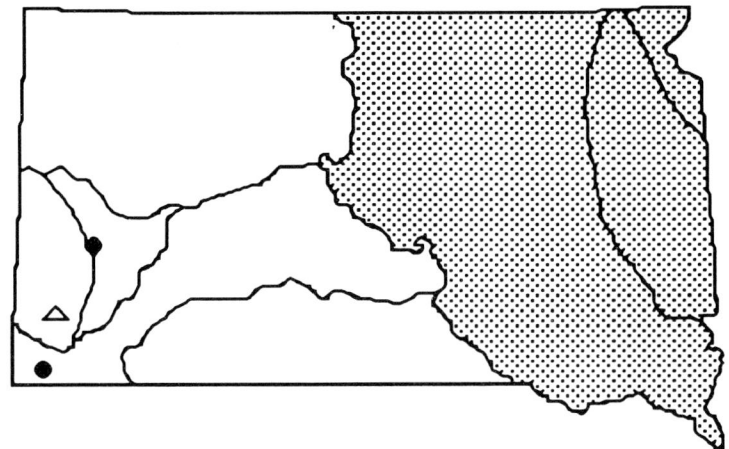

Habitat. Woodlands and residential areas.
Spring migration. Second and third week of May.
  Earliest dates:
    7 May 1933, Aberdeen (George)
    8 May 1975, Brookings (Husmann)
    10 May 1986, Pennington Co. (Whitney and Hafner in Seasons 1986c)
  Latest dates:
    22 May 1974, Highmore (Harter)
    22 May 1982, Huron (Johnson 1983a)
    23 May 1909, Sioux Falls area (Larson 1925)
    25 May 1975, Brown Co. (Rose and Hill in Seasons 1975b)
Summer.
  Only record:
    26 Jun–4 Jul 1988, Custer Co. (Peterson)
Fall migration. Last 3 weeks of Sep and the first week of Oct.
  Earliest dates:
    2 Sep 1986, Minnehaha Co. (Hoeger in Seasons 1987a)
    7 Sep 1941, Sodak Park (Harris 1963)
    7 Sep 1976, Brookings Co., banded (Holden in Seasons 1977a)
  Latest dates:
    18 Oct 1957, Milbank, banded (Elliott)
    19 Oct 1988, Brown Co. (Prisbe in Seasons 1989a)
    27 Oct 1984, Brown Co. (Tallman and Prisbe in Seasons 1984a)
Other W River record.
  29 Sep 1983, Fall River Co. (Peterson in Seasons 1984a)

YELLOW-RUMPED WARBLER *Dendroica coronata* (Linnaeus)

Status. 2 races occur. Myrtle form (*D. c. coronata*): abundant migrant E; fairly common spring and rare fall migrant in Black Hills. Audubon's form (*D. c. auduboni*): common summer resident in Black Hills and in wooded buttes of Harding Co; rare migrant E of Missouri River (6 spring observations). Both forms casual in winter.

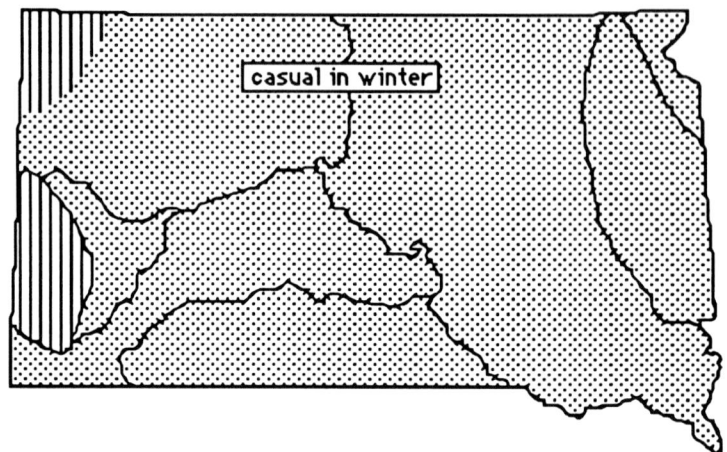

Habitat. Deciduous woodlands E; coniferous forests W.
Spring migration. Last 2 weeks of Apr – first 3 weeks of May.
  Earliest dates:
    23 Mar 1980, Shannon Co. (Homoya)
    28 Mar 1989, Brown Co. (Branson and Montgomery in Seasons 1989c)
    2 Apr 1963, Hyde Co. (Harter 1968a)
    2 Apr 1979, Brown Co. (Kesseler in Seasons 1979c)
  Latest dates (Myrtle Warbler):
    25 May 1955, Milbank (Elliott 1955)
    25 May 1957, Brookings (Holden)
    16 Jun 1987, Walworth Co. (Springer in Seasons 1987d)
Nesting (Audubon's Warbler). Last week of May – mid-Jul.
  Earliest dates:
    8 Jun 1947, Horse Thief Lake, female gathering nesting material (Sutton in Pettingill and Whitney 1965)
    12 Jun 1969, Custer Co., adult feeding young just out of nest (Edie)
    12 Jun 1968, North Cave Hills, nest with eggs (Baylor and Rosine 1970)

Latest dates:
- 16 Jul 1958, South Hell Canyon, adults feeding 2 young (Carter 1958b)
- 22 Jul 1974, North Cave Hills, adult feeding fledgling (Springer)
- 26 Jul 1952, Black Hills area, adults carrying food (Behrens in Gammell and Gammell 1952)

Fall migration. Last 2 weeks of Sep and first 3 weeks of Oct.

Earliest dates (Myrtle Warbler):
- 19 Aug 1934, Silvertip Peak in Black Hills (Cahalane in Pettingill and Whitney 1965)
- 26 Aug 1986, Minnehaha Co. (Skadsen in Seasons 1987a)
- 30 Aug 1964, Highmore (Harter)
- 30 Aug 1986, Gregory Co. (Steffen)

Yellow-rumped Warbler banding recoveries

Latest dates: Late dates are not listed because of birds attempting to winter.

Winter. Fewer than 10 records exist for December.

Jan – Feb records:
- 16 Dec 1986 – 13 Feb 1987, Huron (Johnson 1987)
- 29 Dec 1974 – 2 Mar 1975, Rapid City (Bachmann et al. in Seasons 1975a)
- 4 Feb 1983, Gregory Co. (Steffen 1983)

BLACK-THROATED GRAY WARBLER *Dendroica nigrescens* (Townsend)

Status. Casual. No specimens, but one good photograph.

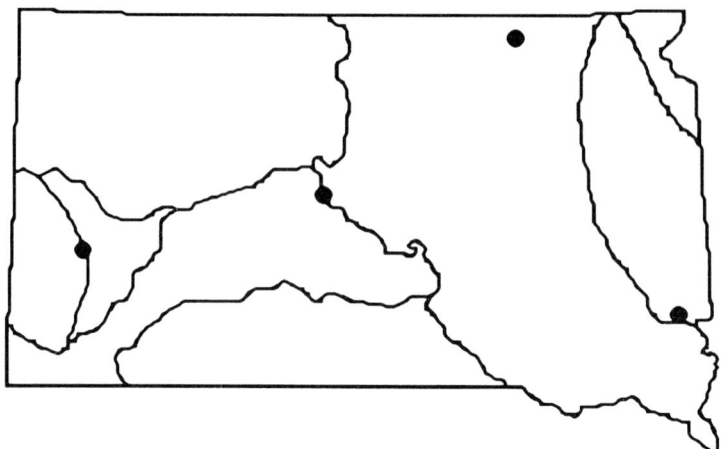

Habitat. Woodlands and residential areas.
Spring migration.
  Only records:
    2 May 1973, near Oahe Dam, photographed (Rose 1975a)
    22 May 1948, Sioux Falls (Donahoe 1949)
Fall migration.
  Only records:
    4 Aug 1973, Rapid City (Baylor 1975)
    1 Sep 1986, Brown Co. (Prisbe and Tallman 1987)

TOWNSEND'S WARBLER *Dendroica townsendi* (Townsend)

Status. Accidental. No specimens. Listed by Over and Thoms (1946) as a possible migrant but without substantiating information.
Only record:
  1 Sep 1984, Lacreek NWR (Paulson and Coons 1984)

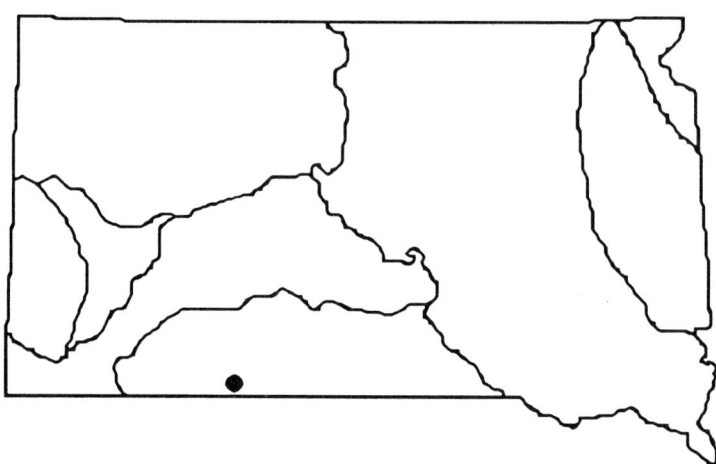

BLACK-THROATED GREEN WARBLER *Dendroica virens* (Gmelin)

Status. Uncommon migrant E; accidental fall migrant W.

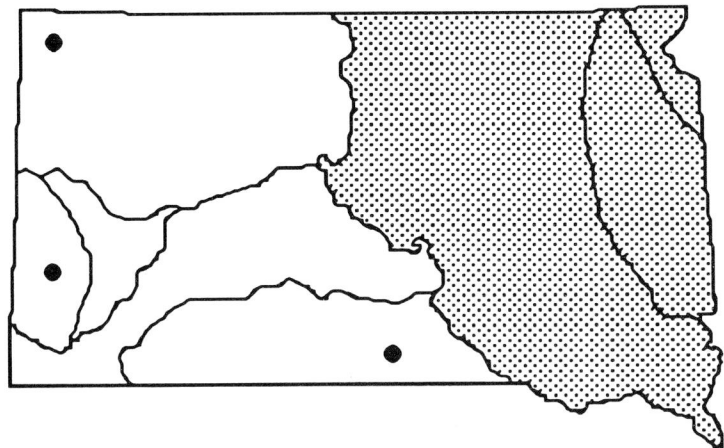

Habitat. Deciduous woodlands and conifers.
Spring migration. Second and third week of May.
   Earliest dates:
      26 Apr 1981, Deuel Co. (Stava in Seasons 1981c)
      28 Apr 1981, Brown Co. (Tallman in Seasons 1981c)
      1 May 1953, Union Co. (Stephens et al. 1955)
      1 May 1957, Minnehaha Co. (Krause)
      1 May 1973, Pierre (Rose)
   Latest dates:
      23 May 1953, Sioux Falls (Krause)
      24 May 1957, Brookings Co. (Holden)
Fall migration. Late Aug – Sep.
   Earliest dates:
      22 Aug 1974, Sheridan Lake (Zimmer)
      23 Aug 1988, Brown Co. (Tallman)
      30 Aug 1975, Lincoln Co. (Blankespoor in Seasons 1975d)
   Latest dates:
      20 Oct 1955, Winner, banded (Wagar)
      20 Oct 1974, Highmore (Harter)
      30 Oct 1980, Brown Co. (Tallman 1981)
      13 Nov 1982, Sanborn Co. (Rogers in Seasons 1983b)
Other W River record.
      12 Oct 1980, Harding Co. (Rogers in Seasons 1981a)

BLACKBURNIAN WARBLER *Dendroica fusca* (Muller)

Status. Uncommon migrant E. Accidental spring migrant W and accidental summer resident in Black Hills.

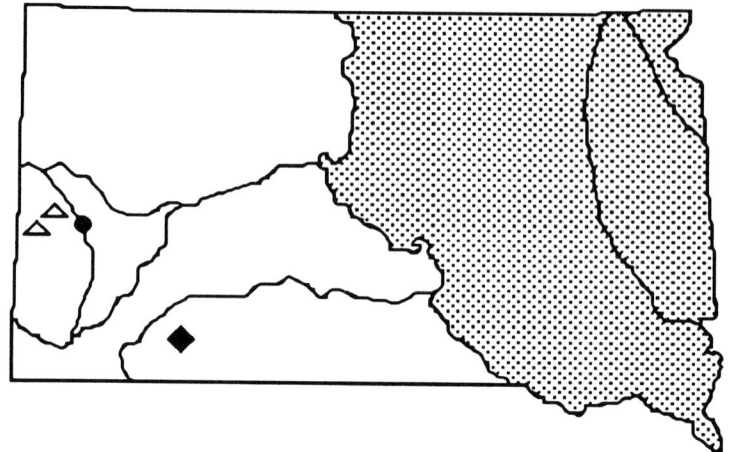

Habitat. Deciduous or coniferous forests.
Spring migration. Second and third week of May.
  Earliest dates:
    1 May 1952, Minnehaha Co. (Krause)
    1 May 1987, Brown Co. (Prisbe)
    3 May [year], Vermillion (Bent 1953)
  Latest dates:
    29 May 1965, Sioux Falls, banded (Rogge and Rogge)
    31 May 1979, Grant Co. (Harris and Spomer in Seasons 1979c)
    2 Jun [year],, Yankton (Bent 1953)
  W River dates:
    17 May 1903, Pine Ridge Indian Reservation (Tullsen in Visher 1912a)
    26 May 1971, Rapid City (Southmayd in Seasons 1971c)
Summer. No nest known.
  Only records:
    2 Jul 1967, Black Fox Campground, 2 singing constantly and perhaps on territory, photographed (Rose in Serr 1967c)
    24 Jul 1980, Roughlock Falls (Bock)
Fall migration. Last half of Aug – mid-Sep.
  Earliest dates:
    11 Aug 1987, Deuel Co. (Harris in Seasons 1988a)
    17 Aug 1979, Brown Co., banded (Tallman 1979)
    19 Aug 1986, Roberts Co. (Harris)

Latest dates:
17 Sep 1959, Minnehaha Co. (Krause 1959a)
17 Sep 1969, Sanborn Co., specimen (Harris)
23 Sep 1982, Brown Co. (Tallman in Seasons 1983a)
5 Oct 1969, Brookings Co. (Edie)

YELLOW-THROATED WARBLER *Dendroica dominica* (Linnaeus)

Status. Accidental in spring E. No specimens.
Records.
19 Apr 1964, Spink Co. (Rose 1966)
23–25 Apr 1960, Sioux Falls (Krause 1960)

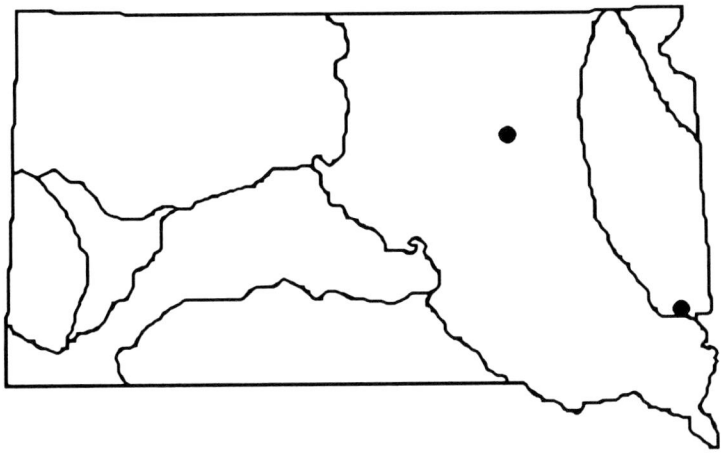

PINE WARBLER *Dendroica pinus* (Wilson)

Status. Rare migrant extreme E. No specimens, but 1 dead, KSOO TV tower near Flandreau, 14 Sep 1965 (Pierce 1969).

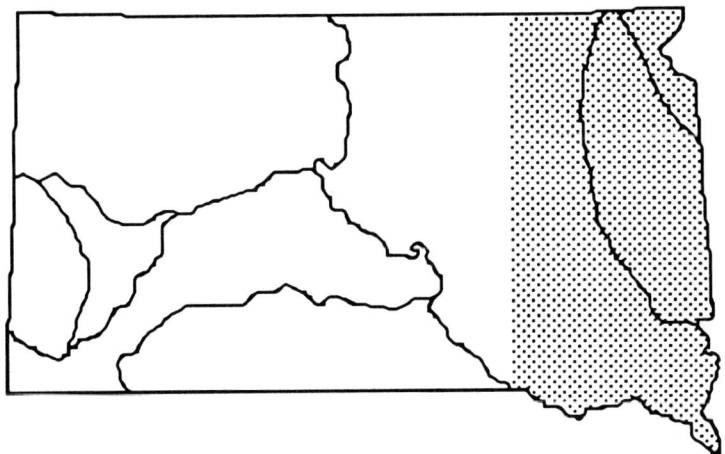

Habitat. Usually associated with pines.
Spring migration. Last 3 weeks of May.
Earliest dates:
2 May 1951, Madison (Habeger 1956b)

7 May 1977, Brookings Co., singing (Holden in Seasons 1977c)
9 May 1958, Brookings Co. (Holden)
Latest dates:
21 May 1950, Madison (Habeger 1950)
23 May 1982, Brookings Co. (Pengra in Seasons 1982c)
23 May 1959, Sioux Falls (Krause)

Fall migration. Late Aug – first 3 weeks of Sep.
Earliest dates:
6 Aug 1987, Roberts Co. (Harris in Seasons 1988a)
19 Aug 1986, Roberts Co. (Harris in Seasons 1987a)
21 Aug 1933, Aberdeen (George)
Latest dates:
21 Sep 1955, Milbank, banded (Elliott 1955)
21 Sep 1962, Brookings, banded (Holden)
22 Sep 1965, Sioux Falls, banded (Rogge and Rogge)
4 Oct 1971, Sioux Falls, singing (Krause)

PRAIRIE WARBLER *Dendroica discolor* (Vieillot)

Status. Casual. No specimens.
Records:
5 May 1990, Beadle Co. (Rogers in Seasons 1990c)
18 May 1962, Sioux Falls (Krause)
11—20 Jun 1976, Wind Cave NP (Palmer)
20 Aug 1977, Lawrence Co. (Rosche and Rosche)
3 Sep 1972, Faulk Co. (Wagar)
7 Sep 1961, near Milbank (Elliott 1961c)

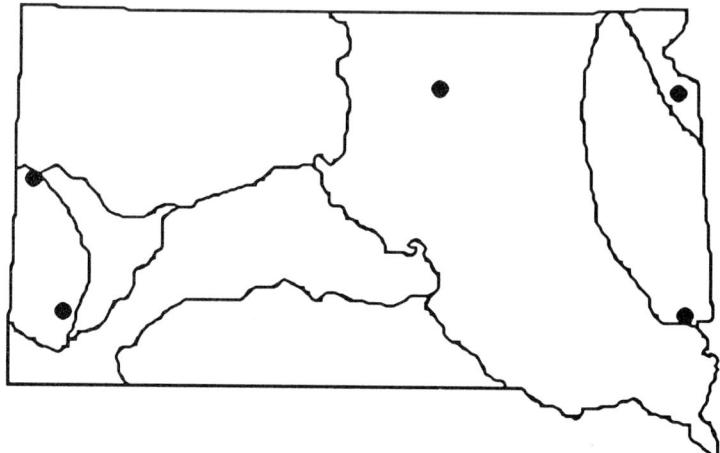

PALM WARBLER *Dendroica palmarum* (Gmelin)

Status. Common migrant E; rare migrant W.

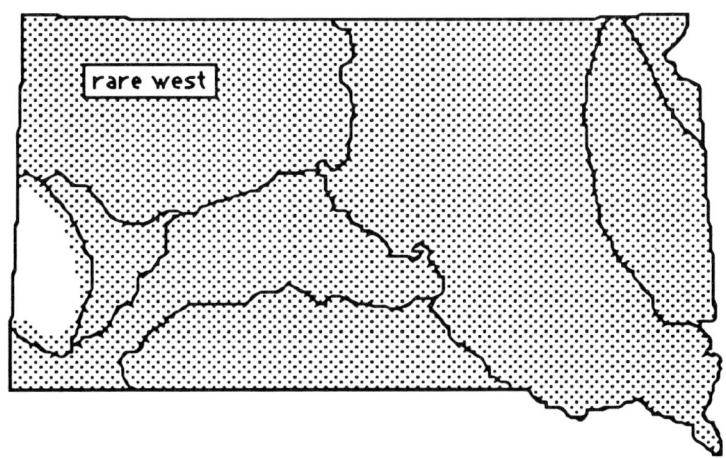

Habitat. Wooded areas or near water.

Spring migration. First half of May.
   Earliest dates:
      16 Apr [year], Huron (Bent 1953)
      17 Apr 1963, Rapid City (Pettingill and Whitney 1965)
      23 Apr 1961, Hyde Co. (Harter 1968a)
   Latest dates:
      22 May 1957, Brookings Co. (Holden)
      23 May 1953, Farm Island (SDOU)
      25 May [year], Sioux Falls (Bent 1953)

Fall migration. Late Aug – Sep.
   Earliest dates:
      24 Aug 1977, Hyde Co. (Harter in Seasons 1978a)
      30 Aug 1934, Wind Cave NP (Cahalane in Pettingill and Whitney 1965)
      8 Sep 1961, Highmore (Harter)
   Latest dates:
      13 Oct 1974, Highmore (Harter)
      14 Oct 1972, Pierre (Rose)
      3 Nov 1967, Jackson Co. (Harris)

BAY-BREASTED WARBLER *Dendroica castanea* (Wilson)
Status. Uncommon migrant E. Accidental migrant W.

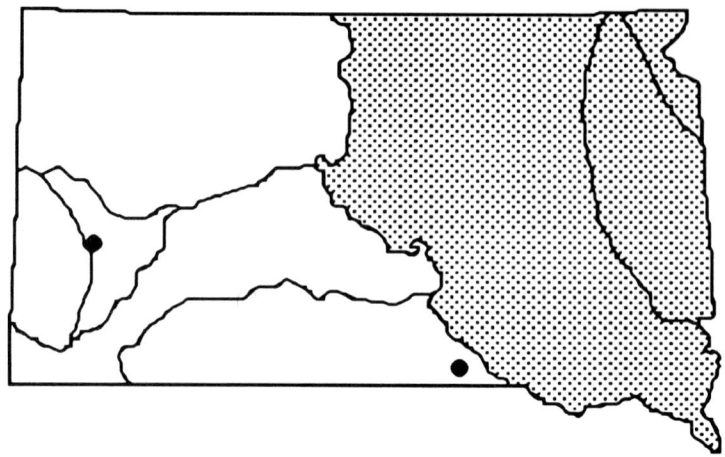

Habitat. Deciduous woodlands.
Spring migration. Third and fourth week of May.
  Earliest dates:
    3 May 1981, Brookings Co. (Holden in Seasons 1981c)
    8 May 1986, Deuel Co. (Harris in Seasons 1986c)
    10 May 1971, Sioux Falls (Krause)
  Latest dates:
    31 May 1964, Highmore (Harter 1964)
    31 May 1968, Roberts Co. (Harris)
    5 Jun 1979, near Colman (Vinland)
Fall migration. Sep.
  Earliest dates:
    11 Aug 1987, Deuel Co. (Harris in Seasons 1988a)
    19 Aug 1986, Deuel Co. (Harris)
    25 Aug 1976, Roberts Co. (Harris in Seasons 1977a)
  Latest dates:
    8 Oct 1980, Brookings Co. (Taylor in Seasons 1981a)
    10 Oct 1933, Aberdeen (George)
    24 Oct 1974, Highmore (Harter 1974b)
W River records.
    12 May 1984, Gregory Co., banded (Steffen in Seasons 1984c)
    22 May 1971, Rapid City (Green in Seasons 1971c)

BLACKPOLL WARBLER *Dendroica striata* (Forster)

Status. Common to abundant migrant E; rare migrant W, absent from higher Black Hills.

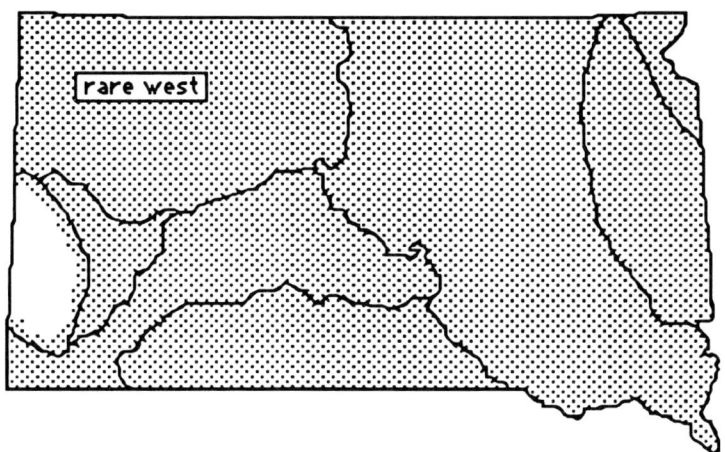

Habitat. Deciduous woodlands.
Spring migration. Second and third week of May.
  Earliest dates:
    1 May 1981, Brown Co. (Tallman in Seasons 1981c)
    3 May 1955, Minnehaha Co. (Krause)
    3 May 1980, Day Co. (Tallman in Seasons 1980c)
    3 May 1986, Lincoln Co. (Holden in Seasons 1986c)
  Latest dates:
    20 Jun 1971, Lake Co. (Holden)
    23 Jun 1976, Rapid City (Bachmann in Seasons 1976d)
    30 Jun 1961, Vermillion (R. R. Nelson)
Fall migration. Late Aug – Sep.
  Earliest dates:
    11 Aug 1987, Deuel Co. (Harris in Seasons 1988a)
    18 Aug 1986, Roberts Co. (Harris)
    25 Aug 1976, Roberts Co. (Harris in Seasons 1977a)
  Latest dates:
    20 Sep 1980, Brown Co. (Tallman 1981)
    24 Sep 1983, Brown Co. (Tallman in Seasons 1984a)
    28 Sep 1986, Grant Co. (Gilman and Rose)

CERULEAN WARBLER *Dendroica cerulea* (Wilson)

Status. Casual spring migrant E. May breed in Lincoln Co. (Springer and Skadsen 1986). No specimens.

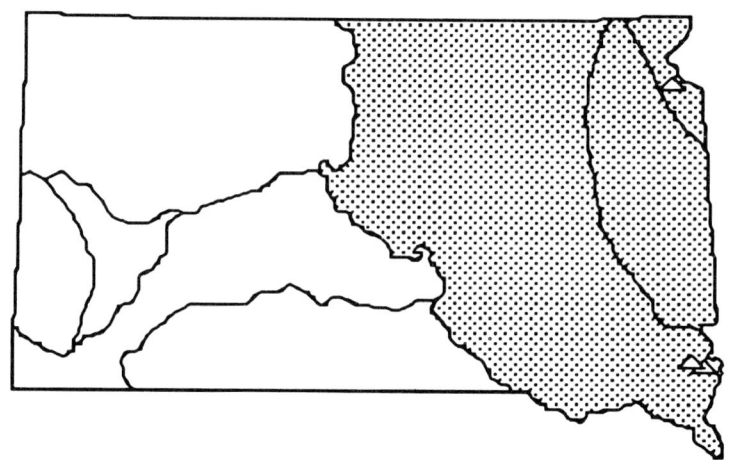

Habitat. Mature woodlands.
Spring migration. Second – third weeks of May.
  Earliest dates:
    10 May 1979, Brookings Co. (Froiland in Seasons 1979c)
    13 May 1958, Brookings Co. (Holden)
    14 May 1950, Madison (Habeger 1950)
  Latest dates:
    22 May 1957, Union Co. (Youngworth 1957)
    22 May 1966, Huron (L. Johnson)
    25–27 May 1985, Lincoln Co. (Harris et al. in Springer and Skadsen 1986)
Summer. No nests known.
  Records:
    5 Jun 1986, Lincoln Co., singing (Skadsen in Seasons 1986d)
    5–6 Jun 1989, Roberts Co., singing (Harris in Seasons 1989d)
    10 Jun 1982, Lincoln Co. (Blankespoor in Springer and Skadsen 1986)
    15 Jun – 5 Jul 1985, Lincoln Co. (Skadsen and Lehman in Springer and Skadsen 1986)
    19 Jun – 2 Jul 1990, Roberts Co., singing (Harris)

BLACK-AND-WHITE WARBLER *Mniotilta varia* (Linnaeus)

Status. Common migrant. Breeding records from Farm Island, Black Hills, and Rosebud; summer records from NE, Campbell, Corson, Dewey, Harding, Sanborn, E Meade, and Shannon counties and the Missouri River and its tributaries.

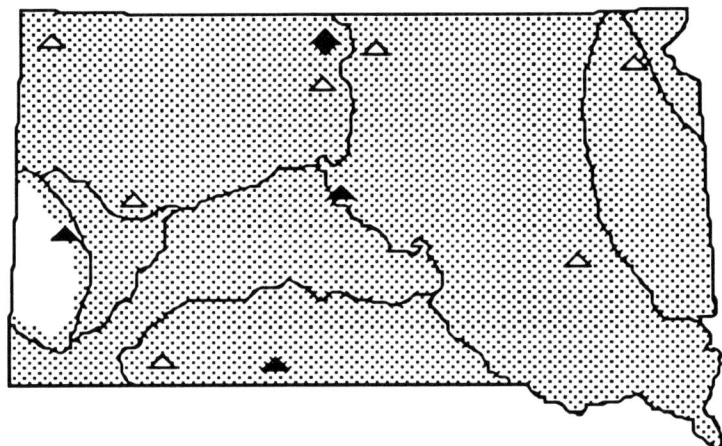

Habitat. Deciduous woodlands.
Spring migration. First 3 weeks of May.
 Earliest dates:
  21 Apr 1970, Sioux Falls (Krause)
  21 Apr 1971, Sioux Falls (Krause and Blankespoor)
  24 Apr 1981, Deuel Co. (Stava in Seasons 1981c)
Nesting. Jun and Jul. Singing males have been heard at Sica Hollow SP (Springer and Harris), near White Owl in Meade Co. (Tallman in Seasons 1983d) and Sanborn (Harris), Dewey (Holden), and Harding (Springer) counties.
 Earliest date:
  21 Jun 1948, near Rapid City, singing male with enlarged testes collected (Dilger in Pettingill and Whitney 1965)
 Latest dates:
  5 Jul 1981, near Rapid City, 1 adult and 2 young (Baker in Seasons 1981d)
  8 Jul 1959, 5 miles NW of Rosebud, adult with fledgling (Whitney)
  22 Jul 1979, Farm Island, adult carrying food (Backland)

Fall migration. Last week of Aug – first 3 weeks of Sep. Early dates may represent resident birds.
  Latest dates:
    25 Sep 1966, Beadle Co. (Johnson)
    29 Sep 1980, Brown Co. (Tallman 1981)
    2 Oct 1977, Pierre (Hill in Seasons 1979a)

AMERICAN REDSTART *Setophaga ruticilla* (Linnaeus)

Status. Common migrant. Locally common summer resident W in suitable habitat; breeds very locally in SE and in Roberts and Marshall counties.

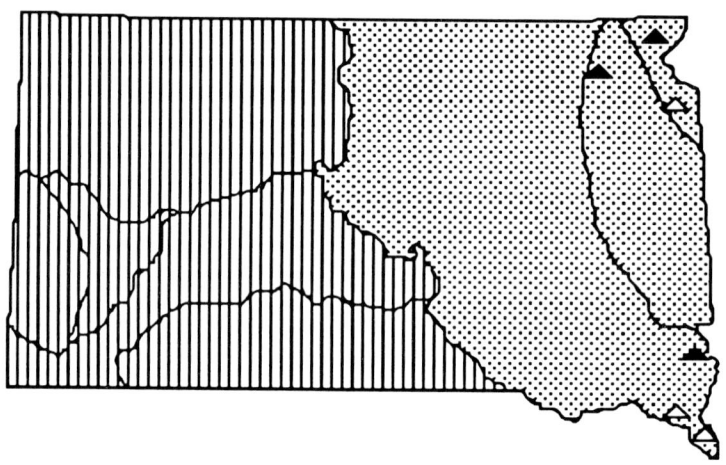

Habitat. Second growth deciduous woodlands.
Spring migration. Last 3 weeks of May.
  Earliest dates:
    26 Apr 1981, Deuel Co. (Stava in Seasons 1981c)
    2 May 1965, Sturgis (Wagar)
    3 May 1959, Brookings Co. (Holden)
    3 May 1964, Sioux Falls (Krause)
Nesting. Last week of May – mid-Jul.
  Earliest dates:
    15 Jun 1985, Lincoln Co., nest with young (Springer and Skadsen 1986)
    20 Jun 1985, Dewey Co. nest with young (Springer)
    23 Jun 1941, Roberts Co., nest with young (Harris 1963)
Summer records:
    3 Jun 1965, Deuel Co. (Springer)
    12 Jun 1959, Union Co. (Youngworth)
    12 Jun 1985, Clay Co. (Springer)
  Latest dates:
    1 Jul 1950, Spearfish, adults feeding 2 fledglings (Haight 1950)
    13 Jul 1978, Todd Co., female feeding young (Springer)

American Redstart banding recoveries

20 Jul 1958, Roughlock Falls, adults feeding young (Carter 1958a)

Fall migration. Last half of Aug – Sep.
Latest dates:
15 Oct [year], Faulkton (Bent 1953)
15 Oct 1983, Brookings Co. (Husmann in Seasons 1984a)
23 Oct 1981, Brown Co., banded (Tallman in Seasons 1982a)

PROTHONOTARY WARBLER *Protonotaria citrea* (Boddaert)

Status. Rare visitor in the SE. Probably nested rarely in Union Co. Accidental W.

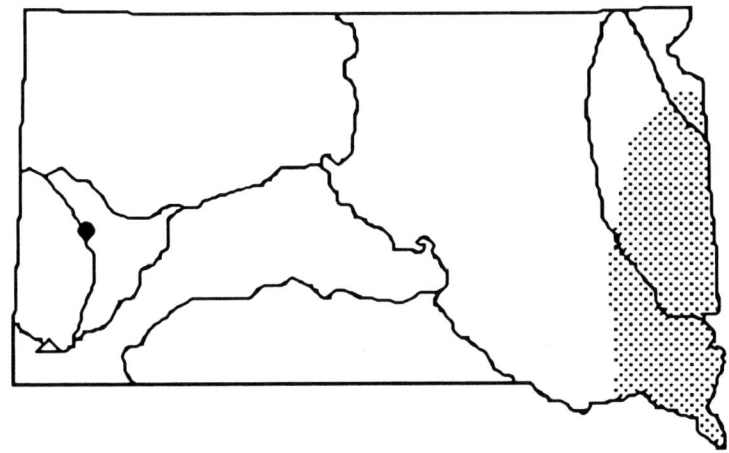

Habitat. Swampy river bottoms and low-lying woods.
Spring migration. Second – third week of May.
Earliest dates:
2 May 1988, Deuel Co. (Harris in Seasons 1988c)
4 May 1953, Sioux Falls (Krause)
11 May 1929, McCook Lake, collected (Kubichek in Stephens et al. 1955)
Latest dates:
21 May 1931, Union Co. (Youngworth)
21 May 1950, Oakwood Lakes (Rollings)
24 May 1950, Madison (Habeger 1950)
25 May 1931, Union Co., collected (Stephens et al. 1955)
Nesting. No nests known, despite the statement, "...we know that it breeds in the McCook Lake, South Dakota area" (Stephens and Youngworth 1957).
Summer records:
4 Jun 1922, Union Co. (Taylor in Stephens et al. 1955)
11 Jun 1982, Hot Springs, specimen (Murdock 1982)
18 Jun 1931, Union Co., specimen (Stephens et al. 1955)
28 Jun 1932, Union Co. (Youngworth)

Fall migration.
Only dates:
1 Sep 1984, Rapid City (Husmann 1985)
6 Sep 1917, McCook Lake (Hayden in Stephens et al. 1955)
28 Sep 1954, Sioux Falls (Krause)

WORM-EATING WARBLER *Helmitheros vermivorus* (Gmelin)

Status. Casual spring and accidental fall visitor E. Accidental W.

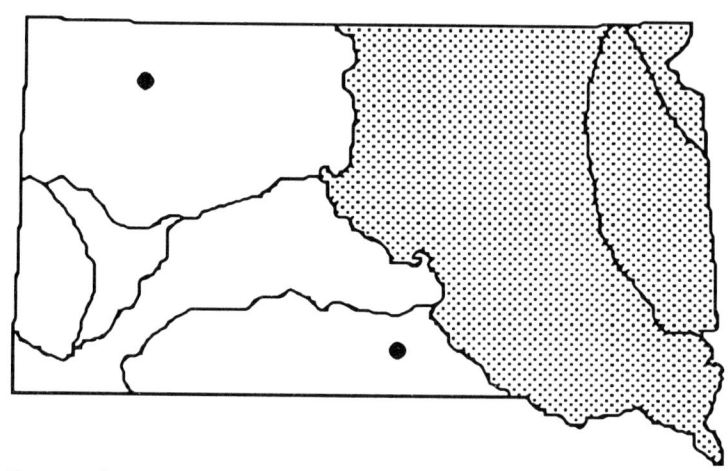

Habitat. Second-growth deciduous woodlands.
Spring migration. Second – third week of May.
Earliest dates:
2 May 1982, Sand Lake (Edens in Seasons 1982c)
2 May 1988, Brown Co., banded (Tallman in Seasons 1988c)
5 May 1970, Tripp Co. (Harris 1971b)
5 May 1982, Brown Co., specimen (Tallman in Seasons 1982c)
Latest dates:
22 May 1954, Milbank (Wagar 1958)
23 May 1965, Farm Island, banded and photographed (Rogge and Rogge 1965a)
27 May 1990, Day Co., banded (Skadsen in Seasons 1990c)
Fall migration.
Only record:
13 Aug 1983, Huron (Johnson 1983b)
Other W River record.
7 May 1988, Perkins Co. (Griffiths et al. in Seasons 1988c)

OVENBIRD *Seiurus aurocapillus* (Linnaeus)

Status. Fairly common migrant. Uncommon to fairly common summer resident in suitable habitat.

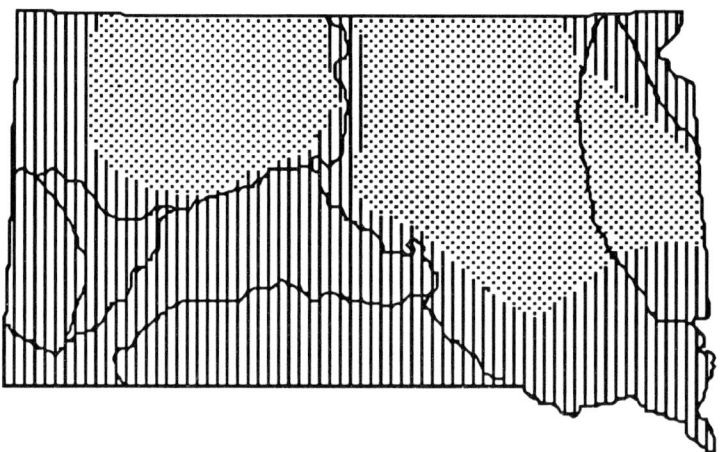

Habitat. Woodlands.
Spring migration. Second and third weeks of May.
  Earliest dates:
    26 Apr 1974, Brookings Co., 1 banded (Holden)
    1 May 1954, Sioux Falls (Krause)
    4 May 1965, near Brookings (Springer)
Nesting. Probably in late May – mid-Jul. During June and July, singing males or nests have been found in the NE coulees (Harris, Holden, and Springer), Sodak Park (Harris), Farm Island (Harris and Holden), Lincoln Co. (Springer), Little Moreau SP (Holden), Shannon Co. (Homoya), and near Rosebud (Timken, Springer).

  Earliest dates:
    31 May 1987, near Blackhawk, nest with 5 eggs (Riner)
    15 Jun 1969, Slim Buttes, pair courting (Baylor and Rosine 1970)
    23 Jun 1989, Slim Buttes, nest with 2 eggs and 2 young (Melius)
  Latest dates:
    3 Jul 1970, Slim Buttes, feeding young (Springer)
    12 Jul 1990, Meade Co., adult carrying food (Whitney)
    14 Jul 1978, Harding Co., pair with 2 fledged young (Springer)

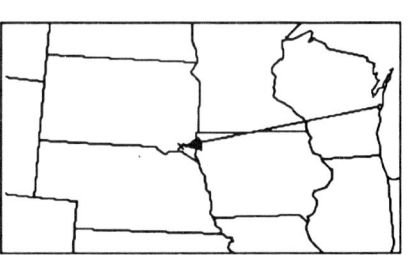

Ovenbird banding recoveries

Fall migration: Mid-Aug – Sep.
  Latest dates:
    19 Oct 1960, Brookings, banded (Holden)
    25 Oct 1958, Armour, dead (Crutchett 1958)
    30 Oct 1977, Hyde Co. (Harter in Seasons 1978a)

NORTHERN WATERTHRUSH *Seiurus noveboracensis* (Gmelin)

Status. Uncommon migrant, most common along E border. Rare migrant in Black Hills, Harding, and Fall River counties.

Habitat. Deciduous woodlands along streams.

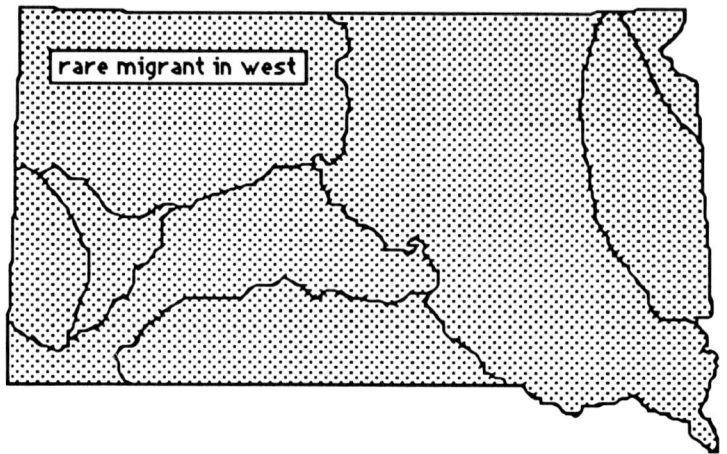

Spring migration. First – second week of May.
  Earliest dates:
    24 Apr 1942, Roberts Co. (Harris 1964)
    26 Apr 1973, Yankton (Hall)
    30 Apr 1955, Sioux Falls (Krause)
  Latest dates:
    29 May 1955, Webster (Dahling 1956)
    29 May 1959, Brookings (Holden)

Fall migration. Mid-Aug – Sep.
  Earliest dates:
    6 Aug 1987, Roberts Co. (Harris in Seasons 1988a)
    10 Aug [year], Faulkton (Bent 1953)
    11 Aug 1938, Day Co. (Dahling 1956)
    11 Aug 1972, Faulk Co. (Wagar)
  Latest dates:
    1 Oct 1980, Union Co. (L. Anderson)
    11 Oct 1984, Brookings Co. (Husmann in Seasons 1985a)
    22 Oct 1985, Brown Co., banded (Tallman)

LOUISIANA WATERTHRUSH *Seiurus motacilla* (Vieillot)

Status. Casual visitor SE. No specimens.

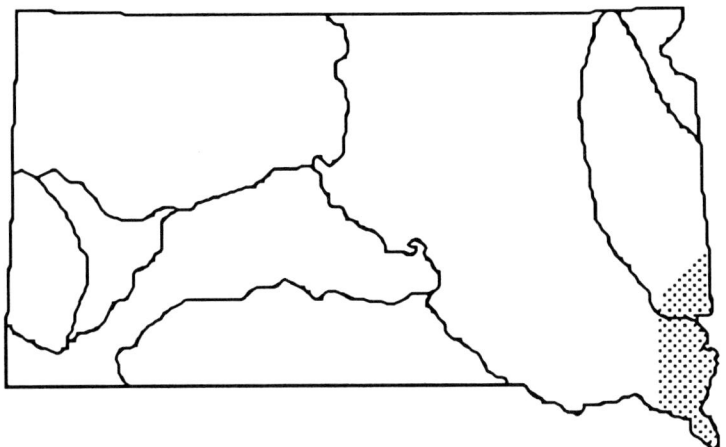

Habitat. Wooded areas along streams.

Spring migration. Second and third weeks of May.
  Earliest dates:
    28 Apr [year], Sioux Falls (Bent 1953)
    7 May 1927, Union Co. (Bailey in Stephens et al. 1955)
    8 May 1987, Minnehaha Co. (Skadsen and Hoeger in Seasons 1987c)
  Latest dates:
    17 May 1956, Union Co. (Youngworth)
    17 May 1957, Brookings (Holden)
    19 May 1923, Union Co. (Bailey in Stephens et al. 1955)
    24 May 1924, Union Co. (Bailey in Stephens et al. 1955)

Fall migration. Early Sep.
  Records:
    3 Sep 1939, Union Co. (Laffoon in Stephens et al. 1955)
    8 Sep 1907, Sioux Falls area (Larson 1925)

KENTUCKY WARBLER *Oporornis formosus* (Wilson)

Status. Casual visitor S and E. No specimens

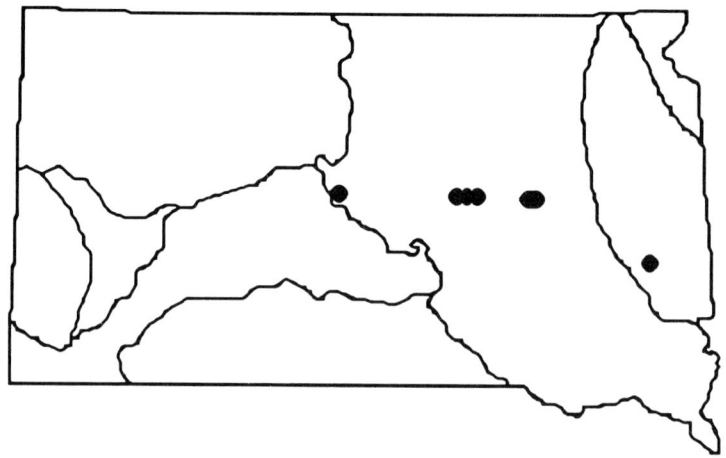

Spring migration.
 Only records:
  15 May 1983, Madison (Buckman 1983)
  18 May 1974, Pierre (Rose 1975c)
Fall migration.
 Only dates:
  29 Aug 1974, Highmore (Harter)
  3 Sep 1970, Huron (Johnson 1970b)
  10 Sep 1961, Highmore (Harter 1969)
  15 Sep 1966, Highmore (Harter 1969)
  16–18 Sep 1963, Huron (Johnson 1963b)

CONNECTICUT WARBLER *Oporornis agilis* (Wilson)

Status. Rare spring and accidental fall migrant E.

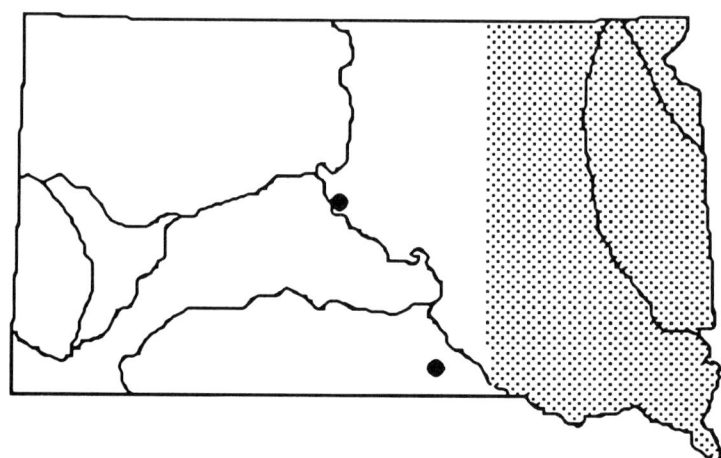

Habitat. Brushy woodlands.
Spring migration. Last 2 weeks of May.

Earliest dates:
  12 May 1949, Madison (Habeger 1950)
  15 May 1958, Brookings (Holden)
  18 May 1982, Brown Co., specimen (Tallman in Seasons 1982c)
Latest dates:
  1 Jun 1958, Winner, banded (Wagar)
  1 Jun 1959, Brookings, banded (Holden)
  9 Jun 1967, Oakwood Lakes, banded (Rogge and Rogge)
  10 Jun 1971, Oakwood Lakes, banded (Rogge and Rogge)
Fall migration.
Only records:
  30 Jul 1988, Grant Co. (Prisbe in Seasons 1988d)
  27 Aug 1972, Minnehaha Co. (Krause)
  1 Sep 1985, Brown Co., banded and photographed (Tallman in Seasons 1986a)
  20 Sep 1972, Pierre (Rose)

MOURNING WARBLER *Oporornis philadelphia* (Wilson)

Status. Fairly common migrant E. Rare migrant W.

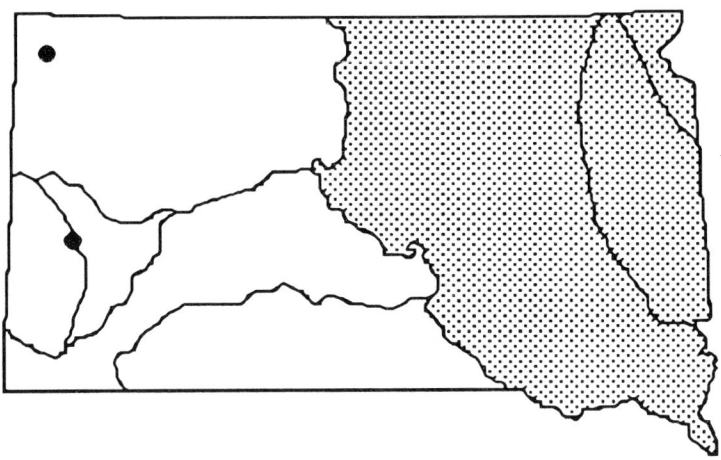

Habitat. Dense undergrowth.
Spring migration. Last 2 weeks of May.
Earliest dates:
  3 May 1981, Deuel Co. (Stava in Seasons 1981c)
  7 May 1963, Sioux Falls (Krause)
  13 May 1972, Hyde Co. (Harter)
Latest dates:
  4 Jun 1967, Canyon Lake area (Rose and Southmayd in Seasons 1967c)
  5 Jun 1965, Sioux Falls (Krause)
  6 Jun 1946, Brookings, banded (Wagar)
  6 Jun 1970, Cresbard, banded (Wagar)

Fall migration. Last week of Aug – Sep.
Earliest dates:
30 Jul 1988, Grant Co. (Prisbe in Seasons 1988d)
15 Aug 1987, Minnehaha Co. (Hoeger in Seasons 1988a)
15 Aug 1990, Brown Co., banded (Tallman)
Latest dates:
12 Oct 1960, Sioux Falls, banded (Findley)
12 Oct 1980, Brookings Co. (Taylor in Seasons 1981a)

MACGILLIVRAY'S WARBLER *Oporornis tolmiei* (Townsend)

Status. Uncommon summer resident in Black Hills. Rare migrant in extreme W and casual in E.

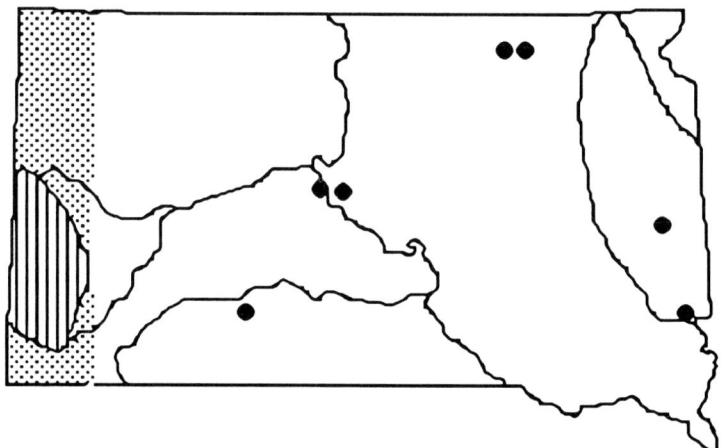

Habitat. Deciduous thickets.
Spring migration. Second – third week of May.
Earliest dates:
9 May 1987, Jackson Co., banded (Graupmann in Seasons 1987c)
13 May 1961, Rapid City, specimen (Whitney)
15 May 1985, Brown Co., banded (Tallman in Seasons 1985a)
16 May 1968, Oahe Reservoir, banded (Rogge and Rogge)
Latest dates (outside Black Hills):
2 Jun 1970, Farm Island, banded (Rogge and Rogge)
7 Jun 1979, Brown Co., specimen (Tallman 1979)
9 Jun 1967, Oakwood Lakes, banded (Rogge and Rogge)
Nesting. Last week of May – mid-Jul.
Earliest date:
20 Jun 1973, Spearfish Canyon, pair at nest (Hays)
Latest dates:
2 Jul 1956, Palmer Gulch, adults feeding fledgling (Eastman in Pettingill and Whitney 1965)
5 Jul 1958, Jewel Cave NM, adults feeding 2 fledglings (Carter 1958b)
10 Jul 1970, Custer Co., nest with young (Edie)

Fall migration. Sep.
  Latest dates:
    23 Sep 1965, Sioux Falls, banded (Rogge and Rogge)
    23 Sep 1979, Pennington Co. (Whitney in Seasons 1980a)
    27 Sep 1955, Cave Hills (Whitney 1957)

COMMON YELLOWTHROAT *Geothlypis trichas* (Linnaeus)

Status. Common to abundant summer resident.

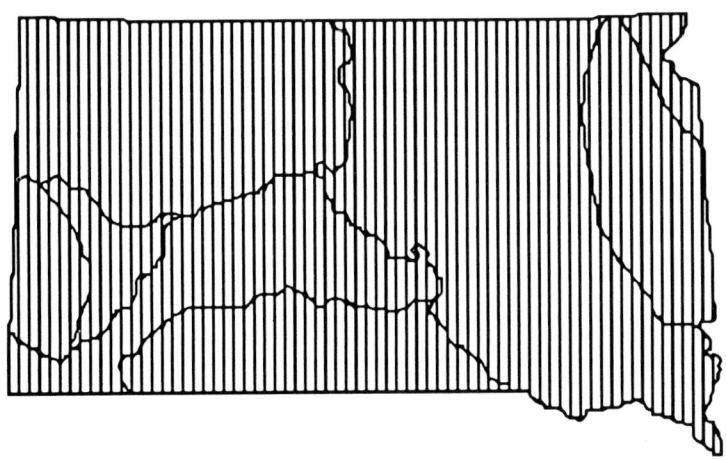

Habitat. Dense marsh vegetation, streamside thickets, and moist grasslands.
Spring migration. Second and third weeks of May.
  Earliest dates:
    26 Apr 1973, Yankton (Hall)
    27 Apr 1962, Rapid City (Behrens in Pettingill and Whitney 1965)
    28 Apr 1989, Fall River Co. (Peterson in Seasons 1989c)
Nesting. Jun to early Aug.
  Earliest dates:
    9 Jun 1968, Sanborn Co., 2 nests with 4 and 5 eggs (Harris)
    17 Jun 1947, near Roughlock Falls, nest with 5 eggs (Sutton in Pettingill and Whitney 1965)
    25 Jun 1962, Watertown area, nests with 5 eggs (Moriarty 1964a)
  Latest dates:
    4 Aug 1966, Sica Hollow, adult feeding young (Springer)
    16 Aug 1977, Hyde Co., male feeding fledgling (Harter in Seasons 1977d)
Fall migration. Late Aug – Sep.
  Latest dates:
    26 Oct 1955, Milbank, banded (Elliott)
    26 Oct 1957, Winner, banded (Wagar)
    28 Oct 1987, Deuel Co. (Harris in Seasons 1988a)

HOODED WARBLER *Wilsonia citrina* (Boddaert)

Status. Casual spring visitor E, chiefly in S. Accidental migrant W.

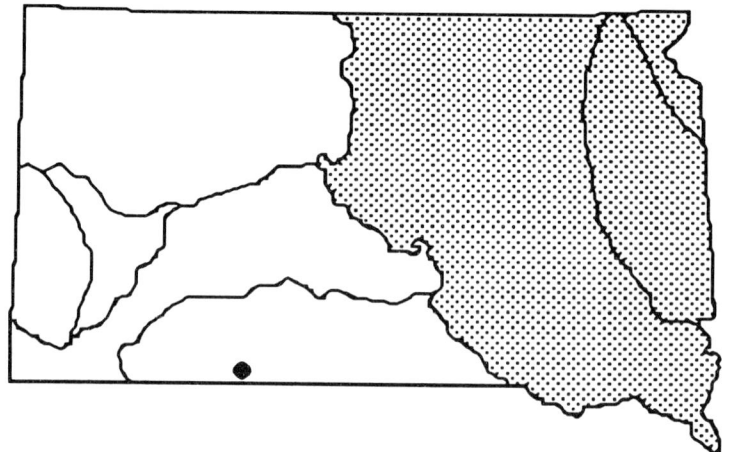

Spring migration. Late Apr – mid-May.
Earliest dates:
  12 Apr 1948, Sioux Falls (Krause)
  26 Apr 1974, near Pierre, male photographed (Rose 1975b)
  29 Apr 1974, near Pierre, female (Rose 1975b)
  29 Apr 1979, Brown Co. (Downs in Seasons 1979c)
Latest dates:
  15 May 1968, Yankton Co., specimen (Anderson in Harris 1969a)
  15 May 1976, Brookings Co., banded (Holden in Seasons 1976c)
  16 May 1981, Brookings Co. (Buckman in Seasons 1981c)
  17 May 1973, Lacreek, banded (Fjetland 1973)

WILSON'S WARBLER *Wilsonia pusilla* (Wilson)

Status. Fairly common migrant E; uncommon migrant W. Accidental summer.

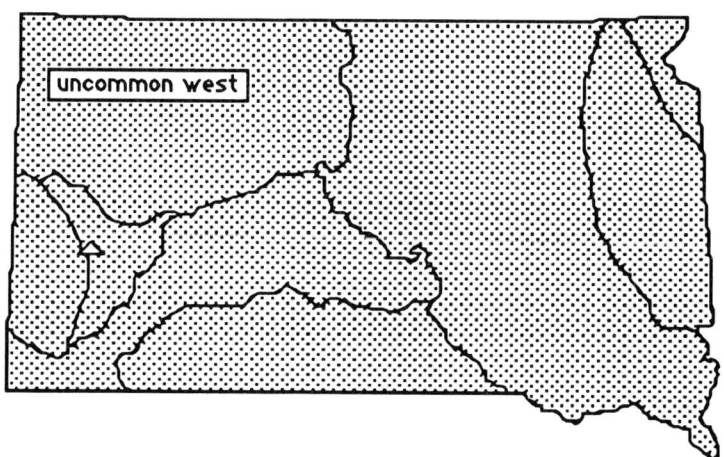

Habitat. Low, shrubby growth.
Spring migration. Second and third week of May.
  Earliest dates:
    18 Apr 1971, Rapid City (Green)
    20 Apr 1987, Brown Co. (Tallman in Seasons 1987c)
    23 Apr 1990, Fall River Co. (Peterson in Seasons 1990c)
  Latest dates:
    27 May 1962, Farm Island (SDOU)
    27 May 1966, Farm Island (J. W. Johnson and L. Johnson)
    28 May 1973, Pierre (Rose)
    1 Jun 1975, Hyde Co. (Harter in Seasons 1975b)
Summer.
  Only record:
    10 Jul 1977, Rapid City (Hays in Seasons 1977d)
Fall migration. Mid-Aug – Sep.
  Earliest dates:
    8 Aug 1963, Highmore (Harter)
    12 Aug 1970, Rapid City (Southmayd)
    17 Aug 1959, Milbank, banded (Elliott 1959)
  Latest dates:
    22 Oct 1955, Milbank, banded (Elliott)
    26 Oct 1975, Rapid City (Seasons 1975d)
    30 Oct [year], Faulkton (Bent 1953)

CANADA WARBLER *Wilsonia canadensis* (Linnaeus)

Status. Uncommon migrant E; accidental W. Accidental summer.

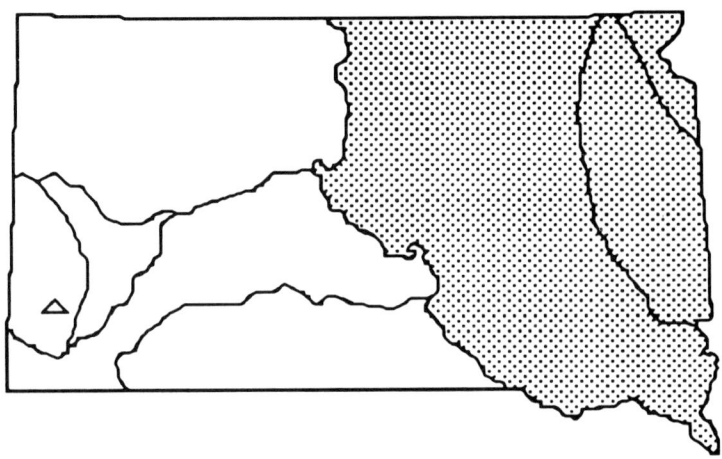

Habitat. Woodlands and brushy areas.
Spring migration. Second week – end of May.
Earliest dates:
  6 May 1983, Brookings Co. (Taylor in Seasons 1983c)
  9 May 1986, Deuel Co. (Harris in Seasons 1986c)
  13 May 1972, Sioux Falls (Krause)
Latest dates:
  1 Jun 1967, Oakwood Lakes, banded (Rogge and Rogge)
  2 Jun 1971, Brookings (Edie)
  3 Jun 1933, Brown Co. (George)
Fall migration. Late Aug – late Sep.
Earliest dates:
  28 Jul 1988, Custer Co. (Harris and Peterson in Seasons 1988d)
  14 Aug 1987, Brown Co. (Montgomery in Seasons 1988a)
  18 Aug 1986, Roberts Co. (Harris)
Latest dates:
  16 Oct 1969, Brookings (Edie)
  20 Oct 1971, Highmore (Harter)
  29 Oct 1981, Brown Co., banded (Tallman in Seasons 1982a)

YELLOW-BREASTED CHAT *Icteria virens* (Linnaeus)

Status. Fairly common summer resident W. Uncommon migrant and probably a local breeder E.

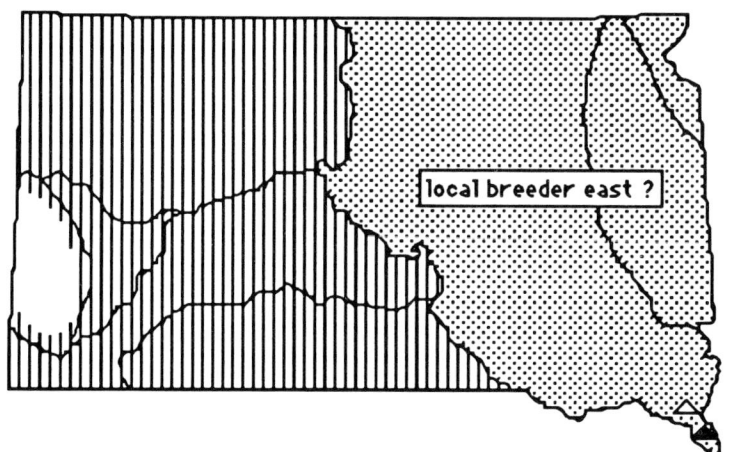

Habitat. Deciduous woodlands with thickets.
Spring migration. Second and third weeks of May.
  Earliest dates:
    2 May 1968, Tilford, specimen (Behrens)
    7 May 1965, Rapid City, specimen (Whitney)
    8 May 1965, Farm Island, banded (Findley)
  Latest dates (outside breeding area):
    27 May 1985, Lincoln Co. (Springer and Skadsen 1986)
    7 Jun 1967, Brown Co. (Timken)
    9 Jun 1983, Brown Co., banded (Tallman in Seasons 1983c)
Nesting. Late May – early Jul. E breeding season records: 13 Jun 1959, Union Co. (Youngworth) and summer 1929, nesting, Union Co. (Bennett).
  Earliest dates:
    27 May 1962, Farm Island, nest with eggs (Holden)
    3 Jun 1932, near Chamberlain, nest with 5 eggs (Lee in Whitney 1955)
    28 Jun 1968, Farm Island, nest (Harris)
  Latest dates:
    3 Jul 1978, Badlands, nest with 3 eggs (Spomer in Seasons 1978d)
    14 Jul 1954, Rapid City, adults feeding fledgling (Pettingill and Whitney 1965)
    15 Jul 1981, Wind Cave NP, 3 fledglings (Hetlet)
Fall migration. Sep.
  Earliest dates (outside breeding area):
    26 Aug 1961, Highmore (Harter)
    28 Aug 1984, Codington Co. (Gilman in Seasons 1985c)
    4 Sep 1987, Brown Co., banded (Tallman in Seasons 1988a)
  Latest dates:
    9 Oct 1957, Winner, banded (Wagar)
    11 Oct 1976, Hyde Co. (Harter in Seasons 1977a)
    20 Oct [year], Faulkton (Bent 1953)

SUBFAMILY THRAUPINAE: Tanagers

SUMMER TANAGER *Piranga rubra* (Linnaeus)

Status. Casual spring visitor E, accidental W. Considered by Reagen (1908) to be rare summer resident in Mellette Co. Accidental fall.

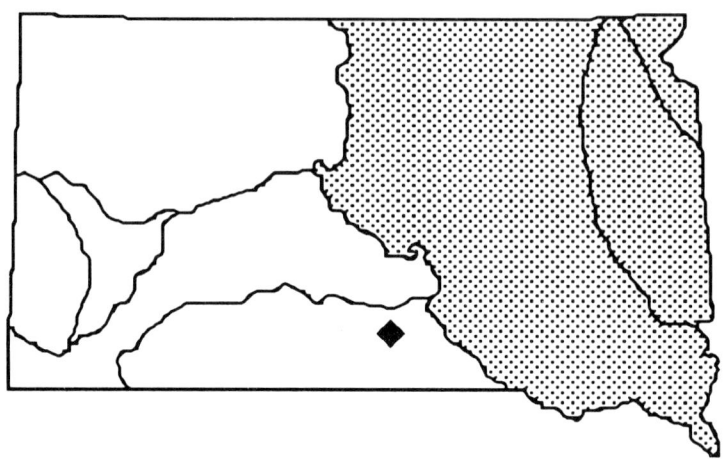

Spring migration. Mid-May.
  Earliest dates:
    25 Apr 1990, Custer Co. (Johnston)
    30 Apr 1961, Woodland Cemetery, Sioux Falls (Rogge and Rogge 1965b)
    5 May 1977, Pierre (Nagel in Seasons 1977c)
  Latest dates:
    23 May 1975, Pierre (Rose in Seasons 1975b)
    26 May 1984, Brown Co., banded (Tallman in Seasons 1984c)
    30 May 1965, Oakwood Lakes, banded (Rogge and Rogge 1965b)

Fall migration.
  Only record:
    7 Sep 1986, Deuel Co. (Harris 1987)

SCARLET TANAGER *Piranga olivacea* (Gmelin)

Status. Uncommon summer resident E, most often seen in migration. Rare migrant and possible breeder W.

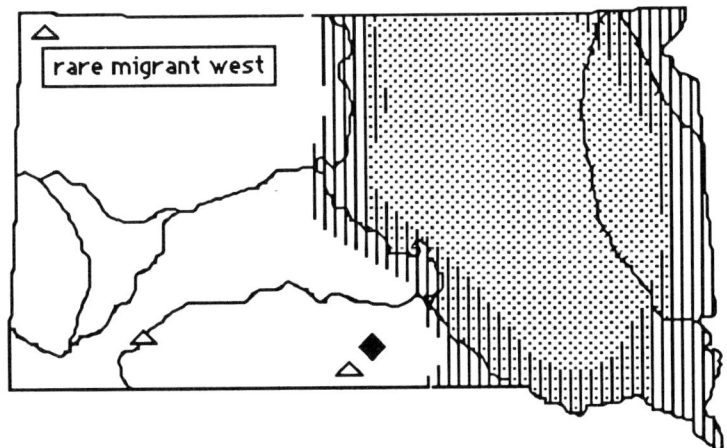

rare migrant west

Habitat. Wooded coulees of the Coteau des Prairies and along wooded streams and rivers, timbered hills bordering Missouri River Valley, and other forested areas (e.g., Newton Hills and Sica Hollow).

Spring migration. Second and third week of May.
Earliest dates:
3 May 1981, Union Co. (Hall in Seasons 1981c)
4 May, Yankton (Bent 1958)
7 May 1985, Lincoln Co. (Skadsen in Seasons 1985c)

Nesting. Jun – Jul. No recent nests found but many Jun and Jul observations in Marshall and Roberts Co. suggest that they nest. Elsewhere, observed in the summer at Farm Island SP (Rogge and Rogge et al.), in SE Mellette Co. (Reagan 1908), Todd Co. at Ghost Hawk Campground on 24 Jun 1972 (Rosche), on White River in Pine Ridge Reservation on 12–13 Jun 1967 (B. Anderson), and in Harding Co. on 14 Jun 1980 (M. Erickson) and 31 May 1985 (Melius).

Earliest date:
14 Jun 1985, Lincoln Co., building nest (Springer and Skadsen 1986)

Latest dates:
5 Jul 1924, Union Co., nest (Stephens et al. 1955)
11 Jul 1967, Sodak Park, male feeding fledgling while female building nest (Harris 1967b)

Fall migration. Last 3 weeks of Sep.
Latest dates:
29 Sep 1969, Brookings (Edie)
29 Sep 1973, Huron (Johnson)
17 Oct 1987, Brown Co., banded (Tallman in Seasons 1988a)
7 Nov 1951, Huron (Kettelle 1951)

WESTERN TANAGER *Piranga ludoviciana* (Wilson)

Status. Common summer resident in Black Hills and in wooded buttes of Harding Co. Records from Shannon (Tullsen 1911), Bennett (R. Peterson), Jackson (Over and Thoms 1946), and Todd (Rosche) counties, where current status unknown. Casual visitor E, with 1 nesting record.

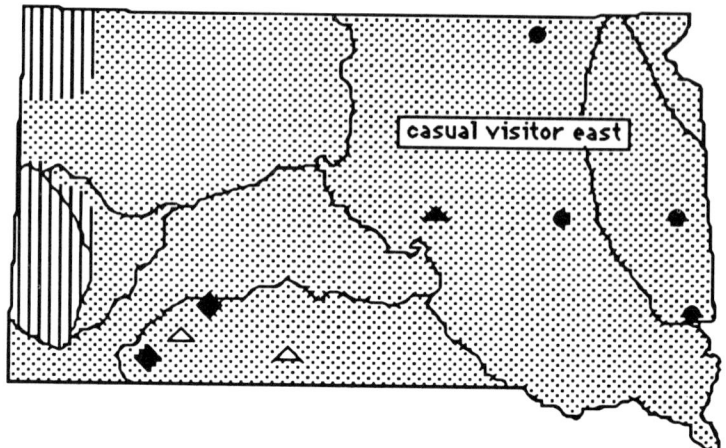

Habitat. Primarily Ponderosa Pine forests and occasionally in secondary deciduous trees in ravines or along streams.

Spring migration. Second and third week of May.
  Earliest dates:
    5 May 1964, Sturgis (Wagar)
    7 May 1964, Brown Co. (Hart 1964)
    7 May 1990, Minnehaha Co. (Hoeger in Seasons 1990c)
    8 May 1975, Pennington Co. (Black Hills Audubon Society in Seasons 1975b)
  Late E River records:
    19 May 1984, Brown Co. (SDOU in Seasons 1984c)
    21 May 1965, Cactus Hills near Sioux Falls (Schleuter and Froiland 1965)
    25 May 1958, near Lake Campbell, female (Cooper in Holden 1958)

Nesting. Jun and Jul. Only E record: Summer 1976, Highmore, 4 young fledged (Drew fide Harter in Seasons 1976d); of interest: 29 Aug 1977, Brookings Co., immature banded (Holden in Seasons 1978a).
  Earliest dates:
    10 Jun 1925, Cascade Springs, nest with 4 eggs (McIntosh in Whitney 1955)
    15 Jun 1989, Lawrence Co., building nest (Riner and Serr)
    24 Jun 1988, Meade Co., adult carrying food (E. Miller)
  Latest date:
    20 Aug 1959, Rapid City, adult feeding full-grown immature (Pettingill and Whitney 1965).

Fall migration. First 3 weeks of Sep.
  Latest dates:
    3 Oct 1976, Rapid City (Bachmann in Seasons 1977a)
    5 Oct 1969, Rapid City, banded (Rose)
    25 Nov 1954, Huron (Johnson)

SUBFAMILY CARDINALINAE: Cardinals, Grosbeaks, and Buntings

NORTHERN CARDINAL *Cardinalis cardinalis* (Linnaeus)

Status. Uncommon to common permanent resident E. N limit of range variable, occasionally breeding in NE, Aberdeen, and Pierre. Rare visitor W.

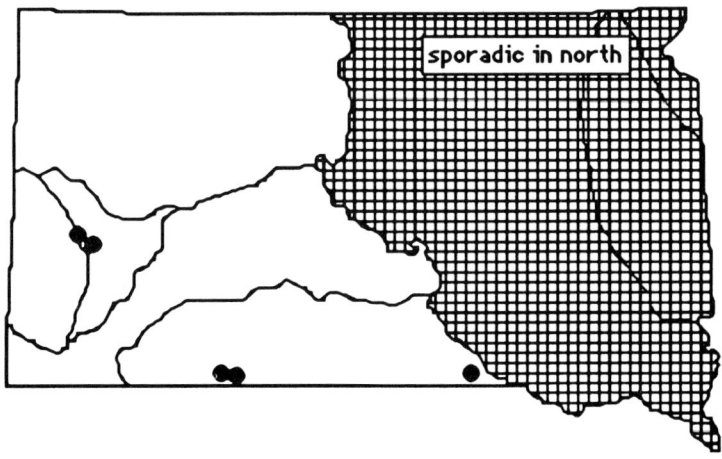

Habitat. Woods and residential areas with thickets. Often nests in residential areas.

Nesting. Mid-Apr – Aug.

Earliest dates:
  21 Apr 1955, Sioux Falls, nest building (Krause)
  23 Apr 1971, Sioux Falls, nest building (Krause)
  24 Apr 1956, Sioux Falls, nest with 3 young (Krause)

Latest dates:
  4 Jul 1957, Big Stone City, nest with hatching eggs (Riss 1957)
  8 Jul 1954, Canton, nest building (five eggs and start of incubation on 16 Jul) (Nelson 1955)
  24 Aug 1971, Huron, fledgling under close feeding supervision of adult female (banded by J. W. Johnson on 16 Oct and found dead on 10 Nov)

W River records:
7–14 Jun 1967, Rapid City (Davies et al. in Serr 1967b)
late Dec 1954 – 2 May 1955 near Rapid City (Hyde 1955)
14 Apr 1955, Lacreek NWR (Krumm 1955b)
11 May 1969, Lacreek NWR (Rose)
22 Dec 1975 and 1978/79 winter, Burke (Steffen 1979)

Winter. Regular in winter as far north as Brookings, occasionally further N.

ROSE-BREASTED GROSBEAK *Pheucticus ludovicianus* (Linnaeus)

Status. Fairly common summer resident E. Casual migrant and rare summer resident W, except fairly common in SE Gregory Co. Not present in higher Black Hills. Where Rose-breasted and Black-headed Grosbeak ranges overlap, species hybridize extensively (West 1962; Anderson and Daugherty 1974). Hybrids are occasionally seen on E and W borders of state.

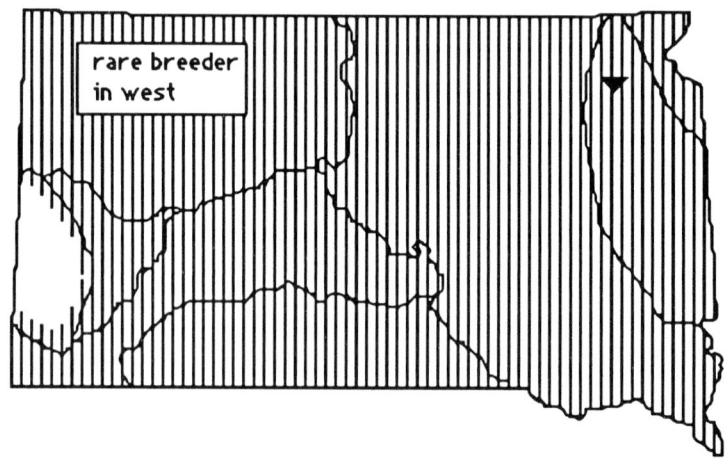

Habitat. Woods and residential areas.
Spring migration. First 3 weeks of May. Unusual concentration: 12 May 1972, Sioux Falls, 40 (Krause).
Earliest dates:
26 Apr 1975, Day Co. (Chilson 1976)
27 Apr 1950, Brookings (Wagar 1958)
28 Apr 1986, Lincoln Co. (Skadsen in Seasons 1986c)
Nesting. Last of May – Jul.
Earliest dates:
16 May 1948, Union Co., pair mating and building nest (Findley)
26 May 1968, Sanborn Co., pair building nest (Harris)
4 Jun 1950, Roberts Co., pair building nest (Findley)
Latest dates:
13 Jul 1967, Roberts Co., adult feeding fledgling (Harris)
14 Jul 1981, Brown Co., adult male and fledgling (Tallman in Seasons 1981d)

W River summer records:
  5 Jun 1970, Slim Buttes, singing male (Springer)
  6 Jun 1969, Rapid City, 2 males, 1 banded (Rose)
  17 Jun 1973, Buffalo, singing male (Springer)
  26 Jun 1953, Rapid City (Behrens in Pettingill and Whitney 1965)
  4 Jul 1977, Rapid City (Baker)
Fall migration. Sep. Unusual concentration: 18 Sep 1982, Minnehaha Co., 40–50 (Hoeger in Seasons 1983a).
  Latest dates:
    19 Oct 1963, Lincoln Co., banded (Findley)
    19 Oct 1986, Minnehaha Co. (Skadsen in Seasons 1987a)
    20 Oct 1987, Pennington Co. (Whitney and Tallman 1988)
Winter.
  Only record:
    10 Nov 1974 – 10 Jan 1975, Day Co. (Chilson 1976)

BLACK-HEADED GROSBEAK *Pheucticus melanocephalus* (Swainson)

Status. Common summer resident from Missouri Valley W. Not present in higher Black Hills. Casual visitor E. See comments on hybridization under Rose-breasted Grosbeak.

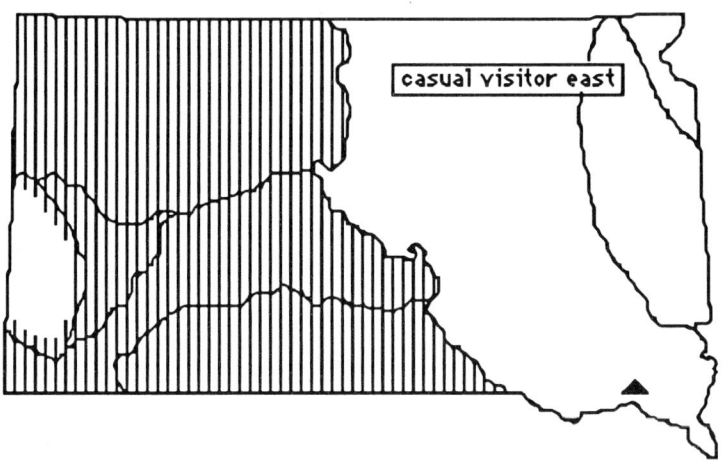

Habitat. Deciduous thickets along rivers and streams.
Spring migration. Second and third weeks of May.
  Earliest dates:
    29 Apr 1975, Pierre (Rose in Seasons 1975b)
    2 May 1974, Pierre (Rose)
    5 May 1973, Pierre (Rose)
    5 May 1978, Perkins Co. (Hinds in Seasons 1978c)

Nesting. Jun – first half of Aug. Moriarty (1965b) reported eggs laid in late May and early Jun in the Missouri River bottoms. E River breeding record: 7 Jul 1931, Yankton Co. (Youngworth 1932a).
   Earliest dates:
   28 May 1925, near Rapid City, nest with 4 eggs collected (McIntosh in Whitney 1955)
   5 Jun 1972, Little Moreau SRA, nest with eggs (Holden)
   7 Jun 1973, Spearfish, nest with 3 eggs (Hays)
   Latest dates:
   28 Jul 1987, Rapid City, adults feeding 2 young (Eckmann)
   2 Aug 1988, Belle Fourche, newly fledged young (Weyler)
   6 Aug 1954, Rapid City, nest with small young (Pettingill and Whitney 1965)
Fall migration. Mid-Aug – mid-Sep.
   Latest dates:
   28 Sep 1968, between Scenic and Wall (Serr 1971b)
   4 Oct 1980, Gregory Co. (Steffen in Seasons 1981a)
   20–27 Oct 1976, Highmore (Harter in Seasons 1977a)

BLUE GROSBEAK *Guiraca caerulea* (Linnaeus)

Status. Fairly common summer resident S and uncommon N. Rare summer resident in lower elevations of Black Hills and Fall River Co. Summer records in the Mobridge area (Randall 1956b), Harding (Griffiths in Seasons 1987a) and Dewey counties (Short 1961, Rose in Seasons 1972c).

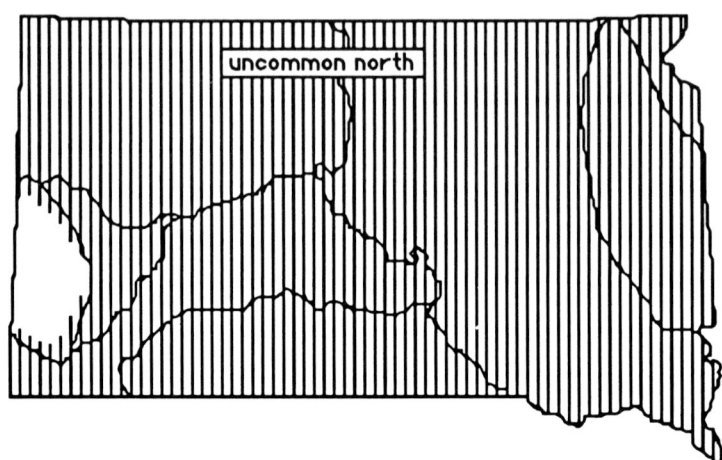

Habitat. Shrubby areas along streams and river beds and brushy draws.
Spring migration. Last half of May.
   Earliest dates:
   2 May 1987, Yankton Co. (Hall in Seasons 1987c)
   8 May 1987, Bennett Co. (Melius in Seasons 1987c)
   11 May 1967, Buffalo Co. (Harris)

Nesting. Jun – first half of Aug.
  Earliest dates:
    9 Jun 1981, Lincoln Co., abandoned nest with 4 eggs and 1 cowbird egg (L. Anderson)
    23 Jun 1958, Delmont, nest with 2 young and 1 egg (Jenny 1958)
    2 Jul 1970, near Smithwick, nest with 1 egg (Springer)
  Latest dates:
    8 Aug 1948, near Pickstown, nest with young in early feathering stage (Weaver 1949)
    21 Aug 1958, near Huron, male feeding 2 young (Johnson 1958)
    21 Aug 1948, Spink Co., nest with young (Stephens et al. 1955)
Fall migration. Last half of Aug.
  Latest dates:
    24 Sep 1980, Gregory Co., banded (Steffen 1981b)
    24 Sep 1984, Charles Mix Co. (Harris)
    25 Sep 1976, Bon Homme Co. (Hall in Seasons 1977a)
    27 Sep 1975, Lincoln Co. (Eckert in Seasons 1975d)

LAZULI BUNTING *Passerina amoena* (Say)

Status. Common summer resident W. Rare visitor E. Reported in summer from Clay (Agersborg 1885), Yankton (Youngworth 1934), Bon Homme (Johnson), and Day (Youngworth 1935) counties, but breeding unconfirmed. Where the 2 species overlap, the Indigo and Lazuli Buntings interbreed (Sibley and Short 1959).

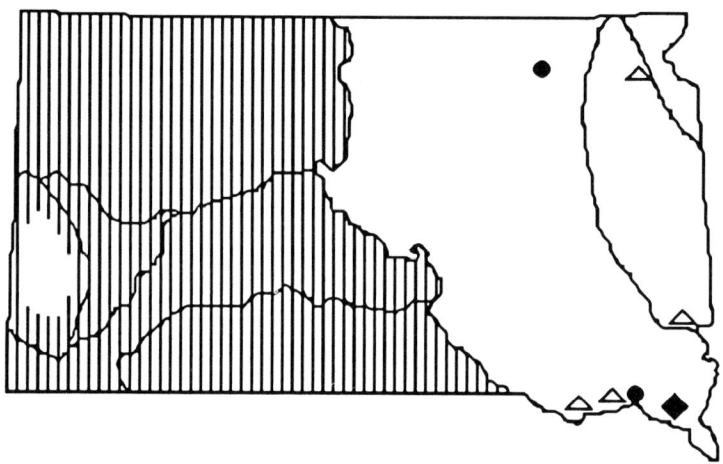

Habitat. Deciduous thickets along waterways and occasionally in residential areas.
Spring migration. Second – third week of May. Unusual concentration: 17–25 May 1984, Brown Co., 6 observed and 2 banded (Tallman and SDOU in Seasons 1984c)

Earliest dates:
  25 Apr 1965, Rapid City (Southmayd and C. Yarger)
  1 May 1986, Yankton Co. (Kronner in Seasons 1986c))
  3 May 1964, Rapid City (Behrens)
Nesting. Late May – Jul.
  Earliest dates:
    25 May 1963, Pierre, pair copulating (Whitney)
    7 and 8 Jun 1954, Rapid City, pairs copulating (Pettingill and Whitney 1965)
    14 Jun 1925, near Hot Springs, 4 eggs collected (McIntosh in Whitney 1955)
  Latest dates:
    24 Jul 1911, near Hot Springs, brood (Visher 1912b)
    31 Jul 1983, Custer Co., nest with 1 egg and 2 young (Goebel)
    7 Aug 1973, Rapid City, adult feeding young (Whitney)
E summer records:
  First week of Jun 1935, Yankton Co., male with female Indigo (Youngworth 1959b)
  21 Jul 1954, Minnehaha Co. (Findley 1954)
Fall migration. Probably last half of Aug.
  Latest dates:
    4 Sep 1950, Rapid City (Behrens in Pettingill and Whitney 1965)
    13 Sep 1961, Sturgis, banded (Wagar)
    16 Sep 1973, Rapid City (Whitney)

INDIGO BUNTING *Passerina cyanea* (Linnaeus)

Status. Uncommon to common local summer resident E. Less common summer resident W. See comments on hybridization under Lazuli Bunting.

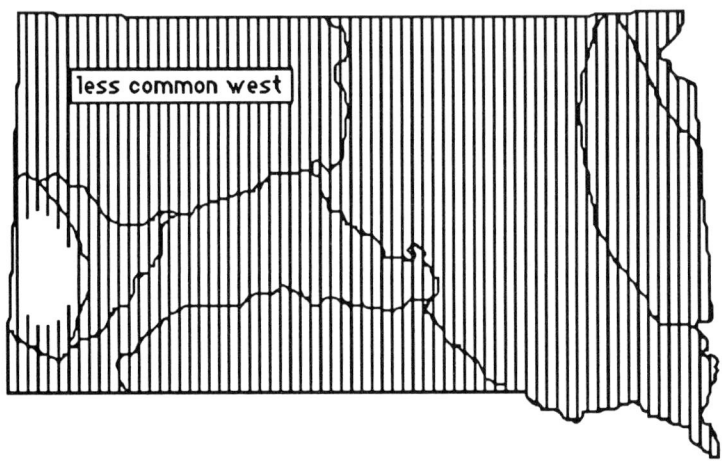

Spring migration. Second – third week of May.
  Earliest dates:
    18 Apr 1976, Clay Co. (Yankton Bird Club in Seasons 1976c)
    22 Apr 1989, Kingsbury Co. (Reinking et al. in Seasons 1989c)
    27 Apr 1984, Brookings Co. (Husmann et al. in Seasons 1984c)
Nesting. Jun – Jul.
  Earliest dates:
    4 Jul 1975, Clay Co., nest with 3 cowbird eggs (Hoover in Seasons 1975c)
    12 Jul 1964, Huron, nest with downy young (Johnson and Johnson 1964)
  Latest dates:
    21 Jul 1975, Pennington Co., fledgling (Williams in Seasons 1975c)
    4 Aug [year], near Blackhawk, 2 broods (Visher 1909)
Fall migration. Sep.
  Latest dates:
    8 Oct 1949, Lacreek NWR (Krumm in Gammell and Gammell 1950)
    9 Oct 1983, Gregory Co., banded (Steffen 1984)
    14 Oct 1984, Brown Co., banded (Tallman in Seasons 1985a)

DICKCISSEL *Spiza americana* (Gmelin)

Status. Common to abundant summer resident, most common E, locally uncommon W. Absent from higher Black Hills. Yearly numbers fluctuate greatly.

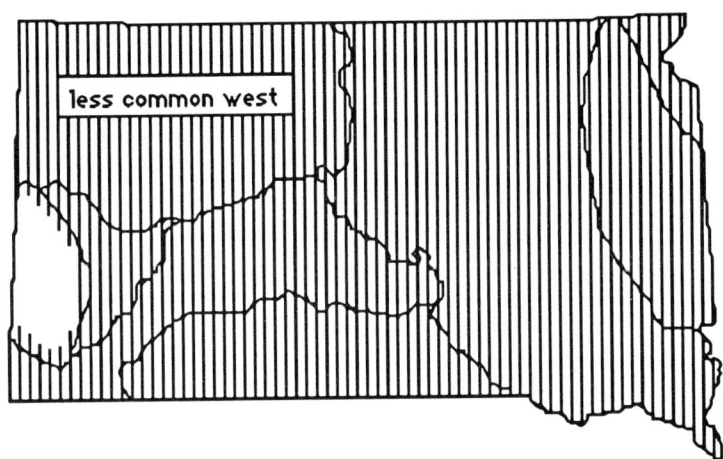

Habitat. Native prairies, clover, alfalfa, and weedy fields.
Spring migration. Last half of May – first week of Jun.
  Earliest dates:
    29 Apr 1978, Deuel Co. (Harris in Seasons 1978c)
    4 May 1952, Roberts Co. (Harris)
    6 May 1951, Minnehaha Co. (Krause)
    6 May 1972, Minnehaha Co. (Krause and Blankespoor)
    6 May 1986, Davison Co. (McLaird in Seasons 1986c)

Nesting. Mid-Jun – Jul.
  Earliest dates:
    30 May 1956, Lincoln Co., pair copulating (Findley)
    Mid Jun, Codington Co., females flushed from nests (Moriarty 1961)
    Late Jun 1903, Lacreek NWR, nest with 4 eggs (Tullsen 1911)
  Latest dates:
    26 Jul 1985, Charles Mix Co., adult with flightless young (Skadsen in Seasons 1985d)
    30 Jul 1987, Minnehaha Co., nest with 4 eggs (Blankespoor)
    5 Aug 1973, Yankton, fledglings (Hall)
Fall migration. Late Jul – Aug.
  Latest dates:
    7 Oct 1979, Yankton Co. (Wilcox and Hall in Seasons 1980a)
    28 Oct 1984, Day Co. (Rabenberg in Seasons 1985a)
    6 Dec 1979, Brookings Co., banded (Holden 1980b)

SUBFAMILY EMBERIZINAE: Towhees, sparrows, juncos and longspurs

GREEN-TAILED TOWHEE *Pipilo chlorurus* (Audubon)

Status. Casual visitor. No specimens.
Records:
  5-26 Jan 1956, Huron (Johnson 1956)
  8 and 9 May 1971, Rapid City (Baylor in Seasons 1971c)
  10-13 May 1967, Rapid City, photographed and banded (Rose and Whitney in Serr 1967c)
  11 May 1967, Fairburn (Smith in Serr 1967c)
  13 May 1970, Rapid City (Rose)
  30 May 1965, Rapid City (Hyde in Serr 1967c)
  7 Jun-late Jul 1987, Pennington Co. (Rosche)

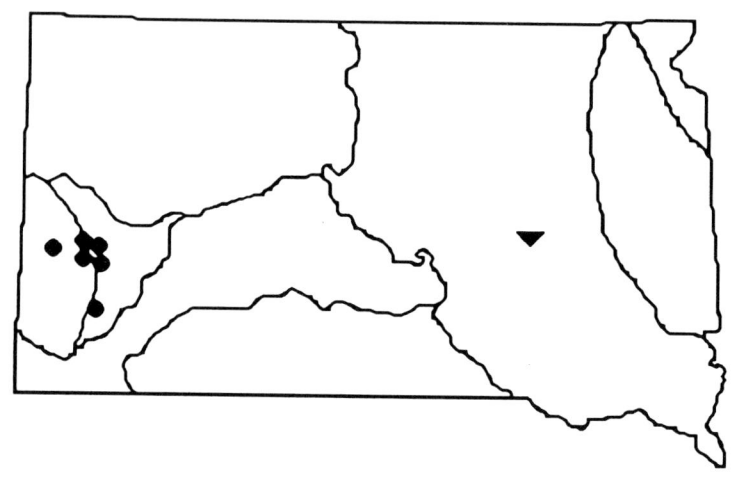

RUFOUS-SIDED TOWHEE *Pipilo erythrophthalmus* (Linnaeus)

Status. Two easily recognizable races occur. The spotted-backed *P. e. arcticus* is a common breeder, chiefly from the Missouri River Valley W, but is a fairly common migrant E; occurs rarely in summer in Lincoln Co. (M. Skadsen and Springer), and is absent from the higher Black Hills. The plain-backed *P. e. erythrophthalmus* undoubtedly nests in suitable habitat in the SE but only 1 breeding record exists. A gap lies between the nesting ranges of these races across E-central SD (Sibley and West 1959). Youngworth (1935) reported the more numerous W race migrated later through the NE than E birds. Both forms casually winter, with records of both races from E and W.

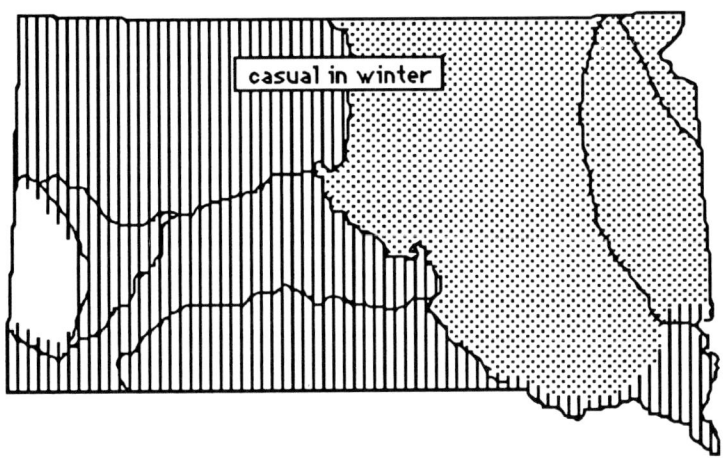

Habitat. Woods with brushy undergrowth.
Spring migration. Last week of Apr and first week of May.
Earliest dates:
  3 Mar 1981, Perkins Co. (Hinds and Hinds in Seasons 1981c)
  25 Mar 1963, Rapid City (Hyde)
  28 Mar, Yankton (Bent 1968)
Nesting. Late May –Jul.
Earliest dates:
  28 May 1924, Rapid City, set of 4 eggs collected (Lee in Whitney 1955)
  28 May 1966, Farm Island, nest with 4 eggs (Holden)
  14 Jun 1985, Lincoln Co., 2 E race fledglings (Springer and Skadsen 1986)
Latest dates:
  22 Jul 1954, Rapid City, recently-fledged young (Pettingill and Whitney 1965)
  27 Jul 1956 Rapid City, occupied nest (Behrens in Pettingill and Whitney 1965)
  13 Aug 1976, Harding Co., feeding fledged young (Springer)

Fall migration. Last week of Sep – first 3 weeks of Oct.
 Latest dates:
   14 Nov 1977, Deuel Co. (Harris in Seasons 1978a)
   24 Nov 1978, Yankton Co. (Hall in Seasons 1979a)
   24 Nov 1978, Hot Springs (Rosche 1982)
Winter. Casually winters, chiefly in S, but several N records (race not specified):
   17 Dec – 1 Jan 1978, Deuel Co. (Lesher in Seasons 1978b)
   Dec – Jan 1985, Brown Co. (Luce in Seasons 1985b)
   28 Jan 1989, Brown Co. (Prisbe)

CASSIN'S SPARROW *Ammophila cassinii* (Woodhouse)

Status. Accidental.
Only record:
   12 Jun 1977, Fall River Co. (Rosche 1982)

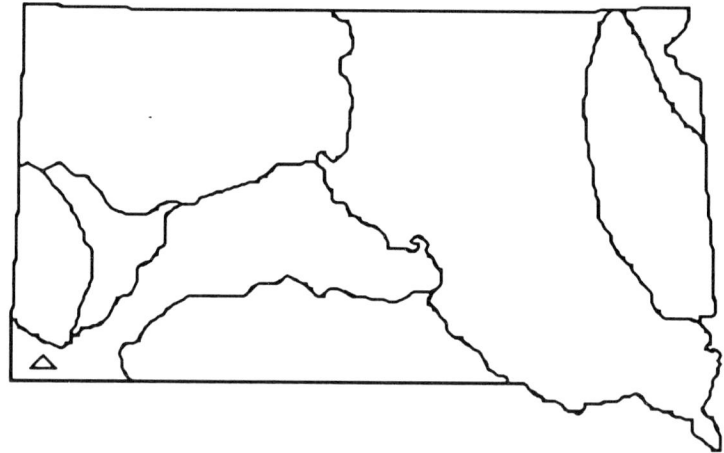

AMERICAN TREE SPARROW *Spizella arborea* (Wilson)

Status. Abundant migrant; regular winter, most common S. Absent from the higher Black Hills.

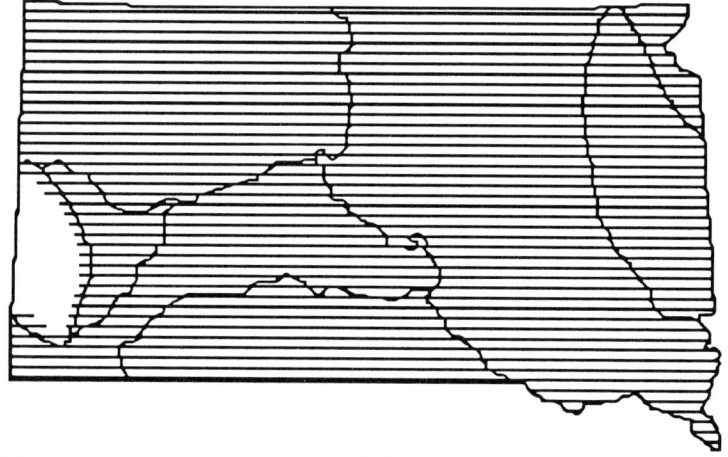

Habitat. Thickets and residential feeding stations.

Spring migration. Mid-Mar – mid-Apr. Peak migration: 28 Mar 1953, 300 in Wall Lake area (Findley); 30 Mar 1971, over 400 in Minnehaha Co. (Krause and Blankespoor in Seasons 1971d).
Latest dates:
   10 May 1960, Brookings Co. (Holden)
   11 May 1952, Sioux Falls (Krause)
   16 May 1972, Rapid City (Katterjohn)
Fall migration. Mid-Oct – mid-Nov. Peak migration: 28 Oct 1951, Moody Co., hundreds (Findley); 25–31 Oct 1962, Brookings Co., 120 banded (Holden).
Earliest dates:
   15 Sep 1934, Alexandria, banded (Wagar)
   18 Sep 1969, Rapid City (Burton)
   20 Sep 1987, Gregory Co. (Steffen in Seasons 1988a)
Winter. Regular but numbers variable.

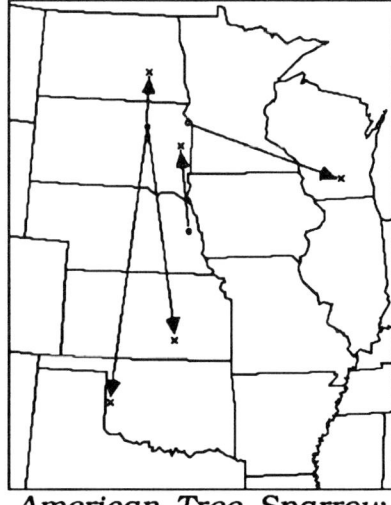
American Tree Sparrow banding recoveries.

CHIPPING SPARROW *Spizella passerina* (Bechstein)

Status. Common to abundant summer resident. Accidental winter.

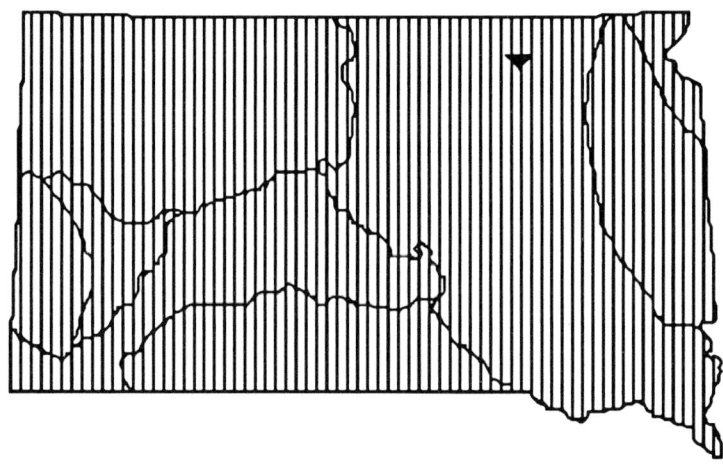

Habitat. In the Black Hills: principally open forests of pine, spruce, and other conifers. Elsewhere: woods and residential areas, especially with conifers.

Spring migration. Late Apr – mid-May.
Earliest dates:
28 Mar 1950, Spearfish (Haight 1950)
1 Apr 1987, Codington Co. (Gilman in Seasons 1987c)
2 Apr 1958, Rapid City (Pettingill and Whitney 1965)

Nesting. Mid-May – mid-Aug.
Earliest dates:
13 May 1951, Sioux Falls, pair mating (Findley)
16 May 1971, Brookings Co., nest with eggs (Holden)
1 Jun 1981, Pennington Co., nest building (Baylor and Baylor 1986)
Latest dates:
25 Jul 1955, Rapid City, fledglings just out of nest (Pettingill and Whitney 1965)
4 Aug 1978, Fall River Co., adult and 2 fledged young (Springer)
12 Aug 1971, Brookings Co., newly-fledged young banded (Holden)

Fall migration. Late Aug – early Oct.
Latest dates:
31 Oct 1983, Gregory Co., banded (Steffen 1984)
1 Nov 1955, Sioux Falls (Krause)
7 Nov 1987, Codington Co. (Gilman in Seasons 1988a)

Winter. Aberdeen CBC and at feeder through December 1981 (Montgomery in Seasons 1982a).

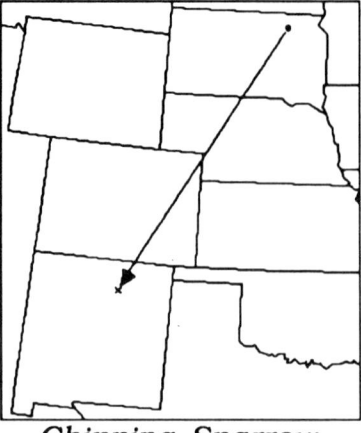

Chipping Sparrow banding recoveries.

CLAY-COLORED SPARROW *Spizella pallida* (Swainson)

Status. Fairly common summer resident along Coteau des Prairies and N Missouri Coteau, accidental elsewhere E. Abundant migrant E; common W. Status in Black Hills uncertain.

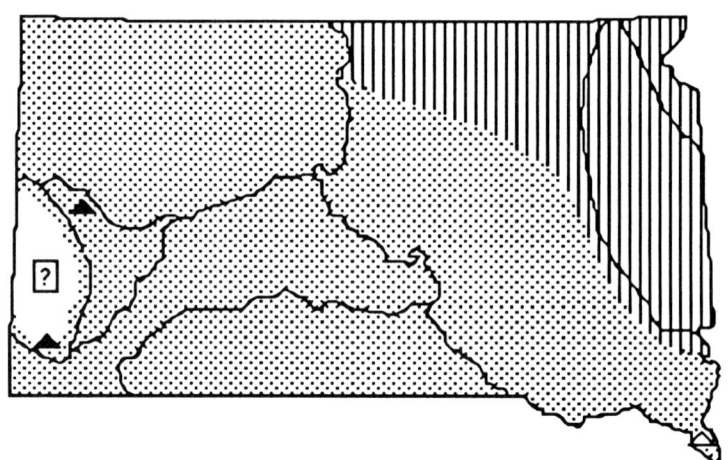

Habitat. E: Brushy prairies and shrubby edges of shelterbelts. Black Hills: Deciduous woodlands and shrubby thickets.

Spring migration. First and second weeks of May. Unusual numbers: 5–15 May 1971, Rapid City, up to 200 in flocks (Serr 1971b); 8 May 1963, Day Co., hundreds (Moriarty 1963).

Earliest dates:
   20 Apr 1948, Sioux Falls (Krause)
   20 Apr 1961, Brookings Co. (Holden)
   23 Apr 1969, Meade Co. (Whitney)
   23 Apr 1980, Brown Co. (Tallman in Seasons 1980c)
   23 Apr 1989, Brown Co. (Tallman in Seasons 1989c)

Latest dates:
   24 May 1957, Brookings Co. (Holden)
   25 May 1957, Rapid City (Pettingill and Whitney 1965)
   7 Jun 1970, Buffalo (Springer)

Nesting. Last half of May – Jul. Breeding season record outside normal range: 18 Jul 1956, Union Co. (Youngworth).

Earliest dates:
   21 May 1961, Day Co., nest with 4 eggs (Holden)
   ca. 10 Jun, Codington co., nests found with eggs (Moriarty 1964c)
   11 Jun 1987, Minnehaha Co., nest with 4 eggs (Springer in Seasons 1987d)

Latest dates:
   28 Jun 1969, Sica Hollow, 1 building nest and 1 feeding young out of nest (Springer)
   1 Aug 1874, Custer Co., adults feeding full-grown young (Grinnell 1875)
   16 Aug 1986, Meade Co., adult with young (Baker in Seasons 1987a)

Fall migration. Mid-Aug – first week of Oct.

Earliest dates:
   10 Aug 1951, Rapid City (Behrens in Pettingill and Whitney 1965)
   21 Aug 1958, Rapid City (Behrens in Pettingill and Whitney 1965)
   22 Aug 1972, Brookings (C. Taylor)

Latest dates:
   15 Oct 1970, Cresbard, banded (Wagar)
   18 Oct 1966, Brookings (Springer)
   20 Oct 1956, Rapid City (Behrens in Pettingill and Whitney 1965)

BREWER'S SPARROW *Spizella breweri* Cassin

Status. An uncommon summer resident in Butte, Harding, and extreme SW Fall River counties. Seen in migration at Pine Ridge (Homoya) and 2 at Pierre, 20 May 1974 (Rose). Accidental winter.

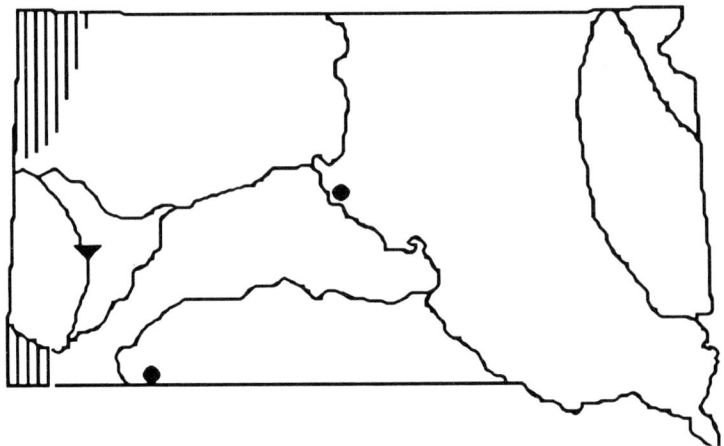

Habitat. Sage prairie dominated by Big Sage, *Artemisia tridentata*.

Spring migration. First half of May.
  Earliest dates:
    23 Apr 1989, Fall River Co. (Peterson in Seasons 1989c)
    30 Apr 1981, Harding Co. (Rogers in Seasons 1981c)
    1 May 1981, Fall River Co. (Rosche in Seasons 1981c)

Nesting. Jun and Jul.
  Earliest dates:
    24-25 May 1986, Fall River Co., 4 nests with 3-4 eggs (Peterson and Peterson 1986)
    2 Jun 1977, Butte Co., 3 nests (Hays in Seasons 1977d)
    9 Jun 1967, Harding Co., nest with 4 eggs (Grant)
  Latest dates:
    3 Jul 1972, Harding Co., nest with 4 young (Springer)
    26 Jul 1967, Harding Co., adult carrying food E (Baylor and Rosine 1970)
    13 Aug 1976, Harding Co., feeding newly fledged young (Springer)

Fall migration. Sep.
  Earliest dates:
    12 Sep 1967, Rapid City, specimen (Rose fide Sutton in Whitney 1972)
    13 Sep 1973, Rapid City (DeFord)
    15 Sep 1966, Rapid City (Southmayd)
  Latest date:
    27 Sep 1966, Rapid City (Southmayd)
    2 Oct 1976, Rapid City (Palmerton and Palmerton in Seasons 1977a)

Winter.
  Only record:
    24 Dec 1968, Meade Co. (Rose)

FIELD SPARROW *Spizella pusilla* (Wilson)

Status. Uncommon summer resident, except common SE and along Missouri River and its tributaries. Largely absent from the Coteau des Prairies except on E edge; probably absent in Missouri Coteau. Irregular summer resident in Black Hills foothills and uncommon migrant W. Accidental winter.

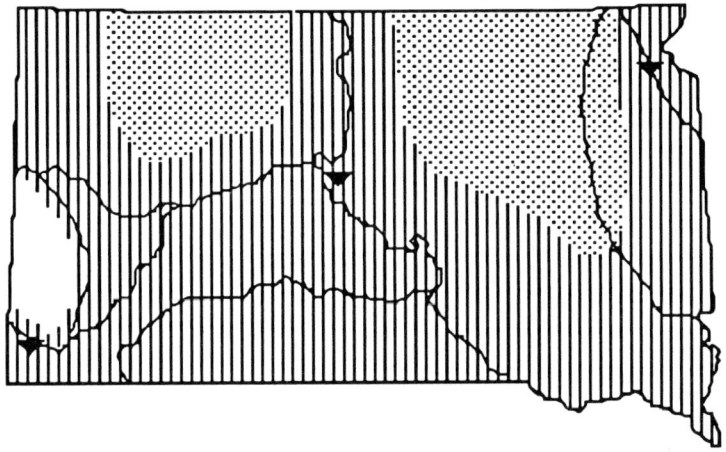

Habitat. Dry, weedy and brushy fields with thickets or trees.
Spring migration. Mid-Apr – mid-May.
  Earliest dates:
    22 Mar 1980, Codington Co. (Herrig in Seasons 1980c)
    25 Mar 1967, Rapid City (Rose)
    4 Apr 1982, Brookings Co., banded (Holden in Seasons 1982c)
  Latest dates in Black Hills area where migrant:
    14 May 1931, near Rapid City (Dille in Pettingill and Whitney 1965)
    14 May 1935, Wind Cave NP (Suter in Pettingill and Whitney 1965)
Nesting. Last half of May – Jul.
  Earliest dates:
    24 May 1923, Lake Hendricks, nest with 5 eggs (SDSU nest collection)
    30 May 1969, Roberts Co., nest with 3 young (Harris)
    8 Jun 1948, Rapid City, 3 or 4 singing males, 1 collected with fully-enlarged testes (Pettingill and Whitney 1965)
  Latest dates:
    15 Jul 1978, Harding Co., fledged young (Springer)
    20 Jul 1979, Yankton Co., nest with 3 eggs (Hall 1980)

Fall migration. Mid-Sep – mid-Oct.
  Earliest dates:
    11 Sep 1980, Brown Co. (Tallman 1981)
    13 Sep 1956, Canton (Mallory 1956)
    14 Sep 1965, Flandreau, dead (Pierce 1969)
  Latest dates:
    25 Oct 1982, Yankton Co. (Hall in Seasons 1983a)
    28 Oct 1979, Deuel Co. (Harris in Seasons 1980a)
    18 Nov 1984, Huron (Johnson in Seasons 1985b)
Winter. Reports without substantiating details are considered unreliable.
  CBC Report:
    Hot Springs and Wilmot.
  Other records:
    1–4 Jan 1979, Pierre, banded (Hill 1979)

VESPER SPARROW *Pooecetes gramineus* (Gmelin)

Status. Common summer resident and migrant. Accidental winter.

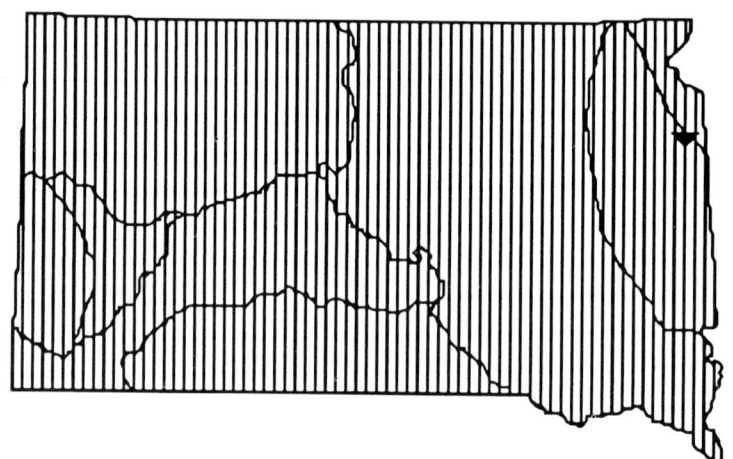

Habitat. Dry grasslands, prairies, field edges, and roadsides.
Spring migration. Mid-Apr – mid-May.
  Earliest dates:
    8 Mar 1986, Union Co. (Anderson in Seasons 1986c)
    30 Mar 1963, Minnehaha Co. (Krause)
    1 Apr 1978, Brookings Co. (Holden in Seasons 1978c)
Nesting. May – Jul.
  Earliest dates:
    13 May 1964, Day Co., nest with 5 eggs (Springer)
    20 May 1975, Deuel Co., nest with 5 eggs (Harris in Seasons 1975c)
    27 May 1967, Roberts Co., nest with 4 eggs (Harris)
  Latest dates:
    1 Jul 1959, Gilly's Grove., nest with 4 young (Holden)
    15 Jul, Codington Co., young leaving nest (Moriarty 1966)
    18 Jul 1959, Jewel Cave NM, 3 immatures (Carter 1958b)

Fall migration. Sep – mid-Oct.
  Latest dates:
    29 Oct 1984, Hutchinson Co. (Anderson in Seasons 1985c)
    30 Oct 1971, Minnehaha Co. (Krause and Blankespoor)
    3 Nov 1979, Deuel Co. (Harris in Seasons 1980a)
Winter.
  Only record:
    1 Dec 1982, Deuel Co. (Stava and Harris in Seasons 1983b)

LARK SPARROW *Chondestes grammacus* (Say)

Status. Common summer resident W; rare migrant and summer resident E.

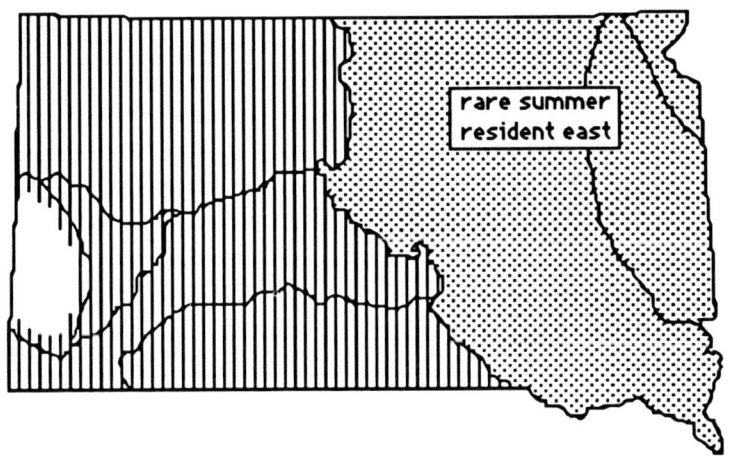

Habitat. Grasslands with scattered shrubby thickets. Often associated with sagebrush. Sometimes nests in open woodlands.
Spring migration. Last week of Apr and first week of May.
  Earliest dates:
    8 Mar 1986, Custer Co. (Parker in Seasons 1986c)
    3 Apr 1951, Stanley Co. (Blankenship et al. 1953)
    6 Apr 1987, Pennington Co. (Glass in Seasons 1987c)
Nesting. May – Jul.
  Earliest dates:
    1 May, Clay Co., full clutch of eggs (Agersborg 1885)
    17 May 1956, Rapid City, pair copulating (Pettingill and Whitney 1965)
    20 May 1955, Lincoln Co., bird carrying nesting material (Findley)
  Latest dates:
    17 Jul 1978, Harding Co., pair with 3 young (Springer)
    28 Jul 1967, Sanborn Co., fledgling (Harris)
    13 Aug 1976, Harding Co., pair with 1 young (Springer)

Lark Sparrow banding recoveries.

336 TOWHEES, SPARROWS, JUNCOS, AND LONGSPURS

Fall migration. Mid-Aug – mid-Oct. Peak migration: 26 Sep 1961, Marshall co., hundreds in Marshall Co. (Jonkel 1961).
  Latest dates:
   28 Oct 1934, Wind Cave NP (Cahalane in Pettingill and Whitney 1965)
   12 Nov 1950, Brookings Co. (Findley)
   15 Nov [year], Faulkton (Bent 1968)

BLACK-THROATED SPARROW *Amphispiza bilineata* (Cassin)

Status. Accidental.
Only record:
  Last 2 weeks of Dec 1971, Vermillion, photographed (Wetmore 1972)

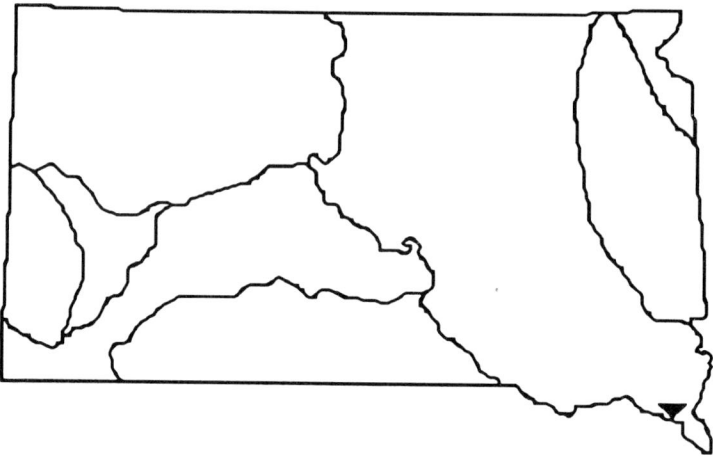

LARK BUNTING *Calamospiza melanocorys* Stejneger

Status. Often abundant summer resident W 2/3 of state, except uncommon to rare in higher Black Hills; a sporadic migrant and summer resident in E third; annual population fluctuations across range.

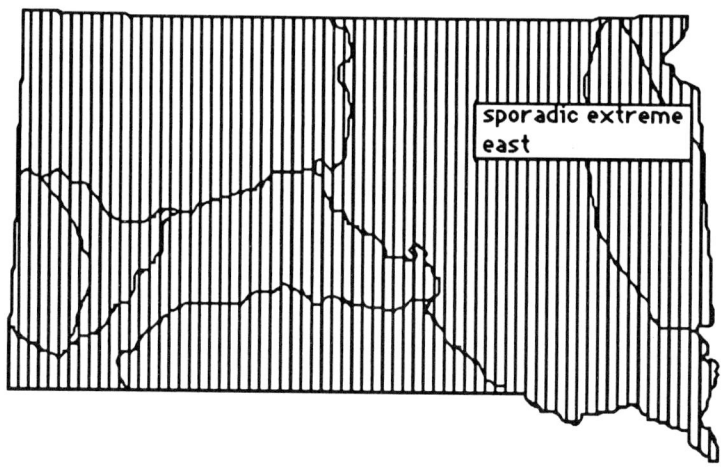

Habitat. Open, dry grasslands.
Spring migration. Second and third weeks of May. Unusual concentration: 11 May 1989, Custer Co., 300 (Melius in Seasons 1989c)
  Earliest dates:
    17 Apr 1967, Meade Co. (Serr)
    20 Apr 1951, Stanley Co. (Blankenship et al. 1953)
    26 Apr 1970, New Underwood (Black Hills Audubon Society)
Nesting. Late May – Jul.
  Earliest dates:
    26 May–15 Jun 1951, Stanley Co., 5 nests with 3 or 4 eggs (Blankenship et al. 1953)
    29 May 1937, Tripp Co., nest with 1 egg (Moos)
    6 Jun 1965, Spink Co., nest with 4 young (Jonkel)
  Latest dates:
    13 Aug 1976, Harding Co., feeding young (Springer)
    25 Aug 1971, Minnehaha Co., young (Krause and Blankespoor)
    29 Aug 1972, Minnehaha Co., young (Krause and Blankespoor)
Fall migration. Mid-Aug – mid-Sep.
  Latest dates:
    19 Oct 1972, Harding Co. (Whitney)
    7 Nov 1958, Pickerel Lake (Fiksdal 1958)
    9 Nov 1963, near Mosher (Springer)

SAVANNAH SPARROW *Passerculus sandwichensis* (Gmelin)

Status. Uncommon summer resident, except rare in Black Hills. Common spring and fall migrant E; uncommon to rare W.

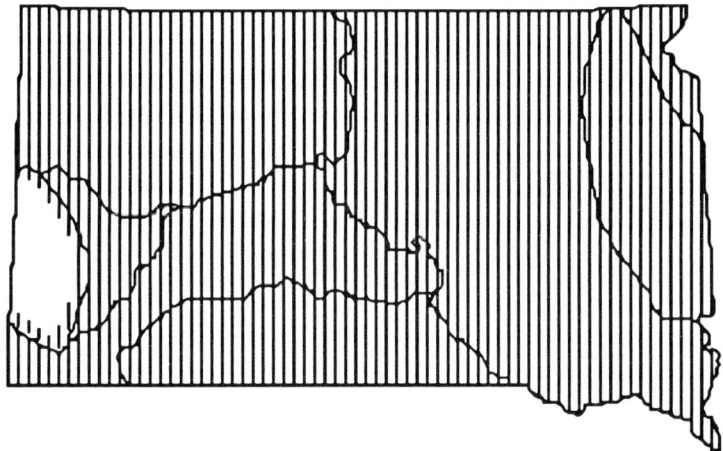

Habitat. Pastures, wet meadows and prairies.
Spring migration. Mid-Apr – first week of May.
  Earliest dates:
    4 Apr 1962, Brookings Co. (Holden)
    5 Apr 1948, Minnehaha Co. (Krause)
    6 Apr 1989, Brown Co. (Prisbe in Seasons 1989c)

Nesting. Last half of May – Jul.
  Earliest dates:
    12 Jun 1969, Miner Co., agitated adults with food (Harris)
    12 Jun 1968, near Roscoe, nest with 4 eggs (Duebbert)
    10 Jul 1967, near Roscoe, fledged young (Duebbert)
  Latest dates:
    24 Jul 1973, Harding Co., flying young and anxious adult (Springer)
    3 Aug 1967, Sanborn Co., female carrying food (Harris)
    5 Aug 1986, Day Co., young in nest (Skadsen 1987d)
Fall migration. Mid-Sep – mid-Oct.
  Latest dates:
    1 Nov 1975, Yankton Co. (Hall in Seasons 1975d)
    1 Nov 1979, Deuel Co. (Harris in Seasons 1980a)
    2 Nov [year], Yankton (Bent 1968)
    15 Nov 1985, Gregory Co. (Skadsen)

BAIRD'S SPARROW *Ammodramus bairdii* (Audubon)

Status. Uncommon to fairly common summer resident in the N tier of counties (Harding, Perkins, Corson, McPherson, Faulk, Dewey, and Edmunds). Possibly bred formerly in Beadle and Hand counties (Cartwright et al. 1937). Singing males observed in Haakon, Lyman, and Bennett counties in late May 1978 (Kantrud and Faanes 1979). Probably uncommon but infrequently detected migrant elsewhere.

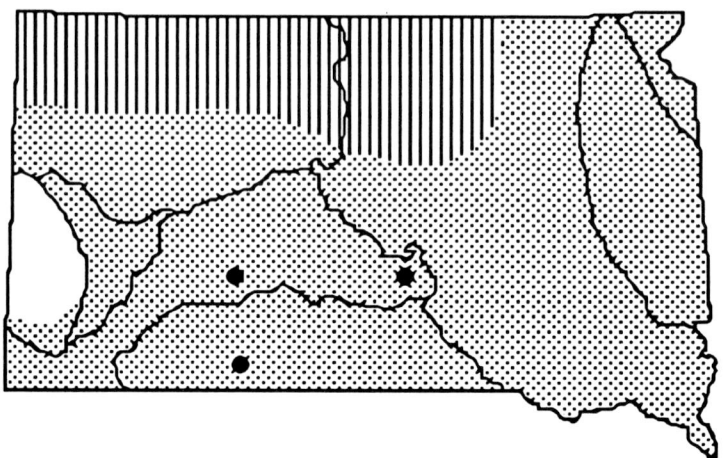

Habitat. Native prairie.
Spring migration. Last week of Apr – first week of May.
  Earliest dates:
    3 Apr 1973, Cresbard, banded (Wagar)
    12 Apr 1972, Cresbard, banded (Wagar)
    25 Apr 1972, Cresbard, banded (returned 17 Apr 1973) (Wagar)

Nesting. Jun – early Jul.
Earliest dates:
  13 Jun 1972, McPherson Co., 2 nests (1 with 3 eggs and 1 with 5 young) (Duebbert and Lokemoen)
  16 Jun 1967, McPherson Co., nest with 2 eggs and 2 cowbird eggs (Duebbert and Lokemoen)
  26 Jun 1967, Roscoe area, brood nearly fledged (Duebbert 1968)
Latest dates:
  22 Jul 1974, Harding Co., nest with 2 young (Springer)
  24 Jul 1973, Harding Co., nest with 4 eggs (Springer)
Fall migration. Sep and Oct.
Latest dates:
  15 Oct [year], Faulkton (Bent 1968)
  15 Oct 1959, Union Co. (Youngworth)
  20 Oct 1971, Sturgis, banded (Wagar)
  25 Oct 1958, Winner, banded (Wagar)

GRASSHOPPER SPARROW *Ammodramus savannarum* (Gmelin)

Status. Uncommon to common summer resident.

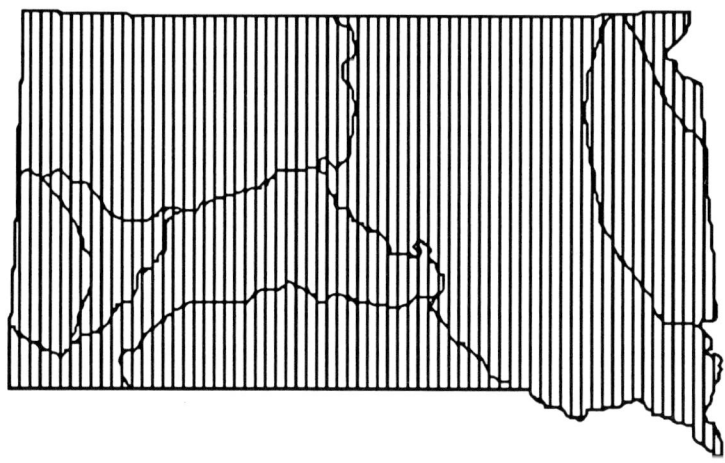

Habitat. Dry grassland and hayfields.
Spring migration. Last week of Apr – mid-May.
Earliest dates:
  11 Apr, Hermosa (Bent 1968)
  18 Apr 1951, Stanley Co. (Blankenship et al. 1953)
  18 Apr 1975, Day Co. (Rose in Seasons 1975b)
Nesting. Jun – mid-Aug.
Earliest dates:
  12 Jun – 26 Jun 1951, Stanley Co., 4 nests with 4 or 5 eggs (Blankenship et al. 1953)
  12 Jun 1965, Altamont Prairie, nest with 4 eggs (Springer)
  26 Jun 1975, Wind Cave NP, nest with 5 eggs (Eckert in Serr 1975)

Latest dates:
- 24 Jul 1973, Harding Co., adults with fledged young (Springer)
- 27 Jul 1967, Jerauld Co., nest with 2 eggs and 2 young (Harris)
- 21 Aug 1987, Yankton Co., adult carrying food (Hall)

Fall migration. First 3 weeks of Sep.

Latest dates:
- 13 Oct 1976, Yankton Co. (Hall in Seasons 1977a)
- 13 Oct 1987, Clay Co. (Hall in Seasons 1988a)
- 21 Oct 1971, Pierre, banded (Rose)
- 24 Oct 1989, Marshall Co. (Harris in Seasons 1990a)

HENSLOW'S SPARROW *Ammodramus henslowii* (Audubon)

Status. Casual summer visitor in E quarter of state.

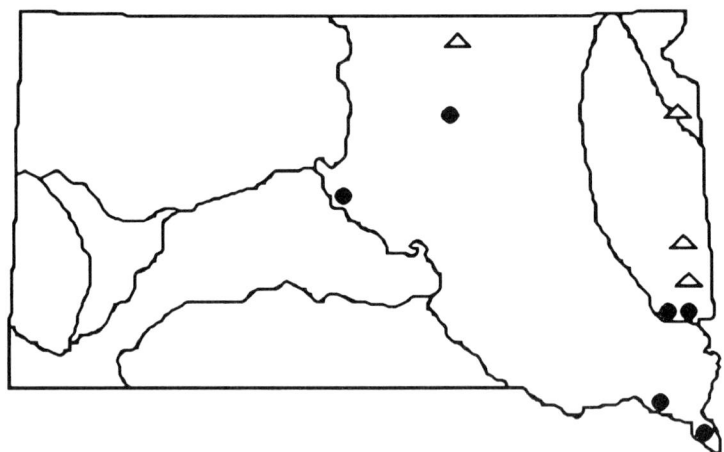

Habitat. Wet meadows, weedy fields, and prairie.

Spring migration. First 2 weeks of May.

Only dates:
- 13 Apr 1941, Pierre, banded (Wagar)
- 29 Apr [year], Sioux Falls and Vermillion (Bent 1968)
- 4 May 1921, Clay Co., specimen (Over)
- 6 May [year], Vermillion (Bent 1968)
- 17 May 1953, Union Co. (Felton and Youngworth)

Nesting. No nesting data. Listed as summer resident in Minnehaha (Larson 1925) and Bon Homme counties (Johnson 1958).

Summer records.
- Ca.15 Jun 1984, McPherson Co. (Weigle and Ewert in Seasons 1984d)
- 16 Jun 1882, Moody Co., 3 specimens (Jencks in Brewster 1891)
- 11, 12 Jun and 3 Jul 1965, Altamont Prairie (Springer 1965a)
- 10 Jul 1965, Brookings Co. (Springer)

Fall migration. Sep – mid-Oct.
Only dates:
1 Sep, Faulkton (Bent 1968)
6 Sep 1971, Sioux Falls (Krause and R. R. Nelson)
22 Oct 1971, near Humboldt (Krause and Blankespoor)
1 Nov, Faulkton (Bent 1968)

LE CONTE'S SPARROW *Ammodramus leconteii* (Audubon)

Status. Uncommon migrant and rare summer resident E; Accidental W.

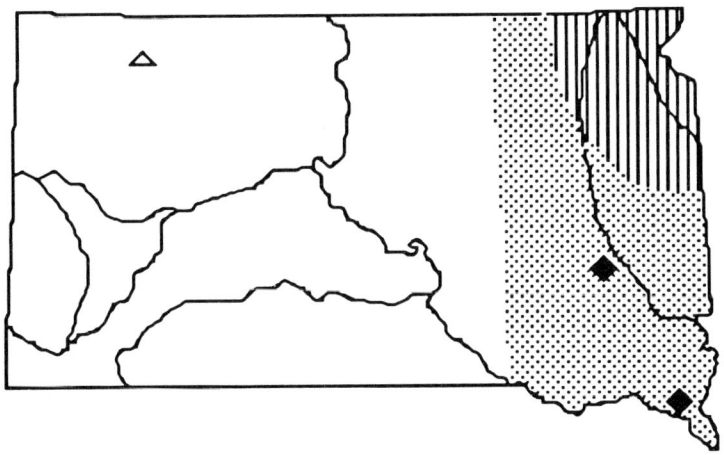

Habitat. Wet meadows and marsh edges.
Spring migration. Last week of Apr – first 2 weeks of May.
Earliest dates:
25 Mar 1977, Gavin's Point (Hall in Seasons 1977c)
11 Apr, Yankton (Bent 1968)
17 April 1976, Yankton Co. (Yankton Bird Club in Seasons 1976c)
Nesting. Jun – Jul.
Earliest Dates:
Jun 1890, Miner Co., set of 4 eggs collected (Patton in Walkinshaw 1937)
19 Jun 1883, Clay Co. with 5 eggs ready to hatch (Agersborg 1885)
25 Jun 1955, Day Co., nest (C. Johnson)
Latest dates:
6 Aug 1986, Day Co., adult with food and fledged young (Skadsen in Seasons 1986d)
Fall migration. Last week of Sep – first half of Oct.
Latest dates:
22 Oct 1971, near Humboldt (Krause and Blankespoor)
26 Oct 1975, Clay Co. (Hall in Seasons 1975d)
28 Oct 1981, Deuel Co. (Harris in Seasons 1982c)
W River Record.
7 Jun 1970, Perkins Co. (J. W. Johnson)

SHARP-TAILED SPARROW *Ammodramus caudacutus* (Gmelin)

Status. Rare migrant E. Several summer records but nesting unconfirmed.

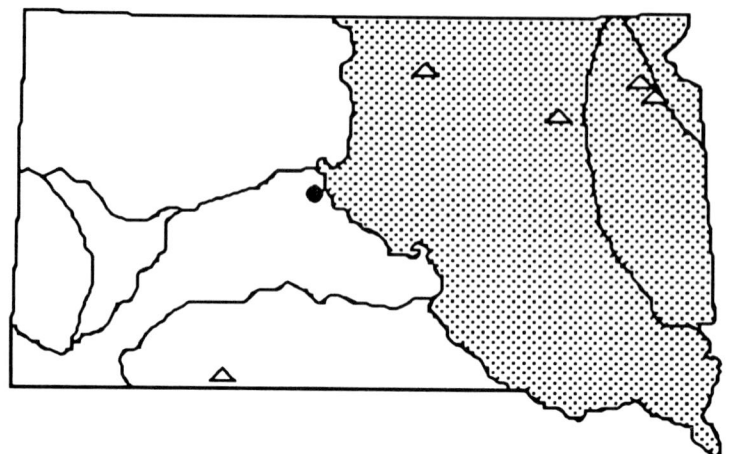

Habitat. Marshes and lake edges.

Nesting. No nests known. Thought to nest around Bitter Lake (Chilson 1957).

Spring migration. Second – third weeks of May.
Only dates:
  29 Apr, Vermillion (Bent 1968)
  9 May 1951, Stanley Co. (Blankenship et al. 1953)
  18 May 1981, McPherson Co. (Tallman and Zusi in Seasons 1981c)
  23 May 1966, Day Co. (Rose)

Summer records.
  6 Jun 1976, Spink Co. (Martsching 1984)
  7 Jun 1931, Rush Lake, specimen (Youngworth 1935)
  15 and 20 Jul, 2 Aug 1971, near Roscoe (Kantrud)
  30–31 Jul 1977, Lacreek NWR (Lohoefener and Ely 1978)

Fall migration. Last half of Sep – first half of Oct.
Latest dates:
  27 Sep 1959, Oakwood Lakes (Findley)
  28 Sep 1984, Sanborn Co. (Rogers in Seasons 1985a)
  20 Oct, Sioux Falls (Bent 1968)

FOX SPARROW *Passerella iliaca* (Merrem).

Status. Uncommon migrant E; rare migrant W. Accidental summer. Casual winter.

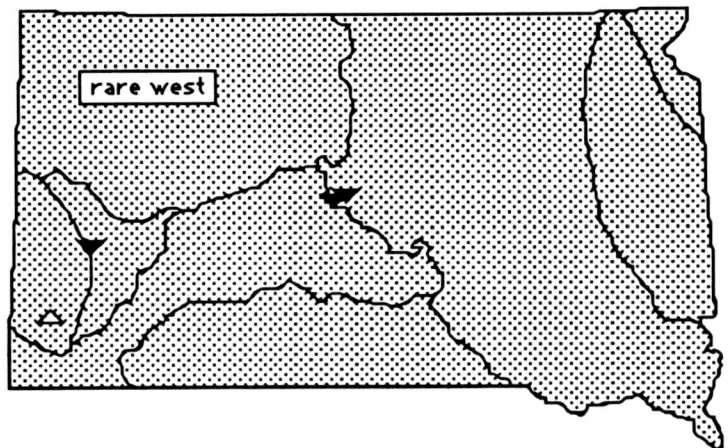

Habitat. Brushy woods, including shrubbery in residential areas.
Spring migration. Last 3 weeks of Apr and first week of May.
  Earliest dates:
    15 Mar 1979, Brookings Co. (Taylor in Seasons 1979c)
    15 Mar 1988, Brookings Co. (Holden in Seasons 1988c)
    18 Mar 1979, Deuel Co. (Harris in Seasons 1979c)
    18 Mar 1989, Jackson Co. (Graupmann in Seasons 1989c)
  Latest dates:
    12 May 1973, Rapid City (DeFord)
    14 May 1969, Rapid City, banded (Rose)
    18 May 1957, Freeman (Kaufman 1958)
Summer record.
    25 Jun 1965, near Custer (Baylor 1966)
Fall migration. Late Sep – Oct.
  Earliest dates:
    6 Sep 1987, Brown Co. (Prisbe in Seasons 1988a)
    11–12 Sep 1975, Badlands (Wilt in Seasons 1975d)
    21 Sep 1972, Brookings Co. (C. Taylor)
  Latest dates:
    14 Nov 1962, Lincoln Co., banded (Findley)
    20 Nov 1986, Brown Co. (Nelson in Seasons 1987a)
    22 Nov 1971, Brookings Co. (Holden)
Winter.
    7–25 Dec 1972, Pierre (Rose)
    19 Dec 1973, Rapid City (Whitney)
    6 Jan 1975, Pierre (Rose)

SONG SPARROW *Melospiza melodia* (Wilson)

Status. Common summer resident, except uncommon to rare NW. Irregular uncommon winter resident S.

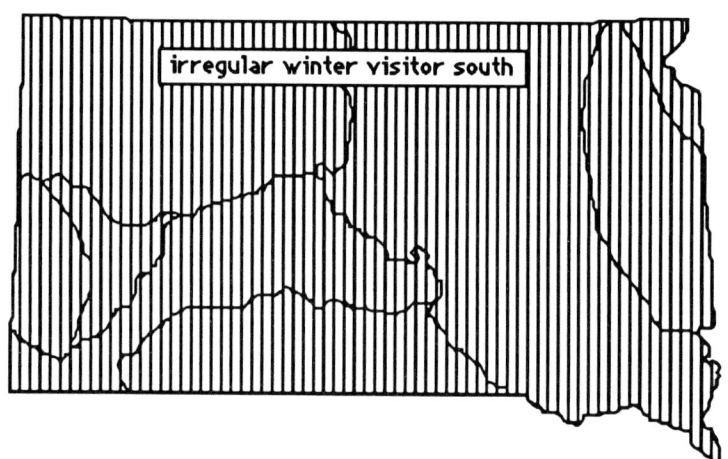

Habitat. Thickets, often near water.
Spring migration. Mid-Mar – mid-Apr. Early spring birds may have wintered.
Nesting. Mid-May – mid-Aug.
Earliest dates:
  14 May 1986, Day Co., adult carrying food (Skadsen in Seasons 1986d)
  19 May 1973, Deuel Co., nest with 5 eggs (3 cowbird eggs) (Harris)
  20 May 1975, Deuel Co., nest with 5 eggs (Harris in Seasons 1975c)
Latest dates:
  24 Jul 1960, Rhodes Fork, adult carrying food (Pettingill and Whitney 1965)
  21 Aug 1968, Huron, nest with well-feathered young (3 Aug 1968, 4 eggs; 17 Aug, 4 young) (J. W. Johnson)
Fall migration. Oct – mid-Nov. Late fall records may be of birds attempting to winter.
Winter. Occasionally winters, most often in S.
Northern CBC reports.
  Milbank and Pierre.

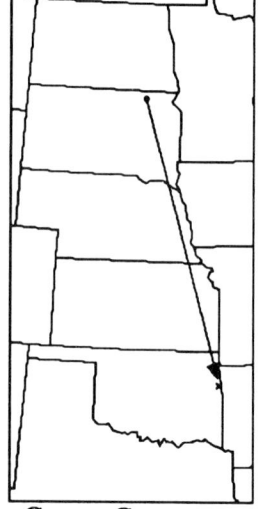

Song Sparrow banding recoveries

LINCOLN'S SPARROW *Melospiza lincolnii* (Audubon)

Status. Uncommon to fairly common migrant.

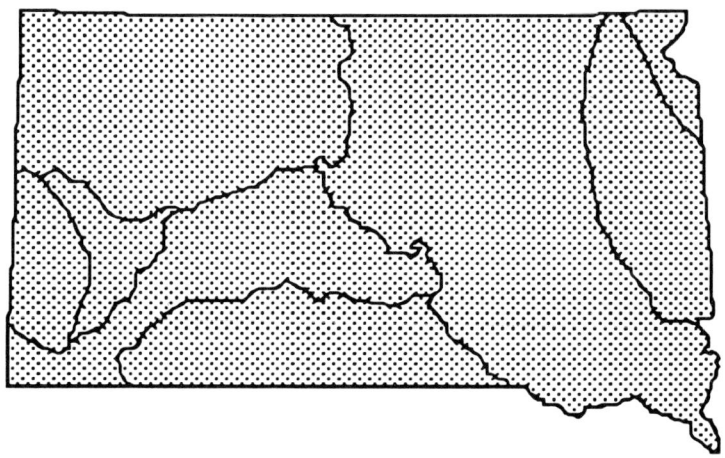

Habitat. Thickets and residential shrubbery.
Spring migration. Late Apr – mid-May.
  Earliest dates:
    6 Apr 1977, Rapid City (Seasons 1977c)
    8 Apr 1971, Brookings Co. (Holden)
    12 Apr 1967, Brookings Co. (Springer)
    12 Apr 1986, Codington Co. (Gilman in Seasons 1986c)
  Latest dates:
    26 May 1989, Brown Co. (Prisbe in Seasons 1989c)
    28 May 1935, Alexandria, banded (Wagar)
    2 Jun 1960, Brookings Co., banded (Holden)
Fall migration. Sep – mid-Oct.
  Earliest dates:
    18 Aug 1972, Minnehaha Co. (Krause and Blankespoor)
    25 Aug 1972, Faulk Co. (Wagar)
    26 Aug 1977, Hyde Co. (Harter in Seasons 1978a)
  Latest dates:
    27 Oct 1966, Hyde Co. (Harter 1969)
    27 Oct 1963, Lincoln Co., banded (Findley)
    29 Oct 1982, Sanborn Co. (Rogers in Seasons 1983b)
    5 Nov 1977, Fall River Co. (Rosche)

Lincoln's Sparrow banding recoveries.

SWAMP SPARROW *Melospiza georgiana* (Latham)

Status. Uncommon to common summer resident E. Locally common Lacreek NWR. Accidental winter. Old record in Harding Co.: 22 Aug 1910 (Visher 1914) and breeding season records in Todd Co. (Springer in Seasons 1989d) and Sully Co. (Springer in Seasons 1990d).

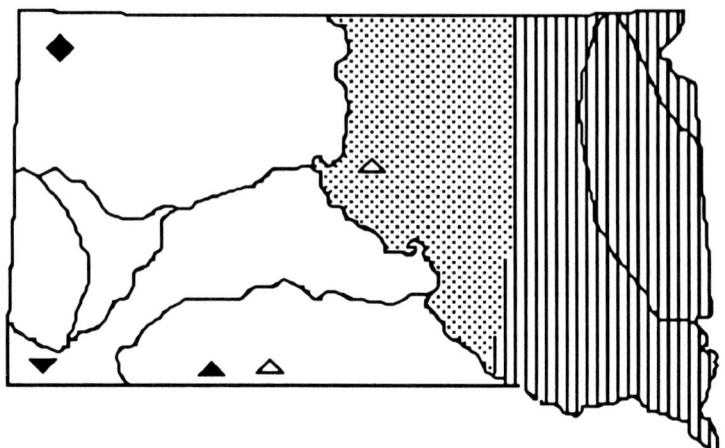

Habitat. Brushy edges of marshes, swamps, and wet meadows.
Spring migration. Last half of Apr.
Earliest dates:
   8 Apr 1984, Codington Co. (Gilman in Seasons 1984c)
   11 Apr 1958, Brookings Co. (Holden)
   13 Apr 1952, Union Co., specimen (Stephens et al. 1955)
Nesting. Last half of May – Jul. Only 2 nest records despite many summer observations.
Earliest dates:
   May or Jun 1882, Flandreau, eggs collected (Bailey in Chapman 1950)
   10 Jun 1921, Sanborn Co., nest with 5 eggs (Patton in Over Museum)
   12 Jun 1969, Miner Co., agitated pair (Harris)
Latest dates:
   29 Jul 1966, Roberts Co., 2 fledglings (Harris)
   3 Aug 1986, Deuel Co., adults with food, young heard calling (Harris in Seasons 1986d)
Fall migration. Mid-Sep – mid-Oct.
   Latest dates:
   30 Oct 1981, Bon Homme Co. (Hall in Seasons 1981a)
   4 Nov 1979, Yankton Co. (Rogge and Rogge in Seasons 1980a)
   6 Nov 1957, near Milbank (Elliott)
Winter.
Only record:
   18 Dec 1976 – 29 Jan 1977, Fall River Co. (Rosche 1982)

WHITE-THROATED SPARROW *Zonotrichia albicollis* (Gmelin)

Status. Common migrant E; rare W. Rare and irregular winter resident E. Casual in lower Black Hills.

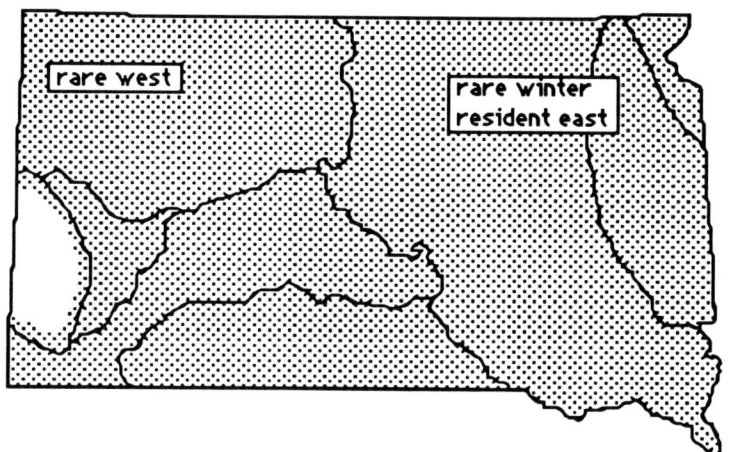

Habitat. Woodlands and residential areas.

Spring migration. Late Apr – mid-May.
  Earliest dates:
    11 Mar 1966, Brookings (Edie)
    22 Mar, Yankton (Bent 1968)
    28 Mar 1957, Brookings Co. (Holden)
  Latest dates:
    24 May 1957, Brookings Co. (Holden)
    24 May 1975, Hyde Co. (Harter in Seasons 1975b)
    26 May, Sioux Falls (Bent 1968)

Fall migration. Mid-Sep – mid-Nov. Latest fall dates may represent birds attempting to winter.
  Earliest dates:
    4 Sep 1988, Brown Co. (Tallman in Seasons 1989a)
    7 Sep 1987, Brown Co. (Prisbe in Seasons 1987a)
    9 Sep 1976, Hyde Co. (Harter in Seasons 1977a)
    9 Sep 1980, Brookings Co. (Taylor in Scasons 1981a)
    9 Sep 1988, Faulk Co. (Springer)

Winter. Often remains through December. Present entire winter 1978–79, Deuel Co. (Harris in Seasons 1979b).
  CBC reports.
    Brookings, Canton, Hot Springs, Pierre, Sioux Falls, Yankton, and Rapid City.
  Other records.
    Remained through winter at Highmore (1976–77) (Harter in Seasons 1977b), Deuel Co.

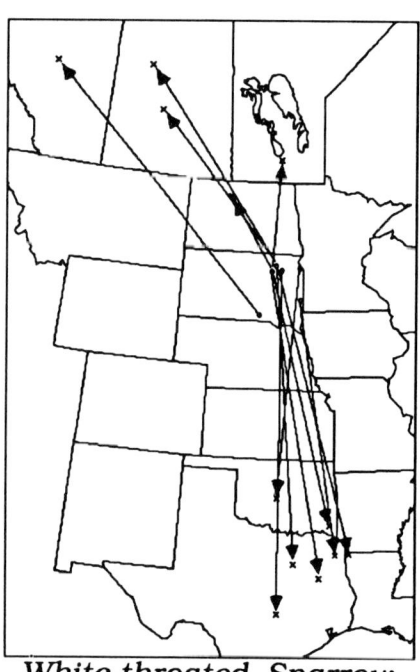

White-throated Sparrow banding recoveries.

(1978–79) (Harris in Seasons 1979b), and Day Co. (1983–84) (Koerner in Seasons 1984b).

WHITE-CROWNED SPARROW *Zonotrichia leucophrys* (Forster)

Status. Common migrant; rare winter resident, usually S. 2 races, the White-crowned Sparrow (*Z. l. leucophrys*), with black lores, and the Gambel's Sparrow (*Z. l. gambelii*), with white lores, occur in about equal numbers in the extreme E. Gambel's Sparrows occur more frequently W.

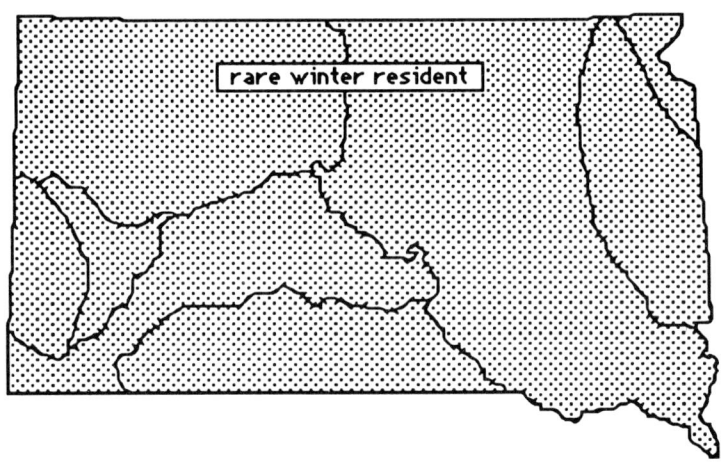

Habitat. Woods, thickets, and residential areas.
Spring migration. Mid-Apr – mid-May.
  Earliest dates:
    26 Mar 1962, Perkins Co. (Hinds 1968)
    2 Apr 1967, Rapid City, banded (Rose)
    3 Apr [year], Faulkton (Bent 1968)
  Latest dates:
    22 May 1935, Alexandria, banded (Wagar)
    26 May 1957, Winner, banded (Wagar)
    14 Jun [year], Faulkton (Bent 1968)
Fall migration. Mid-Sep – Oct.
  Earliest dates:
    11 Sep 1955, Rapid City (Pettingill and Whitney 1965)
    11 Sep 1961, Highmore (Harter 1962)
    12 Sep 1988, Hughes Co. (Springer in Seasons 1989a)
Winter. Occasionally remains into Dec.

CBC reports.
  Huron, Madison, Pierre, Rapid City, Sioux Falls, and Spearfish.

Post Dec records.
  3 Dec 1966 – rest of winter, Rapid City (Bachmann in Serr 1967a)
  Winter 1963–64, few, Belle Fourche (Weyler 1964)
  20 Jan 1982, Day Co. (Koerner in Seasons 1983b)

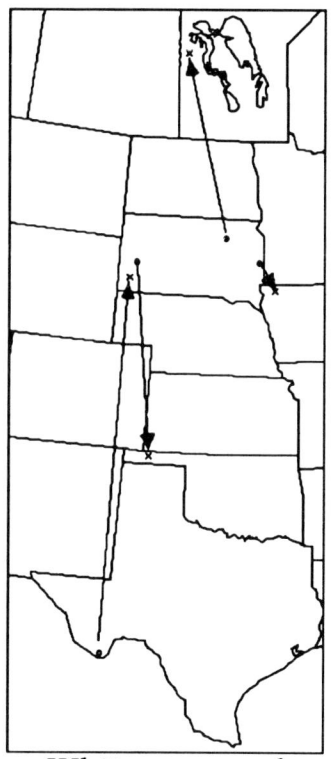

White-crowned Sparrow banding recoveries.

HARRIS' SPARROW *Zonotrichia querula* (Nuttall)

Status. Common to abundant migrant E, uncommon migrant W, and rare migrant and winter resident in lower Black Hills. Uncommon winter resident S, rare N. Casual summer nonbreeder. Absent from higher Black Hills.

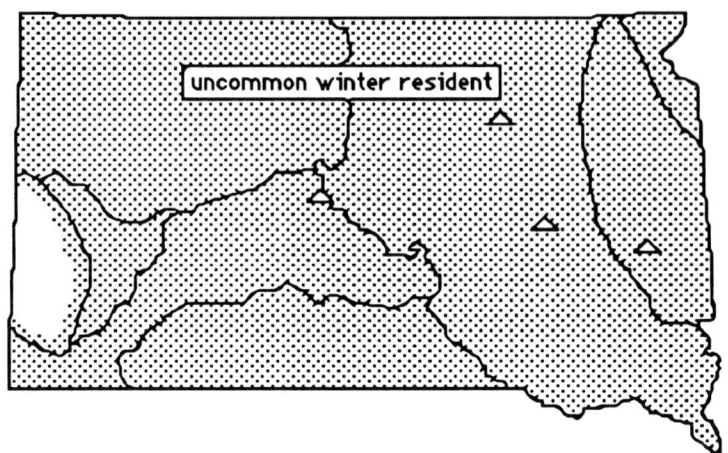

Habitat. Woods and residential areas.

Spring migration. Apr – mid-May. Youngworth (1959a) describes 3 flights: after mid-Mar, in mid-Apr, and in early May. The earliest spring dates are in early March, but these birds may have wintered within the state.

Latest dates:
25 May 1957, Brookings Co. (Holden)
27 May 1953, Redfield (Padrnos 1953a)
30 May 1955, near Milbank (Elliott)

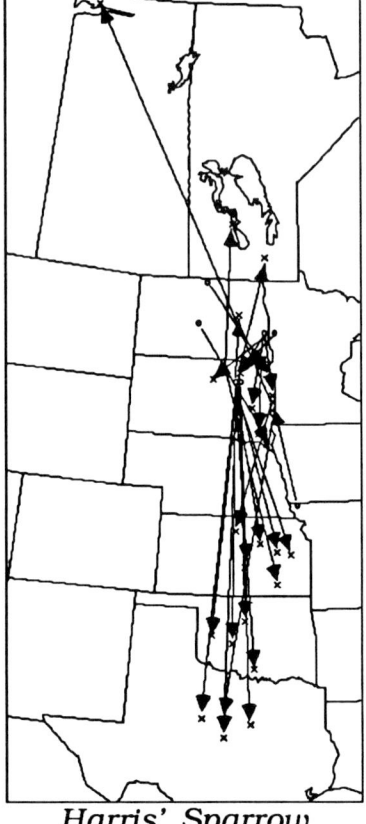

Harris' Sparrow banding recoveries

Summer records.
 12 Jun 1968, Huron, banded (Johnson 1968)
 18 Jun 1968, Spink Co. (Moriarty 1968)
 23 Jun 1929 – Aug, near Arlington (Larson 1930)
 13 Jul 1979, Oahe Dam (Backlund in Seasons 1977a)
Fall migration. Late Sep – mid-Nov.
 Earliest dates:
 12 Sep 1976, Brookings Co. (Holden in Seasons 1977a)
 15 Sep 1974, Pierre (Rose)
 18 Sep, Sioux Falls (Bent 1968)
 Latest dates:
 19 Nov 1972, banded, Brookings Co. (Holden)
 25 Nov 1954, Sioux Falls (Krause)
 27 Nov 1973, Spearfish (Hays)
Winter. Uncommon S, rare N. Has occurred on most CBC counts.

DARK-EYED JUNCO *Junco hyemalis* (Linnaeus)

Status. Five well-marked races occur, but many intergrades make positive field identification difficult. The breeding race, the White-winged Junco, *J. h. aikeni,* is a common permanent resident in Black Hills at all elevations (although most numerous at higher elevations during the breeding season and at lower elevations in winter) and is an uncommon permanent resident in coniferous forests of Harding and Shannon counties. Accidental E (2 Nov 1946, Lake Andes (Stephens and Youngworth 1947)). (See Whitney in Bent (1968) for a review of this species' status). The remaining races (Slate-colored, Oregon, and Pink-sided Juncos) are common migrants and winter residents, although more sporadic N in winter. The Gray-headed Junco, *J. h. caniceps,* is casual in winter in the lower elevations of the Black Hills.

Habitat. Breeds in forests, especially aspen, and widespread in winter and migration.

Spring migration (for nonresidents). Last week of Mar – Apr.

Latest dates:
21 May 1983, Pierre (Steffen et al. in Seasons 1983c)
21 May 1986, Brown Co. (Prisbe in Seasons 1986c)
28 May 1981, Day Co. (Husmann in Seasons 1981c)

Nesting. Late May – early Jul in lower elevations and Jun – late Jul at higher elevations.

Earliest dates:
20 May 1924, Dark Canyon, nest with 4 eggs collected (Lee in Whitney 1955)
27 May 1928, above Pactola, 2 nests containing 4 eggs each (Over and Clement 1951)
30 May 1928, above Pactola, nest with young which left on 5 Jun (Over and Clement 1951)

Latest dates:
20 Jul 1987, near Rapid City, adult feeding fledgling (Eckmann)
22 Jul 1928, Harney Peak 7100', nest with well-incubated eggs collected (Less in Whitney 1955)
1 Aug 1874, near Harney Peak, many broods just fledged (Grinnell 1875)

Fall migration (for non residents). Oct – mid-Nov.

Earliest dates:
17 Aug 1934, Wind Cave National Park (Cahalane in Pettingill and Whitney 1965)
22 Aug 1969, near Custer (Edie)
5 Sep 1982, Brown Co., banded (Tallman in Seasons 1983a)

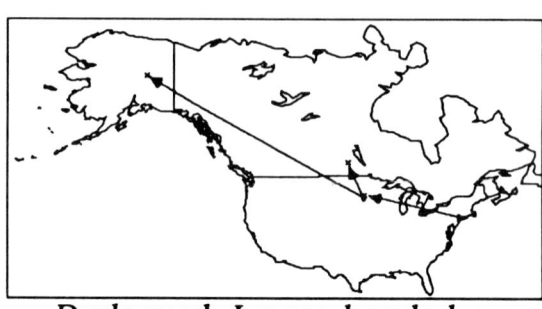

Dark-eyed Juncos banding midwest USA recoveries.

Dark-eyed Juncos banded or recovered outside the midwest United States.

White-winged Junco banding recoveries.

MCCOWN'S LONGSPUR *Calcarius mccownii* (Lawrence)

Status. Rare migrant through W tier of counties. Formerly abundant summer breeding bird in Harding Co. (Visher 1914). Also bred at Whitewood (Visher 1909). Scattered, mostly old, records elsewhere in state. Status of this species was reviewed by Krause in Bent (1968).

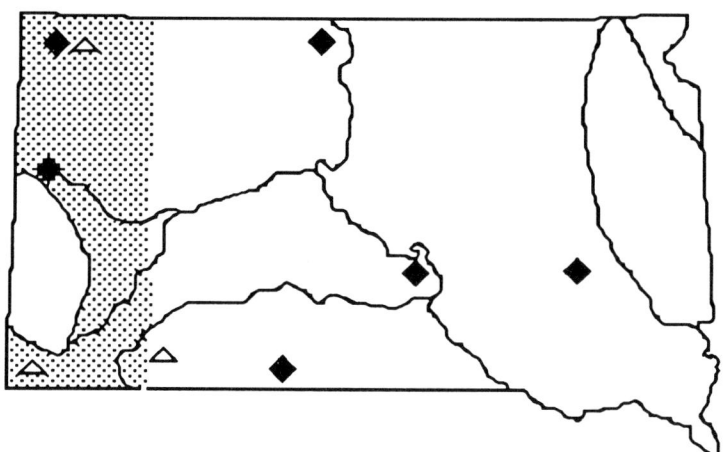

Habitat. Shortgrass prairies, stubble fields.
Spring migration. Late Mar – Apr.
  Earliest dates:
    7 Apr 1907, Lyman Co. (Larson 1907)
    16 Apr 1982, Fall River Co. (Rosche in Seasons 1982c)
    19 Apr 1983, Fall River Co. (R. Peterson)
Nesting. May – Jul. Seen 7 Jun 1970, Harding Co. (Harris and Springer in Baylor and Rosine 1971), 10 Jul 1981, Fall River Co. (Rosche 1982), and 20 Jul 1967, Shannon Co. (K. Evans).
  Only date:
    16 Jul 1910, Harding Co., nest with just-hatched young (Visher 1914)
Fall migration. Sep and Oct.
  Earliest dates:
    after 10 Aug 1911, old Pine Ridge Indian Reservation (Visher 1912a)
    22 Aug 1967, Pennington Co. (K. Evans)
  Latest dates:
    25 Oct 1975, Fall River Co. (Rosche)
    29 Oct 1979, Custer Co. (Parker in Seasons 1980a)
    27 Nov 1982, Fall River Co. (Rosche and Rosche in Seasons 1983a)
Other records away from far W
  Grand River Agency (Hoffman 1877)
  Sanborn Co. (Visher 1913a)

354 TOWHEES, SPARROWS, JUNCOS, AND LONGSPURS

LAPLAND LONGSPUR *Calcarius lapponicus* (Linnaeus)

Status. Abundant migrant and winter visitor. Black Hills and SW status uncertain.

Habitat. Fields and prairies.

Spring migration. Late Feb – mid-Apr. Unusual concentrations: 4 Mar 1955, Armour-Delmont area, hundreds found dead after blizzard (Crutchett and Crutchett 1955); 13 Mar 1971, Wall Lake, flock of several thousand (Krause and Blankespoor in Seasons 1971c).

Latest dates:
29 Apr 1896, Miner Co., specimens (Patton)
2 May 1959, Sioux Falls (Krause)
10 May 1930, Spearfish, specimen (Haight 1952)

Fall migration. Mid-Oct and Nov. Unusual concentrations: 4 Nov 1955, near Milbank, thousands migrating against a SE wind (Elliott 1955).

Earliest dates:
13 Sep 1977, Deuel Co. (Harris in Seasons 1978a)
17 Sep 1988, Butte Co. (Springer in Seasons 1989a)
8 Oct 1964, near Parmelee (Springer)

Winter. Unusual concentrations: 6 Jan 1938, Union Co., 300 found dead after storm (Stephens et al. 1955); 26 Jan 1954, Walworth Co. thousands (Randall 1956a); 29–31 Jan 1952, Lacreek NWR, tremendous concentrations (Krumm 1952a); 14 Feb 1967, between Hartford and Forestburg, 36 flocks ahead of blizzard (Jonkel 1967).

SMITH'S LONGSPUR *Calcarius pictus* (Swainson)

Status. Rare spring and common fall migrant NE. Abundant migrant in 1879 in Ft. Sisseton area (McChesney 1890).

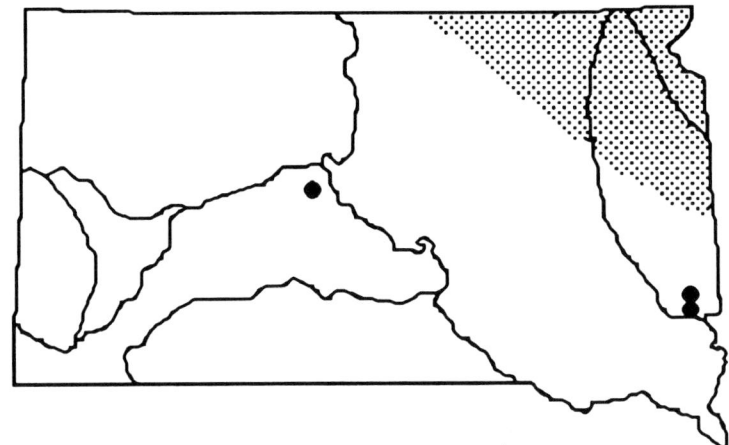

Habitat. Short grass prairie and stubble fields.
Spring migration. Late Apr though late May.
  Earliest dates:
    6 Apr 1978, Deuel Co. (Harris in Seasons 1978c)
    15 Apr 1986, Deuel Co. (Harris in Seasons 1986c)
    23 Apr 1974, Deuel Co. (Harris)
  Latest dates:
    1 May 1951, Stanley Co. (Blankenship et al. 1953)
    19 May 1951, Minnehaha Co. (Findley)
Fall migration. Late Sep – Oct.
  Earliest dates:
    23 Sep 1950, The Dells (Findley)
    23 Sep 1979, Deuel Co. (Harris and Monson in Seasons 1980a)
    11-28 Oct 1974, along Coteau des Prairies from Clear Lake area N to Roberts Co., flocks of 20 – 40 (Harris 1974a)
  Latest dates:
    4 Nov 1978, Deuel Co. (Harris in Seasons 1979a)
    4 Nov 1984, Deuel Co. (Harris in Seasons 1985a)
    5 Nov 1986, Deuel Co. (Harris in Seasons 1987a)
    7 Nov 1975, Deuel Co. (Harris in Seasons 1975d)

CHESTNUT-COLLARED LONGSPUR *Calcarius ornatus* (Townsend)

Status. Common summer resident W and NE in appropriate habitat; no recent records from SE. Formerly rare summer resident in Clay Co. (Agersborg 1885; Visher 1915).

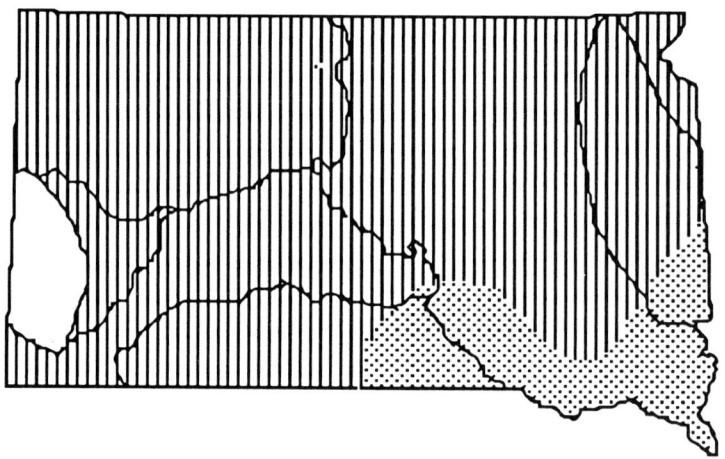

Habitat. Shortgrass prairies and stony pastures.
Spring migration. Mid-Apr – mid-May.
  Earliest dates:
    11 Mar 1982, Wind Cave NP (Cavigelli)
    13 Mar 1985, Jackson Co. dead male (Graupmann in Seasons 1985c)
    23 Mar 1982, Deuel Co. (Harris in Seasons 1982c)
Nesting. May – mid-Aug.
  Earliest dates:
    28 Apr 1965, Codington Co., female lining nest, clutch of 4 eggs on 7 May, eggs hatched on 18 May, and young fledged on 1 Jun (Moriarty 1965c)
    19 May 1968, Hyde Co., nest with 6 eggs (P. Jonkel)
    22 May 1894, Miner Co., nest with eggs (Patton)
  Latest dates:
    22 Jul 1967, Gardner Lake, nest with 3 eggs (Baylor and Rosine 1970)
    27 Jun 1968, near Roswell, male feeding nearly-grown bird (Rogge and Rogge 1968)
    29 Jul 1985, Deuel Co., nest with 3 young (Harris)
Fall migration. Sep.
  Latest dates:
    10 Oct 1982, Miner Co. (Anderson in Seasons 1983a)
    10 Oct 1982, Stanley Co. (Harris in Seasons 1983a)
    13 Oct 1968, Hyde Co. (Harter 1969)
    13 Oct 1975, Deuel Co. (Harris in Seasons 1975d)

SNOW BUNTING *Plectrophenax nivalis* (Linnaeus)

Status. Winter visitor in irregular numbers; most common E, accidental Black Hills.

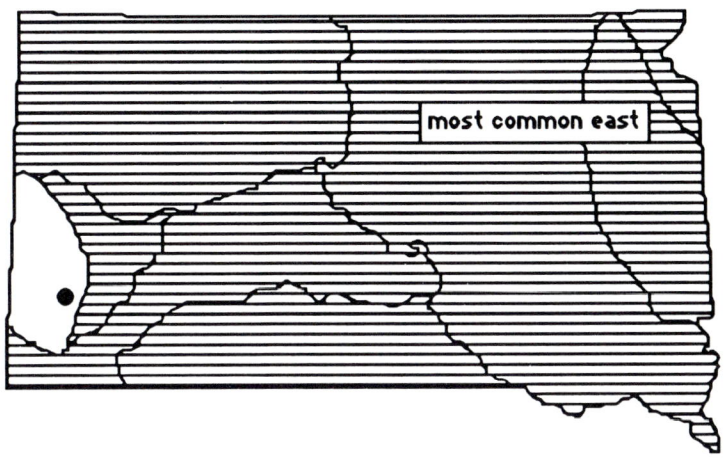

Habitat. Prairies and fields.

Spring migration. Mid-Feb – Mar. Unusual concentration: 8 Mar 1956, over 550, Milbank (Elliott).
  Latest dates:
    4 Apr 1975, Deuel Co. (Harris)
    4 Apr 1986, Codington Co. (Skadsen in Seasons 1986c)
    6 Apr 1957, Minnehaha Co. (Krause)
    8 Apr 1978, Pennington Co. (Whitney in Seasons 1978c)

Fall migration. Late Oct – Nov.
  Earliest dates:
    24 Sep 1960, near Milbank (Elliott 1961a)
    22 Oct 1955, near Milbank (Elliott 1955)
    22 Oct 1977, Deuel Co. (Harris in Seasons 1978c)

Winter. Irregular, occasionally abundant, winter visitor across state, reported most often E.

Black Hills record:
  6 Nov 1982, Wind Cave NP (Peterson in Seasons 1983a)

SUBFAMILY ICTERINAE: Meadowlarks, Blackbirds and Orioles

BOBOLINK *Dolichonyx oryzivorus* (Linnaeus)

Status. Fairly common summer resident E. Uncommon and irregular summer resident W during wet years.

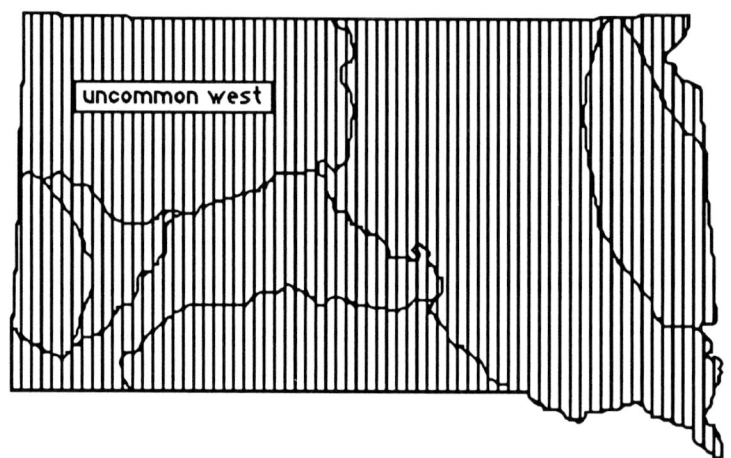

Habitat. Tall grass prairies, meadows and haylands.
Spring migration. Second – third week of May.
  Earliest dates:
    20 Apr 1984, Turner Co. (Wilcox in Seasons 1984c)
    29 Apr [year], Faulkton (Bent 1958)
    1 May 1983, Deuel Co. (Stava in Seasons 1983c)
Nesting. Late May – Jul.
  Earliest date:
    8 Jun 1969, Sanborn Co., nest with eggs (Harris)
  Latest dates:
    9 Jul 1968, near Howard, nest with 6 eggs (Fuller)
    24 Jul 1973, near Ralph, pair and female feeding 2 sets of young (Springer)
    30 Jul 1973, pair with fledgling, Rapid Valley (Serr and Bachmann)
Fall migration. Late Aug – Sep. Unusual concentration: 8 Sep 1965, Lacreek NWR, several hundred (Russell 1966).
  Latest dates:
    9 Oct, Sioux Falls (Bent 1958)
    16 Oct 1979, Brown Co. (Montgomery and Tallman in Seasons 1980a)

RED-WINGED BLACKBIRD *Agelaius phoeniceus* (Linnaeus).

Status. Abundant summer resident. Uncommon winter E, casual W.

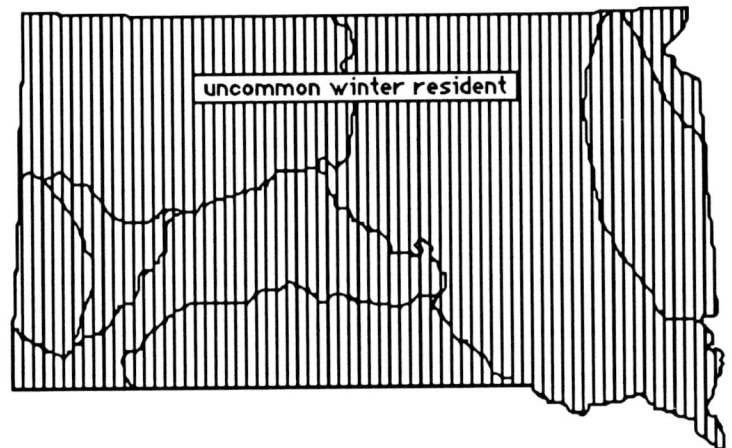

Habitat. Swamps, marshes, and wet thickets; often frequents feedlots. Sometimes nests in shrubs over dry land.

Spring migration. Mid-Mar – first week of Apr. Early spring dates may be wintering birds.

Nesting. Mid-May – Aug.
Earliest dates:
12 May 1964, Brown Co., first egg in nest (Besser et al 1987)
19 May 1965, Brown Co., first egg in nest (Besser et al 1987)
19 May 1987, Lake Andes NWR, building nest (Springer)
21 May 1963, Brown Co., first egg in nest (Besser et al 1987)
Latest dates:
30 Jul 1967, Sanborn Co., nest with 1 egg and 3 young (Harris)
3 Aug 1965, Brown Co., last nestling fledged (Besser et al. 1987)
6 Aug 1966, Brown Co., last nestling fledged (Besser et al. 1987)

Fall migration. Mid-Oct – Mid-Nov. Late fall dates may be of birds attempting to winter.

Winter. Unusual concentration: mid-Jan, near Madison, ca. 2000 (Strauss et al. 1961). Observed every year on CBC.

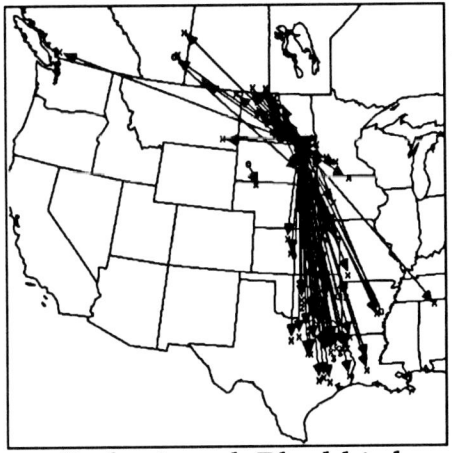

Red-winged Blackbird banding recoveries.

360 MEADOWLARKS, BLACKBIRDS, AND ORIOLES

EASTERN MEADOWLARK *Sturnella magna* (Linnaeus)

Status. Fairly common summer resident at Lacreek NWR and adjacent valley meadows in the narrow strip of sandhills in South Dakota. Rare visitor elsewhere. Formerly nested Minnehaha Co. (Larson 1925).

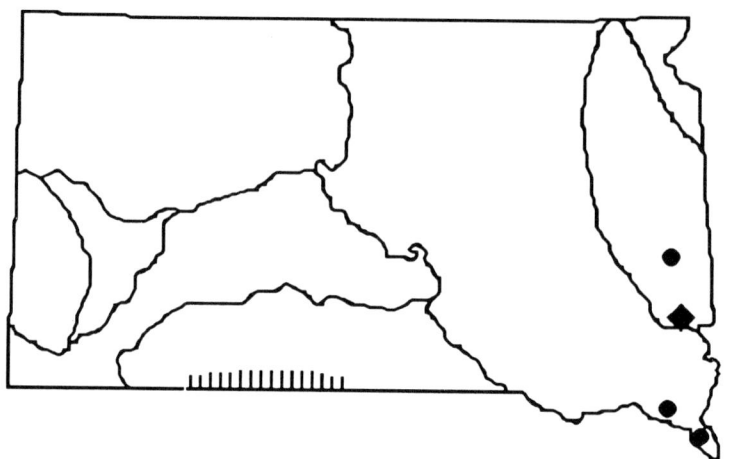

Habitat. Lowland meadows.
Spring migration. Last half of Mar – first of Apr.
  Earliest dates:
    1 Mar 1988, Brookings Co. Sandell in Seasons 1988c)
    10 Mar 1972, Lacreek NWR (Fjetland)
    25 Mar 1956, McCook Lake (Chapman and Krause)
    2 Apr 1971, Lacreek NWR (Fjetland)
Nesting.
  Only record:
    24 May 1990, Shanon Co., nest with eggs (Peterson in Seasons 1990d)
Fall migration. Oct.
  Only date:
    14 Oct 1982, Clay Co. (Hall in Seasons 1983a)

WESTERN MEADOWLARK *Sturnella neglecta* Audubon

Status. Abundant summer resident. Casual winter.

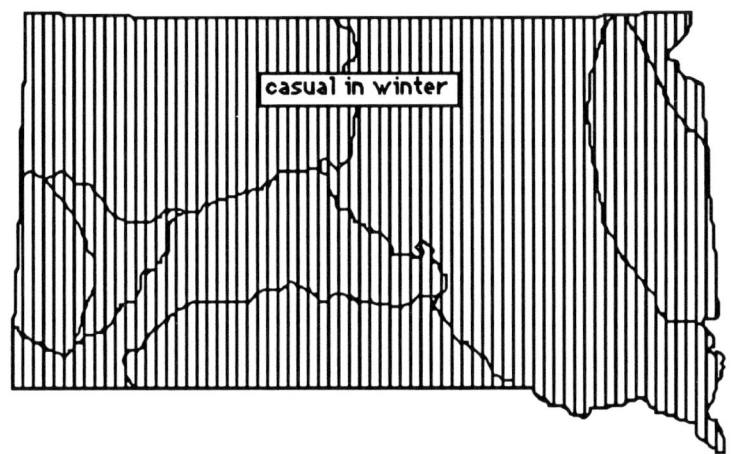

Habitat. Grasslands and prairies.
Spring migration. Last half of Mar – first of Apr.
  Earliest dates:
    17 Feb 1959, Bennett Co. (Whitney)
    22 Feb 1966, Brown Co. (Rose 1967)
    23 Feb 1981, Brookings Co. (Holden in Seasons 1981c)
Nesting. May – mid-Jul.
  Earliest dates:
    27 Apr 1911, Douglas Co., nest with 5 eggs (Walker)
    11 May 1951, Stanley Co., nest with 4 eggs (Blankenship et al. 1953)
    13 May 1886, Huron, nest with 5 eggs (Cheney)
    13 May 1967, Sanborn Co., nest with 2 eggs (Harris)
  Latest dates:
    24 Jul 1973, Harding Co., adult feeding young (Springer)
    7 Aug 1983, Hyde Co., fledgling just out of nest (Harter in Seasons 1984a)
    13 Aug 1976, Harding Co., adult feeding young (Springer)
Fall migration. Oct. Late dates may be birds attempting to winter.
Winter. Most have departed by the end of Nov but has been recorded on 12 CBC. Seen in winter as far N as Perkins and Brown counties.

YELLOW-HEADED BLACKBIRD *Xanthocephalus xanthocephalus* (Bonaparte)

Status. Common to abundant summer resident E; migrant W, breeding in suitable habitat. Does not nest in the Black Hills. Rare winter in E.

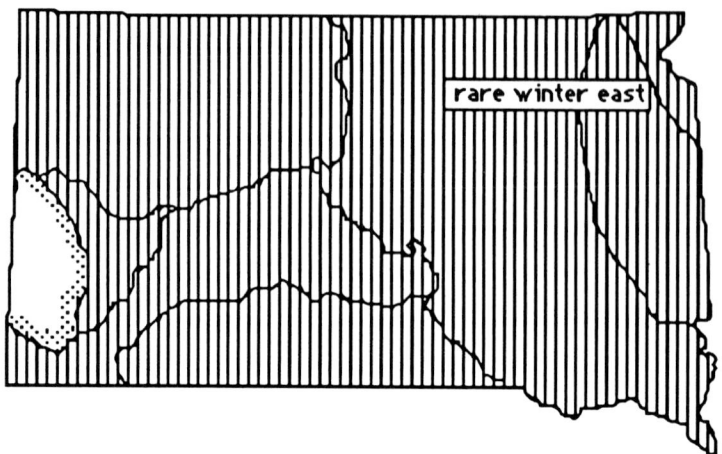

Habitat. Deeper sloughs, reedy marshes, lakes; forages in feedlots.

Spring migration. Mid-Apr – first week of May.
  Earliest dates:
    7 Mar 1973, Yankton (Hall)
    14 Mar 1978, Brown Co. (Hill in Seasons 1978c)
    17 Mar 1938, Roberts Co. (Harris 1964)

Nesting. Last of May – Jun.
  Earliest dates:
    5 Jun 1968, near Roscoe, 4 nests with from 1 to 3 eggs (Duebbert)
    7 Jun 1968, Sanborn Co., nest with 4 eggs and 9 Jun 1968, nest with 3 eggs (Harris)
  Latest dates:
    17 Jul 1977, Lacreek NWR, 4 young (Lohoefener and Ely 1978)
    23 Jul 1978, Brule Co., adults feeding young (Springer)
    24 Jul 1973, Harding Co., adults with young (Springer)

Fall migration. Late Sep – Oct. Late fall birds may be attempting to winter.

Winter.
  CBC reports:
    Sand Lake, Lake Co., Wilmot, Brookings Co., Deuel Co., Waubay, and Pierre.
  Post Dec records.
    4 Jan 1986, Brown Co. (Tallman)
    14 Jan 1978, Hughes Co. (Backlund fide Harris in Seasons 1978b)

RUSTY BLACKBIRD *Euphagus carolinus* (Muller)

Status. Uncommon migrant E and irregular winter resident; few records W. Absent from higher Black Hills.

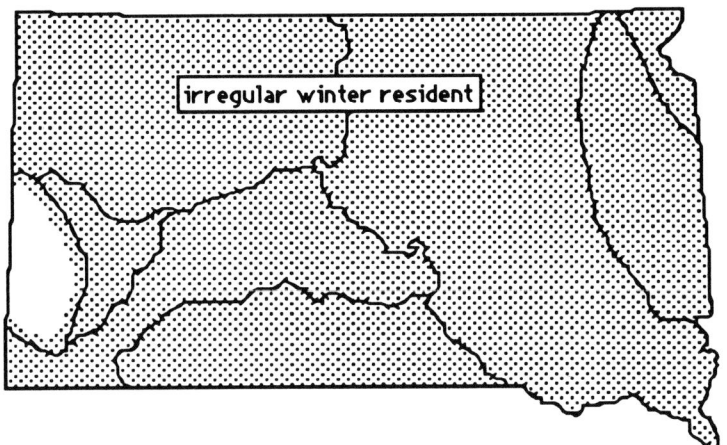

Habitat. Deciduous woodlands usually near water and along sloughs; winters near feedlots.

Spring migration. Last half of Mar – first part of Apr.
  Earliest dates:
    1 Mar 1983, Hutchinson Co. (Anderson in Seasons 1983c)
    2 Mar 1956, Sioux Falls (Krause)
    3 Mar 1969, Rapid City (Rose)
  Latest dates:
    28 Apr 1984, Brookings Co. (Baker and Tallman in Seasons 1984c)
    4 May 1961, Brookings Co. (Holden)
    16 May [year], Aberdeen (Bent 1958)

Fall migration. Oct and Nov.
  Earliest dates:
    14 Sep 1977, Meade Co. (Whitney in Seasons 1978a)
    29 Sep 1931, Union Co. (Youngworth)
    4 Oct 1972, Sioux Falls (Krause and Blankespoor)

Winter. Recorded at least once at almost all CBC. Winters at Sand Lake NWR and was recorded in the winter of 1985–86 in Fall River Co. (Rosche).

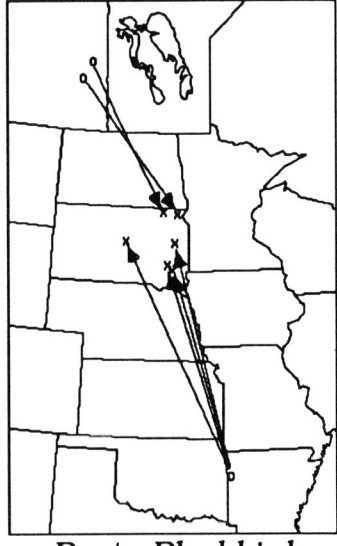

Rusty Blackbird banding recoveries.

BREWER'S BLACKBIRD *Euphagus cyanocephalus* (Wagler)

Status. Fairly common summer resident in the far W. Rare breeder in NE (near Ft. Sisseton and Clear Lake) (Youngworth 1935, Peterson 1954, Harris in Seasons 1987d) and probably Roberts Co. (Buckman). Formerly bred in Clay Co. (Agersborg 1885). Rare migrant and winter resident E.

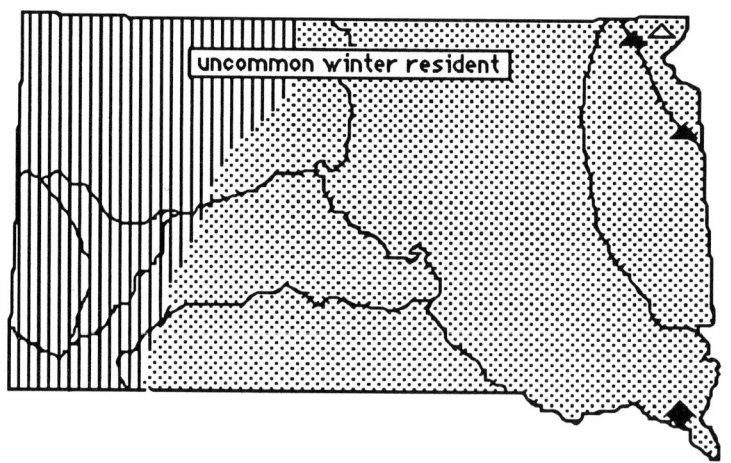

Habitat. Short grass prairies broken by brushy draws; fields and pastures with thickets; winters near feedlots.

Spring migration. Black Hills: Mid-Apr – first week of May. E: Mid-Mar – first week of Apr.

Earliest dates:
10 Mar 1953, near Clear Lake (Peterson 1954)
10 Mar 1985, Lincoln Co. (Skadsen in Seasons 1985c)
10 Mar 1987, Shannon Co. (Dagelen)

Nesting. Last week of May – Aug.

Earliest dates:
4 Jun 1969, Pennington Co., nest with 3 young (Whitney)
6 Jun 1956, Pennington Co., nest with 6 recently hatched young (Pettingill and Whitney 1965)
16 Jun 1973, Harding Co., female feeding young (Springer)

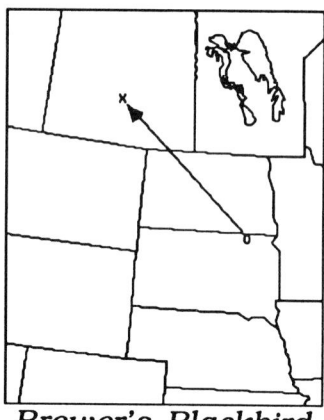

Brewer's Blackbird banding recoveries.

Latest dates:
14 Jul 1978, Harding Co., adult feeding young (Springer)
22 Jul 1974, Harding Co., adult feeding young (Springer)
6 Aug 1960, Redfern Burn, 6 fledged young (Behrens in Pettingill and Whitney 1965).

Fall migration. Mid-Sep – Oct. Late fall dates may be wintering birds.

Winter. Uncommon in feedlots around Sand Lake NWR. Recorded at least once on most CBC.

GREAT-TAILED GRACKLE *Cassidix mexicanus* (Gmelin)

Status. Accidental.
Only record:
  14–15 May 1988, Yankton Co., photographed (Van Sickle et al. in Seasons 1988c)

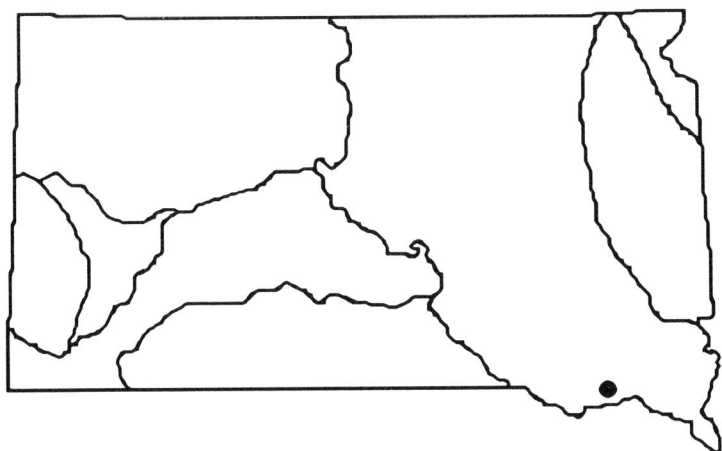

COMMON GRACKLE *Quiscalus quiscula* (Linnaeus)

Status. Abundant summer resident. Absent in higher Black Hills except in towns. Rare winter, most often S.

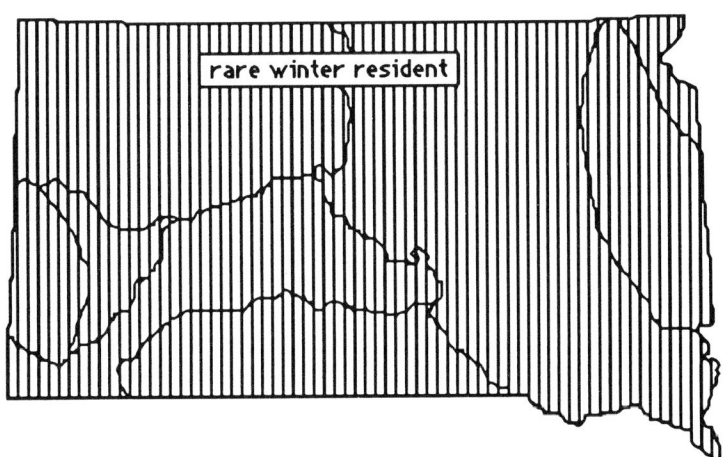

Habitat. Shelterbelts, marshes, woodlands and residential areas.
Spring migration. Mid-Mar – mid-Apr. Early spring dates may be wintering birds.
Nesting. May into Jul.
  Earliest dates:
    8 Apr 1965, Brookings Co., building nests (Springer)
    19 Apr 1967, Meade Co., building nest (Whitney)
    20 Apr 1964, Brookings Co., building nests (Springer)
  Latest dates:
    15 Jul 1978, Harding Co., carrying food (Springer)
    24 Jul 1973, Harding Co., adult and fledged young (Springer)
    24 Jul 1977, feeding young (Lohoefener and Ely 1978)

Fall migration. Mid-Sep – Oct. Latest dates may be birds attempting to winter.

Winter. Seen almost every year in small numbers on CBC.

Post-Dec records:
 1 Jan 1986, Brown Co. (Tallman)
 3 Jan 1987, Brown Co. (Tallman)
 22 Jan 1976, Day Co. (Chilson)

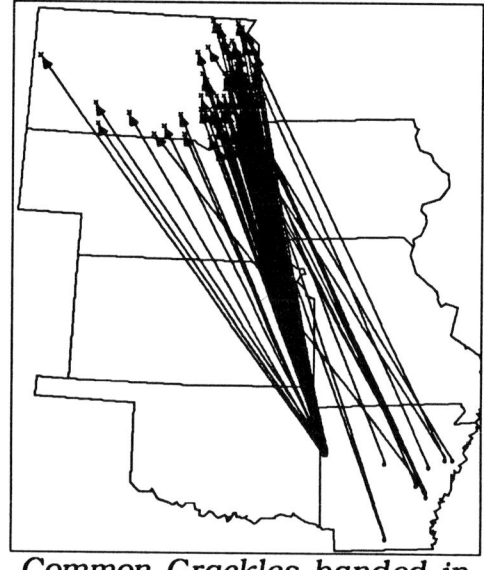

Common Grackles banded in Arkansas and recovered in South Dakota.

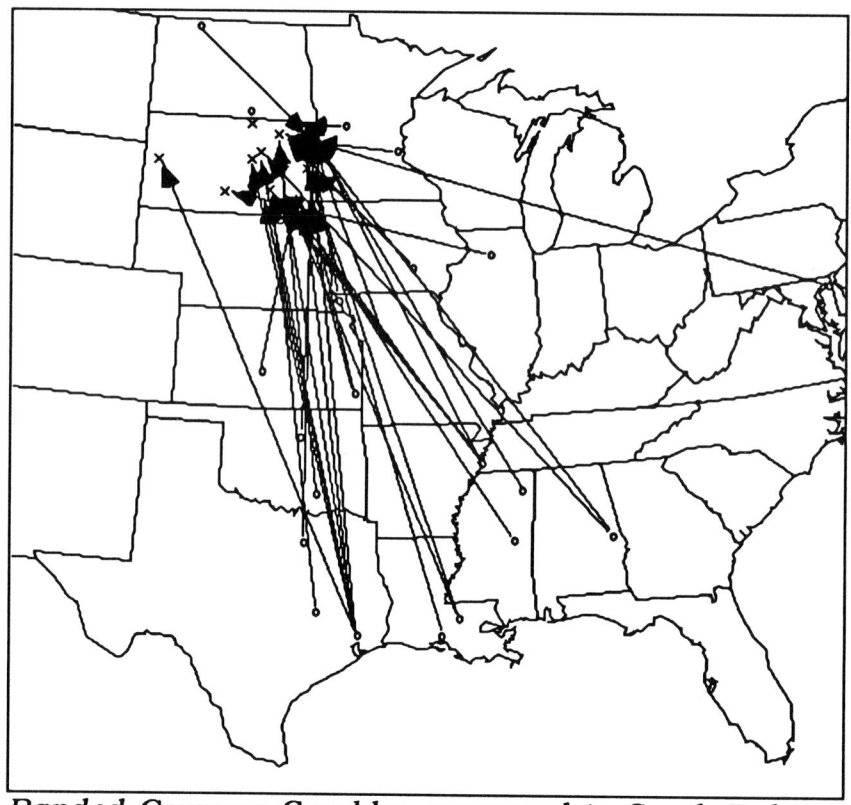

Banded Common Grackles recovered in South Dakota.

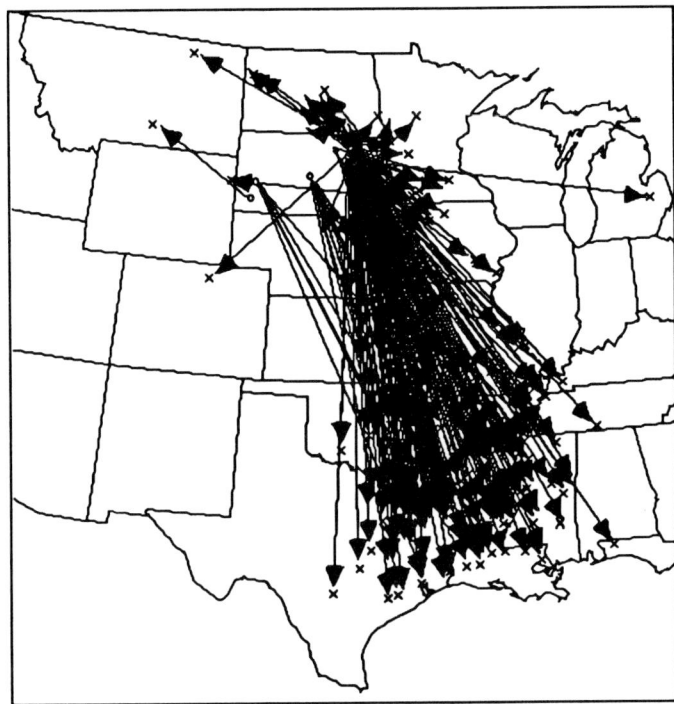
Common Grackle banding recoveries outside South Dakota.

BROWN-HEADED COWBIRD *Molothrus ater* (Boddaert)

Status. Abundant summer resident, except fairly common summer resident in Black Hills. Casual winter.

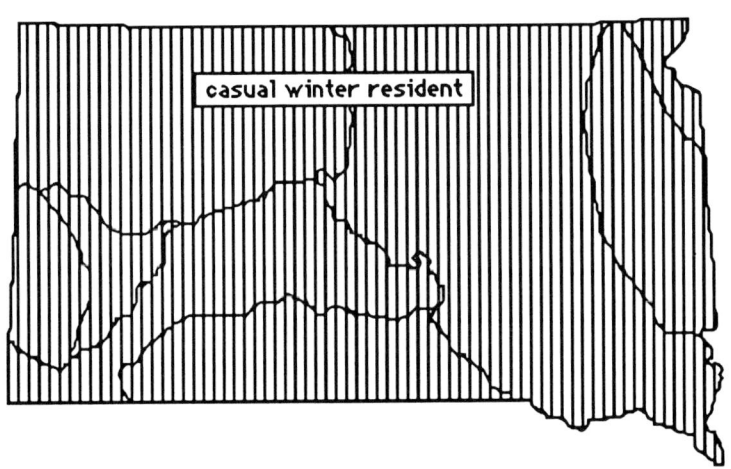

Habitat. Open woodlands, fields, feedlots, and residential areas.
Spring migration. Mid-Apr – first week of May.
  Earliest dates:
    12 Mar 1985, Turner Co. (Anderson in Seasons 1985a)
    21 Mar 1987, Sanborn Co. (Rogers in Seasons 1987c)
    25 Mar 1966, Minnehaha Co. (Springer)
    25 Mar 1972, Sioux Falls (Krause)
    25 Mar 1978, Deuel Co. (Harris in Seasons 1978c)

Nesting. Mid-May – mid-Aug.
   Earliest dates:
   29 Apr 1952, Sioux Falls, 1 egg, Pine Siskin nest (Krause)
   18 May 1968, Union Co. 2 eggs in cardinal nest (Harris)
   20 May 1975, Deuel Co., 1 egg in Vesper Sparrow nest (Harris in Seasons 1975c)
   Latest dates:
   26 Jul 1958, Jewel Cave NM, Audubon's Warbler feeding immature (Carter 1958b)
   3 Aug 1986, Day Co., young fed by American Goldfinch (Skadsen in Seasons 1987a)
   18 Aug 1972, near Humboldt, young fluttering wings beside Lark Bunting (Krause and Blankespoor)
Fall migration. Mid-Sep – mid-Oct. Late fall birds may be attempting to winter.
Winter.
   CBC reports:
   Brookings, Deuel, Lake Andes, Madison, Pierre, Sand Lake, Sioux Falls, Wilmot, and Yankton.

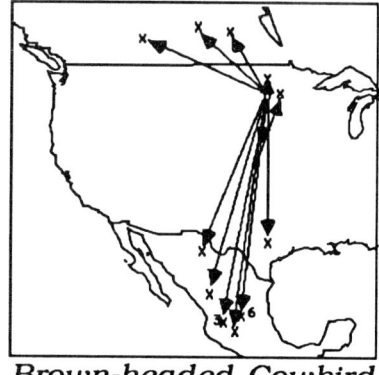

Brown-headed Cowbird banding recoveries.

ORCHARD ORIOLE *Icterus spurius* (Linnaeus)

Status. Fairly common summer resident, except uncommon Black Hills foothills.

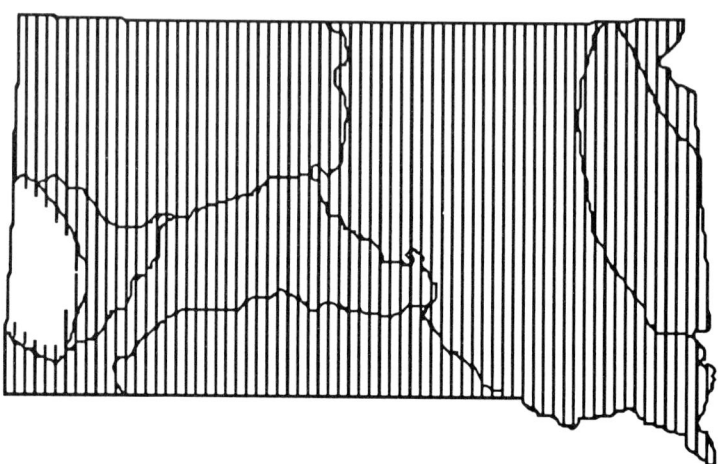

Habitat. Woodlands and residential areas.
Spring migration. Last half of May.
   Earliest dates:
   29 Apr 1978, Yankton Co. (Hall and Wilcox in Seasons 1978c)
   2 May 1975, Pierre (Rose in Seasons 1975b)
   3 May 1938, Roberts Co. (Harris 1964)
   3 May 1964, Sioux Falls (Krause)

Nesting. Mid-May – late Jul.
Earliest dates:
26 May 1966, Rapid City, courtship display (Baylor 1966)
30 May 1973, Highmore, nest building (Harter)
6 Jun 1970, Perkins Co., nest building (Whitney)
Latest dates:
12 Jul 1934, Alexandria, fledgling banded (Wagar)
12 Jul 1977, Todd Co., adults feeding young (Lohenofener and Ely 1978)
22 Jul 1974, Harding Co., adult feeding fledgling (Springer)
17 Aug 1975, Hyde Co., adult feeding 2 fledglings (Harter in Seasons 1975c)
Fall migration. Last week of Jul – mid-Aug.
Latest dates:
28 Aug 1971, Sioux Falls (Krause)
6 Sep 1977, Hyde Co. (Harter in Seasons 1977a)
15 Sep 1975, Hyde Co. (Harter in Seasons 1975d)

NORTHERN ORIOLE *Icterus galbula* (Linnaeus)

Status. Two races occur: *I. g. galbula* (Baltimore Oriole): uncommon to common summer resident E; uncommon spring migrant W; *I. g. bullockii* (Bullock's Oriole): fairly common summer resident W, most common in Black Hills foothills and along White, Cheyenne, and Little Missouri Rivers; accidental migrant SE. Accidental winter. Most South Dakota birds are variously intermediate between the 2 extremes and should not be assigned to either race (Anderson 1969, 1971).

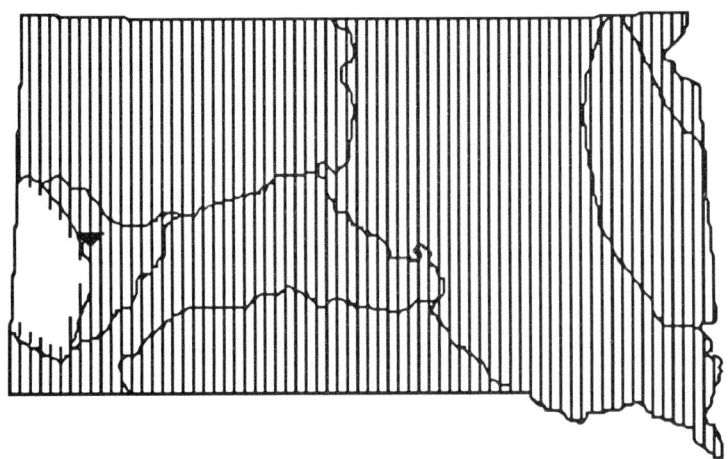

Habitat. Woodlands and residential areas.
Spring migration. First 2 weeks of May E; last half of May W.
Earliest dates:
17 Apr 1898, Elk Point (Hoffman)
20 Apr 1955, Sand Lake (Podoll 1963)
22 Apr 1954, Madison (Habeger 1956a)

Nesting. Mid-May – Aug.
Earliest dates:
21 May 1965, Mitchell, female building nest, feeding young, 22 Jun (Crutchett and Hall 1966)
3–28 Jun 1973, Rapid City, nest building to fledging of 4 (Bachmann)
4 Jun 1911, Douglas Co., nest with 5 eggs (Walker)
Latest date:
21 Jul 1961, Rapid City, female feeding full-grown immature (Whitney)
3 Aug 1978, Fall River Co., adult with 2 young (Springer)
9 Aug 1966, Cascade Springs, nest with young (Edie)

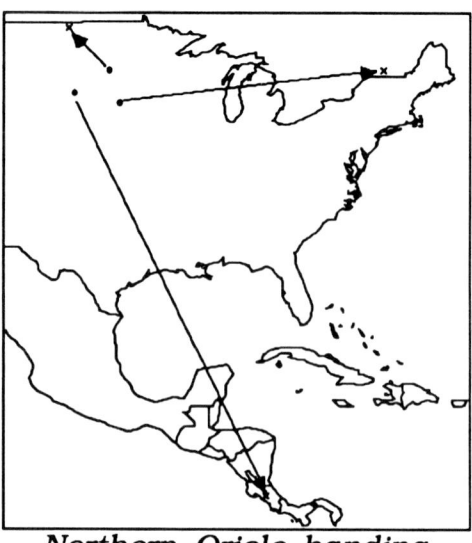
Northern Oriole banding recoveries

Fall migration. Last week in Aug – first 3 weeks of Sep.
Latest dates:
3 Nov 1941, Wilmot (Harris 1963)
5 Nov 1982, Clay Co. (Lemons in Seasons 1982d)
11 Nov 1965, Watertown (Duffner)

Winter.
CBC report:
Rapid City.

FRINGILLIDAE: Finches

ROSY FINCH *Leucosticte arctoa* (Pallas)

Status. Sporadic, occasionally abundant, winter visitor in Black Hills and Badlands. Accidental winter elsewhere.

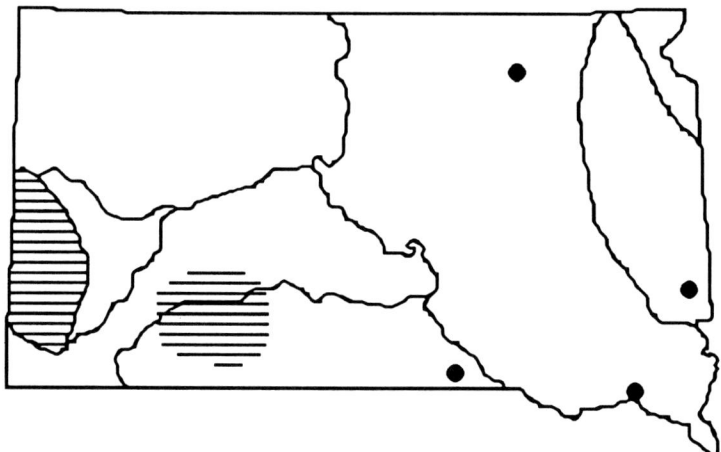

Habitat. Weedy areas, stubble fields, and roadsides.

Spring migration. Apr.
Latest dates:
  8 Apr 1984, Badlands NP (Glass 1986)
  10 Apr 1965, Spearfish (Springer)
  24 May 1954, Custer Co. (Heumphreus 1954)
Fall migration. Mid-Oct – mid-Nov.
Earliest dates:
  19 Oct 1977, Rapid City (Kovorik fide Serr in Seasons 1978c)
  20 Oct 1956, Pennington Co. (Pettingill and Whitney 1965)
  22 Oct 1988, Meade Co. (Miller in Seasons 1989a)
Winter. Many records in Black Hills and Badlands region.
CBC report:
  Rapid City.
E records:
  9 Nov 1980, Moody Co. (Wells in Seasons 1981a)
  14 Nov 1972 – 1 Feb 1973, Aberdeen, photographed (Arbogast 1974)
  Late Dec 1960 – 15 Mar 1961, Volin, photographed (Lien et al. 1961)
  2 Dec 1972 – Mar 1972, Burke (Frank in Steffen 1973)

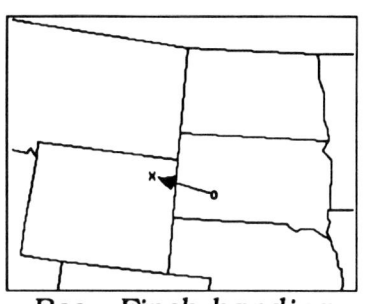

Rosy Finch banding recoveries.

PINE GROSBEAK *Pinicola enucleator* (Linnaeus)

Status. Uncommon and irregular winter visitor. Casual visitor during all seasons in Black Hills.

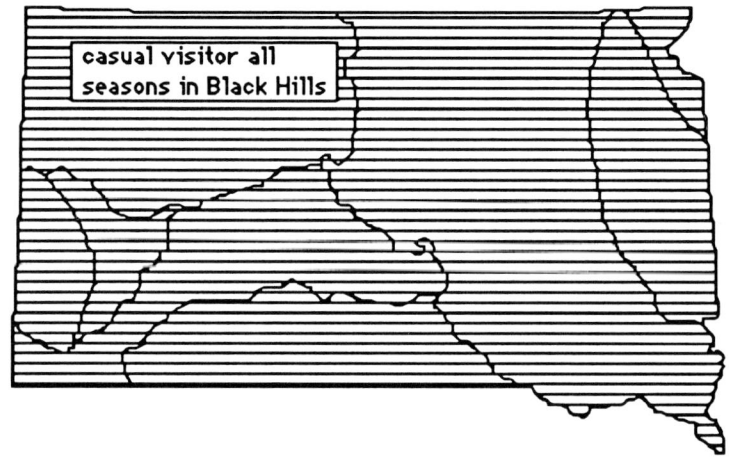

Habitat. Black Hills area: spruce and Box Elder. E: conifers and fruit trees.
Spring migration. Possibly mid-Feb – mid-Mar.
Latest dates:
  27 Mar 1970, Sioux Falls (Krause)
  27 Mar 1981, Custer Co. (Parker in Seasons 1981c)
  5 Apr 1970, Spearfish Canyon (Black Hills Audubon Society in Serr 1970)

Summer records.
- 28 May 1899, Hot Springs (Cary 1901)
- 1 Jun 1977, Rapid City, pair (Brodsky in Seasons 1977d)
- 6 Jun 1963, Jewel Cave NM, pair (V. Harris in Pettingill and Whitney 1965)
- 15 Jul 1942, Palmer Gulch (R. Elliott)
- 24 Jul 1952, Palmer Gulch (Behrens)
- 28 Jul 1952, Silver City (Behrens in Pettingill and Whitney 1965)

Fall migration. Last week of Oct – first half of Nov.
Earliest dates:
- 9 Sep 1974, Pierre (Rose)
- 21 Sep 1961, Highmore (Harter 1962)
- 25 Oct 1969, Brookings Co. (Shaw)

Winter. Not reported every year but may be common when present. Reported at most E CBC.

PURPLE FINCH *Carpodacus purpureus* (Gmelin)

Status. Irregular, often common, winter resident E, uncommon W. Black Hills status uncertain.

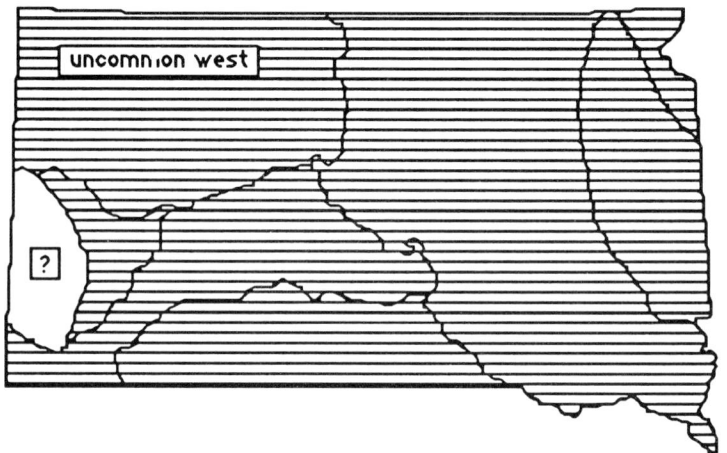

Habitat. Woodlands and residential areas.
Spring migration. Mid-Mar – mid-Apr.
Latest dates:
- 12 May 1984, Brookings Co. (Holden in Seasons 1984c)
- 13 May 1953, Sioux Falls (Krause)
- 16 May 1984, Codington Co. (Harris in Seasons 1984c)

Fall migration. Mid-Oct – mid-Nov.

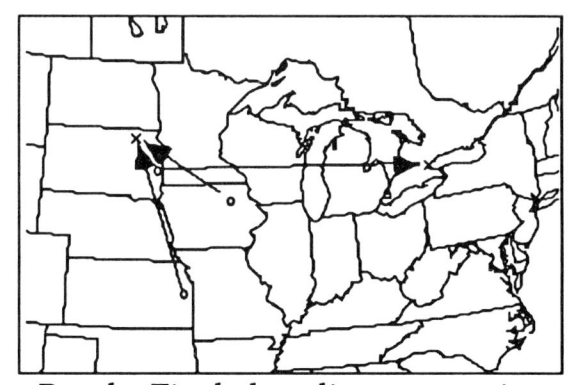

Purple Finch banding recoveries

Earliest dates:
- 28 Aug 1976, Brookings Co. (Taylor in Seasons 1977a)
- 28 Aug 1981, Brown Co., immature banded (Tallman in Seasons 1982a)
- 3 Sep 1976, Roberts Co. (Harris in Seasons 1977a)

Winter. Seen almost every year on CBC's.

CASSIN'S FINCH *Carpodacus cassinii* Baird

Status. Fairly common winter and summer resident in Black Hills. Accidental elsewhere.

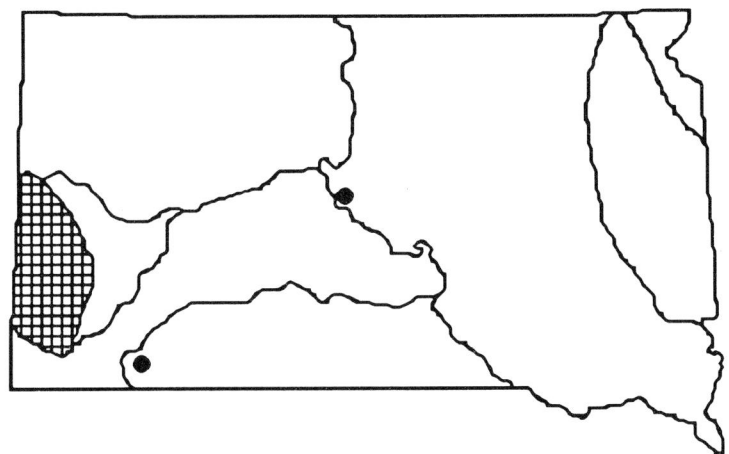

Habitat. Woodlands and residential areas.

Nesting. Many summer records but most breeding unconfirmed.
Only record:
- 11 July 1984, Custer Co., begging young (Peterson in Seasons 1984d)

Records E of Black Hills.
- 8 Apr 1973, Pierre, banded (Rose)
- 19 Jan – 7 May 1980, Shannon Co. (Homoyá)

HOUSE FINCH *Carpodacus mexicanus* (Muller)

Status. Species expanding range into both ends of state, presumably from both the E and W United States First reported 30 Dec 1966 at Mitchell (Harris 1970). Increasingly reported. First reported nesting in 1989 (Peterson and Peterson 1989). Widely reported across E in 1990. Movements seem to be sporadic.

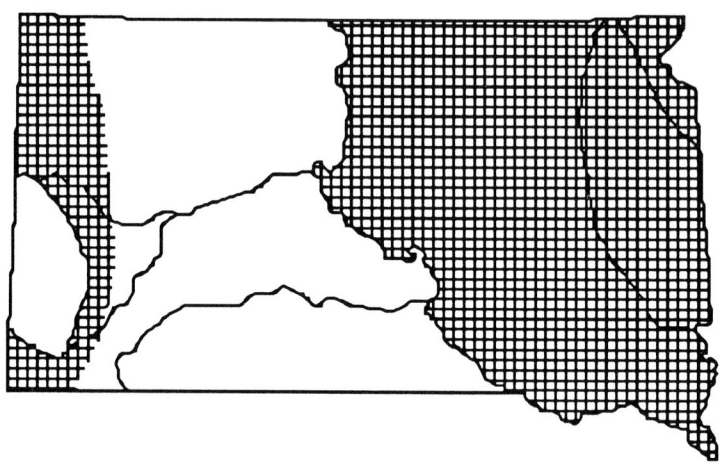

Habitat. Residential areas.

Breeding.

Records to 1989:

28 May 1989, Fall River Co., nest with 2 young (Peterson and Peterson 1989)

22 Jun 1989, Brookings Co., female with 3 begging young (Harris in Seasons 1989d)

Summer 1989, Minnehaha Co., juvenile with down (Blankespoor 1989)

RED CROSSBILL *Loxia curvirostra* Linnaeus

Status. Irregular and often common visitor, any time of year, regular, but unpredictable, breeder in the Black Hills and buttes of Harding Co., less frequently elsewhere.

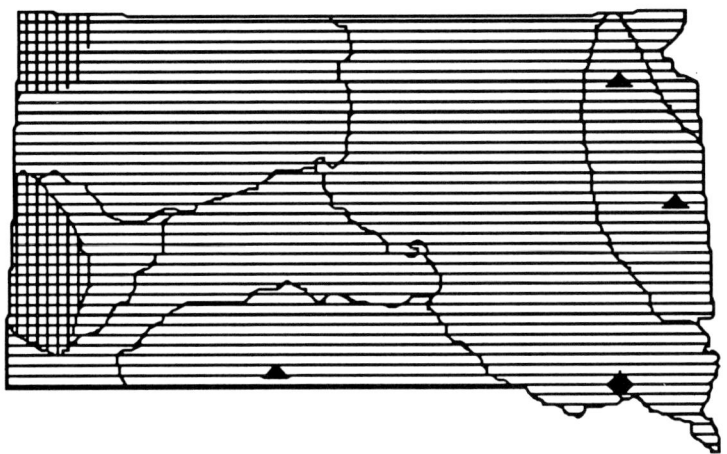

Habitat. Coniferous forest.
Spring migration. Extremely irregular.
Nesting.
  Earliest dates:
    23 Dec 1964, Pennington Co., specimen with greatly enlarged ovary (Pettingill and Whitney 1965)
    20 Jan 1965, Sheridan Lake, female building nest (Whitney)
    18 Feb 1961, Rapid City, nest with 3 fresh eggs (Pettingill and Whitney 1965)
  Latest date:
    6 Aug 1957, Palmer Gulch, nest being built (Eastman in Pettingill and Whitney 1965)
  Breeding records E of Black Hills:
    25 Mar 1920, Yankton, female nest building, 2 eggs on 29 Mar (Larrabee 1920)
    24 Mar 1987, Day Co., nest with 3 young (Skadsen in Seasons 1987c)
    24 May 1973, Brookings Co., young at feeder (C. Peterson)
    1 Jun 1969, Todd Co., newly-fledged young collected, and several pairs feeding young (B. Anderson)
Fall migration. Mid-Sep – mid-Nov. July records in NE may represent early migrants.
  Earliest dates:
    10 Aug 1977, Reliance (Thietje in Seasons 1977a)
    10 Aug 1972, near Webster (Chilson 1972)
    20 Aug 1987, Brown Co., banded (Tallman)
Winter. A 3-year invasion cycle in E South Dakota has been suggested (N. Holden). Occasionally reported across state on CBC.

WHITE-WINGED CROSSBILL *Loxia leucoptera* Gmelin

Status. Sporadic, uncommon, winter visitor E, rare W. Possible summer resident in Black Hills.

Habitat. Pine and spruce trees.
Spring migration. Mid-Mar – mid-Apr.
  Latest dates:
    10 May 1990, Brown Co. (Tallman)
    13 May 1972, Sioux Falls (Krause and Blankespoor)
Nesting season. Over and Thoms (1946) say that young birds occurred in Black Hills during breeding season.
  Other records:
    Jul 1964, Cheyenne Crossing, 1 (Harter)
    Jun or Jul 1955, Meade Co. N of Rapid City (Short 1961)
    1 Jun 1976, Pennington Co., 40–50 (Buckman 1976a)
    1 Jun 1982, Sylvan Lake, 100+ (Holden in Seasons 1982)
    13 Jun 1990, Pennington Co., 100+ (Peterson in Seasons 1990d)
Fall migration. Mid-Oct – Nov.
  Earliest dates:
    22 Jul 1989, Brown Co., juvenile. (Tallman and Tallman in Seasons 1989d)
    17 Aug 1969, Highmore (Harter 1970)
    27 Aug 1981, Burke (Steffen in Seasons 1982a)
    9 Sep 1979, Deuel Co. (Harris in Seasons 1980a)
Winter. A tendency toward a 3-year invasion cycle (Holden).
  CBC reports:
    Brookings, Pierre, Aberdeen, Deuel, Hot Springs, Watertown, and Wilmot.

COMMON REDPOLL *Carduelis flammea* (Linnaeus)
Status. Irregular, absent to abundant, winter visitor.

Habitat. Trees, thickets, and weedy fields.
Spring migration. Mar.
  Latest dates:
    13 Apr 1982, Brown Co. (Montgomery in Seasons 1982c)
    14 Apr 1970, Brookings (O. Cooper)
    10 May 1966, Brown Co. (Rose 1967)
Fall migration. First half of Nov.
  Earliest dates:
    3 Oct 1976, Spink Co. (Martsching 1984)
    12 Oct 1986, Day Co. (Bryant in Seasons 1987a)
    17 Oct 1981, Deuel Co. (Harris in Seasons 1982a)
    17 Oct 1977, Deuel Co. (Harris in Seasons 1978a)
Winter. Recorded on almost all CBC.

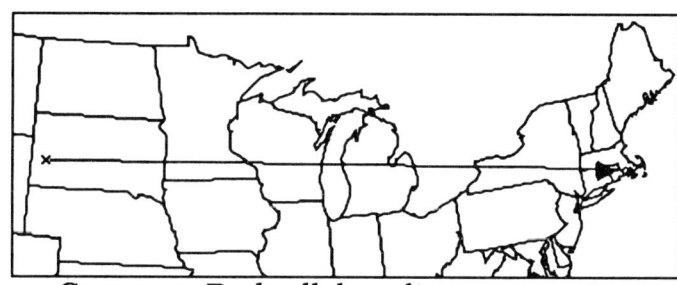

Common Redpoll banding recoveries.

HOARY REDPOLL *Carduelis hornemanni* (Holboll)

Status. Rare winter visitor in E and Black Hills. Usually not recorded before Jan. Status in W prairies unknown.

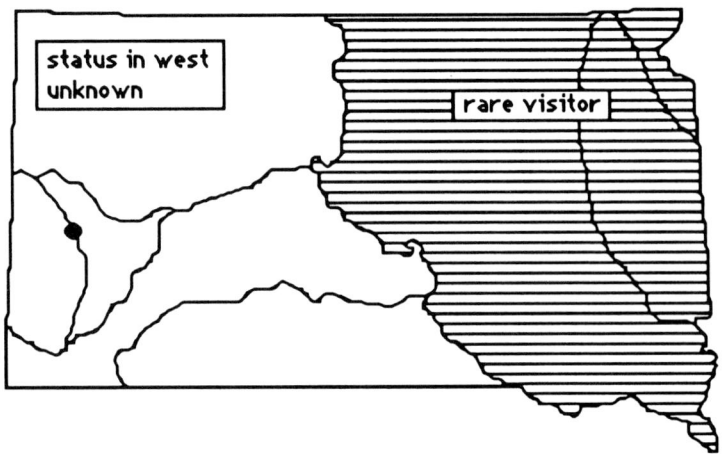

Habitat. Trees, thickets, and weedy fields.

Spring migration. Last half of Mar.
  Latest dates:
    20 Mar 1971, Waubay NWR (Johnson 1972)
    20 Mar 1978, Clear Lake (Harris in Seasons 1978c)
    22 Mar 1969, Huron (Johnson and Johnson 1969)
    22 Mar 1970, Brookings (O. Cooper)

Fall migration. Jan.
  Earliest dates:
    1 Nov 1984, Codington Co. (Harris in Seasons 1985a)
    7 Jan 1970, Brookings (O. Cooper)
    8 Jan 1958, Watertown (Moriarty 1957)
    9 Jan 1972, Huron (Johnson)

Winter.
  CBC reports.
    Pierre and Waubay.

Black Hills records.
    25 Feb and 3 Mar 1969, Rapid City, photographed (Rose)
    1 Mar 1974, Rapid City (Whitney)
    15 and 18 Feb 1978, Pennington Co. (Whitney)

PINE SISKIN *Carduelis pinus* (Wilson)

Status. Abundant permanent resident in Black Hills, possibly migrating to lower elevations in winter. Irregular, uncommon summer resident and irregular, absent to abundant, winter resident throughout rest of state.

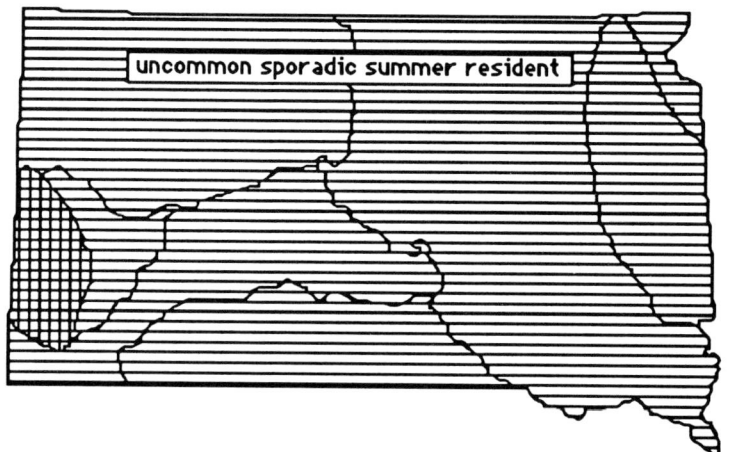

Habitat. Woodlands and residential areas, preferring conifers for breeding.

Spring migration. Since a few siskins nest in E after large numbers winter, migration dates are omitted. Most wintering birds migrate in Apr. E breeding birds are absent in late summer.

Nesting. Black Hills: Apr – Jul; E: Mar – early May

Black Hills earliest dates:
  27 Mar 1988, Meade Co., adult feeding fledged young (E. Miller)
  25 Apr 1954, Rapid City, pair building nest (Whitney)
  23 May 1989, Pennington Co., young just fledged (Biltoft)

Black Hills latest dates:
  8 Jul 1962, Black Fox Campground, copulating pair (Whitney)
  13 Jul 1975, Palmer Gulch, 2 young (Whitney in Seasons 1975c)
  6 Aug 1957, Pennington Co., fledgling banded (Wagar)

E Earliest dates:
  17 Mar 1973, Deuel Co., nest with 1 egg (Harris)
  1 Apr 1973, Deuel Co., nest with 3 eggs (Harris)
  4 Apr 1961, Brookings Co., nest with eggs (O. Cooper and Holden)

E Latest dates:
  26 Apr 1926, Yankton Co., nest with 2 young recently hatched on 6 May, fledged between 17–19 May (Larrabee 1937)
  27 Apr 1970, Woonsocket, nest (Harris)
  29 Apr 1952, Minnehaha Co., nest with 3 eggs, and 2 fledged young photographed on 9 May 1953 (Krause 1953, 1954)
  5 and 7 May 1970, Minnehaha Co., 2 nests being built (Krause)

380 FINCHES

Fall migration. Mid-Oct – mid-Nov.
  Earliest dates:
    11 Sep 1969, Highmore (Harter)
    12 Sep 1977, Brookings Co. (Holden in Seasons 1978a)
    19 Sep 1977, Hyde Co. (Harter in Seasons 1977a)
Winter. Has been recorded on all CBC.

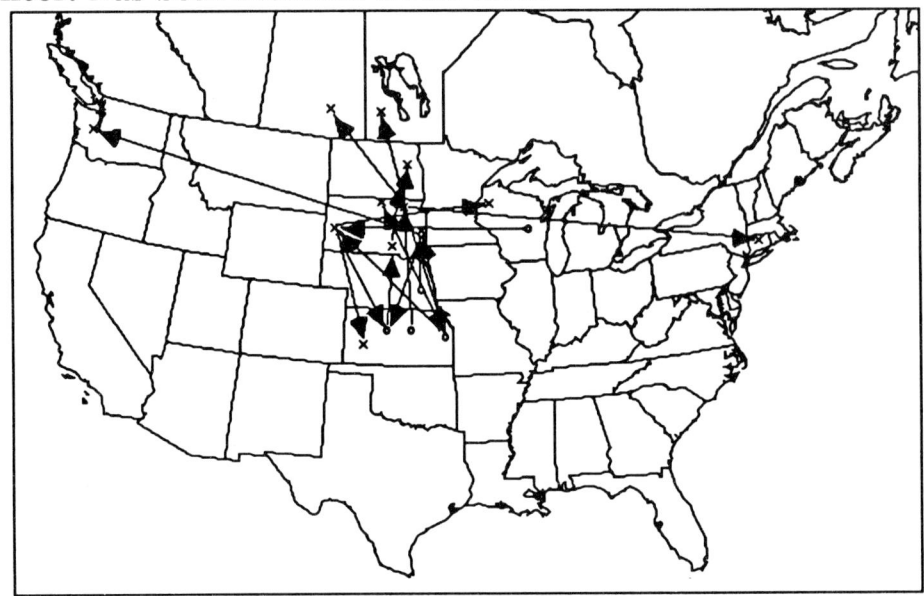

Pine Siskin banding recoveries

LESSER GOLDFINCH *Carduelis psaltria* (Say)

Status. Accidental. Over and Thoms (1921, 1946) list without documentation the species as rare and nesting in Sanborn Co.

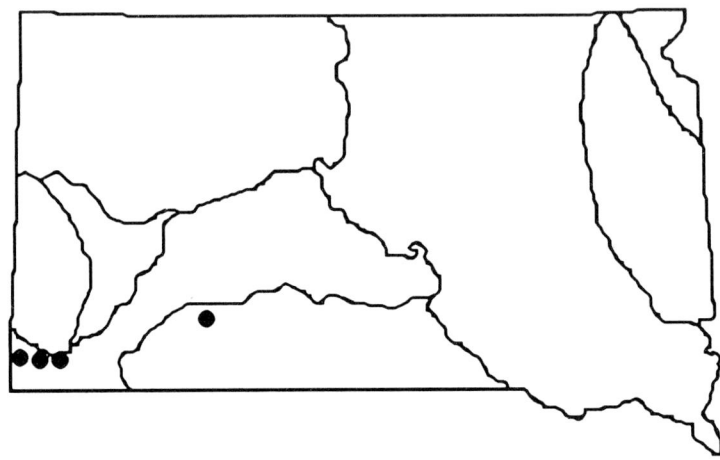

Records.
  5 May 1988, Jackson Co. (Shuler)
  8 Jul – 10 Sep 1969, Hot Springs (Twomey 1969)
  6 Aug – 2 Sep 1982, Fall River Co. (Murdock in Peterson 1984)
  2–5 Sep 1983, Fall River Co. (Peterson 1984)

AMERICAN GOLDFINCH *Carduelis tristis* (Linnaeus)

Status. Fairly common to common summer resident, except higher Black Hills. Irregular, uncommon to abundant, winter resident.

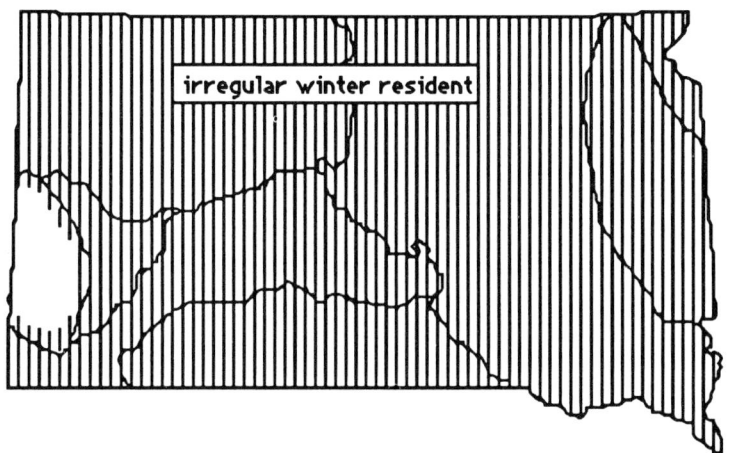

Habitat. Woodlands, residential areas, weedy fields and pastures.

Migration. Since this species breeds and also winters, early and late migration dates are omitted. However, most birds migrate in mid-Apr – mid-May and from mid-Oct – mid-Nov.

Nesting. Jul into Sep.

Earliest dates:
13 Jul 1966, Lake Madison, nest with 1 egg and 1 cowbird egg (Harris)
18 Jul 1968, Sanborn Co., nest with 5 eggs (Harris)
25 Jul 1955, Rapid City, nest with 3 newly-hatched young (Pettingill and Whitney 1965)

Latest dates:
25 Aug 1962, Codington Co., nest with eggs (Moriarty)
4 Sep 1967, Huron, fledgling (Johnson and Johnson 1968)
11 Sep 1967, Rapid City, 4 young fledged (Bachmann)

Winter. Most common in S. Recorded on almost all CBC's.

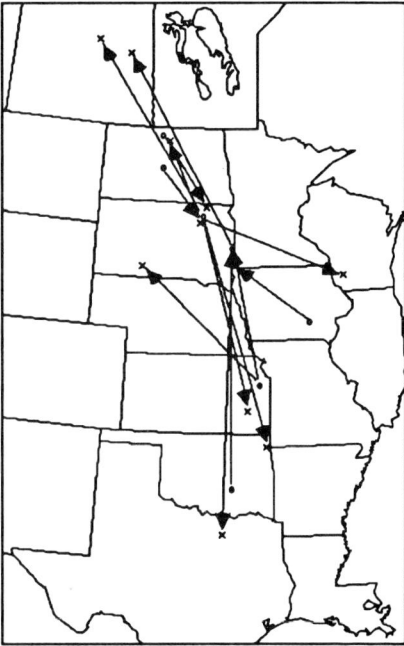

American Goldfinch banding recoveries

EVENING GROSBEAK *Coccothraustes vespertinus* (Cooper)

Status. Common migrant and winter resident in Black Hills. Rare summer resident N Black Hills. Irregular, uncommon winter visitor elsewhere.

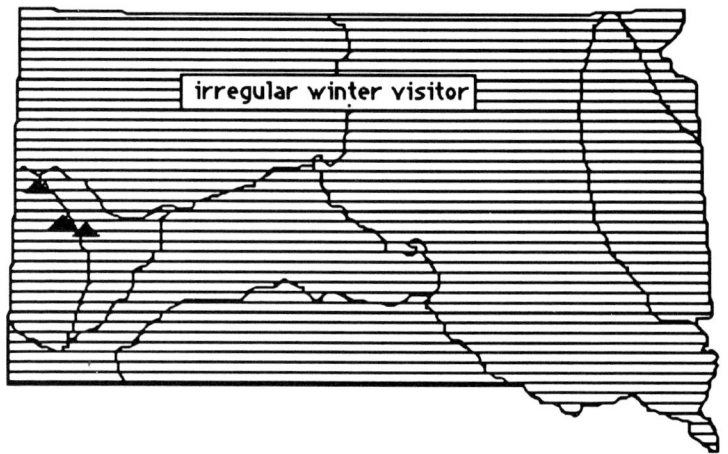

Habitat. Migration and winter: Woodlands and residential areas. Breeding: spruce forests.

Spring migration. Apr.
  Latest dates:
    25 May 1962, Hyde Co. (Harter 1969)
    28 May 1957, Hot Springs (Whitney)
    1 Jun 1973, Belle Fourche (Weyler)

Nesting. May – Jul.
  Earliest dates:
    11 Jun 1947, Spearfish Canyon 3 specimens in breeding condition (Edwards in Pettingill and Whitney 1965)
  Latest dates:
    17 Jul 1969 Rapid City, adults bringing young to feeder (Rose)
    24 Jul 1968, Rapid City, adults bringing young to feeder (Rose)

Fall migration. Nov. Earliest dates are given for areas E of Black Hills.
  Earliest dates:
    27 Aug 1986, Codington Co. (Gilman in Seasons 1987a)
    18 Sep 1977, Badlands (Wilt in Seasons 1977a)
    1 Oct 1980, Brown Co. (Montgomery in Seasons 1981a)

Winter. Recorded on most CBC.

PASSERIDAE: Old World Sparrows

HOUSE SPARROW *Passer domesticus* (Linnaeus)

Status. Common to abundant permanent resident. Uncommon in large towns in Black Hills. First reported in 1884 at Milltown (Cooke 1888). Entered Mellette Co. by 1908 (Reagen 1908).

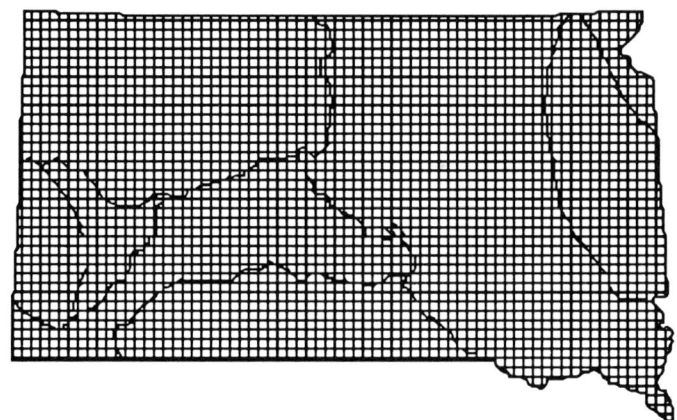

Habitat. Usually near human habitation.
Nesting. Late Mar – Jul.
  Earliest dates:
    6 Mar 1987, Brown Co., carrying nesting material (Tallman)
    11 Mar 1987, Brown Co., completed nest, no eggs (Tallman)
    30 Mar 1961, Rapid City, 3 males and a female collected in breeding condition (Pettingill and Whitney 1965)
  Latest dates:
    18 Jun 1989, Brown Co., 4 nestlings banded (Tallman)
    14 Jul 1956, Rapid City, nest with young (Pettingill and Whitney 1965)
    12 Aug 1988, Tripp Co., adult feeding fledged young (Springer)

REFERENCES CITED

Adolphson, Donald G. 1965. Snowy Owl Observations in Eastern South Dakota, Winter 1964–65. SDBN 17:344-35.
—1966a. Supplemental Observations of Snowy Owls in South Dakota. SDBN 18:34.
—1966b. Open-country Buteo Nesting. SDBN 18:54–56.
—1967. Snowy Owl Observations Winter 1966–67. SDBN 20:83.
—1969a. West River Owl Notes. SDBN 21:21–22.
—1969b. Snowy Owls, 1967–68. SDBN 21:33.
—1969c. 1969 West River Owl Notes. SDBN 21:67–68.
— and Marion Adolphson. 1966. Mourning Dove Nesting in a Shelterbelt near Huron, S. Dak. SDBN 18:5–6.
— and — 1968. Size, Distribution, and Population of Three Colony Nesting Species in South Dakota. SDBN 20:4–10.
— and George M. Jonkel. 1965. 16 Years of Snowy Owl Records from S. Dak. SDBN 17:63–66.
Agersborg, G.S. 1885. The Birds of Southeastern Dakota. Auk 2:276–289.
Allen, Robert P. 1952. The Whooping Crane. National Audubon Society, Research Report No. 3, 246 pp.
American Ornithologists' Union. 1983. Check-list of North American Birds. 6th edition. Lawrence, KS, 691 pp.
—1985. Thirty-fifth Supplement to the American Ornithologists' Union Check-list of North American Birds. Auk 102:680–686.
—1989. Thirty-seventh Supplement to the American Ornithologists' Union Check-list of North American Birds. Auk 106:532–538.
Anderson, Bertin W. 1969. Hybridization in Flickers, Grosbeaks and Orioles in South Dakota. Ph. D. Thesis, Univ. of South Dakota, 140 pp.
—1971. Man's Influence on Hybridization in Two Avian Species in South Dakota. Condor 73:342–347.
— and Raymond J. Daugherty. 1974. Characteristics and Reproductive Biology of Grosbeaks (*Pheucticus*) in the Hybrid Zone in South Dakota. Wilson Bull. 86:1–11, col. pl.
Anderson, Edwin C., 1933. First Record of Golden-winged Warbler for South Dakota. Wilson Bull. 45:157–158 [reprinted in SDBN 2:13,1950].
Anderson, Leon L. 1984. Ross' Goose in Eastern South Dakota. SDBN 36:77–79.
Anonymous. 1956. Scissor-tailed Flycatcher. SDBN 8:31.
—1962. Check-list of the Birds of Wind Cave National Park, South Dakota, 26 pp. (mimeo).
—1964. Barred Owl Found near Yankton. SDBN 16:98.
—1967. Mountain Chickadee at Rapid City. SDBN 19:19.
—1976. Christmas Count Notes. SDBN 28:8–11
Antonides, Bill. 1989. Barred Owl Injured in Aberdeen. SDBN 41:26–27.
Arbogast, Margery R. 1974. Gray-crowned Rosy Finch (Hepburn's Form) at Aberdeen. SDBN 26:21.

Audubon, Maria R. 1897. Audubon and His Journals. 2 vol.N.Y.: Scribners, 532 and 554 pp.
Backlund, Doug. 1989. American Dippers in Spearfish Canyon. SDBN 41:63.
—1990. Common Poor-will Nest in Tripp County. SDBN 42:61.
Baird, Spencer F. 1885. Birds. In: Reports of Explorations and Surveys to Ascertain the Most Practicable and Economical Route for a Railroad from the Mississippi River to the Pacific Ocean. Vol. 9, Part 2. Washington, D.C., War Dept., 1005 pp.
Baker, Jocelyn L. 1979. Blue-gray Gnatcatcher in Rapid City. SDBN 31:49.
—1980. Mating Ritual of an American Bittern. SDBN 32:56.
—1987. Ross' Geese West River. SDBN 39:41–42.
Banko, Winston E. 1960. The Trumpeter Swan, Its History, Habits and Population in the United States. North American Fauna No. 63, 214 pp.
Barr, Claude A. 1937. The Mockingbird in Western South Dakota. Wilson Bull. 49:270–275.
—1961. Sage Thrashers East of Smithwick. SDBN 13:17.
Bartelt, Paul E. 1977. Management of the American Goshawk in the Black Hills. M.A. Thesis, Univ. of South Dakota, 102 pp.
Baylor, L.M. 1959. First Sight Record of Vermilion Flycatcher (*Pyrocephalus rubinus*) in South Dakota. SDBN 11:13–14.
—1966. Some Black Hills Observations. SDBN 18:52–53,62.
—1969. Bonaparte's Gull at Rapid City. SDBN 21:20.
—1971a. Barrow's Goldeneye Winters at Rapid City. SDBN 26:79–80.
—1973. Clark's Nutcracker and Mountain Chickadee: Rare Visitors at a Rapid City Feeding Station. SDBN 25:64–65.
—1975a. Black-throated Gray Warbler at Rapid City. SDBN 27:14–15.
—1975b. Barrow's Goldeneye for a Second Winter at Rapid City. SDBN 27:70.
— and Mary E. Baylor. 1986. Observations of Nesting Chipping Sparrows. SDBN 38:96–97.
—, —, and Florence L. Baylor. 1983. Great Crested Flycatchers in Pennington County. SDBN 35:69.
—, Thomas M. Hays, Ruth Palmerton and Leighton Palmerton. 1987. Common Mergansers Breeding in Pennington County, South Dakota. SDBN 39:37–38.
— and Willard Rosine. 1970. Summer Birds of Harding County, South Dakota:1967–69. SDBN 22:36–48,57.
—, —, and Fred Wild. 1972. Notes on Four Nesting Species in the Black Hills. SDBN 24:4–6.
Bean, Larry L. 1973. Winter Waterfowl Ecology in Yankton, Clay and Union Counties, South Dakota. M.A. Thesis, Univ. of South Dakota, 61 pp.
Behrends. John F. 1966. A Population and Territorial Study of the Great Horned Owl, *Bubo virginianus*, along the Ver-

million River, Clay County, South Dakota. M.A. Thesis, Univ. of South Dakota, 52 pp.

Bent, Arthur Cleveland. 1926. Life Histories of North American Marsh Birds. U.S. Nat. Mus. Bull. 135, 392 pp.

—1929. Life Histories of North American Shore Birds (Part 2). U.S. Nat. Mus. Bull. 146, 412 pp.

—1937. Life Histories of North American Birds of Prey (Part 1). U.S. Nat. Mus. Bull. 167, 409 pp.

—1948. Life Histories of North American Nuthatches, Wrens, Thrashers, and Their Allies. U.S. Nat. Mus. Bull.195, 475 pp.

—1949. Life Histories of North American Thrushes, Kinglets, and Their Allies. U.S. Nat. Mus. Bull. 196, 452 pp.

—1950. Life Histories of North American Wagtails, Shrikes, Vireos and Their Allies. U.S. Nat. Mus. Bull. 197, 411 pp.

—1953. Life Histories of North American Wood Warblers. U.S. Nat. Mus. Bull. 203, 734 pp.

—1958. Life Histories of North American Blackbirds, Orioles, Tanagers, and Allies. U.S. Nat. Mus. Bull. 211, 549 pp.

—1968. Life Histories of North American Cardinals, Grosbeaks, Buntings. Towhees, Finches. Sparrows, and Allies (Parts 1,2,3). U.S. Nat. Mus. Bull.237, 1889 pp

Berkey, G. B. 1985. The Spring Migration, March 1–May 31, 1985, Northern Great Plains Region. Amer. Birds 39: 317–319.

—1989a. The Spring Season, March 1–May 31, 1989, Northern Great Plains Region. Amer. Birds 43:497–499.

—1989b. The Nesting Season, June 1–July 31, 1989, Northern Great Plains Region. Amer. Birds 43:1332–1334.

Besser, J. F., O. E. Bray, Jr., J. W. DeGrazio, D. L. Gilbert, R. R. Martinka, and D. A. Dysart. 1987. Productivity of Red-winged Blackbirds in South Dakota. Prairie Nat. 19:221–232.

Betts, Barry. 1971. Varied Thrush in Beadle County. SDBN 23:81.

Bever, Wendell. 1962. Scissor-tailed Flycatcher in Lyman County. SDBN 14:65.

Bingaman, W. H. 1912. Nesting of the Sprague's Pipit. Oologist 29:398–399.

Bjerke, Dan. 1984. Swans and Gulls at Orman Dam. SDBN 36:27–28.

Blair, Charles L., and Frank Schitoskey, Jr. 1982. Breeding Biology and Diet of the Ferruginous Hawk In South Dakota. Wilson Bull. 94:46–54.

Blankenship, L. H., I. G. Bue, and W. H. Marshall. 1953. Spring Migration and Nesting Data in Stanley County, South Dakota. SDBN 5:10–13.

Blankespoor, G. 1984. Mississippi Kite Sighted in Minnehaha County. SDBN 36:11–12.

—1985. Whooping Crane Migration in South Dakota. SDBN 37:4–9.

—1986. [Photograph of Common Snipe nest.] SDBN 38:1.

—1989. House Finches Breed in Sioux Falls. SDBN 41:63.

Breckenridge, W.J. 1933. Pomarine Jaeger in South Dakota. Wilson Bull. 45:79.
Brewster, William. 1891. Description of Seven Supposed New North American Birds. Auk 8:139-149.
Buckman, Robert D. 1976a. White-winged Crossbills in Pennington County. SDBN 28:60.
— 1976b. Cinnamon Teal, Goshawk, Osprey in Lake County. SDBN 28:66-67.
— 1979. The President's Page. SDBN 31:45-47.
— 1983. Kentucky Warbler in Lake County. SDBN 35:50.
Bull, John. 1974. Birds of New York State. Doubleday: Garden City. 655 pp.
Buller, Raymond J. 1967. Sandhill Crane Study in the Central Flyway. U. S. Fish and Wildlife Service, Spec. Scien. Report-Wildlife No. 113, 17 pp.
Burgess, Harold. 1975. Long-tailed Jaeger: New Record for South Dakota. SDBN 27:69.
— 1976. Unusual Bird Sightings at Lacreek National Wildlife Refuge. SDBN 28:66.
Burns, Frank L. 1911. A Monograph of the Broad-winged Hawk (*Buteo platypterus*). Wilson Bull. 23:139-320.
Burroughs, Raymond D. 1961. The Natural History of the Lewis and Clark Expedition. Michigan State Univ. Press, 340 pp.
Call, Daniel J. 1967. A Study of Hawk Populations in Clay County, South Dakota, M.A. Thesis, Univ. of South Dakota, 55 pp.
— 1975. Seasonal Hawk Population Densities in Southeastern South Dakota. Proc. S.D. Acad. Sci. 54:172-177.
Carter, Dennis. 1958a. Summer Records from the Black Hills. SDBN 10:36,40.
—1958b. Survey of the Birds of Jewel Cave National Monument. SDBN 10:56-57,60-62,67.
Cartwright, B.W., T.M. Shortt, and R. D. Harris. 1937. Baird's Sparrow. Trans. Royal Can. Institute 21:153-198.
Cary, Merritt. 1901. Birds of the Black Hills. Auk 18:231-238.
Chapman, Herman F. 1950. An Early Egg Collector. SDBN 2:11,15.
—1951. Composite List of Birds Observed at Vermillion, Clay County, S.D., May 6, 1951, on Annual Field Trip of SDOU. SDBN 3:29.
—1952. King Rails near Freeman, S.D. SDBN 4:42.
— and Mrs. Herman Chapman. 1954. Nest and Young of Sage Hen in N.W. So. Dak. SDBN 6:36.
Chapman, Mrs. H.F. 1949. Black-necked Stilt. SDBN 1:34.
Chilson, Herman P. 1957. Bitter Lake-A Refuge? SDBN 9:41.
—1966. Little Blue Heron in Day County. SDBN 18:16.
—1968. Knickerbocker's 1869 List of the Birds of Fort Wadsworth, Dakota Territory. SDBN 20:32-42.
—1972. Red Crossbills near Webster. SDBN 24:85-86.
—1973. Emperor Geese in Marshall County. SDBN 25:11.
—1976. Grosbeaks at Pickerel Lake: Winter Record for Rose-breasted Grosbeak. SDBN 28:7,14.

Clawson, M. E. 1989. Woodcock Nesting in Gregory Co. SDBN 41: 44
Cooke, Wells W. 1888. Report on Bird Migration in the Mississippi Valley in the Years 1884 and 85. USDA, Div. Econ. Ornith. Bull. 2, 313 pp.
—1906. Distribution and Migration of North American Ducks, Geese, and Swans. Biol. Surv. Bull. 26, 90 pp.
—1912. Distribution and Migration of North American Shorebirds. Biol. Surv. Bull. 35 (revised), 100 pp.
—1914. Distribution and Migration of North American Gulls and Their Allies. U.S. Dept. Agric. Bull. 128, 50 pp.
Coonrod, Bruce. 1981. A Band-tailed Pigeon at Pierre. SDBN 33:59.
—1982. Late Warbler Migration. SDBN 34:41.
Cooper, J.G. 1860. Birds Collected on the Survey. Chapter 1. Land Birds. Pages 140–226 in Part 3, Zoological Report No. 3, Report of Exploration and Surveys to Ascertain the most Practicable and Economical Route for a Railroad from the Mississippi River to the Pacific Ocean, 1853–55. Vol. 12, Book 2, 36th Congress, 1st Session, Senate.
—1869. The Fauna of Montana Territory (Part). Amer. Nat. 3:78–84.
Coues, Elliott. 1874. Birds of the Northwest. U.S. Geol. Surv. of Terr., Misc. Publ. 3, 791 pp.
—1878. Swallow-tailed Kite in Dakota in Winter. Bull. Nuttall Orn. Club 3:147.
Crutchett, Charles P. 1957. Barrow's Goldeneye at Armour. SDBN 9:27.
—1958. Ovenbird in Douglas County. SDBN 10:47.
—1961. Notes on Nest of Short-eared Owl. SDBN 13:85–86,102.
—1962. Blue-winged Warblers Sighted at Armour, S.D. SDBN 14:37.
— and Mrs. Charles Crutchett 1955. Longspurs Killed in Storm. SDBN 7:15.
— and Willis Hall 1966. Baltimore Oriole of Unusual Color. SDBN 18:28–33,25.
Dahling, Mrs. Ury. 1956. Notes from a Notebook. SDBN 8:9.
DeVries, Velma. 1963. Birding along White River. SDBN 15:55–58.
—1965. Early Parula Warbler near Belvidere. SDBN 17:69–70.
Donahoe, John D. 1949. Black-throated Gray Warbler. SDBN 1:35.
—1950. Gyrfalcon in Northeastern South Dakota. SDBN 2:14.
Drewien, Roderick C., and Robert H. Johnson. 1968. Cooperative Study of the Northeastern South Dakota Resident Canada Goose Population, 1964–1967. S.D. Dept. of Game, Fish and Parks and U.S. Fish and Wildlife Service, Unpublished Report. 27 pp.
— and Rollin D. Sparrowe. 1966. Nesting and Production of the Mourning Dove in Eastern South Dakota, 1965. SDBN 18:33–44.

Duebbert, Harold F. 1968. Breeding Birds in the Roscoe, South Dakota Area in 1967. SDBN 20:28–29.
— and John T. Lokemoen. 1973. Horned Grebe Breeding Records in North-central South Dakota. SDBN 25:20–21.
Dunstan, Thomas C. 1970. Post-fledging Activities of Juvenile Great Horned Owls as Determined by Radio-telemetry. Ph.D. Thesis, Univ. of South Dakota, 110 pp.
— and Byron E. Harrell. 1973. Spatio-temporal Relationships between Breeding Red-tailed Hawks and Great Horned Owls in South Dakota. Raptor Res. 7:49–54.
Edie, Esther R. 1975. Carolina Wren in Brookings County. SDBN 27:17–18.
Edwards, Ray O., Jr. 1969. Lesser Nighthawk in Badlands National Monument. SDBN 21:19.
Elliott, Lowry. 1955. Bird Haven Diary. SDBN 7:60.
—1957a. Early Bank Swallow Nesting. SDBN 9:46.
—1957b. Crested Flycatchers Nest at Waubay. SDBN 9:47.
—1959. Notes from Bird Haven Area. SDBN 11:57–58.
—1961a. Bird Haven Notes. SDBN 13:41.
—1961b. Least Tern at Rush Lake. SDBN 13:92.
—1961c. Prairie Warblers at Bird Haven. SDBN 13:102.
—1963a. Bird Haven Notes...Fall of 1962. SDBN 15:8–9.
—1963b. Tufted Titmouse in Northeastern S.D. 15:16.
—1963c. Prairie Falcon and Tufted Titmouse. SDBN 15:42.
—1967a. Birds of Prey, 1960. SDBN 19:4–6,10,13.
—1967b. Bird Haven Notes, 1966 SDBN 19:15,22.
—1967c. Yellow-bellied Flycatcher Banded at Milbank. SDBN 19:18.
—1968. Notes from Bird Haven, 1968. SDBN 20:91.
Erickson, Michael G. 1987. Nest Site Habitat Selection of the Goshawk (*Accipiter gentilis*) in the Black Hills National Forest of South Dakota. M.A. Thesis, Univ. of South Dakota. vi +49 pp.
Evans, Charles D., and Kenneth E. Black. 1956. Duck Production Studies in the Prairie Potholes of South Dakota. U.S. Fish and Wildlife Service, Spec. Scien.Report-Wildlife No. 32, 59 pp.
Evans, Keith E., and Roger R. Kerbs. 1967. Waterfowl and Shorebird Use on Selected Stock Ponds in Jackson County: 1966. SDBN 19:28–30.
Felton, William R., Jr. 1952. Fall and Winter Birds, Union County, South Dakota. SDBN 4:13.
Fiksdal, Mrs. R. Alice. 1958. Summer Notes from Pickerel Lake SDBN 10:45–46.
Findley, J. Scott. 1949. Mockingbirds in South Dakota. SDBN 1:43–44.
—1959. Rock Wren in Yankton Co. SDBN 11:33.
—1961. Barn Owls Nest in Sioux Falls. SDBN 13:98.
— and Mrs. J. S. Findley 1953a. Barrow's Goldeneyes near Sioux Falls. SDBN 5:46.
Findley, Mrs. J. S. 1954. Lazuli Bunting at Sioux Falls. SDBN 6:51.

Fjetland, Conrad A. 1973. Recent Additions to the Lacreek National Wildlife Refuge Bird List. SDBN 25:60–63.
—1975. Common Gallinule in Brown County. SDBN 27:37.
Flake, Lester D., and Raymond L. Linder. 1985. Peregrine Falcon Sighting. SDBN 37:57.
Fowler, Ron. 1987. A Summary of Turkey Restoration in South Dakota. S.D. Dept. of Game Fish and Parks, Unpublished Report. 10 pp.
Fredrickson, Larry F. 1973. Snowy Egrets and White-faced Ibis. SDBN 25:53.
Fuller, Thad. L. 1976. White-faced Ibis Records. SDBN 28:12.
Gammell, Ann M., and Robert T. Gammell. 1952. Northern Great Plains Region. Audubon Field Notes 6:286–288.
Gammell, Robert T., and Mrs. R.T. Gammell 1950. Northern Great Plains Region. Audubon Field Notes 4:21–22.
Gates, Doris. 1960. Whip-poor-will near Hill City. SDBN 12:35.
Gates, John M. 1973. Nesting of Woodcock in Brookings County, South Dakota. SDBN 25:6–7.
Giusti, Jessica. 1982. Active Broad-winged Hawk Nest at Sica Hollow State Park. SDBN 34:18–19.
Glass, Marjorie A. 1986. Rosy Finches in Badlands National Park. SDBN 38:65.
Grant, B.A. 1963. A List of Other Interesting Records from Two Trips through the Dakotas: Summer 1963. SDBN 15:85–86.
Greiner, Dale W., and Bob Neill. 1966. Nesting Record of the Hermit Thrush in the Black Hills. Wilson Bull. 78:321–322.
Grinnell, George Bird. 1875. Zoological Report: Chapter 2. Birds. In: Report of a Reconnaissance of the Black Hills of Dakota Made in the Summer of 1874. By William Ludlow. Washington, D.C.: Engineer Dept., U.S. Army, 121 pp.
Habeger, Ruth. 1950. Spring Observations at Madison, South Dakota. SDBN 2:22–24.
—1956a. A Few Spring Arrival Dates. SDBN 8:25–26.
—1956b. More Spring Arrival Dates. SDBN 8:47.
Haglund, Brent M. 1974. Snowy Egrets in Eastern South Dakota. SDBN 26:58.
Hahn, Paul. 1963. Where is that Vanished Bird? Royal Ontario Museum, Univ. of Toronto Press. 374 pp.
Haight, Cecil P. 1950. Summer Residents of Spearfish, SD. SDBN 2:36–38.
—1952. Birds of the Black Hills (Part 2). SDBN 4:7,10.
—1953. G-C Kinglet at Spearfish. SDBN 5:41.
Hall, Kent. 1976. Yellow Rail in Roberts County. SDBN 28:58.
Hall, Victor M. 1971. Black Brant and Ross' Geese Visit Lacreek National Wildlife Refuge. SDBN 23:32.
Hall, Willis. 1961. Burrowing Owls. Vanishing Bird of the Vanishing Prairie. SDBN 13:29–35.
—1965. Photographing Red-tailed Hawks. SDBN 17:28–33.
—1969. Camera Captures Illusive Woodpecker. SDBN 21:62.
—1975. Black Scoters at Yankton. SDBN 27:39.

—1980. Bell's Vireo, Cowbird, and other Birds of a Plum Thicket: Success and Failure Among Birds. SDBN 32:49–51.
Harris, Bruce K. 1963. South Dakota Bird Records, 1938 to 1963. SDBN 15:79–82.
—1964. Migration Notes from the Whetstone Valley, Roberts County. SDBN 16:87–90.
—1967. The Black-legged Kittiwake in South Dakota. SDBN 19:76–77.
—1968a. Late Breeding Season Record of Tennessee Warbler in Marshall County. SDBN 20:18.
—1968b. 1967 Mockingbird Records—Nesting in Sanborn County. SDBN 20:19–20.
—1968c. Roberts County Notes — Specimen Records for the Barred Owl and Winter Wren. SDBN 20:65–66.
—1968d. Kouf Collection—Yellow-crowned Night Heron and Old Squaw Duck. SDBN 20:66–67.
—1968e. Fulvous Tree Duck, Cinnamon Teal and Black Duck in Miner County. SDBN 20:69–70.
—1969. Wood Thrush Nesting Records from Charles Mix County. SDBN 22:64.
—1970a. Specimen Records for South Dakota. Condor 72:234–244.
—1970b. Clark's Nutcracker in Lyman County. SDBN 22:58.
—1971a. Yellow-bellied Sapsucker Again Nesting at Hartford Beach. SDBN 23:24.
—1971b. Worm-eating Warbler in Tripp County. SDBN 23:53.
—1972. Boreal Chickadee in Deuel Co. SDBN 24:84–85.
—1973a. Notes on the 1972 Hawk Migration in Northeastern South Dakota with Observations on Gyrfalcon, Prairie Falcon and Goshawks. SDBN 25:24–26.
—1973b. Oldsquaw and White-winged Scoter in Deuel County. SDBN 25:65.
—1974a. Specimen records for Smith's Longspur in Deuel and Roberts Counties. SDBN 26:15–17.
—1974b. Magpie Invasion in Northeastern South Dakota Counties. SDBN 26:42.
—1975a. Second Record for the Red Knot in South Dakota. SDBN 27:37–38.
—1975b. Specimen Record for Short-billed Dowitcher in Deuel Co. SDBN 27:38–39..
—1977a. Cooper's Hawk: Third Nest Record in South Dakota. SDBN 29:31–32.
—1977b. Caspian Terns: Unusual Concentrations in Deuel County. SDBN 29:40.
—1977c. Egyptian Goose in Deuel Co. SDBN 29:74–75
—1980a. Unprecedented Numbers of Short-eared Owls in Northeastern South Dakota During the 1978 Breeding Season. SDBN 32:24–27.
—1980b. First State Record of the Louisiana Heron. SDBN 32:81.
—1982a First Confirmed Nesting of the Great Egret in South Dakota. SDBN 34:39–40.

—1982b. 1981 Gull and Tern Nesting in Northeastern South Dakota. SDBN 34:64–65.
—1983. Whitewood Lake Heron and Ibis Breeding Surveys. SDBN 35:4–7.
—1987a. First Confirmed Nesting of the Ruby-throated Hummingbird in South Dakota. SDBN 39:66–67.
—1987b. Summary of Recent South Dakota Pileated Woodpecker Records. SDBN 39:67–68.
—1987c. Summer Tanager in Deuel County. SDBN 39:68–69.
—1987d. Red Knot in Deuel County. SDBN 39:69.
—1987e Carolina Wren in Deuel County. SDBN 39:69.
—1990. The Caspian Tern in Northeastern South Dakota. SDBN 42:84–85.
Harris, Mark. 1972. Sight Record for Scissor-tailed Flycatcher and Magpie in Deuel County. SDBN 24:86.
Hart, Ray S. 1964. Western Tanager at Sand Lake. SDBN 16:74.
— and Curtis Twedt. 1963. Early Nesting Coots and Grebes Observed at Lake Preston on May 1. SDBN 15:61.
Harter, June. 1962. Birds at Highmore , 1961. SDBN 14:22–23.
—1964. Bay-breasted Warbler Studied at Highmore.. SDBN 16:74.
—1967. European Wigeon near Highmore. SDBN 19:90.
—1968a. Hyde County Birds, 1962–67. SDBN 20:12–13,23.
—1968b. Parula Warbler at Highmore. SDBN 20:44–45.
—1969. Some Fall Records for Hyde County. SDBN 21:34–35.
—1970. White-winged Crossbill at Highmore. SDBN 22:127.
—1974a. A Review of Wood Thrush Records in South Dakota. SDBN 26:14; 26.
—1974b. Bay-breasted Warbler in Hyde County. SDBN 26:75.
Harter, Nancy. 1964. Bay-breasted Warbler Studied at Highmore. SDBN 16:74.
Hayden, F. V. 1863. On the Geology and Natural History of the Upper Missouri. Amer. Philosophical Soc. 12 (New Series):1–218.
Hereford, Scott G. 1982. Nest Site Habitat and Productivity of the Red-tailed Hawk (Buteo jamaicensis) in Northwest South Dakota. M.A. Thesis, Univ. of South Dakota. ii + 64 pp.
Heumphreus, Mary S. 1954. Gray-crowned Rosy Finch. SDBN 6:51.
Hill, Richard L. 1976. Virginia Rail: Winter Record in Jones County. SDBN 28:40.
—1979. First Winter Record for the Field Sparrow in South Dakota. SDBN 31:65.
Hilley, David. 1980a Common Gallinule on Lake Andes National Wildlife Refuge. SDBN 32:11.
—1980b. Lesser Sandhill Crane in Charles Mix County. SDBN 32;11.
Hills, Charles S. 1949. Fulvous Tree Duck. SDBN 1:35–36.
Hillman, Conrad N., and Warren W. Jackson. 1973. The Sharp-tailed Grouse in South Dakota. S. D. Dept. of Game, Fish and Parks, Tech. Bull., 364 pp.

Hinds, Alfred. 1968. Some Birds of Southwestern Perkins County SDBN 20:53-57.
Hoffman, W.J. 1877. List of Birds Observed at Grand River Agency, Dakota Ter., From Oct. 7th 1872, to June 7th, 1873. Proc. Bos. Soc. Nat. Hist. 18:169-175.
Holden, Nelda. 1958. Townsend's Solitaire in Brookings County SDBN 10:45.
—1962. Whip-poor-will in Brookings County. SDBN 14:18.
—1964. Turkey Vulture in Brookings County. SDBN 16:52.
—1966. Farm Island Banding, 1956. SDBN 18:35,47.
—1972. Boreal Chickadee in Brookings county. SDBN 24:83.
—1980a. Winter Wren in Northern Black Hills. SDBN 32:55.
—1980b. Late Fall Record for the Dickcissel. SDBN 32:56.
— and David Holden. 1968. Chuck-Will's-Widow in Southeastern South Dakota, SDBN 27:15-16.
Hoover, Karolyn J. 1975. Whimbrel in Clay County. SDBN 27:15-16.
Houston, C. Stuart. 1971. Northern Great Plains Region. American Birds 25:761.
Hughlett, Charles A. 1962. Whooping Crane Sighted Near Martin, South Dakota. SDBN 14:57-58.
Huntley, Clarence W. 1970. A Comparative Population and Behavioral Study of Two Tyrannus Species in Clay County, South Dakota. M.A. Thesis, Univ. of South Dakota, 39 pp.
Husmann, Kenneth H. 1981. Rough-winged Swallow Nest in Building. SDBN 33:59.
—1985. Live Prothonotary Warbler in South Dakota. SDBN 37:14-15.
Hyde, Mrs. A.L. 1955. Cardinal in the Hills. SDBN 7:29.
Jave, John. 1984. Unusual Birds at Lake Andes National Wildlife Refuge. SDBN 36:12-13.
Jenny, Elice. 1958. Blue Grosbeaks. SDBN 10:40.
Jervis, Carlyn J. 1979. Chestnut-sided Warbler in Custer County. SDBN 31:37.
Johnson, Blanche Battin. 1983. Ani Seen at Huron. SDBN 35:8.
—1987. Winter Yellow-rumped Warbler at Huron. SDBN 39:71.
Johnson, Carl M. 1958. Birds of Bon Homme County, 1932. SDBN 10:52-55.
— and J. Scott Findley. 1959. Piping Plover Nests Near Yankton. SDBN 11:34-35.
Johnson, J. O. 1956a. [Photo of Ruddy Duck Nest]. SDBN 8:21,26.
—1956b. [Photo of Marbled Godwit Young]. SDBN 8:37,47.
Johnson, James W. 1956. Green-tailed Towhee at Huron. SDBN 8:67.
—1958. Blue Grosbeaks near Huron. SDBN 10:22-23.
—1960. Cuckoo Feeding Young at Huron. SDBN 12:60-61.
—1962. Golden-winged Warbler at Huron. SDBN 14:90.
—1963a. Yellow-crowned Night Heron at Huron. SDBN 15:41-42.
—1963b. Kentucky Warbler at Huron. SDBN 15:92-93.
—1965. Hawk Roost Near Huron. SDBN 17:17-18.
—1967. The Life of Our Martins: Chapter IV. SDBN 19:7-12; 22.

—1968. Late Harris' Sparrow at Huron. SDBN 20:65.
—1970a. A Western Kingbird Family. SDBN 22:122–125.
—1970b. Kentucky Warbler at Huron. SDBN 22:126.
—1972. Curve-billed Thrasher Still Lingers Near Gann Valley. SDBN 24-21.
—1973. Curve-billed Thrasher at Gann Valley. SDBN 25:53.
—1983a. Black-throated Blue Warbler Sightings at Huron. SDBN 35:9.
—1983b. Worm-eating Warbler at Huron. SDBN 35:69.
—1984. Pinyon Jay at Huron. SDBN 36:10–11.
— and Blanche Johnson. 1985. Northern Saw-Whet Owls at Huron. SDBN 37:78–79.
— and Lucille Johnson. 1959. Pinion Jay at Huron. SDBN 11:35.
— and — 1964. Indigo Buntings at Huron. SDBN 16:97–98.
— and — 1968. Wolsey. SDBN 20:64.
— and — 1969. Hoary Redpolls at Huron. SDBN 21:68–69.
— and — 1970. Late Nashville Warbler at Huron. SDBN 22:127–128.
— and — 1976. Brewster's, Golden-winged Warblers at Huron. SDBN 28:58–59.
Johnson, M. C. 1891. The Cuckoo in South Dakota. Oologist 8:176.
Johnson, Robert R. 1972. Hoary Redpolls at Waubay Refuge. SDBN 24:42.
Johnson, Sara Jane. 1969. A Population, Territory, and Voice Recognition Study of the Screech Owl, *Otus asio*, along the Missouri River, Clay County, South Dakota. M.A. Thesis, Univ. of South Dakota, 64 pp.
Jones, Sheridan R. 1908. Preliminary Report on the Flora and Fauna of the Eastern Part of the Rosebud Reservation, Now Known as Gregory County. S. D. Geol. Surv., Bull. No. 4, 229 pp.
Jonkel, George. 1961. Apparent Migration of Lark Sparrows. SDBN 13:98.
—1965. South Dakota Wintering Eagle Inventories. SDBN 17:61–62.
—1967. Lapland Longspur Observations. SDBN 19:41.
— and Jean Jonkel. 1960. Gray Jay at Huron. SDBN 12:88–89.
Kantrud, Harold A., and Craig A. Faanes. 1979. Range Expansion of Baird's Sparrow in South Dakota. Prairie Naturalist 11:111–112.
Kaufman, Katherine. 1957. Richardson's Owl in Freeman. SDBN 9:66.
—1958. Fox Sparrow at Freeman. SDBN 10:13.
Keck, S.W. 1952. Black-necked Stilt in Central S.E. South Dakota. SDBN 4:15.
Kettelle, Mary. Aberdeen 1951. Late Fall Scarlet Tanager at Huron. SDBN 3:61.
Knopf, Sharon Gullickson. 1974. Wood Thrush Nesting Behavior. SDBN 26:4–13.
Krause, Herbert. 1951. Bewick's Wren at Sioux Falls. SDBN 3:13.
—1953. Pine Siskin at Sioux Falls. SDBN 5:41.

—1954. Preliminary Notes on the Pine Siskin in S.D. SDBN 6:41-42,48.
—1955a. Gyrfalcon. SDBN 7:48.
—1955b. Winter Wren at Sioux Falls. SDBN 7:58–59.
—1956. Ornithology in South Dakota before Audubon. Proc. S.D. Acad. Sci. 35:198–201.
—1959. Unusual Migration Waves at Sioux Falls. SDBN 11:72-75,79.
—1960. The Yellow-throated Warbler in Southeastern South Dakota. SDBN 12:48–49 and 62.
— and Willard Rosine. 1955. Peregrine Falcon Near Wall Lake SDBN 7:45–46.
Krumm, Kenneth. 1952a. Lacreek Refuge Notes. SDBN 4:14.
—1952b. White Pelicans at Lacreek Refuge. SDBN 4:28–29.
—1955a. Brown Pelican at Lacreek Refuge. SDBN 7:27.
—1955b. Cardinal at Lacreek Refuge. SDBN 7:29–30.
—1955c. Cinnamon Teal at Lacreek. SDBN 7:47.
—1955d. Least Bittern at Lacreek. SDBN 7:47.
Lambeth, David O. 1989. The Autumn Migration, August 1–November 30 1988, Northern Great Plains Region. American Birds 43:121–123.
Larrabee, Austin. P. 1920. Nesting of the Red Crossbill. Proc. S.D. Acad. Sci. 5:20–22 [Reprinted 1950, SDBN 2:55–56].
—1932. The Barn Owl Nesting in Southeastern South Dakota. Wilson Bull. 44:38.
—1937. Nesting of the Pine Siskin in South Dakota and Kansas. Wilson Bull. 49: 116.
Larsen, Wallace L. 1983. Groove-billed Ani in Pierre. SDBN 35:7.
Larson, Adrian. 1907. A Preliminary List of the Birds of Western Lyman County, South Dakota. Wilson Bull. 19:113–118.
—1912. Notes from Sioux Falls, South Dakota (Spring of 1911). Wilson Bull. 24:53–54.
—1925. The Birds of Sioux Falls, South Dakota, and Vicinity. Wilson Bull. 37:18–38,72–76.
—1930. Summer Occurrence of the Harris's Sparrow in South Dakota. Wilson Bull. 42:54.
—1931. The Brown Pelican in South Dakota. Wilson Bull. 43:308.
Law, Bonar D. 1964. Wood Ibis Northeast of Mitchell. SDBN 16:91.
Leach, James T. 1977. Lacreek Area Trumpeter Swan Behavior and Migration Study. M.A. Thesis, Univ. of South Dakota, 66 pp.
Levi, Lorna R., and Herbert W. Levi. 1954. Arctic Three-toed Woodpecker Nests in Hills. SDBN 6:49.
Lewis, Meriwether, and William Clark. 1904–1905. Original Journals of the Lewis and Clark Expedition, 1804–1806, R.G. Thwaites, Ed. 8 vols. New York: Dodd Mead [not seen; New York: Antiquarian Press, 1959 reprint seen].
Lien, Evelyn, William Youngworth, and Willis Hall. 1961. The Gray-crowned Rosy Finch at Volin. SDBN 13:36, 44:25.
Lind, Gordon S. 1976. Cattle Egret in Spink County. SDBN 28:67.

Lock, Ross A., and John S. Schuckman. 1973. A Bald Eagle Nest in Nebraska. Nebr. Bird Rev. 41:76–77.
Lohoefener, Ren, and Charles A. Ely. 1978. The Nesting Birds of Lacreek National Wildlife Refuge. SDBN 30:24–30.
Lokemoen, John T., and Harold F. Deubbert. 1976. Ferruginous Hawk Nesting Ecology and Raptor Populations in Northern South Dakota. Condor 78:464–470.
Lundquist, Arthur R. 1934. The Starling in Day County, South Dakota. Wilson Bull. 46:62.
—1949. The Waubay Lake Colonies of Double-crested Cormorants. SDBN 1:8–10.
—1950. Florida Gallinules. SDBN 2:60.
—1952. Grebes in the Lake Region. SDBN 4:42–43.
Mack, Gene. 1979. White-tailed Kite: New South Dakota Record. SDBN 31:38–39.
Maher, Jeremiah Leo, III. 1982. Nest Site Habitat and Productivity of the Prairie Falcon (*Falco mexicanus*) in Harding County, South Dakota. M.A. Thesis, Univ. of South Dakota, vii + 68 pp.
Mallory, W.B. 1915. Chronicles of the Nest Builders. Bird-Lore 17:274–277.
—1956. Field Sparrows in Town. SDBN 8:51.
Martsching, Paul. 1984. South Dakota Bird Observations. SDBN 36:26–27.
Maximilian, Prince of Wied, See Wied, Prince Maximilian of.
McChesney, Charles E. 1879. Notes on the Birds of Fort Sisseton, Dakota Territories. Bull. U.S. Geol. and Geog. Surv. of the Territories 5:71–103.
McCrow, V. Pat. 1974. Reproduction of White Pelicans in South Dakota in 1973. Proc. SD Acad. Sci. 53:135–152.
McIntosh, Arthur C. 1928. Biological Features of Cascade Valley and Vicinity. Black Hills Engineer 16:68–83. Section on birds reprinted in SDBN 9:36–38,44.
McPhillips, Kelly B. 1980. Spring 1980 Woodcock Nest on Sioux River Floodplain, Brookings County. SDBN 32:82–83.
—1981. Green Heron Nest at Paul L. Errington Memorial Marsh. SDBN 33:16–18.
Montgomery, Everett C. 1981. Birds Observed during the 1981 Fall Meeting. SDBN 33:73.
— and Dan Tallman. 1979. Fall Migrating Mountain Bluebird near Aberdeen. SDBN 31:65–66.
Moos, Louis L. 1937. Interesting Records of Birds of Western South Dakota. J. Minn. Ornith. 1:11–12.
Moriarty, L. J. 1951. Richardson's Owl in N.E. South Dakota. SDBN 3:13.
—1954. Lawrence's Warbler. SDBN 6:32.
—1957. Snowy Owls, Crossbills, Redpolls at Watertown. SDBN 9:66.
—1960. Birds' Nests of South Dakota. Chimney Swift. SDBN 12:83,90.
—1961. Birds' Nests of South Dakota. Dickcissel. SDBN 13:71,78.

—1962a. Birds' Nests of South Dakota. Common Crow; Marsh Hawk; Harrier. SDBN 14:36.
—1962b. Caspian Terns, Bonaparte Gulls, Common Egret at Watertown. SDBN 14:91–92.
—1963a. A Perfect Spring Day—Waubay. SDBN 15:61–62.
—1963b. A Plover Day—Waubay. SDBN 15:64.
—1963c. Birds' Nests of South Dakota. Catbird and Grasshopper Sparrow. SDBN 15;83.
—1964a. Birds' Nests of South Dakota. Yellow-throat and Tree Swallow. SDBN 16:40.
—1964b. Birds' Nests of South Dakota. American Coot. SDBN 16:95.
—1965a. Late Snowy Owls. SDBN 17:47.
—1965b. Birds' Nests of South Dakota. American Redstart, Eastern Bluebird and Black-headed Grosbeak. SDBN 17:59,66.
—1965c. A Study of the Breeding Biology of the Chestnut-collared Longspur (*Calcarius ornatus*) in Northeastern South Dakota. SDBN 17:76,79.
—1966. Birds' Nests of South Dakota. Vesper Sparrow. SDBN 18:10.
—1968. Late Harris' Sparrow in Spink County. SDBN 20:65.
Mortimer, J. 1976. Winter Record for Wilson Phalarope. SDBN 28:37.
Murdock, Kathrine P. 1982. Prothonotary Warbler in Hot Springs. SDBN 34:96.
Nelson, Mrs. C.J. 1955. Whodunit? SDBN 7:13–14.
Nelson, Delbert A. 1972. Notes on the White-eyed Vireo. SDBN 24:45–46.
Nelson, Ronald R. 1963. Golden-crowned Sparrow near Sioux Falls. SDBN 15:41.
—1971a. Common Gallinule in Clark County. SDBN 23:101.
—1971b. White-eyed Vireo in Eastern South Dakota. SDBN 23:102.
Olsen, David L. 1968. Raven at Lake Andes. SDBN 20:18.
Olson, Kent. 1965. Nest of Horned Lark Found near Rifle Lake. SDBN 17:71.
Oolman, John, and Gil Blankespoor. 1977. Least Bittern: Breeding Record in Lincoln County. SDBN 29:37.
Over, W. H., and G.M. Clement. 1951. Nesting of the White-winged Junco in the Black Hills of South Dakota. Wilson Bull. 42:28–31. [Reprinted in SDBN 3:7–9.]
— and Craig S. Thoms. 1921. Birds of South Dakota. S.D. Geol. and Nat. Hist. Surv. Bull. 9, 142 pp.
— and Craig S. Thoms. 1932. Additional Bird Records for South Dakota. Wilson Bull. 44:47–49.
— and Craig S. Thoms. 1946. Birds of South Dakota. Revised Edition. Univ. of S.D. Museum, Natural History Series, No. 1, 210 pp.
Packard, Fred M. 1949. Yellow Rail in South Central South Dakota. SDBN 1:12. [Reprint of Nebr. Bird Rev. 16:94, 1948, with additional comment].

Padrnos, H.V. 1953a. Harris's and other Sparrows at Redfield. SDBN 5:39.
—1953b. Notes from Redfield. SDBN 5:67–68.
Parrish, Barry. 1980. Red-bellied Woodpecker Nest in Brookings. SDBN 32:81–82.
Patton, Frank A. 1926. Our Trip to the Eagle's Nest. The Oologist 43:31–31. [Condensation printed in SDBN 4:55, 1952.]
Paulson, Debra D., and John Coons. 1984. First South Dakota Record for Townsend's Warbler. SDBN 36:75–76.
— and Carolyn H. Sieg. 1984. Long-eared Owls Nesting in Badlands National Park. SDBN 36:72–75.
Peterson, Alfred. 1953. Shore Birds in 1953. SDBN 5:56–57 and 62–63,71.
—1954. Brewer's Blackbird. SDBN 6:50–51.
—1955. Piping Plover. SDBN 7:46–47.
—1957. Spring Shore Birds, 1957. SDBN 9:22–23.
—1958. Knots in Deuel County. SDBN 10:14–15.
—1959. Migration Dates, Spring of 1958. SDBN 11:26–31.
—1960a. Shorebird Migration in Northeastern South Dakota. SDBN 12:10–12,17.
—1960b. 1930 Nesting Record of Common Terns. SDBN 12:59.
—1961a. Fall Shorebirds, 1957. SDBN 13:40,49.
—1961b. Shore Birds in 1961. SDBN 13:84,101–102.
—1962a. Shore Birds in 1955. SDBN 14:33–35.
—1962b. Shore Birds. 1962. SDBN 14:76–78.
—1963a. Shore Birds in 1956. SDBN 15:4–6.
—1963b. Migration Dates, Fall of 1958. SDBN 15:30–31.
—1963c. Ruddy Turnstones. SDBN 15:54,59.
—1964. Shore Birds in 1959. SDBN 16:84–86.
—1965. Shore Birds in 1960. SDBN 17:14–15.
Peterson, Carol. 1978. Hawk Owl: First South Dakota Record. SDBN 30:33.
Peterson, Lyle E., and Arthur H. Richardson. 1975. The Wild Turkey in the Black Hills. S.D. Dept. of Game, Fish and Parks, Bull. 6, 51 pp.
Peterson, Richard A. 1983. Pygmy Nuthatches Nesting in the Southern Hills. SDBN 35:53–54.
—1984. Lesser Goldfinches in Fall River County. SDBN 36:28–29.
—1985. Evidence of Nesting Clark's Nutcrackers. SDBN 37:58.
—1986. Birds of Black Hills Old Growth Forest. SDBN 38:35–37.
—1988. Clark's Nutcracker Nesting. SDBN:40:94–95.
— and Juanita Peterson. 1986. Brewer's Sparrow Nests. SDBN 38:98–99.
— and — 1989. House Finch Nesting in Edgemont. SDBN 41: .
Pettingill, Olin Sewell, Jr., and Nathaniel R. Whitney, Jr. 1965. Birds of the Black Hills. Cornell Laboratory of Ornithology, Spec. Pub. No. 1, 139 pp.
Phillips, Allen, Joe Marshall and Gale Monson. 1964. The Birds of Arizona. Tucson: Univ. of Arizona Press, 220 pp.
Pierce, Max. 1969. Tall Television Tower and Bird Migration. SDBN 21:4–5.

Podoll, Elmer. 1963. Spring Arrival Dates at Sand Lake National Wildlife Refuge. SDBN 15:36–38.
Prisbe, D. George. 1987. Vermilion Flycatcher and Gray Jay at Sand Lake NWR. SDBN 39:64.
— and Dan A. Tallman. 1986. Black-throated Gray Warbler at Aberdeen. SDBN 38:99.
Pulkrabek, Merritt, and Daniel O'Brien. 1974. An Inventory of Raptor Nesting in Harding County, South Dakota—1974. Pittman-Robertson Project W-95-R-8 [S.D. Dept. of Game, Fish and Parks, Report]. 5 pp.
Pulliam, Jim. 1961. Summer Record of Sandhill Crane in South Dakota. SDBN 13:98–99.
Purdy, Scott, Gary Purdy and John Purdy. 1985. First South Dakota Record for the Olivaceous Cormorant. SDBN 37:77.
Randall, Robert N. 1953. Birds of the Fort Randall Reservoir Area. SDBN 5:68–69.
—1956a. Highway Mortality of Winter Birds. SDBN 8:4.
—1956b. Blue Grosbeak. SDBN 8:31.
Rapid City Journal. 18 May [probably 1897]. Article stating that R. B. Hughes observed a female Common Merganser with 6 ducklings in Rapid Creek.
Reagen, Albert B. 1908. The Birds of the Rosebud Indian Reservation, South Dakota. Auk 25;462–467.
Reeves, Milt. 1961. Ring-necked Duck in South Dakota. SDBN 13:43–44.
Ring, Carol, Steve Stampfli, and Barry Parrish. 1987. Broad-winged Hawks Nesting in the Northern Black Hills. SDBN 39:60–63.
Riss, Elanor G. 1957. Northern Nesting of Cardinals. SDBN 9:43–44.
Roberts, Frank, and Mary Roberts. 1951. Winter Visitants at Pine Ridge. SDBN 3:30.
Roberts, Thomas Sadler. 1932. Birds of Minnesota. Minneapolis: Univ. of Minn. Press, 2 Vol., 821 pp.
—1958. A Manual for the Identification of the Birds of Minnesota and Neighboring States. Minneapolis: Univ. of Minn. Press, 280 pp.
Rogers, Bob. 1981. Winter Wren Sighted in Northern Black Hills. SDBN 33:38–39.
— 1989. June Brown Creeper Sighting in Lincoln County. SDBN 41:13.
Rogge, Charles. 1950. Snowy Owl in South Dakota. SDBN 2:4–7.
—1964. Bald Eagles at Yankton. SDBN 16:73.
— and Gladyce Rogge. 1965a. Worm-eating Warbler Banded at Farm Island, East of Pierre. SDBN 17:69.
— and — 1965b. Summer Tanager at Oakwood Lakes. SDBN 17:89–90.
— and — 1968. Chestnut-collared Longspur in Miner County. SDBN 20:64.

— and —1970. Avocet, Traill's Flycatcher, Swainson's Thrush, and Whip-poor-will Observations in Perkins and Walworth Counties. SDBN 17:103.
— and — 1978, Common Gallinule in Custer County. SDBN 30:39.
— and — 1983. Warbling Vireo in El Salvador and a 1982 Banding Report. SDBN 35:54-55
Rosche, Richard C. 1982. Birds of Northwestern Nebraska and Southwestern South Dakota. Published by the author,. Chadron, NE, 100 pp.
Rose, B.J. 1966. Yellow-throated Warbler near Armdale. SDBN 18:20.
—1967. 1966 Bird Records for Brown county, South Dakota. SDBN 19:31-33.
—1968. A History of Introduced Game Birds in South Dakota. Unpublished paper. 2 pp.
—1969a. Stranger Seen at Fairburn. SDBN 21:86.
—1969b. Chestnut-sided Warbler at Rapid City. SDBN 21:92.
—1969c. First Cassin's Kingbird Record for South Dakota. SDBN 21:91-92.
—1969d. Sage Thrasher in Pennington County. SDBN 21:92.
—1974. Glaucous Gulls in South Dakota. SDBN 26:48-49.
—1975a Black-throated Gray Warbler at Pierre. SDBN 27:15.
—1975b. Hooded Warblers at Pierre. SDBN 27:18.
—1975c. Kentucky Warbler at Pierre. SDBN 27:39.
Rose, Walter A., and Paul F. Springer. 1975. Boreal Owl Taken Near Watertown. SDBN 27:64-65.
Rothrock, E.P. 1943. Geology of South Dakota. Part I. The Surface. S.D. State Geol. Survey, Bull. 13, 88 pp.
Russell, Jean. 1968. Pileated Woodpecker near Oahe. SDBN 20:95-96.
Russell, Robert P. 1966. Observations Across South Dakota. SDBN 18:17-19.
Schleuter, Jan, and Tom Froiland. 1965. Western Tanager at Cactus Hills, East Edge of Sioux Falls. SDBN 17:72.
Schoonover, Lyle J. 1962. Cattle Egret, Glossy Ibis, and Least Bittern at Sand Lake. SDBN 14:57.
Schroeder, James R. 1970. First Black-legged Kittiwake Specimen for South Dakota. SDBN 22:81.
Schwalbach, Monica, George Vandel, and Ken Higgins. 1986. Status, Distribution, and Production of the Interior Least Tern and Piping Plover along the Mainstem Missouri River in South Dakota, 1986. SD Game Fish and Parks Report 86-10. 22 pp.
Scott, Merial, and Nathaniel R. Whitney, 1977. Broad-winged Hawk Nesting in the Black Hills. SDBN 29:72.
Serr, Esther. 1967a. Rare Species Come to Feeding Stations in Rapid City. SDBN 19:19.
—1967b. Summer Seasons in the Black Hills. SDBN 19:55,69.
—1970. Summary of Unusual Sightings in the Black Hills and Prairie Slopes. SDBN 22:126.
—1971a. Water Development as Related to Birds in the Badlands, Western South Dakota. SDBN 23:64-70.

—1971b. 1971 Spring Migration for South Dakota. SDBN 23:72–78,81.
—1975. The Nesting Season, June 1 – July 31, 1975, Northern Great Plains. American Birds 29:995–999.
Sharps, Jon C., and Dan O'Brien. 1984. Peregrine Falcon Reintroduction in the Black Hills, South Dakota, 1977–1980. S.D. Dept. of Game, Fish and Parks, Completion Report, 12 pp.
Short, Lester L., Jr. 1961. Notes on the Bird Distribution in the Central Plains. Nebr. Bird Rev. 29:2–22.
Sibley, Charles G., and Lester L. Short, Jr. 1959. Hybridization in the Buntings (Passerinia) of the Great Plains. Auk 76:443–463.
— and David A. West. 1959. Hybridization in the Rufous-sided Towhees of the Great Plains. Auk 76:326–338.
Sieg, Carolyn Hull. 1990. Northern Saw-whet Owl Sighting in Meade Co. SDBN 42:15.
Siljenberg, Adelene M. 1975. White-faced or Glossy Ibis in Clay County. SDBN 27:54–55.
Skadsen, Dennis. 1986a. Late and Uncommon Gulls at Fort Randall Dam. SDBN 38:65–67.
—1986b. Injured Prairie Falcon near Bristol. SDBN 38:98.
—1987a. Black Terns Nesting in Roberts County. SDBN 39:12.
—1987b. Le Conte's Sparrow Breeding in Day County. SDBN 39:13–14.
—1987c. Late Savannah Sparrow Nesting in Day County. SDBN 39:44–45.
—1987d. New Breeding Locations for the Common Tern, Ring-billed Gull, and California Gull in NE South Dakota. SDBN 39:65–66
—1988. Breeding Records and Observations of South Dakota's Rare Birds Heritage List 1965–1987. Part Two. SDBN 40:36–55.
Skadsen, Mark. 1986. First South Dakota Tricolored Heron Nest. SDBN 38:95.
—1987. Blue-gray Gnatcatcher Builds Nest in Lincoln County. SDBN 39:38–39.
Sloan, Norman F. 1982. Status of Breeding Colonies of White Pelicans in the United States through 1979. American Birds 36:250–254.
Smith, Mrs. Harold 1967. Curve-billed Thrasher Winters at Fairburn. SDBN 19:18.
Smith, Randy L. 1981. Hooded Merganser Nesting in Brookings County. SDBN 33:15.
—1982. Further Records of Nesting Hooded Mergansers. SDBN 34:63.
South Dakota Ornithologists' Union. 1956. Check-list of South Dakota Birds. SDBN 8:13–19.
Spawn, Gerald B. 1935. Some Shore Birds Collected in South Dakota. Wilson Bull. 47:72.
—1950. American Eider in Eastern S.D. SDBN 2:62.
—1952. King Rails Breed in Moody County. SDBN 4:42.

Spinner, K., and E. Spinner. 1978. Young Saw-whet Owls in Roberts Co. SDBN 30:50.
Spomer, Bob. 1981. Scissor-tailed Flycatcher in Brookings County. SDBN 33:14.
Spomer, Ron. 1979. Say's Phoebes Nesting in Hutchinson County. SDBN 31:64–65.
—1980. Oldsquaws on the Missouri. SDBN 32:59.
—1981. Long-billed Curlews and Sprague's Pipits near Pierre. SDBN 33:78
Springer, Paul F. 1965a. Tall and Midgrass Prairie, Breeding Survey 51. Audubon Field Notes 19:618–619.
—1965b. Whooping Cranes Near Pollock. SDBN 17:45–46,86.
—1987. Report of the Rare Bird Records Committee. SDBN 40:67–70.
— and Mark Skadsen. 1986. Unusual Birds in Newton Hills State Park: Late Spring and Summer 1985. SDBN 38:7–16.
—1990. 1989 Report of the Rare Bird Records Committee. SDBN 42:10–14.
Steenhof, K., S. S. Berlinger, and L. H. Fredrickson. 1980. Habitat Use by Wintering Bald Eagles in South Dakota. J. Wildl. Manage. 49:437–442.
Steffen, Galen. 1973. Possible Mountain Bluebird Sighted near Burke. SDBN 25:13.
—1977. Least Bittern at Burke Lake. SDBN 29:40–41.
—1979. Cardinals in Gregory County. SDBN 31:38.
—1981a. Summer Records of Red-breasted Nuthatches in Gregory County. SDBN 33:41.
—1981b. Late Fall Date for the Blue Grosbeak in Gregory County. SDBN 33:60.
—1981c. Possible Nesting of Green Herons at Burke Lake. SDBN 33:61.
—1982a. Great Egret Observed in Gregory County. SDBN 34:17.
—1982b. Spring Sighting of the Black Scoter in Gregory County. SDBN 34:18
—1983a. Early Spring Date for the Say's Phoebe and Early Fall Date for the Osprey in Gregory Co. SDBN 35:10.
—1983b. Goshawk Late Spring Date. SDBN 35:26.
—1983c. Wintering Yellow-rumped Warblers in Gregory County. SDBN 35:27
—1983d. Arctic Horned Owl Sighted in Burke. SDBN 36:49.
—1984. 1983 Late Fall Dates. SDBN 36:49.
—1985. Late Date for Osprey at Burke Lake. SDBN 37:35.
—1986. White-winged and Surf Scoters on Burke Lake SDBN 38:67–68.
— and Jocelyn L. Baker. 1986. Early Date for the Rough-legged Hawk. SDBN 38:64–65.
—, Erika Tallman and Dan A. Tallman. 1981. Early Dates for Mourning Dove Nests in Gregory and Brown Counties. SDBN 33:60.
Stephens, T.C. 1914. The Red Phalarope in Iowa. Wilson Bull. 26:103.

—1916. Red Phalarope in South Dakota (A Correction). Wilson Bull. 28:92.
—1918. Notes on the Birds of South Dakota, with a Preliminary List for Union County . Proc. Iowa Acad. Sci. 25:85–104.
—1920. Bird Records of the Past Two Winters, 1918–1920 in the Upper Missouri Valley. Proc. Iowa Acad. Sci. 27:395–407.
— and William Youngworth. 1947. Late Fall and Winter Bird Records, for 1941 to 1947, in the Upper Missouri Valley. Proc. Iowa Acad. Sci. 54:373–378.
— and — 1957. The Birds of Dakota County Nebraska. Nebr. Ornith. Union, Occ. Papers, No. 3, 28 pp.
—, — and W.R. Felton, Jr. 1955. The Birds of Union County, South Dakota. Nebr. Ornith. Union, Occ. Papers, No. 1, 35 pp.
Stewart, Robert E. 1975. Breeding Birds of North Dakota. Fargo, N.D.: Tri-College Center for Environmental Studies, 295 pp.
Storer, R. W., and G. L. Neuchterlein. 1985. An Analysis of Plumage and Morphological Characteristics of the two Color Forms of the Western Grebe. Auk 102:102–119.
Stoudt, Jerome H. 1968. Delineation of Primary Canvasback Migration and Wintering Habitat. Bureau of Sport Fisheries and Wildlife, Northern Prairie Wildlife Research Center, Jamestown, N.D. Progress Report, Project A-10.2, 24 pp.
Strauss, Mrs., Mrs. Wesley M. Beardsley and Ruth Habeger. 1961. Red-wing Blackbirds near Madison. SDBN 13:21.
Strom, Roger F. 1981. Great Egret in Tripp County. SDBN 33:38.
Swanton, John Reed. 1952. The Indian Tribes of North America. Bur. Amer. Ethnol., Bull. 145, 726 pp.
Taber, Richard D. 1971. Criteria of Sex and Age. Pages 324–401 in Wildlife Management Techniques, 3rd Ed Rev., Robert H. Giles, Jr., Ed. Washington, D.C.: Wildlife Society, 633 pp.
Tallman, Dan A. 1979. Unusual Migrants at Aberdeen. SDBN 31:48–49.
—1981. Can Ornithology be Taught in the Fall? SDBN 33:30–33.
—1982. House Finches in South Dakota. SDBN 34:19–20.
—1983. Probable Arctic Horned Owl at Aberdeen. SDBN 35:27–28.
—1987. Unusual Northern Saw-Whet Owl Numbers at Aberdeen. SDBN 39:16.
—1989. Siskin and Other Banding at Two Locations in Aberdeen, South Dakota: 1983–1987. SDBN 41:4–9.
—1990. Banding Recoveries of South Dakota Birds. Part 1: Woodpeckers, Swifts, and Flycatchers. SDBN 42:4–6.
—, Charlann Suel, and Robert Brown. 1983. An Analysis of the Avifauna of an Isolated Ponderosa Pine Forest in Eastern Meade County, South Dakota. SDBN 35:44–50.
Terry, Merwin M., III. 1976. The Ethology of a Bald Eagle Population Wintering Along the Missouri River in South

Dakota and Nebraska. M.A. Thesis, Univ. of South Dakota, 47 pp.

Town, Ralph H. 1967. Northern Phalarope at Lake Andes. SDBN 19:40.

—1968. Old-squaw Ducks, Immature Swan, and Sandhill Cranes at Lake Andes. SDBN 20:43.

Trautman, Carl G. 1960. Evaluation of Pheasant Nesting Habitat in Eastern South Dakota. Trans. N. Amer. Wildlife Conf. 25:202–213.

Tullsen, H. 1911. My Avian Visitors: Notes from South Dakota. Condor 13:89–104.

Twomey, Katherine. 1969. Lesser Goldfinch Observed in the Hot Springs Area. SDBN 21:93.

—1981. Band-tailed Pigeon at Hot Springs. SDBN 33:78.

Van Bruggen, Theodore. 1976. The Vascular Plants of South Dakota. Iowa State Univ. Press, Ames. 538 pp.

Van Dyk, John. 1989. Adult Black-legged Kittiwake in Summer. SDBN 41:11–12.

Van Sickle, Steve. 1989. Copulating Screech Owls in Yankton. SDBN 41:14.

Visher, Stephen Sargent. 1909. A List of the Birds of Western South Dakota. Auk 26:144–153.

—1910. Notes on the Sandhill Crane. Wilson Bull. 22:115–117.

—1912a. A List of the Birds of the Pine Ridge Reservation. S.D. State Geol. and Biol. Surv. Bull. 5:109–121.

—1912b. A Preliminary List of the Summer Birds of Fall River County, Southwestern South Dakota. Wilson Bull. 24:1–6.

—1912c. Northern Eider in South Dakota, A New Record for the Interior of North America. Auk 29:359–336.

—1913a. An Annotated List of the Birds of Sanborn County, South Dakota. Auk 30:561–573.

—1913b. Corrections to a Preliminary List of the Summer Birds of Fall River County, Southwestern South Dakota. Wilson Bull. 25:38–39.

—1914. List of the Birds of Harding County. In A Preliminary report on the Biology of Harding County, Northwestern South Dakota. S.D. Geol. Surv. Bull. 6:68–87.

—1915. A List of the Birds of Clay County, Southeastern South Dakota. Wilson Bull. 27:321–335.

—1949. Bird Study in South Dakota. SDBN 1:4–7.

Wagar, Harold T. 1958. 25 Years of Spring Dates. SDBN 10:23–25.

Waldstein, Sam. 1977. First Nest Records for Cattle Egrets and Snowy Egrets in South Dakota. SDBN 29:72.

Wallenstrom, Rolf L. 1968. American Scoter in McPherson County. SDBN 20:92.

Weaver, Gertrude. 1949. Blue Grosbeak's Nest in South Dakota. Iowa Bird Life 19:15–16 [Reprinted in SDBN 1:13, 1949].

Weaver, Kenneth L. 1982. Summer Bird Records from the Southern Black Hills. SDBN 34:66–67.

Wells, Darrel, and Lois Wells. 1983. Herons, Egrets, and Ibis Nesting at Lake Preston. SDBN 35:52–53.

West, David A. 1962. Hybridization in Grosbeaks (*Pheucticus*) of the Great Plains. Auk 79:399–424.
Wetmore, Mark. 1972. A Black-throated Sparrow in Vermillion. SDBN 24:20, photo 24;1.
Weyler, Irma. 1964. Fall to Winter in Belle Fourche. SDBN 16:27–29.
—1971. in Daily Belle Fourche Post, 31 Aug 1971.
Whitney, N.R., Jr. 1955. A Catalogue of Eggs. SDBN 7:21–22,26,30–32.
—1957. A Day in Harding County. SDBN 9:39.
—1958. Whimbrel (Hudsonian Curlew) in South Dakota. SDBN 10:28.
—1960. Observations on the Life of the White-winged Junco. SDBN 12:24–25 and 41.
—1972. Notes on Some Significant Specimens of South Dakota Birds. SDBN 24:3.
—1977. Blue-gray Gnatcatcher at Rapid City. SDBN 29:16.
—1982. Twenty-five Years of Pinyon Jay Studies. SDBN 34:29–30.
— and Dan A. Tallman. 1988. Late Rose-breasted Grosbeaks and Other Late Migrants at Rapid City and Aberdeen. SDBN 40:19–20.
Wied, Prince Maximilian of. 1839–41. Reise in das Innere Nord-America in den Jahren 1932 bis 1934. Coblenz: J. Haelscher, 2 vols. (Original not seen; translation, 1843. Travels in the Interior of North America. London: Ackermann. 520 pp., and reprinted in Vol. 22 and 24 of Early Western Travels 1798–1846, R. G. Thwaites, Ed. 1906. Cleveland: Clark).
Wilcox, Juli. 1977. Tufted Titmouse at Yankton. SDBN 29:39.
Wild, Fred.1973. Goshawk Nests in the Black Hills. SDBN 25:22–23.
Wright, A. H. 1915. Early Records of the Wild Turkey. V. Auk 32:348–366.
Wurttemberg, Duke Paul Wilhelm of. 1835. Erste Reise nach dem nordlichen Amerika in den Jahren 1822 bis 1824. Stuttgart and Tubingen: J.G. Cotta, 345 pp. [Translation, 1973. Travels in North America 1822–1824. Norman: Univ. of Okla. Press, 456 pp.; also South Dakota Historical Collections 19:6–474, 1938].
Youngworth, Wm. 1932a. Recent Bird Notes from Southern South Dakota. Wilson Bull. 44:43.
—1932b. The Yellow-throated Vireo in South Dakota. Wilson Bull. 44:233.
—1934. Field Notes from the Sioux City, Iowa, Region. Wilson Bull. 46:62.
—1935. Birds of Fort Sisseton, S.D. A Sixty Year Comparison. Wilson Bull. 47:209–235.
—1944. The Starling in South Dakota, North Dakota and Minnesota. Iowa Bird Life 14:76.
—1949. Union County Notes. SDBN 1:34.
—1953. The Western Grebe in South Dakota. SDBN 5:58–61.
—1957. Union County Spring Notes. SDBN 9:28–29.

—1958. A Summer Tanager Comes to South Dakota. SDBN 10:13.
—1959a. The Harris' Sparrow in the Missouri River Valley. SDBN 11:64–67,79.
—1959b. The Lazuli Bunting along the Western Border of Iowa: A Summary. Iowa Bird Life 29:2–5, pl.
—1960a. Least Tern. SDBN 12:70–71,96.
—1960b. The Tennessee Warbler as an Abundant Migrant. SDBN 12:50–52.

SPECIES INDEX AND CHECKLIST

☐ Ani, Groove-billed	168	
☐ Smooth-billed	x	
☐ Avocet, American	116	
☐ Bittern, American	14	
☐ Least	15	
☐ Blackbird, Brewer's	364	
☒ Red-winged	359	
☐ Rusty	363	
☒ Yellow-headed	362	
☒ Bluebird, Eastern	250	
☒ Mountain	251	
☐ Bobolink	358	
☐ Bobwhite, Northern	100	
☐ Brant	35	
☐ Bufflehead	60	
☒ Bunting, Indigo	324	
☒ Lark	336	
☒ Lazuli	323	
☐ Snow	357	
☐ Canvasback	48	
☐ Cardinal, Northern	319	
☐ Catbird, Gray	260	
Chickadee,		
☐ Black-capped	232	
☐ Boreal	233	
☐ Mountain	233	
☐ Chat, Yellow-breasted	315	
☐ Chuck-will's-widow	183	
☐ Chukar	92	
☐ Coot, American	106	
Cormorant,		
☐ Double-crested	12	
☐ Olivaceous	13	
☐ Cowbird, Brown-headed	367	
☐ Crane, Sandhill	107	
☐ Whooping	108	
☐ Creeper, Brown	238	
☐ Crossbill, Red	375	
☐ White-winged	376	
☒ Crow, American	230	
☐ Cuckoo, Black-billed	166	
☐ Yellow-billed	167	
☐ Curlew, Eskimo	124	
☐ Long-billed	125	
☐ Dickcissel	325	
☐ Dipper, American	246	
☐ Dove, Inca	x	
☒ Mourning	164	
☐ Ringed Turtle	x	
☐ Rock	163	
☐ Dowitcher, Long-billed	140	
☐ Short-billed	139
☐ Duck, American Black	39
☐ Ring-necked	51
☐ Ruddy	66
☐ Wood	37
☐ Dunlin	136
☒ Eagle, Bald	70
☒ Golden	84
☒ Egret, Cattle	21
☒ Great	17
☒ Snowy	18
☐ Eider, Common	55
☐ Falcon, Peregrine	88
☒ Prairie	90
☐ Finch, Cassin's	373
☒ House	374
☒ Purple	372
☐ Rosy	370
☒ Flicker, Northern	198
☐ Flycatcher, Acadian	205
☐ Alder	205
☐ Cordilleran	209
☐ Dusky	208
☐ Great Crested	212
☐ Least	207
☐ Olive-sided	201
☐ Scissor-tailed	216
☐ "Traill's"	205
☐ Vermilion	212
☐ Western	209
☐ Willow	206
☐ Yellow-bellied	204
☐ Gadwall	46
☐ Gnatcatcher, Blue-gray	249
☐ Godwit, Hudsonian	126
☐ Marbled	127
☐ Goldeneye, Barrow's	60
☐ Common	59
☐ Golden-Plover, Lesser	111
☒ Goldfinch, American	381
☐ Lesser	380
☒ Goose, Canada	35
☐ Egyptian	x
☐ Emperor	x
☐ Greater White-fronted	31
☐ Ross'	33
☐ Snow	32
☐ Goshawk, Northern	75
☒ Grackle, Common	365
☐ Great-tailed	365
☐ Grebe, Clark's	9

SPECIES INDEX AND CHECKLIST

- [x] Eared 6
- [ ] Horned 4
- [ ] Pied-billed 3
- [ ] Red-necked 5
- [ ] Western 8
- [ ] Grosbeak, Black-headed 321
- [ ] Blue 322
- [ ] Evening 382
- [ ] Pine 371
- [ ] Rose-breasted 320
- [ ] Grouse, Blue 94
- [ ] Ruffed 95
- [ ] Sage 96
- [x] Sharp-tailed 98
- [ ] Gull, Bonaparte's 149
- [ ] California 152
- [ ] Franklin's 147
- [ ] Glaucous 156
- [ ] Herring 154
- [ ] Iceland 156
- [x] Laughing 147
- [x] Ring-billed 151
- [ ] Sabine's 157
- [ ] Thayer's 155
- [ ] Gyrfalcon 89
- [x] Harrier, Northern 72
- [ ] Hawk, Broad-winged 77
- [ ] Cooper's 74
- [ ] Ferruginous 82
- [ ] Red-shouldered 76
- [x] Red-tailed 80
- [ ] Rough-legged 83
- [ ] Sharp-shinned 73
- [ ] Swainson's 78
- [x] Heron, Great Blue 16
- [x] Green-backed 22
- [x] Little Blue 19
- [x] Tricolored 21
- Hummingbird,
- [ ] Broad-tailed 187
- [ ] Calliope 187
- [x] Ruby-throated 186
- [ ] Rufous 188
- [x] Ibis, White 26
- [ ] White-faced 26
- [ ] Jaeger, Pomarine 146
- [ ] Long-tailed 146
- [x] Jay, Blue 226
- [ ] Gray 225
- [ ] Pinyon 227
- [x] Steller's 227
- [ ] Junco, Dark-eyed 351
- [ ] Gray-headed 351
- [ ] White-winged 351
- [x] Kestrel, American 86
- [x] Killdeer 114
- [x] Kingbird, Cassin's 213
- [x] Eastern 215
- [x] Western 214
- [x] Kingfisher, Belted 189
- Kinglet,
- [ ] Golden-crowned 247
- [ ] Ruby-crowned 248
- Kite,
- [ ] Am. Swallow-tailed 69
- [ ] Black-shouldered 69
- [ ] Mississippi 70
- [ ] Kittiwake, Black-legged 157
- [ ] Knot, Red 129
- [x] Lark, Horned 217
- Longspur,
- [ ] Chestnut-collared 356
- [ ] Lapland 354
- [ ] McCown's 353
- [ ] Smith's 355
- [ ] Loon, Common 1
- [ ] Red-throated 1
- [ ] Magpie, Black-billed 229
- [x] Mallard 40
- [x] Martin, Purple 218
- [x] Meadowlark, Eastern 360
- [x] Western 361
- [ ] Merganser, Common 63
- [ ] Hooded 62
- [ ] Red-breasted 65
- [ ] Merlin 87
- [ ] Mockingbird, Northern 261
- [ ] Moorhen, Common 105
- [x] Nighthawk, Common 181
- [ ] Lesser x
- Night-Heron,
- [ ] Black-crowned 23
- [ ] Yellow-crowned 25
- Nuthatch,
- [ ] Brown-headed x
- [ ] Pygmy 237
- [x] Red-breasted 235
- [x] White-breasted 236
- [ ] Nutcracker, Clark's 228
- [ ] Oldsquaw 55
- [x] Oriole, Baltimore 369
- [ ] Bullock's 369
- [ ] Northern 369
- [x] Orchard 368
- [ ] Osprey 68
- [ ] Ovenbird 305

SPECIES INDEX AND CHECKLIST 409

- ☐ Owl, Barn 169
- ☐   Barred 175
- ☐   Boreal 179
- ☐   Burrowing 174
- ☐   Great Gray 176
- ☐   Great Horned 171
- ☐   Long-eared 177
- ☐   Northern Hawk 173
- ☐   Northern Saw-whet 179
- ☐   Short-eared 178
- ☐   Snowy 172
- ☐ Parakeet, Carolina 166
- ☐ Partridge, Gray 91
- ☐ Parula, Northern 284
- ☐ Pelican, American White 10
- ☐   Brown 11
- ☐ Phalarope, Red 145
- ☐   Red-necked 144
- ☐   Wilson's 143
- ☒ Pheasant, Ring-necked 93
- ☐ Phoebe, Eastern 210
- ☐   Say's 211
- ☐ Pigeon, Band-tailed 163
- ☐   Passenger 165
- ☐ Pintail, Northern 41
- ☐ Pipit, American 265
- ☐   Sprague's 266
- ☐   Water 265
- ☐ Plover, Black-bellied 110
- ☐   Mountain 115
- ☐   Piping 113
- ☐   Semipalmated 112
- ☐   Snowy 112
- ☐ Poorwill, Common 182
- ☐ Prairie-Chicken, Greater 97
- ☐ Quail, California 101
- ☐ Rail, King 102
- ☐   Virginia 103
- ☐   Yellow 102
- ☒ Raven, Common 231
- ☐ Redhead 50
- ☐ Redpoll, Common 377
- ☐   Hoary 378
- ☐ Redstart, American 302
- ☒ Robin, American 258
- ☐ Ruff 139
- ☐ Sanderling 129
- ☐ Sandpiper, Baird's 134
- ☐   Buff-breasted 138
- ☐   Least 132
- ☐   Pectoral 135
- ☐   Semipalmated 130
- ☐   Solitary 120
- ☐   Spotted 122
- ☐   Stilt 137
- ☐   Upland 123
- ☐   Western 131
- ☐   White-rumped 133
- ☐ Sapsucker, Red-naped 194
- ☐   Yellow-bellied 193
- ☐   Williamson's 195
- ☐ Scaup, Greater 52
- ☐   Lesser 53
- ☐ Scoter, Black 56
- ☐   Surf 57
- ☐   White-winged 58
- ☐ Screech-Owl, Eastern 170
- ☒ Shrike, Loggerhead 270
- ☒   Northern 269
- ☐ Shoveler, Northern 45
- ☐ Siskin, Pine 379
- ☐ Snipe, Common 141
- ☐ Solitaire, Townsend's 252
- ☐ Sora 104
- ☐ Sparrow, American Tree 328
- ☐   Baird's 338
- ☐   Black-throated 336
- ☐   Brewer's 332
- ☐   Cassin's 328
- ☒   Chipping 329
- ☐   Clay-colored 330
- ☐   Field 333
- ☐   Fox 343
- ☐   Golden-crowned x
- ☒   Grasshopper 339
- ☐   Harris' 350
- ☐   Henslow's 340
- ☐   House 383
- ☒   Lark 335
- ☐   Le Conte's 341
- ☐   Lincoln's 345
- ☐   Savannah 337
- ☐   Sharp-tailed 342
- ☒   Song 344
- ☒   Swamp 346
- ☒   Vesper 334
- ☐   White-crowned 348
- ☐   White-throated 347
- ☒ Starling, European 271
- ☐ Stilt, Black-necked 116
- ☐ Stork, Wood 28
- ☒ Swallow, Bank 222
- ☒   Barn 224
- ☐   Cliff 223
- ☐   N. Rough-winged 221
- ☒   Tree 219

410 SPECIES INDEX AND CHECKLIST

☐	Violet-green	220	☐	Connecticut	308
☐ Swan, Mute		31	☐	Golden-winged	280
☐	Trumpeter	30	☐	Hooded	312
☐	Tundra	29	☐	Kentucky	308
☒ Swift, Chimney		184	☐	MacGillivray's	310
☒	White-throated	185	☐	Magnolia	287
☐ Tanager, Scarlet		317	☐	Mourning	309
☐	Summer	316	☐	Myrtle	290
☐	Western	318	☐	Nashville	283
☐ Teal, Blue-winged		43	☐	Orange-crowned	282
☐	Cinnamon	44	☐	Palm	297
☐	Green-winged	38	☐	Pine	295
☐ Tern, Black		162	☐	Prairie	296
☐	Caspian	158	☐	Prothonotary	303
☐	Common	159	☐	Tennessee	281
☐	Forster's	160	☐	Townsend's	292
☐	Least	161	☐	Wilson's	313
☐ Thrasher, Brown		263	☐	Worm-eating	304
☐	Curve-billed	264	☐	Yellow	285
☐	Sage	262	☐	Yellow-rumped	290
☐ Thrush, Gray-cheeked		254	☐	Yellow-throated	295
☐	Hermit	256	☐ Waterthrush, Louisiana		307
☐	Swainson's	255	☐	Northern	306
☐	Varied	259	☐ Waxwing, Bohemian		267
☐	Wood	257	☒	Cedar	268
☐ Titmouse, Tufted		234	☐ Wheatear, Northern		x
☐ Towhee, Green-tailed		326	☐ Whimbrel		124
☐	Rufous-sided	327	☐ Whip-poor-will		183
☒ Turkey, Wild		99	☐ Whistling-Duck, Fulvous		28
☐ Turnstone, Ruddy		128	☐ Wigeon, American		47
☐ Veery		253	☐	Eurasian	x
☐ Vireo, Bell's		273	☐ Willet		121
☐	Philadelphia	277	☐ Woodcock, American		142
☐	Red-eyed	278		Woodpecker,	
☐	Solitary	274	☐	Black-backed	197
☐	Warbling	276	☒	Downy	195
☐	White-eyed	272	☒	Hairy	196
☐	Yellow-throated	275	☐	Lewis'	190
☐ Vulture, Black		x	☒	Pileated	200
☒	Turkey	67	☒	Red-bellied	192
☐ Warbler, Audubon's		290	☒	Red-headed	191
☐	Bay-breasted	298	☐	Three-toed	197
☐	Black-and-white	301	☐ Wood-Pewee, Eastern		203
☐	Black-throated Blue	289	☒	Western	202
☐	Black-throated Gray	292	☐ Wren, Bewick's		242
☐	Black-throated Green	293	☒	Canyon	240
☐	Blackburnian	294	☐	Carolina	241
☐	Blackpoll	299	☒	House	242
☐	Blue-winged	279	☐	Marsh	245
☐	Canada	314	☒	Rock	239
☐	Cape May	288	☐	Sedge	244
☐	Cerulean	300	☐	Winter	243
☐	Chestnut-sided	286	☐ Yellowthroat, Common		311

☐ Yellowlegs, Greater   118 ☐   Lesser   119

THE SOUTH DAKOTA ORNITHOLOGISTS' UNION

The South Dakota Ornithologists' Union is a statewide group for all with the interest in birds; both the serious enthusiast and the more casual bird lover are welcome. The SDOU was founded in 1949 and immediately began publishing a quarterly journal to record observations, *South Dakota Bird Notes*. Quarterly seasonal reports from all over the state and summaries of the Christmas Bird Counts provide a view for the reader of the changing bird world. The SDOU also publishes a biannual newsletter, *The Lark Bunting*. Our organization holds two statewide meetings each year, one in the fall for papers and reports, and one in the spring or early summer for field trips; both events give an opportunity for participants to visit different habitats in the state. After many years of preparation by the Checklist Committee, the SDOU has published *The Birds of South Dakota*.

Membership is open to all. Information on the organization and its publications is available from: Nelda Holden, Treasurer, SDOU, Rt. 4, Box 252, Brookings SD 57006 or from Dan Tallman, Editor, SDOU, Northern State University, Aberdeen, SD 57401.